Autodesk Inventor R4 Fundamentals: Conquering the Rubicon

Elise Moss

autodesk
authorized author

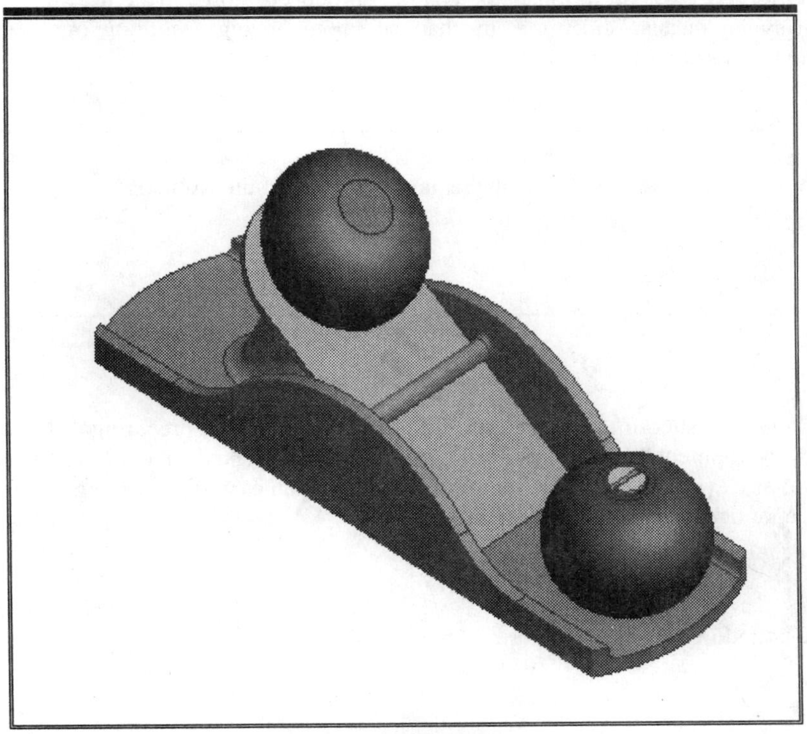

SDC
PUBLICATIONS

Schroff Development Corporation

www.schroff.com

Schroff Development Corporation
P.O. Box 1334
Mission, KS 66222
(913) 262-2664
www.schroff.com

Trademarks
The following are registered trademarks of Autodesk, Inc.: AutoCAD, AutoCAD Mechanical Desktop, Inventor, Autodesk, AutoLISP, AutoCAD Design Center, Autodesk Device Interface, and HEIDI
Microsoft, Windows, Word, and Excel are either registered trademarks or trademarks of Microsoft Corporation.
All other trademarks are trademarks of their respective holders.

Moss, Elise
Autodesk Inventor R4 Fundamentals: Conquering the Rubicon/
Elise Moss

ISBN 1-58503-066-X

The author and publisher of this book have used their best efforts in preparing this book. These efforts include the development, research, and testing of material presented. The author and publisher shall not be held liable in any event for incidental or consequential damages with, or arising out of, the furnishing, performance, or use of the material herein.

Printed and bound in the United States of America.

Preface

RUBICON: ancient name of a stream in central Italy that flowed into the Adriatic Sea a short distance north of Ariminum (modern Rimini). The modern Rubicone River, which rises near San Marino, is usually identified as the ancient Rubicon. In the 1st century BC, the Rubicon River formed the boundary between Italy and the Roman province of Cisalpine Gaul. In 49 BC, Julius Caesar made his famous crossing of the Rubicon; as the Roman Senate had forbidden him to enter Italy with an army, this action initiated civil war between his forces and those of Pompey the Great. The phrase "to cross the Rubicon" has come to mean the taking of a step by which one is committed to a hazardous enterprise; and, once committed, there is no return.

Rubicon was Autodesk's code name for their new software, Inventor. This was a hazardous enterprise for Autodesk. They literally started over with this product. The highly successful AutoCAD and Mechanical Desktop relied on software code that had become bulky and slow, incapable of handling large assemblies and the demands of parametric modeling. It was a risky business – abandoning highly successful software code and embarking in a new direction.

As a professor at a community college, my students often express their fears and trepidation about learning a new software program, especially a parametric modeling program. For some, it is their first time in front of a computer. Not unlike Julius Caesar, they must confront the twin evils of self-doubt and the fear of failure.

The primary goal of this text is not only to assist the beginner and intermediate user in "crossing the Rubicon", but also to CONQUER it. The text includes in-depth descriptions of the toolbars, dialog boxes, user options, and the modeling process. This text is not meant to replace tutorial instruction, but meant to act as a reference guide for the software, to fill in the gaps of Inventor's on-line help, and to ease the student into becoming a more productive user.

The files used in this text are accessible from the Internet at www.schroff1.com/inventor.

We value customer input. Please contact us with any comments, questions, or concerns about this text.

Elise Moss
Applied Technologies Department
De Anza College
21250 Stevens Creek Blvd
Cupertino, CA 95014
elise_moss@mossdesigns.com

Acknowledgements

This book would not have been possible without the support of some key Autodesk employees. A special thanks to Susie Chang, Derrick Smith, Alan Jacobs, Rebecca Bell, Lynn Allen, Melrose Ross, Denis Cadu, Carolyn Gavriloff, and David Koel.

Additional thanks to the board and members of the Silicon Valley AutoCAD Power Users, a dedicated group of Autodesk users, for educating me about the needs and wants of CAD users.

My deep appreciation to Dr. Martha Kanter, President of DeAnza College; Dr. Steven Silletti, Dean of Applied Technology; Michael Engle, Gary Lamit, and Sally Larson for their guidance and support.

The effort and support of the editorial and production staff of Schroff Development Corporation is gratefully acknowledged. I especially thank Stephen Schroff for his helpful suggestions regarding the format of this text.

Finally, truly infinite thanks to Ari for his encouragement and his faith.

Table of Contents

Lesson 3
User Interface (continued)

Lesson 4
The Standard Toolbar

Lesson 5
The Features Toolbar

Lesson 6
Sketch Tools

Lesson 7
The Solids Toolbar

Lesson 8
The Precise Input Toolbar and the Collaboration Toolbar

Lesson 9
Sheet Metal Tools

Lesson 10
Hole Features

Lesson 11
Constructing Geometry

Lesson 12
Adding Fillets and Chamfers

Lesson 13
Patterns

Lesson 14
Lofting

Lesson 15
Creating a Base Sweep

Lesson 16
Creating Sheet Metal Parts

Lesson 17
Creating a Basic Part

Lesson 18
Drawing Management

Lesson 19
Drawing Annotation Toolbar

Lesson 20
Orthographic Views

Lesson 21
Auxiliary Views

Lesson 22
Section Views

Lesson 23
Detail Views

Lesson 24
Drafting Standards

Lesson 25
Assembly Tools

TIP: All the drawing files used in this text can be downloaded for free from the Schroff Development Corporation website at http://www.schroff1.com/inventor/.

Lesson 26
Bottom Up Assembly

Lesson 27
Top Down Assembly

Lesson 28
Presentations

Lesson 29
Assembly Drawings

week 1 12
chapter 1, 2, 11,
1-14 — 1-18

Lesson 1

Parametric Modeling Fundamentals – Quick Start

Learning Objectives

When you have completed this lesson, you will be able to:

- Create simple parametric models
- Understand the Basic Parametric Modeling Process
- Create Rough Sketches
- Understand the "Shape before Size" Approach
- Use the view commands
- Create and modify dimensions

In Inventor, the parametric part modeling process involves the following steps:

1. Create a rough two-dimensional sketch.
2. Apply geometric constraints as needed
3. Apply dimensions
4. Extrude/revolve/sweep
5. Add additional features, such as holes, fillets, chamfers, and shells.
6. Analyse and refine the model
7. Create the drawing layout.

Start Inventor by double-clicking on the Inventor icon on the desktop.

A window will come up. On the left side, we see four icons: Getting Started, New, Open, and Projects. Depending on which left icon is highlighted, the options in the main window change. Verify that the 'New' icon is highlighted.

Inventor uses new file extensions. Refer to the table below to assist you in determining the type of file being created and accessed.

File Extension	File Type
*.ipt	Part File/Sheet Metal Part (3D model)
*.iam	Assembly File (3D model)
*.idv	Design View File
*.ipj	Project File
*.idw	Drawing Layout (2D paper space)
*.ipn	Presentation (3D model/Scene/Rendering)
*.ide	Design Element

Select the Standard.ipt icon and press 'OK'.

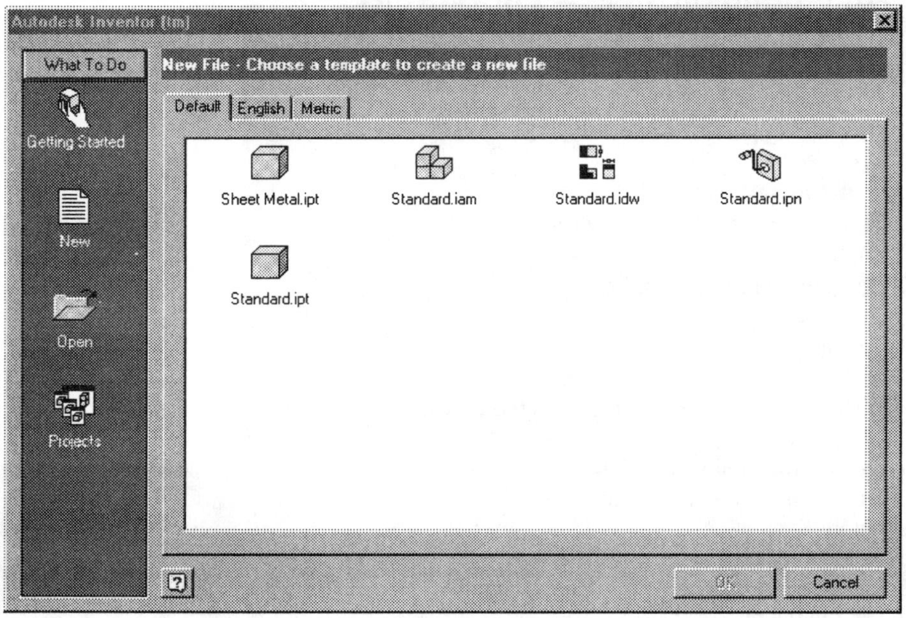

The files displayed and used in the Start-Up dialog are templates. These templates contain default drafting standards.

We will start with a rough sketch. Keep the following guidelines in mind when creating a rough sketch.

- Create a sketch that is proportional to the desired shape.
- Keep sketches simple. Leave out fillets, rounds, and chamfers…those can be added later.
- Exaggerate the geometric features of the desired shape. Remember your sketch is parametric - you can adjust the size when we start adding dimensions. It's easier to go from big to small than vice versa.
- Draw the geometry so it does not overlap. Inventor looks for a closed polygonal shape. Overlapping lines can create confusion and errors.

Creating a rough sketch

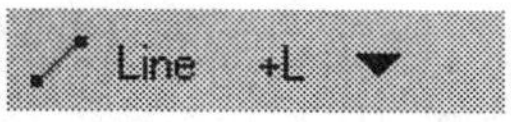

1. Select the LINE icon from the Sketch Toolbar by clicking on it with the left-mouse button. This will activate the Line command.

TIP: The +L next to the Line icon means that typing the letter L on the keyboard will also initiate the Line command. This similar to the command alias 'L' used in AutoCAD.

The Message box located in the top middle of the menu and in the lower left corner of the screen will change to indicate we are now in 'line' mode. Use the Message box as a help. Inventor expects us to identify the starting location of a line. To switch to arc mode, merely hold down the left-mouse button and move the mouse to form an arc.

2. Move the mouse near the lower left corner of the Drawing Screen and create a freehand sketch as shown below. Create the sketch by starting at Point 1 and ending at Point 7. Do not be concerned by the actual size of the sketch. Do not worry about keeping the lines perfectly horizontal or vertical as Inventor automatically keeps lines orthogonal.

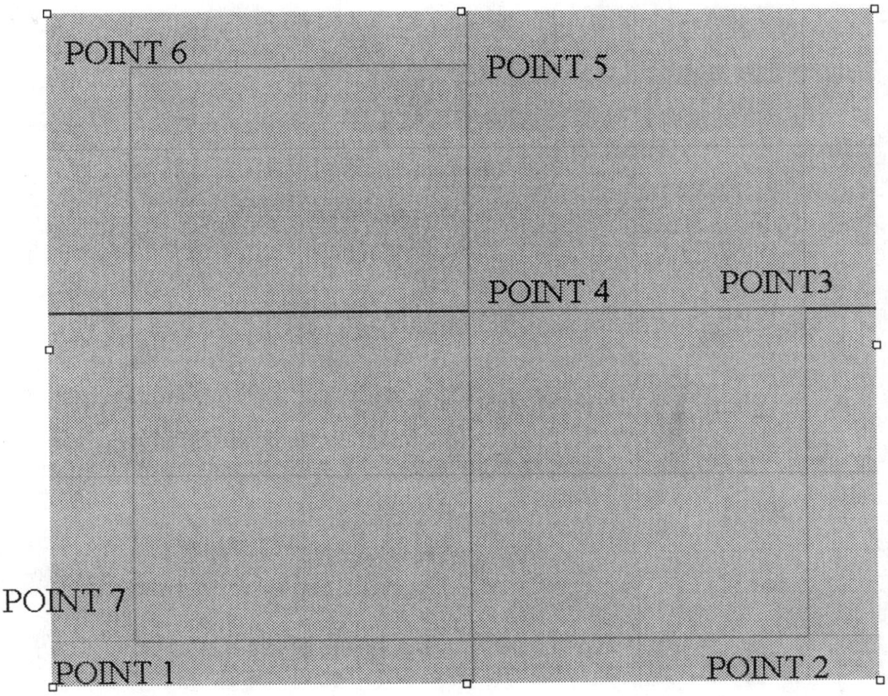

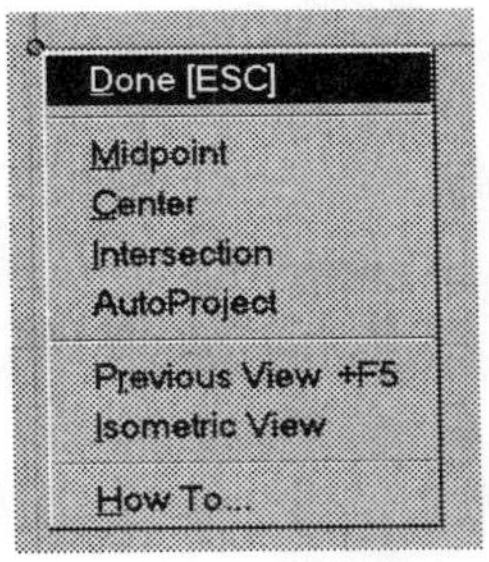

While in the LINE command, we can right-click the mouse to get the pop-up shown. When we are done with the sketch, we right-click the mouse and select 'Done'. Notice that we have the option to select Midpoint, Center, Intersection or AutoProject to help us in our sketching.

Dimensioning a Sketch

Select the dimension tool by left-picking the Dimension icon with the mouse. Then select the line to dimension. Finally move the mouse away from the line being dimensioned and select the dimension location. To modify the dimension, left pick on the dimension and an edit box appears.

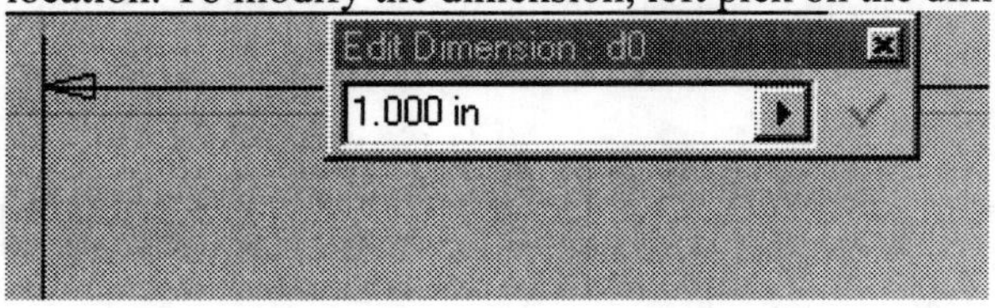

Place your mouse inside the text box and enter the desired dimension.
Select the green check mark when done editing.

Repeat Step 3 applying the dimensions shown below.

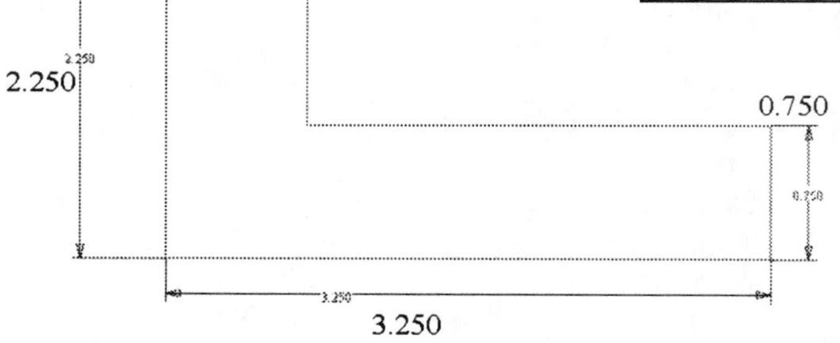

TIP: Typing the letter D on the keyboard will also initiate the DIMENSION command.

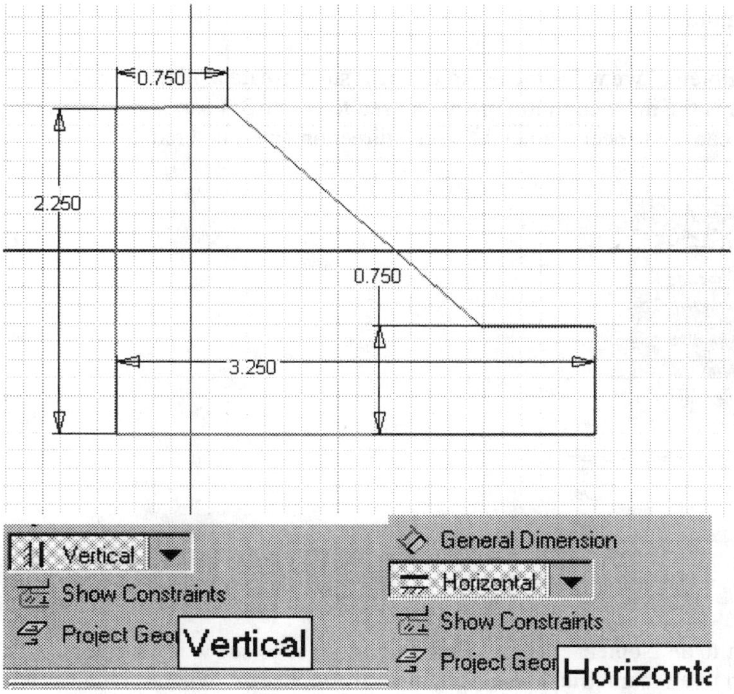

What if your sketch turns out like this?
Time to use geometric constraints.
Add a vertical constraint to the slanted line.
Add a horizontal constraint to the upper line.
If your sketch is different, apply the constraints as needed.

TIP: If you do not wish constraints to automatically be added with your geometry, hold down the CONTROL key as you sketch.

Completing the Sketch

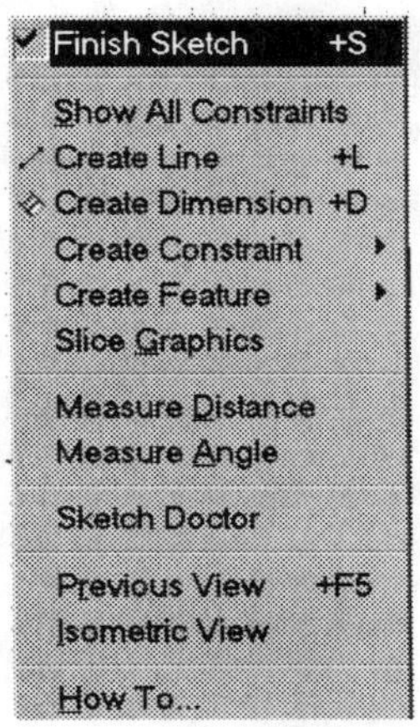

Right click the mouse and Select 'Done' to finish adding dimensions/constraints. Right click the mouse and Select 'Finish Sketch' to indicate we are done defining our geometry.

TIP: The +S next to the Finish Sketch icon means that typing the letter S on the keyboard will also initiate the Finish Sketch command.

Completing the Base Solid Feature

Now that the 2-D sketch is completed, we will proceed to the next step: create a 3D part from the 2D profile. Extruding a 2D sketch is the most common methods used to create 3D parts. We can extrude planar faces along a path. We can also specify a height value, direction and a tapered angle.

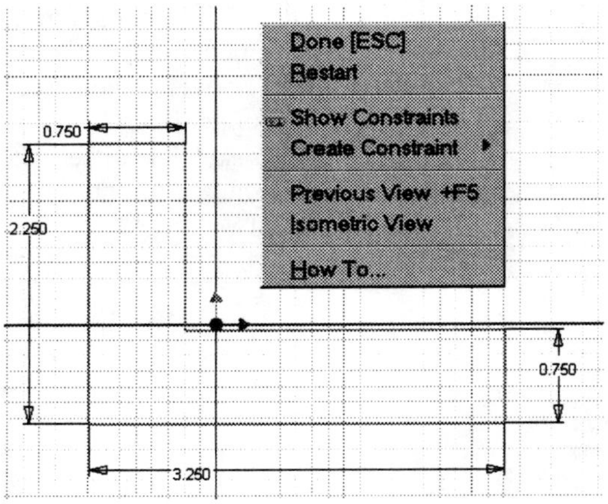

Before we extrude, let's switch to an Isometric View. That will allow us to see what is going to happen more easily. To switch to an Isometric View, right click the mouse anywhere in the Drawing Screen area and select 'Isometric View' from the pop-up menu. We select by highlighting 'IsometricView' and picking with the left mouse button.

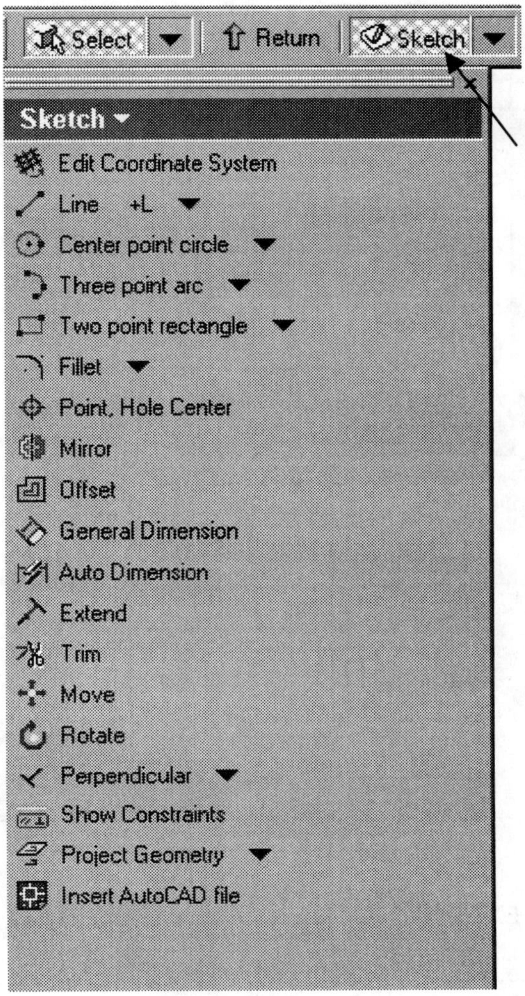

We still see the Sketch tools and we need to switch to the Feature tools. To do that, press the Sketch button located above the Sketch toolbar.

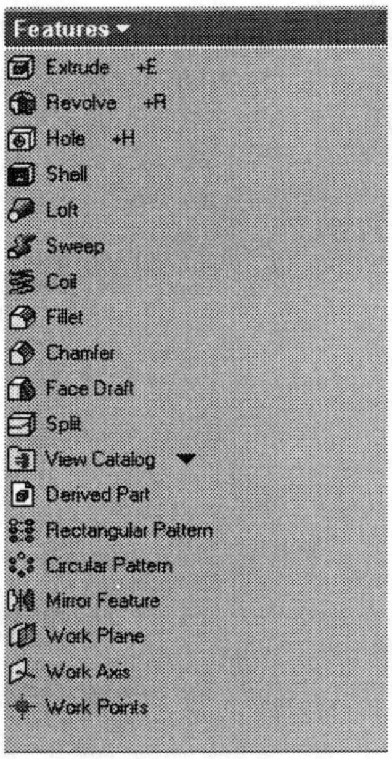

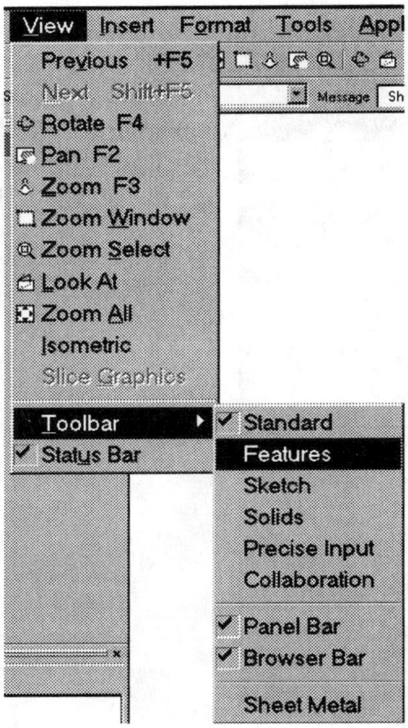

The Features toolbar should appear.

TIP: To hide the text next to the tool icons, switch to EXPERT mode. Select the panel bar, right click and select EXPERT.

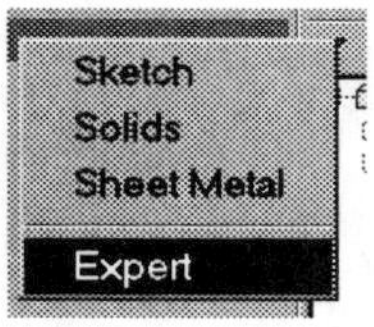

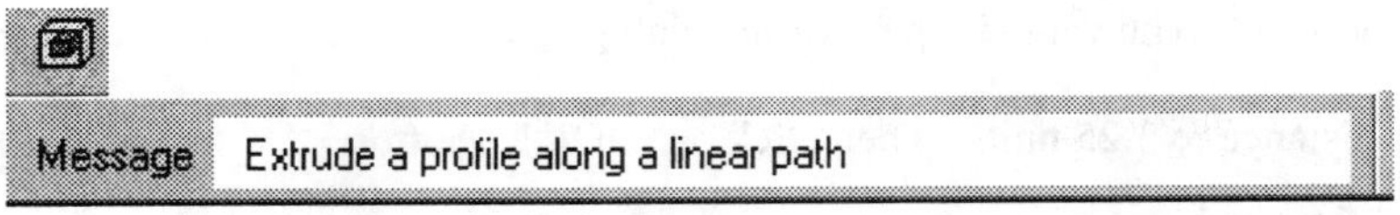

We select the Extrude icon located in the Features toolbar. Note that when we move the mouse over the Extrude icon, the message changes in the Message box to indicate what the Extrude icon does. The Extrude icon is selected by picking it with the left mouse button.

TIP: The +E next to the Extrude icon means that typing the letter E on the keyboard will also initiate the EXTRUDE command.

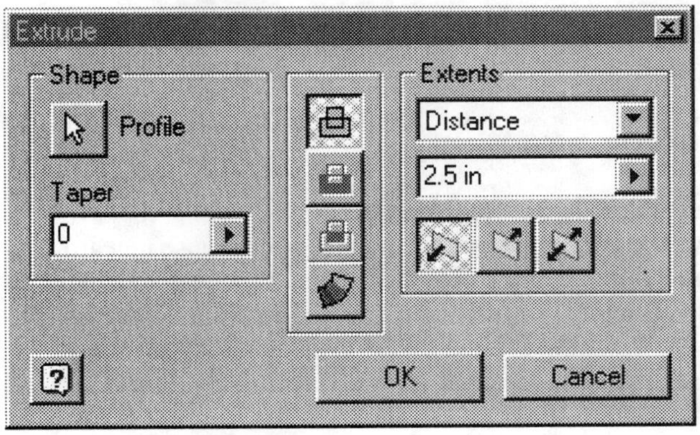

Select 'Distance' under Extents and enter '2.5' as the value.
Refer to the dialog box shown.

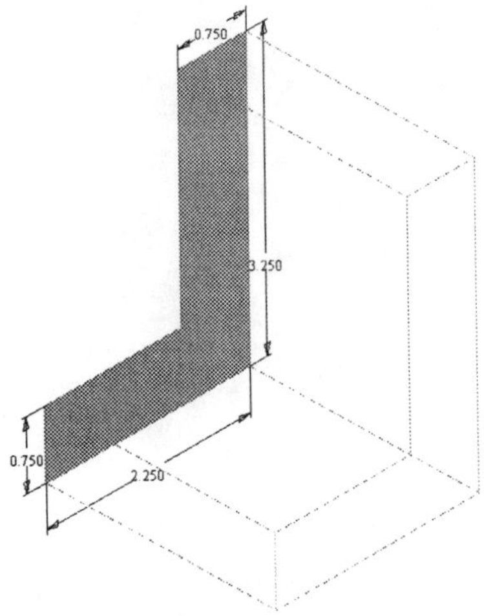

We see a preview of what the extrude will look like. Note that we can modify the distance by using the mouse in the Drawing Screen area.

To do this, simply place the mouse near one of the outer corners and hold down the left mouse button. Now drag the mouse back and forth. The value in the Extrude dialog box will automatically update.

Using your mouse, set your distance to 3.25 units. Then click on the 'OK' button.

Our extruded part.

Dynamic Viewing Functions – Realtime Zoom

 Click on the Zoom Realtime icon in the Standard toolbar area.
Inside the Drawing Screen area, hold down the left mouse button and move the mouse upward. Next move the mouse downward. Note how the size of the object changes. We are not actually scaling or modifying the part size. We are changing our perspective view. Imagine holding a part at arms-length and then moving the part closer to our face. This is what the Zoom Realtime does.

Right-click the mouse.

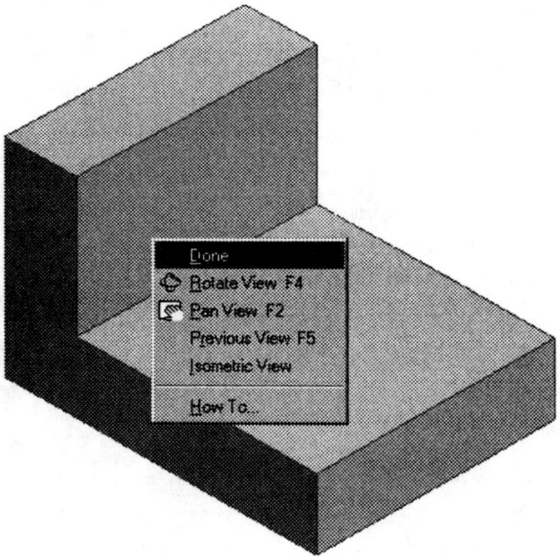

A pop-up menu appears that provides several View Options. Select the 'Pan View' option.

Our mouse icon changes from an arrow to a small hand. Imagine a piece of paper on our desk and using our hand to move the paper around the tabletop. This is what 'pan' does. The size of our object does not change, but we can shift its position inside our Drawing Screen area.

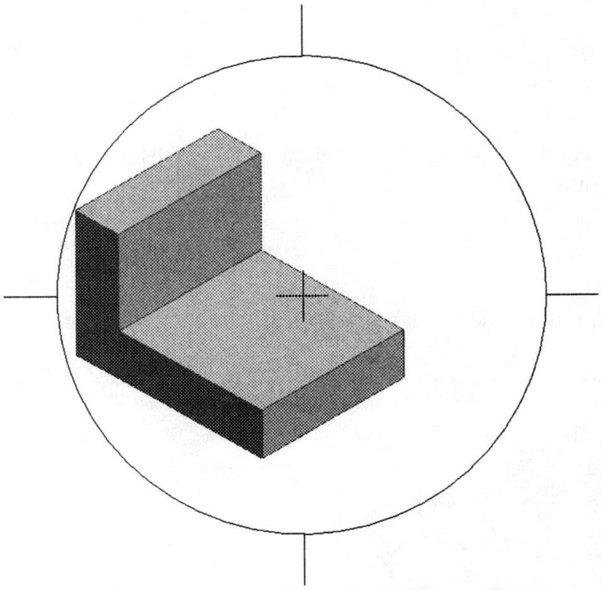

Right-click the mouse again and select 'Rotate View'. The 'Rotate View' displays an arcball, which is a circle divided into four quadrants. This enables us to manipulate the view of 3D objects by clicking and dragging with the left-mouse button.

Inside the arcball, press down the left-mouse button and drag it up and down to rotate about the X-axis.

Move the cursor to different locations on the screen, such as outside the arcball or on one of the four small tickmarks, and experiment with the real-time dynamic rotation feature.

Note: The graphics card installed on the computer system as well as the amount of memory installed will affect how well the dynamic rotation feature works.

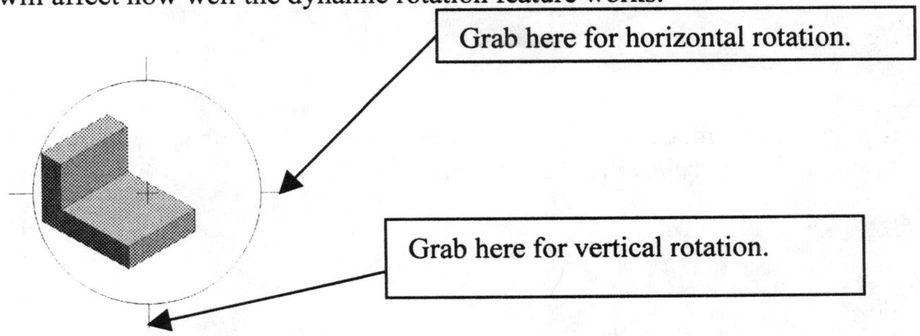

TIP: To rotate the model in the horizontal direction, grab one of the horizontal bars. To rotate the model in the vertical direction, grab one of the vertical bars.

Use the 3D Rotate button on the Standard toolbar to:

- Rotate a part or assembly in the graphics window
- Display standard isometric and orthographic views of a part or assembly.

Rotation can be around the center mark, free in all directions, or around the X or Y axes in the 3D Rotate symbol view. You can rotate the view while other tools are active.

TIP: The 3D Rotate tool remembers the last mode used when you exit the command. When the command is active, press the spacebar to switch modes.

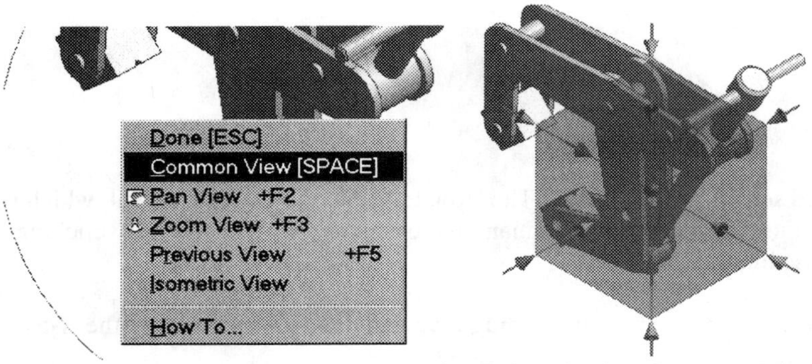

To switch to Common View mode, right click and select Common View from the menu or press the space bar. Common View mode allows the user to quickly switch view orientations. Simply pick on the arrow to select the desired view.

Changing the Appearance of the Model

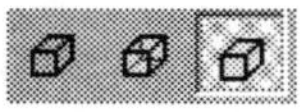

Inventor comes with three modes for model appearance: Wire frame, Hidden, and Shaded. To change the mode, use the left mouse button to select the desired mode.

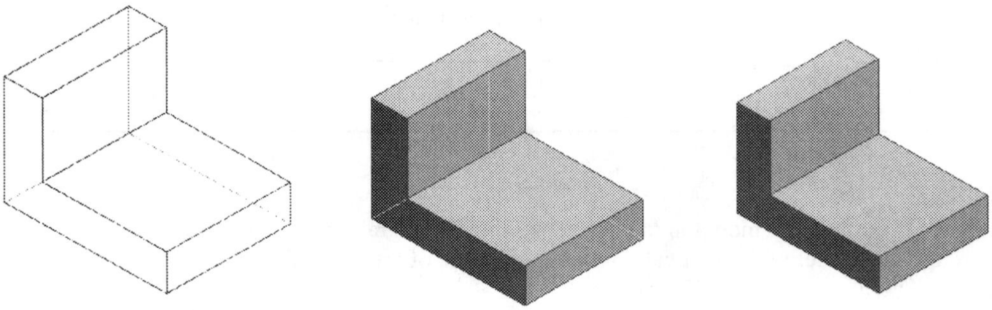

Our model in all three modes: Wire frame, Hidden Edge, and Shaded.

Save the file as 'lesson1.ipt'.

Review Questions

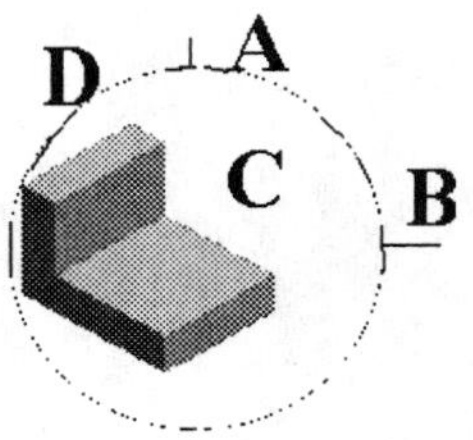

1. Select the area to rotate the model in a horizontal direction.

2. The shortcut key to place a General Dimension is:

   A. I
   B. G
   C. D
   D. GD

3. To edit or modify a dimension:

   A. Left pick on a dimension and type in the edit box.
   B. Right pick on a dimension and select Edit from the menu.
   C. Select the Edit Dimension tool.
   D. Select Edit Dimension from the Menu.

4. To quickly switch to an Isometric View:

   A. Right click anywhere in the drawing window and select 'Isometric View' from the menu.
   B. Select the Isometric View tool from the View toolbar.
   C. Select the 3D Orbit tool, right click and select 'Isometric View.'
   D. Select Isometric View from the View menu.

5. To draw a line, you should be in this mode:

   A. Sketch
   B. Features
   C. Solids
   D. Assembly

6. The three modes of appearance for a model are:

   A. Wire Frame, Hidden, Shaded with Edges On
   B. Wire Frame, Shaded, Colored
   C. Wire Frame, Hidden, Rendered
   D. Wire Frame, Hidden, Shaded

7. To prevent constraints from automatically being added to a sketch:

   A. Turn off constraint mode under Options.
   B. Hold down the CONTROL key while sketching.
   C. Hold down the ALT key while sketching.
   D. You can not prevent constraints from being added.

8. The file extension for an Inventor part file is:

   A. ipt
   B. dwg
   C. iam
   D. ipn

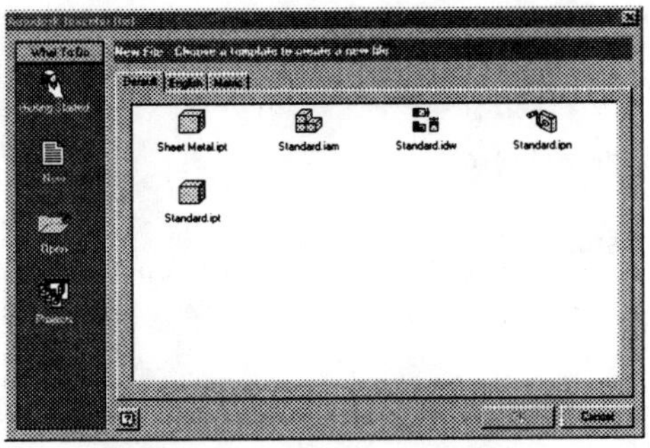

9. The files displayed in the start up dialog are:

   A. Dummy files
   B. Blank files
   C. Templates with default settings
   D. Transparent files – they don't exist, they are just icons used for starting a new file

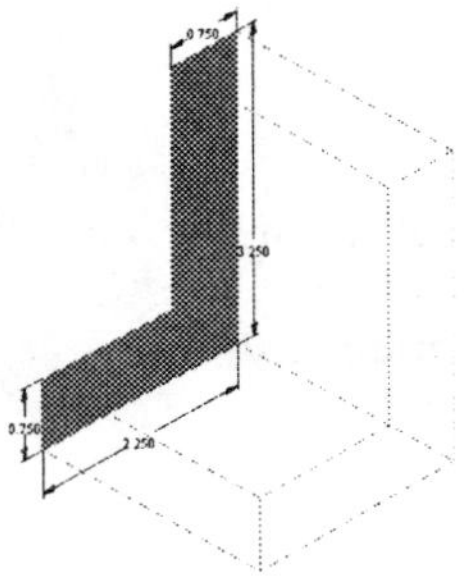

10. To change the extrusion distance:

    A. Modify the value in the distance edit box of the Extrude dialog box
    B. Use the mouse to drag the extrusion into position
    C. Right click on the extrusion and enter a value.
    D. A & B but not C.

ANSWERS: 1) B; 2) C; 3) A; 4) A; 5) A; 6) D; 7) B; 8) A; 9) C; 10) D

Lesson 2

Work Features

Learning Objectives

When you have completed this lesson, you will:

- Have an understanding of Work Planes, Work Axis, and Work Points
- Be able to create a Work Features
- Be able to modify a Work Features

In most 3-D geometric modelers, 3-D objects are located and defined in what is usually called **world space** or **global space**. This space is usually a 3-D **Cartesian coordinate system** that the user cannot modify.

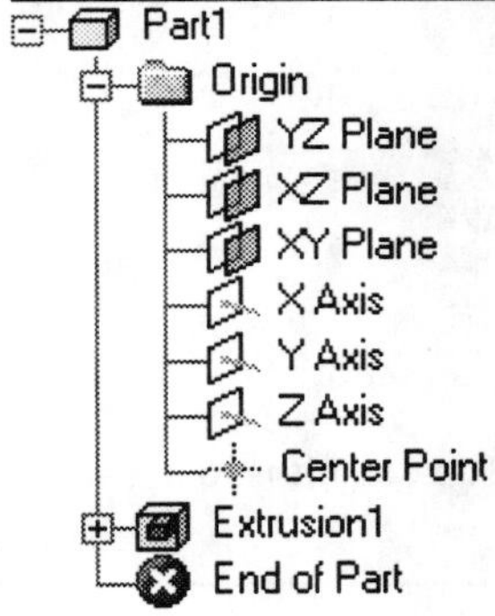

If we create a new part file in Inventor, we first look in the Browser area. There we see that Inventor automatically created an XY Plane, an XZ Plane, a YZ Plane, an X axis, a Y axis, a Z axis, and a Center Point.

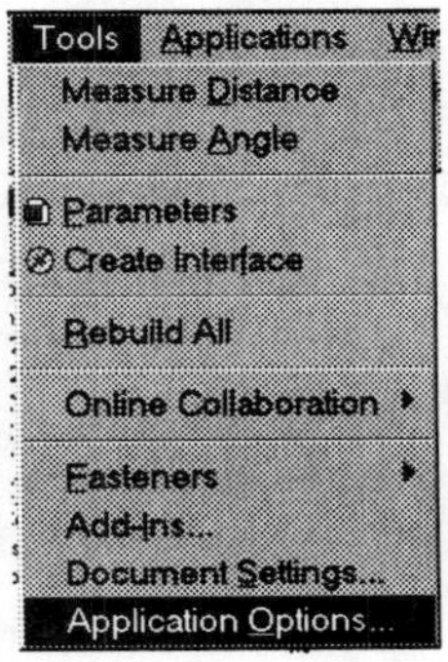

To explore further, we go to the menu and select Tools->Application Options.

An Options Dialog box will appear.
Select the Part tab.

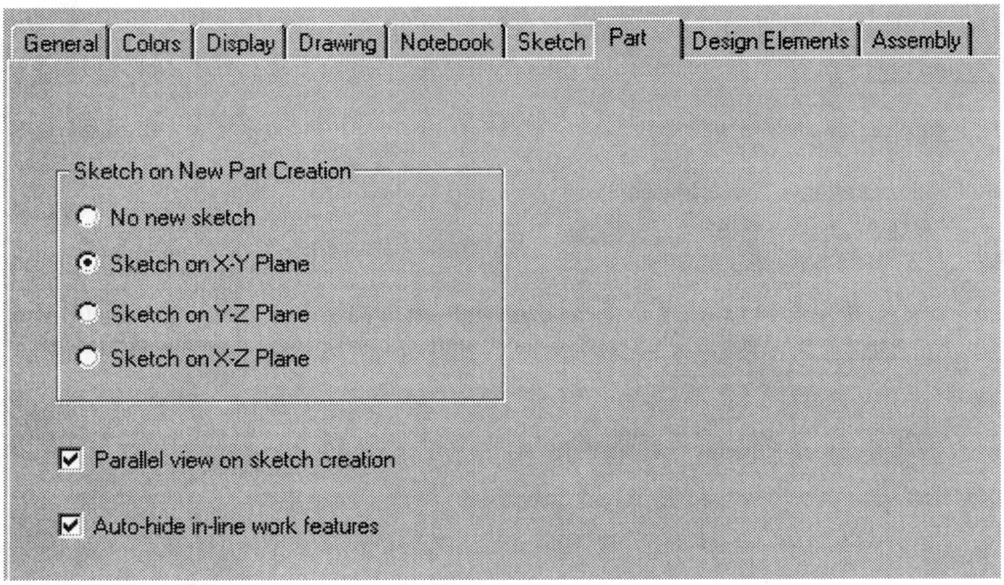

Note that we can select which plane we would like to start all new part creation. The default is to use the XY plane.

TIP: Enable the box that says 'Parallel view on sketch creation' to automatically switch to PLAN view when starting a sketch.

If we switch to Isometric View (right-click the mouse and select 'Isometric View'), then highlight each plane in the Browser; we see each plane highlighted in our Drawing Screen area.

The XY Plane should be considered the Front Plane. The XZ Plane should be considered the Top Plane. The YZ Plane should be considered the Right Side Plane.

TIP: It may be helpful to beginners to change the names of the planes in your browser and save a part template file with the new names.

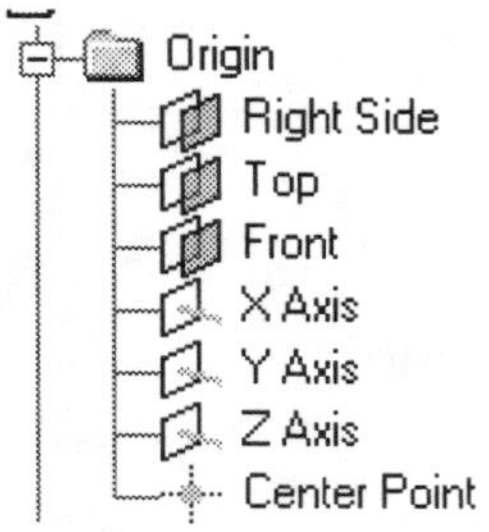

The names of the planes can be changed by left clicking on top of the text.

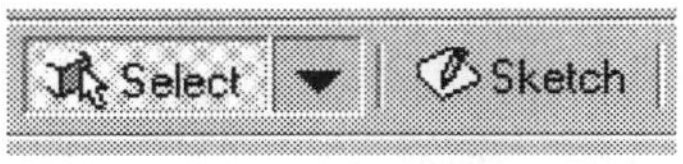

To draw a sketch on a specific plane, make sure 'Select' is enabled and Sketch is disabled in the Command Bar.

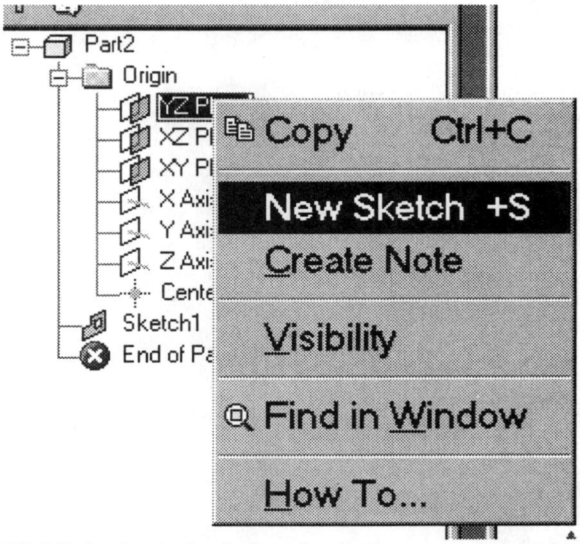

Highlight the desired plane in the Browser, then right-click the mouse to bring up the pop-up menu. Select 'New Sketch' and the sketch plane will automatically switch to that selected plane.

A work plane is an infinite construction plane that is parametrically attached to a part. Work planes can be placed at any orientation in space, offset from existing part faces, or rotated around an axis or edge in a part face. A work plane can be designated as a sketch plane and can be dimensioned or constrained to other features.Selecting different geometry combinations yields different work plane orientations. Each work plane has its own internal coordinate system. The order in which geometry is selected determines the origin and positive directions the coordinate system axes.

A work plane can be created in-line, while you are using another work feature command. You can create a work plane when the feature command expects you to select a point, line, or plane. When you activate the work plane tool in-line, to respond to the feature command, it terminates as soon as the work plane is created.

TIP: If shading is on, work planes are translucent; otherwise they are transparent.

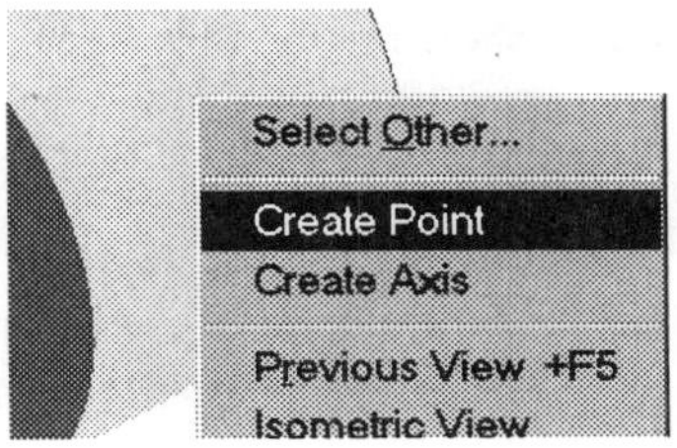

When you select any work feature tool, a right click will bring up a menu that allows the user to switch between work feature creation tools.

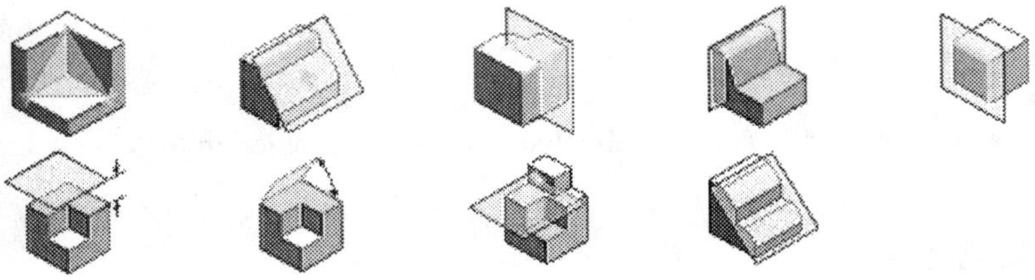

There are several different types of work plane options available in Inventor.

- 3 Point
- Tangent to a Face through an Edge
- Normal to an Axis through a Point
- Normal to a Face through an Edge
- Two Coplanar Edges
- Offset
- Face-Angle
- Parallel to a Face through a Point
- Tangent to a Curve Parallel to a Face

1. Open the lesson1.ipt file created in Lesson 1.

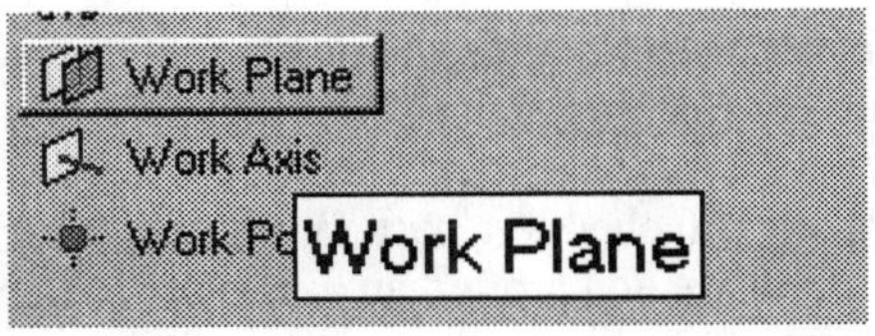

The Features toolbar needs to be visible to access the Work Plane tool. Refer to Lesson 1 on how to bring up the Feature toolbar.

Creating Edge/Edge Work Plane

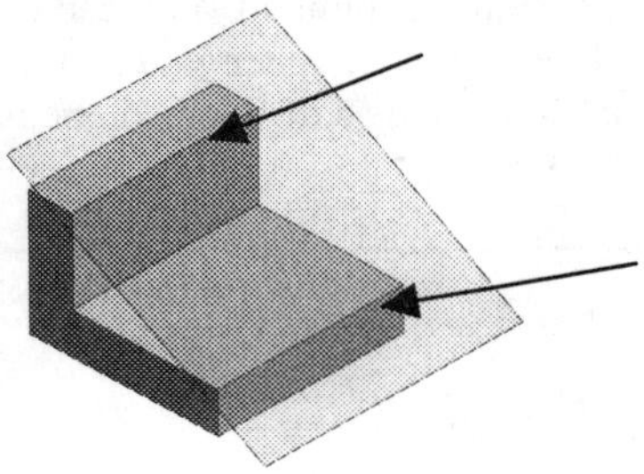

Select the Work Plane tool. Pick the two edges indicated. Use the messages shown in the Message bar to aid you in construction of the work plane.

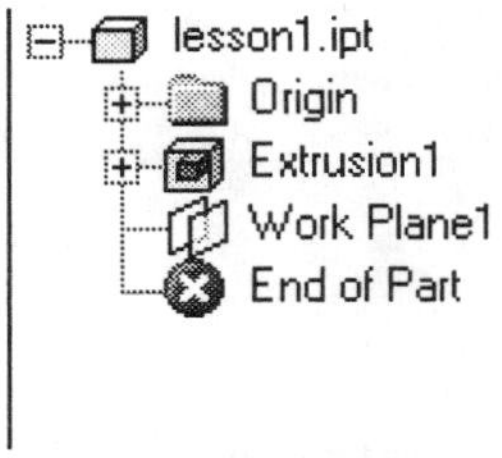

You will see the new Work Plane defined in the Browser.

Modifying a Work Plane

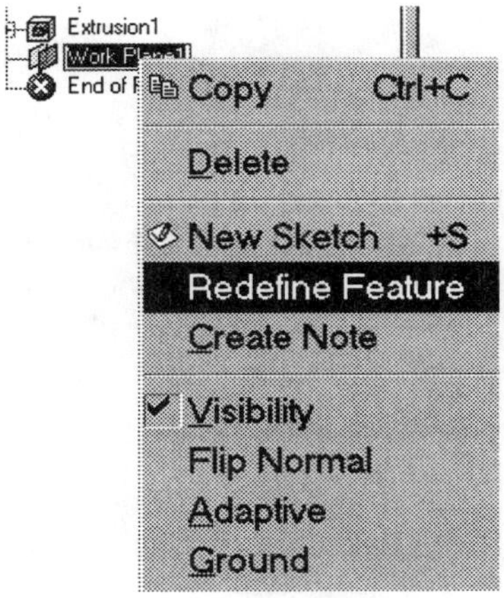

Some modeling software packages require the user to delete work planes that are improperly defined. Inventor allows the user to redefine work planes easily.

Highlight the Work Plane in the Browser. Right click and select 'Redefine Feature.'

Creating Edge/Angle Work Plane

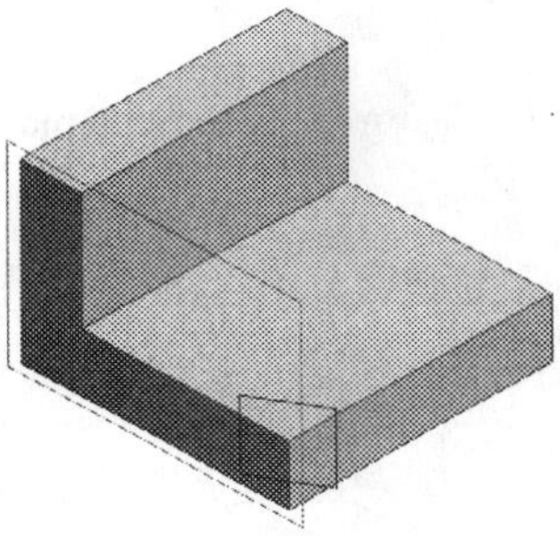

Select the edge shown. Click twice to see the message displayed.

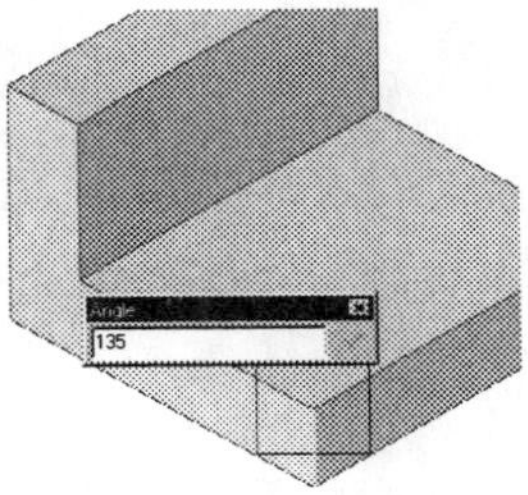

An Angle edit box appears. Type in different values, i.e. 135, 45, 25, and 30. Observe how the plane updates as each value is entered. Type in 60 and then press the green check mark to end the definition.

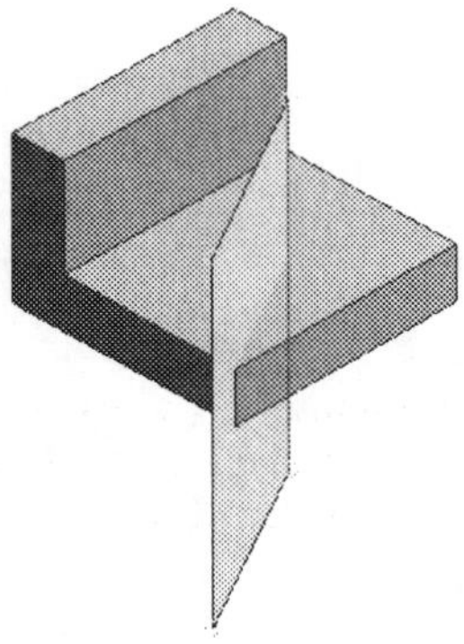

Select the plane created by placing the mouse over the work plane and holding down the left mouse button. Move the mouse up and down and observe how the plane moves along with the mouse.

When the plane is positioned to your satisfaction, release the left mouse button.

Creating an Offset Work Plane

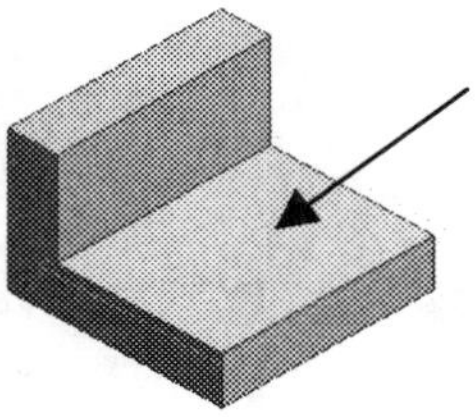

Highlight the Work Plane in the Browser. Right click and select 'Redefine Feature.' Select the plane indicated. With the left mouse button held down, move the work plane up.

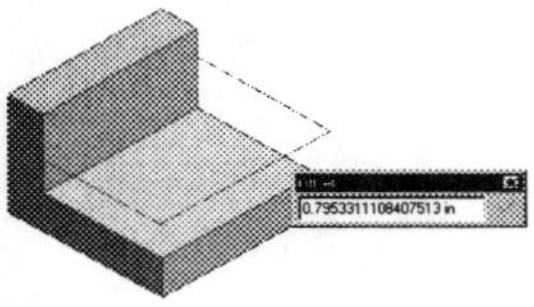

An Offset edit box appears. You have the option of using the mouse to place the work plane or entering a value in the edit box. Type various values in the edit box and observe how the work plane automatically updates. Finish by typing the value '2' and clicking the green check mark.

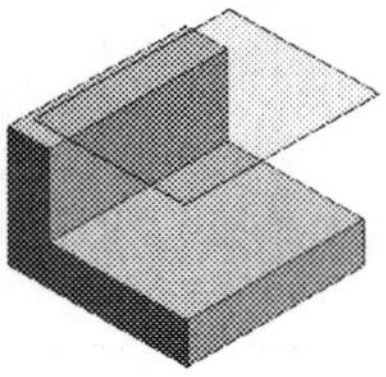

 **Work Axis**

A work axis is a construction line of infinite length that is parametrically attached to a part. Access: Click the Work Axis tool on the Feature toolbar.

A work axis can be created in-line, while you are using another work feature command. You can create a work axis when the feature command expects you to select a point, line, or plane. When you activate the work axis tool in-line to respond to the feature command, the work axis tool terminates as soon as the axis is created.

A work axis can be created using the following methods:

- Through a revolved or cylindrical feature
- Two points
- Two intersecting planes
- Perpendicular to a point

To create a work axis using two points:

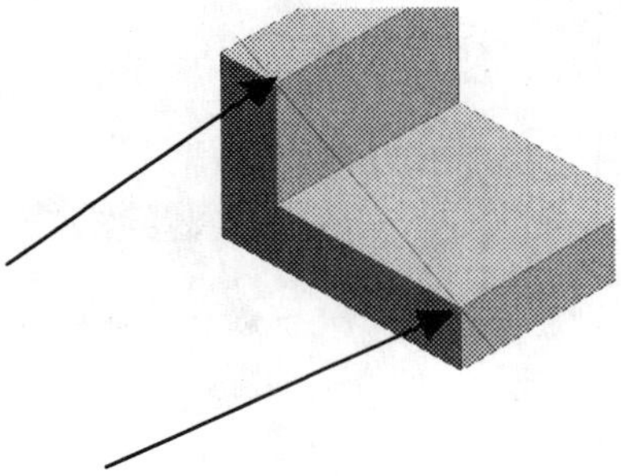

Select the Work Axis tool. Pick two points. The points will highlight to aid in selection.

TIP: A work axis created with two points will have its positive direction oriented in the direction from the first point selected to the second point.

To create a work axis through a point:

Select the top plane of the bracket by picking on it with the left mouse button. Right click and select 'New Sketch' from the pop up menu to create a 'New Sketch'.

Select the Point tool and locate a point as shown.

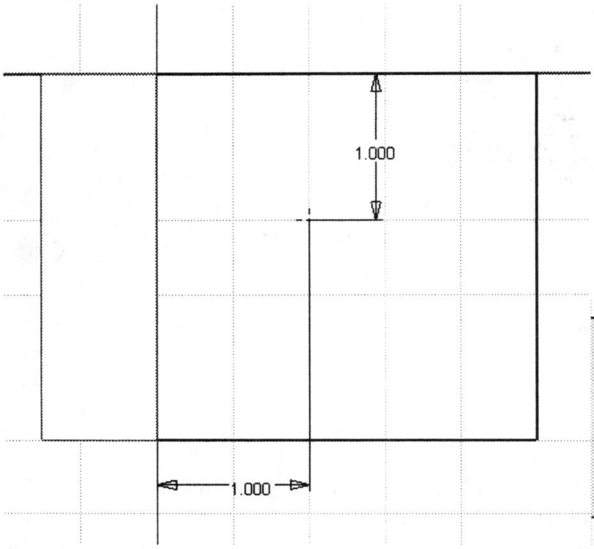

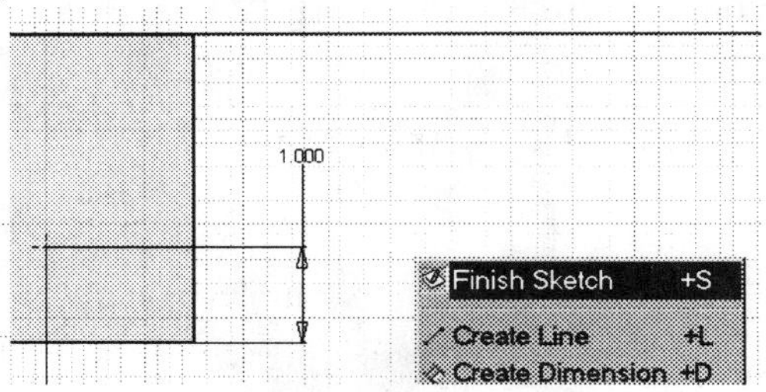

Right click and select 'Done'. Right click again and select 'Finish Sketch'.
Switch back to an Isometric View by right clicking and selecting 'Isometric View.'

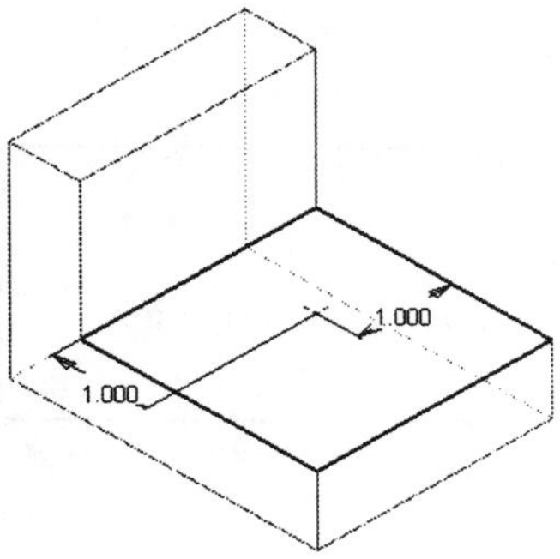

Select the Work Axis tool.

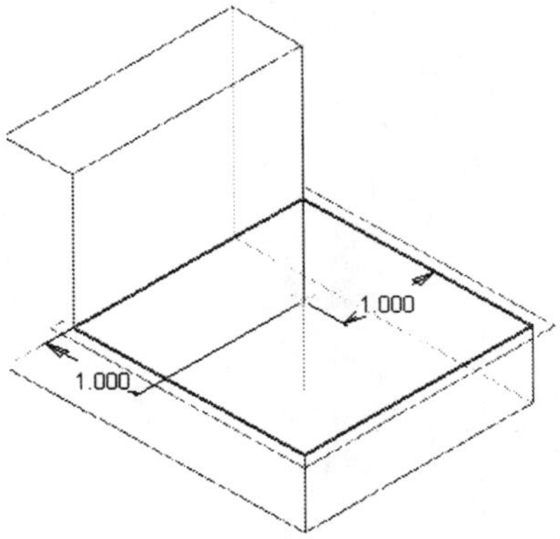

Select the point and a Work Axis will be placed.

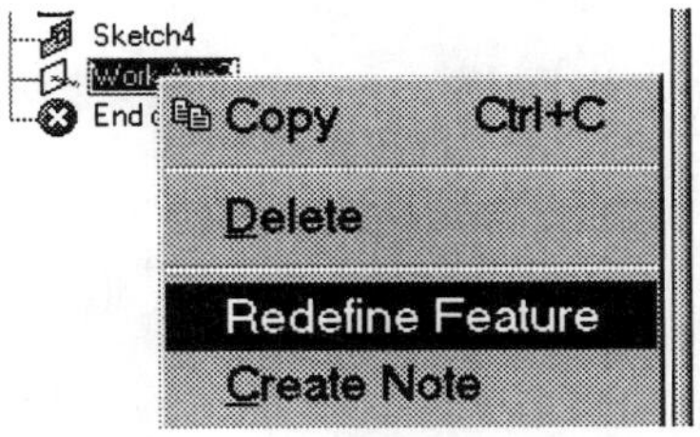

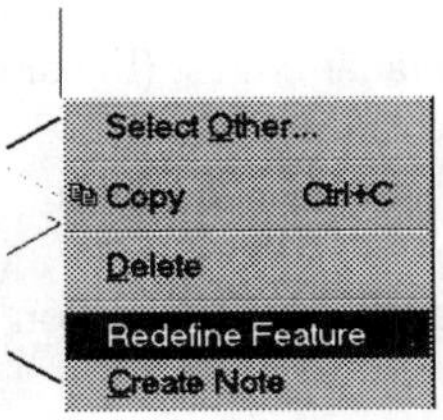

To modify or delete the work axis, simply select the work axis in the browser or in the drawing window; right click and select the desired option.

Work Points

A work point is a parametric construction point that can be placed anywhere on part geometry or in 3D space. A work point can be created in-line, while you are using another feature command. You can create a work point when you need to select a point, line, or plane. When you create a work point in-line, to respond to the feature command, it terminates as soon as the work point is created.

When you create work points independent of a feature command, you can create multiple work points.

You can move the cursor over the model to highlight valid work point locations.

Click one of the following geometric elements of the active part or feature to place the work point:

- Midpoint of a curve or an edge
- Endpoint of a curve or an edge
- Center of an arc, circle, or ellipse
- Planar face or work plane

Work points can be created using the following methods:

- Intersection of three planes
- Offset from two edges
- Projected from a plane
- Two projected edges
- Intersection of any plane and edge
- Intersection of any two edges
- Intersection of any three planes
- Projected intersection of two coplanar edges, (linear or curved)

Save the file as 'lesson2.ipt' using the 'Save Copy As' option under File.

TIP: When you use 'Save Copy As' your current file's name does not change nor is the current file saved. You are saving a copy of the current file under a new name.

Review Questions

1. Inventor automatically creates all of the following features EXCEPT:

   A. XY Plane
   B. XZ Plane
   C. Origin
   D. Z axis

2. When creating a new part, the default sketch plane is:

   A. XY Plane
   B. XZ Plane
   C. YZ Plane
   D. There is no default sketch plane.

3. To have the view automatically switch to PLAN view when starting a sketch:

   A. Enable 'Parallel view on Sketch Creation' under the Part tab in the Options dialog
   B. Use the 'Look At' tool.
   C. Use the '3D Rotate' tool.
   D. Type '9'.

4. To sketch on a the XZ plane:

   A. Highlight the XZ plane in the browser, right click and select 'New Sketch'.
   B. You can only sketch on the XZ plane if there is a feature located on that plane.
   C. Delete all existing features, start a new part file and set the default sketch plane to XZ Plane.
   D. Go to Options and select XZ Plane.

5. Work Planes are visible when:

   A. Visibility is turned ON and Hidden mode is ENABLED.
   B. Visibility is turned OFF and Shaded mode is ENABLED.
   C. Visibility is turned ON and Wire Frame mode is ENABLED.
   D. Visibility is turned ON and Shaded mode is ENABLED.

6. When placing a work feature, such as Work Plane, the user can switch to create a Work Axis by:

   A. Select the Work Axis tool.
   B. Press the space bar.
   C. Press the tab key.
   D. Right click and select Work Axis from the menu.

7. Work Planes can be created in all the ways listed below EXCEPT:

   A. 3 Point
   B. Projected two offset planes
   C. Offset
   D. Face-Angle

8. The Work Features tools are located on:

   A. The Sketch Toolbar
   B. The Assembly Toolbar
   C. The Features Toolbar
   D. The Drawing Annotation Toolbar

9. To modify a Work Feature:

   A. Select the Work Feature in the browser, right click and select 'Edit'.
   B. Select the Work Feature in the drawing window, right click and select 'Edit'.
   C. Select the Work Feature in the browser or the drawing window, right click and select 'Redefine Feature'.
   D. Select 'Modify' from the menu and then select the work feature.

10. A work axis created with two points:

   A. Has the positive direction oriented in the direction from the first point to the second point.
   B. Has the positive direction oriented in the direction from the second point to the first point.
   C. Has the positive direction oriented in the direction of the Z axis.
   D. Has no positive/negative direction. It's an axis.

ANSWERS: 1) C; 2) A; 3) A; 4) A; 5) D; 6) D; 7) B; 8) C; 9) C; 10) A

Lesson 3

User Interface

Learning Objectives

Upon completion of this lesson, the user will be able to:

- Enable/Disable Toolbars
- Control Display Colors
- Modify System Settings

Autodesk Inventor adheres to Microsoft Windows standards and features user interface elements common to Windows-based applications.

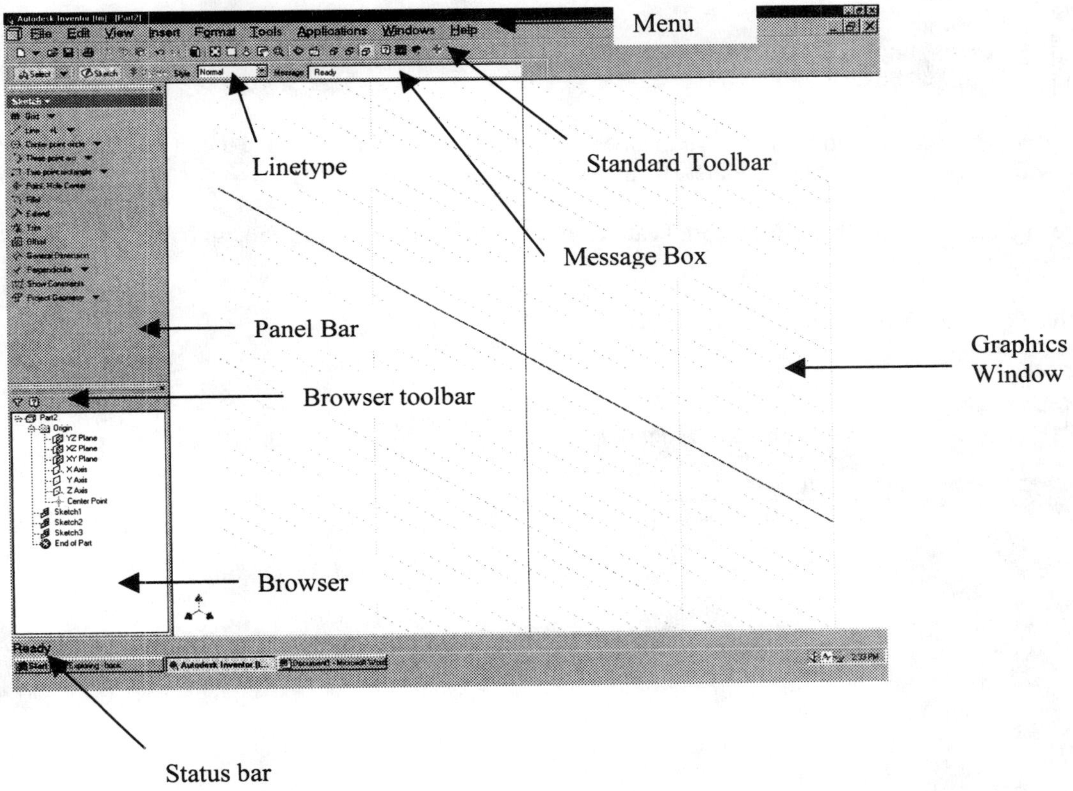

The user interface within Inventor is completely customizable. Experiment by pulling and dragging the toolbars and placing them in different areas of the screen.

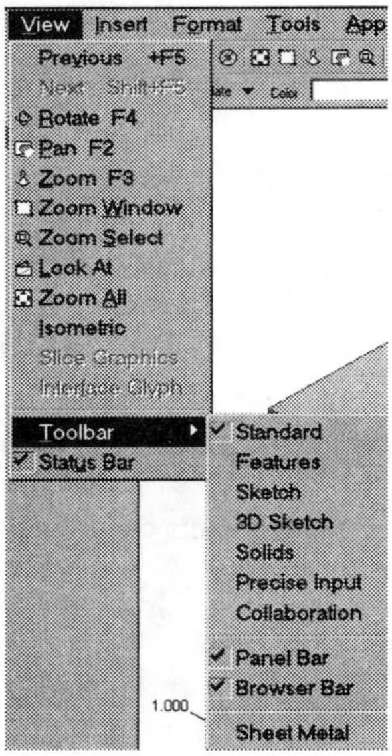

You can access the various toolbars through the menu using View->Toolbar. Disable the Status Bar and notice how it disappears. Disable the Panel Bar and the Browser Bar.

There are eight standard toolbars: Standard, Features, Sketch, 3D Sketch, Solids, Precise Input, Collaboration, and Sheet Metal.

Enable the Sketch toolbar and then enable the panel bar.
Compare the two.

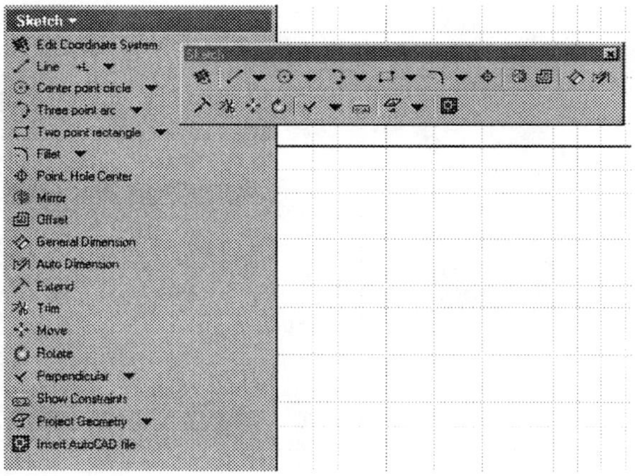

Note how the Sketch toolbar takes up less space than the Panel Bar. The Panel Bar has more information.

TIP: Use the Panel Bar while you are learning. Once you gain familiarity with the various icons, disable the Panel Bar and enable the toolbars to conserve space on your desktop.

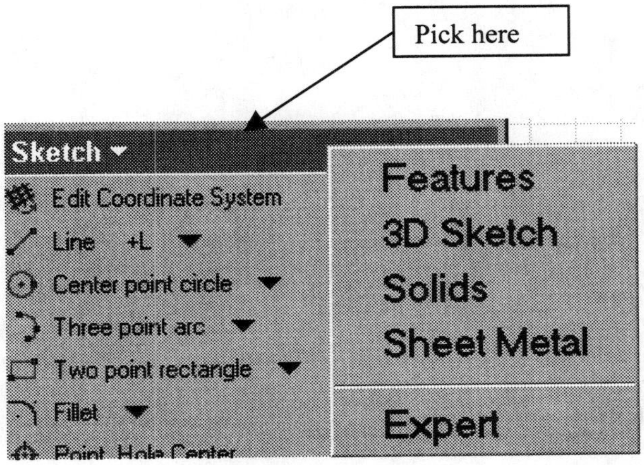

TIP: A left mouse pick on the grey bar at the top of the panel bar allows the user quickly to switch between Panel Bars.

The Properties Dialog Box

Selecting the Properties item from the File Menu allows the user to set up file statistics as well as material properties for sheet metal parts.

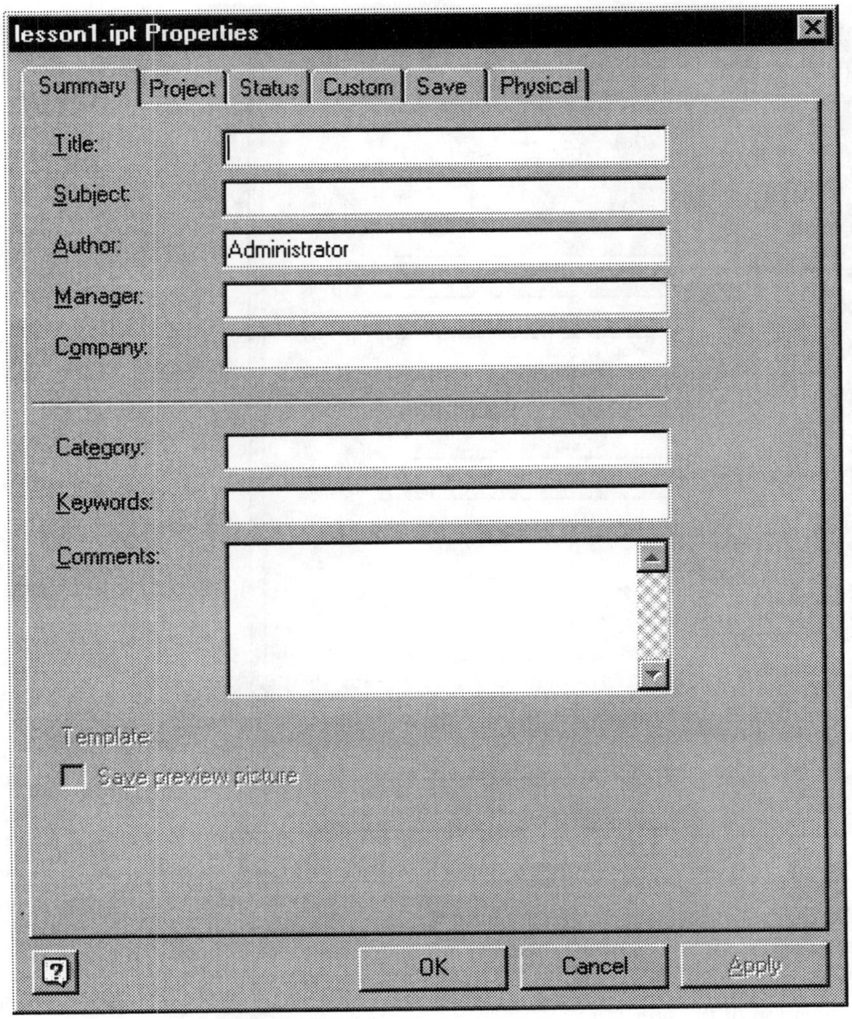

Summary Tab

The Summary window defines summary properties for the selected part, assembly, drawing, or template file. You can use summary properties to classify and manage your Autodesk Inventor files, search for files, create reports, and automatically update title blocks and parts lists in drawings and bills of materials in assemblies. Enter the desired information in the boxes.

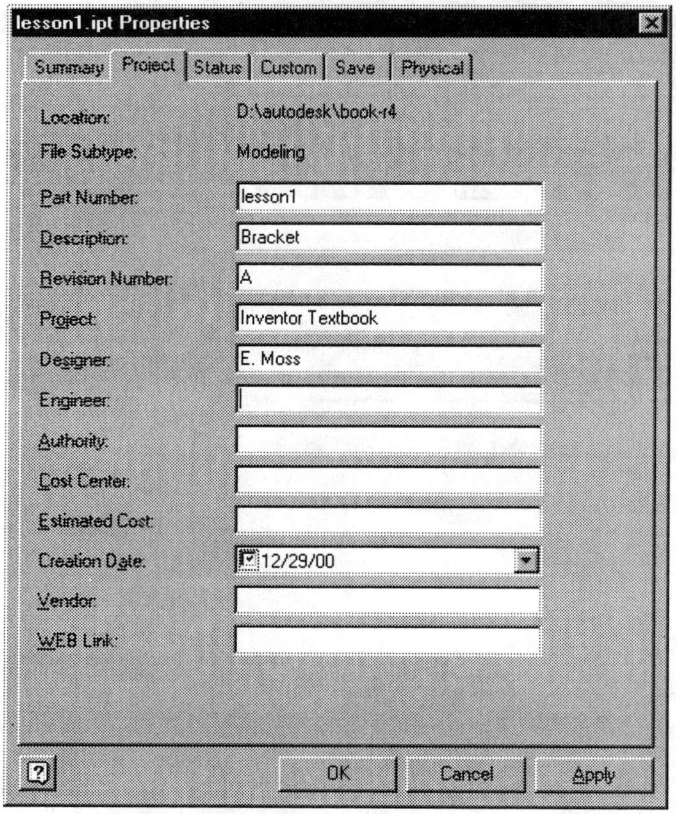

Project Tab

The Project window allows the user to embed additional data into the file. This information can be extracted for use in a document control system or used when performing a search for a specific file.

Location	Displays the location of the selected file.
File Subtype	Displays the Autodesk Inventor file type for the selected file.
Part Number	Specifies the part number. If you do not enter a part number, the file name is automatically assigned as the part number.
Description	Adds a description for a part or assembly file.
Revision Number	Specifies the revision number of the file.
Project	Specifies a project name.
Designer	Specifies the name of the drafter/designer.
Engineer	Specifies the name of the cognizant engineer.
Authority	Specifies the name of the project/team leader.
Cost Center	Specifies a cost center.
Estimated Cost	Assigns a cost to the file. Enter a real number.
Creation Date	Shows the date that Autodesk Inventor created the file. To change the date, click the arrow and select a new date.
Vendor	Manufacturer or supplier name for components obtained from a third party.
WEB Link	Displays a Web site address.

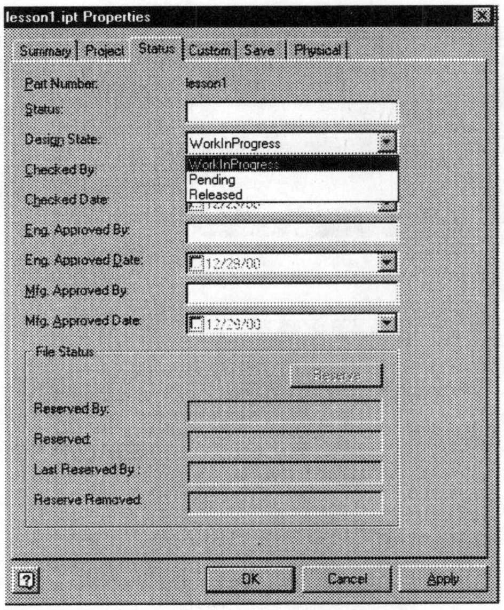

Status Tab

The Status Window can be incorporated into an Engineering Control process. Files could be attached to an ECO and signed off in this window by appropriate personnel.

Part Number	Displays the Part Number that is set on the Project tab.
Status	Sets the status for the file. You can enter any status classification.
Design State	Design State allows the user to set where the file is in process. Options are Work In Progress, Pending or Released.
Checked By	Names the person who checked the file.
Checked Date	Shows the date that the file was checked. To change the date, click the arrow and select a date.
Eng Approved By	Names the person who approved the file for Engineering.
Eng Approved Date	Shows the date that the file was approved in Engineering. To change the date, click the arrow and select a date.
Mfg Approved By	Names the person who approved the file for Manufacturing.
Mfg Approved Date	Shows the date that the file was approved for Manufacturing. To change the date, click the arrow and select a date.
File Status	Shows the reservation status of the file for collaborative projects. You can also set the reservation status. To use the reservation option, you must first select the Multi User option in Autodesk Inventor. Select Tools>Options>General tab and then select the Multi User check box. Reserve/Unreserve Sets the file status. When you change the status to Reserved, your name and the current date are entered in the appropriate boxes. Click the button to switch the status. Reserved By If the file is currently reserved shows the name of the person who reserved it. Reserved If the file is currently reserved, shows the date that it was reserved. Last Reserved By Shows the user name of the last person to reserve the file if the file is not currently reserved. Reserve Removed Shows the date that the reserve status was removed from the file if the file is not currently reserved.

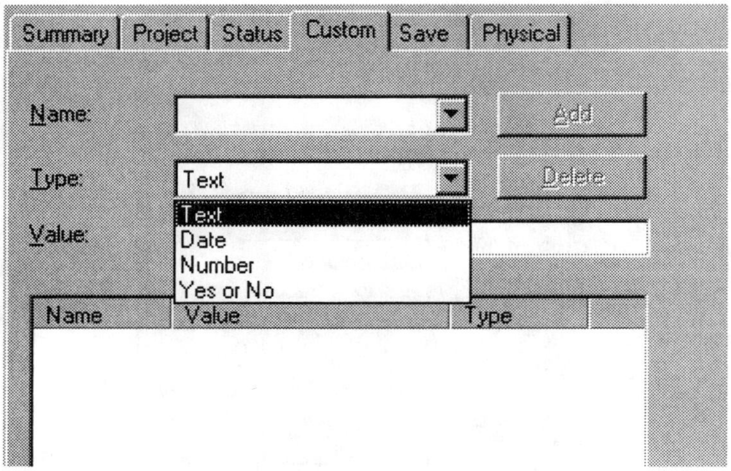

Custom Tab

Adds custom properties to the selected part, assembly, drawing, or template file. You can use custom properties to classify and manage your Autodesk Inventor files, search for files, create reports, and automatically update title blocks and parts lists in drawings and bills of materials in assemblies.

Name	Specifies a name for a new custom property or selects an existing custom property for editing. Enter the name or click the arrow and select from the list.
Type	Sets the data type for the property. Click the arrow and select from the list. Options include Text, Date, Number, and Yes or No.
Value	Specifies the value for the property in the selected file. The value must conform to the selected data type.
Properties	Lists the custom properties currently defined in the selected file.
Add/Modify	Updates the Properties List with the changes to Name, Type, or Value.
Delete	Deletes the selected property from the Properties list.

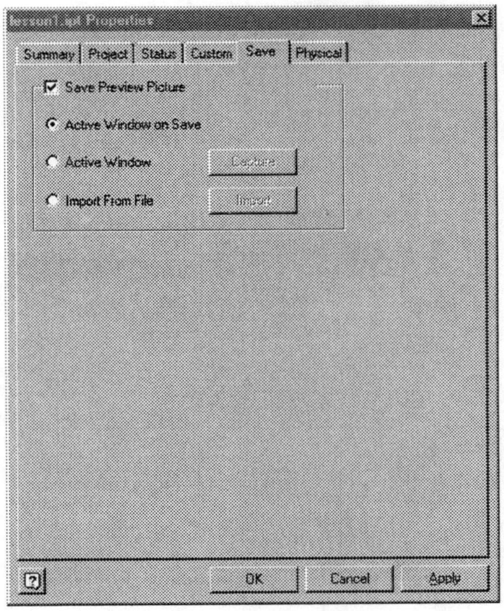

Save Tab

You can show a thumbnail image of the model in the preview pane on the File Open dialog. Specifies the origin of the preview image of the model.

Save Preview Picture	Saves a thumbnail image of the model so that it appears on the File Open dialog box. The default is on. In order to select any remaining options, this option must be selected.
Active Window on Save	Sets thumbnail image to the view in the graphics window when the file is saved.
Active Window	Click Capture button to set thumbnail image to the view in the active graphics window.
Import From File	Imports thumbnail BMP image from a file. Click Import to browse to the file containing the image. Image must be 120 x 120 pixels.

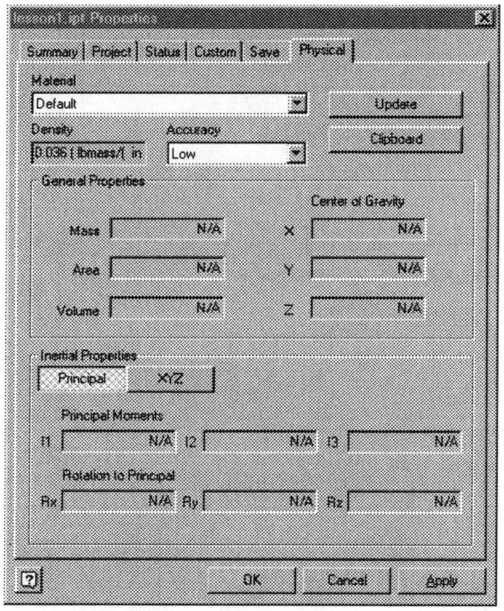

Physical Tab

The Physical Tab allows the user to assign physical properties to sheet metal for use in later analysis. This tab calculates physical and inertial properties for a part or assembly to demonstrate how differences in materials, analysis tolerances, and other values affect the model.

If you only need to calculate mass, surface area, and volume, you do not need to click Update. They are automatically calculated.

Physical properties are affected whenever you add, delete, or modify a feature on a part or add or delete a part from an assembly. Any time a change has occurred, you must click Update to recalculate. If required components are not loaded into memory, a message asks if you want to load them. When physical properties are up to date, the Update button is dimmed.

The clipboard is used to move a physical properties report to the Clipboard in Rich Text Format. You can open the report in a text editor and print it.	
Material	Material properties inherited from a part are used in calculations. Lists materials from the application material table. Material list is specified in default template files or in custom template files that specify custom materials.
Density	Lists the density for the selected material. The density of the default material is 1 kg/m^3.
Accuracy	Specifies the degree of accuracy for physical property calculations. The default setting is Low but you may specify greater level.
General Properties calculates mass, surface area, and volume of the selected part or assembly. Units are set to a default scheme during Autodesk Inventor installation. For files created using a template, units are those set in the template.	
Mass	Mass in default units or, if applicable, the units specified in the template.
Area	Surface area of the selected part or assembly.
Volume	Volume of the selected part or assembly.

<table>
<tr><td>Center of Gravity</td><td>Lists the x, y, z coordinates of the center of gravity of the selected component, relative to the assembly origin.</td></tr>
<tr><td colspan="2">Click Principal or XYZ to select the method for calculating inertial properties. Select a component and calculate physical properties to show results based on the component in its current state. Edit the occurrence and then calculate physical properties to show results in the assembly context.</td></tr>
<tr><td>Principal Moments</td><td>Calculates principal moments of inertia.</td></tr>
<tr><td>Rotation to principal</td><td>Calculates rotation to principal relative to the XYZ reference frame.</td></tr>
<tr><td>Mass Moments</td><td>Calculates mass moments relative to the XYZ reference frame.</td></tr>
</table>

TIP: You can search on materials to locate parts and assemblies that meet specified criteria. Searches are performed using the Design Assistant.

Projects

Inventor is unique in that it encourages the user to organize files into projects. Users may balk at first, but once you get into the habit of organizing your files into folders and subdirectories for each project you will appreciate the ease and efficiency created in locating and managing your files.

Projects are set up under File->Projects.

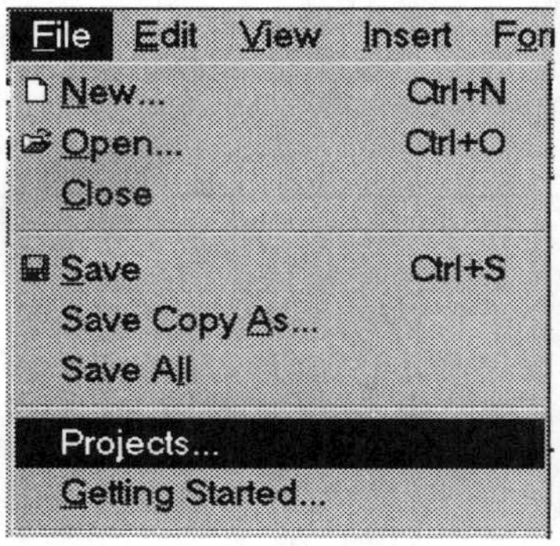

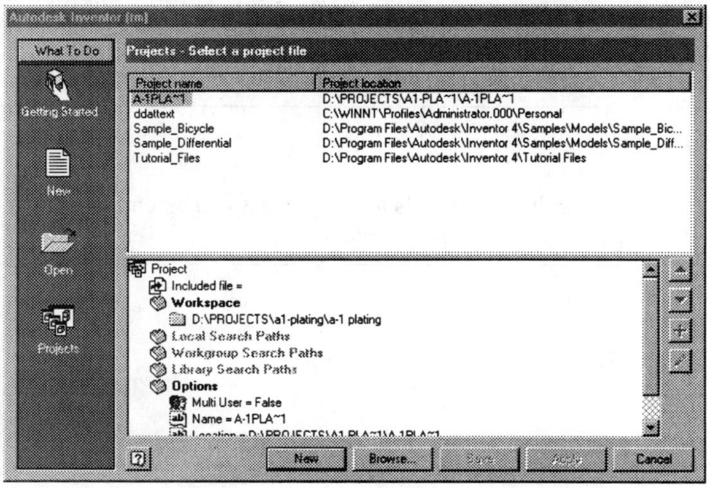

Projects are really just shortcut files that allow the user quickly to select the subdirectory where files are located.

Setting Up a Project

Select the New button in the Projects Dialog box.

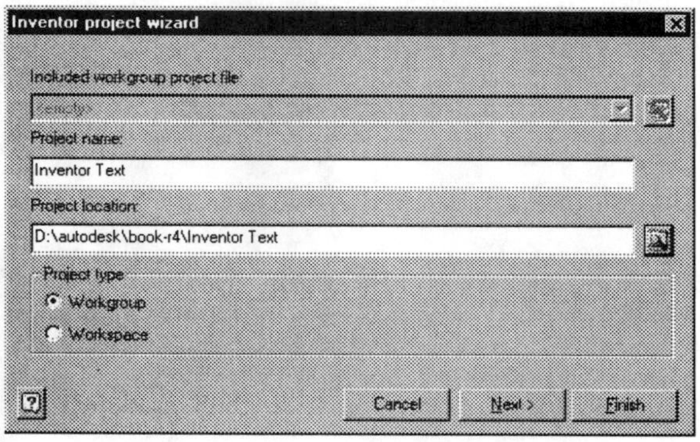

Project Name	Specifies a name for a new project. The name is applied to a new folder that is the location for the project and to the project file (.ipj) that specifies the valid file locations for the project. Enter a meaningful name.
Project Location	Specifies an existing folder in which to place the new project folder. Enter the full path to the folder or click Browse to find the desired folder.

You can set up a project as a work space or as a work group. Specifying a project as a Work Group means that files in that directory may be shared by a group. Inventor allows users to copy files into their work space (check them out), modify them, and then check them back in. Specifying a project as a work space assumes that a single user will be accessing the files.

Press the Next button.

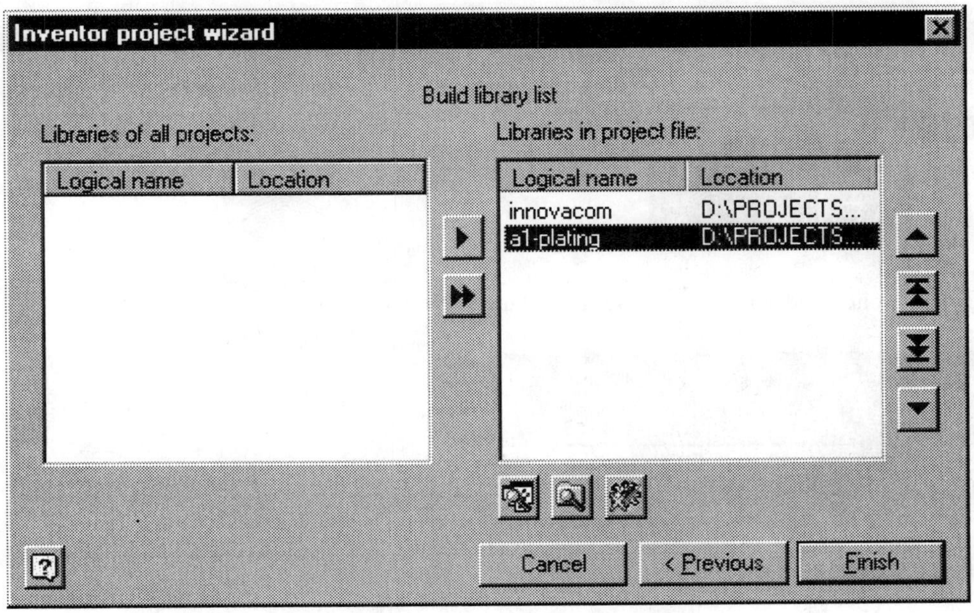

The next dialog box allows the user to specify subdirectories of other Inventor files that may be accessed for the current project.

Press Finish.

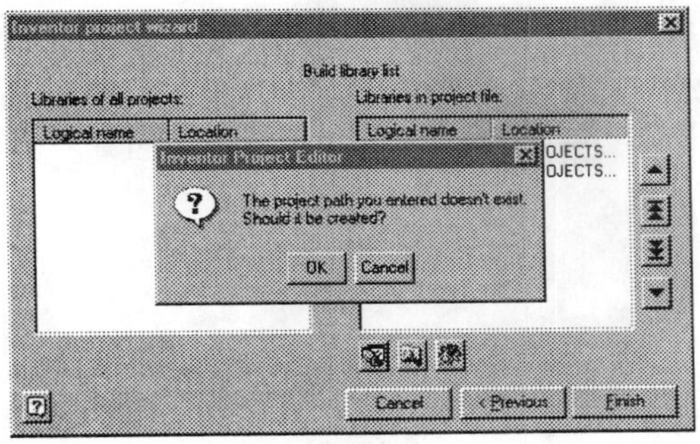

You will be asked if you want to create a new project path. Press 'OK'.

Project files are just text files. They are not mysterious at all. Locate the project file you just created in the directory you specified.

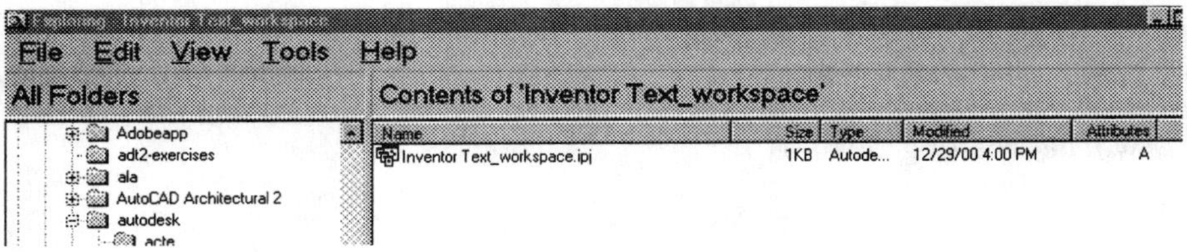

You can use WINDOWS Explorer to locate your project file. Remember project files have a *.ipj file extension.

Highlight the file. Right click and select 'Edit'. This will launch Notepad.

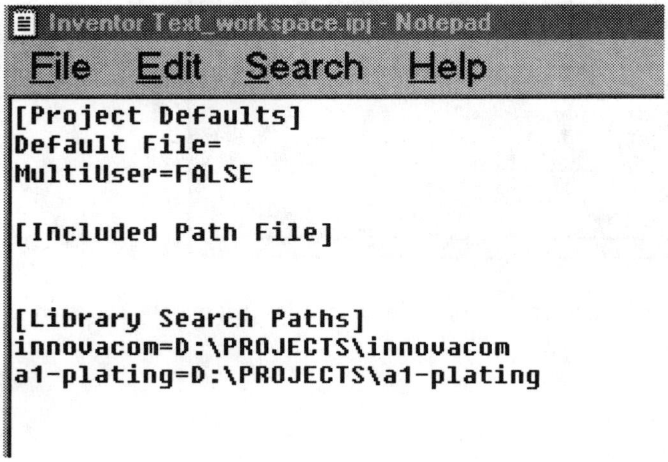

You can use the Notepad editor to modify the project file if you decide to change the location of your project files. This is faster and easier than setting up a new project file every time you decide to move part and assembly files around.

Options Dialog

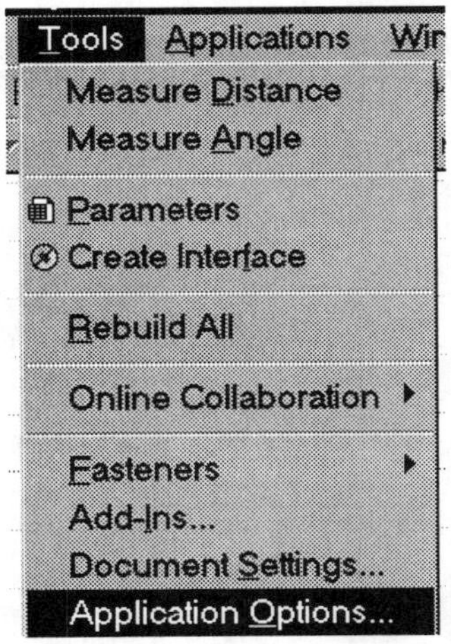

Users can set options using the Options dialog box. It is accessed under the Tools menu.

The tabs are:

- General
- Colors
- Display
- Drawing
- Notebook
- Sketch
- Part
- Design Elements
- Assembly

The Options dialog controls the color and display of your Autodesk Inventor work environment, the behavior and settings or files, the default file locations, and a variety multiple-user functions.

TIP: To apply changes immediately, click Apply. Unapplied changes become effective when you click OK and close the dialog box.

General Options

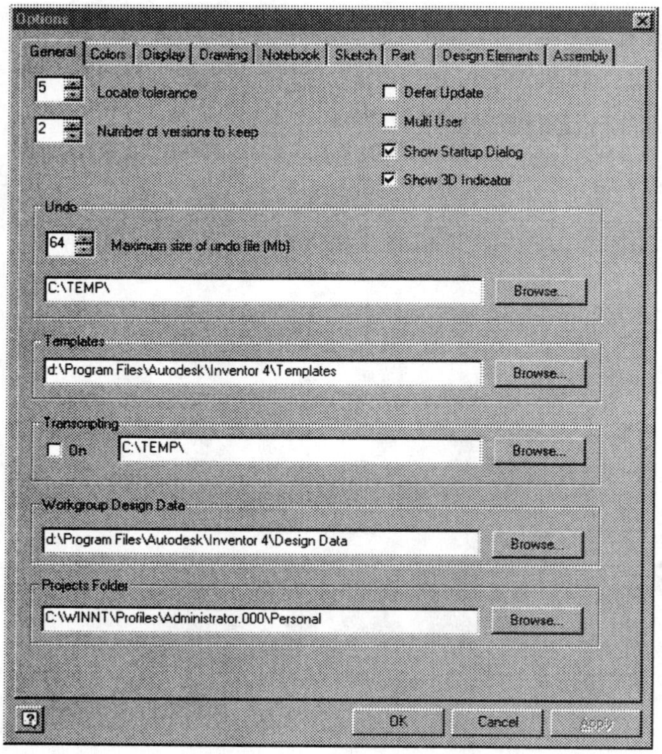

Locate Tolerance	Sets the distance (in pixels) from which clicking will select an object. Enter a number from 1 to 10 or click the up or down arrow to select the distance.
Number of Versions to keep	Sets the number of versions of a model to store in a model file. Enter a number from 1 to 10 or click the up or down arrow to select the number.
Defer Update	Sets preference for updating assemblies when you edit components. Select the box to defer updates of an assembly until you click the Update button for the assembly file. Clear the check box to update an assembly automatically after you edit a component.
Multi user	Enables safeguards when multiple users edit files. Select the check box to use the file reservation system and warnings. Clear the check box if safeguards are not needed.
Show Startup dialog	Shows the Startup dialog box each time Autodesk Inventor is opened. Select the check box to display the Startup dialog box. Clear the check box to open Autodesk Inventor without showing the dialog box.
Show 3D Indicator 	In a 3D view, displays an XYZ axis indicator in the bottom left corner of the graphics screen. Select the check box to display the axis indicator or clear the check box to turn it off. The red arrow indicates the X axis, the green arrow indicates the Y axis, and the blue arrow indicates the Z axis. In assemblies, the indicator shows the orientation of the top-level assembly, not the component being edited.

TIP: A version of the model is created each time the file is saved. When the maximum number of versions is reached, the oldest version of the model is discarded each time a new version is saved. You can open and restore any existing version of the model.

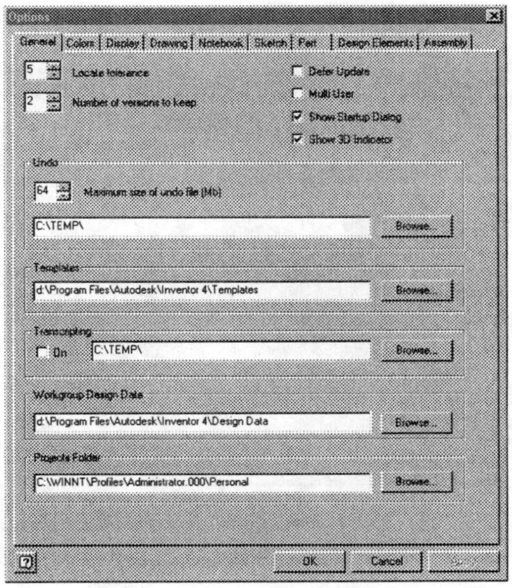

Undo	Maximum Size of Undo File (Mb)	Sets the size of the temporary file that tracks changes to a model or drawing so that actions can be undone. When working with large or complex models and drawings, you may need to increase the size of this file to provide adequate Undo capacity. Enter the size, in megabytes, or click the up or down arrow to select the size. Note: For best results, increase or decrease the file size in 4-Mb increments.
	Path	Specifies the location of the temporary file that tracks changes to a model or drawing so that actions can be undone. To change the location, enter the new path or click Browse to search for and select the path.
Templates	Specifies the location of template files. To change the location, enter the new path or click Browse to search for and select the path.	
Transcripting	Sets the options for transcripting. When transcripting is on, all of the work that you do as you build a model is recorded and can be replayed at a later time.	
	On	Turns on transcripting functionality. Select the check box to use transcripting; clear the check box to turn it off.
	Path	Specifies the location for transcripting files. To change the location, enter the new path in the box, or click Browse to search for and select the path.

Opening a Previous File Version

Select File -> Open.

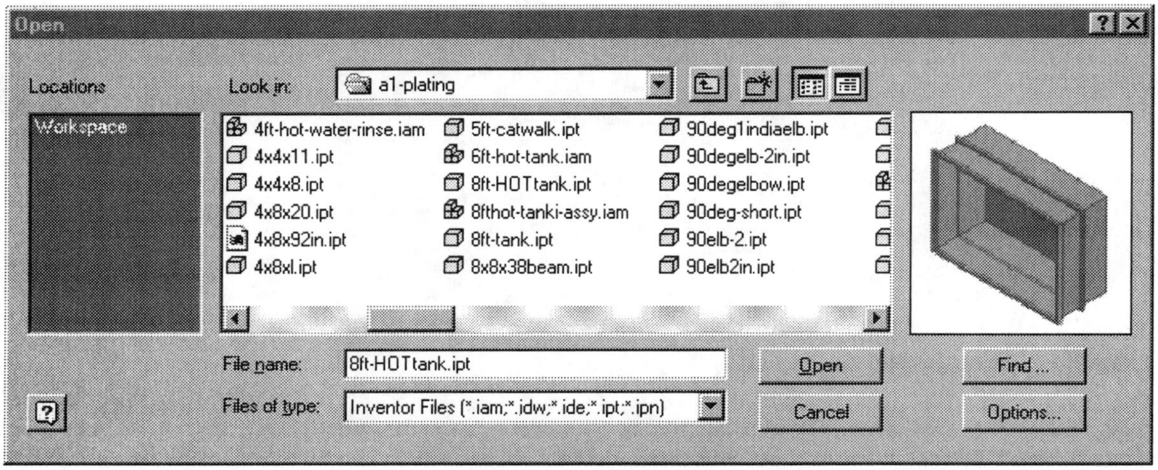

Select the Options button.

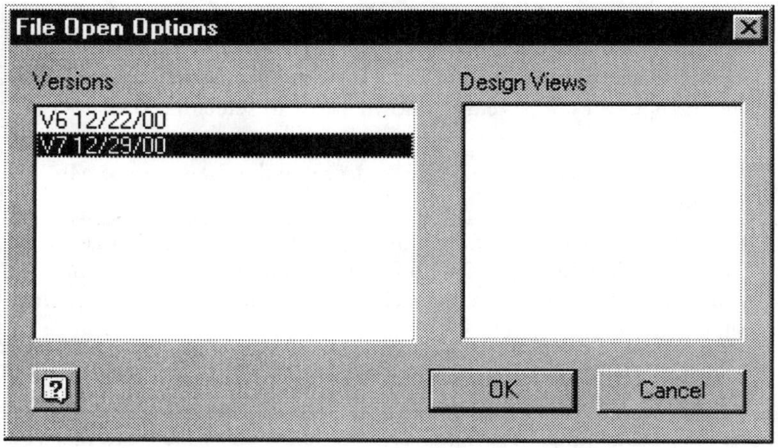

Note that there are two versions of the file stored. Version 6, which was saved on 12/22/00, and Version 7, which was saved on 12/29/00. No design views were stored with either file. Simply highlight the desired file version and press 'OK'.

Color Options

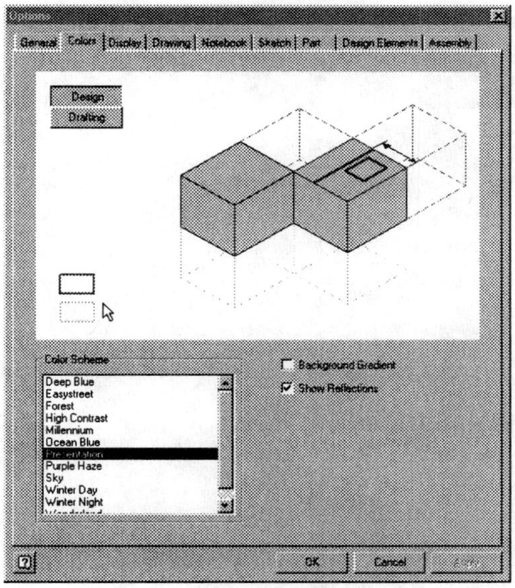

Select the 'Color' tab.
Highlight the various colors and note how the display changes. When you find a color you like, select 'Apply'.

Select 'OK'.

Sets the background color for the graphics window.

Design/Drafting	Displays the effect of the color choice in either the design or the drafting environment. Click Design or Drafting to view the effect of the active color choice in the view box.
Color Scheme	Lists the available color schemes. Click to select from the available schemes. The view box displays the result of your selection.
Background Gradient	Applies a saturation gradient to the background color. Select the check box to apply the gradient; clear the check box to apply a solid background color.
Show Reflections	Adds a reflected image to parts when they are assigned highly reflective color and lighting styles.

TIP: To preview your selections in the graphics window before closing the dialog box, click Apply.

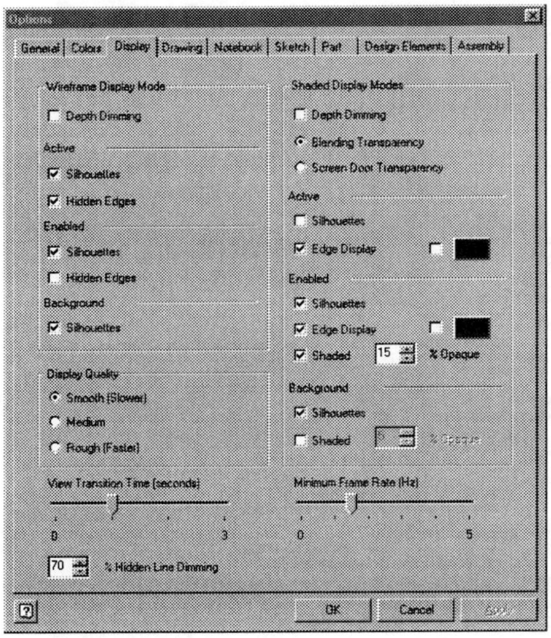

Display Options

Customizes the wire frame and shaded display of models and assemblies.

Sets the preferences for wire frame display of the model.	
Depth Dimming	Sets a dimming effect to better convey the depth of a model. Select the check box to turn on depth dimming; clear the check box to turn it off.
Active	Sets the preferences for wire frame display of a part or of the active components in an assembly. Silhouettes enable the display of silhouettes. Select the check box to display silhouettes; clear the check box to suppress the display.Hidden Edges dims the display of edges hidden behind other geometry. Select the check box to dim the display of hidden edges; clear the check box to display the hidden edges in full intensity.
Enabled	Sets the preferences for wire frame display of a typical enabled component in an assembly. Silhouettes enable the display of silhouettes. Select the check box to display silhouettes; clear the check box to suppress the display. Hidden Edges dims the display of edges hidden behind other geometry. Select the check box to dim the display of hidden edges; clear the check box to display the hidden edges in full intensity.
Background	Sets the preferences for wire frame display of parts that are not enabled in an assembly. Silhouettes enable the display of silhouettes. Select the check box to display silhouettes; clear the check box to suppress the display.
Display Quality	Sets the resolution for the display of the model. Generally, the smoother the resolution, the longer it takes to redisplay the model when changes are made. When working with a very large or complex model, you may want to lower the quality of the display to speed up operation. For example, Rough setting temporarily simplifies detail on large parts but updates faster while Smooth setting temporarily simplifies fewer details but updates slower.

Shaded Display Modes	Sets the preferences for shaded display of the model.	
	Depth Dimming	Sets a dimming effect to better convey the depth of a model. Select the check box to turn depth dimming on; clear the check box to turn it off.
	Transparency	Sets the quality of the transparency display. If you do not have a 3D graphics board, the screen door display option speeds up operation. Blending specifies a high quality transparency display that is achieved by averaging the colors of overlapping objects. Screen Door specifies a lower quality transparency display that is achieved by using a pattern that allows the color of the hidden object to show through.
	Active	Sets the preferences for shaded display of a part or of the active components in an assembly. Silhouettes enable the display of silhouettes. Select the check box to display silhouettes; clear the check box to suppress the display. Edge Display sets the display of edges. Select the check box to display edges in a contrasting color; clear the check box to display edges in the same color as faces. If Edge Display is selected, you can change edge color by clicking on the color pad and choosing a color from the Color dialog box.
	Enabled	Sets the preferences for shaded display of a typical enabled component in an assembly. Silhouettes enables the display of silhouettes. Select the check box to display silhouettes; clear the check box to suppress the display. Edge Display sets the display of edges when shaded display is selected for enabled components. Select the check box to display edges in a contrasting color; clear the check box to display edges in the same color as faces. If Edge Display is selected, you can change edge color by clicking on the color pad and choosing a color from the Color dialog box. Shaded enables contrasting shading for enabled components except the active component when a single component is activated in an assembly. Select the check box to enable the shading; clear the check box to display enabled but not active components in wireframe. % Opaque if Shaded is selected, you can set the opacity for the shading. Enter the percent opaque or click the up or down arrow to select the value.
	Background	Sets the preferences for shaded display of components that are not enabled in an assembly. Silhouettes enable the display of silhouettes. Select the check box to display silhouettes; clear the check box to suppress the display. Shaded enables contrasting shading, rather than outline presentation, for background components. Select the check box to enable the shading; clear the check box to display background components in outline. % Opaque if Shaded is selected, you can set the opacity for the shading. Enter the percent opaque or click the up or down arrow to select the value.

View Transition Time	Controls the time required to smoothly transition between views when using viewing tools (such as Isometric View, Zoom All, Zoom Area, Look At, and so on). Zero transition time causes transition to be abrupt, which might make it difficult to understand changes in position and orientation. Three sets the greatest amount of time to transition between views.
Minimum Frame Rate	With complex views (such as very large assemblies), use this setting to specify how slowly you are willing to update the display during interactive viewing operations (like Rotate, Pan, and Zoom). Autodesk Inventor tries to maintain the frame rate you set, but to do so, may need to simplify or discard parts of the view. All parts are restored to the view when movement ends. Set zero to always draw everything in the view, regardless of the time required. Set one to have Autodesk Inventor try to draw the view at least one frame per second; set five to draw at least five frames per second. Note: Usually, this setting has no effect on views because they update more quickly than this rate.
% Hidden Line Dimming	Sets the percent of dimming for hidden edges when one or more of the Hidden Edges check boxes is selected. Enter the percentage of dimming to apply or click the up or down arrow to select the value.

Drawing Options

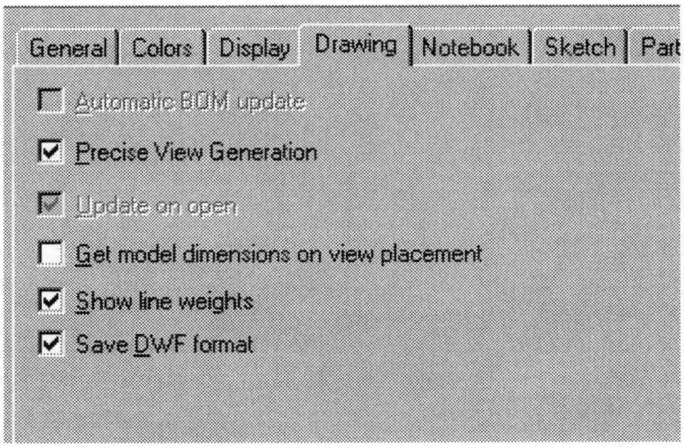

Sets the drawing options. To use an option, select its check box.

Precise View Generation	Enables or disables the placement of precise geometry in drawing views. If the check box is selected, drawing views are displayed with their full precision when they are placed. If the check box is cleared, drawing views are placed with an approximation of the geometry (to allow for faster operation) and can be updated later.
Get model dimensions on view placement	Sets the default for the Dimensions option in the Create View dialog boxes. If the check box is selected, the Dimensions option in Create View is automatically selected so that applicable model dimensions are added to drawing views when they are placed. If this box is cleared, you must manually select Dimensions in Create View dialog boxes to add the model dimensions when placing drawing views.
Show line weights	Enables the display of unique line weights in drawings. If the check box is selected, visible lines in drawings are displayed with the line weights defined in the active drafting standard. If the check box is cleared, all visible lines are displayed with the same weight. This setting does not affect line weights in printed drawings.
Save DWF Format	DWF is the format used to create drawings that can be placed on web pages.

TIP: To display full precision for an imprecise view, right-click the view and choose Make View Precise from the menu. A precise view cannot be changed to imprecise

Enable 'Get model dimensions' to automatically have dimensions appear when placing drawing views.

Notebook Options

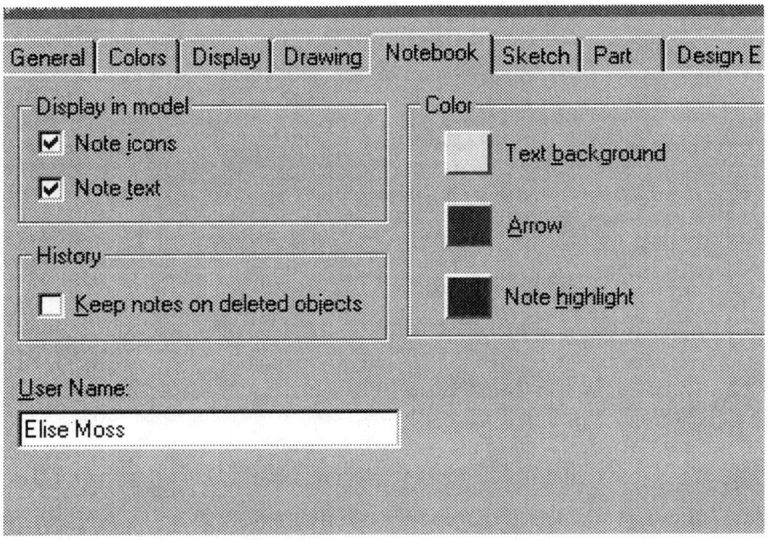

Controls the display of design notes in the Engineer's Notebook.

Display in Model	Sets the display of note indicators in the model.	
	Note Icons	Displays note icons in the model. Select the check box to display design note to display icons in the graphics window. Clear the check box to suppress the display of an icon. .
	Note Text	Displays note text in pop-up windows in the model. Select the check box to display the text of a design note when the cursor pauses over a note symbol. Clear the check box to suppress the display of note text.
History	Sets archival options for design notes.	
	Keep Notes On Deleted Objects	Retains notes attached to deleted geometry. Select the check box to save notes attached to geometry that is deleted. Clear the check box to delete notes when associated geometry is deleted.
Color	Sets the colors of elements in design notes. The color pad next to each item shows the current color setting. To change the color for an item, click the color pad to open the color dialog box and select the color.	
	Text Background	Sets the background color for the comment boxes in design notes.
	Arrow	Sets the color for arrows in design notes.
	Note Highlight	Sets the color for the highlighted component in note views.
User Information	Sets the default information that is included in a design note.	
	Name	Sets the name to include in design note comments. Enter the name.

TIP: If you attach multiple notes to a single item, only the first note displays a symbol
Changing the user name affects only those notes created after the change is made. You cannot change a name on an existing note.

Sketch Options

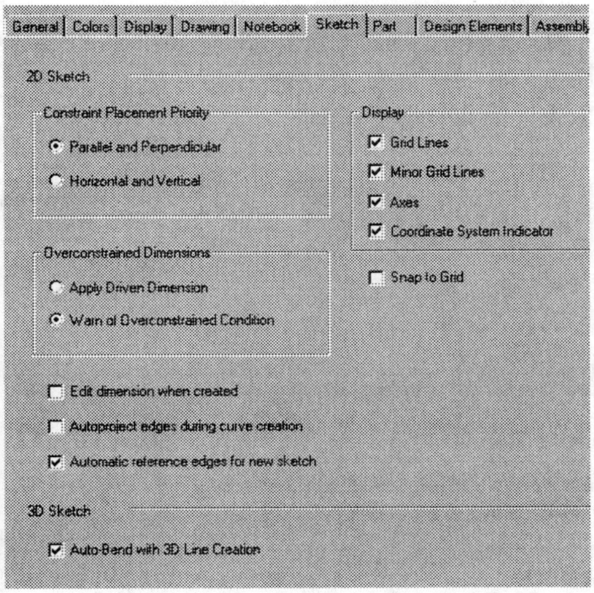

Sets the sketch options.

Constraint Placement Priority	Sets the preferred constraint type for automatic placement of constraints. Select one of the options. Parallel and Perpendicular Applies constraints that define the relationships among geometry, without regard to the coordinates of the sketch grid. Horizontal and Vertical Applies grid-specific constraints that define the orientation of sketch geometry in relationship to the sketch coordinates.
Overconstrained Dimensions	Sets the preferred behavior for dimensions on overconstrained sketches. Apply Driven Dimension Applies a non-parametric dimension enclosed in parentheses. Dimension updates when the sketch changes, but cannot resize the sketch. Warn of Overconstrained Condition Displays warning message when a dimension will overconstrain a sketch. Click OK to place the dimension or Cancel to prevent creating the dimension.
Edit dimension when created	Presents the dimension edit box when a dimension is created.
Automatic reference edges for new sketch	If this is enabled, whenever you create a new sketch the edges of the plane selected will be projected as reference geometry to be used as part of the new sketch.

Part Options

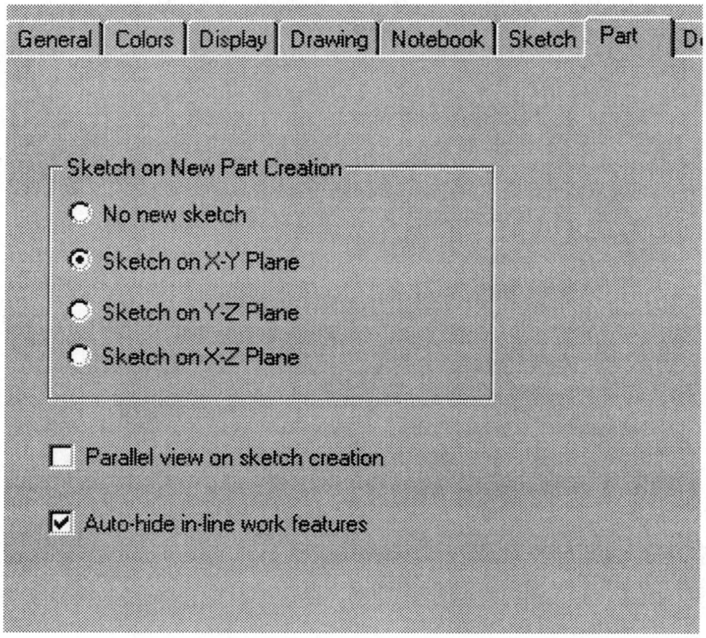

Sets the defaults for creating new parts.

Sketch on New Part Creation	Sets the preference for creating the sketch when a new part file is created. Select one of the options: No New Sketch disables automatic sketch creation when creating a new part. Sketch on X-Y Plane sets X-Y as the sketch plane when creating a new part. Sketch on Y-Z Plane sets Y-Z as the sketch plane when creating a new part. Sketch on X-Z Plane sets X-Z as the sketch plane when creating a new part.
Parallel view on sketch creation	Automatically reorients the view to be planar to the screen when Sketch mode is activated. Select the check box to enable automatic reorientation; clear the check box to sketch in the current orientation.
Auto-hide in-line work features	When this is enabled, the user will not see the lines of in-line features.

Design Element Options

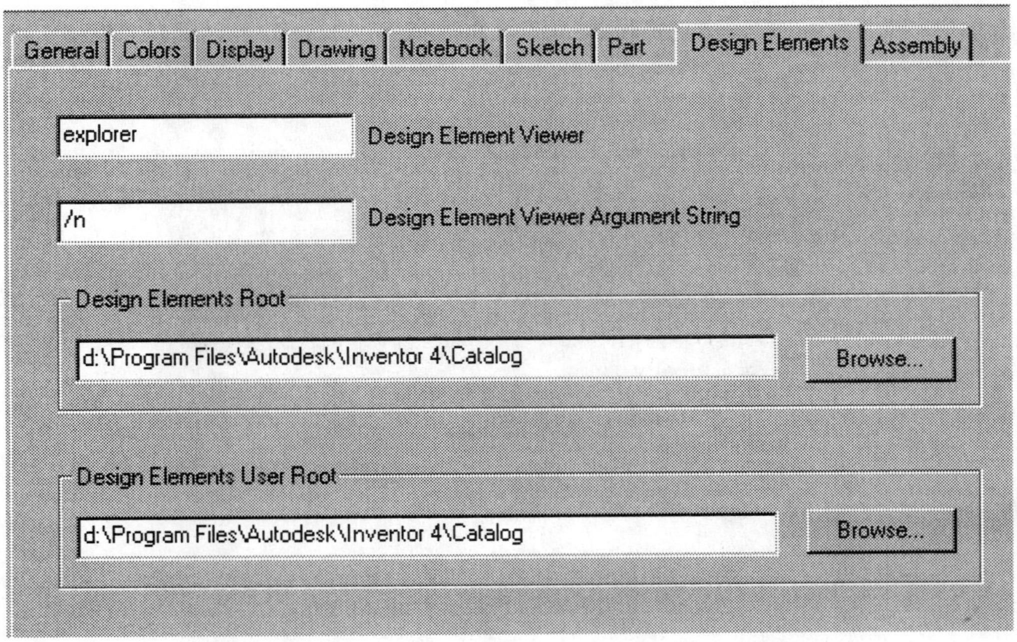

Design Element Viewer	Specifies the viewer application used to manage the design element files. Enter the name of the executable file for the viewer application in the box. The default is Windows Explorer.
Design Element Viewer Argument String	Sets the viewer command line arguments for run-time options. The default is /n. Windows Explorer opens with the folder specified in the Design Elements Root box. Note: To find out if your viewer application supports command line arguments, refer to the Help for your viewer.
Design Elements Root	Specifies the location of design element files used by the View Catalog dialog box. The location can be on your local computer or on a network drive accessed by other users. Enter the path in the box or click Browse to search for and select the path. The default path is the path to the Catalog folder installed with Autodesk Inventor.
Design Elements User Roots	Specifies the location of Design Element files used by both the Create Design Element and Insert design element dialog boxes. The location can be on your local computer or on a network drive accessed by other users. Enter the path in the box or click Browse to search for and select the path. The default path is the path to the Catalog folder installed with Autodesk Inventor. If desired, you can define a Design Elements Root location on a network drive that can be accessed by others in your company and a Design Elements User Root location on your computer hard drive. Note: Use Windows shortcuts to quickly access other folders. For example, you can place a shortcut to a shared folder on a network in your Design Elements User Root folder.

Use the Browse button to locate the design element files.

TIP: It is a good idea to locate any custom files, such as design elements, away from the standard Inventor directories. Otherwise, if you have to re-install Inventor or when you perform an upgrade, you may lose your work.

Assembly Options

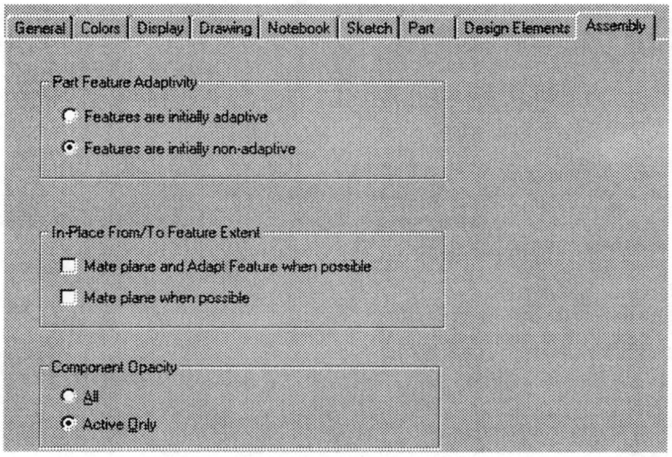

Sets the preferences for creating assemblies.

Part Feature Adaptivity	Sets the default adaptive status for creating new features. You can change the adaptive status after creating a feature. An adaptive feature will change in response to assembly constraints, allowing the assembly to determine final size. Only those details that are left underconstrained can change. For example, if an undimensioned rectangle is extruded to create a block, the length and height of the block can adapt, if required, to assembly constraints. If the height of a sketch is dimensioned, but the length is not, then only the length can adapt. To set the default status, select one of the options. Features Are Initially Adaptive sets the default status for all new features to adaptive. Features Are Initially Non-Adaptive sets the default status for all new features to non-adaptive.
In-Place From/To Feature Extent	When creating a part in place in an assembly, you can set options to control feature termination. Mate plane and adapt feature when possible constructs an adaptive relationship automatically. When the plane on which feature is constructed changes size or position, the in-place feature adapts. Mate plane when possible constructs the feature to the desired size and mates it to the plane, but does not allow it to adapt.
Component Opacity	Controls how parts in an assembly are viewed when editing a single component within an assembly. The default is to dim all components except the one being modified.

Review Questions

1. To turn off the 3D indicator in the drawing window:
   - A. Go to Tools->Options->Display
   - B. Go to Tools->Options->Part
   - C. Go to Tools->Options->General
   - D. Go to Tools->Options->Design Elements

2. In the 3D Indicator, the red arrow is:
   - A. the X axis
   - B. the Y axis
   - C. the Z axis
   - D. the active sketch plane

3. The maximum number of versions of a file that can be saved is:
   - A. 1
   - B. 2
   - C. 5
   - D. 10

4. To change the units used in a file:
   - A. Go to Tools->Options->Units
   - B. Go to File->Properties->Units
   - C. Go to Tools->Options->General
   - D. Go to File->Properties->Physical

5. In assembly mode, the 3D indicator indicates the orientation of:

   - A. The active part
   - B. The active assembly
   - C. The base part of the assembly
   - D. The active sketch plane

6. The Options tab to select to set the color of the drawing window:

   - A. General
   - B. Colors
   - C. Display
   - D. Drawing

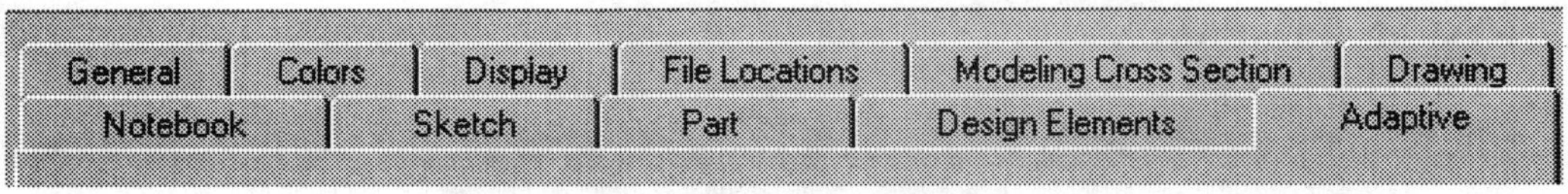

7. The tab to select the set the sketch plane to be used when creating a new part:

    A. General
    B. Sketch
    C. Part
    D. Design Elements

8. The tab to select to determine how constraints are applied.

    A. General
    B. Sketch
    C. Part
    D. Design Elements

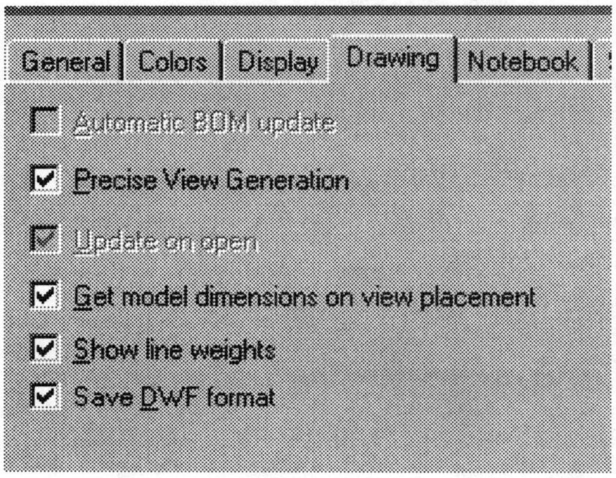

9. You place a check mark next to 'Get model dimensions on view placement'. This accomplishes the following:

    A. Model dimensions will automatically update when placing a view.
    B. Model dimensions will become visible when placing a drawing vew.
    C. Model dimensions will become visible when rotating a model.
    D. Model dimensions will automatically be erased when placing a drawing view.

10. The information entered in the Properties dialog box may be used in:

    A. Parts lists
    B. Title blocks
    C. Mass Analysis
    D. All of the above

ANSWERS: 1) C; 2) A; 3) D; 4) B; 5) C; 6) B; 7) C; 8) B; 9) B; 10) D

week 2
chapter
4-5-6, 7
Review
1-2, 11, 12
Date
1-21 — 1-26

Lesson 4

The Standard Toolbar

The Standard toolbar looks similar to the Microsoft Windows standard toolbar. The first icon shows a blank piece of paper indicating that it opens a new file.

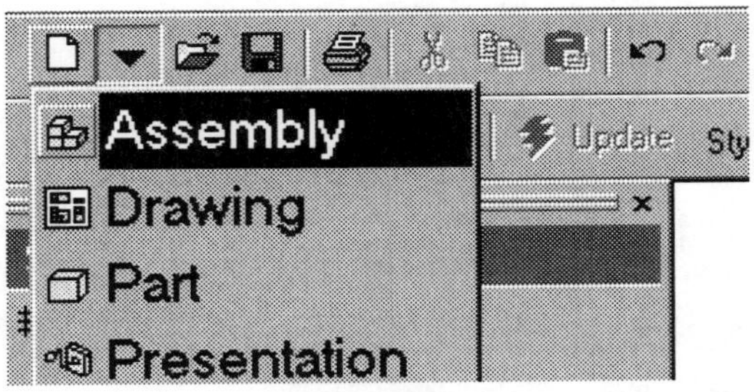

However, immediately to the right of the blank sheet of paper is an arrow. Pressing down on that arrow reveals four options: Assembly, Drawing, Part, or Presentation. So, when starting a new file, first specify whether to create an assembly, drawing, presentation or part file. Clicking on the blank sheet of paper will bring up Inventor's Start Up dialog box.

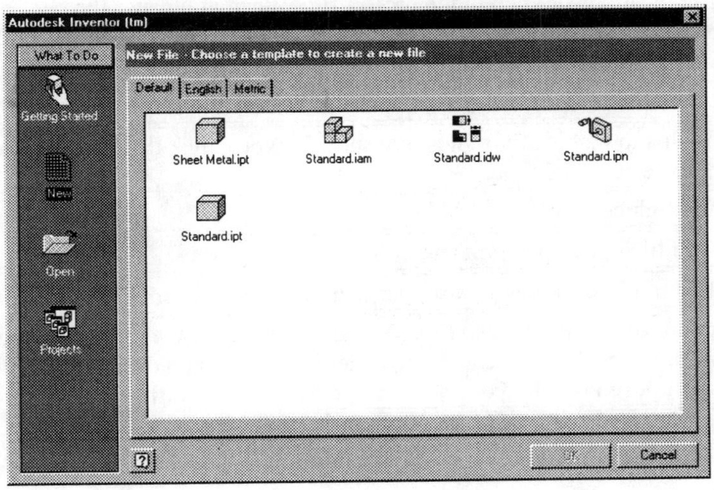

TIP: Using the pull-down arrow reduces the number of steps required to create a new file, so that is the preferred method when starting a new file.

The Open folder opens an existing file. Pressing this icon brings up a browser window that allows the user to locate the file.

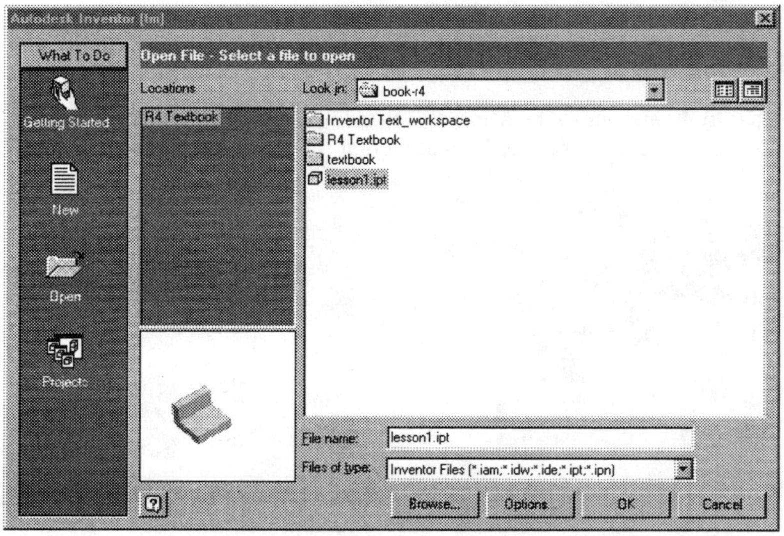

Look in	Shows path of the active directory.
Locations	Shows file locations defined in the project file. When you pause the cursor over a path type, the ToolTip shows the path. Click to change to the folder. The folder tree and files are listed in the main window of the dialog box.
File name	Specifies the file to open, enter a file name or select a file from the listed files.
File of type	Filters file list to include only files of a specific type. Click the arrow to show list, then highlight to select a file type.
Open	Opens highlighted file.
Cancel	Cancels the file open operation and closes the dialog box.
Find	Opens the Find Files dialog box so that you can search for files based on file properties.
Options	Opens an options dialog box so that you can set the options for the selected file. If the file is an Autodesk Inventor file, you can specify the file version and design view (if applicable) to open. If you are importing a file, you can set import options specific to the type of file.
Reserved by	Shows the name of the person who has reserved the file or allows you to reserve the file. Available only if the Multi User option is on.
Reserve	When you open a file, click to reserve the file.
Clear	When you open a file, click to clear the name of the person who has reserved the file.

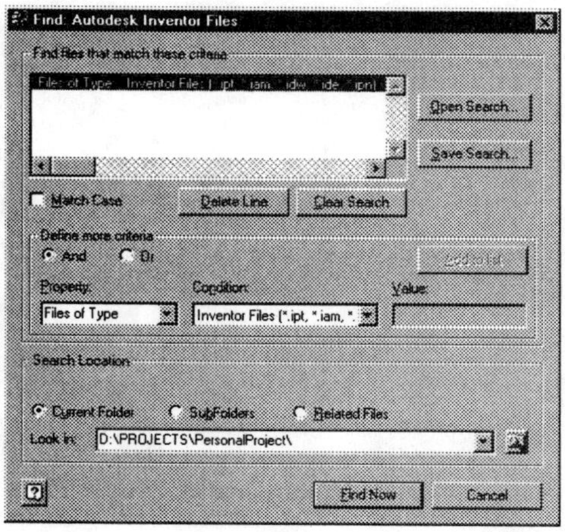

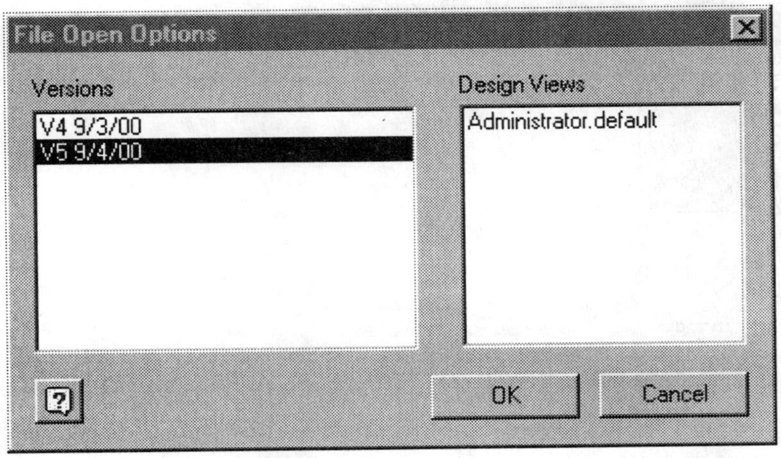

The File Open Options dialog box is accessed by highlighting a file in the Open dialog and then pressing the 'Options' button.

Versions	Lists the available versions of the selected file. Select a version from the list. Note: To increase or decrease the number of versions that are saved, specify the Number of Versions to Keep option in the Tools>Options>General tab.
Design Views	If the selected file is an assembly, lists the available design views. Select a design view from the list.

Inventor tracks up to ten different versions or revisions of each model and assembly. This allows the user to roll back to a prior version easily.

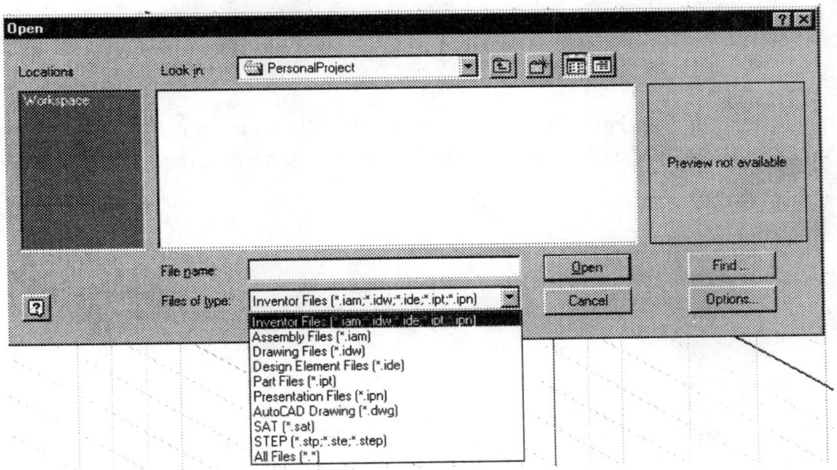

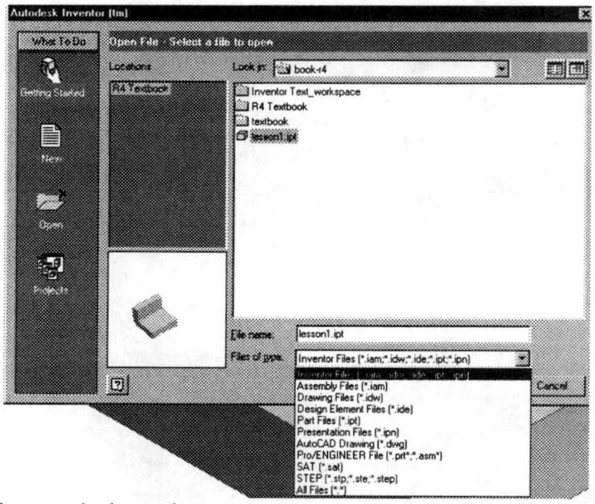

In the 'Files of type' drop-down window, the user can access a list of the file types Inventor can open. Drawings of types other than Inventor, i.e. .iam, .idw, .ide, .ipt, are not fully supported in Release 1, but Release 2 and above will fully support dwg files from AutoCAD or Mechanical Desktop and other file types as well. Release 4 allows users to open Pro/Engineer files. Pro/Engineer files can be modified and saved as Inventor files.

The next seven buttons are familiar to most users: Save, Print, Cut, Copy, Paste, Undo, and Redo.

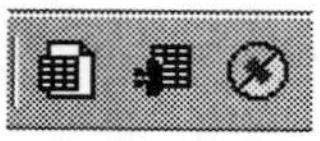

The next three buttons are specific to Inventor. They are Parameters, iPart Table, and Create Interface.

Parameters

The parameters button, located between the Standard Windows icons and the Viewing icons, is used for table driven parts. More information on creation and management of table driven parts can be found in my intermediate level textbook.

iPart Table

The Ipart Table allows the user to convert the existing part into a part linked to an Excel-type spreadsheet.

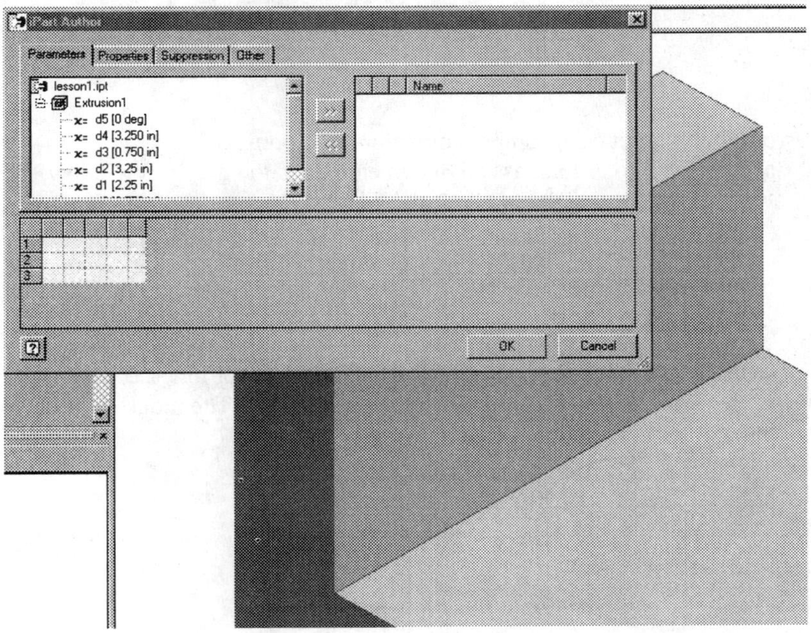

The iPart Author allows the user to select existing dimensions and define them as variables. More information on how to use the iPart Author can be found in my intermediate level textbook.

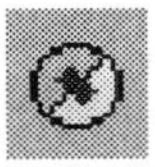

Create Interface

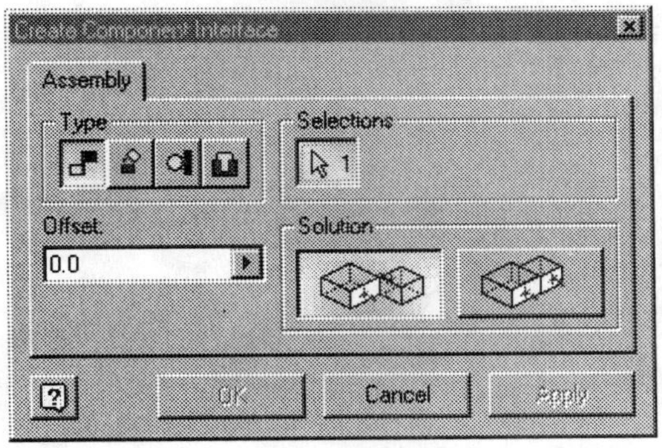

The Create Interface button launches the Create Component Interface. This allows the user to set edges, faces, or axes for use in assembling parts. By pre-selecting where assembly constraints are to be made, assembling parts together is faster and easier.

The next five buttons are grouped together because they all have to do with viewing options.

Zoom All

The first button, which has four arrows pointing in each compass direction, is 'Zoom All'.
Pressing the button expands or shrinks the view to encompass all drawn entities in the graphics window.

Zoom Window

The next button is 'Zoom Window'.
To create the window, pick a point with the left mouse button. This will be the upper or lower corner of the window. Drag the mouse across the area you wish to zoom in. Pick the next corner. The mouse will draw a light window to indicate the area that will be captured in the zoom.

Dynamic Zoom

The middle button is a 'Dynamic Zoom' that allows the user to zoom in or out by moving the mouse. The user selects the Dynamic Zoom, then holds the left mouse down while moving the mouse up and down. A left click of the mouse selects the current view. If the user needs additional help adjusting the view, a simple right click of the mouse will bring up a submenu.

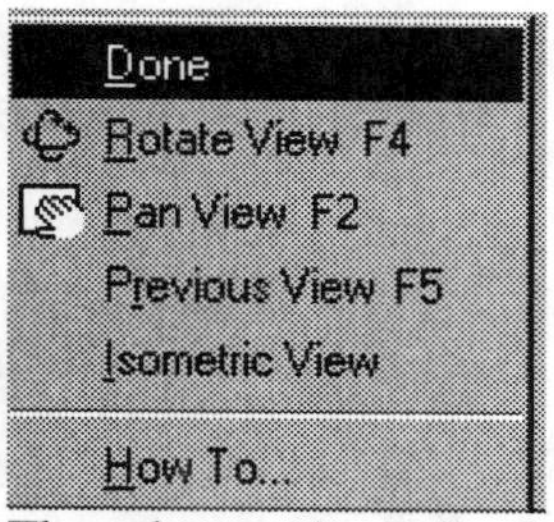

The submenu is similar to the drop-down menu in AutoCAD and provides the user with an abbreviated view menu.

Pan Mode

The icon showing a hand on a piece of paper indicates 'Pan' mode. This allows the user to shift the view without changing the scale of the object. Hold down the left mouse button and move the mouse from left to right to adjust the view.

Zoom Selected

The final view icon is 'Zoom Selected'. Press this button, then pick on the feature desired to zoom into and the window will automatically take you there. This is an excellent tool when working on complex parts or assemblies; something that other CAD users will envy. If Inventor is unable to determine which feature was selected, an alert box will appear and Inventor will take you to its best guess, which is usually close enough for you to continue working.

The next section of the Standard toolbar also comes under View menu topics.

3D Rotate

The first icon, which resembles a sphere, is Inventor's 3D orbiter. This tool allows us to rotate our object in 3D space seamlessly.

When first activated, a crosshair target figure will appear. The user can grab any pole and rotate by that pole. Additionally, a right mouse click will bring up a submenu.

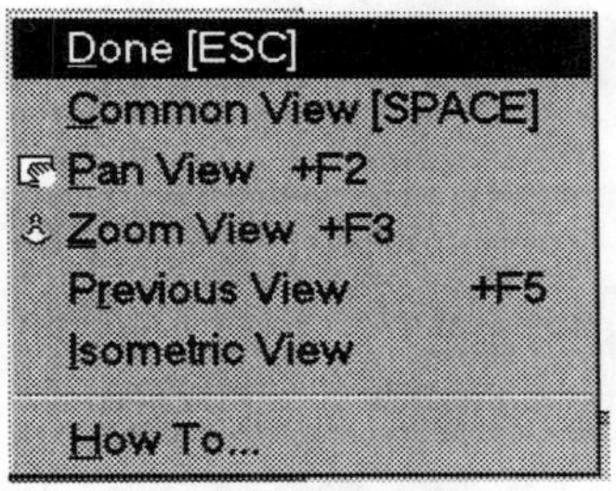

The Rotate Submenu

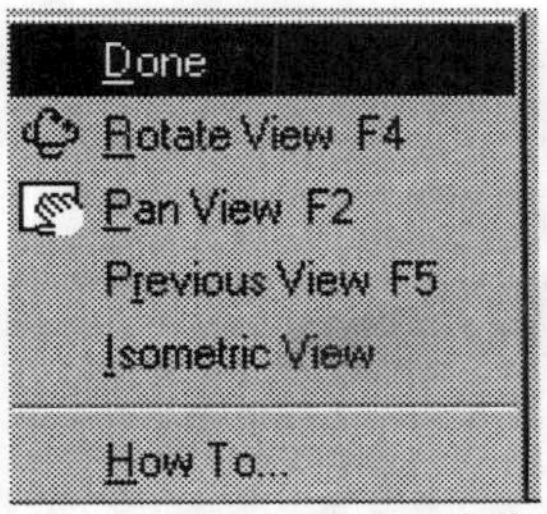

The Dynamic Zoom Submenu

Compare the submenus depending on whether you are in Rotate mode or Dynamic Zoom mode.

When the object is positioned as desired, a left mouse click sets the view.

Starting in Inventor R2, a new orbit feature called Common View was introduced.

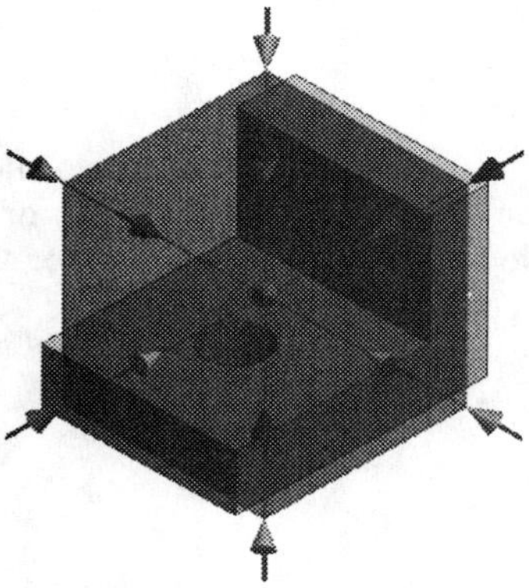

Selecting this option brings up a box with arrows at the vertices and centered on each plane. Selecting an arrow will automatically orient the view accordingly. This can be a quick way of rotating and orienting your model.

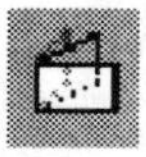

Look At

The second icon, which resembles a projected plane, is the 'Look At' tool. This tool will automatically switch the view to a plan view of the selected plane or feature of an object, allowing for quick editing.

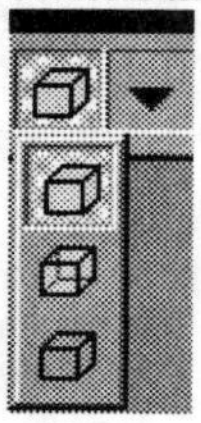

Display

The last icon is a drop-down that controls the appearance of our objects, Wire Frame, Hidden Edge, or Shaded. Modifying the appearance can affect the ease of editing.

TIP: Pressing the SPACE bar when the Rotate command is active switches from COMMON mode to FREE ROTATE mode.

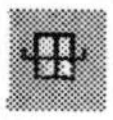

Section All Parts

This tool allows the user to create a sectioned view that can be used in a drawing.

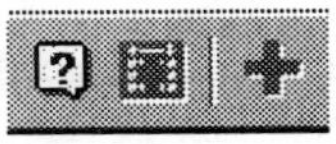

The last three icons in the Standard toolbar are Design Support System tools.

Help

The balloon with the question mark brings up 'Help'.
This can also be brought up by pressing F1.

Visual Syllabus

The icon with a table and a question mark brings up the DesignProf Visual Syllabus, an on-line learning tool for new users. The syllabus will walk the beginner through just about any task they want to do.

Design Doctor

The final icon button is normally grayed out. The cross indicates the Design Doctor. This is a remarkable tool to walk the user through any problems or conflicts, which may occur during the design process. The icon is only enabled if Inventor detects a modeling or assembly error.

Standard Toolbar

Button	Tool	Function	Special Instructions
	Parameters	Allows the user to create a part using a spreadsheet to control dimensions and features	
	iPart Author	Creates a spreadsheet for an existing part	
	Create Interface	Allows the user to pre-set edges, faces, or axes to be used for assembly constraints	
	Zoom All	Zoom in or out so everything is visible in the graphics window	
	Zoom Window	Zoom in so the selected viewing area fills the graphics window	Pick two corners to designate the window
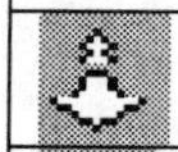	Dynamic Zoom	Drag to zoom in or out	Use F3 to activate
	Pan	Drag to reposition the model in the graphics window – does not zoom in or out	Use F2 to activate
	Zoom Selected	Zooms in or out so selected geometry fits in graphics window	
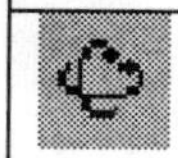	3D Rotate	Change the viewing perspective of the model	Use F4 to activate. Use spacebar to toggle rotation modes
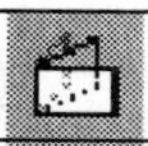	Look At	Select geometry for a PLAN view	
	Wire Frame display	Display the model as a wire frame	
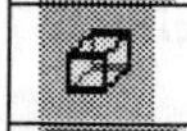	Hidden Edge display	Display the model as a shaded solid with hidden edges visible	
	Shaded Display	Display the model as a shaded solid	Default display setting
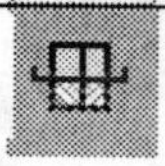	Section All Parts	Allows the user to create a sectioned 3D view of a part or assembly.	
	Help	Brings up Help	Use F1 to activate
	Visual Syllabus	Animated tutorials	
	Design Doctor	Diagnose and fix part and assembly errors and problems	Is grayed out unless errors occur

Review Questions

1. The three display modes in Inventor are:

   A. Shaded, Wire Frame, Hidden Edge
   B. Shaded, Wire Frame, Shaded with Edges On
   C. Wire Frame, Hidden, Rendered
   D. Wire Frame, Shaded, Rendered

2. The function key to activate Dynamic Zoom is:

   A. F1
   B. F2
   C. F3
   D. F4

3. The function key to bring up Help is:

   A. F1
   B. F2
   C. F3
   D. F4

4. The tool to select geometry and then automatically switch to a PLAN view of that geometry is:

   A.  Look At
   B.  Zoom Selected
   C.  Zoom Window
   D.  Dynamic Zoom

5. To switch from Common to Free Rotate when Rotate is active:

   A. Use TAB key
   B. Use Control key
   C. Use Shift key
   D. Use SPACE bar

6. The toolbar to select to bring up Visual Syllabus:

   A. 
   B. 
   C. 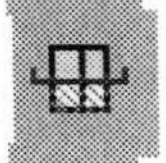
   D. 

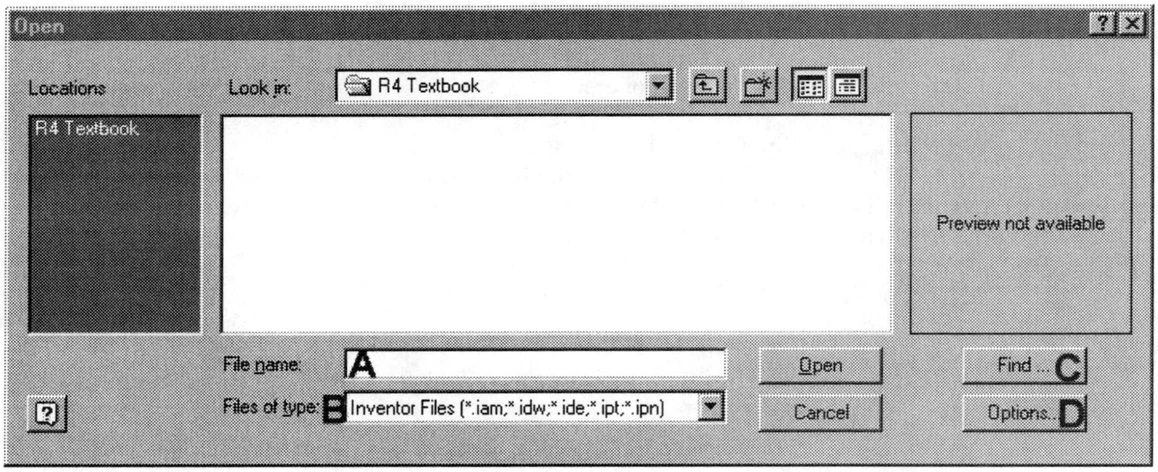

7. The button to select to search for a file.
8. The button to select to see an AutoCAD dwg file

9. The user highlights a file and presses the Options button. The Options button allows the user to:

   A. Select which version of the file to open
   B. Which version of Inventor to use to edit the file
   C. Enable partial file loading
   D. Set the default settings for units, physical properties, and display

10. The Design Doctor tool is:

   A. Normally inactive
   B. Normally active
   C. Used to check a design for interference
   D. Used to recover corrupted files

Lesson 5

The Features Toolbar

The Features toolbar has six sections. They are Sketched feature tools, Thread, Placed feature tools, Design Element tools, Pattern Feature tools, and Work features.

The Sketched feature tools use sketched geometry to build features.
The Thread tool maps the image of a thread onto a cylindrical face.
The Placed feature tools add finishing touches to existing features.
Design element tools create or add predefined features to a model.
Pattern feature tools add multiple instances of existing features.
Work features create work planes, work axes, or work points that you can used to define other features in a model.

You'll notice that when you start your part most of the Features tool bar is grayed out. That's because Inventor automatically disables any tools you don't need until you need them. Those tools will become available once you have created the appropriate features.

Sketched Feature Tools

The eight options of this section are Extrude, Revolve, Hole, Shell, Rib, Loft, Sweep and Coil.

Extrude

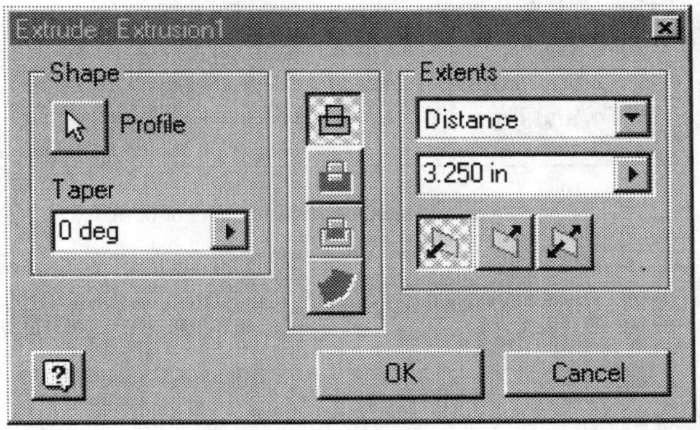

The Shape button selects a profile to extrude. If there are multiple profiles and none are selected, click Profile and then click on one or more profiles in the graphics window.

Inventor allows you to extrude more than one profile at a time. When you select a profile it will highlight to indicate that it is part of the selection set. To remove a profile from the selection set, hold down Ctrl and click a profile. If your selection set is not what you want and you were unable to de-select a profile, just press on the Cancel button and start over.

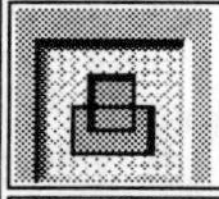	Join Adds the volume created by the extruded feature to another feature.
	Cut Removes the volume created by the extruded feature from another feature.
	Intersect Creates a new feature from the shared volume of the extruded feature and another feature. Material not included in the shared volume is deleted.
	Surface Creates a 3D surface.

The four buttons in the middle of the Extrude dialog box control the type of extrusion. The top button performs a 'Join' operation. The second button performs a 'Cut'. The third button performs an 'Intersect'. The bottom button creates a surface. You can drag the previewed profile using your mouse to determine the distance you want to extrude or enter a value into the dialog box under extents. The operation is automatically previewed in the graphics window.

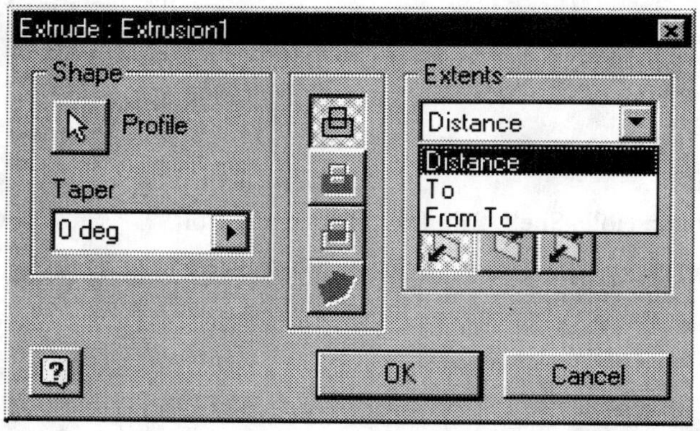

Under the Extents section of the dialog box, there is a drop down that allows you to define how far you want to extrude the profile. Your options are Distance, To, and From To.

Distance Default method. Establishes the depth of extrusion between start and end planes. For a base feature, shows negative or positive distance of extruded profile or entered value. The extrusion end face is parallel to the sketch plane.
To Allows you to select an ending face or plane on which to terminate the extrusion. You may terminate the feature on the selected face, or on a face that extends beyond the termination plane. In an assembly, the face or plane may be on another part. After you select the termination plane, choose one of the following: • Click the left button to terminate the feature entirely on the selected face. • Click the right button to terminate the feature on the selected plane and the extended face.
From - To Allows you to select beginning and ending faces or planes on which to terminate the extrusion. In an assembly, the faces or planes may be on other parts. Not available for base features.

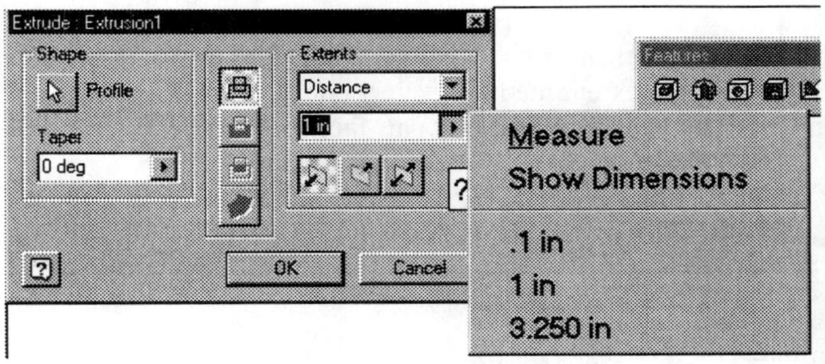

Inventor automatically saves your most common values. You can also measure objects on the fly to determine what value you want to use. You can use the Show Dimensions to select an existing dimension on the model to be used for the feature being defined.

The buttons on the bottom of the Extents section determine the direction for the extrusion. Inventor will automatically preview, so you can see if you have selected the correct direction.

The Taper Angle sets a taper angle of up to 180 degrees for the extrusion (normal to the sketch plane). The taper extends equally in both directions. If a taper angle is specified, a symbol in the graphics window shows the fixed edge and direction of taper.

TIP: To taper a feature in only one direction, create an extruded feature with no draft, then use the Face Draft tool to add draft to a specific face.

Revolve

A revolve is done similarly to an Extrude. First you create the sketch using the Sketch toolbar. Then select the Revolve button from the Features toolbar. The Revolve dialog box will appear. Select the profile to revolve. Define the centerline or axis you wish to revolve around by picking the axis button and then selecting the appropriate centerline or axis. The axis may be a work axis, a construction line, or a normal line. The axis of revolution can be part of the profile or offset from it. The profile and axis must be coplanar.

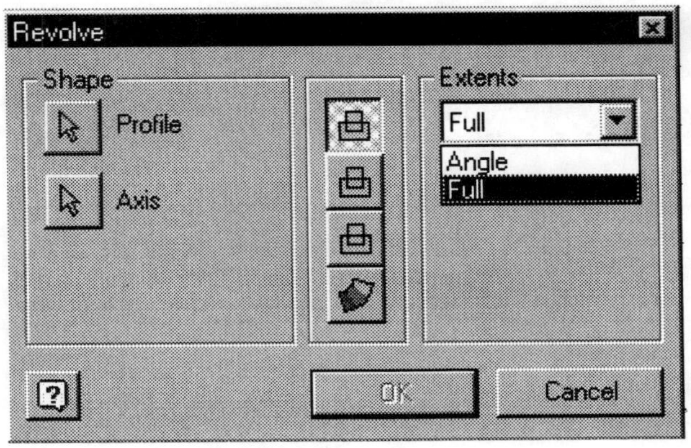

Under Extents, you determine the method for the revolution and set the angular displacement of the profile around a centerline. Click the drop-down arrow to list the extent methods, select one, and enter a value. Revolutions can be a specific distance or can terminate on a work plane or part face.

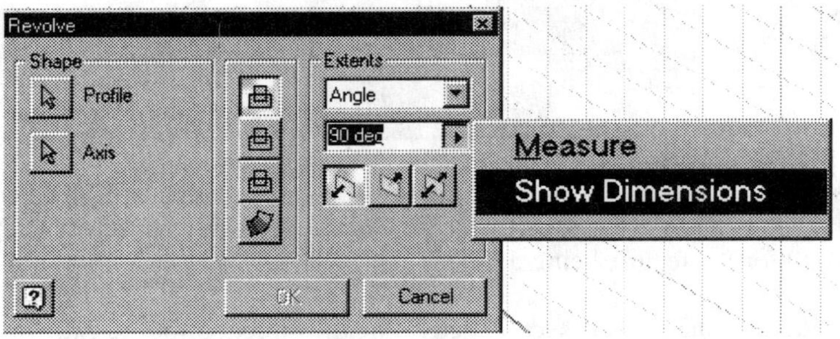

For the angle, you can measure for an angle, show dimensions to help you determine a value or simply type in an angle.

Finally, you can determine the direction for the revolve. Inventor will preview the revolve so you can decide if you have defined it properly before pressing 'OK'.

Creating a Revolve

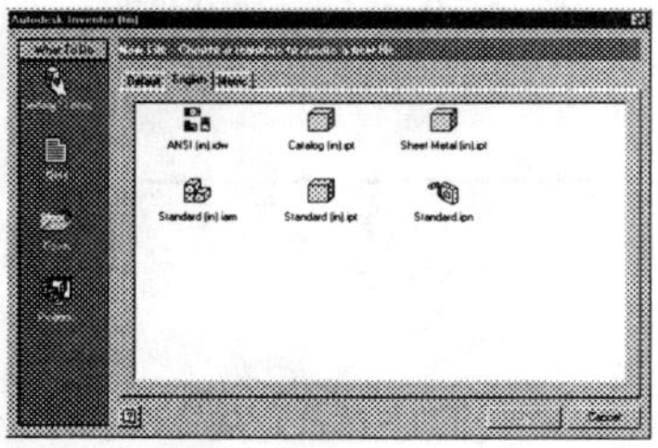

Go to File->New.
We begin our part by opening a new part under the English tab to ensure that our units are in inches.
Left-click on Standard(in).ipt.

Press 'OK'.

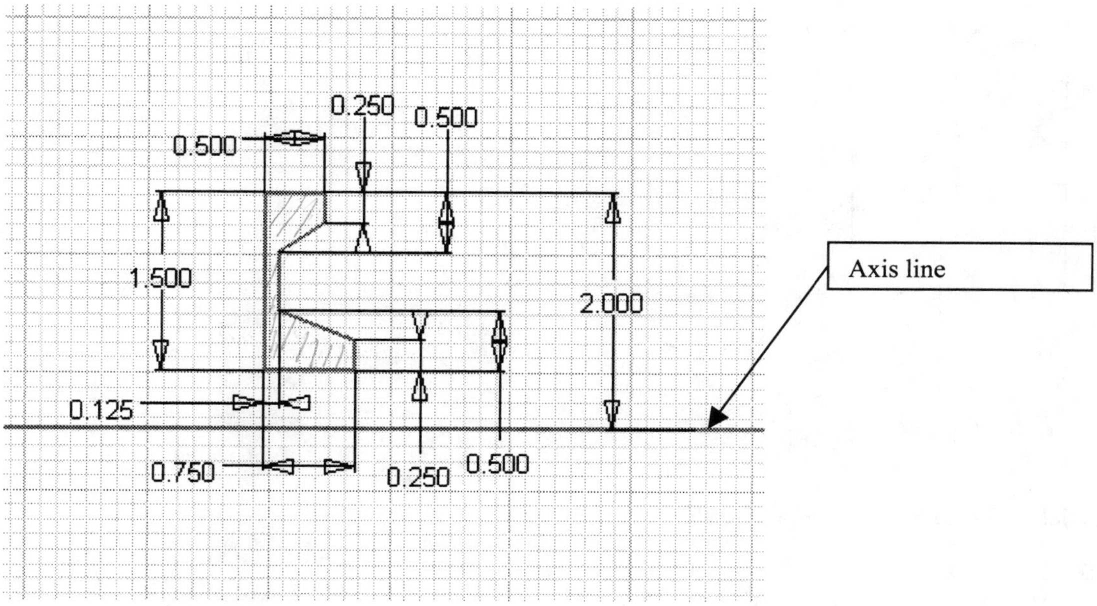

Draw the sketch shown. Note the axis line. This will be used to revolve around.
Inventor R4 comes with three line types: Normal, Construction, and Centerline.
We can identify the axis line as a centerline by selecting it and then selecting Centerline from the drop down.

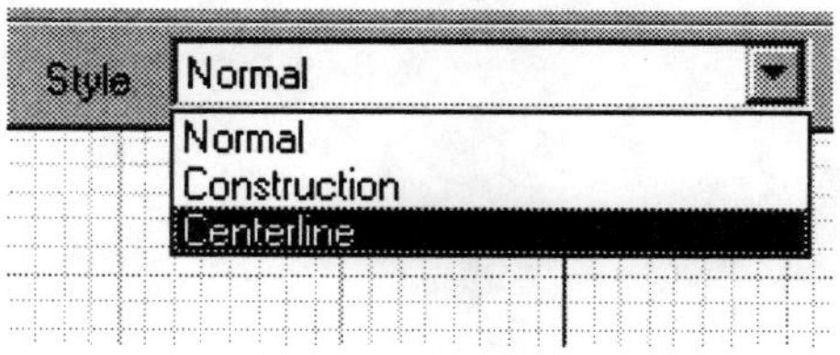

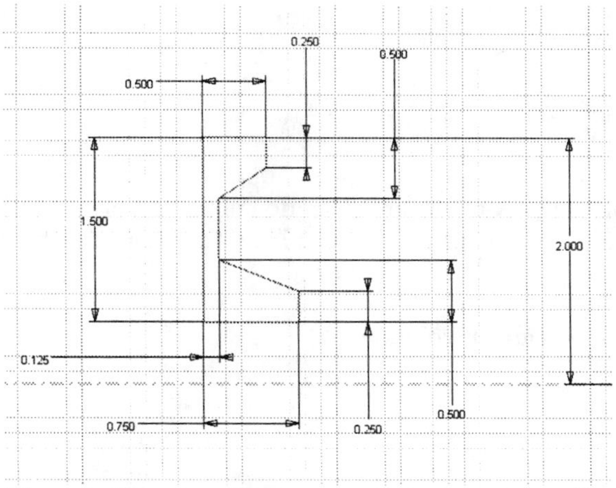

The axis line now changes appearance to a centerline.

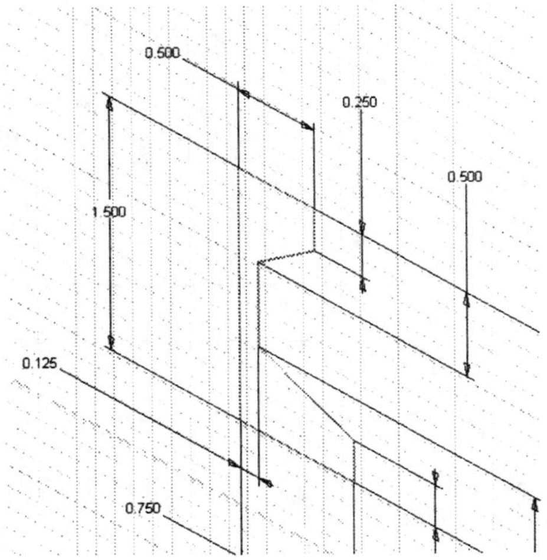

Right click and switch to 'Isometric View'.

Select the Revolve icon in the Features toolbar.

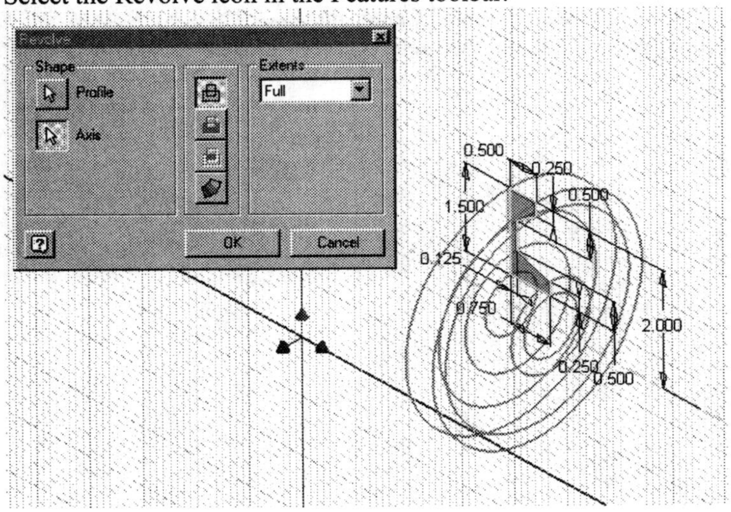

Verify that the correct profile is highlighted. If it is not, left-pick on the profile button in the Revolve dialog box and select the sketch. Because we defined our axis line as a centerline, Inventor automatically knows how to revolve our profile.

In the Extents drop-down, select 'Full' for a complete 360-degree revolution.

Press 'OK'.

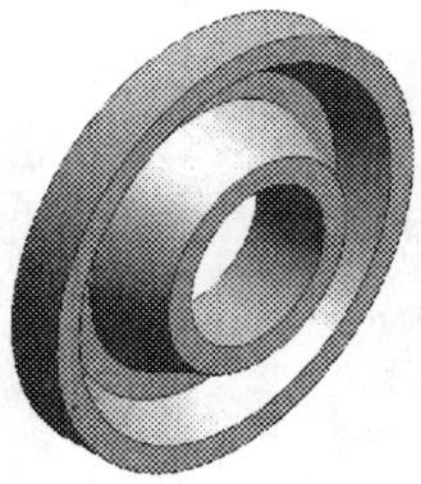

Save this part as 'wheel.ipt'. We will be using this part later in the text when we create patterns.

Hole

The Hole tool creates parametric drilled; counter bored, or countersunk hole features. A single hole feature can represent multiple holes with identical configurations (diameters and termination methods). Different holes can be created from the same, shared hole-pattern sketch.

Before you place a hole, you have to place a point or hole center using the Sketch toolbar. Place the point, constrain it's location and then you can proceed to the Features toolbar. You can also select endpoints or center points on existing geometry as hole centers.

Inventor's hole dialog box is extremely advanced and has several 'Gee Whiz' features. You can actually click inside the dialog box and modify the dimensions there. You can define more than one hole at a time simply by selecting on those hole centers and adding them to the selection set. So, for maximum efficiency, you can place all your hole centers using the sketch tool and then extrude them using the hole feature tool all in one shot.

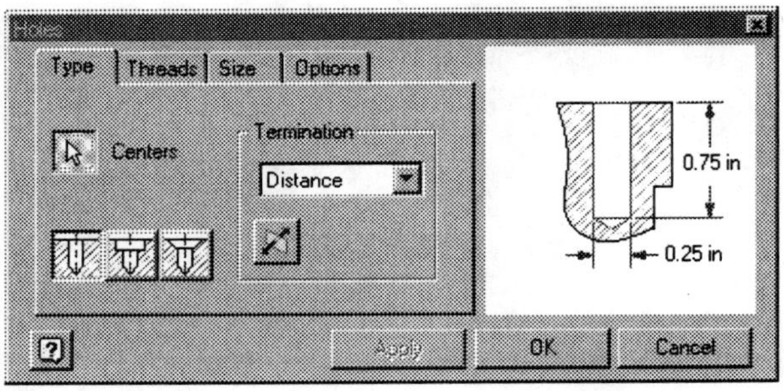

Hole Types

The Type Tab selects hole centers and specifies hole type.		
Centers	Hole center points are automatically selected. Click to select endpoints or center points of geometry as hole centers.	
Hole type		Drilled holes are flush with the planar face and have a specified diameter. This is the default.
	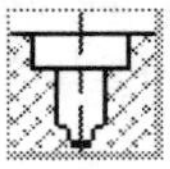	Counterbored holes have a specified diameter, counterbore diameter, and counterbore depth.
	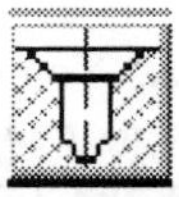	Countersunk holes have a specified diameter, countersink diameter and countersink depth.
Termination	Distance	Defines the termination method for the hole. Uses a positive value for the hole depth. Depth is measured perpendicular from the planar face.
	Through All	Extends a hole through all faces.
	To	Terminates a hole at the specified planar face.
Flip	Reverses direction of the hole.	

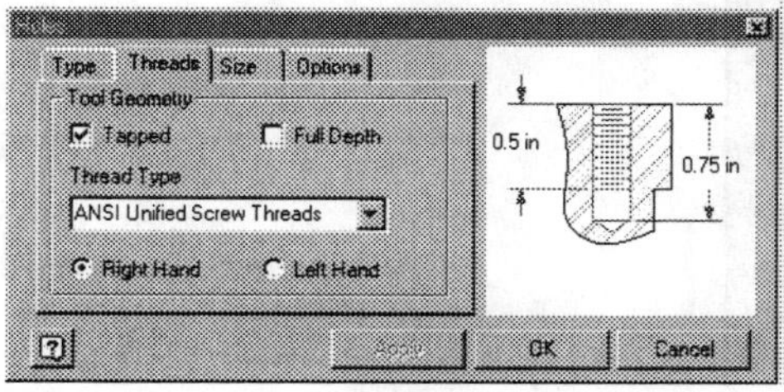

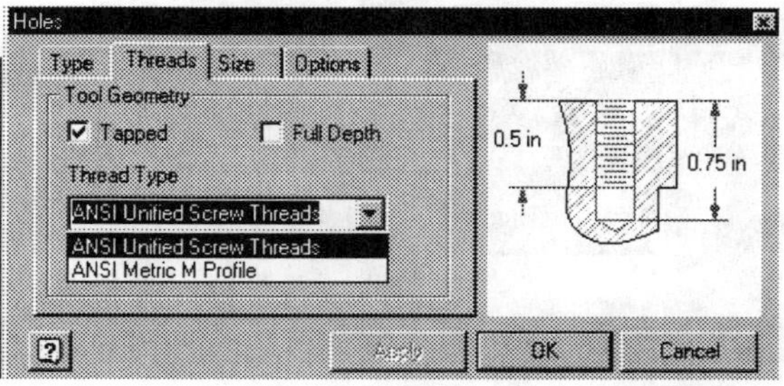

Hole Threads

The Threads Tab sets values to define tapped holes. The hole is previewed according to the values you specify.	
Tapped	Select the check box to define hole threads.
Full Depth	Select the check box to specify threads the full depth of the hole.
Thread Type	Either ANSI or Metric. The default depends on which the user selected when Inventor was installed.
Right Hand/Left Hand	Determines the direction of thread.

The threads will not appear in your model, but the information will be used when you move into the drawing stage of your design. It will save you time and frustration to define any tapped holes here rather than relying on memory.

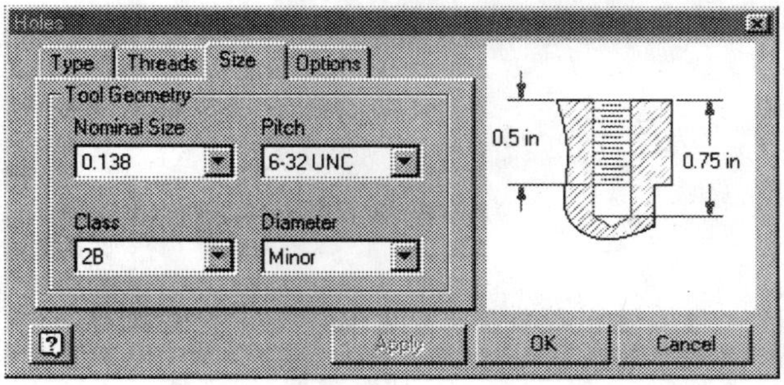

Hole Size

The nominal size and pitch callout pull downs display standard threads depending on whether the user set the drawing as metric or standard. The drafting standard can only be changed in a drawing file. You can decide to switch to a metric thread when you create your drawing file. Use Tools->Drafting Standards to set your options.

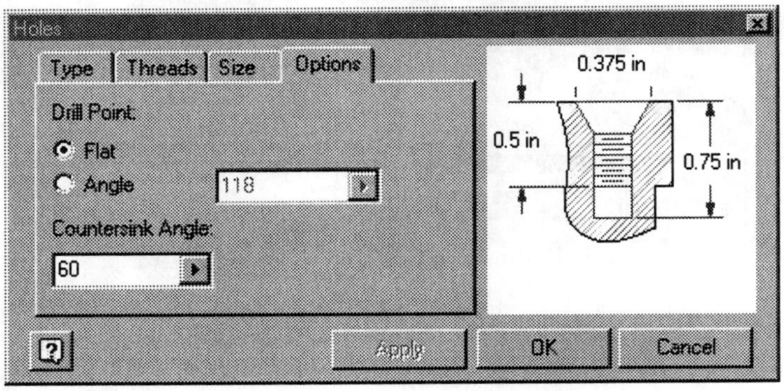

Hole Options

The Options tab defines the angle for countersunk holes and defines angle or flat tip for drill points.	
Countersink Angle	For countersunk holes, click the down arrow to specify the angle of the countersunk head or select geometry on the model to measure a custom angle. The positive direction of the countersink taper is measured counterclockwise from the hole axis, normal to the planar face.
Drill Point	Sets the angle of the drill-point taper to the end of the hole. Select Flat or Angle point. Click the down arrow to specify angle dimension or select geometry on the model to measure a custom angle, if applicable.

This dialog box grays out the Countersink Angle option unless Countersink is selected under Type.

Shell

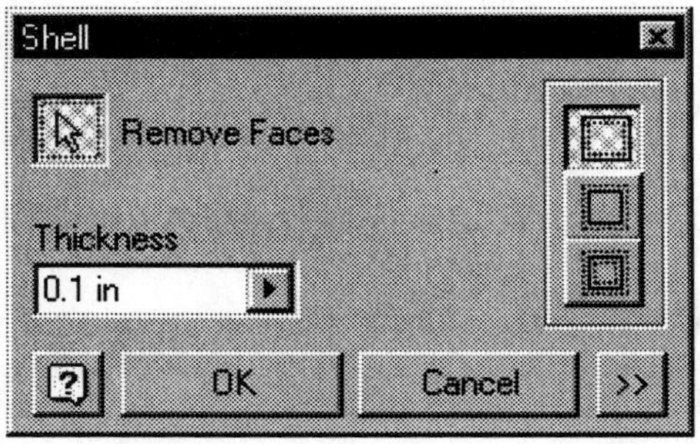

The Shell tool removes material from a part interior, creating a hollow cavity with walls of a specified thickness.

Remove Faces	Selects part faces to remove, leaving the remaining faces as the shell walls. Click to activate the part, then select the faces to remove. To reclaim a face, press and hold Ctrl and select the face. Selected faces are removed. Thickness is applied to remaining faces to create shell walls. If no part faces are selected for removal, the shell cavity is entirely enclosed within the part.
Direction	 Inside Offsets the shell wall to the part interior. The external wall of the original part becomes the external wall of the shell  Outside Offsets the shell wall to the exterior of the part. The external wall of the original part is the internal wall of the shell.  Both Sides Offsets the shell wall equal distances to the inside and outside of the part. Adds half of the shell thickness to the thickness of the part.
Thickness	Specifies the thickness to be applied uniformly to shell walls. Part surfaces not selected for removal become shell walls. If you need to use the thickness value in a parameter table, you can highlight the value in the box, then right-click to cut, copy, paste, or delete it.

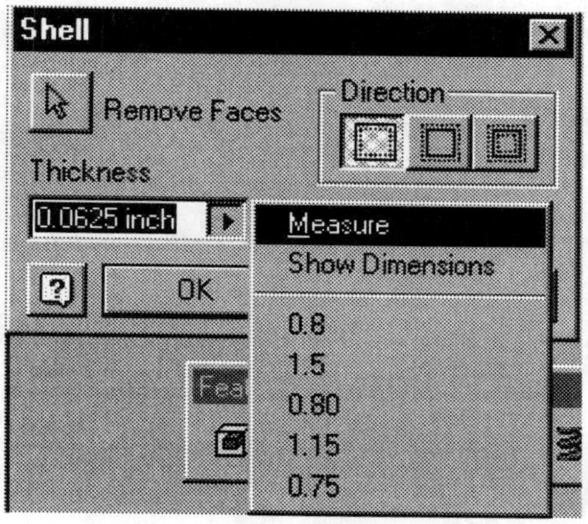

The drop down on the Thickness bar allows you to measure a distance to determine the shell thickness or display dimensions to assist you in determining which thickness value to use. Inventor stores the most common values and displays them to aid you in making a choice.

The three direction buttons from left to right are Inside, Outside or Both.

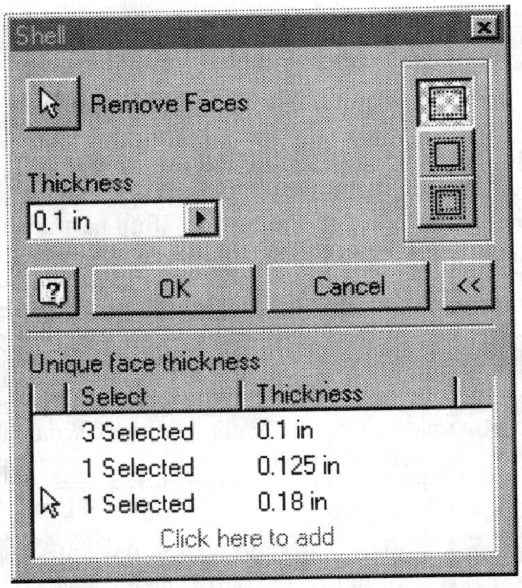

Pressing on the double arrow button located on the lower right of the Shell dialog box enlarges the dialog box, providing the user with the ability to define sides with different thickness values. To remove items from the unique face thickness list, highlight and press the 'Delete' key in your keyboard.

TIP: To reclaim a face, press and hold Ctrl and select the face.

Rib

A Rib is a special type of extruded feature created from an OPEN sketched contour. It adds material of a specified thickness in a specified direction between the contour and an existing part.

Adding a Rib

Open the file created in Lesson 1.

We start by creating an offset work plane in the middle of the bracket.

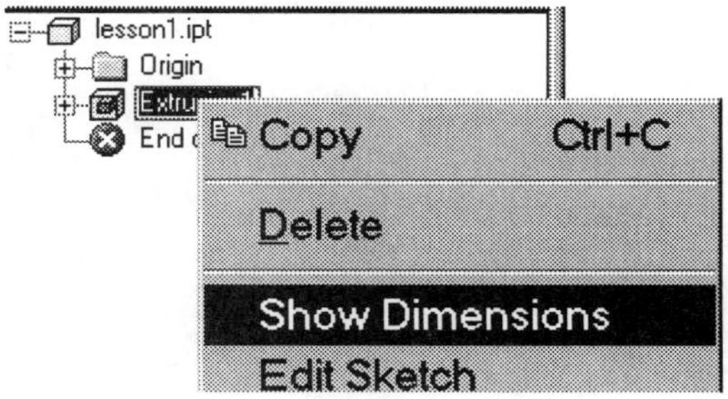

Highlight the extrusion in the browser. Right click and select 'Show Dimensions'.

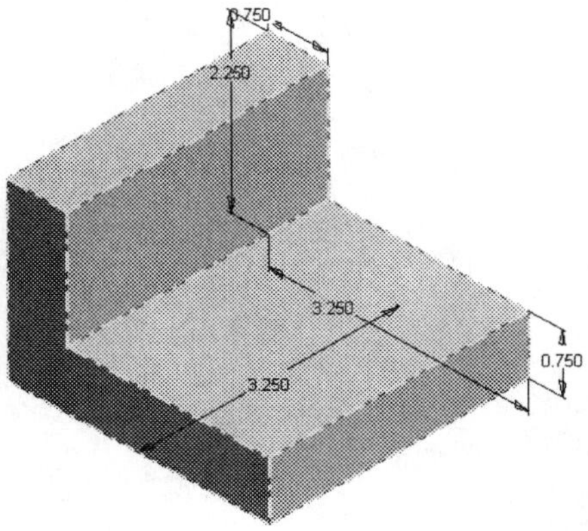

The extrusion's dimensions are now visible. We see that the width is 3.25 units.

Select the Work Plane tool from the Features toolbar.

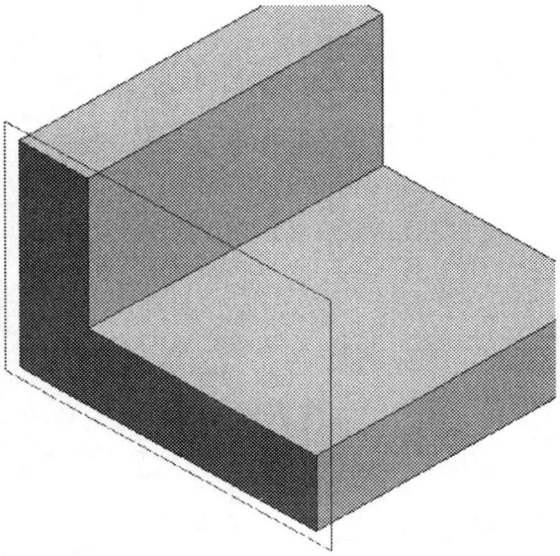

Select the face shown and start dragging the work plane into the part.

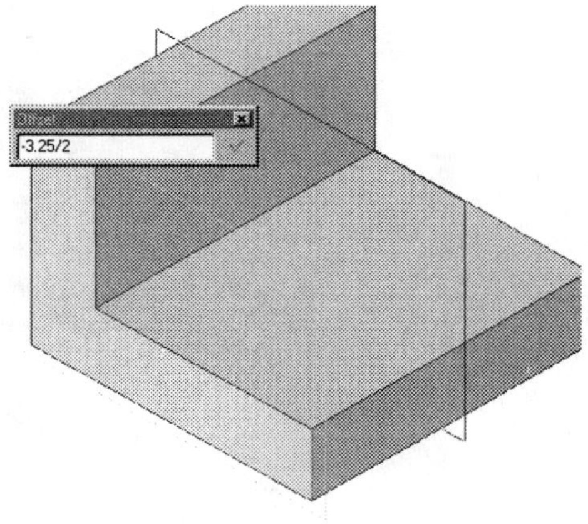

The Offset edit box should appear. Enter the value –3.25/2. The part was extruded 3.25 units.

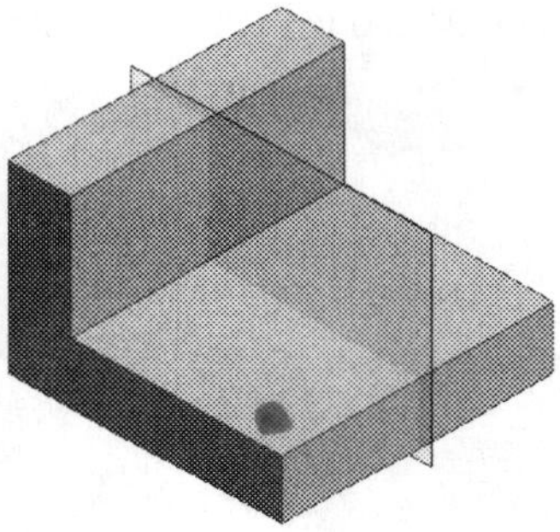

Our work plane now bisects the part. Select the work plane. Right click and select 'New Sketch.'

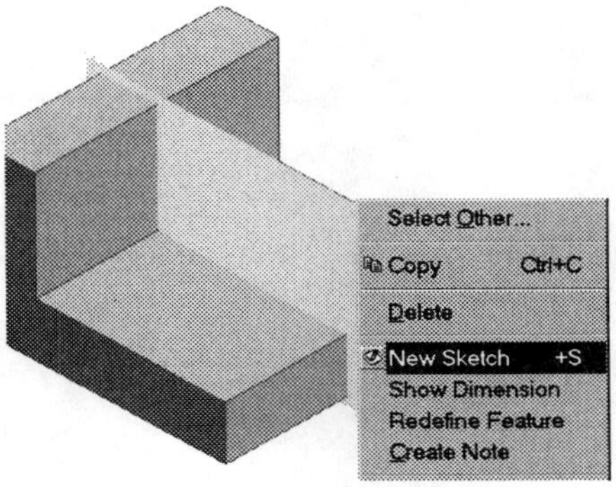

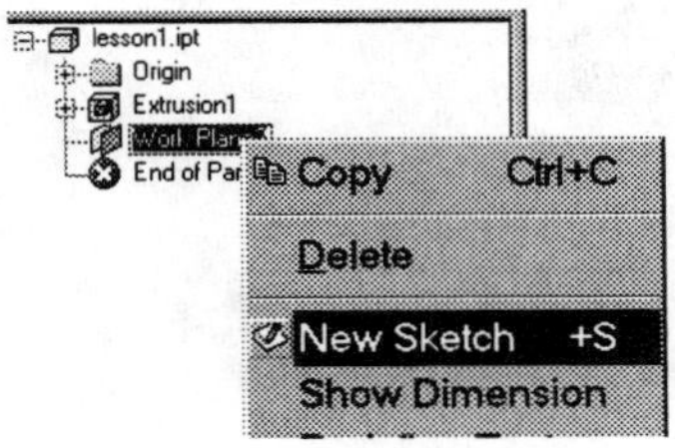

TIP: You can select the work plane for the New Sketch in the browser or in the graphics window.

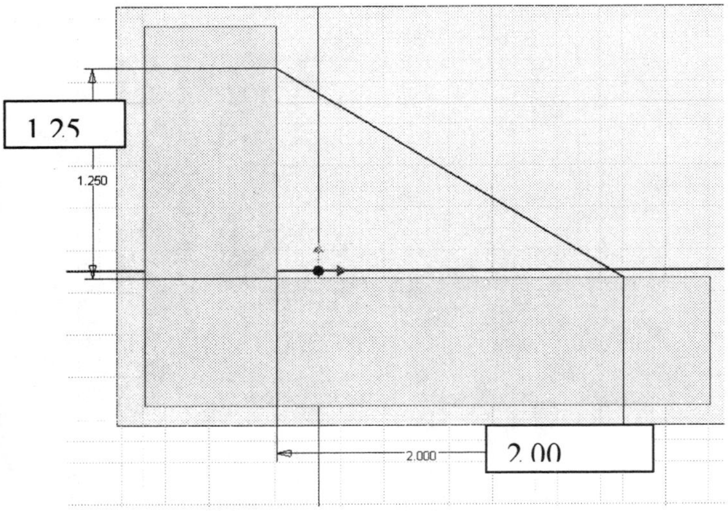

Draw a single slanted line as shown. Add coincident constraints for the horizontal and vertical endpoints and then dimension.

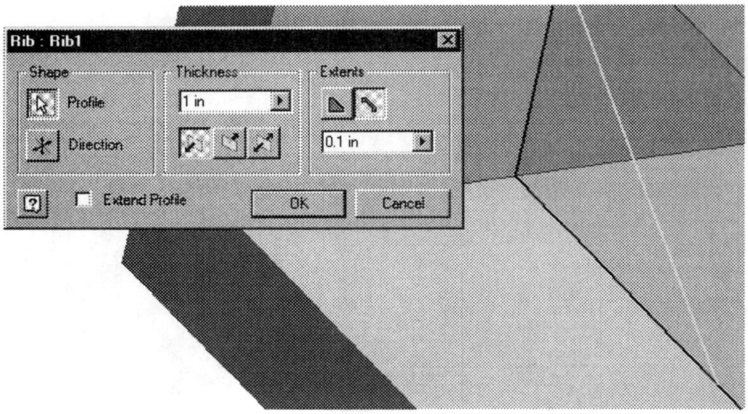

Select the Rib tool.
Set the thickness to 1 in.
Disable the 'Extend Profile' box.
Set the Extents to Finite and set the value to 0.1 in.
Press 'OK'.

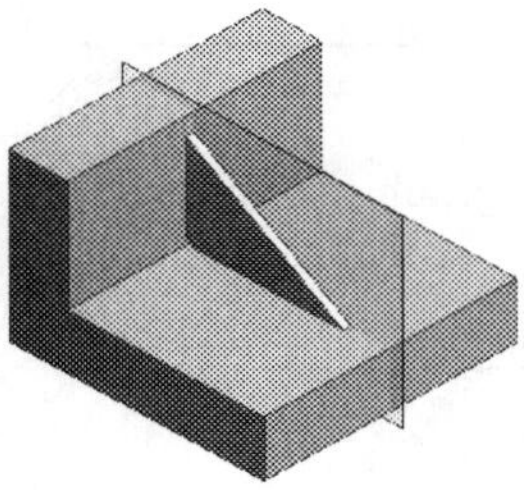

Our bracket with the rib added.
Save the part using 'Save Copy As' 'bracketwrib.ipt'. (Remember this does not save the current file!)

Loft

Loft features are created by blending the shapes of two or more profiles on work planes or planar faces. You can include the following in a loft feature:

- Sketches created on work planes offset from one another by a distance. The planes are usually parallel to one another, but any planes that are not perpendicular can be used.
- An existing planar face, as the beginning or end of a loft.
  To use an existing face as the beginning or end of a loft, create a sketch on that face (inserts a sketch icon in the browser). You do not need to draw anything in the sketch, but creating the sketch makes the edges of the face selectable for the loft.

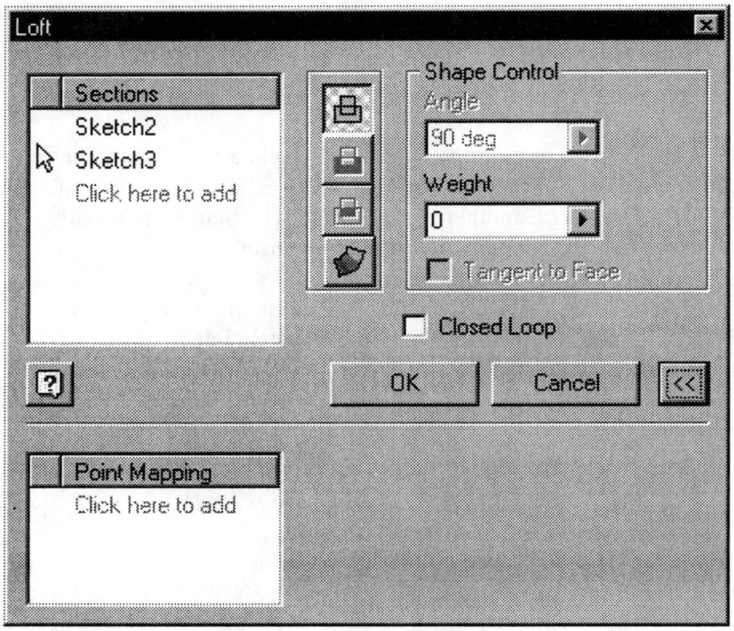

Sections	Specifies the profiles to include in the loft. Click in the row then click two or more profiles. Your selection is identified in the dialog box by sketch number, and a new row is added. To remove a section, highlight and press the 'Delete' key on the keyboard.
Shape Control	Angle Represents the angle between the sketch plane and the faces created by the loft at the sketch plane. The default value is 90 degrees. Weight A unitless value that controls how the angle affects appearance of the loft. A large number creates a gradual transition, while a small number creates an abrupt transition. Large and small values are relative to the size of your model Tangent to Face Constrains profiles created on a planar face to be tangent to the face. (Angle is not selectable if Tangent to Face is selected.)
Point Mapping	Selects a point on a sketch to use as the starting point for the loft surface. Selecting mapping points aligns profiles linearly along the points to minimize

Sweep

Sweep creates a feature by moving a sketched profile along a planar path. A sweep feature requires two unconsumed sketches, a profile and a path, on intersecting planes.

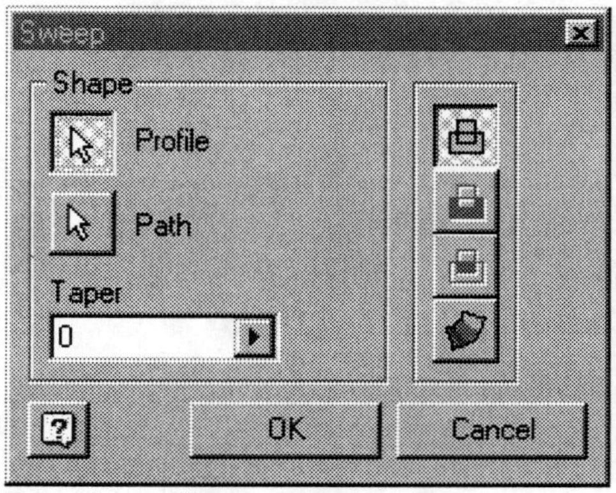

Base Sweep Feature

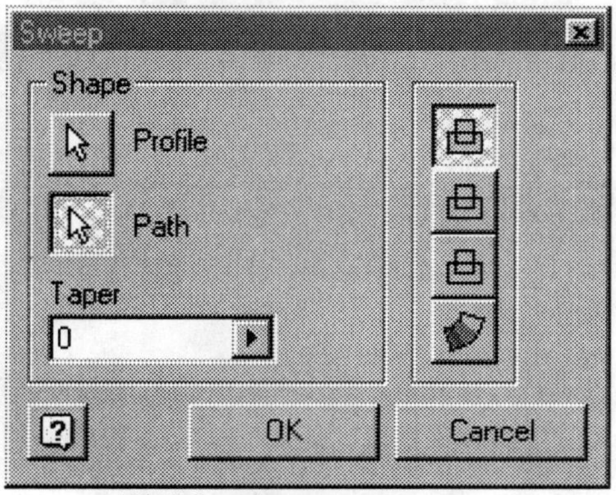

All Other Sweeps

<table>
<tr><td>Profile</td><td>Selects one or more profiles to sweep along the specified path. Profiles may be nested but may not intersect. To select multiple profiles, press Ctrl and continue to select.</td></tr>
<tr><td>Path</td><td>Sets the trajectory and endpoints of the swept feature. The profile remains normal to the path at all points.</td></tr>
<tr><td>Operation</td><td>Specifies whether the sweep joins, cuts, or intersects with another feature. Not available for base features, but required for all other sweep features. The dialog box on the left appears for base features. The dialog box on the right appears for all other sweep features.</td></tr>
<tr><td>Taper</td><td>Sets taper angle for sweeps normal to the sketch plane. If taper angle is specified, a symbol shows the fixed edge and direction of taper. Not available for closed paths.
<table>
<tr><td>Positive Angle</td><td>Positive taper angle increases the section area as the sweep moves away from the start point.</td></tr>
<tr><td>Negative Angle</td><td>Negative taper angle decreases the section area as the sweep moves away from the start point.</td></tr>
<tr><td>Nested Profiles</td><td>The sign (positive or negative) of the taper angle is applied to the outer loop of nested profiles; inner loops have the opposite sign.</td></tr>
</table>
</td></tr>
</table>

 Coil

Our last Sketch feature tool is Coil. Start by creating the profile for the coil, usually a circle or rectangle. Then press the Coil tool button.

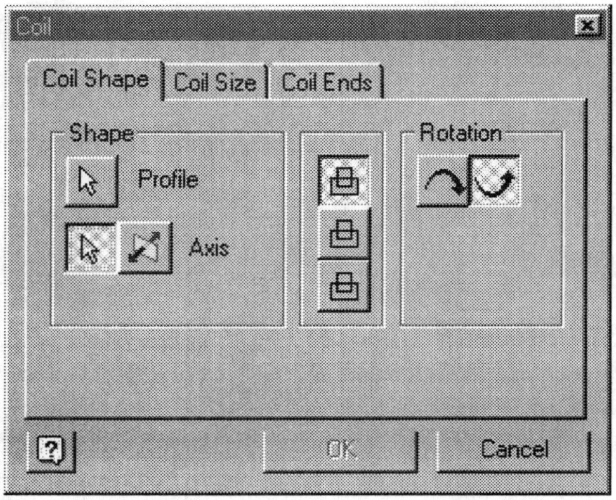

Select the profile we have created. We can adjust whether the coil will be created clockwise or counterclockwise using the Rotation button. Inventor previews our selection so we can decide if the selection is correct. The axis can either be defined using an existing sketch, edge or, if the profile is a circle, selecting the circle profile will automatically set it to the center.

The Coil Shape Tab selects a profile and axis and specifies the direction of coil rotation. Profile and axis must be in the same sketch unless the axis is a work axis.	
Shape	Profile Selects a single profile automatically. If multiple profiles exist, you must specify one. Axis A straight line or work axis that defines the axis of revolution. It cannot intersect the profile.
Operation	Specifies whether the coil Joins, Cuts, or Intersects with the base feature. Not available if the coil is the base feature (first feature in the file). Join Adds the volume created by the coil feature to another feature. Cut Removes the volume created by the coil feature from another feature. Intersect Creates a new feature from the shared volume of the coil feature and another feature. Material not included in the shared volume is deleted.
Rotation	Specifies if the coil rotates clockwise or counterclockwise.

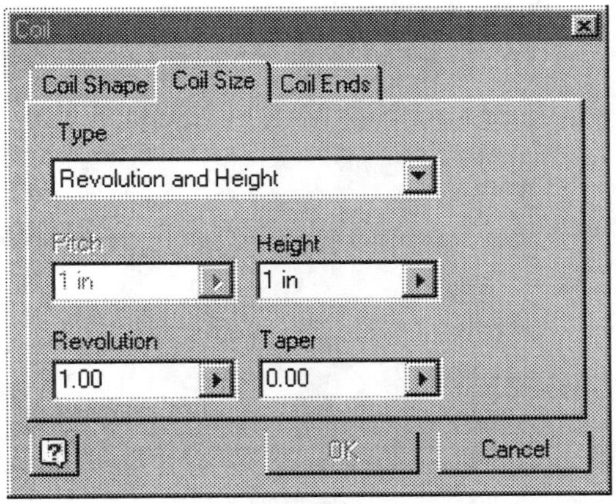

The Coil Size Tab specifies how the coil is created by specifying Pitch, Revolution, and/or Height. Specify two of the three parameters; the third parameter is calculated.	
Type	Selects which pair of parameters to specify: Pitch and Revolution, Revolution and Height, Pitch and Height, or Spiral.
Pitch	Specifies the elevation gain for each revolution of the helix.
Height	Specifies the height of the coil from the center of the profile at the start to the center of the profile at the end.
Revolution	Specifies the number of revolutions for the coil. Must be greater than zero but may include a fraction (for example, 1.5 turns). The number of revolutions includes the end conditions, if specified.
Taper	Specifies the taper angle, if desired, 1 for all coil types except Spiral.

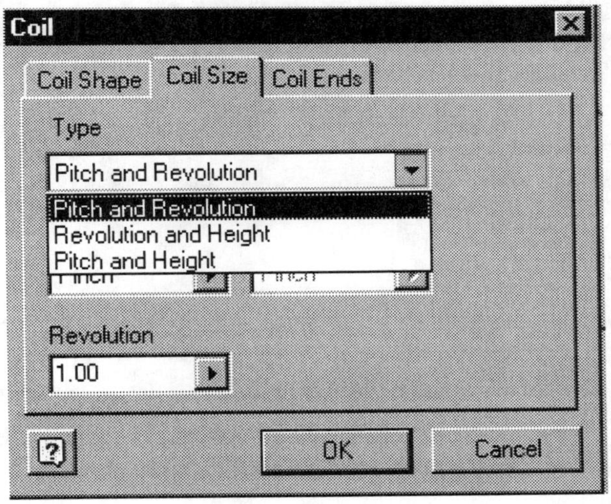

We can define a coil using Pitch and Revolution, Revolution and Height, or Pitch and Height. To modify the values, place the mouse cursor inside the edit box and type the desired value.

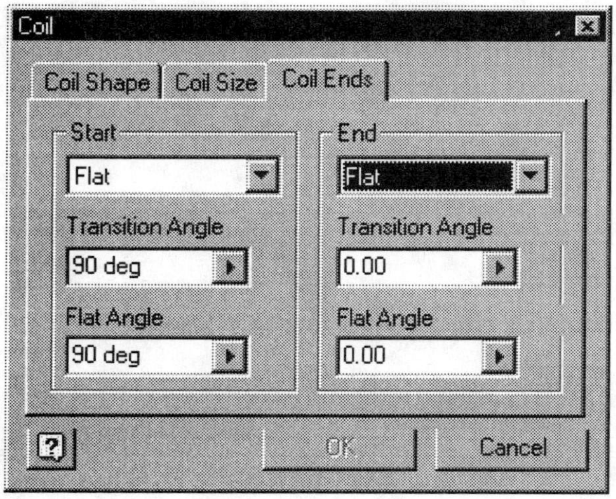

The Coil Ends tab specifies End conditions for the Start and End of the coil. Only the helix is flattened, not the profile of the coil.	
Natural or Flat	Click down arrow to specify Natural or Flat for both ends of the coil. Ends can have dissimilar end conditions.
	Transition angle The distance (in degrees) over which the coil achieves the transition (normally less than one revolution). The example shows the top with a natural end and the bottom end with a one-quarter turn transition (90 degrees) and no flat angle.
	Flat angle The distance (in degrees) the coil extends after transition with no pitch (flat). Provides transition from the end of the revolved coil to a flattened end. The example shows the same coil as above, but with a half-turn (180 degree) flat angle specified.

Thread Tool

This tool maps a bitmap of a thread onto a cylindrical feature.

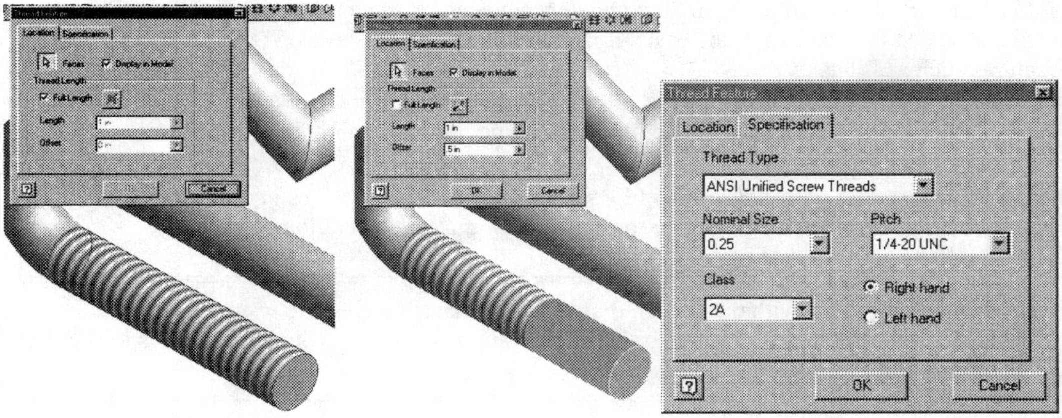

Location	
Faces	Select the faces to apply the bitmap
Display in Model	When this is enabled, the bitmap is visible.
Full Length	Adds threads to the entire length when enabled. When Full Length is disabled, the user can specify a length and an offset from an end.
Specification	
Thread Type	User can select ANSI or Metric. The default depends on which standard was selected during installation.
Nominal Size	User can select the diameter of the thread from a drop down list.
Pitch	User can select pitch from a drop down list.
Class	User can select from a drop down list.
Right/Left Hand	Determines the direction of the thread.

Placed Feature Tools

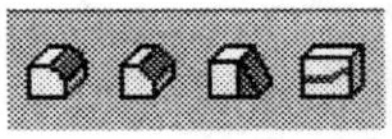

Our Placed Feature Tools are FILLET, CHAMFER, FACE DRAFT, and SPLIT.

 **FILLET**

You can include a fillet in your design by adding a 2D fillet when sketching. A 2D sketched fillet and a fillet feature can produce models that are identical in appearance. Although the results look the same, the model with the fillet features has several advantages:

- A fillet feature can be edited, suppressed, or deleted independent of the extrusion feature, without returning to the original sketch.
- If the remaining edges are to be filleted, you have more control over the corners.
- You have more flexibility when performing subsequent operations such as applying face draft.

Because other features may affect fillets and rounds, add the fillets and rounds toward the end of the modeling process. For example:

- It is easier to add draft to a face that intersects with other faces at a sharp angle, so it is better to add draft to a face before adding fillets.
- Fillets can increase the time required to update when feature dimensions change. To work most efficiently, add the features of the basic design early and wait until the end of the process to add features such as fillets.
- Reordering features can cause existing fillet features to produce undesired results. Adding features such as fillets and chamfers at the end of the modeling process can minimize problems.

When filleting adjacent edges, you can add the fillets separately or fillet all edges in one operation. Consider the following when deciding whether to use single or multiple operations:

	When adding fillets with the same radius to three adjacent edges, the result is the same whether you add them separately or in one operation. The most efficient method is to add them in one operation.
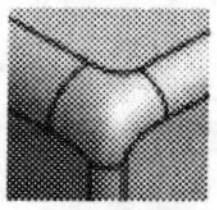	If each edge has a different radius, use a single fillet operation, if possible, to ensure a smooth corner. This situation always results in a blended corner.
	When two edges have the same radius and the third edge has a different radius, use a single fillet operation if possible. If you add the fillets as separate operations, the edge with the larger radius must be filleted first.
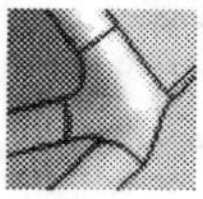	When filleting four or more edges, fillet all edges as a single operation

If a fillet is applied to a single edge, any operation that deletes the edge results in an error condition, since the fillet is no longer valid. If a fillet feature is applied to multiple edges, you can delete an edge and the fillet will update to reflect the change, as long as any edge in the set remains.

You can create constant-radius and variable-radius fillets and fillets of different sizes in a single operation. All fillets and rounds created in a single operation become a single feature.

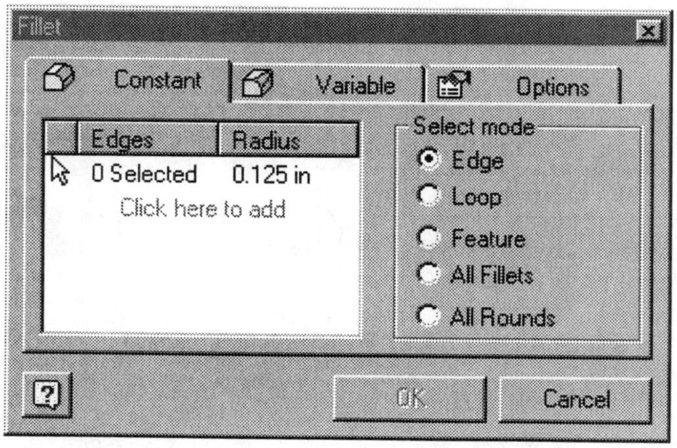

Selecting the Fillet tool brings up the dialog box shown. On the right side, we can set the selection mode of what we want to select. For example, enabling the 'All Fillets' mode, would select all the current fillets defined on the model.

The Constant Tab sets the parameters for adding constant-radius fillets. If necessary, set the options on the Options tab before creating the fillets.	
Edges	Defines a set of edges to fillet. To add edges, select the set from the Edges box, then click the edges in the graphics window. (To remove edges, press Ctrl as you click.) To add another edge set, click the prompt in the last row of the Edges box. Use Select Mode to simplify the selection of edges.
Radius	Specifies the fillet radius for the selected set of edges. To change the radius, click the radius value, then enter the new radius.
Select Mode	Changes the selection method for adding or removing edges from an edge set. Click to select the mode from the list. Edge selects or removes single edges. Loop selects or removes the edges of a closed loop on a face. Feature selects or removes all edges of a feature that do not result from intersections between the feature and other faces. Fillets selects or removes all remaining concave edges and corners. This mode requires a separate edge set. Rounds selects or removes all remaining convex edges and corners. This mode requires a separate edge set.

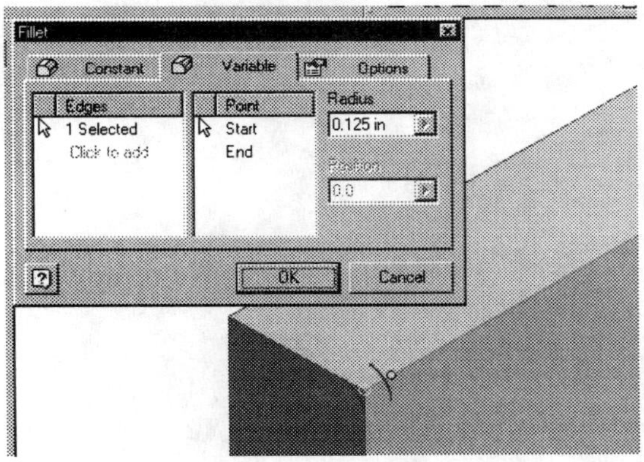

The Variable Tab sets the parameters for adding variable-radius fillets. If necessary, set the options on the Options tab before creating the fillets.	
Edges	Specifies edges to fillet. To add an edge, select the prompt in the Edges box, then click the edge in the graphics window.
Point	Selects the start point, endpoint, or an intermediate point so that you can enter its radius.
Radius	Sets the fillet radius at the selected point. To change the radius, select the point in the point list, then enter the new radius.
Position	Specifies the position of the selected point. To change the position, select the point in the point list, and then enter a value between 0 and 1 as a percentage of the length of the edge.

To create a variable fillet, select the Variable tab. Select an edge. The user is then prompted for a series of points along the edge. As the user picks each point, he can assign a value for the radius at that point.

TIP: To select a single edge without selecting edges that are tangent to it, turn off Automatic Edge Chain on the Options tab.

TIP: To select a single edge segment without selecting edges that are tangent to it, turn off Automatic Edge Chain on the Options tab.

If the selected edge contains multiple tangent edge segments, the position is relative to the start point of individual edge segment on which the point resides.

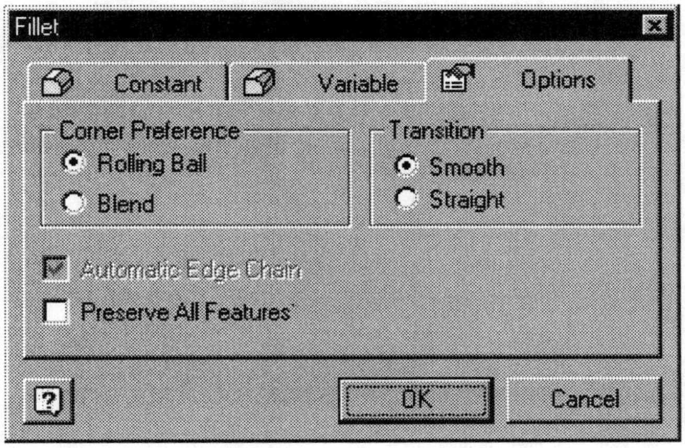

The Options tab sets the corner preference, transition type, and edge chain preference for fillets and rounds. The default settings for these options are correct for most fillet features.		
Corner Preference	Sets the corner style for the fillets. Rolling ball is the default setting.	
		Rolling Ball creates a fillet defined as if a ball had been rolled along the edge and around the corners.
	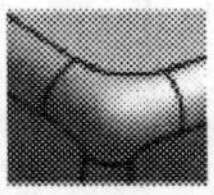	Blend creates a continuous tangent transition between fillets in sharp corners.
Transition	Defines how variable-radius fillets are created between control points. Smooth is the default setting.	
		Smooth creates fillets with a gradual blending transition between the points. The transition is tangent (no rate of change between points).
		Straight creates fillets with linear transitions between the points.
Automatic Edge Chain	When the check box is selected, selecting an edge to fillet selects all tangent edges automatically. When the check box is cleared, only the indicated edge is selected. The default setting is on.	
Preserve All Features	When the check box is selected, all features that intersect with the fillet are checked and their intersections are calculated during the fillet operation. If the check box is cleared, only the edges that are part of the fillet operation are calculated during the operation.	

TIP: To select part of an edge that already has filleted corners, clear the check box.

 Chamfer

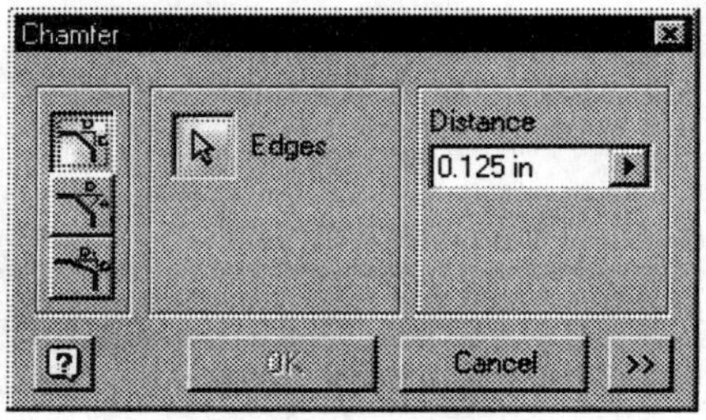

You specify the corner appearance and select edges individually or as part of a chain. All chamfers created in a single operation are one feature.

Method Specifies how the chamfer is constructed	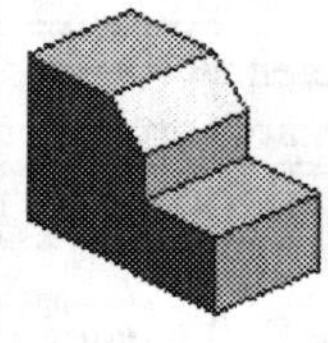	Distance 	Creates a chamfer with the same offset distance from the edge on both faces. Selects a single edge, multiple edges, or chained edges. Corner setback appearance may be specified.
	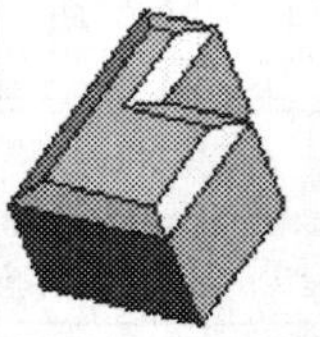	Distance and Angle 	Creates a chamfer defined by an offset from an edge and an angle from one face to the offset. Any/all edges of a selected face may be chamfered at once.
	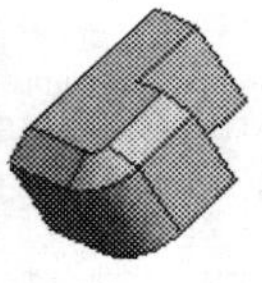	Two Distances 	Creates a chamfer on a single edge with a specified distance for each face. Edges may be chained together.
Edges and Faces Selects one or more edges or faces. Pressing Ctrl while clicking removes geometry from the selection.	Edges	Selects individual edges to chamfer and previews default distance.	
	Face	For chamfers defined by a distance and angle, selects the affected face.	

Flip	For chamfers defined by two distances, flips the direction of the chamfer distances.	
Distance and Angle	Specifies the extent of selected chamfer method.	
	Distance	Specifies offset distance of chamfer from selected edge(s). For chamfer defined by two distances, specifies both offsets.
	Angle	For chamfers defined by a distance and angle, specifies the angle of the chamfer.
If edges intersect at a tangent point, edge chain and setback appearance may be specified.	Edge Chain	Selects all edges that share a tangent point.
	Setback	For the Distance chamfer method, defines corner appearance when three chamfered edges meet at a corner.
		 Chamfer may be joined at a flat intersection (left button).
		 Chamfer may form a corner point at the intersection, as if milled on three edges (right button).

The three modes of chamfers are located on the left side of the dialog box. The top tool is for Equal Distance. The middle tool is for Distance-Angle. The bottom tool is for two different Distance values. Note that on the lower right corner there is a double arrow (More) button.

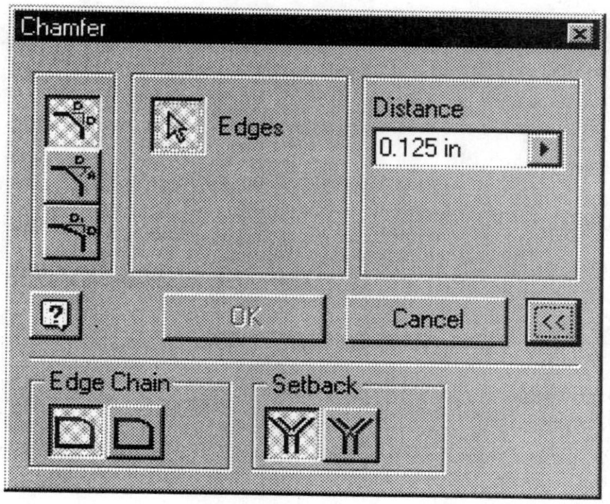

Pressing the double arrow brings up additional chamfer options. The Edge Chain option controls whether the chamfer affects all tangential edges or only the selected edge. The Setback option controls whether or not a setback is added.

Face Draft

A face draft is a slight angle applied to the walls of a part.

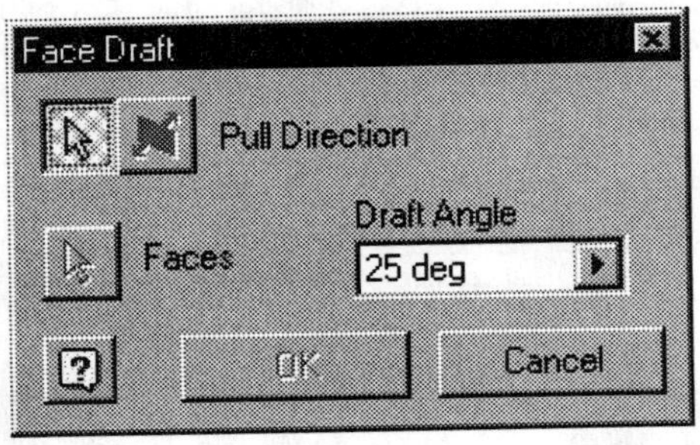

Draft is a taper applied to part faces so that a part can be retrieved from a mold or to cant one or more faces. When designing features for molded or cast parts, you can apply draft by specifying a taper angle for an extrusion or sweep. To add draft to an existing feature or to individual faces, use the Face Draft tool. When applying draft to a face, the relationship between the pull direction and the fixed edge determines the result of the operation.

- If you select a set of tangent continuous faces (like a staircase with fillets at the edges), draft is applied to all faces. In the browser, this draft is labeled TaperShadow.
- If you select a face that is not tangent to another face, draft is applied to that face only. In the browser, this draft is labeled TaperEdge.

Pull Direction	Indicates direction in which a mold is pulled from a part. As you move the cursor in the graphics window, a vector displays normal to a highlighted face or along a highlighted edge. When the vector displays as desired, click to select it and display the direction arrow.	Flip Direction: Reverses the pull-direction arrow. Accept: Accepts the displayed pull direction.
Faces	Specifies the faces to which draft will be applied. As you move the cursor over a face, a symbol indicates the fixed edge for the draft and how the draft will be applied. Click to select the desired fixed edge.	
Draft Angle	Sets the angle of the draft. Enter the angle or choose a calculation method from the drop-down list.	

TIP: The first edge selected determines the curves you can select for draft. For example, if the first edge you select is linear, you cannot select edges with continuous tangency.

Applying a Face Draft

Click the Face Draft tool.

1. To define the pull direction, move the cursor over a feature until the direction vector is aligned with the desired pull direction, then click to select.
2. If necessary, click the Flip Direction button to change the pull direction.
3. Select the faces to draft. As you move the cursor over a face, a symbol indicates the fixed edge and direction for the draft.
4. Enter the draft angle.
5. Click OK.

TIP: To select part of an edge that already has filleted corners, clear the check box.

If a face is tangent to other faces, all tangent faces are highlighted.

Split

Part Splitting is a fast and easy way to create a top and bottom for a box or enclosure. It ensures that the parts mate properly. To create a split, the easiest method is to place an offset work plane at the location for the split and then use the work plane for the split operation. We can split part faces or an entire part and remove one of the resulting sides. This tool allows faces on both sides of the split to have draft applied.

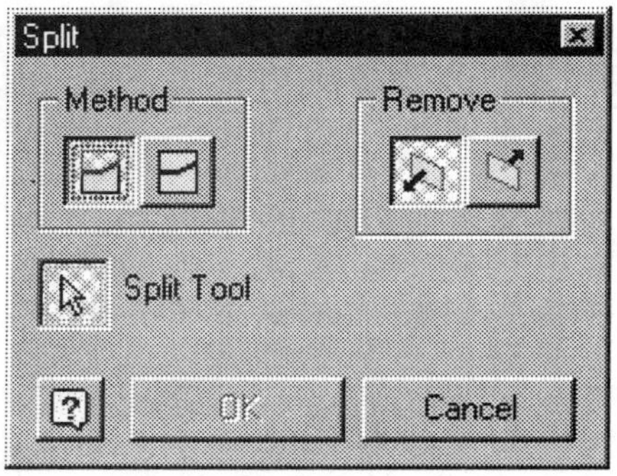

Split Part	Selects part to split and discards one side.
Split Face	Selects one or more faces to split into two pieces.
Split tool	Selects workplane or parting line used to split face or part into two pieces.
All	Selects all faces to split. Click OK.
Selected	Selects faces to split. Click Faces to Split tool, select faces to split, then click OK.
When Split Part method is active, click Side to Remove button to preview, then click OK to remove specified side.	

Selecting the Split tool brings up the dialog box shown. The user has two options under Method: Splitting the Part (left icon) and Splitting a Face (right icon).

The Split tool can be a workplane or sketch a parting line on a workplane or part face. The sketched parting line can include lines, arcs, and splines.

By default, Split removes one side of a split part. If you need to split a part into two parts you can use this procedure:

1. Sketch a parting line on a part face.
2. On the File menu, use Save Copy As to save the part with the parting line and both halves intact.
3. Use the Split tool to split the part and remove the selected half.
4. Use Save Copy As to save the first half of the part.
5. Open the original file, then use the Split tool to remove the other half of the part.
6. Use Save Copy As to save the second half of the part.

Both halves of the part are now saved in separate files.

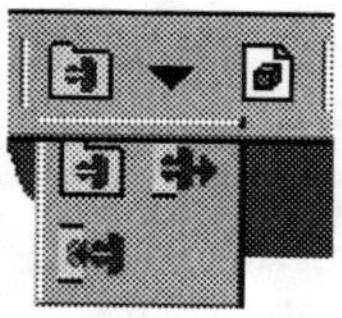

The next section of the Features tool bar contains the Catalog flyout tools and the Derived Component tool.

 **View Catalog**

The Catalog is similar to AutoCAD Design Center. The user can browse a library of parts and blocks that can be inserted into the current file.

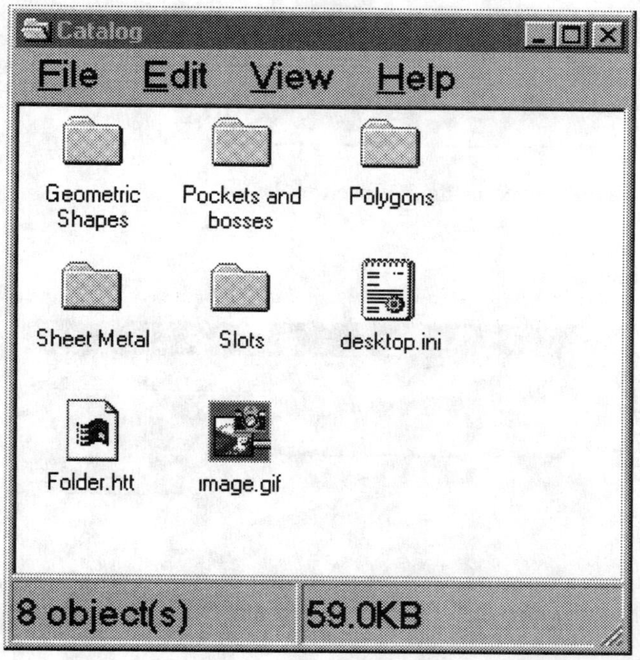

Inventor includes a set of features ready for use. Users can explore the pre-existing library of sketches to save time when constructing their models.

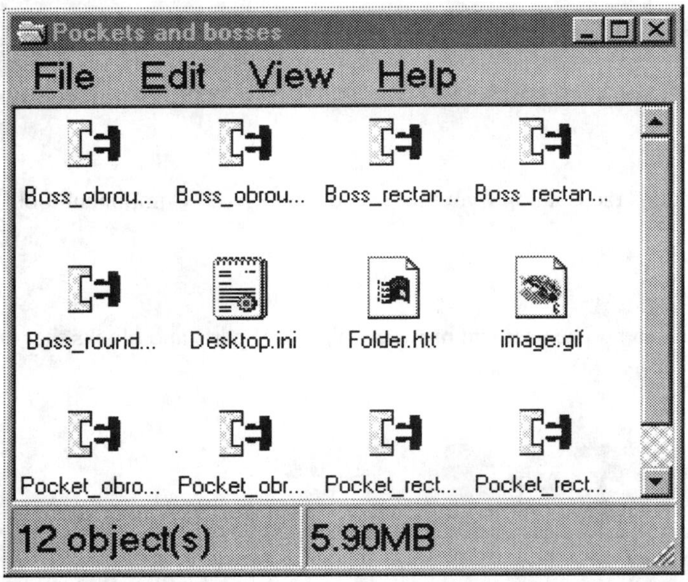

The library features can be previewed using the Insert tool.

 **Insert Design Element**

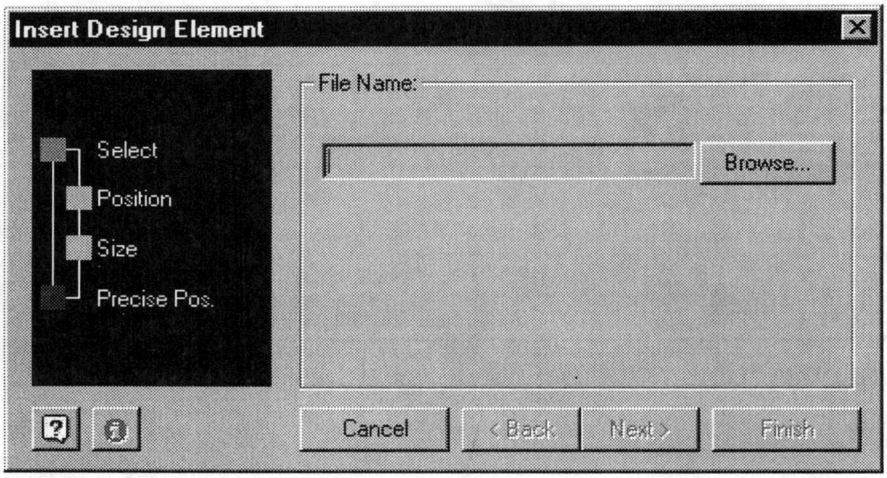

Selecting this tool brings up the dialog box shown. Select the 'Browse' button to locate the element to be added to the model.

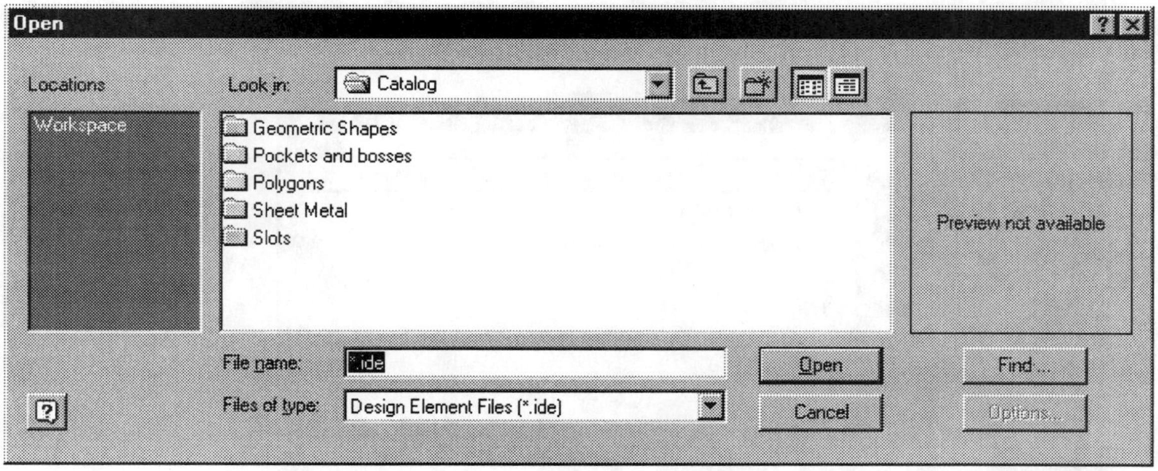

The user can then select the element category.

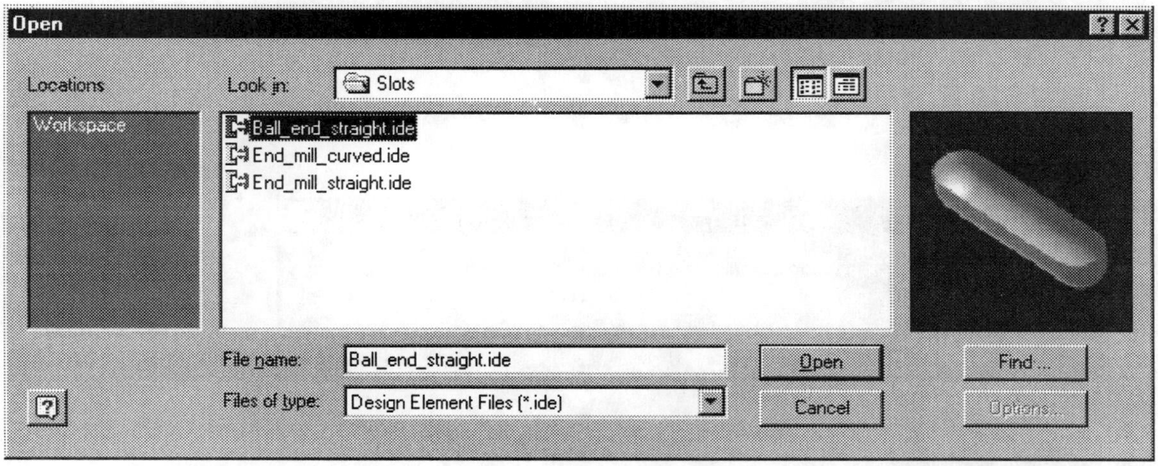

Once we get into the category area, we can preview each element to determine which one we want.

Select the desired element and press 'Open'.

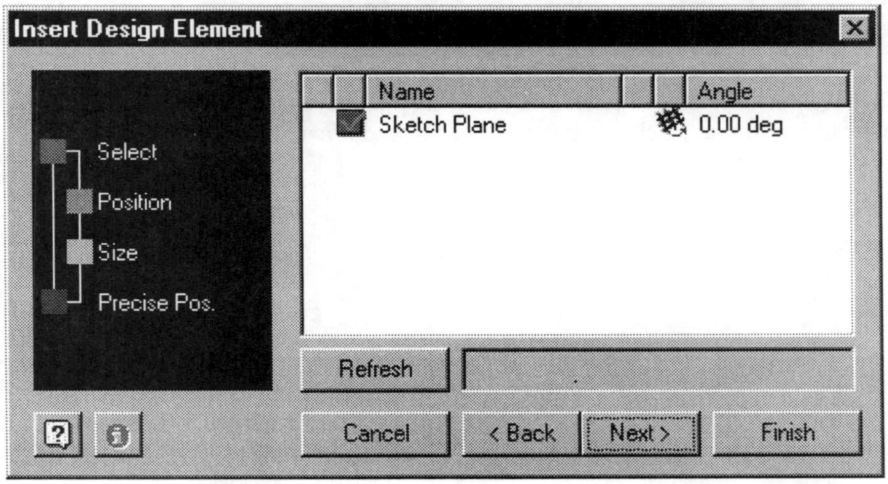

Once the element is selected, the next dialog appears. The user is required to select the plane on the existing model to place the element.

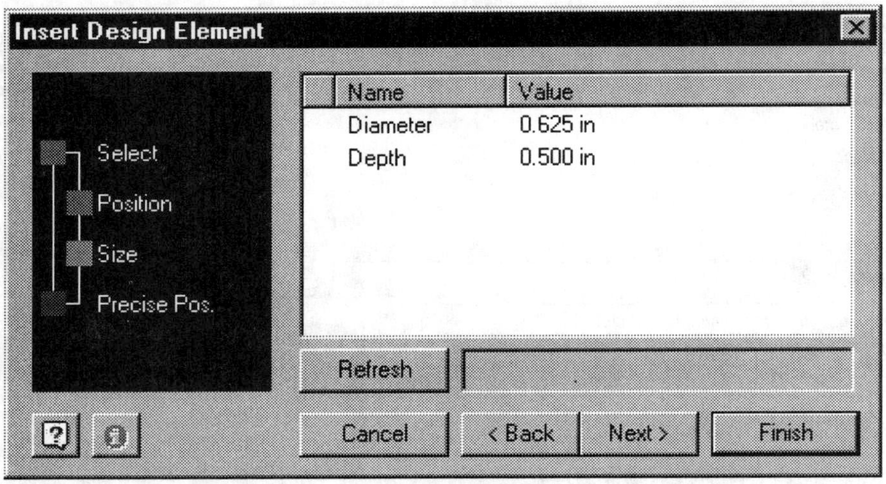

The user is then prompted for the values for the element to be placed. At this time, the user can specify his specifications for the design element.

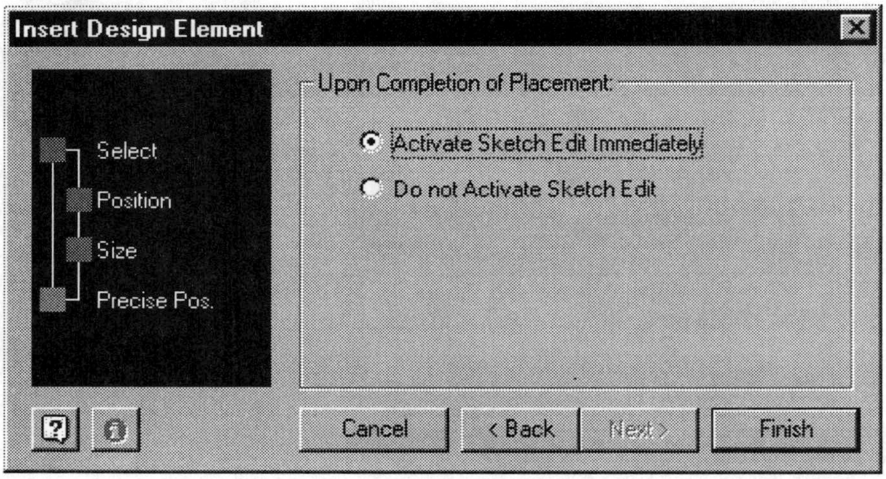

The user is then allowed to set whether to enter Sketch Edit mode immediately upon placement. Entering Sketch Mode allows the user to reposition the element or make further modifications to the basic element.

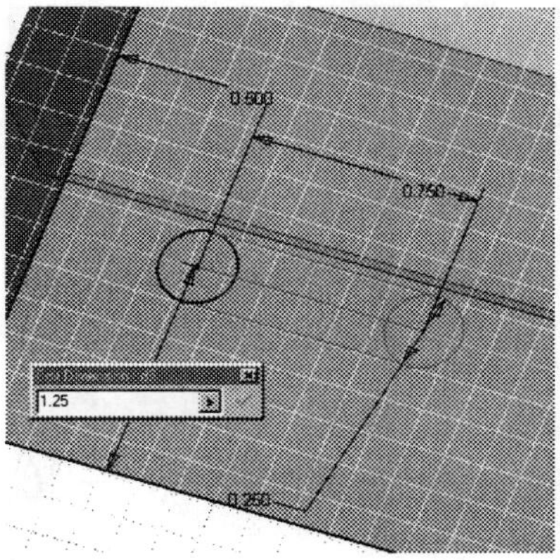

Modifying the inserted element is exactly the same as if we had created the sketch from scratch.

 **Create Design Element**

We start by creating a basic shape. In this case, I've created a basic keyhole slot.

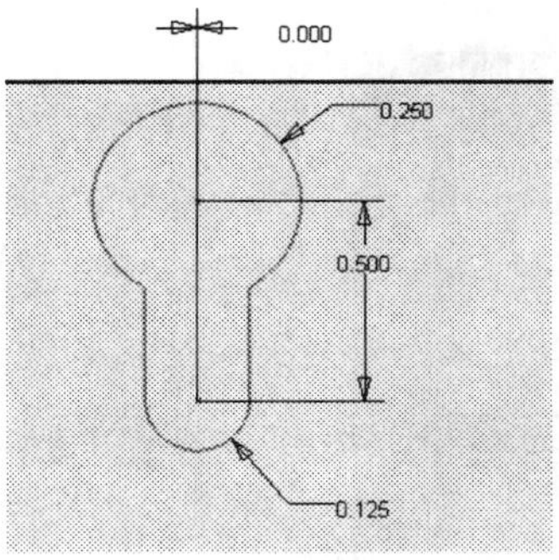

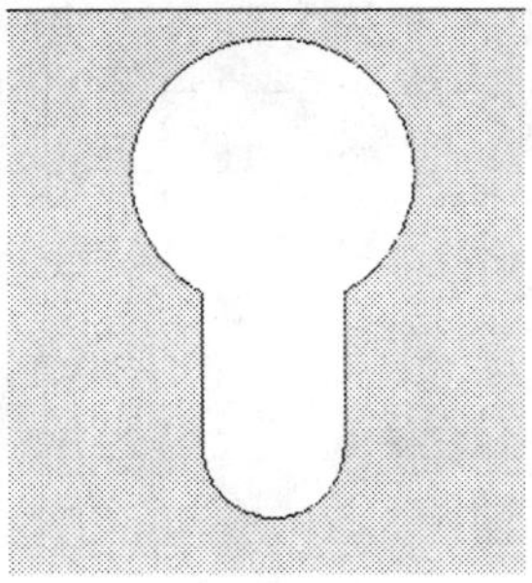

 We use the Create Design Element tool located on the Features toolbar. If you don't see the tool, it is because it is a flyout option under the View Catalog tool.

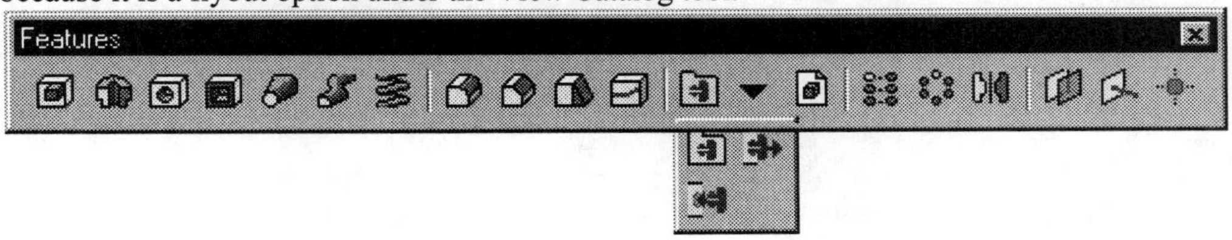

TIP: The sketch must be turned into a feature using Extrude, Revolve, or Sweep BEFORE it can be turned into a design element.

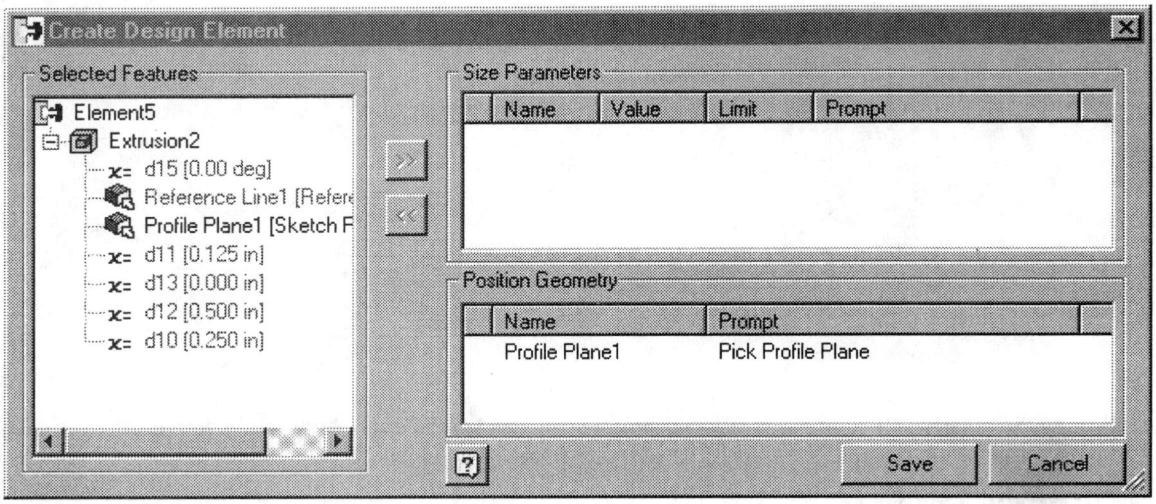

Initiate the Create Design Element command. To select the feature, simply pick it from the Browser. The window with the selected features will fill in as shown.

To define the variable parameters for the design, highlight it and then select the top double arrow. We can rename the parameter to allow useful prompting.

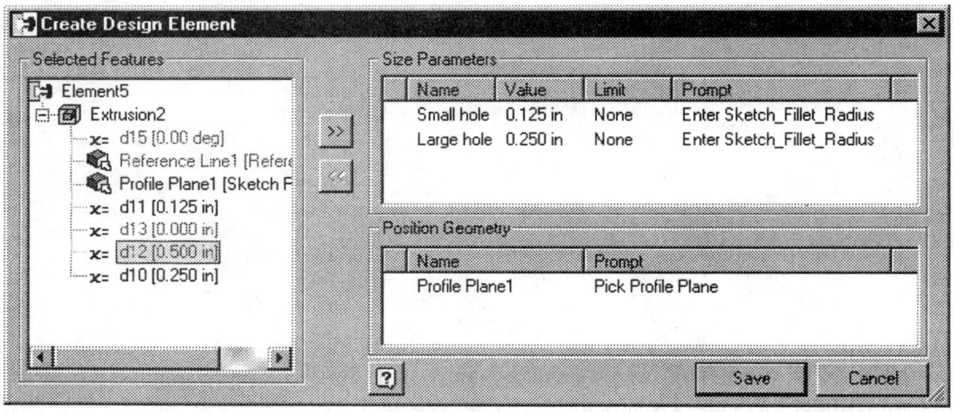

Notice that when a parameter is highlighted, the top double arrow becomes available to insert into the Size Parameters.

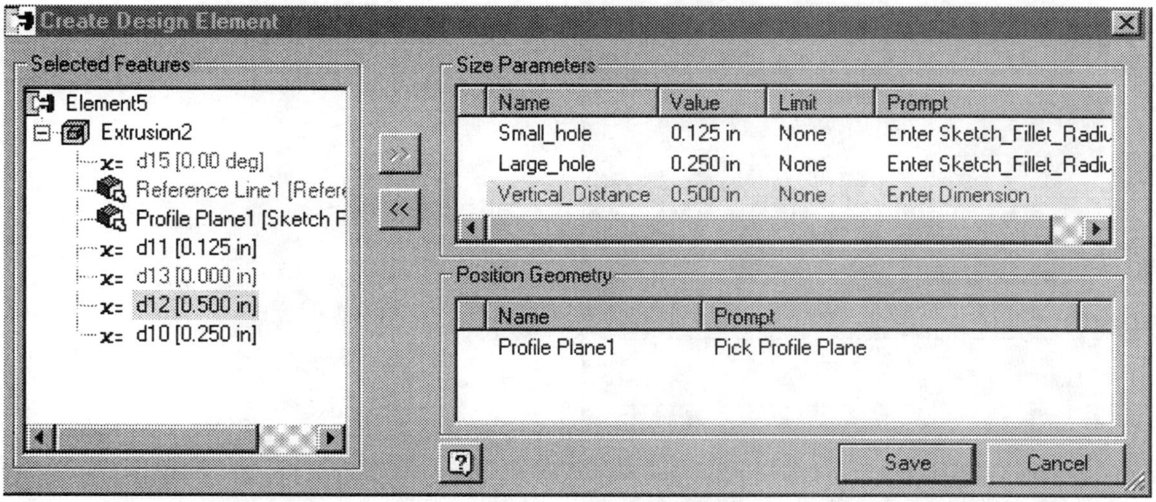

In this example, we have defined the design parameters to be the large hole, the small hole, and the vertical distance between the holes. Notice that the 0.00-inch dimension which forces the holes to line up is omitted at a user-defined parameter. In this way, we can control our design elements and decide which geometries are changeable and which are not.

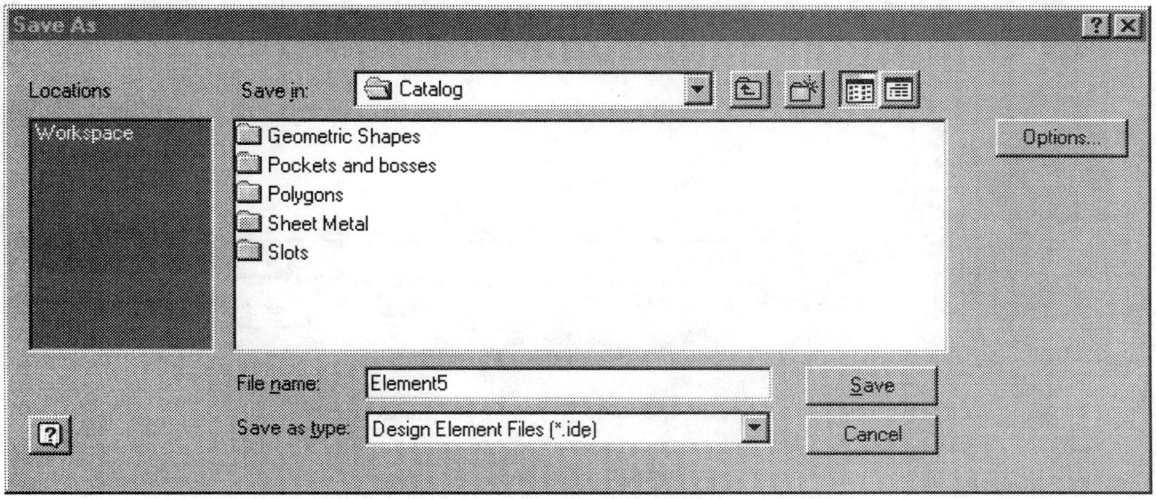

When we press 'SAVE', we get the Catalog. Since this is a keyhole slot, we will place this design element in the Slots Category.

TIP: When naming parameters, you can not use spaces, dashes or other punctuation marks. If you use an invalid character, you will get an error message to provide a proper name.

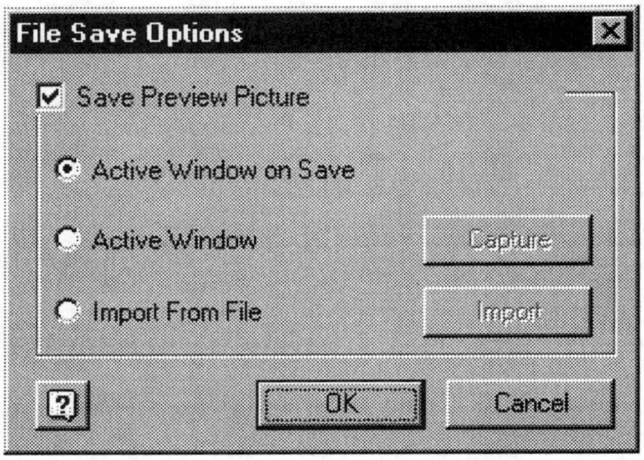

Pressing the Options button on the far right allows the user to set whether or not to create a Preview Picture of the design element and how it should be captured.

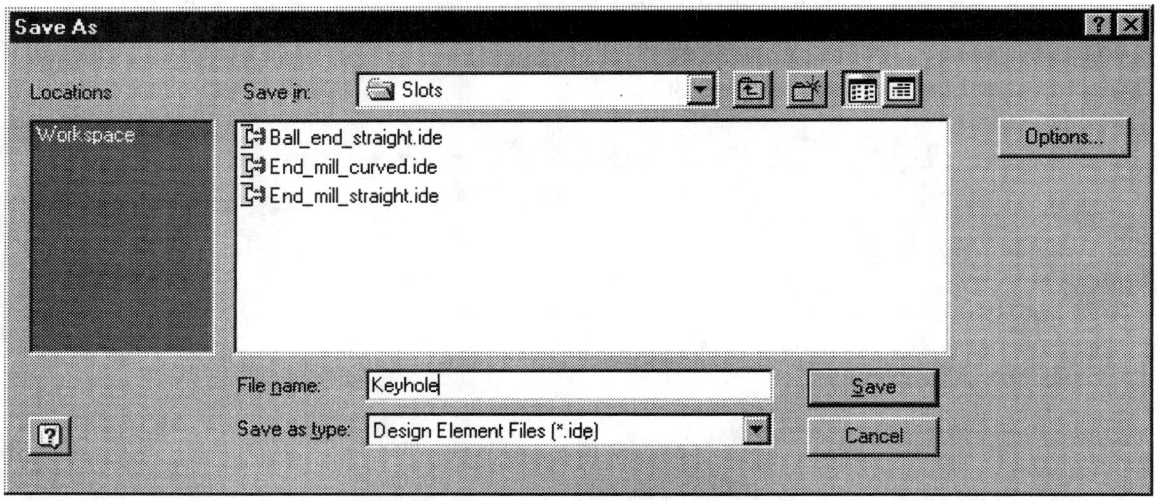

We select the Slots category and assign the filename 'Keyhole' to our design element.

Derived Part

Creates a new derived part using an Autodesk Inventor part as the base part. The derived part can be scaled larger or smaller than the original part or mirrored using any of the origin workplanes of the base part. The location and orientation of the derived body is the same as the base part.	
Access:	Insert>Derived part
Scale factor	Default value is 1.0. Scale factor may be expressed in whole numbers of percentages (expressed with a decimal). Click arrow to select from recently used values.
Mirror body	Mirrors part when check box is selected. Specifies X, Y, or Z origin workplanes as the mirror plane. Click arrow to select plane.

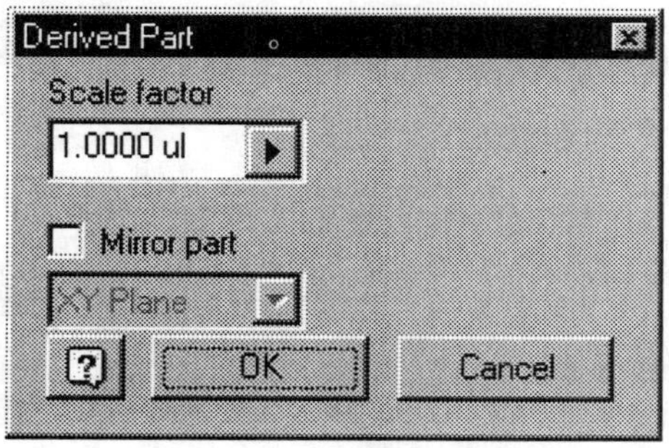

To capture design intent, you can use an Autodesk Inventor part as the basis for a derived part. A derived part is a new part that uses an existing part as its base feature. You can add features to the derived part feature (the base feature), and update it to incorporate changes made to the original part.

You can use the derived part to explore design alternatives and manufacturing processes. You can add features to the derived part feature and create multiple derived parts from one original design. For example:

- A casting blank can be machined several different ways.
- A standard length of tubing can be machined in different configurations.

Changes to the original part do not affect the derived part unless you specifically request an update. For example, you can insert a part into a file as the base feature of the derived part. You can add features to the derived part feature (base feature) to modify it. When you click the Update button on the Command bar, the derived part feature does not update, but all other features update.

To update the derived part feature, right-click on the part in the browser and select Update. Changes made to the original part are reflected in the updated derived part feature.

A derived part is linked to its original part so changes to the original part can be incorporated. You can modify the derived part feature and save the file, but changes to the original part will not affect it unless you specifically update the derived part feature.

You can break the link to the original part if you no longer wish to update the derived part feature. Right-click on the derived part feature in the browser and select Break Link. The derived part feature becomes a regular feature and its changes are saved only in the current file.

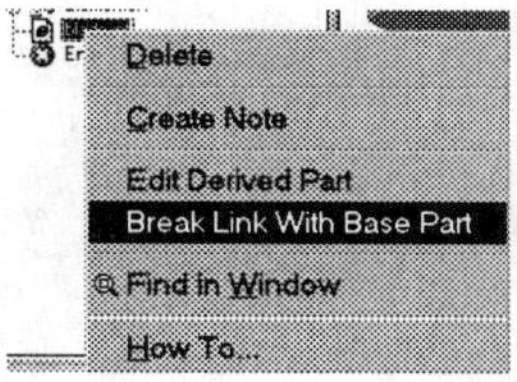

Our next section allows us to pattern or mirror features.

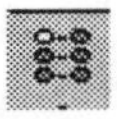 **Rectangular Pattern**

Use the Rectangular Pattern tool on the Feature toolbar to duplicate a feature and arrange the resulting features in a rectangular pattern. You can arrange the features in rows and columns by a specific count and spacing, suppressing individual features if desired.

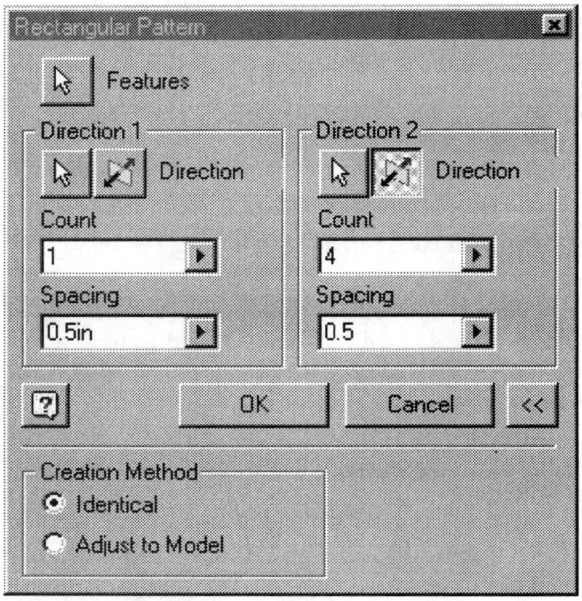

1. Click the Rectangular Pattern tool.
2. Click in the graphics window to select the feature to duplicate and arrange in a pattern.
3. Click Column Placement, then click an edge or work axis to indicate the direction of the column. Click Flip to change the column direction, if desired.
4. Enter the count (number of features) for the column and the spacing between features.
5. If the pattern has multiple rows, Click Row Placement and set the row direction, count, and spacing.
6. If desired, click the More button to set a Creation Method:
    - Choose Identical to create identical features, regardless of termination.

Choose Adjust to Model to terminate features when it encounters a face.

TIP: Patterns created with the Identical method calculate faster than the Adjust to Model method. Using Adjust to Model, the pattern terminates if it encounters a planar face, and may result in a feature whose size and shape differs from the original.

You can suppress individual occurrences in a pattern (except the original feature) to allow the pattern to flow around another feature, an irregular shape, or create a missing-tooth pattern. In the browser, right-click the occurrence and click Suppress.

Circular Pattern

Use the Circular Pattern tool on the Feature toolbar to duplicate a feature and arrange the resulting features in an arc or a circle

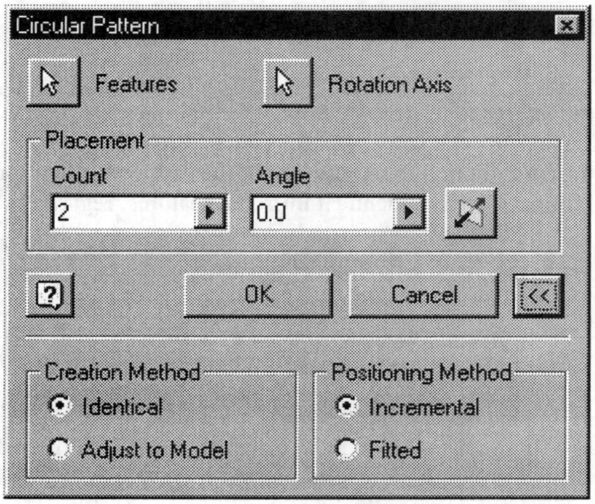

To begin, create the one or more features to include in the pattern.

1. Click the Circular Pattern tool.
2. Select the feature to arrange in a pattern.
3. Click the axis (pivot point of angle) about which occurrences are repeated. The axis can be on a different plane from the feature being patterned.
4. In the Count box, enter the number of occurrences in the pattern.
5. In the Angle box, enter the angle, as follows:
   - For Incremental positioning, the angle specifies the spacing between occurrences.
   - For Fitted positioning, the angle specifies the total area the pattern feature occupies.
6. Click the Flip button to reverse the direction of the pattern, if desired.
7. If desired, click the More button to specify the following options:
   - Under Creation Method, click Identical to create identical features or click Adjust to Model to terminate features when it encounters a face.
   - Under Positioning Method, click Incremental to space occurrences at the angle specified or click Fitted to arrange occurrences within the specified angle.

Click OK.

TIP: Patterns created with the Identical method calculate faster than the Adjust to Model method. Using Adjust to Model, the pattern terminates if it encounters a planar face, and may result in a feature whose size and shape differs from the original.

You can suppress individual occurrences in a pattern (except the original feature) to allow the pattern to flow around another feature, an irregular shape, or create a missing-tooth pattern. In the browser, right-click the occurrence and click Suppress.

Mirror Feature

Use the Mirror tool on the Features toolbar to mirror one or more features at equal distances across a plane.

To begin, create one or more features to mirror. Create a work plane to serve as the mirror plane or, if you prefer, identify a planar face to use.

1. Click the Mirror tool.
2. Click one or more features to mirror.
3. Click Mirror Plane and select a work plane or planar face.
4. If desired, click the More button to choose one of the following Creation Methods:
    - Click Identical to create identical mirrored features, regardless of termination.

Click Adjust to Model to terminate features on model planes.

TIP: Features mirrored with the Identical method calculate faster than the Adjust to Model method. Using Adjust to Model, the mirrored feature terminates if it encounters a planar face, and may result in a feature whose size and shape differs from the original.

Create Work Plane

Use the Work Plane tool on the Feature toolbar to define a work plane using unconsumed sketch geometry, feature vertices, edges, faces, or other work features. Work planes can also be created in-line when a work feature command requires you to select a plane.

Use one or more of the following relationships to define a work plane:

- On geometry (on three points, for example)
- Normal to geometry
- Parallel to geometry
- At an angle to geometry (on a plane and an axis)

1. Click the Work Plane tool.
2. Select appropriate vertices, edges, or faces to define a work plane.

   For offset work planes, drag the work plane to desired location and enter a distance or angle in the Offset dialog box. Click the check mark in the dialog box to accept the preview and create the offset work plane.

If desired, you can create multiple work planes offset from one another at a specific distance or angle. Follow the steps above, selecting the last created work plane as the sketch plane, then drag the new work plane to the desired offset distance.

TIP: If more than one solution is possible, a selection box appears. Click the forward or reverse arrows in the selection box, then click the check mark when the correct solution is previewed.

Work Axis

Use the Work Axis tool on the Feature toolbar to designate unconsumed sketch geometry, points, or a part edge as a work axis. Work axes can also be created in-line as input to other work feature commands.

1. Click the Work Axis tool.
2. Select one of four methods:
    - Select a revolved feature to create a work axis along its axis of revolution.
    - Select two valid points to create a work axis through them.
    - Select a work point and a plane (or face) to create a work axis normal to the plane (or face) and through the point.

Select any two non-parallel planes to create a work axis at their intersection.

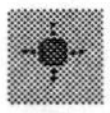

Work Point

Use the Work Point tool on the Feature toolbar to select model vertices, edge and axis intersections, intersections of three non-parallel faces or planes, and other work features as work points.

Work points can also be created as input to other work feature commands that require you to select a point. Work points are partially constrained in place relative to vertices, edges, and other topological characteristics of the parent part or feature.

Feature Tools

Button	Tool	Function	Special Instructions
	Extrude	Extrude a profile normal to the sketch	Can be base feature
	Revolve	Revolve a profile around an axis	Can be base feature
	Hole	Create a hole in a part	Use hole points or line endpoints as hole centers
	Shell	Create a hollow part	Placed feature
	Rib	Creates a rib	Uses an open contour
	Loft	Construct a feature with varying cross sections; can follow a curved path	Requires multiple work planes
	Sweep	Extrude a profile along a curved path	Can be base feature
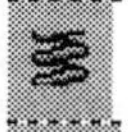	Coil	Extrude a profile along a helical path	Can be base feature
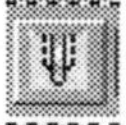	Thread	Maps a bitmap of a thread to a cylindrical face.	
	Fillet	Create a fillet or round edges	Placed feature
	Chamfer	Create a chamfer on selected edges	Placed feature
	Face Draft	Create a draft on selected faces	Placed feature
	Split	Part Split using parting line or spline	
	View Catalog	Open a Catalog of Design Elements	
	Insert Design Element	Add a Design Element	
	Create a Design Element	Create a Design Element from an Existing Feature	
	Derived Part	Create a new derived part from a base part	
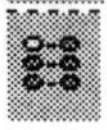	Rectangular Pattern	Creates a rectangular pattern of features	Pattern can be suppressed, items in the pattern can be individualized
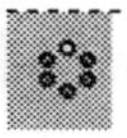	Circular Pattern	Creates a circular pattern around a center	Pattern can be suppressed, items in the pattern can be individualized
	Mirror Feature	Create a mirror image using a plane, line or axis as mirror line	
	Work Plane	Create a work plane	
	Work Axis	Create a work axis	
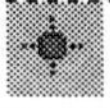	Work Point	Create a work point	Can be used to place holes on curved surfaces

Review Questions

Identify the icon.

1. Hole
2. Extrude
3. Coil
4. Loft

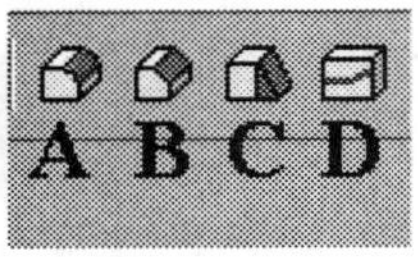

Identify the icon.

5. Part Splitting
6. Face Draft
7. Fillet
8. Chamfer

9. A Derived Part is:

   A. Used to explore different design ideas
   B. A copy of a base part
   C. Can be scaled or mirrored
   D. All of the above

10. The three options for creating a chamfer are:

    A. Equal distance, distance-angle, two distances
    B. Variable, constant, radial
    C. Equal Distance, Variable Distance, Distance-Angle
    D. Two angles, Two Distances, Equal Distance

ANSWERS: 1) B; 2) A; 3) D; 4) C; 5) D; 6) C; 7) A; 8) B; 9) D; 10) A

Lesson 6

Sketch Tools

Inventor's Sketch Tool Bar contains tools for creating the basic geometry to create features and parts.

Edit Coordinate System

We use the Edit Coordinate System to rotate the origin.

We select the Edit Coordinate System tool and then pick on the Origin. Watch the messages shown in the Message box to assist you through tasks. We then select the lower corner of the sketch to reset the origin.

The next section of the Sketch toolbar is the geometry tools, which sketch basic geometric shapes to use for creating features.

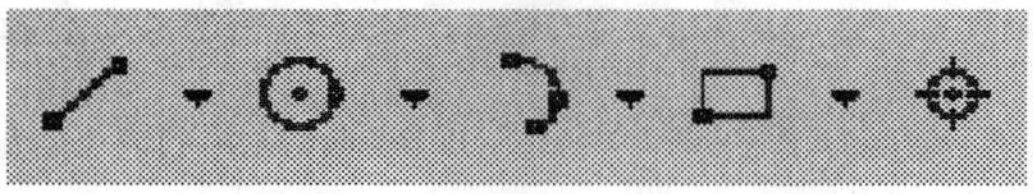

On the surface, the Geometry tools look fairly standard: line, circle, arc, rectangle, and point.

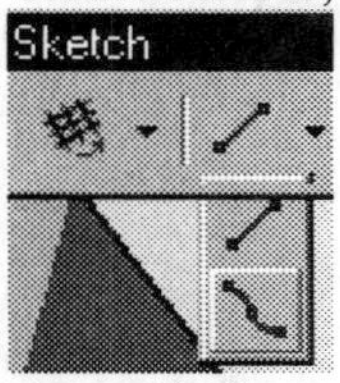

Line/Spline

Let's start with the Line tool. Its drop-down has two options: line or spline. Run the mouse over the button and look in the lower left hand of the screen, a help description will appear describing the tool function. In this case, the tool creates lines and tangent arcs. This means filleted corners can be created without having to exit the line mode and performing a fillet command.

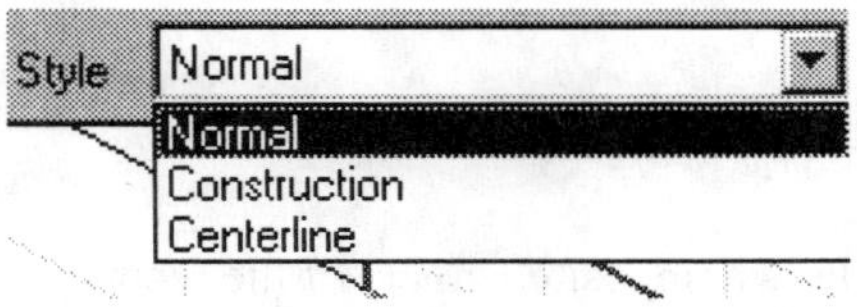

To create a Construction line instead of an object line, select the Construction option under Style.

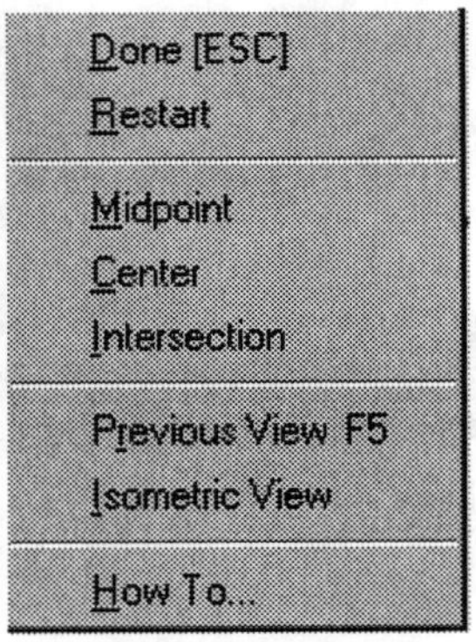

Right click the mouse while in 'Line' mode, this will bring up a submenu to assist in the construction of your sketch.

To create a tangent arc while in 'Line' mode, select an endpoint and hold down the left mouse button. When the arc is located properly, release the left mouse button and Inventor will automatically return to 'Line' mode.

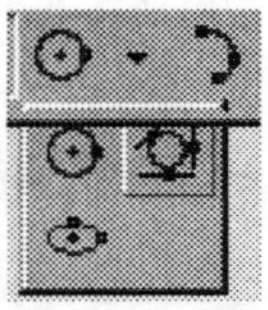

Circle/Ellipse

The default circle tool creates a circle using Center point and radius. Access the drop down toolbar to see that there are two other circle options, ellipse and Tangent, Tangent, Tangent.

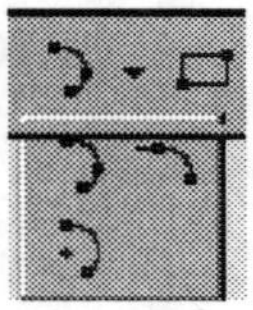

Arc

The default arc tool creates an arc using three points. The drop down toolbar provides two additional options: Center, Start, End and Start, Tangent. All three methods will draw arcs either clockwise or counter-clockwise.

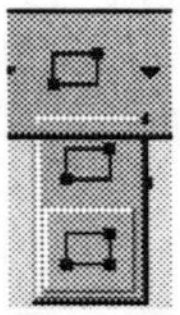

Rectangle

The rectangle tool provides two options. The default is to select the two opposite corners of the rectangle. The second option has the user define the length of one side and then the length of the adjacent side.

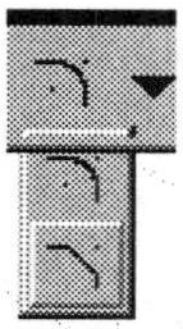

Fillet/Chamfer

The Fillet tool is actually a flyout that includes Fillet and Chamfer. Inventor recommends that it is better to add fillets and chamfers as placed features. The reason is that the user can then suppress fillets for faster regens and to conserve memory. It also makes it easier to modify values. However, there are instances where it is preferable to include the fillet or chamfer in the sketch.

The fillet tool prompts the user to select the edges of the sketch to be modified and brings up a dialog box where the user can modify the radius value. To modify the value of a fillet you've already placed, just double-click using the left mouse button and a dialog box will pop up allowing you to edit the value. Pressing the equal button allows the user to select an existing fillet and apply that fillet's value to the fillet being defined.

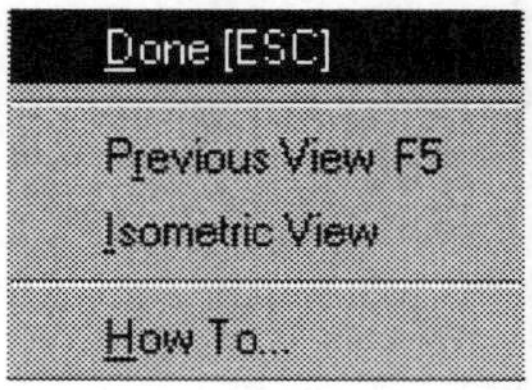

Right-clicking the mouse while in 'Fillet' mode brings up a small dialog box that allows the user to switch views on the fly to allow for easier editing.

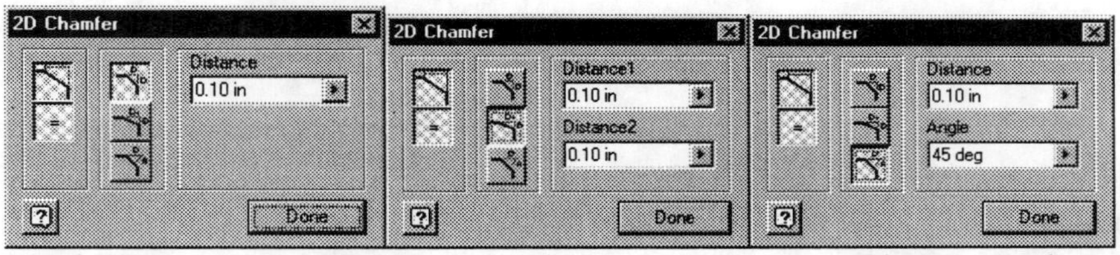

Equal Distance 2 Distance Distance-Angle

Chamfers can be defined in three ways: Equal Distance, 2 Distance, and Distance-Angle.
The user also has the option of selecting an existing chamfer in the sketch and applying that value to the chamfer being defined.

Point, Hole Center

The point tool is used to determine the location of holes as well as points.

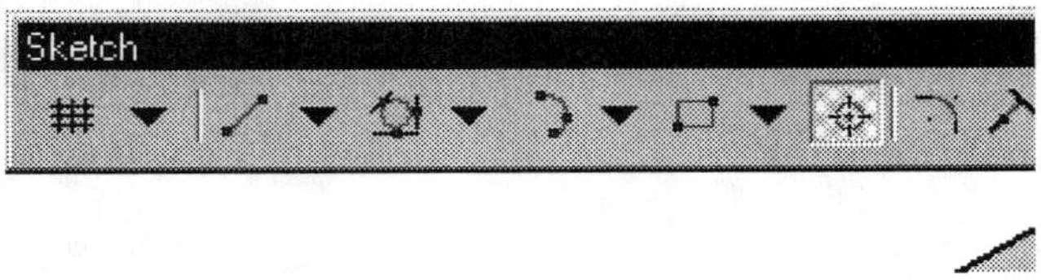

To create a Sketch Point (used to constraint geometry), select the Sketch Point under Style.

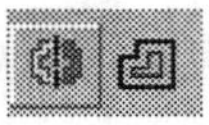

The next section of the Sketch toolbar contains Mirror and Offset.

Mirror

Mirror is a new tool introduced in Release 4.

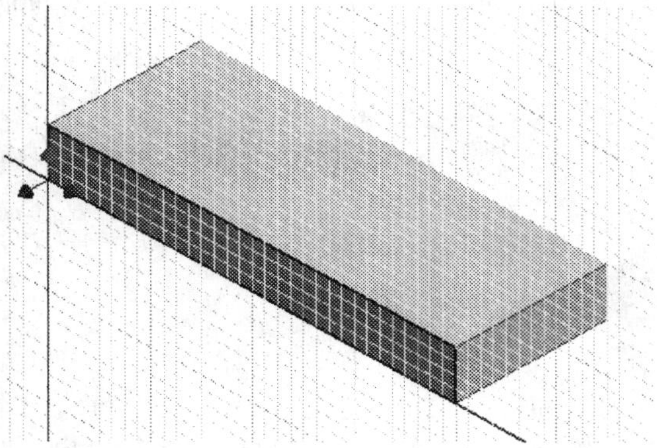

We create a simple block: 4 units by 1.5 units x 0.5 units thick on the top (XZ) plane.

Select the front plane for a New Sketch.

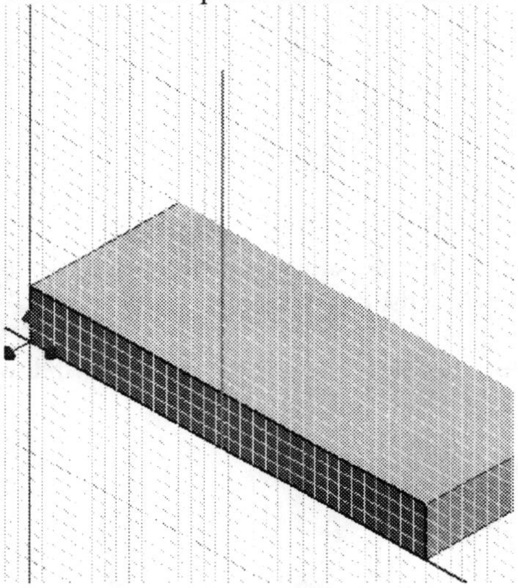

Draw a vertical line roughly in the center of the front side.

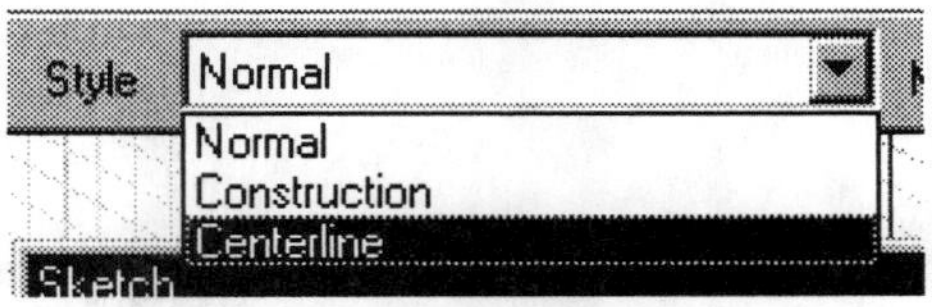

Select the line and change it to a centerline.

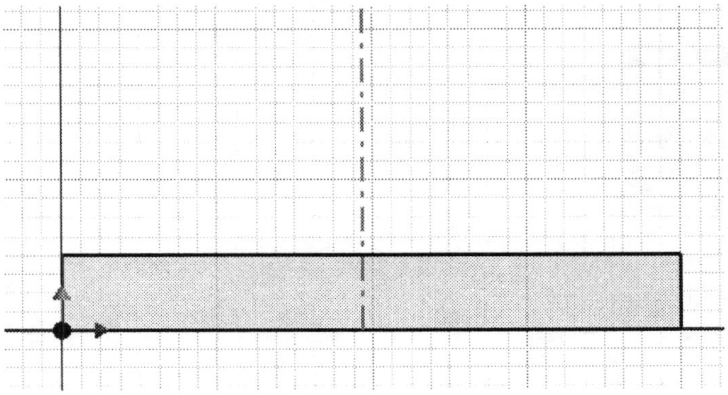

The line now appears as a centerline.

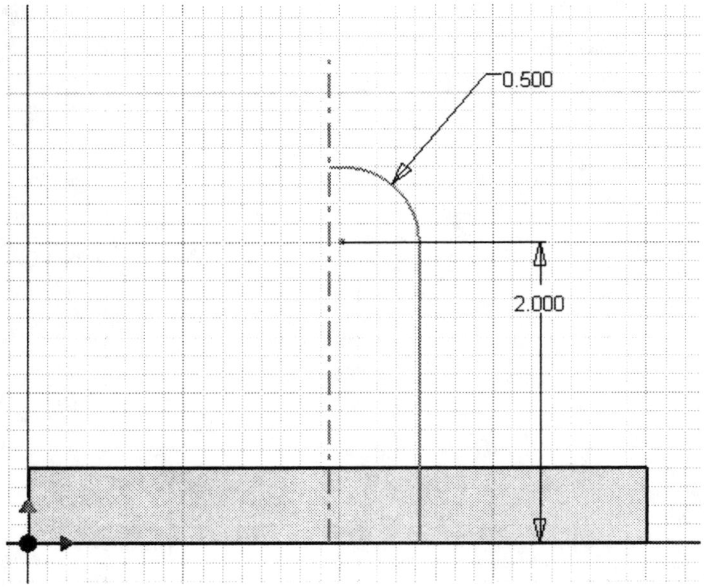

Create the sketch shown. There is a small horizontal line at the bottom of the sketch that will be used to close the profile. Add a coincident constraint between the arc center and the center line.

Select the Mirror tool. Then select the entire sketch. You can select the entire sketch by drawing a window around the sketch and centerline.

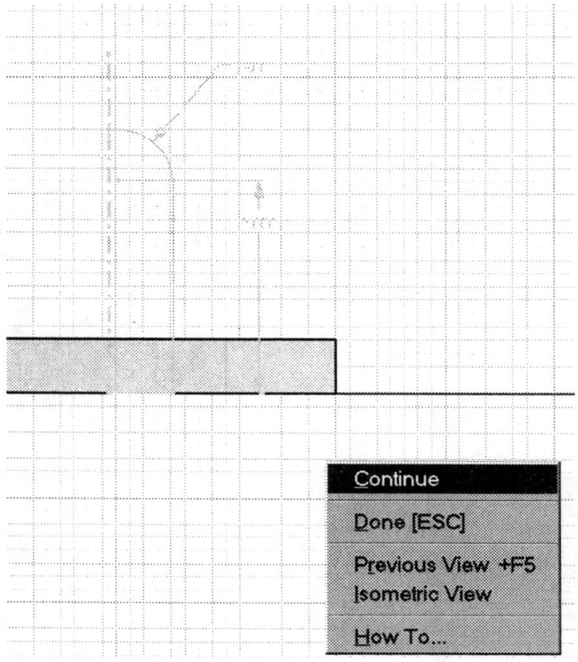

Right click and select 'Continue'.

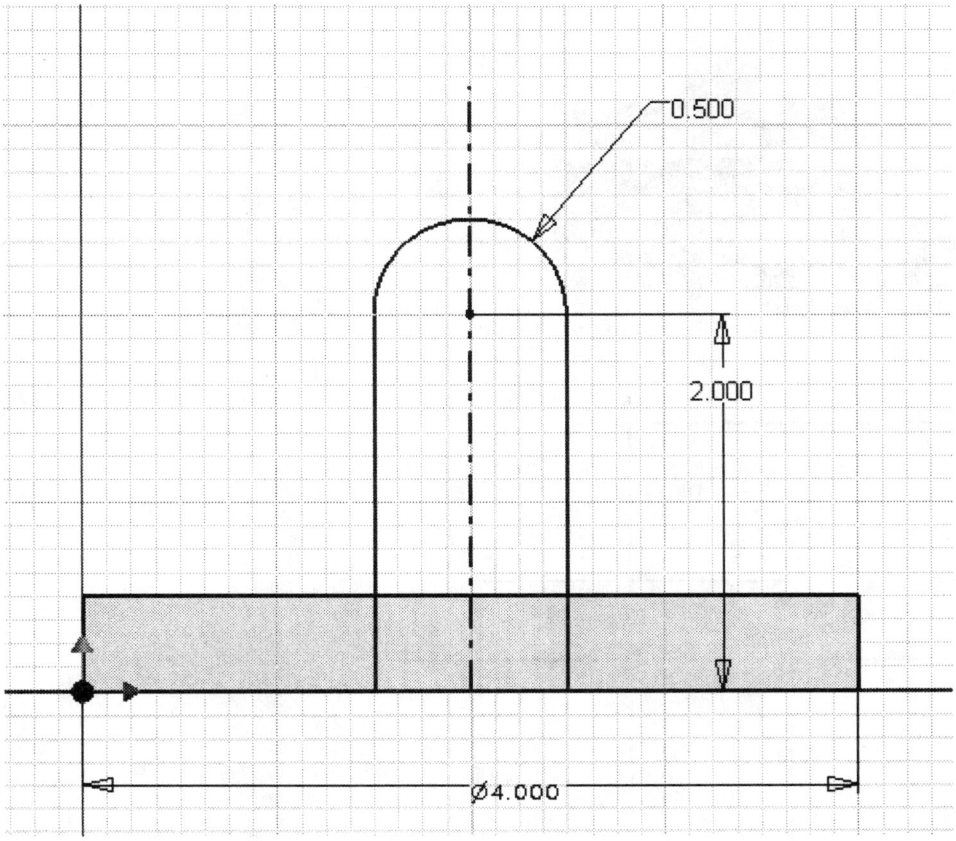

Our geometry is now mirrored.

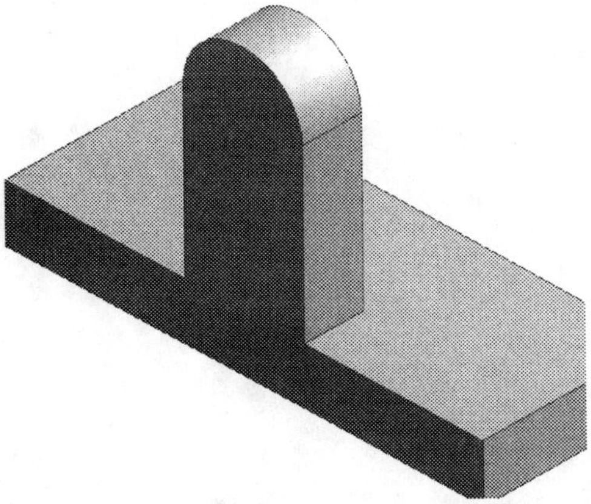

Extrude the geometry into the block a Depth of 0.5 units.

If you have difficulty extruding the profile, there may be some gaps between the arcs and lines. Use the Design Doctor to assist you in creating a closed profile.

Select the top face for a New Sketch.

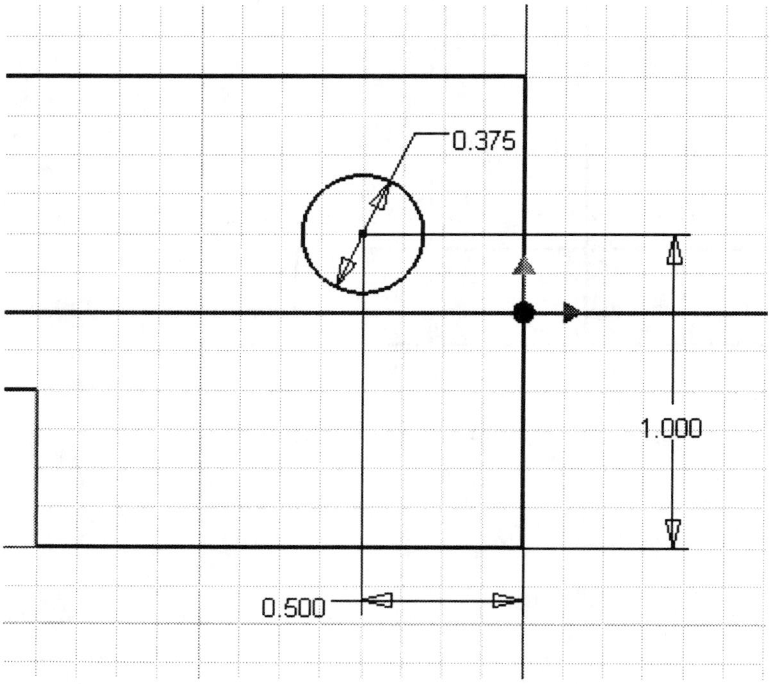

Draw a circle on the right side as shown.

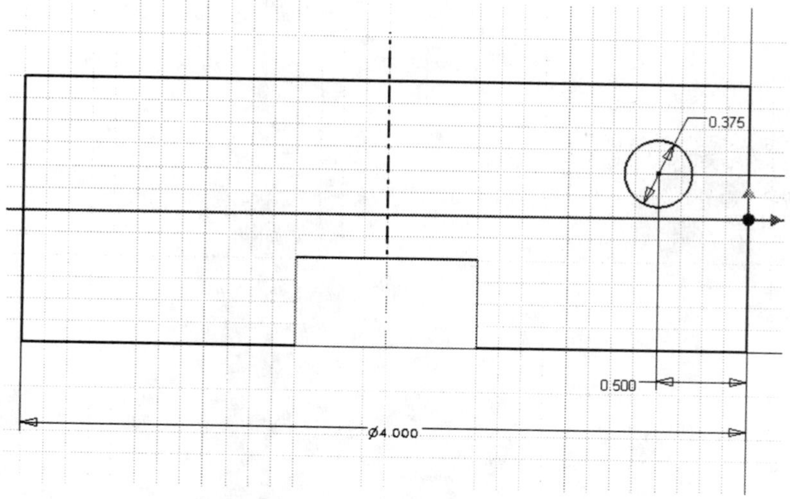

Create a centerline. Draw a vertical line. Select it and set the Style to Centerline. Add a 4.00 dimension to center it on the block.

Select the Mirror tool. Select the Centerline and the circle.

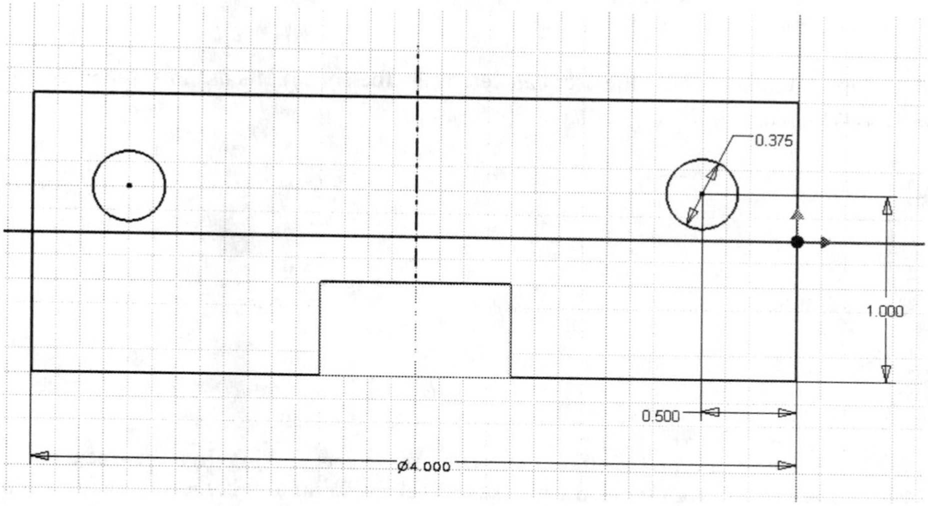

Right click and select 'Done'.

One advantage to mirroring the hole is that you only need to change the dimensions on one hole and both holes will automatically update.

Extrude the holes through all.

Our completed exercise.
Save this as 'Mirror-Exercise.ipt'.

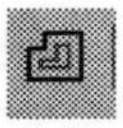

Offset

The offset tool prompts the user to select the object to offset and the user then uses the mouse to drag and drop the offset copy to the approximate location. To constrain the offset object, the user can add dimensions using the dimension tool.

A right mouse click brings up a submenu where the user can determine the constraints used for the offset or change views to facilitate editing.

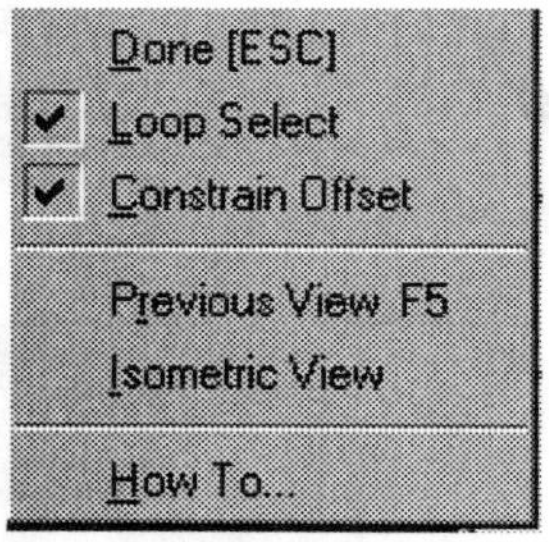

More than one object can be selected at a time for offset. The selected objects will highlight in green. When we have completed our selections, right-click the mouse and select 'Continue' in the submenu. Then drag the offset to the approximate location desired.

The default setting automatically selects loops (curves joined at the endpoints) and constrains the offset curve to be equidistant from the original curve. To offset one or more individual curves or omit the Equal constraint, right-click and clear the checkmarks on Loop Select and Constrain Offset in the submenu.

Our next section contains Dimensioning tools.

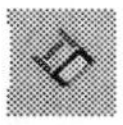

General Dimension

The first icon, which resembles a paintbrush roller, is used for General Dimensioning. Inventor automatically knows whether the object being dimensioned is a line or an arc.

If an arc is being dimensioned, you can right-click the mouse and bring up a sub-menu. This submenu allows you to switch from Radius mode to Diameter mode simply by selecting that option.

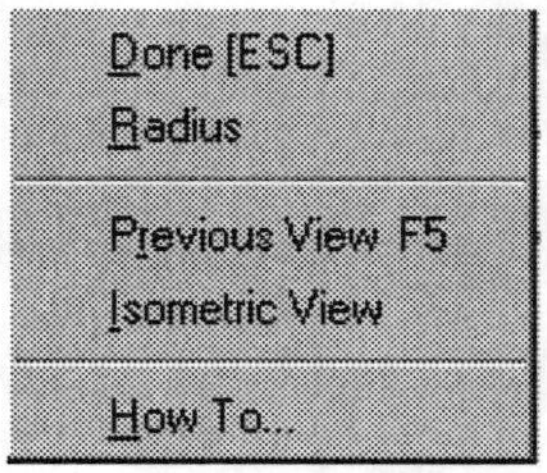

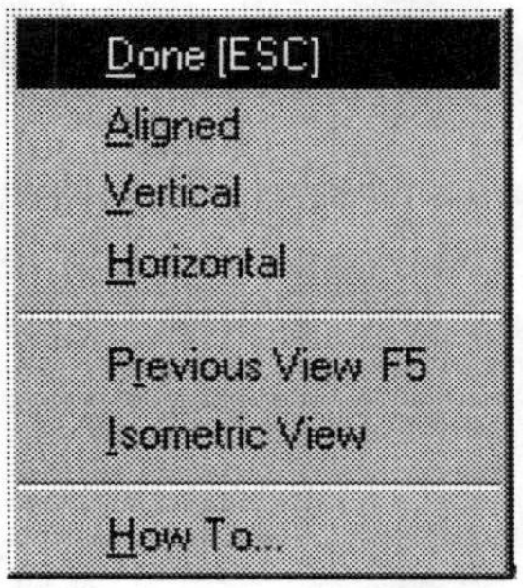

When dimensioning a line, right clicking the mouse will bring up a submenu with the options for aligned, vertical or horizontal linear dimensions.

Simply selecting a dimension and then editing the value in the dialog box that appears will modify any dimension.

Auto Dimension

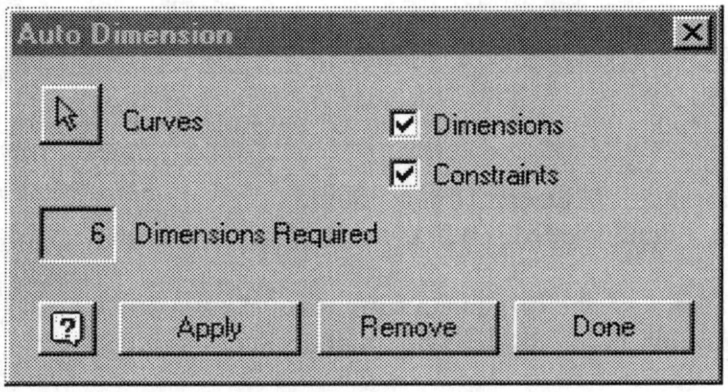

Auto Dimension tells the user how many dimensions are required to fully define a sketch and applies constraints as needed.

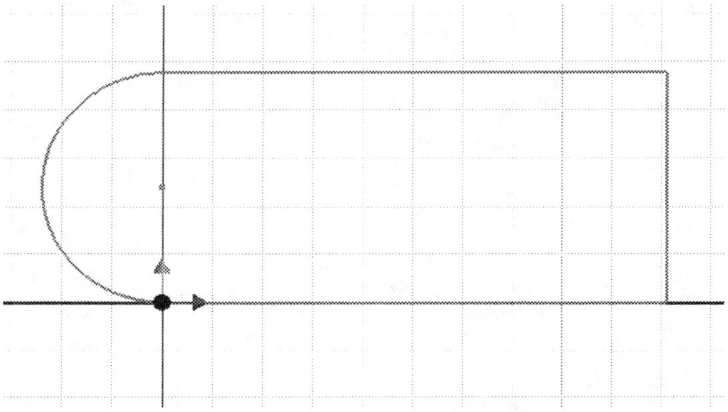

Draw the sketch shown.

Select Auto Dimension.
Press the 'Apply' button.

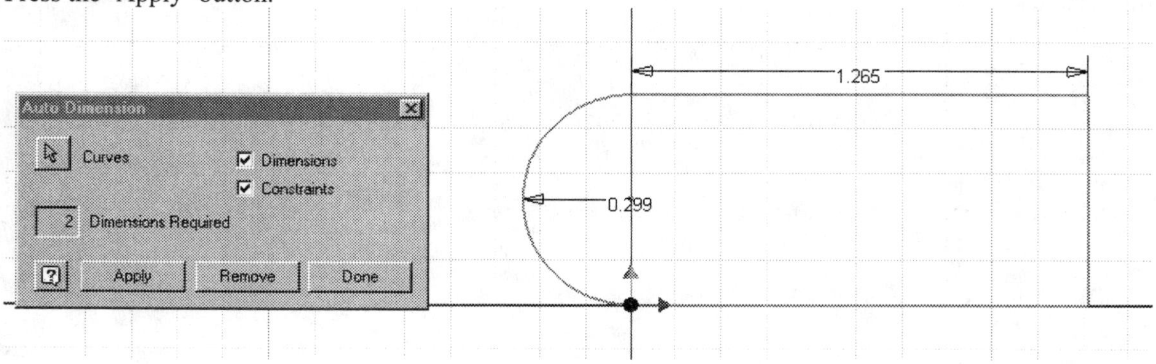

The dimensions appear as shown. (Note: Your dimensions will probably be different depending on how you drew your sketch.)
Press 'Done'.

The dimensions are then placed. You can now select dimensions and edit them as needed.

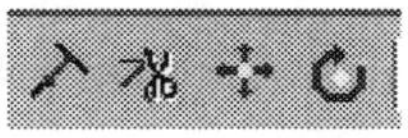

Modify Tools

Our next section contains tools used to modify sketches: Extend, Trim, Move, and Rotate.

Extend

The extend tool works differently than in AutoCAD. The user is prompted for the object to extend. The object then highlights in red and the user moves the mouse to indicate how far to extend the object. Inventor previews the object as modified and the user left-clicks the mouse to accept the modification.

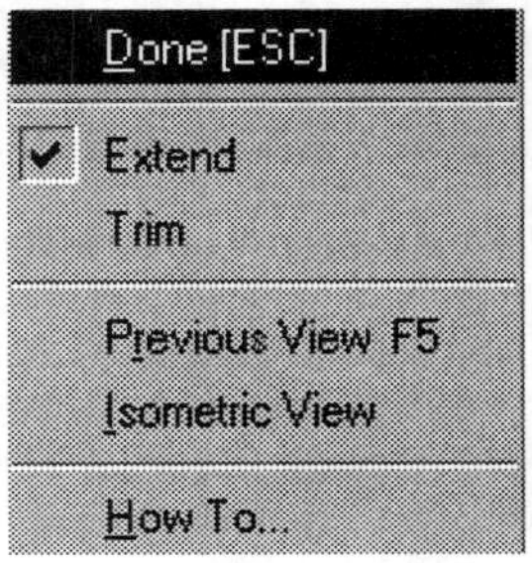

Right-clicking the mouse while in 'Extend' mode will bring up a submenu giving the option to switch to 'Trim' mode or change views.

Trim

The trim tool prompts the user to select the object to trim and automatically uses any intersecting edges as the cutting tool. Inventor previews the modification in red for the user and the user accepts by left clicking the mouse. A right mouse click brings up the same submenu as the extend right mouse click, only with the check mark appearing next to the Trim option. Thus, the user can easily switch from 'Trim' mode to 'Extend' mode.

TIP: Press and hold SHIFT to temporarily enable Trim when in Extend mode or to enable Extend when in Trim mode.

Move

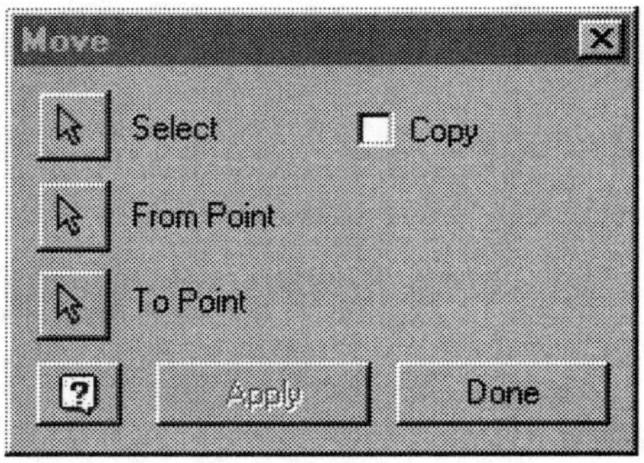

Pressing this tool brings up this dialog box.

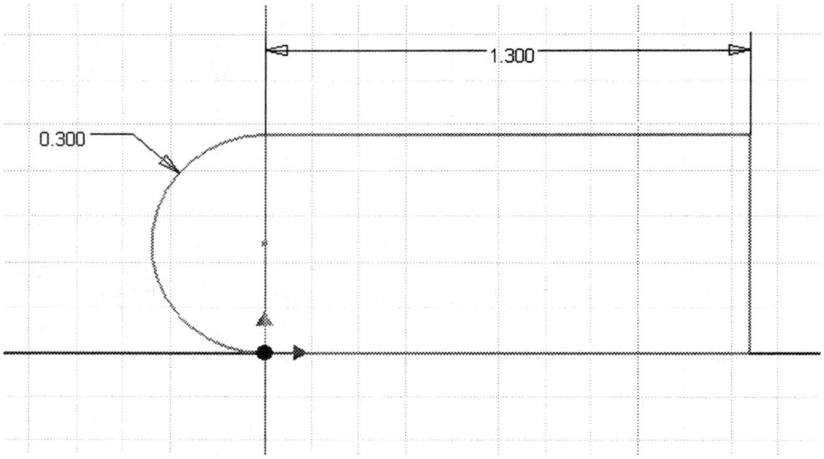

Using the sketch we used for the Auto Dimension exercise, we will use the Move tool to copy the arc.

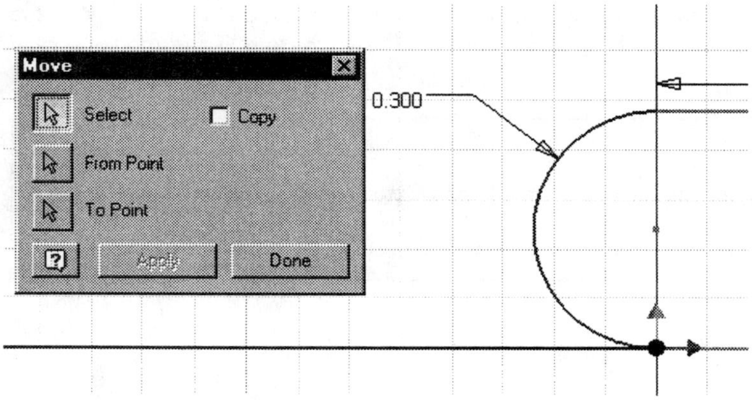

Press the Select button and select the arc. Enable the Copy button.

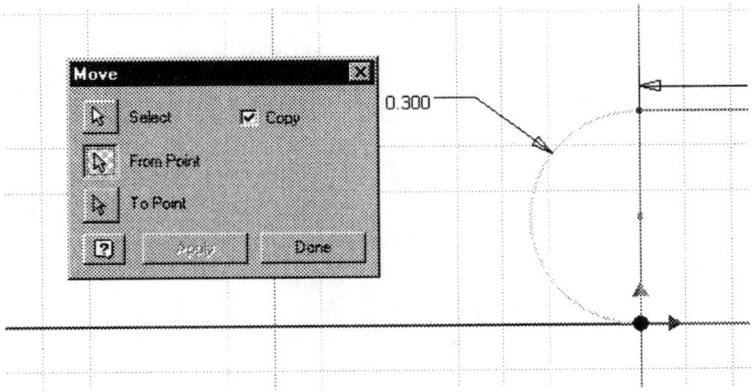

The arc will grey out to indicate it has been selected. Press the From Point button and select the top arc endpoint.

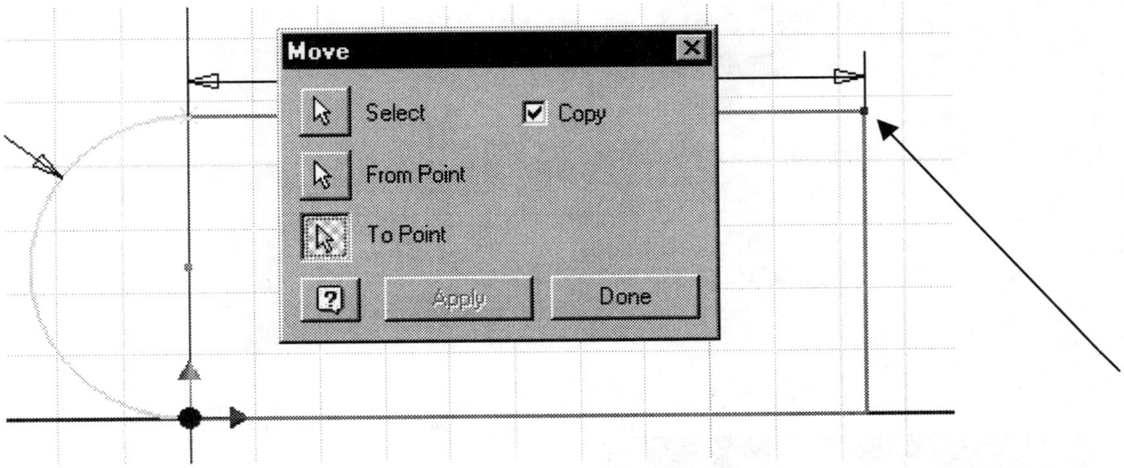

Select the To Point button and Select the top endpoint of the rectangle.

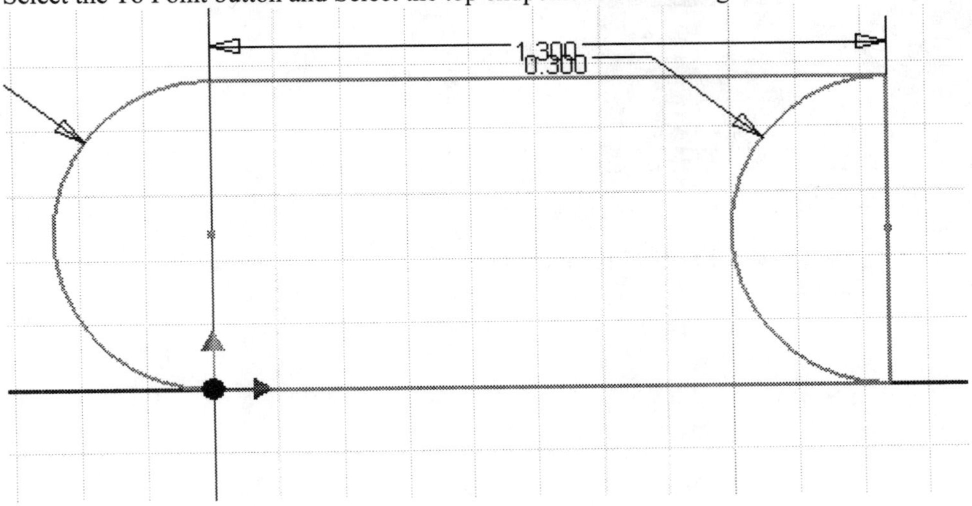

Press 'Apply' and 'Done'.
The arc is now copied to the new position.

Rotate

We will now rotate the sketch we just modified.

Select the Rotate tool.

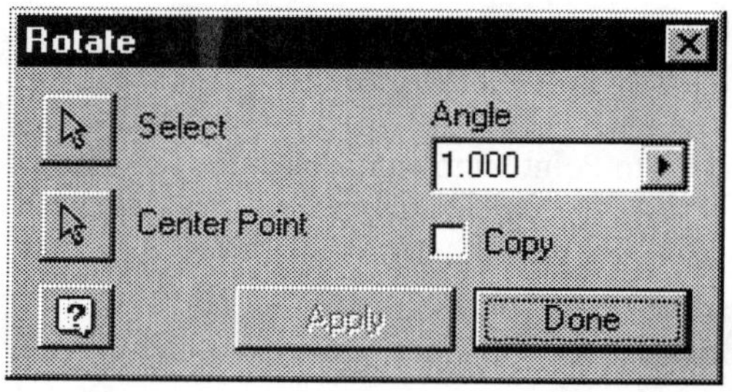

The Rotate dialog box appears.
Press the Select button and window around the entire sketch.

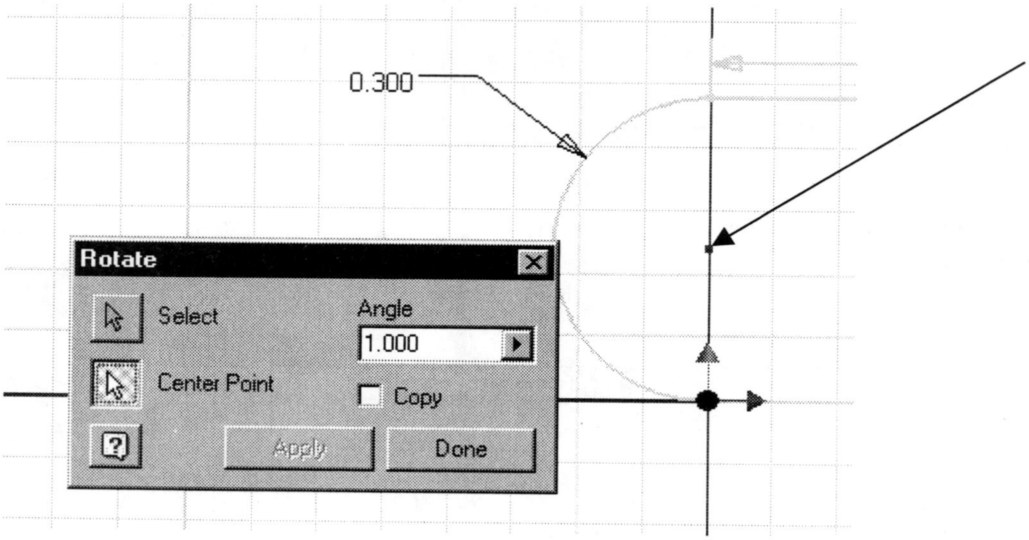

Press the Center point button and select the center point of the left arc.

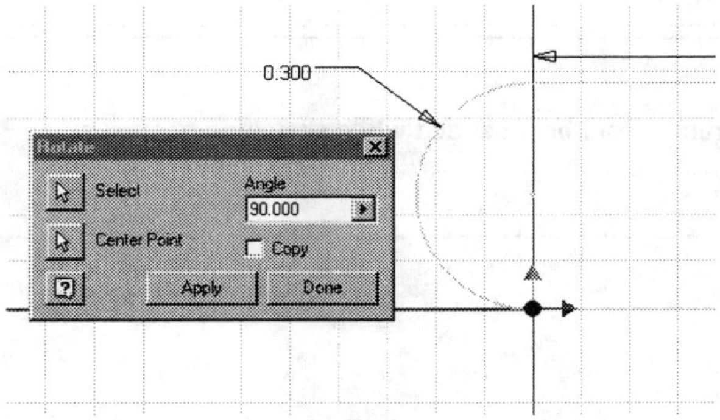

Change the Angle value to 90.
Press 'Apply' and 'Done'.

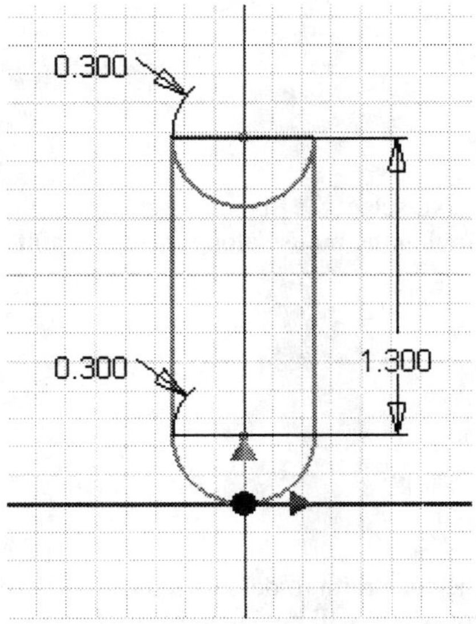

Our rotated sketch.

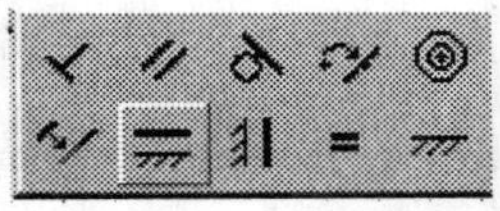

Constraints

The next tool is used for adding geometric constraints. Pressing on the arrow reveals a fly out toolbar with all the available constraints. The top row of constraints from left to right are Perpendicular, Parallel, Tangent, Coincident, and Concentric. The bottom row of constraints from left to right are Collinear, Horizontal, Vertical, Equal, and Fixed.

The Coincident constraint may be used to ensure that two lines form a closed angle with no overlap. The Fixed constraint fixes an object to a location relative to the sketch coordinate system. The other constraints are used in a similar manner to other parametric modeling software.

TIP: Press and hold CONTROL to prevent constraints from being added while sketching geometry.

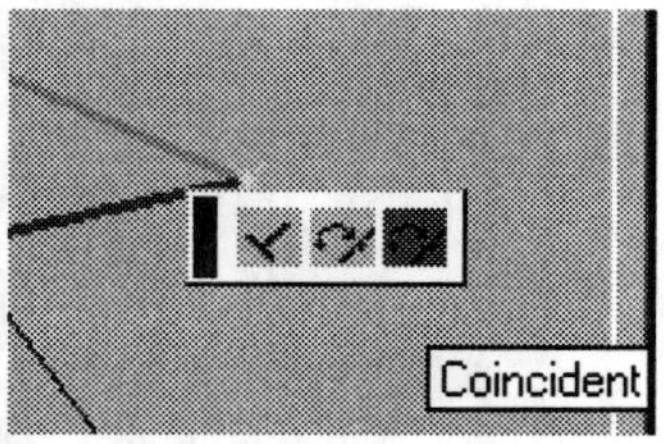

Show/Delete Constraints

To show constraints, press the Show/Delete Constraints tool button. Next, select the object. A small constraint bar will appear displaying the constraints for that object. Moving the mouse along the constraint bar will highlight each constraint.

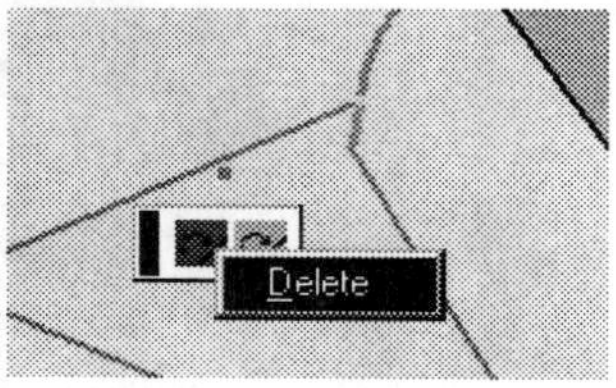

To delete a constraint, enable the constraint bar. Move the mouse to the constraint to delete on the constraint bar (note the highlighted objects to ensure that the correct constraint will be deleted). Right click the mouse and the 'Delete' key will appear. Left click the mouse to accept. If we don't wish to delete, just move the mouse off of the constraint bar and left click anywhere in the window.

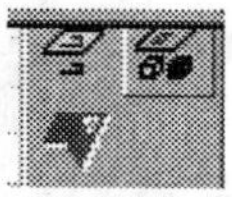

Inventor R4 features three projection tools: Project Geometry, Project Cut Edges, and Project Fat Pattern.

Project Geometry

Our next tool button creates reference geometry by projecting model geometry (edges and vertices), work features, or sketch geometry from another sketch onto the active sketch plane. Reference geometry can be used to constrain other sketch geometry or used directly in a profile or path sketch.

TIP:

- Use the Zoom Window button on the Standard toolbar to zoom in on the area where you are working.
- Set the grid to the spacing needed to quickly line up the sketch elements.
- Check the Snap to Grid setting to more easily place sketch elements.
- To select a group of sketch elements, activate the Select tool, then click in the graphics window and drag a box around the elements.
- Use the dimension tools to set the size of sketched geometry or to add dimensions between the geometry in a sketch and elements in the underlying drawing view.
- When you use dimensions to set the size of elements in a title block or border, the dimensions are hidden when you finish editing.

Project Cut Edges

This tool projects edges cut by the sketch plane onto the current sketch plane.

Project Flat Pattern

This tool is greyed out unless a flat pattern exists. If a flat pattern is available, the user may select a face to project it onto a selected plane.

Insert AutoCAD file

AutoCAD remains the Number One 2D drafting software package in the world. Many companies would like to move into the 3D world, but the ability to use existing AutoCAD drawings is a major concern. This new tool in Inventor Release 4 should go a long way in alleviating those concerns.

To demonstrate how it works, we use a drawing from Nidec's fan catalog, but any AutoCAD drawing will do.

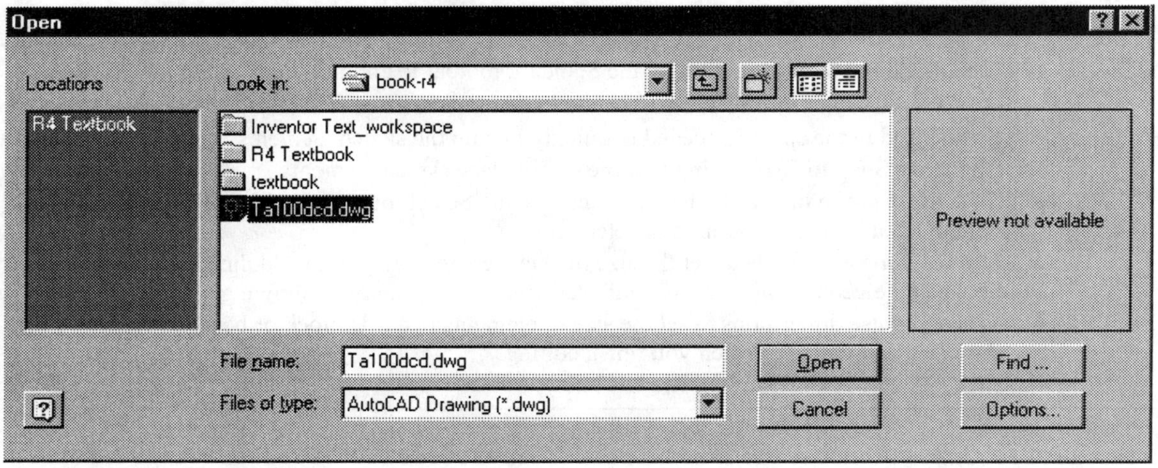

Select the Insert AutoCAD file tool. The browser dialog will come up.

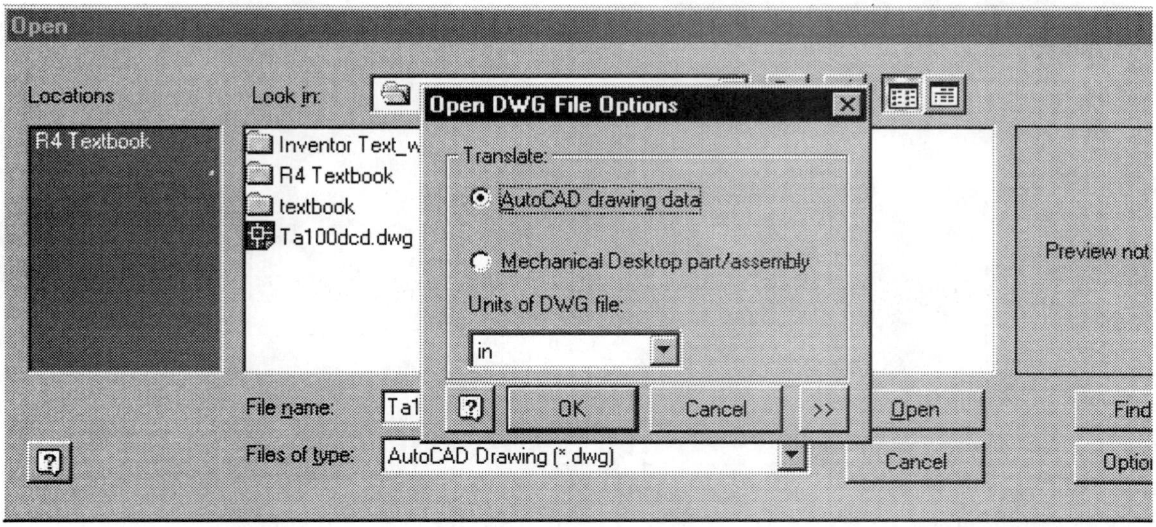

If you select Options, you will get the Open DWG File Options. You have a choice importing a Mechanical Desktop or AutoCAD file.

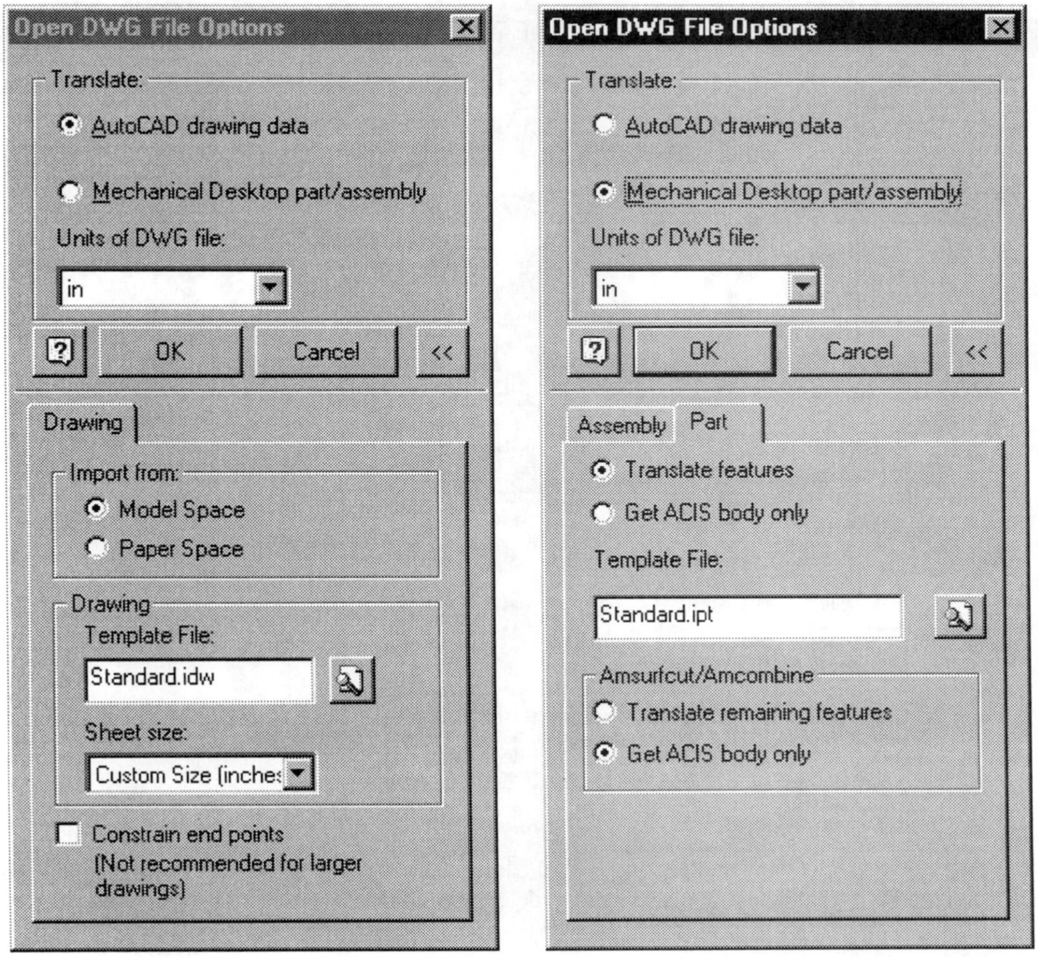

Pressing the More Button provides even more options. Depending on whether the file is an AutoCAD or Mechanical Desktop file, we can determine how Inventor will interpret the data imported.

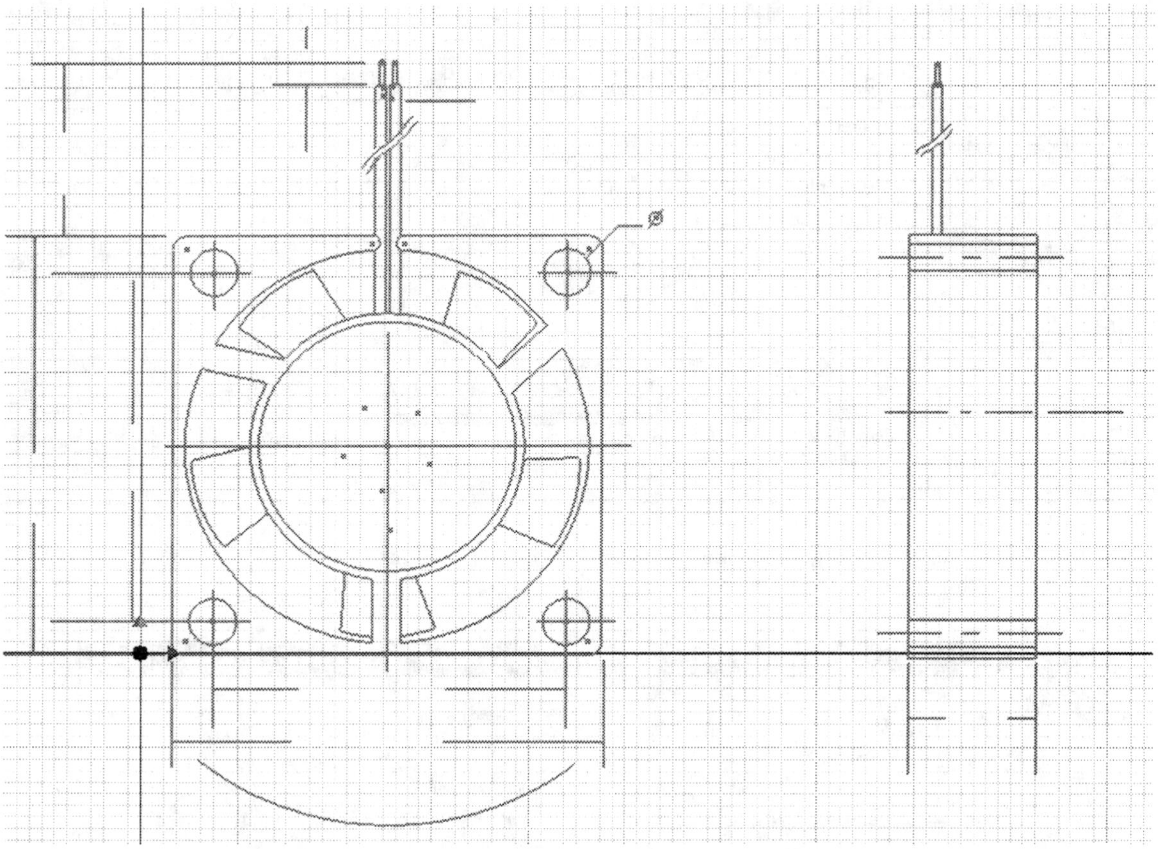

Here is the AutoCAD drawing once the import process is completed.

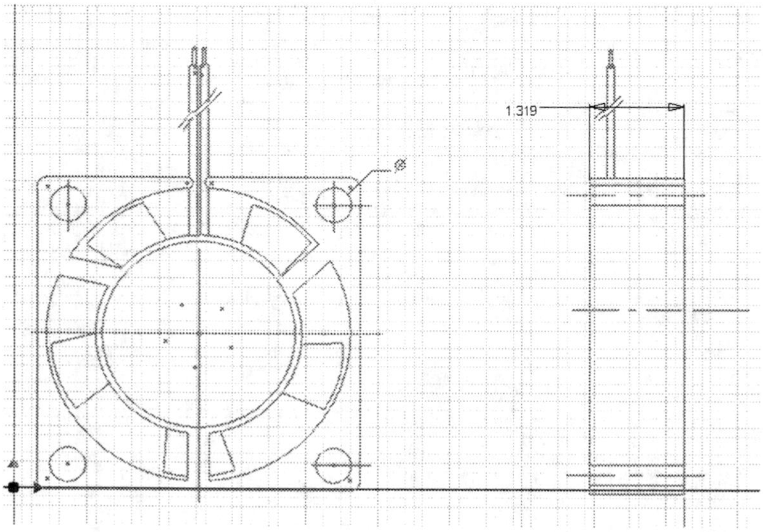

By holding down the Control key and picking with the left mouse, we can select all the dimension lines, then right click and press 'Delete'. We also need to delete the side view.

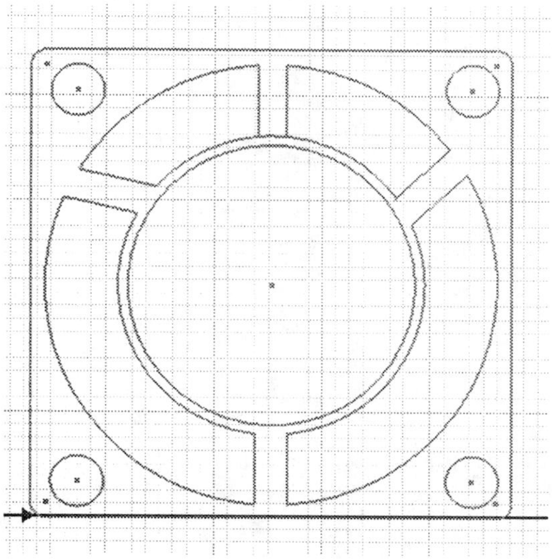

Continue cleaning up the sketch until you have a basic profile. Use the Design Doctor to assist you in creating a closed loop profile.

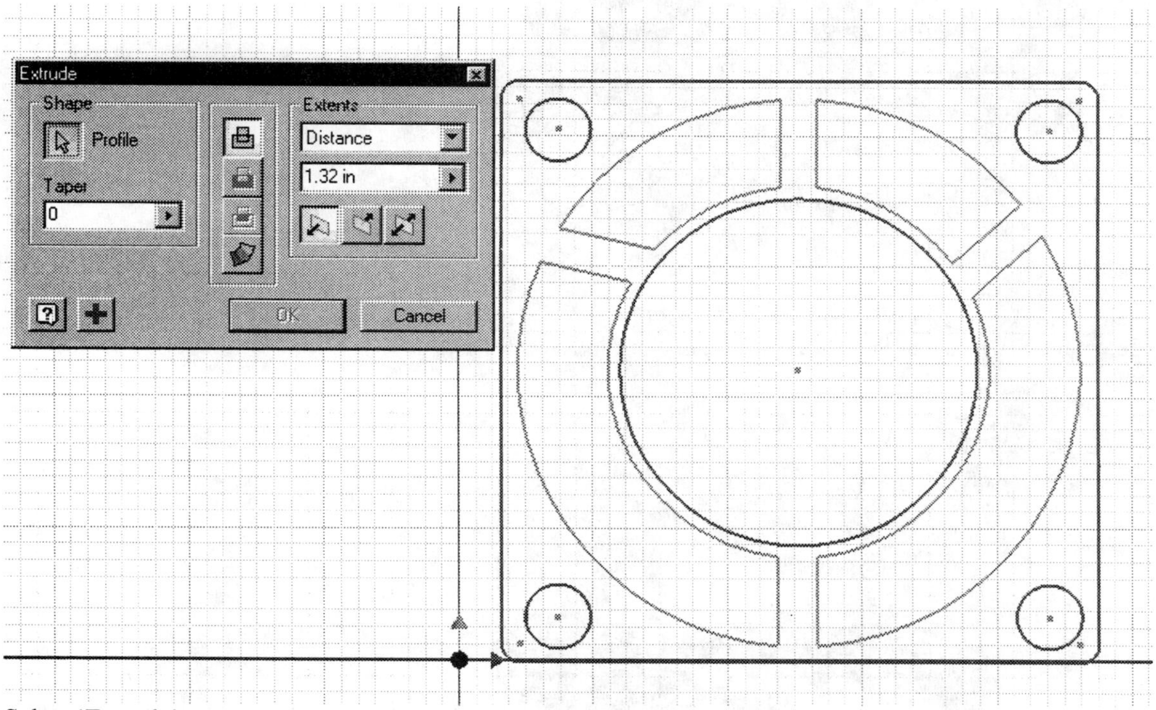

Select 'Extrude'.

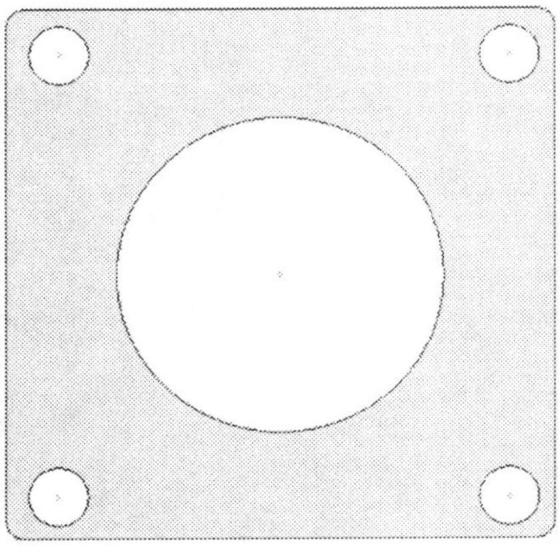

Our base feature.

But what about the cuts for the fan blades?

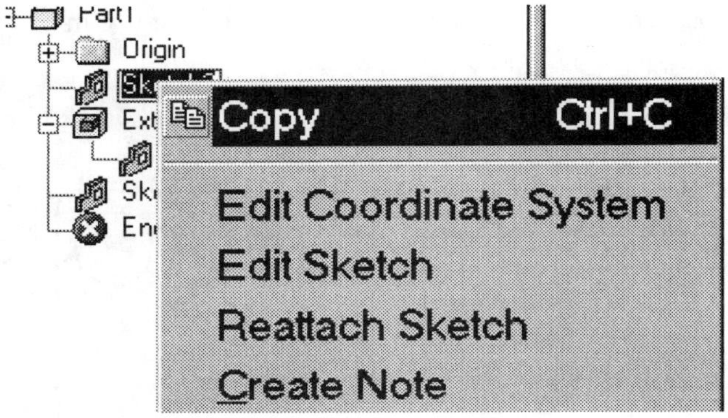

Select the sketch, right click and select ‘Copy’.
Select the front face of the extrusion, , right click and select ‘Paste’.

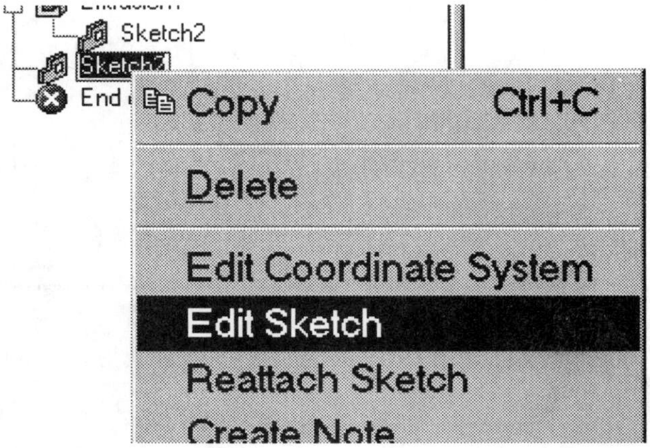

Select the Sketch, right click and select ‘Edit Sketch’.

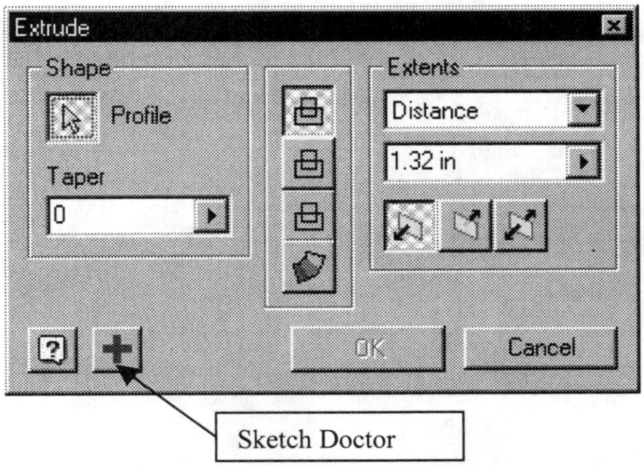

Select the Extrude tool and then select the Sketch Doctor.

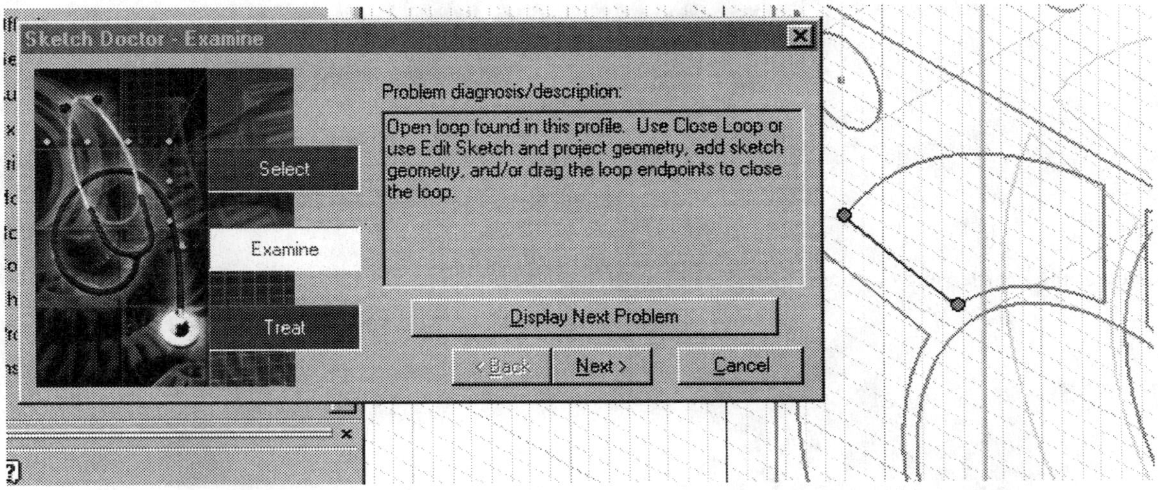

The Sketch Doctor will step you through the process of creating closed profiles of the imported geometries.

Once all the profiles have been resolved, you will be able to select the profiles to extrude.

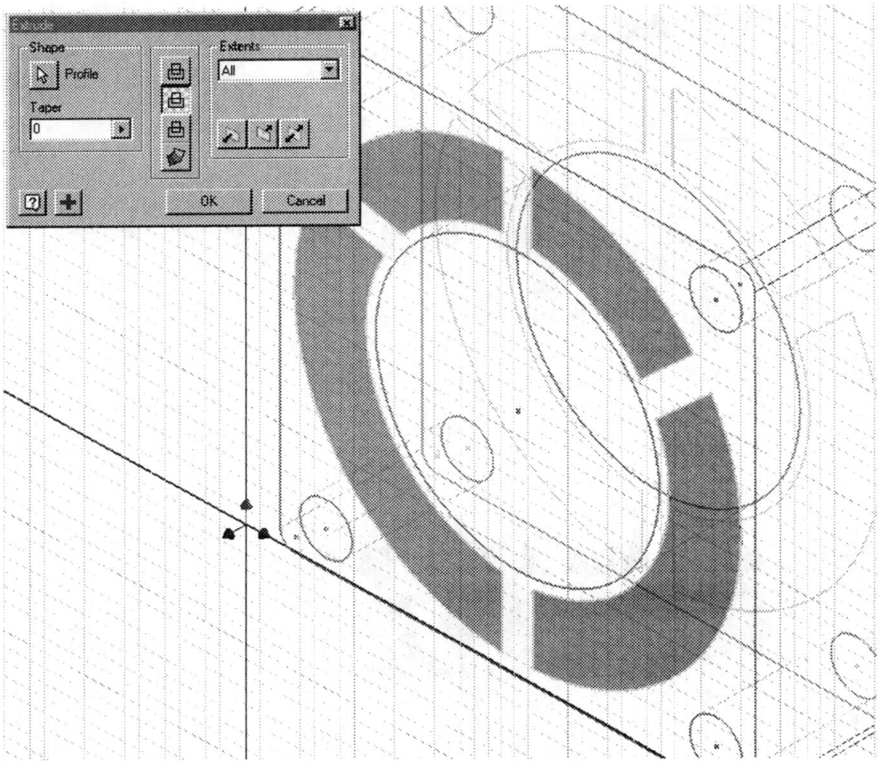

Select the profiles and define as Cuts Through All.

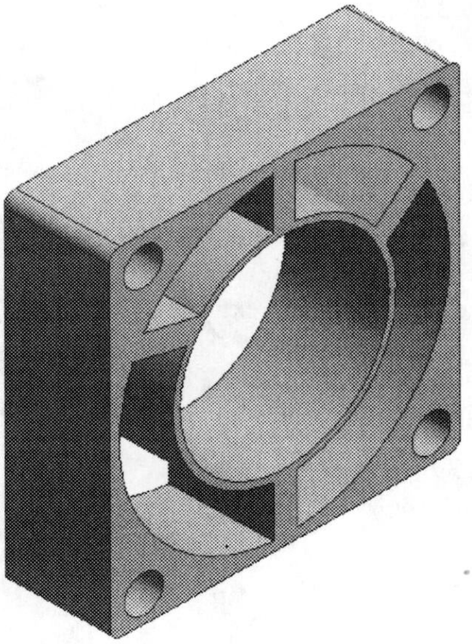

We have successfully transformed an AutoCAD 2D drawing into a 3D Parametric part in minutes.

Reattach Sketch

Use Reattach Sketch to move an existing sketch to a different planar face or work plane than the one on which it originated, then use constraints and dimensions to position it and modify its size as needed.

1. In the browser, select the sketch you want to attach to a face or plane.
2. Right-click and select Reattach Sketch.
3. Click the face or plane on which to attach the sketch.

If the sketch is constrained or dimensioned to the plane on which it originated, the constrained geometry is included when the sketch is moved to a different plane. You can delete extraneous geometry as needed.

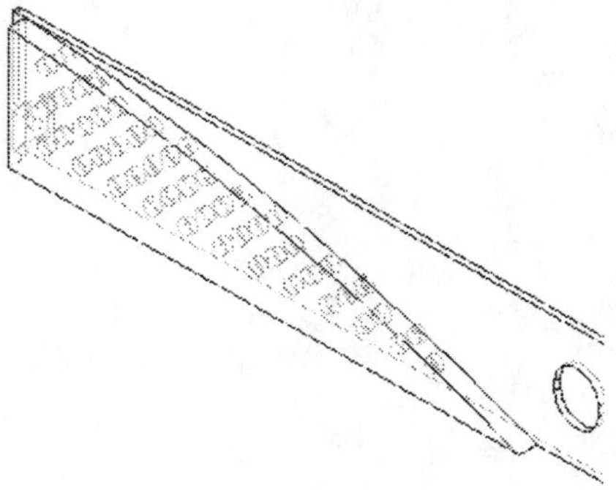

In the model shown, the holes are located on the middle plane, so that they do not go all the way through the part. We can move the holes to the top plane using 'Reattach Sketch' and then edit the feature to ensure that the holes cut through the part. Our other choice would be to delete all the holes and start over.

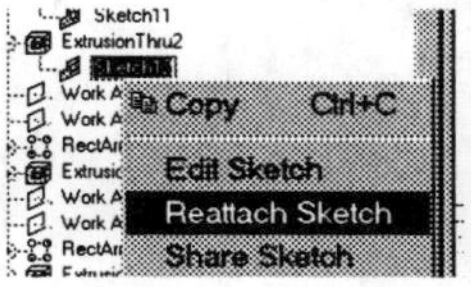

We locate one of the holes to be moved. Right click and select 'Reattach Sketch'.

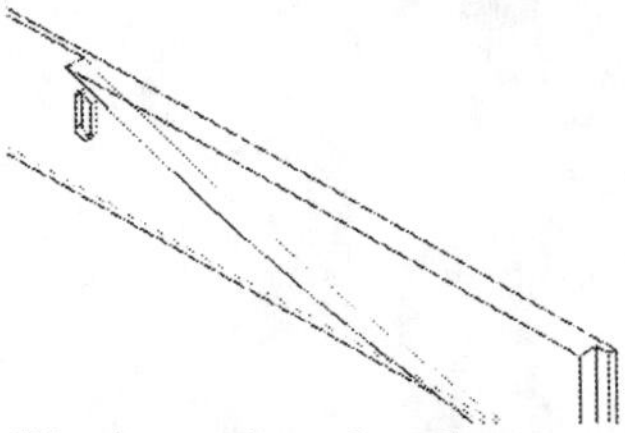

We then select the plane to move the sketch.

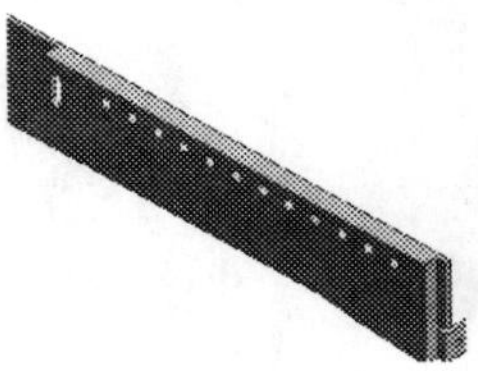

We now see that the holes go through the part.

Cursor Cues

As we create our sketches, we see cursor cues telling us how Inventor is interpreting what we are drawing. By watching for the visual feedback Inventor provides we can create sketches faster and with less edits required.

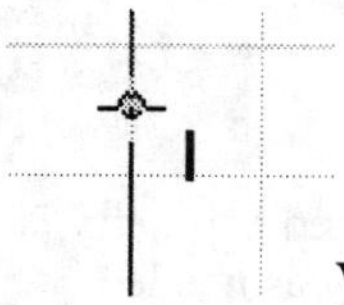
Vertical

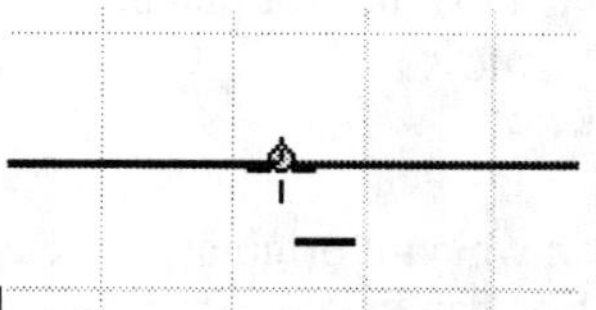
Horizontal

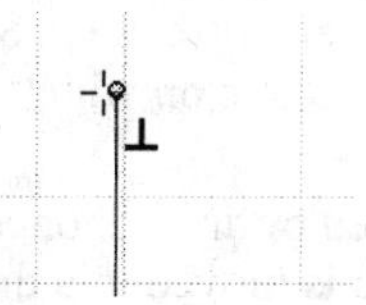
Perpendicular

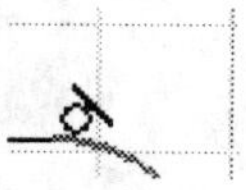
Tangent

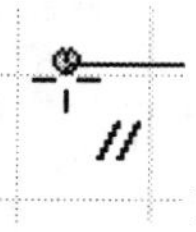
Parallel

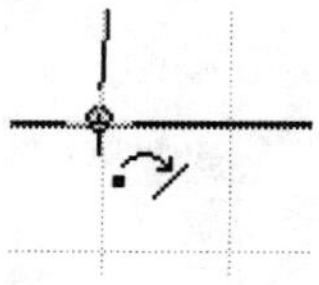
Coincident

Sketch Tools

Button	Tool	Function	Special Instructions
	Edit Coordinate System	Use for creating isometric or angled sketches	
	Line	Create line segment	Select NORMAL or CONSTRUCTION from the Style Menu
	Spline	Create spline	
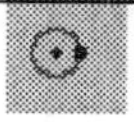	Circle	Create circle using center point and radius	Select NORMAL or CONSTRUCTION from the Style Menu
	Circle	Create circle tangent to three lines or arcs	
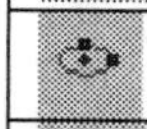	Circle	Create ellipse	
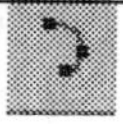	Arc	Create 3 point arc	Select NORMAL or CONSTRUCTION from the Style Menu
	Arc	Create arc with center and two endpoints	
	Arc	Create arc tangent to a line	
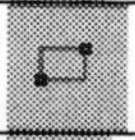	Rectangle	Use corner method to create rectangle	
	Rectangle	Create rectangle with three orthogonal points	
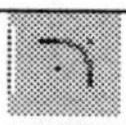	Fillet	Create fillet by entering a radius and selecting two lines or arcs	Radius controlled by dialog box entry
	Chamfer	Create chamfer. Three options available: Equal Distance, Two Distances, and Distance-Angle	
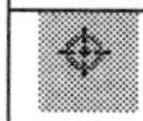	Point, Hole Center	Position the center point for a hole or sketch point	Select Hole Center (default) or Sketch Point from the Style Menu
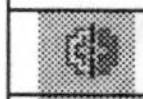	Mirror	Mirrors Geometry about a centerline	Requires Centerline
	Offset	Create parallel lines/curves at a specified distance	
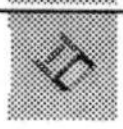	General Dimension	Apply dimensions to sketches	Use the Right click button to select the type of dimension to apply.
	Auto Dimension	Applies dimensions to selected sketch geometry	

Button	Tool	Function	Special Instructions
	Extend	Extend a line/curve to intersect with the nearest line/curve/point.	Press and hold SHIFT to temporarily enable Trim.
	Trim	Trim a line/curve	Press and hold SHIFT to temporarily enable Extend.
	Move	Moves/Copies Selected Geometry to a new location	
	Rotate	Rotates/Copies Selected Geometry to a new location	
	Add Constraint	Perpendicular	
		Parallel	
		Tangent	
		Coincident	May be applied to lines, points, or arcs.
		Concentric	
		Collinear	May be applied to lines or axes
		Horizontal	
		Vertical	
		Equal	
		Fixed	
	Show/Delete Constraint	Show applied constraints or delete existing constraints	Position the cursor over the constraint and select DELETE. Use the OTHER option to cycle through multiple constraints.
	Project Geometry	Project geometry onto another sketch	
	Project cut edges	Project onto a sketch plane all edges of a selected part that intersect the sketch plane	
	Project Flat Pattern	Project a flat pattern onto a selected plane	
	AutoCAD drawing	Inserts an AutoCAD drawing into a sketch	Use Sketch Doctor to create closed profiles

Review Questions

A.  B.  C.  D. 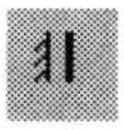

Identify the geometric constraint

1. Vertical
2. Fixed
3. Parallel
4. Coincident

5. The Spline tool is located under this drop-down:

   A. Line
   B. Arc
   C. Circle
   D. Rectangle

6. The three types of arc options are:

   A. 3 Point, Tan-Tan-Tan, Start End Radius
   B. 3 Point, Star t Direction Radius, Start End Radius
   C. 3 Point, Center Two Ends, Tangent
   D. 3 Point, Center Radius, Start End Radius

7. To draw a construction line or circle:

   A. Use the Style drop-down and select Construction
   B. Use the Construction Line/Circle tool
   C. Select the Line/Circle, Right click and enable 'Construction'
   D. While drawing the line, hole down the CONTROL button.

8. To switch to arc mode while using the Line tool:

   A. Hold down the CONTROL key
   B. Left Click and Hold down the left mouse button
   C. Hold down the TAB Key
   D. Right click and select ARC from the menu.

9. To switch from TRIM mode to EXTEND mode:

   A. Hold down the CONTROL key
   B. Press and hold SHIFT
   C. Right click and select EXTEND from the menu.
   D. Hold down the TAB Key

10. To modify a dimension:

    A. Double click on top of the dimension
    B. Select the Edit Dimension tool
    C. Select the Dimension in the browser, right click and select Edit
    D. Select Edit Text from the Modify menu.

ANSWERS: 1) D; 2) B; 3) A; 4) C; 5) A; 6) C; 7) A; 8) B; 9) B; 10) A

Notes:

Lesson 7

The Solids Toolbar

Base solids are models created in other CAD systems and saved in SAT or STEP file format. You open a base solid in Autodesk Inventor as a fixed size base feature (the first one in a file). Unlike Autodesk Inventor models, you cannot access sketches or features used to create a base solid.

In the Solids environment, you use tools to modify an imported base solid. Modifications do not add features to the solid, except for work features used as construction geometry.

TIP: If you are using solids created in MDT4, you need to have Service Pack 3 or greater installed before you can use Inventor's Solid tools to modify the file. These are downloadable for free from Autodesk's website at www.autodesk.com.

Users who have created 3D models in AutoCAD can use Inventor's Solids Modeling ability to modify their solids and even build them into parametric models.

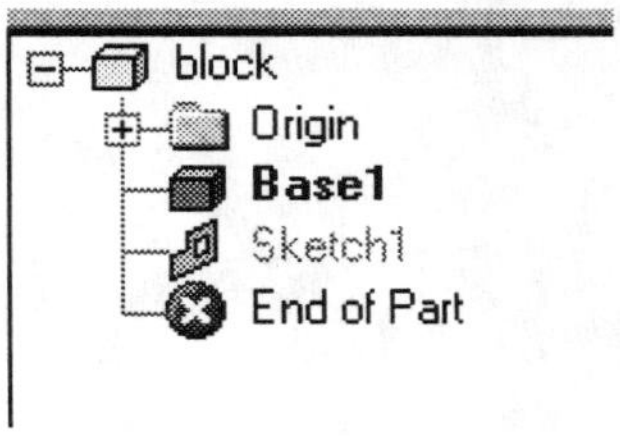

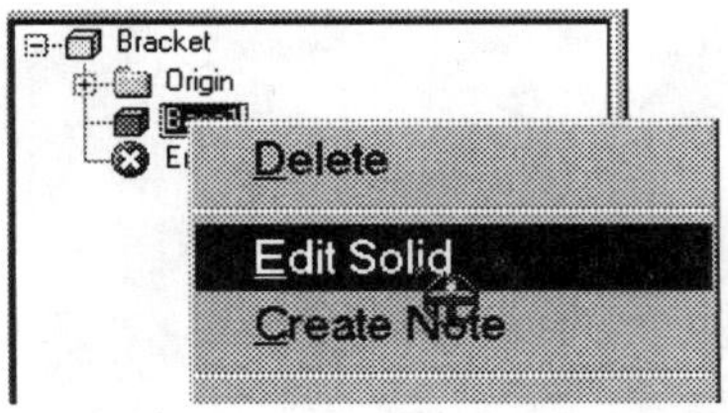

The Solids toolbar is activated by selecting the Base Solid from the browser and double-clicking it. You can also right click on the Base feature, right click and select 'Edit Solid'.

TIP: You will not be able to access any of the tools on the Solids Toolbar unless you have a Base Solid present in your drawing. The tools will be greyed out until the base is activated by a double-click.

Move Face

Use the Move Faces tool on the Solids toolbar to move one or more faces on a base solid. Moved faces are not parametrically located.

TIP: Usually, you select all faces that need to move. Because faces are not parametrically associated, moving them as a group is the easiest way to retain their positions relative to one another.

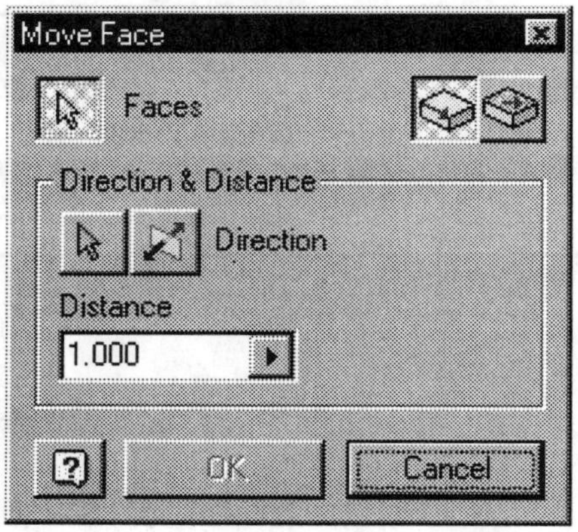

To move faces by direction and distance

1. Click the Move Faces tool.
2. Click the Distance and Direction button.
3. In the graphics window, click an edge or work axis to define the direction. If desired, click Flip to reverse direction.
4. Enter the distance one of these ways:
   - Enter a number or an equation. The equation cannot include a parameter name.
   - Click the arrow to list recent values, then click to select one.
   - Click the arrow to access the Measure tool. The measured value is automatically entered in the distance field.

Click Update to exit the solids environment.

To move a face by a distance in a plane:

1. Click the Move Faces tool.
2. Click one or more faces to move.
3. Click the Planar Move button.
4. In the graphics window, click a plane.
5. Click the Points button, then click two points to define the start and end points.

   The points are projected onto the plane, if necessary, and one or more faces are moved relative to the projected points.

6. Click Update to exit the solids environment.

TIP: Only work points, the end or midpoint of an edge, or the center of a circular edge may be selected. Instead of clicking two points, you can use the Precise Input tool to enter coordinates. For example, click the Relative Coordinates button to relocate the coordinate origin, then enter coordinates relative to the new origin.

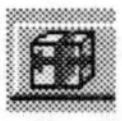

Extend or Contract Body

In the Solids environment, extends or contracts a base solid along an axis. The base solid is resized perpendicular to a selected plane. Extending or contracting a base solid does not add a new feature.

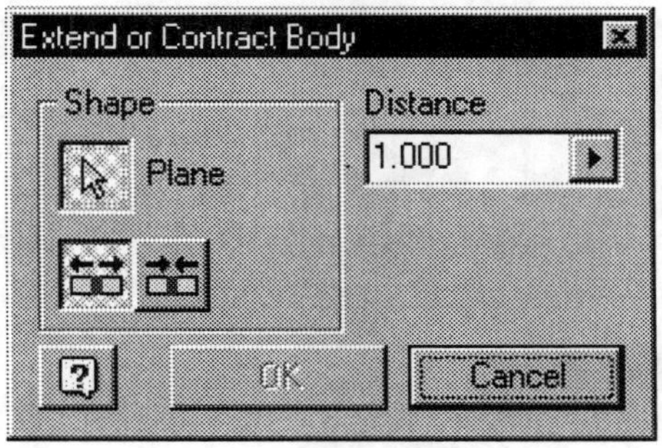

The Plane tool selects a work plane or planar face to identify the section about which the base solid will extend or contract.

The two buttons on the left specify if the base solid extends or contracts equally on both sides of the selected plane by a specified distance. The button on the left extends the solid. The button on the right contracts the solid.

The Distance edit box specifies distance the base solid extends or contracts. May be specified as a number or an equation. You must enter in a value – using the mouse is not an option.

The remaining tools on the Solid toolbar (Work Plane, Work Axis and Work Point) allow the user to add work features for the purposes of adding Inventor features to the model.

Toggle Precise UI

This brings up the Precise Input Toolbar.

Solids Editing Tools

Button	Tool	Function
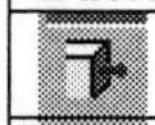	Move Face	Moves one or more faces on a solid
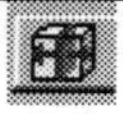	Extend or Contract	Extend or contract a base solid symmetrically about a planar face or work plane
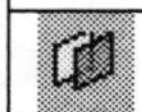	Work Plane	Create a work plane
	Work Axis	Create a work axis
	Work Point	Create a work point
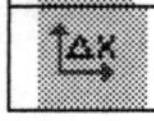	Toggle Precise UI	Brings up the Precise Input Toolbar

Review Questions

1. The Solids tools are used to:

   A. Edit solid models created in AutoCAD and inserted into an Inventor file
   B. Create solid models
   C. Transform solid models into parametric models
   D. All of the above

2. True or False:

You will not be able to access any of the tools on the Solids Toolbar unless you have a Base Solid present in your drawing file.

3. True or False

You can add work features, such as work planes and work points, to a base solid.

4. True or False

You can add a hole feature to your base solid.

5. True or False

You can extend or shorten your base model using Solids tools.

6. To activate the Solids Toolbar:

   A. Go to View->Toolbars->Solids
   B. Highlight the Base solid in the browser, right click and select 'Solids'
   C. Double click on the Base Solid in the browser
   D. Right click in the drawing window and select 'Solids'

ANSWERS: 1) A; 2) T; 3) T; 4) T; 5) T; 6) C

Lesson 8

The Precise Input Toolbar

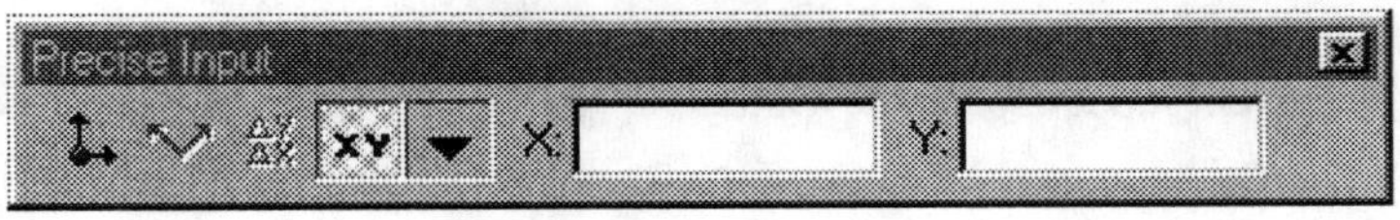

Typically, sketch geometry is dimensioned only after it is created. Precise input allows you to key-in sketch dimension values as you create the geometry. The precise input fields are modified versions of the same edit boxes used in the Equations and Parameters tools. This means that you can enter expressions as well as other algebraic values, with or without units. Note: Relative Orientation is only available for sketches in the Drawing environment.

For those users who like to use coordinate entry, the Precise Input toolbar allows them to continue that method.

Relative Origin

Relative Origin allows you to select a point on your model to define a temporary origin. Your subsequent coordinate inputs are measured from this new origin until you change it. The orientation of the new coordinate system is unchanged, only the origin changes.

Relative Origin will stay active after being used to set a new origin. You can pick an out-of-plane point to define the origin. The point is projected into the plane, and is used to define the origin. This projection is not persistent. The relative origin is reset when you leave sketch mode, or when you click the Relative Origin button again.

To set a relative origin:

1. Click the relative origin button.
2. Select a valid sketch point in the part modeling or drawing environments.

TIP: The coordinate icon displays the current orientation.

The Relative Origin tool is similar to setting the Origin in AutoCAD.

Relative Orientation

Relative Orientation rotates the axes of the current input coordinate system.

To rotate the current input coordinate system:

1. Select an axis, line, or linear edge to define the X axis.
2. The sense of the X axis will be inferred so as to maintain the sense of the current Z axis.
   You can choose out-of-plane lines to set the orientation.
   The line will be projected onto the plane, and the projected line will be used to set the orientation.

TIP: This command will be disabled in part modeling sketching.
This is similar to the SNAP ROTATE option in AutoCAD.

Delta Input

Delta Input allows you to enter sketch dimensions relative to the last point picked or entered in the current coordinate system. The first point of any command is always relative to the origin. Subsequent points are relative to the last selected point when this button is active.

TIP: The setting of this button persists throughout an Inventor session.

This is similar to using a relative coordinate in AutoCAD.

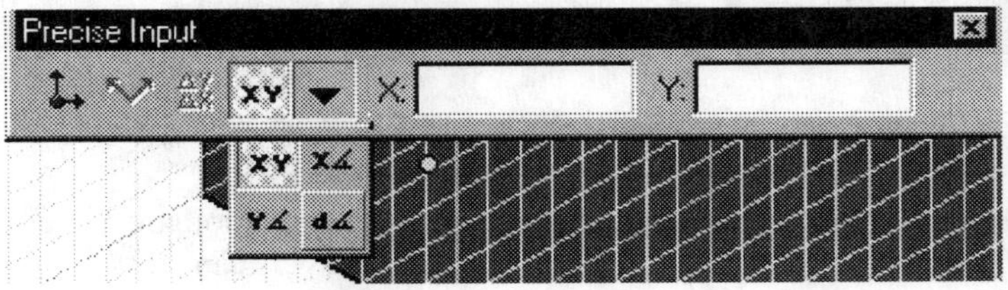

Precise input accepts data in the four formats listed below.

xy Specifies a coordinate by (x,y) point relative to current origin.

x° Specifies a coordinate by x-coordinate and an angle from positive x-axis.

y° Specifies a coordinate by y-coordinate and an angle from positive y-axis.

d° Traditional polar coordinates. Specifies a coordinate by a distance and an angle from positive x-axis.

To change the input type:

1. Click the down arrow to the right of the input type button.
2. Select a format from the fly-out icon menu.

TIP: The (x,y) coordinates reported on the status line reflect the current coordinate system and input method.

The Collaboration Toolbar

Autodesk Inventor provides tools to enable collaboration, cooperative work on a project by more than one person. The tools establish a framework for effective communication so that you and others can work simultaneously in related files.

- A system for defining projects and file locations. A project consists of the local and network folders containing the Autodesk Inventor files, and a project file that identifies these file locations.
- A file reservation system that warns other designers when someone is editing a file.
- The Engineer's Notebook to capture design information and other notes.
- The Design Assistant to track and manage file properties, links between files, and other important information about Autodesk Inventor files.
- Access to Windows® NetMeeting® to exchange ideas in a chat setting and on an electronic whiteboard.

The Collaboration Toolbar interfaces with NetMeeting to allow the user to Add Participants, Delete Participants, Add Directories, Chat, White Board, and Hang Up.

Usually, participants collaborate in a session similar to this:

- The host is working in an assembly and notifies participants that a meeting is needed.
- The host starts a Windows® NetMeeting® session and sets up the host security options.
- Participants start Windows® NetMeeting® on their own computers.
- The host selects Tools>Online Collaboration>Meet Now, then enters information about the participant's computer.
- On the participant's computer, a message signals the start of the meeting.
- A window opens on each participant's computer, showing a working session of Autodesk Inventor.

At the start of the meeting, the host has control of the Autodesk Inventor session. To operate Autodesk Inventor, double-click in the graphics window. On the host's machine, a window displays the request. When the host accepts, you gain control of the session and can operate Autodesk Inventor normally. Other meeting participants follow the same sequence when they want to operate Autodesk Inventor.

Any participant can start a chat or whiteboard session, but only the host can change control of Autodesk Inventor.

Lesson 9

Sheet Metal Tools

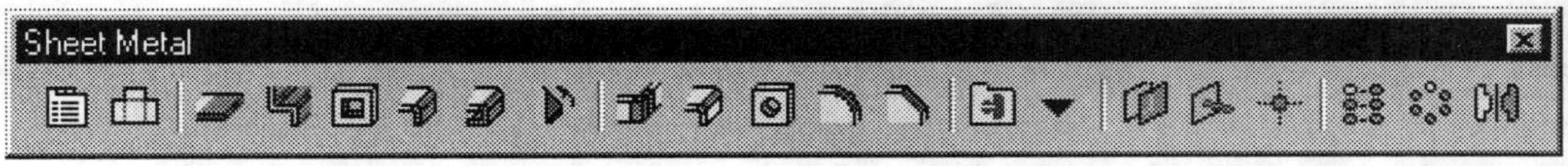

Styles

Sheet metal styles specify default parameters for sheet metal parts. Only the bend radius can be modified when creating a sheet metal part; all other settings must be modified on the Sheet Metal Styles dialog box (to change defaults for all sheet metal parts) or in the Parameters dialog box (to change settings for an individual sheet metal part).

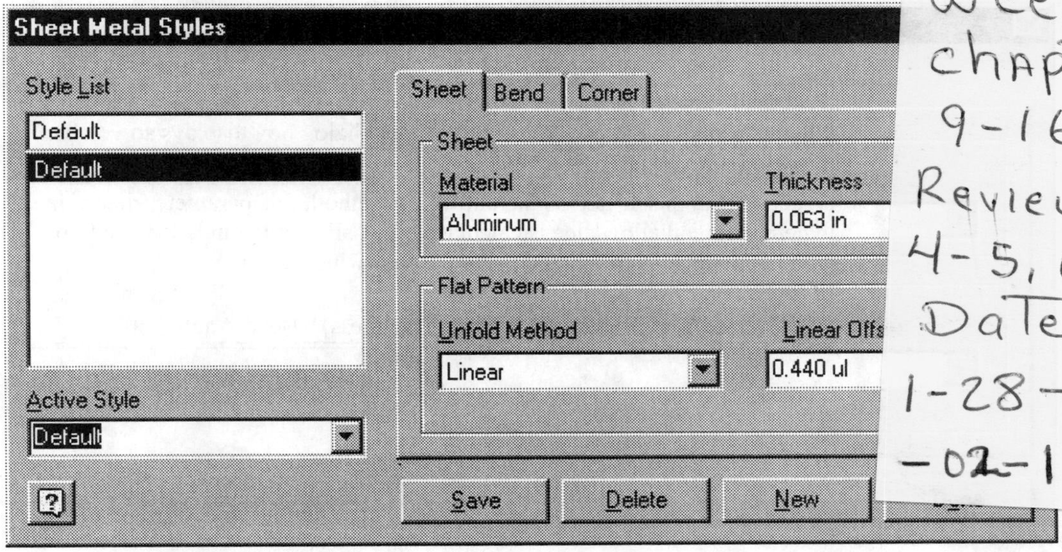

Week 3
chapter
9-16
Review
4-5, 6, 7
Date
1-28 — [illegible]
-02-1

Pressing the Styles tool brings up the dialog box shown.

Under the Sheet Tab, we have several options;

Material	Click the arrow and select a material from the list. This parameter can also be entered on the Physical tab of the Properties dialog box. Select File>Properties>Physical.
Units	Click the arrow and select a system of units from the list. This parameter can also be entered on the Units tab of the Properties dialog box. Select Files>Properties>Units.
Thickness	Sets the sheet metal thickness in decimal units.

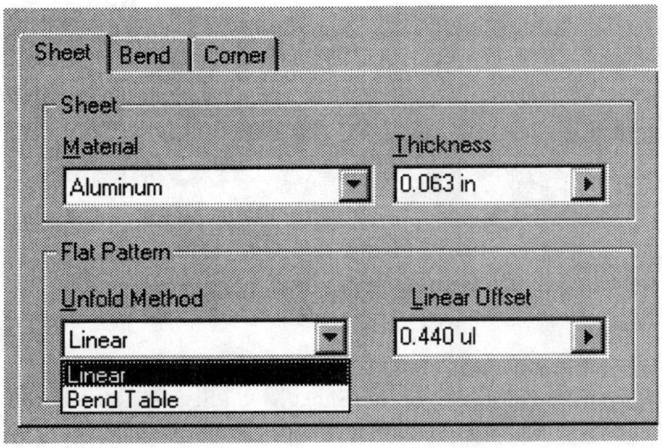

On the right side of the Sheet Tab, we set the Unfold Method for the Flat Pattern.

Unfolding Method	Sets the Linear or Bend Table unfolding method. For Linear, enter a value for the linear offset. For Bend Table, the Open dialog box displays so you can browse to the location of a bend table.
Linear Offset	When Linear is selected as the unfolding method, this parameter determines where the bend allowance is calculated. The allowable range is from 0 to 1. The bend allowance is calculated using the following equation: 2*PI*(Bend Radius + Linear Offset*Thickness)*(Bend Angle/360)

TIP: Users can set up sheet metal styles (similar to dimension styles in AutoCAD) with their favorite sheet metal settings. Create styles by pressing the 'New' button in the Styles dialog box.

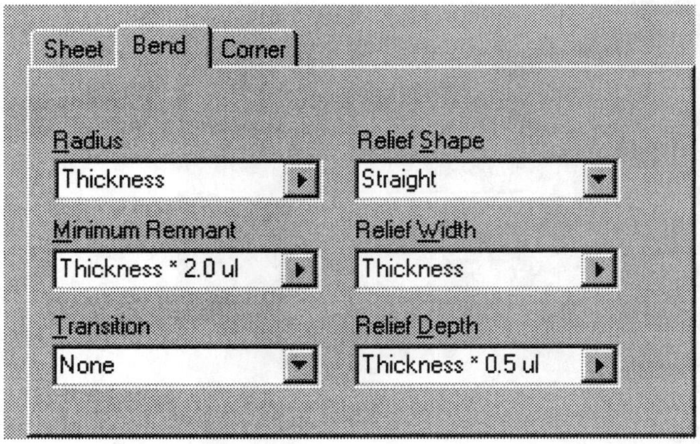

Under the Bend Tab, we have several options:

Bend Radius	Sets value for the default bend radius. This parameter can be overridden on an individual feature.
Bend Relief	Inserts a bend relief if the bend does not extend the full width of a sheet metal face. Select Default Straight (square corners) or Default Round (full radius corners).
Minimum Remnant	Sets the amount of material between the bend relief and the edge of the sheet metal part. If the remnant is less than this value, the width of the bend relief is increased to consume the remnant.
Bend Relief Width	Sets the distance between the edge of the bend and the bend relief. This value is usually determined by the selection of available punches.
Bend Relief Depth	Sets the distance the bend relief extends past the bend zone.

TIP: By using the variable ***Thickness*** multiplied or divided by a value, we can eliminate the amount of editing we need to do. Simply change the value for the Thickness under the Sheet tab and all the values on the Bend tab will automatically update.

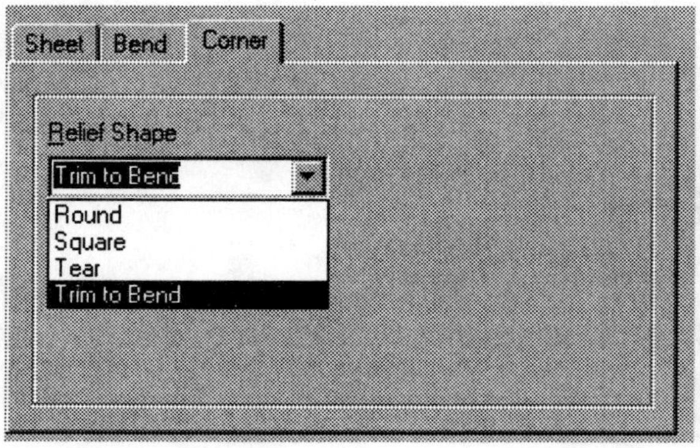

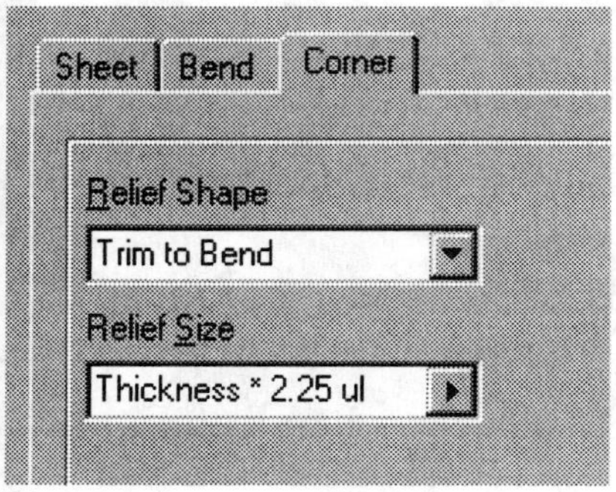

The third tab on the Sheet Metal Settings dialog is Corner.

Relief Shape	Inserts a corner relief when a corner seam is applied and three faces come together in the corner. Select None for no corner relief or Default Round for a circular corner relief.
Relief Size	Sets the corner relief size. Specify a value that extends the corner relief past the bend lines on the largest bend.

TIP: To see the correct corner relief, create a flat pattern.

Flat Pattern

Creates an unfolded representation of a sheet metal part. The flat pattern appears in a separate graphics window from the sheet metal part.

The Flat pattern tool calculates the unfolded state of the 3D model and displays it in a separate graphics window. You can arrange the part window and the flat pattern window so you can view both at the same time. The flat pattern updates automatically when you edit the 3D model, but you cannot edit the part in the flat pattern window.

If you create a model that cannot be unfolded (if the features overlap in the flat pattern, for example), the flat pattern does not update. The flat pattern symbol in the browser is marked.

Features that require material deformation, such as louvers or dimples, cannot be flattened. The flat pattern tool shows the outline of the feature on the flat pattern.

The Drawing Manager uses the flat pattern for the flat pattern view. The flat pattern must be created in the part before you can place a flat pattern view in the drawing

TIP: A flat pattern cannot be created if the part has no bends. If you delete the flat pattern, the drawing will also lose the flat pattern view.

An incorrect flat pattern may be generated if the incorrect face is used as the base face. If this happens, right-click the flat pattern icon in the browser and click Delete. Then, to preselect the face you want to be the base face, click it in the graphics window, and then click the Flat Pattern tool.

Flat patterns are created with MetalBender Solver software from data M Software + Engineering. Their website is http://www.data-m.com/.

Face

The Face command is similar to the Extrude command.

Creates a sheet metal face by adding depth to a sketched profile. The Feature shape is controlled by the sketch shape and any bends or seams between the new sheet metal face and existing sheet metal faces.

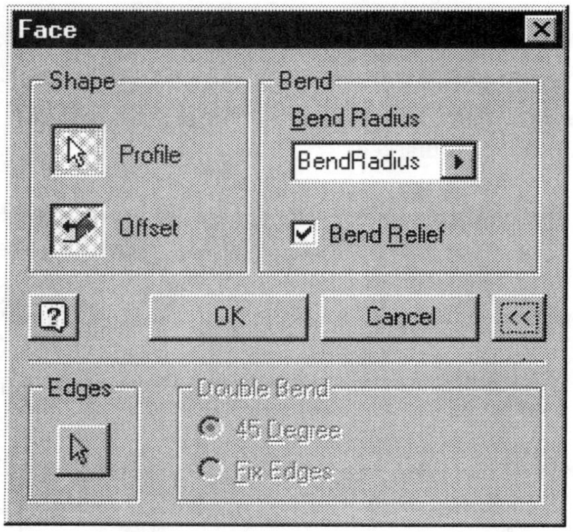

The Shape tool selects a profile to extrude by the sheet metal thickness. If there are multiple profiles, click on one or more profiles in the graphics window. The extrusion of the selected profiles is previewed in the graphics window. Click the Offset button to change the direction of the extrude.

TIP: To select multiple profiles to extrude, position the cursor over the profile and click to select. To unselect, press Ctrl and click profile.

On the right side of the Face Dialog box we specify the bend radius and whether a bend relief is added. If the new sheet metal face is coincident with one existing sheet metal face, a bend is created automatically.

We have two options: Bend Radius and Bend Relief.

The default bend radius is displayed. Enter another value if desired. Select Bend Relief automatically generate bend reliefs. Clear Bend Relief to create a bend without a relief.

Click the More button 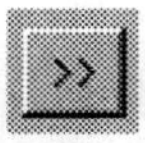 to display the Edges button. Select the intersecting model edge on the existing sheet metal face.

Under the More area we can select a single bend or double bend.

<table>
<tr><td>Single bend</td><td>For a new sheet metal face, you can create a bend to an existing sheet metal face. Select the sheet metal face for the bend if one of the following applies:<ul><li>The profile for the new sheet metal face is coincident with multiple existing sheet metal faces.</li><li>The profile for the new sheet metal face is not coincident with any sheet metal faces.</li></ul>Autodesk Inventor trims or extends the sheet metal faces as required to create the bends.</td></tr>
<tr><td>Double bend</td><td>If sheet metal faces are parallel, but not coplanar, you can create a double bend between the faces. The bends are trimmed so they are tangent or a new sheet metal face is constructed to connect the bends.<table><tr><td>45 Degree</td><td>Sheet metal faces are trimmed or extended as necessary and 45 degree bends are inserted.</td></tr><tr><td>Fix Edges</td><td>Equal bends are added to the existing sheet metal edges.</td></tr></table></td></tr>
</table>

Contour Flange

A contour flange is created using an open profile.

Create a new sheet metal part file.

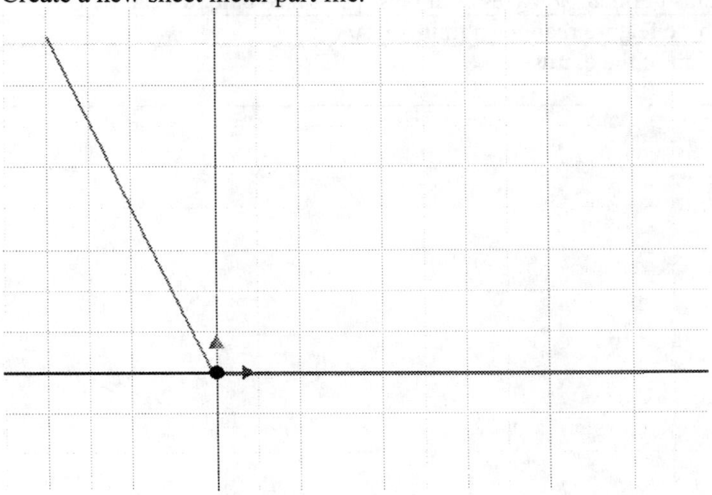

Draw two lines as shown: one horizontal and one at an angle.

Select the Contour Flange tool.

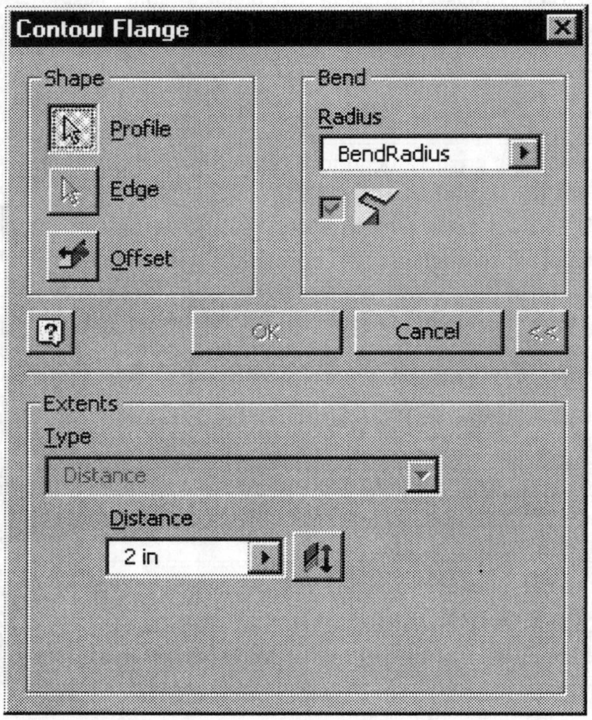

The Contour Flange dialog box comes up.

Shape	
Profile	Select an open profile to be used
Edge	Select the existing edge of a part as the contour
Offset	Select the direction for the offset
Bend	Defaults to Bend Radius defined by Styles or allows the user to enter a value
Extents	If Contour Flange is base feature requires a finite distance.
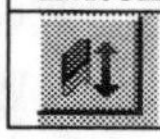	Determines the direction of the extrusion

Our contour flange.

Cut

A cut removes material from a sheet metal face. You sketch a profile on a sheet metal face and then cut through one or more faces. You can use Design Elements to create a library of punch shapes. Cut features can be used with the Design Element, Mirror, Rectangular Array, and Circular Array tools.

You can specify a distance for a cut or it can terminate on a face or workplane. In an assembly, the terminating face or workplane can be on another part.

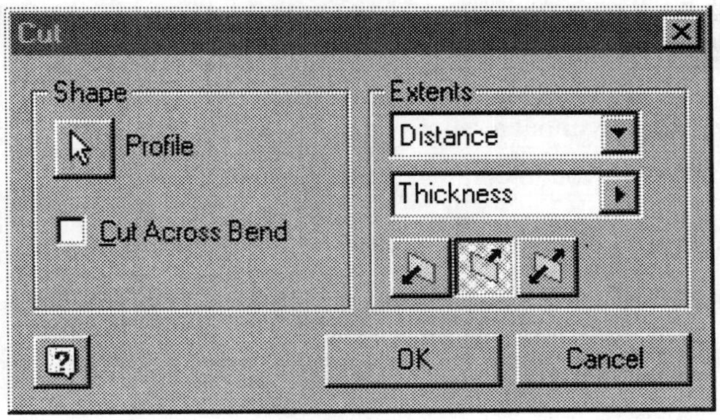

Flange

Creates a flange by adding a sheet metal face and a bend to an existing face. The flange is created the full width of the existing face.

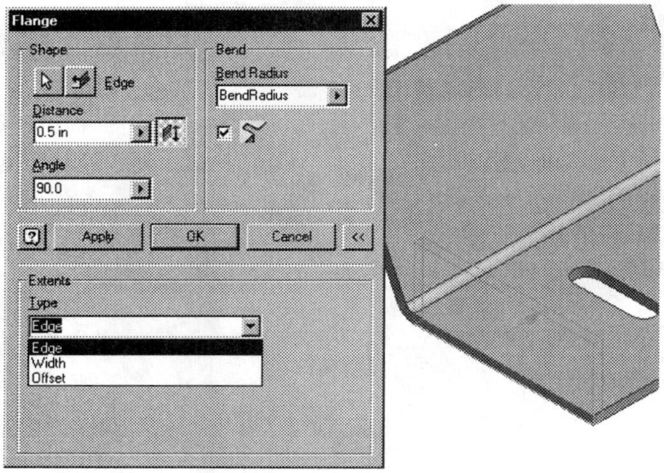

Distance	Enter the distance for the depth of the flange. The distance is measured from the model edge you select for the flange.
Angle	Enter the angle for the flange. The angle must be less than 150 degrees.
Flip Offset	Creates the flange on the inside or the outside of the face. Click to change the position of the flange as needed.
Flip Direction	Changes the side of the face the flange is created on. Click to change direction as needed.
Edge	Selects a model edge for the flange.
Bend radius	Displays the default Bend Radius. Enter another value if desired.
Bend relief	Specifies Bend Relief to automatically generate bend reliefs. Clear the Bend Relief check box to create a bend without a relief.
Apply button	Places specified flange and allows you to continue defining and adding flanges.
OK button	Places specified flange and closes the dialog box.

Hem

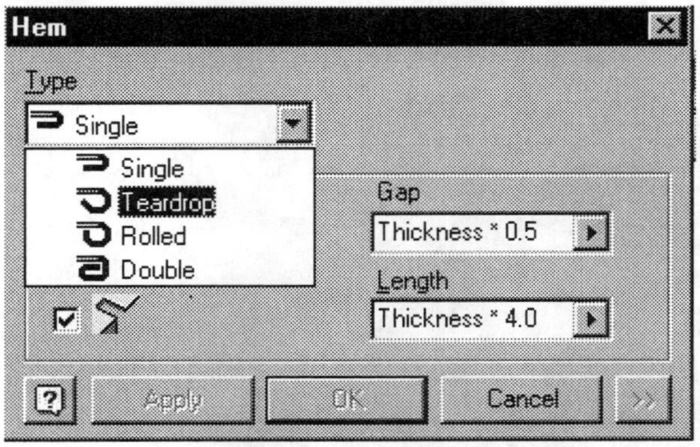

Type	
Hem Style	User can select Single, Teardrop, Rolled, or Double
Shape	Selects profile or edge to be used
Edge	Determines direction of Hem
Radius	Displays the default Bend Radius. Enter another value if desired.
Angle	Sets the angle for the bend; must be greater than 180 degrees
Extents	Edge – Uses the entire selected edge Width – Allows user to set an offset from a point and a width value for the hem Offset – Allows user to offset the hem from two points

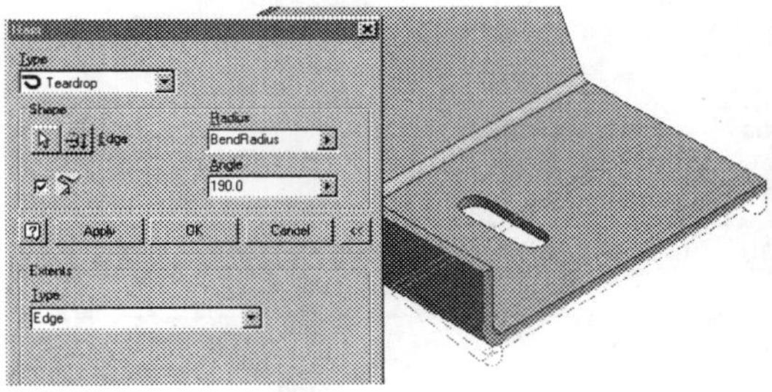

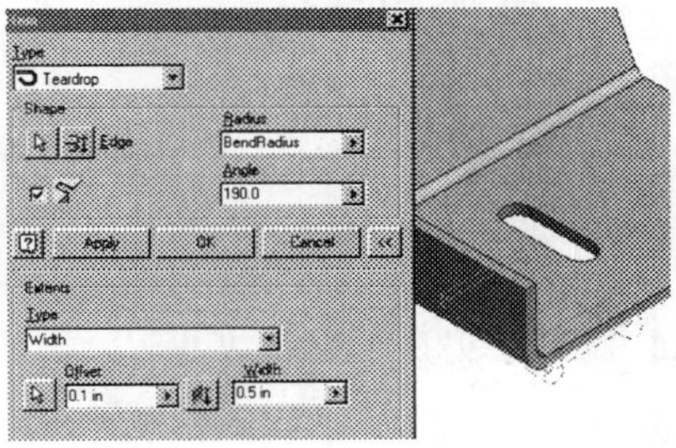

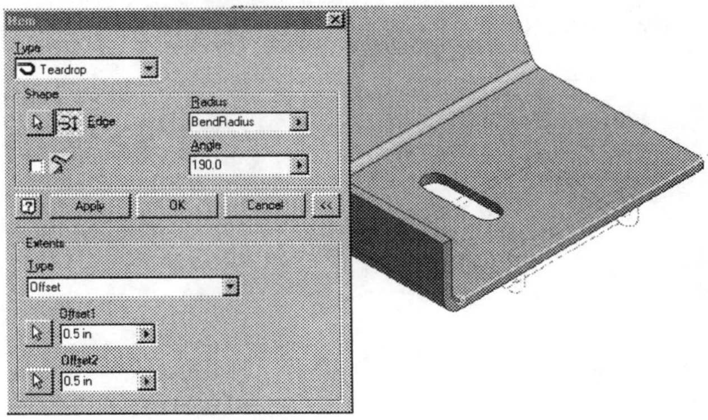

Fold

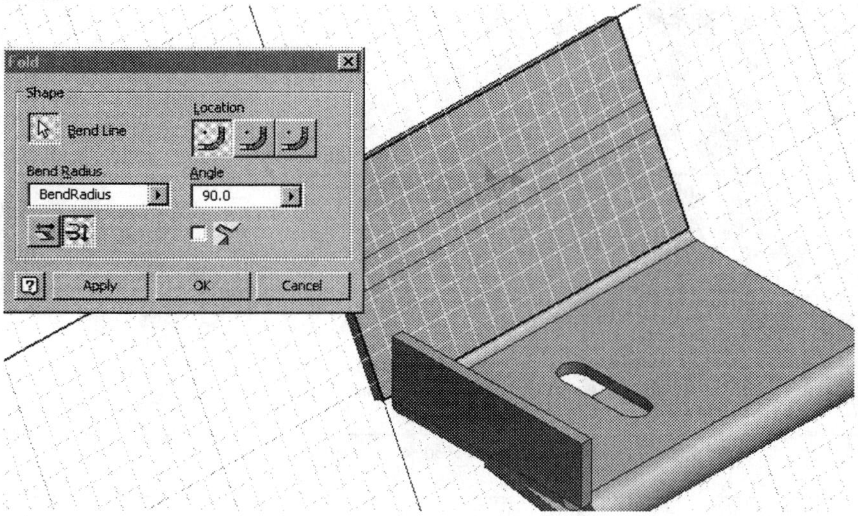

To add a fold to a sheet metal part, select a plane and create a 'New Sketch'. Then draw a line where the fold should be placed. Add dimensions as needed. Select the Fold tool.

Bend line	Sketched line used to locate the fold
Location	Defines how the line selected is to be used: . Centerline of Bend  Start of Bend  End of Bend
BendRadius	Displays the default Bend Radius. Enter another value if desired.
Angle	User defines angle of fold
	Flip Side
	Flip Direction
	Enable/Disable Bend Relief – uses Bend Relief value defined in Style

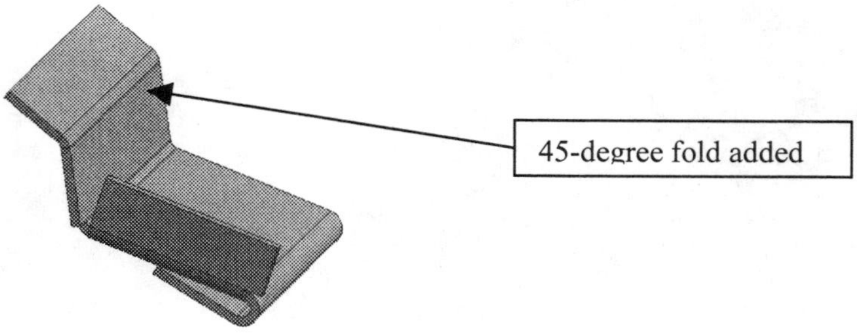

Corner Seam

Use the Corner Seam tool on the Sheet Metal toolbar to add a seam to two sheet metal faces.

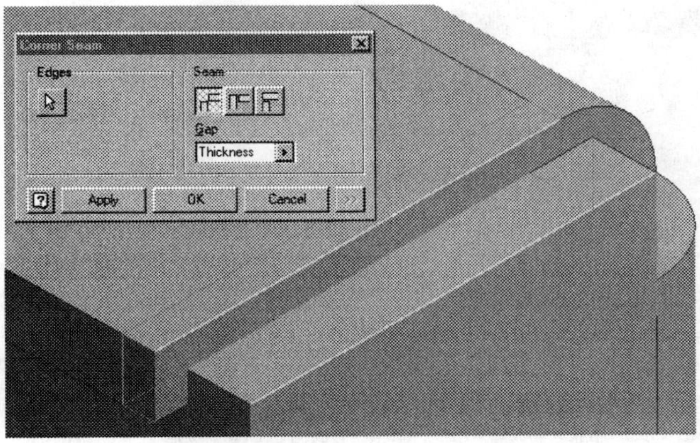

Edges	Selects a model edge on each face.	
Seam	Specifies the overlap (no overlap or one of the faces overlap) condition of the edges. The overlap condition impacts manufacturing. If one face overlaps the other, it must be formed first. Enter a value for the Gap if it is different than the default specified in the Sheet Metal Settings dialog box.	
	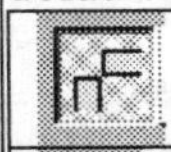	No overlap
		Overlap
	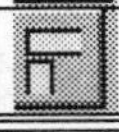	Reverse Overlap
More button	Click the More button to specify adjacent edges for an Aligned Seam. If the faces are coplanar, you can specify these overlap options: Miter joint requires two faces joined by a corner seam before the miter can be applied. Butt joint specifies one face overlapping the other face.	
Apply button	Places specified corner seam and allows you to continue defining and adding corner seams.	
OK button	Places specified corner seam and closes the dialog box.	

1. Click the Corner Seam tool.
2. Select a model edge on each sheet metal face.
3. Under Seam, choose the overlap method.
4. Enter a value for the seam gap. The default is the thickness of the sheet metal.
5. To align the seam gap for miter seams, click the More button and select edges.

Click Apply to continue to add seams or click OK to close the dialog box.

Bend

Adds a bend between two sheet metal faces.

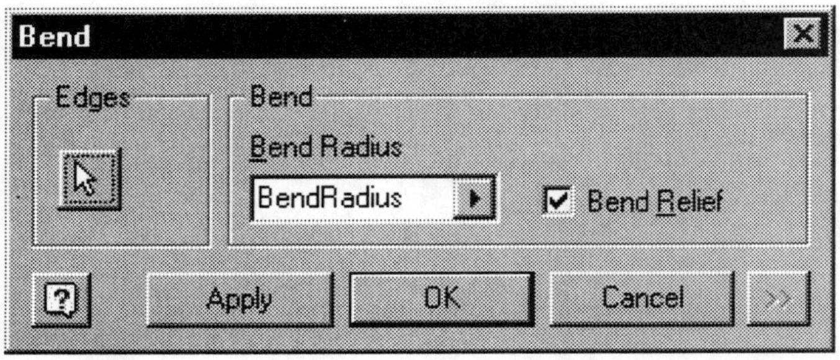

<table>
<tr><td>Edges</td><td>Selects a model edge on each face. The bend is previewed. The sheet metal faces are trimmed or extended as necessary to create the bend.</td></tr>
<tr><td>Bend</td><td>Specifies the radius for the bend. Clear the check mark in the Bend Relief box if you do not want a relief inserted.</td></tr>
<tr><td>More Button</td><td>Click the More button to display the Double Bend options.

If the sheet metal faces are parallel, but not coplanar, you can create a double bend between the faces. The bends are trimmed so they are tangent or a new sheet metal face is constructed to connect the bends.

<table><tr><td>45 Degree Connection</td><td>The sheet metal faces are trimmed or extended as necessary and 45 degree bends are inserted.</td></tr><tr><td>Fix Edges</td><td>Equal bends are added to the existing sheet metal edges.</td></tr></table></td></tr>
<tr><td>Apply button</td><td>Places specified bend and allows you to continue defining and adding corner bends.</td></tr>
<tr><td>OK button</td><td>Places specified bend and closes the dialog box.</td></tr>
</table>

Hole

Refer to Lesson 5 regarding the Hole tool.

Corner Round

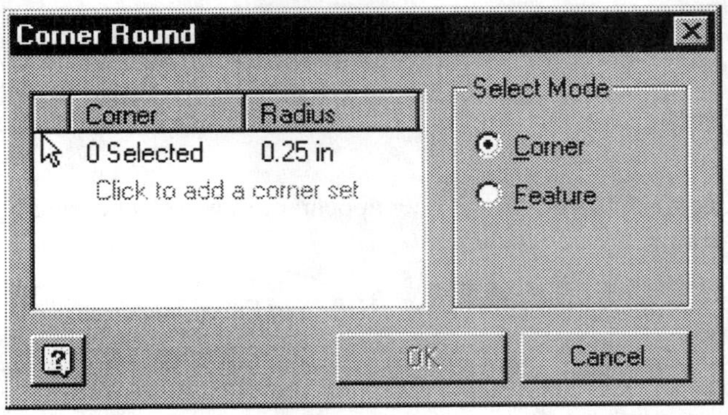

Adds fillets or rounds to one or more corners of a sheet metal part. You can create fillets or rounds of different sizes in a single operation. All fillets and rounds created in a single operation are one feature.

Corner	Defines corners for fillets or rounds. To add corners, select the set from the Corner box, and then select the corners by clicking the model edges in the graphics window. (To remove corners, press Ctrl as you click.) To add another corner set, click the prompt in the last row of the Corner box. Use Select Mode to simplify the selection of edges.
Cut	Specifies the radius for the selected set of corners. To change the radius, click the radius value, then enter the new radius.
Select Mode	Changes the selection method for adding or removing corners from a corner set. Click to select the mode from the list. Corner selects or removes single corners. Feature selects or removes all corners of a feature that do not result from intersections between the feature and other sheet metal faces.

Corner Chamfer

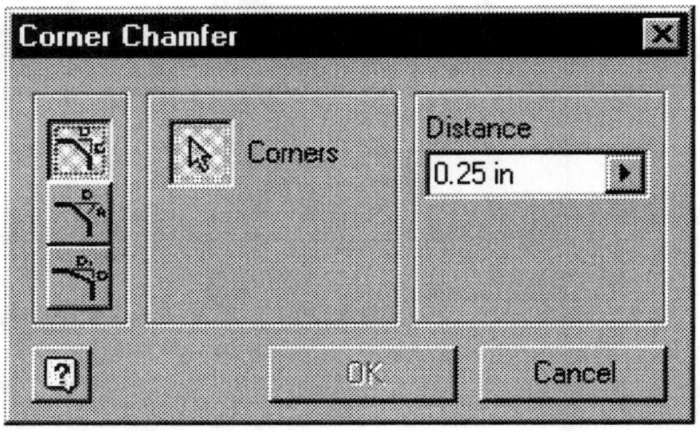

Adds a chamfer on one or more sheet metal corners. You specify the corner appearance and select corners individually. All chamfers created in a single operation are one feature.

The three left buttons determine the method the chamfer is created. The top button is Equal Distance. The middle button is Distance and Angle. The bottom button is Two Distances.

Distance	Creates a chamfer with the same offset distance from the corner on both sheet metal edges. Select a single corner or multiple corners.
Distance and Angle	Creates a chamfer defined by an offset from a sheet metal edge and an angle from that sheet metal edge to the offset. One or both corners of a selected sheet metal edge may be chamfered in one operation.
Two Distances	Creates a chamfer on a single corner with a specified distance for each sheet metal edge. Edges may be chained together.

The Corners button located in the center of the dialog box selects one or more corners or edges.

Edges	Selects individual corners to chamfer and previews default distance.
Face	For chamfers defined by a distance and angle, selects the affected sheet metal edge.
Flip	For chamfers defined by two distances, flips the direction of the chamfer distances.

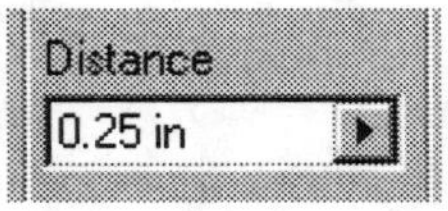

The Distance edit box specifies the extent of selected chamfer method.

Distance	Specifies offset distance of chamfer from selected sheet metal edge. For chamfers defined by two distances, specifies both offsets.
Angle	For chamfers defined by a distance and angle, specifies the angle of the chamfer.

View Catalog

The Catalog is similar to AutoCAD Design Center. The user can browse a library of parts and blocks that can be inserted into the current file.

Inventor includes a set of features ready for use. Users can explore the pre-existing library of sketches to save time when constructing their models.

Design elements are stored in feature files with the **.ide** extension. You can open a feature file to view and edit the design element.

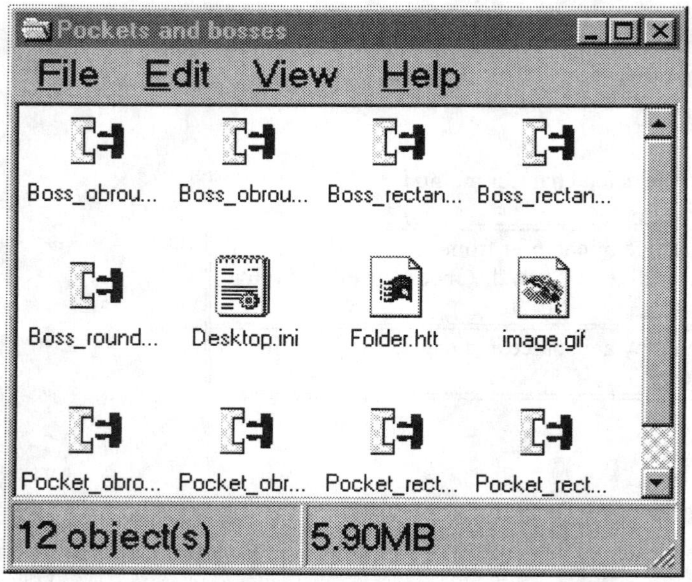

The library features can be previewed using the Insert tool.

Insert Design Element

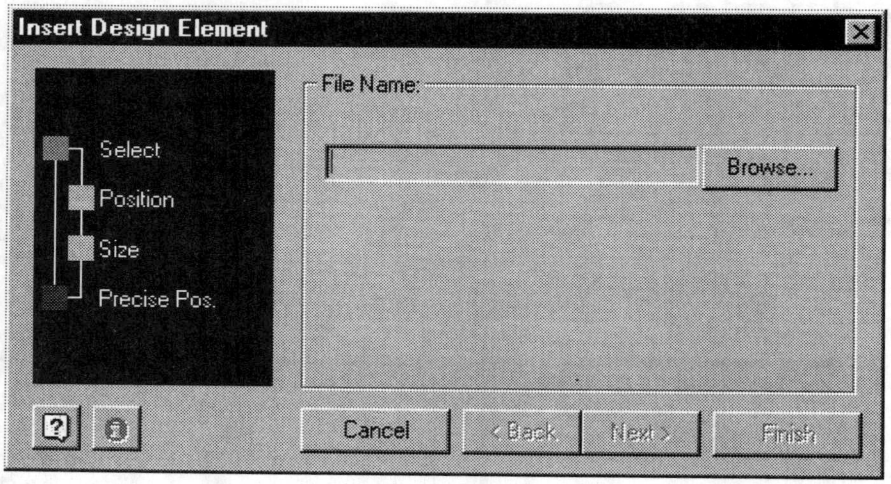

Selecting this tool brings up the dialog box shown. Select the 'Browse' button to locate the element to be added to the model.

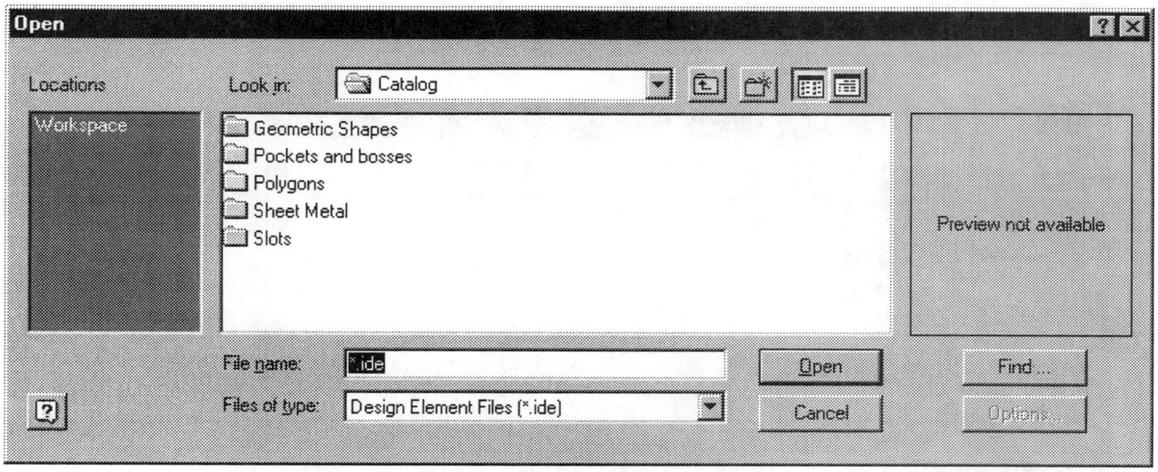

The user can then select the element category.

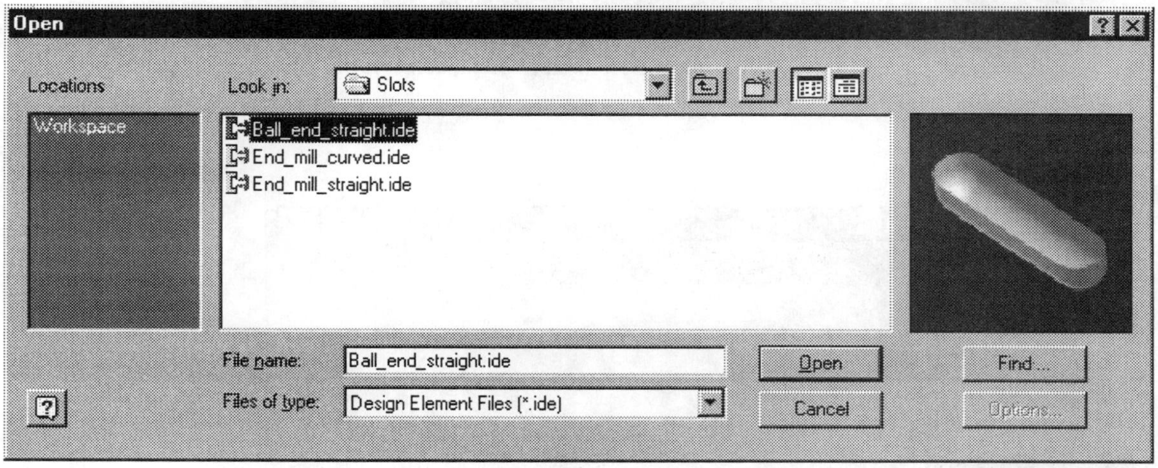

Once we get into the category area, we can preview each element to determine which one we want.

Select the desired element and press 'Open'.

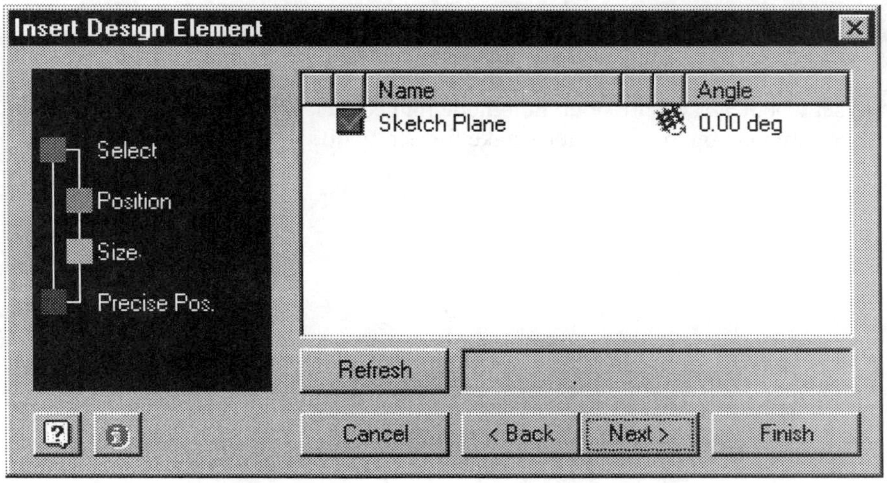

Once the element is selected, the next dialog appears. The user is required to select the plane on the existing model to place the element.

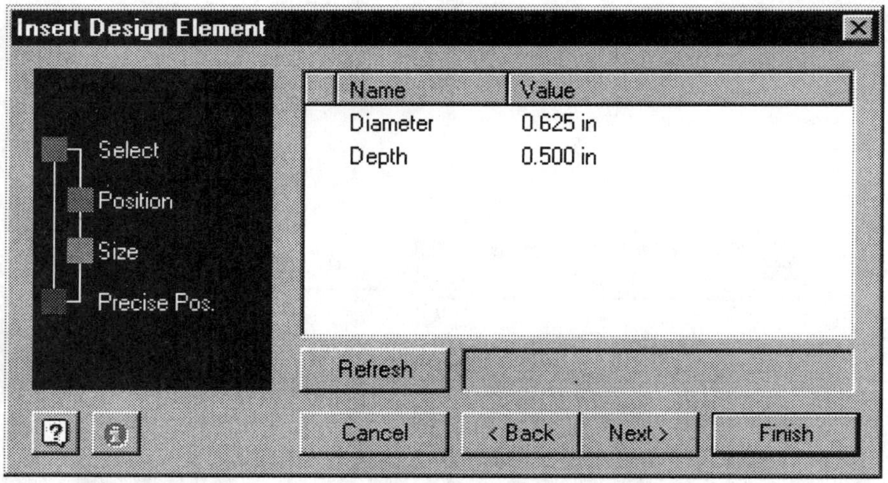

The user is then prompted for the values for the element to be placed. At this time, the user can specify his specifications for the design element.

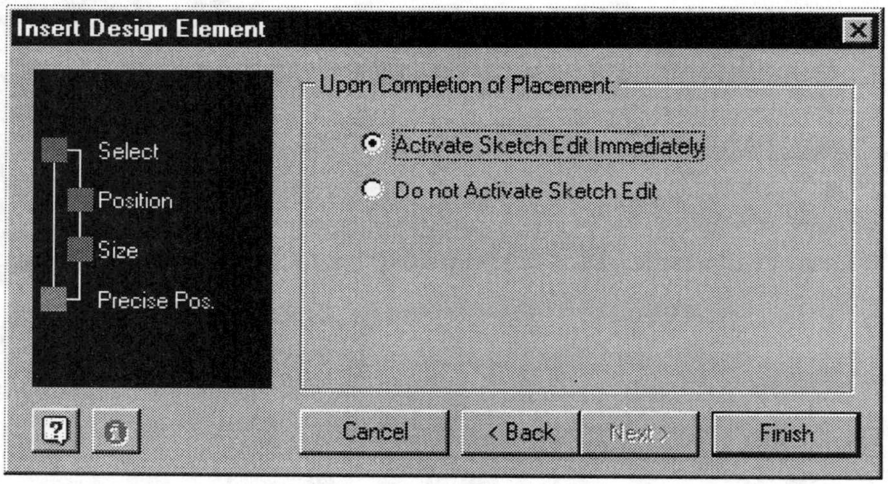

The user is then allowed to set whether to enter Sketch Edit mode immediately upon placement. Entering Sketch Mode allows the user to reposition the element or make further modifications to the basic element.

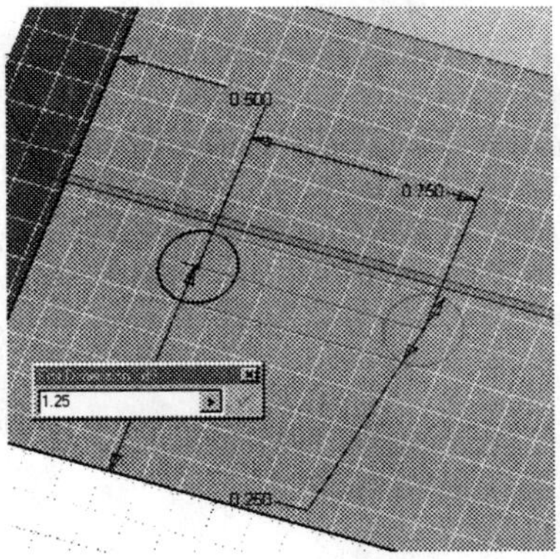

Modifying the inserted element is exactly the same as if we had created the sketch from scratch.

Create Design Element

Use the Create Design Element tool to extract and save a sketched feature in a catalog for future use. If the selected feature has geometrically dependent features, they are automatically selected, but you may delete them using the Create Design Element dialog box. To extract all the features in a part, select the base feature.

1. Select the Create Design Element tool from the pop-up menu.
2. On the model or in the browser, select one or more features to extract.
3. Save the design element with a unique name.

TIP: The sketch must be turned into a feature using Extrude, Revolve, or Sweep BEFORE it can be turned into a design element.

The Create Design Element tool may also be used to RENAME a design element.

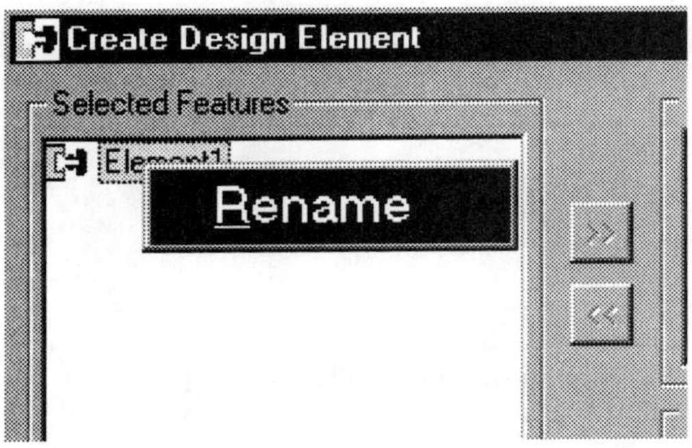

In the Create Design Element dialog box, the feature and the geometry used to create it are listed in the Selected Features tree.

1. Right-click the top level in the feature tree.
2. In the edit box, enter a new feature name.

The new name appears in the browser when you place the design element, but does not change its saved file name. To make the design element easier to use, give similar names to the design element file (.ide) and the design element feature.

TIP: Do not use spaces and other special characters in the feature name. It is included in the parameter name and may be used in equations when placing the design element.

Create Work Plane

Use the Work Plane tool on the Feature toolbar to define a work plane using unconsumed sketch geometry, feature vertices, edges, faces, or other work features. Work planes can also be created in-line when a work feature command requires you to select a plane. Use one or more of the following relationships to define a work plane:

- On geometry (on three points, for example)
- Normal to geometry
- Parallel to geometry
- At an angle to geometry (on a plane and an axis)

1. Click the Work Plane tool.
2. Select appropriate vertices, edges, or faces to define a work plane.

   For offset work planes, drag the work plane to desired location and enter a distance or angle in the Offset dialog box. Click the check mark in the dialog box to accept the preview and create the offset work plane.

If desired, you can create multiple work planes offset from one another at a specific distance or angle. Follow the steps above, selecting the last created work plane as the sketch plane, then drag the new work plane to the desired offset distance.

TIP: If more than one solution is possible, a selection box appears. Click the forward or reverse arrows in the selection box, then click the check mark when the correct solution is previewed.

Work Axis

Use the Work Axis tool on the Feature toolbar to designate unconsumed sketch geometry, points, or a part edge as a work axis. Work axes can also be created in-line as input to other work feature commands.

1. Click the Work Axis tool.
2. Select one of four methods:
    - Select a revolved feature to create a work axis along its axis of revolution.
    - Select two valid points to create a work axis through them.
    - Select a work point and a plane (or face) to create a work axis normal to the plane (or face) and through the point.

Select any two non-parallel planes to create a work axis at their intersection.

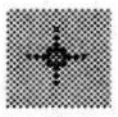

Work Point

Create a work point to constrain other sketch geometry. Work points can be placed anywhere on the active sketch plane.

The last three tools in the Sheet Metal toolbar are the same as the ones used in the Features toolbar. They are Rectangular Pattern, Circular Pattern, and Mirror Feature. Refer to Lesson 5 for more information on these tools.

Sheet Metal Tools

Button	Function	Settings/Options	Special Instructions
	Styles	Sets sheet metals styles	Use the Variable Thickness to specify values under the Bend tab to boost productivity.
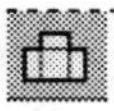	Flat Pattern	Creates a flat pattern of the sheet metal part.	
	Face	Creates a sheet metal face.	Similar to Extrude.
	Contour Flange	Uses an open profile to create a flange	
	Cut	Removes a profile from a sheet metal face.	
	Flange	Creates a flange on a sheet metal edge	
	Hem	Creates several different styles of hems	
	Fold	Creates a fold	Uses a single sketched line
	Corner Seam	Creates a corner seam between two sheet metal faces	
	Bend	Creates a bend between two sheet metal faces	
	Hole	Creates a Hole	This is the same as the Features tool
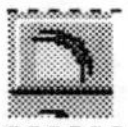	Corner Round	Creates a fillet or round on a corner	
	Corner Chamfer	Creates a chamfer on a corner	
	View Catalog	Open a Catalog of Design Elements	
	Insert Design Element	Add a Design Element	
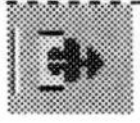	Create a Design Element	Create a Design Element from an Existing Feature	
	Work Plane	Create a work plane	
	Work Axis	Create a work axis	
	Work Point	Create a work point	
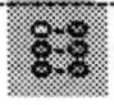	Rectangular Pattern	Create a rectangular pattern of one or more features	
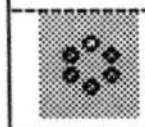	Circular Pattern	Create a circular pattern of one or more features	
	Mirror Feature	Mirror one or more features along a plane	

Review Questions

1. The three tabs on the Sheet Metal Styles dialog box are:

    A. Sheet, Bend, Corner
    B. Material, Bend, Corner
    C. Material, Thickness, Bend
    D. Sheet, Material, Properties

2. The Flat Pattern is used as:

    A. A method to determine problems with the design
    B. A view in a drawing file
    C. A method for designing sheet metal parts
    D. A silverware pattern

3. True-False
   If you delete the flat pattern in a sheet metal file, the flat pattern view will also be deleted in the corresponding drawing file.

4. The file extension for a sheet metal part file is:

    A. spt
    B. iam
    C. idw
    D. ipt

5. The Face command is similar to the command:

    A. Work Plane
    B. New Sketch Plane
    C. Extrude
    D. Extend

6. When adding a bend to a part:

    A. Inventor will automatically trim or extend the perpendicular faces to form the bend
    B. The user must trim or extend the perpendicular faces to form the bend
    C. Inventor will automatically extend perpendicular faces to form a bend, but can not automatically trim.
    D. Inventor will automatically trim perpendicular faces to form a bend, but can not automatically extend.

7. To create a cut in a sheet metal part:

    A. Draw a profile and then Extrude
    B. Draw a profile and then Cut
    C. Draw a profile and then Subtract
    D. Draw a profile and then Intersect

ANSWERS: 1) A; 2) B; 3) T; 4) D; 5) C; 6) A; 7) B

8. To add a flange to a sheet metal part:

   A. Draw the profile, extrude, and then add a bend
   B. Draw the profile, create a face, and then add a bend
   C. Draw the profile, and then use flange (flange will automatically create the bend and bend relief)
   D. Draw the profile, use flange and then bend

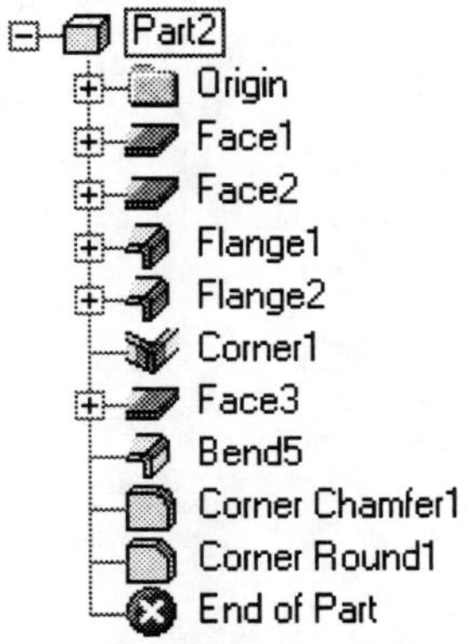

9. A corner seam is indicated in the browser by the prefix:

   A. Face
   B. Flange
   C. Corner Chamfer
   D. Corner

10. The Design Elements tools are available on the Sheet Metal toolbar. Another toolbar where we see these tools is:

   A. Sketch
   B. Feature
   C. Solids
   D. Assembly

ANSWERS: 1) A; 2) B; 3) T; 4) D; 5) C; 6) A; 7) B

NOTES:

Lesson 10

Hole Features

Learning Objectives

Upon completion of this lesson, the user will be comfortable using the Hole dialog box as well as placing and locating points to be used for the hole centers.

In this lesson, we will add a hole to the 'L' bracket created in Lesson 1.

Open the file we saved as 'lesson1.ipt.'

First, we must select the Sketch Plane where we will be locating the hole. Activate the 'Select' button in the Command Bar.

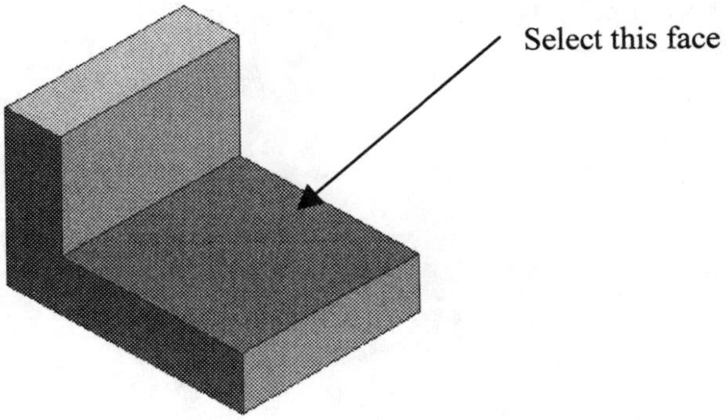

Place the mouse over the face indicated in the figure and left-click the mouse. The face will highlight and change color to indicate it is the active sketch plane.

Inventor will automatically turn on the Sketch toolbar.

Select the Hole Point tool from the Sketch toolbar and place the hole point anywhere on the desired plane. Right-click and select 'Done'. Don't be concerned about locating it exactly; remember we will be adding dimensions to constrain it.

TIP: Use the Look At tool to orient our sketch plane to a PLAN view.

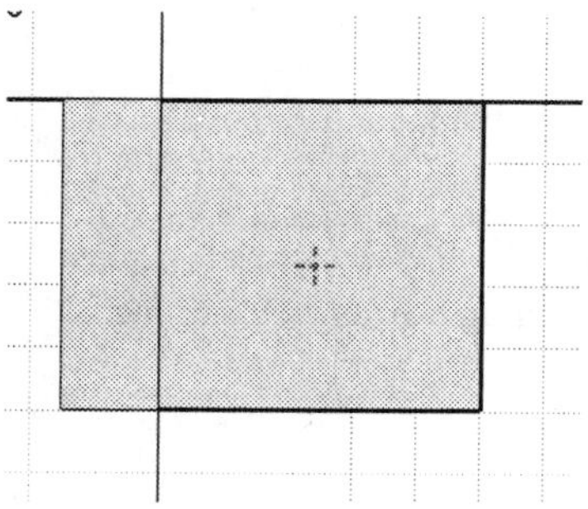

We can use the existing dimensions to help us locate our hole. Highlight the Extrusion in the browser. Right click and select 'Show Dimensions'.

Use the General Dimension tool.

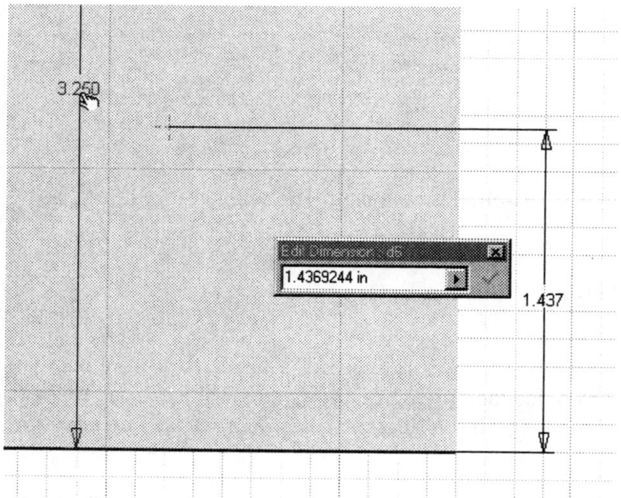

To place the vertical dimension, select the hole point and then select the bottom edge of the model by left-picking the mouse. The selected side will highlight in red. Next move the mouse away from the part and place the dimension.

Modify the dimension by left-picking on it.
Pick inside the edit box and then pick the 3.25 vertical dimension displayed.

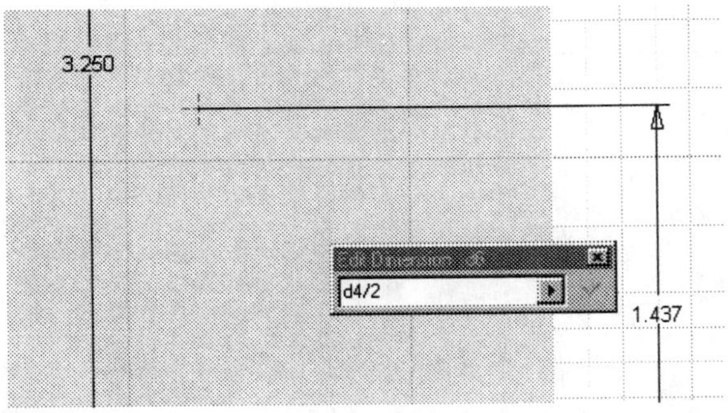

The dimension id appears in the edit box. Add /2 to locate the hole in the middle of the part.
Press the green check mark.

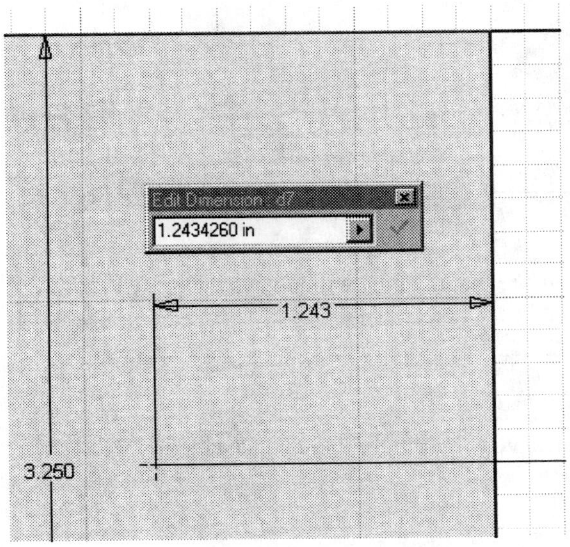

Apply the horizontal dimension by selecting the point and the right side edge.
We will use the existing dimensions again.
Select the 3.25 horizontal dimension, then type a -, then select the .75 horizontal dimension then divide by 2.

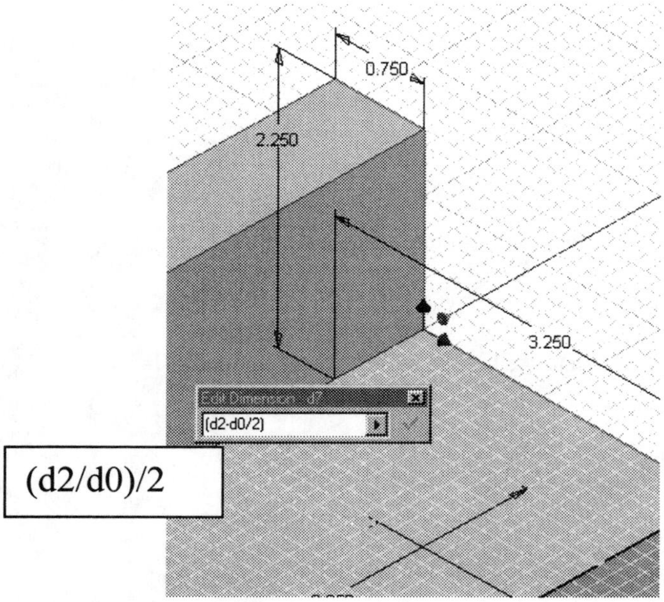

TIP: By using the existing dimensions of the part, we ensure that the hole will always be located at the midpoints; thus capturing design intent.

Once the hole point is located properly, switch to isometric view by right-clicking and selecting 'Isometric View.'

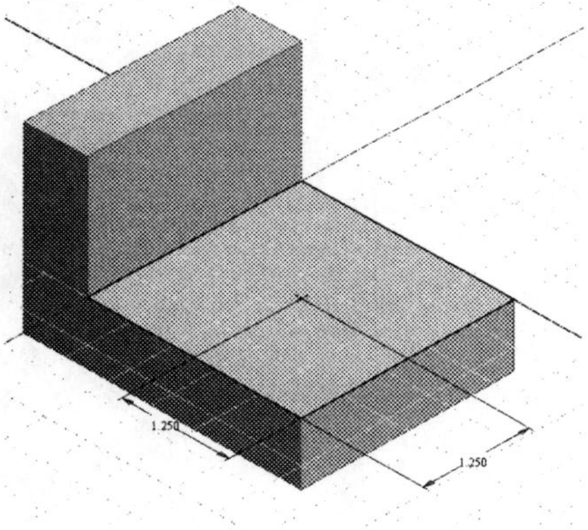

Note that Inventor automatically updates our formulas to show the actual values for our dimensions. Right-click and select 'Finish Sketch'.

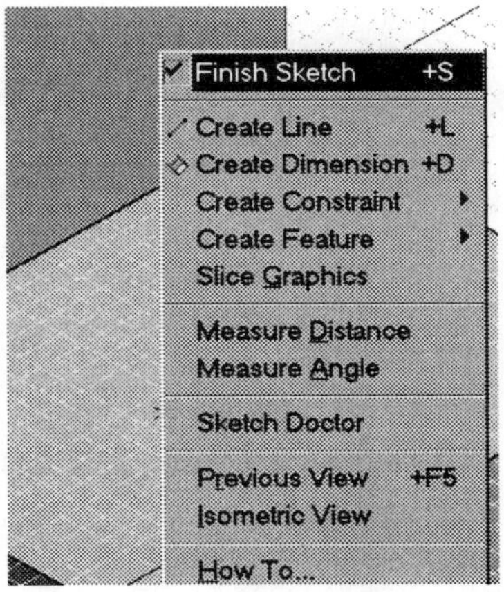

When we select 'Finish Sketch', the Sketch tools are replaced by the Feature tools in the Panel Bar.

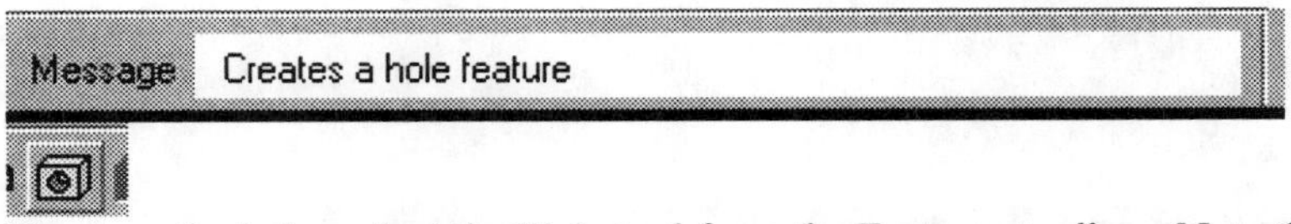

To place the hole, select the Hole tool from the Features toolbar. Note that when our mouse is over the Hole Icon, the Message in the Command Bar updates to indicate what the Hole tool does.

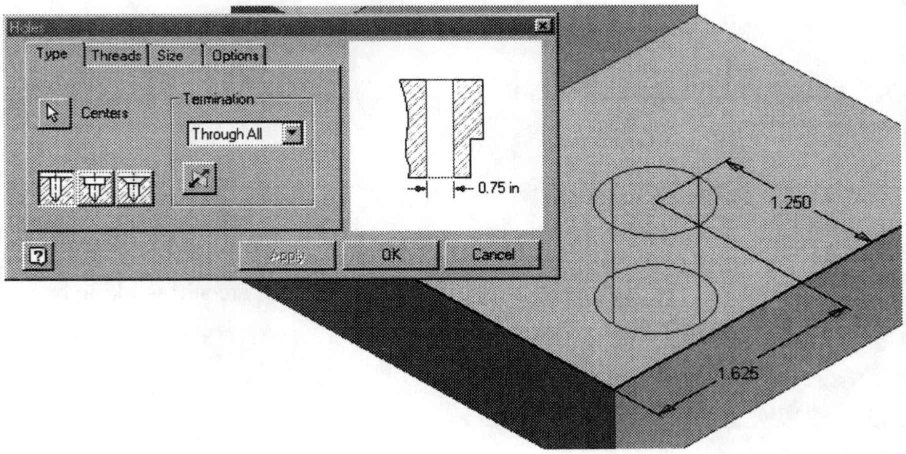

Select 'Through All' for the Termination type. To change the value of the diameter, left-click with the mouse over the diameter value and type '0.75'.

We see the hole previewed in our Drawing Screen area. Once the settings in our Holes dialog box are correct, press 'OK'.

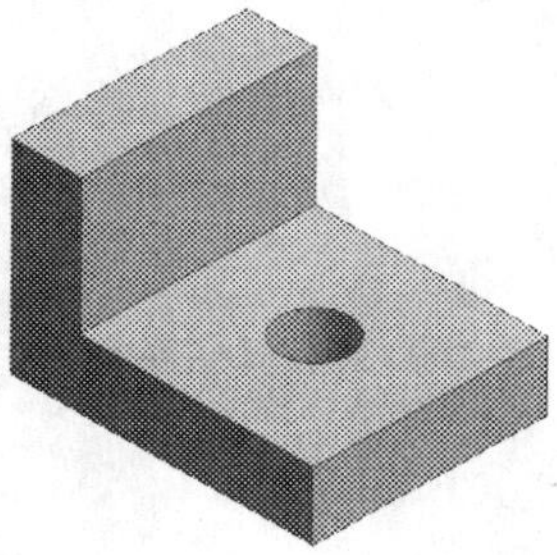

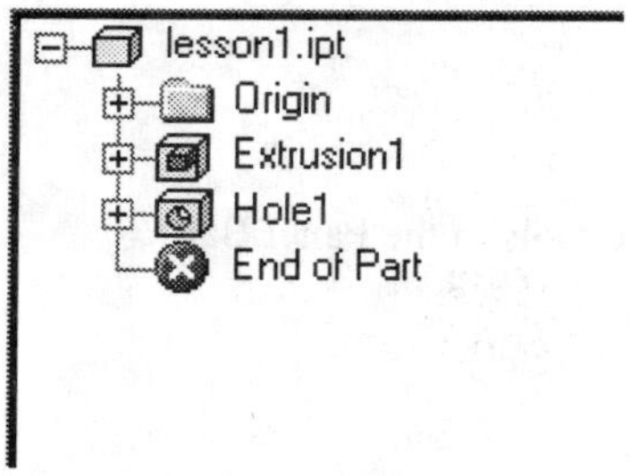

Notice that a Hole now appears in the browser.

Select 'Save Copy As' under the File menu.
Type in 'L-bracket' for our part name and locate the directory where we wish to save the file.
Note that this does not change the name of the file we are currently working in. We are still working on the Lesson1.ipt file.

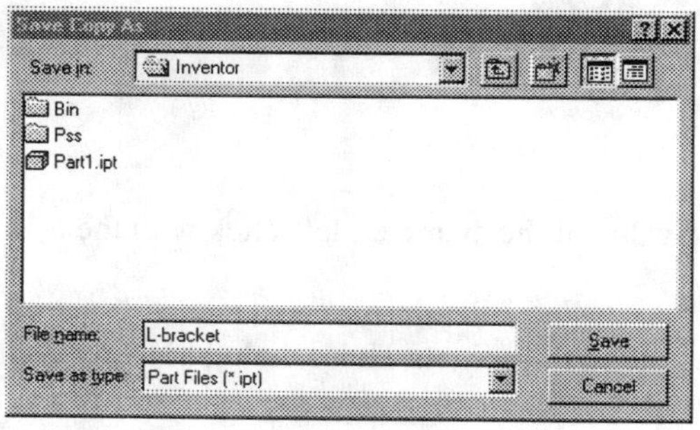

Press the 'Save' button.

Edit Hole

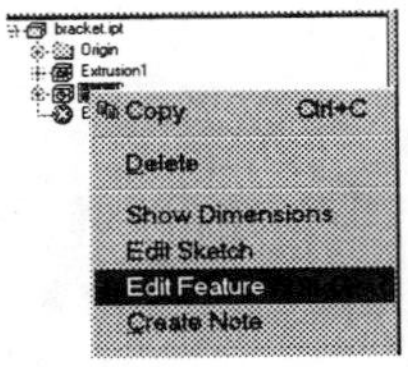

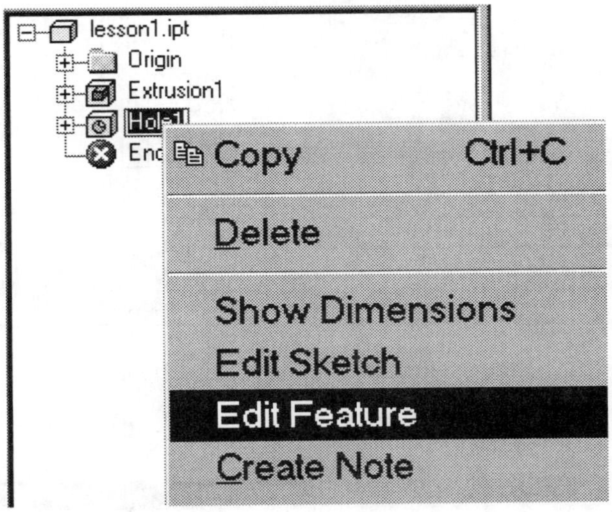

We can modify the hole by highlighting the hole in the browser, right click and select 'Edit Feature'

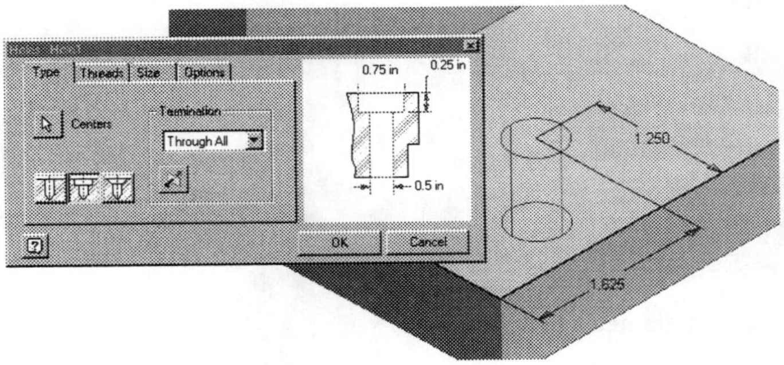

The Hole dialog box appears as well as the dimensions locating our hole.

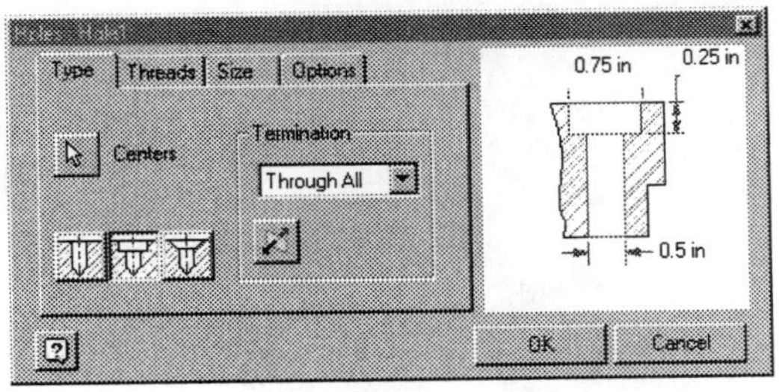

Select the counter bore option. Termination should be set to Through All. Counter bore depth should be 0.25 in. Counter bore diameter should be 0.75 and thread diameters set to 0.50.

Select the Threads tab.

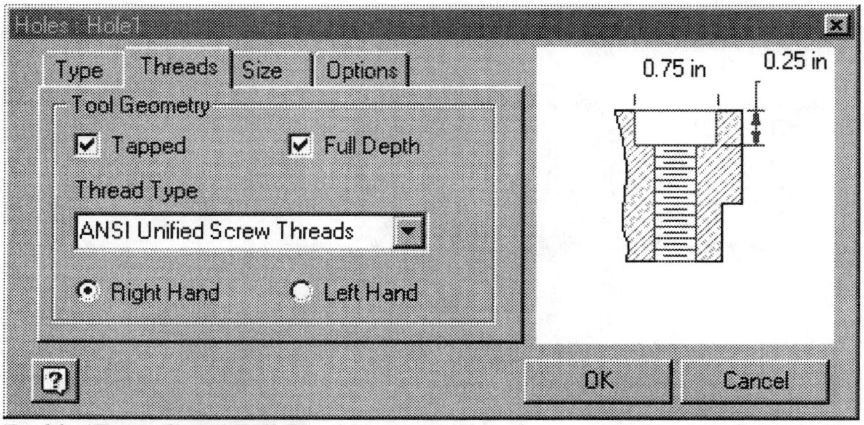

Enable 'Tapped' and Full Depth.
Set the Thread Type to ANSI and the thread direction to Right Hand.

Select the Size Tab.

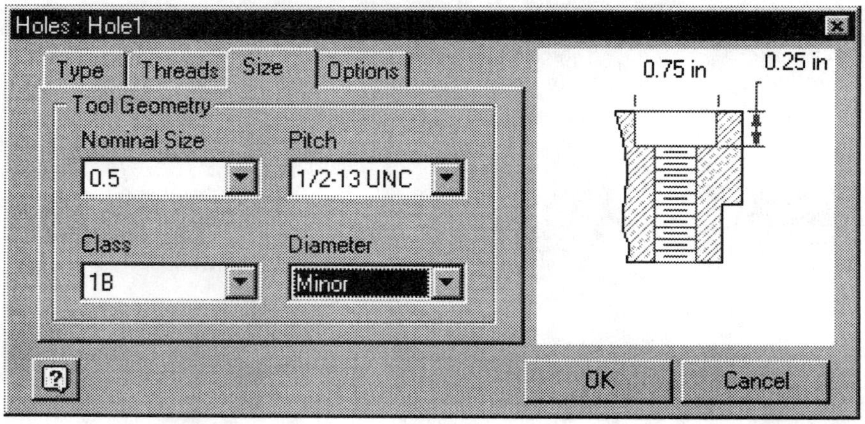

Set the Pitch to ½-13 UNC. Set the class to 1B and diameter to Minor.

Press 'OK'.

Notice how in R4, we can now see the threads assigned to our hole.

TIP: The Hole updates to the new definition immediately. The user does not need to select the Update tool to see the change. The hole notation we defined will be used when we create our drawing views.

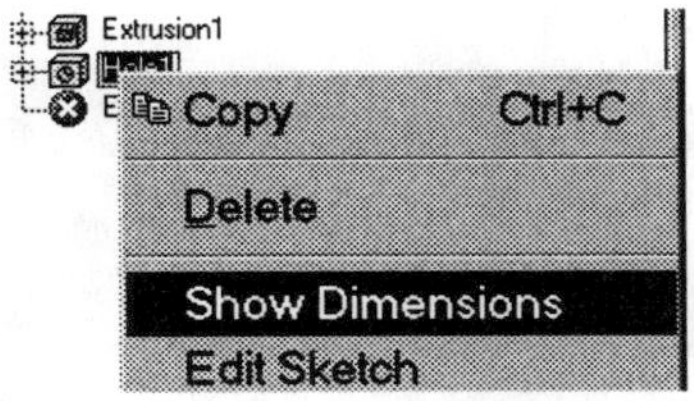

Go to the browser. Highlight the hole, right click and select 'Show Dimensions'.

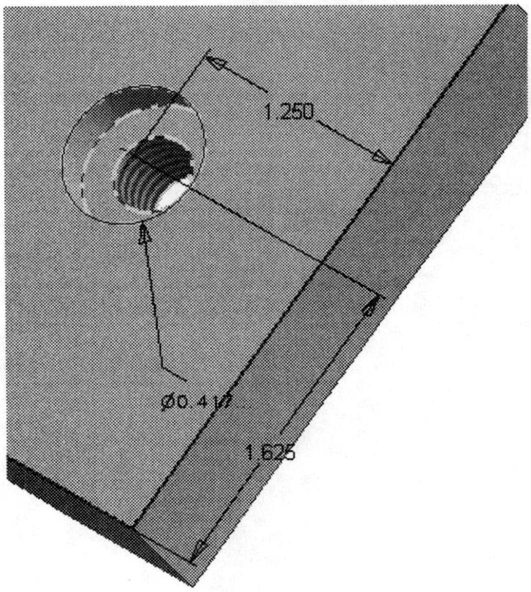

The dimensions for the hole appear in the graphics window.
Select the 1.625 dimension and change it to 1.5.

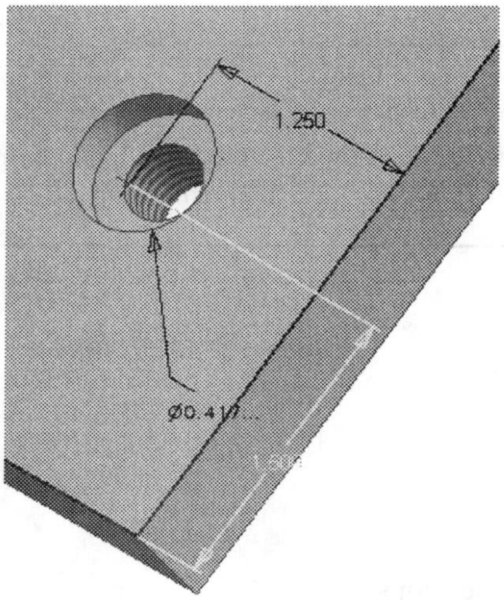

Notice that the dimension remains grayed in the graphics window and the hole location is unchanged.

Select the 'Update' button located in the upper left of the screen.

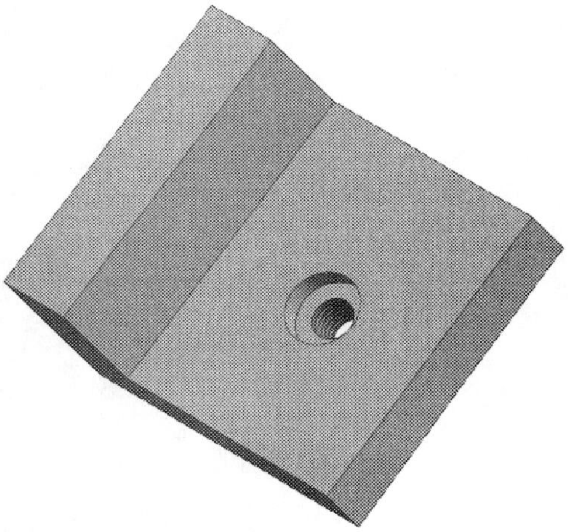

The hole now updates to the new location.

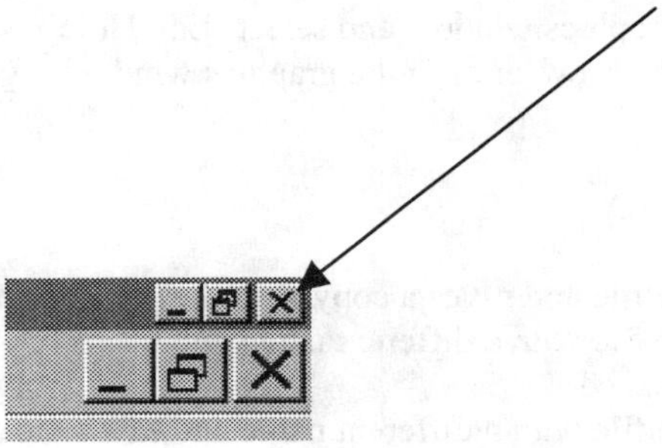

To exit Inventor:

- Go to File->Exit
- Press the small 'x' on the upper right corner of the screen

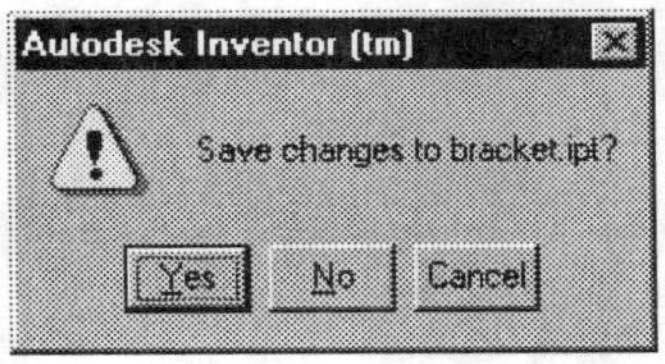

The user will be prompted if he wants to save changes.

But – note we are saving changes to bracket.ipt, NOT L-bracket.ipt.
That is because Inventor did not automatically rename our file to L-bracket when we performed the 'Save Copy As', instead we remained in our original file.

TIP: Save Copy As does not rename your open file. It creates a copy of your file with a new name. If you wish to work in the new renamed file, you need to close your current file and open the new copy.

Review Questions

1. Before a hole can be created the user must first place and locate:

   A. A work point
   B. A Point, Hole Center
   C. A circle
   D. A drill

2. To modify a hole:

   A. Select the hole in the browser, right click and select 'Modify'
   B. Select the hole in the graphics window, right click and select 'Edit'
   C. Right click in the graphics window and select 'Edit Hole'
   D. Select the hole in the browser or in the graphics window, right click and select 'Edit Feature'

3. The menu option 'Save Copy As':

   A. Renames the active file and saves a copy with the previous name
   B. Saves a copy of the file with a different name and keeps the active file open with the same name and unsaved
   C. Saves a copy of the file with a different name and saves the active file. The user continues working on the active file.
   D. Renames the active file and saves it

4. The three types of holes that can be placed are:

   A. Drill, Counter bore, and Counter sunk
   B. Through, blind, and mid-plane
   C. Drill, angled, and flat
   D. Threaded, unthreaded, and curled

5. True or False

In Inventor R4, we can see threads when they are applied to hole or cylindrical features.

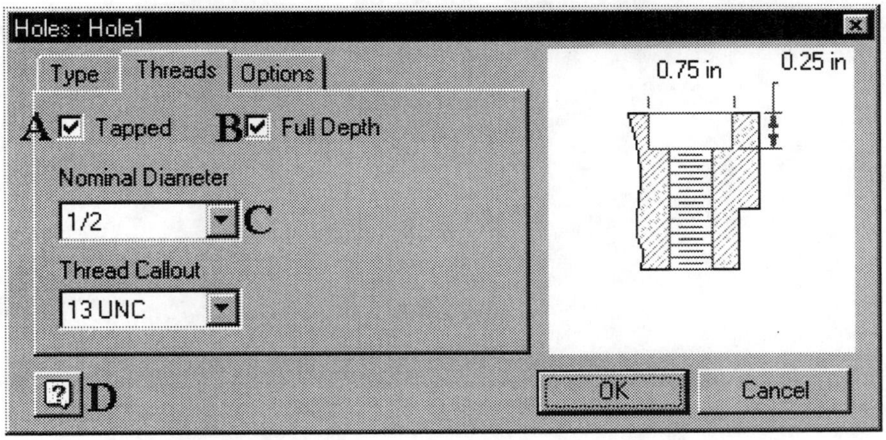

6. Select here to add threads to a hole.
7. Select here to have the threads go the entire depth of the body part of the hole
8. Select here to bring up context-driven help

9. The Options tab is selected to control:

   A. The angle of countersunk holes
   B. The angle of the drill point
   C. The depth of the hole
   D. A & B, but not C

ANSWERS: 1) B; 2) D; 3) B; 4) A; 5) T; 6) A; 7) B; 8) D; 9) D

NOTES:

Lesson 11

Constructing Geometry

Learning Objectives

In this lesson, the user reviews some of the fundamentals of parametric modeling.
Tools used include:

- Dimension
- Extrude
- Rectangle
- Hole

In Parametric Modeling, the first solid feature is called the **Base Feature**. This is the primary shape or profile of the feature. Depending on the design, additional features are then added to the design.

Some of the considerations involved when creating a model:

- Design intent – determine the functionality of the design, identify the feature that is central to the design and make this feature the base feature.

- Order of features – consider the order of features required for the design, how will the design be built up. Do we need one feature to be created before another feature can be defined?

- Ease of making modifications – select the feature that is the least likely to be changed as the base feature.

In this lesson, we will create another part called 'Bracket'.
This part will be using metric dimensions so we need to set up our part as a metric part.

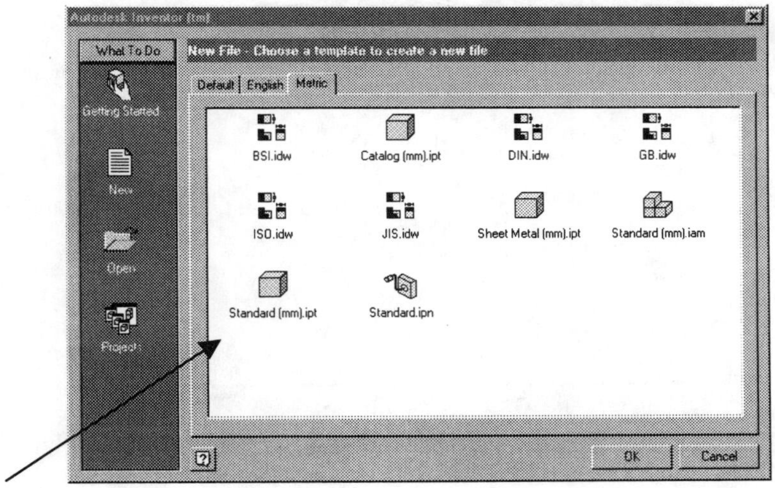

Go to File->New.
Next select the Metric Tab on the New dialog box.
Highlight the standard.ipt icon by clicking on it with the left mouse button.
Select 'OK'.

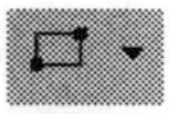

Step 1:
Create the base feature by sketching a rectangle. Use the rectangle tool from the Sketch toolbar.
Select it by picking it with the left mouse button. Locate the rectangle by selecting one corner using the left mouse button and then pick with the left mouse button for the opposite corner.

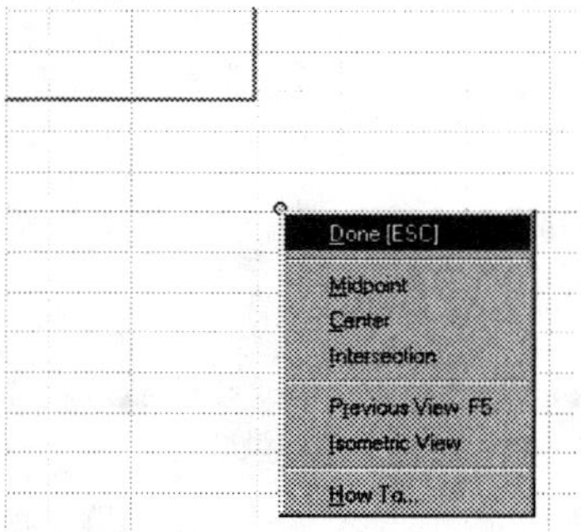

Once the rectangle has been placed, right-click the mouse and select 'Done'.

Next place dimensions using the Auto Dimension tool.
Select 'Apply' and 'Done'. Then edit the dimensions as shown.

The rectangle should be 75 units wide and 50 units high as shown.

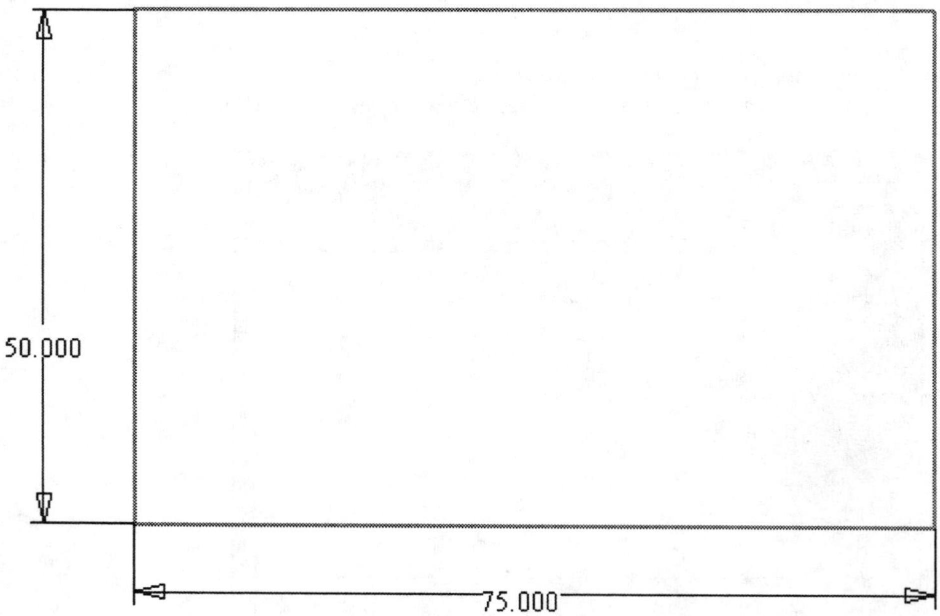

Switch to Isometric View by right-clicking the mouse and selecting 'Isometric View'.
Right-click and Select 'Finish Sketch'.

TIP: You can also initiate the Finish Sketch command by pressing *S* on the keyboard.

In the Features toolbar, select the Extrude icon (or type *E*)
In the Extrude popup window, enter 15 as the extrusion distance.

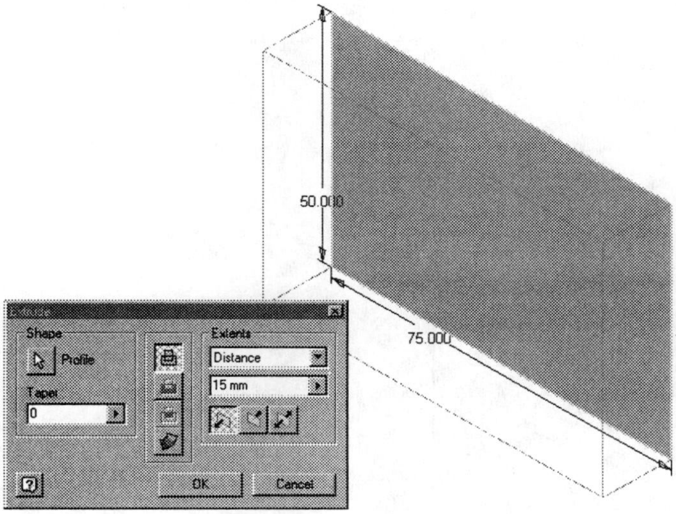

Press ‘OK’.

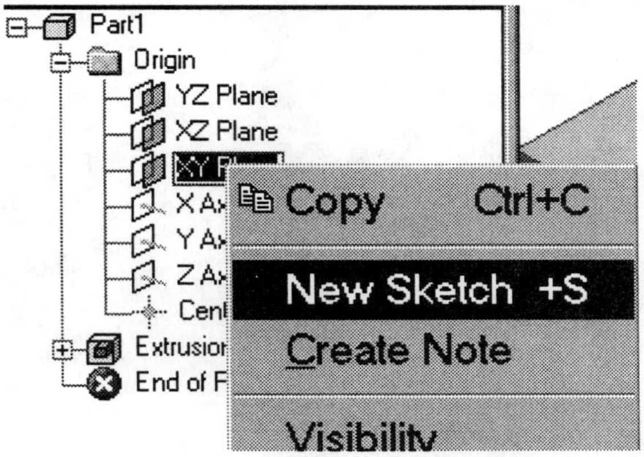

Highlight the XY plane in the Browser. Right click and select ‘New Sketch’.

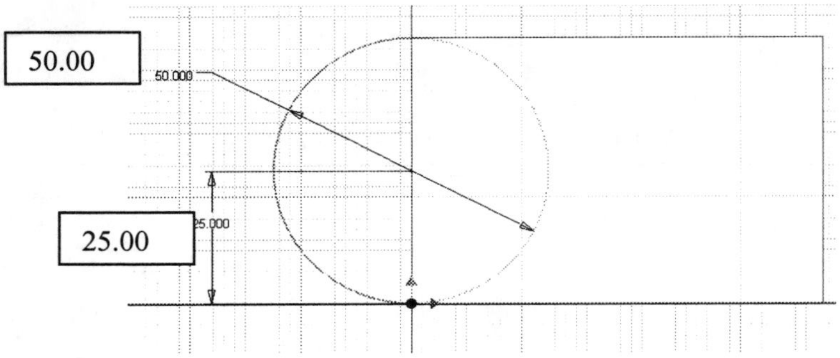

Add a circle using the dimensions shown.
Switch to 'Isometric View'.

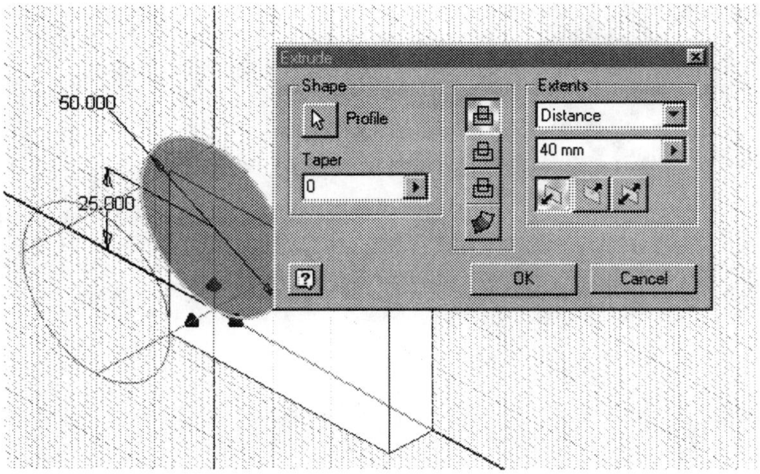

Select the 'Extrude' icon.
Use the 'Join' option (the top button in the middle of the Extrude dialog box).
Set the Extents to 'Distance'.
Enter a value of '40'.
The dialog box should appear as shown.
Click on 'OK' to proceed with the Join operation.

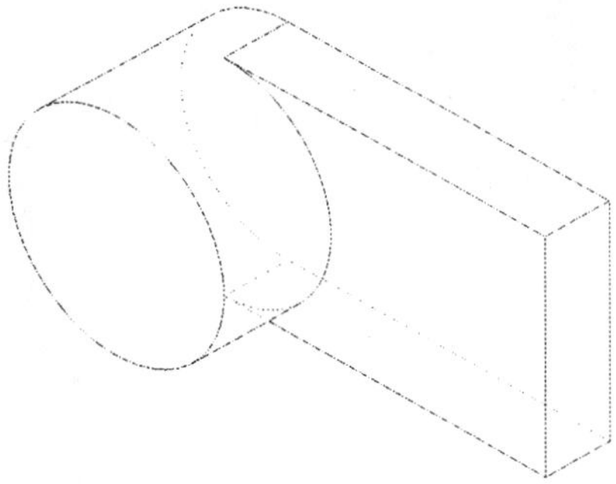

Creating a Hole

Next we will add a hole concentric to the circular feature just made.

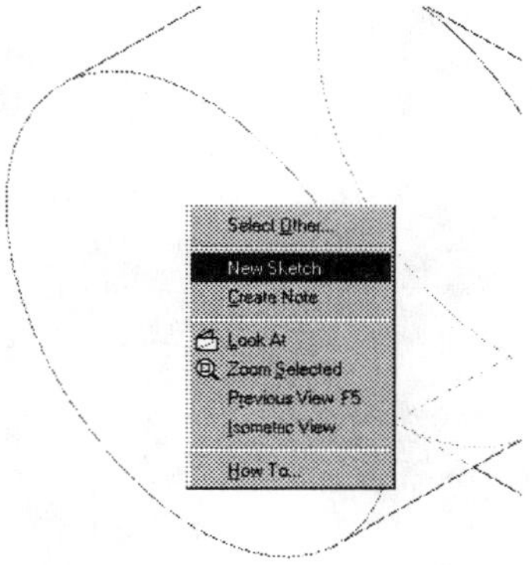

Pick the top of the cylinder with the left mouse so that it highlights.
Then right-click and select 'New Sketch' from the popup menu.

Inventor will automatically activate the Sketch toolbar.

Select the hole point tool. Right click and select the Center option to place the hole point at the center of the cylinder. In the message box, we are prompted to select the center of an arc or the midpoint of a line. Select the center of the cylinder.

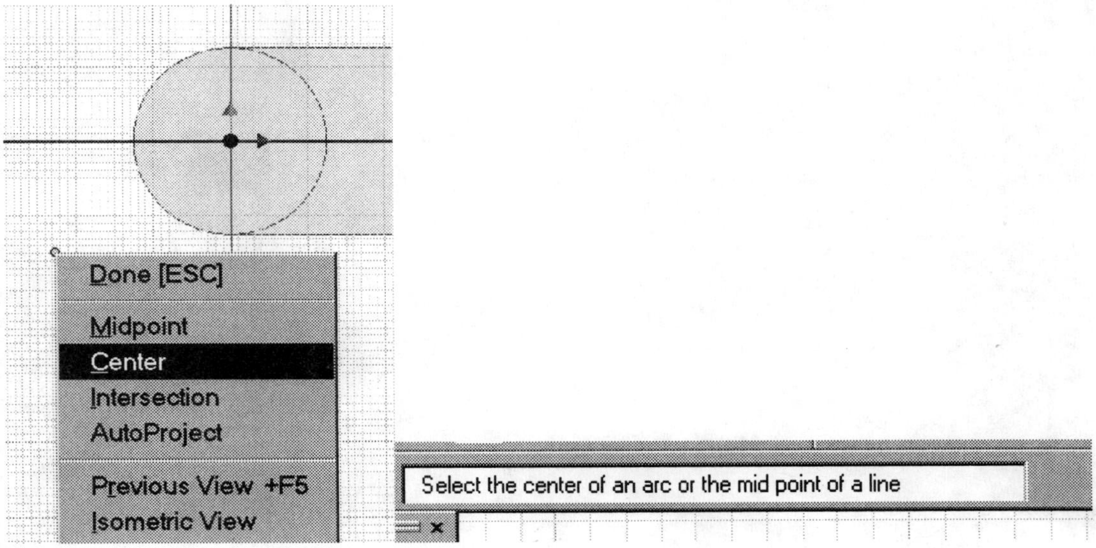

Switch to an 'Isometric View' by right-clicking the mouse and selecting 'Isometric View'.

Add a hole using the Hole tool on the Features toolbar.

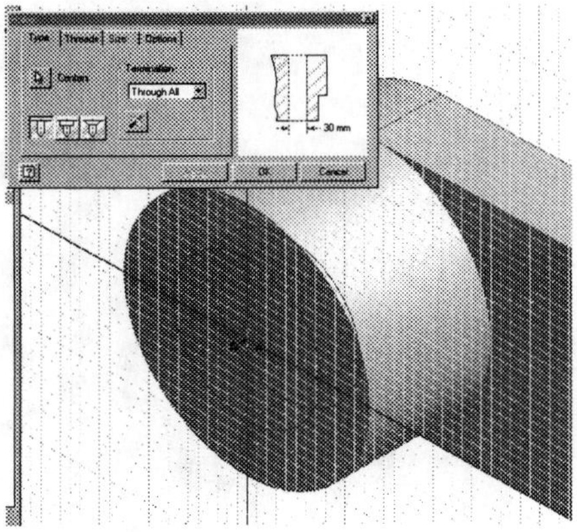

In the Holes dialog box, select a 'Through All' termination and set the diameter to '30'. The diameter can be changed by left-picking on the diameter value and entering a new value.

Press 'OK'.

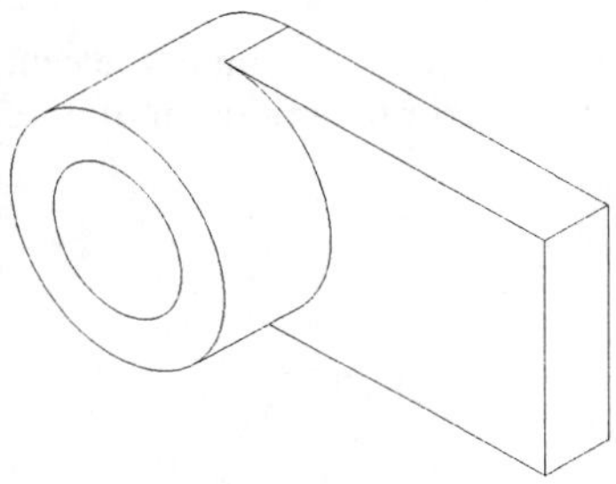

Adding a Cut Feature

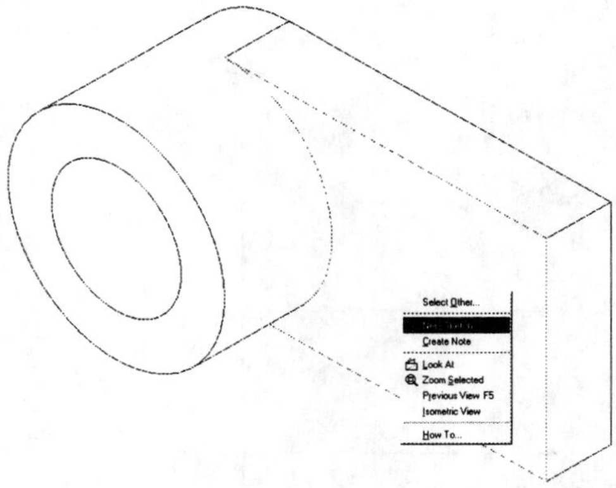

Select the plane shown so that it highlights. Right-click and select 'New Sketch'.

Inventor will automatically activate the Sketch toolbar.

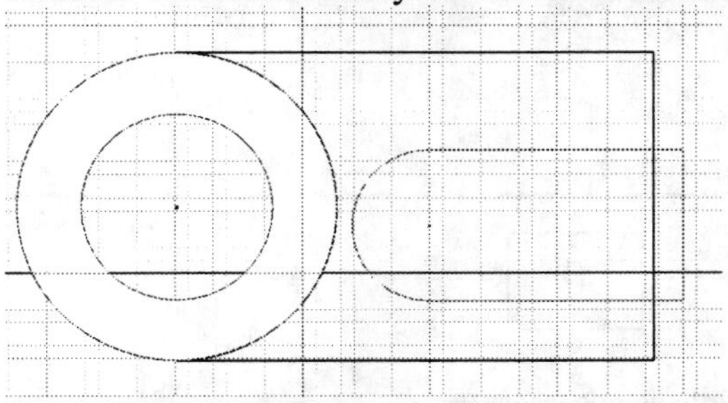

Create the sketch shown. To switch to 'arc' mode, press down the left mouse button and move the mouse in the correct direction to form the arc. To close the figure, right-click and select 'Done'.

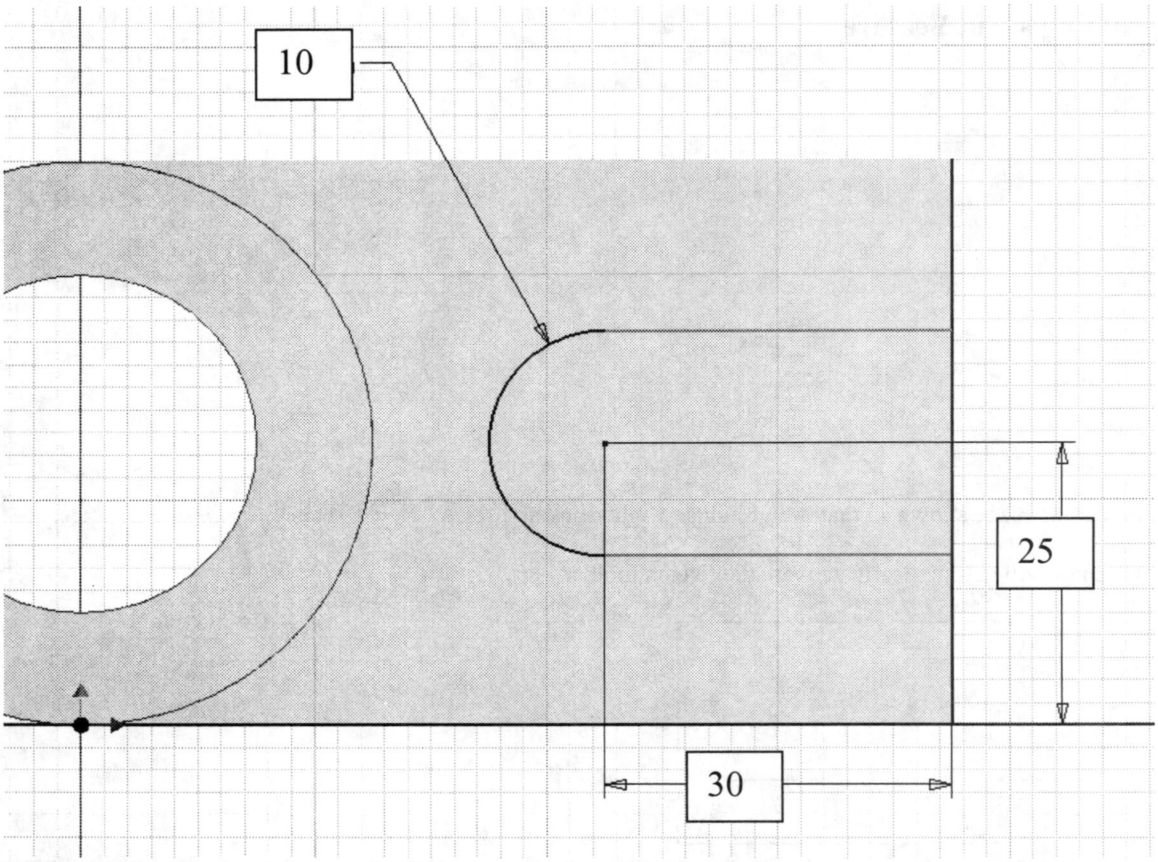

Dimension the sketch as shown. Apply geometric constraints as necessary.
For example, a collinear constraint between the right vertical line and the edge of the bracket., Tangent constraints between the arc and the two horizontal lines, and vertical/horizontal constraints.

Select 'Done' and switch to Isometric View.

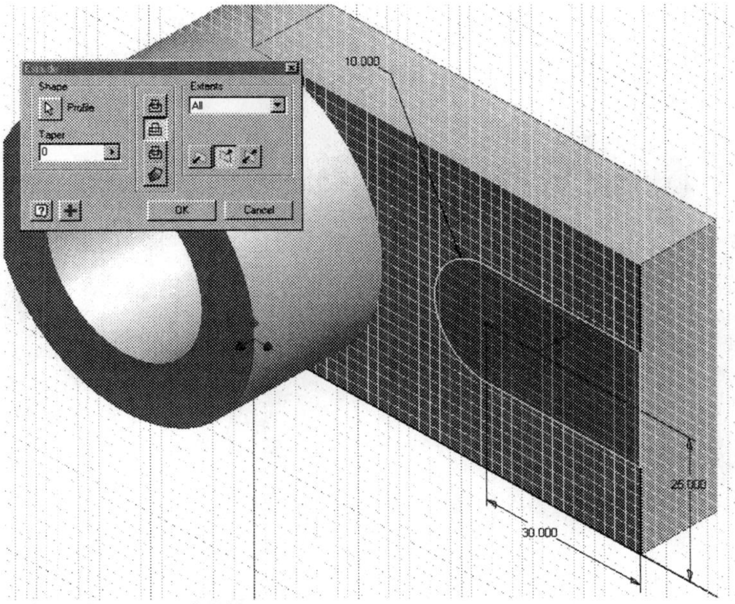

Select the 'Extrude' icon.
The correct profile should be highlighted. If it is not, select the arrow next to Profile and pick the correct profile.
Activate the 'Cut' option. This is the middle button in the Extrude dialog box.
Extents should be set to 'All'.
The direction arrow should indicate that the cut will be going through the part.
Press 'OK'.

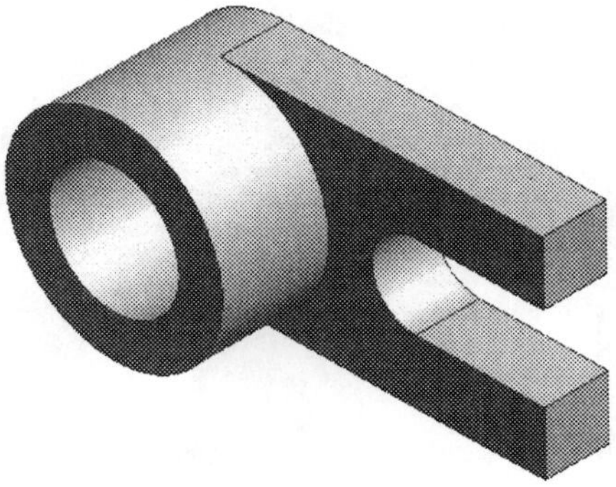

Some users are going to be annoyed by this isometric view of the part.
The reason it looks like this is because the base sketch was drawn on the XY or Front Plane.
We could use the 'Reattach Sketch' tool, but we would have to redefine all our sketches to the correct orientating planes. Another method would be to use the 'Redefine Isometric View' under 3D Common Space Rotation.

Save the completed model as 'lesson11.ipt'.

Notes:

Lesson 12

Adding Fillets and Chamfers

Learning Objectives

Upon completion of this lesson, the user will be familiar with the fillet and chamfer tools.

We can use the bracket created in the previous lesson to practice adding chamfers and fillets.

Select 'open' and locate the 'lesson11.ipt' file.

Constant Fillet

To add a constant fillet, select the Fillet tool from the Features toolbar.

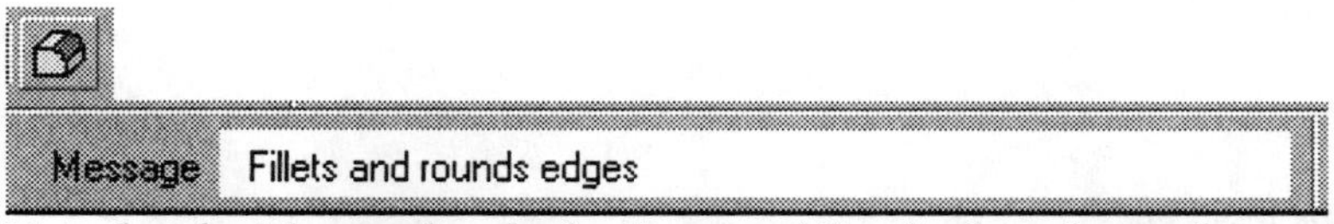

Note that the Message box in the Command Bar displays that we have selected the Fillet tool.

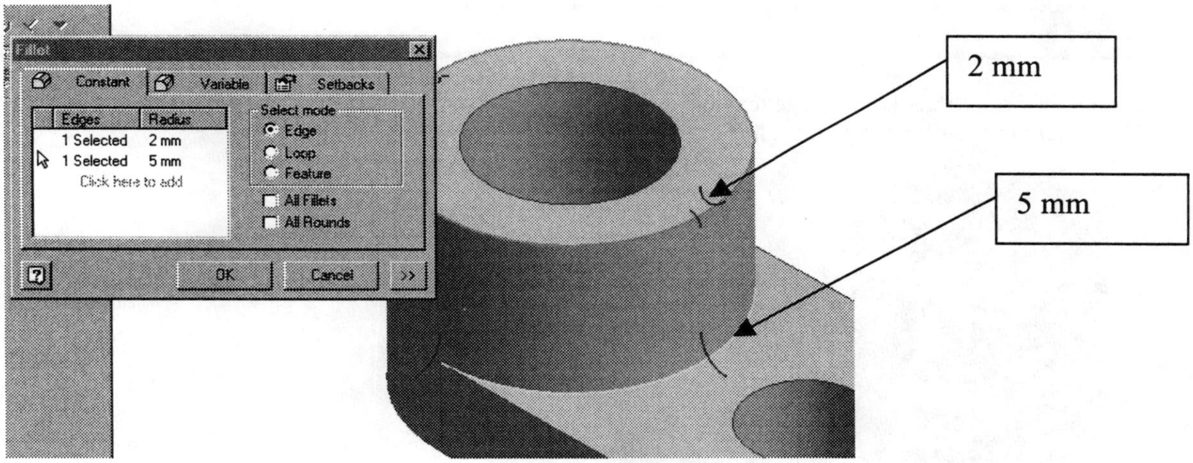

The Fillet dialog box appears Highlight inside the box where it lists edges and then select the top edge of the cylinder. We should see the edge of the cylinder highlight in green and the number of edges change from 0 to 1. Accept the value of 2. Pick the line below it to add another edge. Select the bottom edge of the cylinder as shown. Set that fillet to 5 mm. Verify that 'Edge mode' is enabled under 'Select Mode'.

Press 'OK'.

Our model with the fillets added.

The chamfer tool acts similar to the fillet tool.

Chamfer – Equal Distances

We will chamfer the two ends of the bracket.

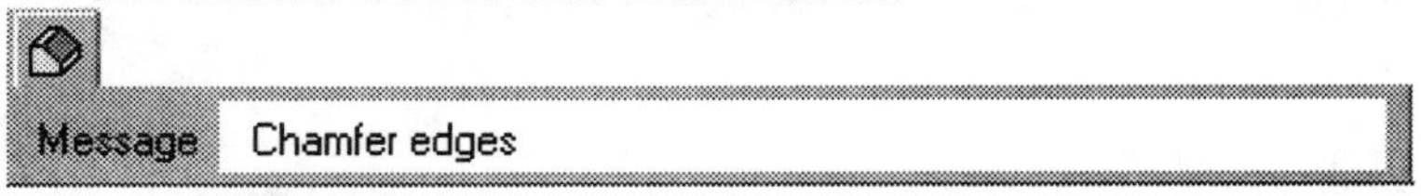

Again, we notice that the Message text changes when our mouse rolls over the Chamfer tool.
We select the chamfer tool using a left-pick.

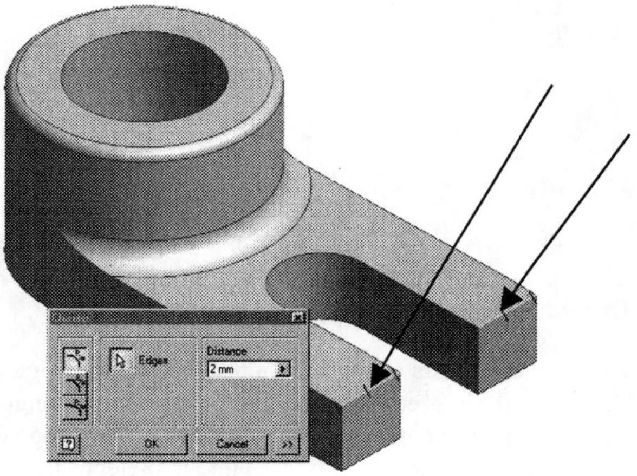

The Chamfer dialog box appears.
Select the two edges shown.
We will use the top Chamfer option, which is Equal Distance.
We will accept the default distance of 2mm.
Press 'OK'.

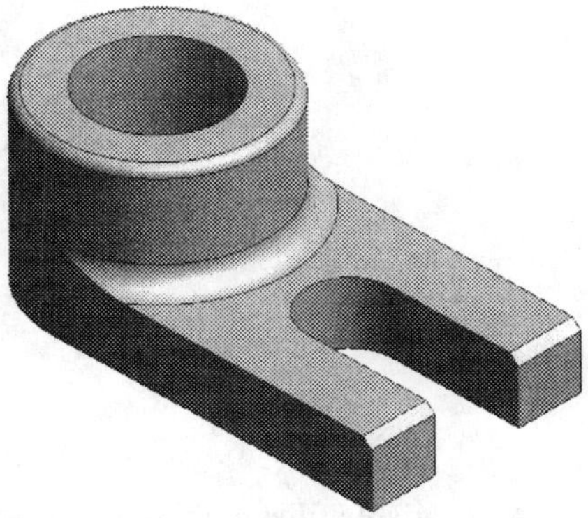

Our model with the chamfers added.

Modify Chamfer

We note that the chamfer appears too small, so we would like to edit the value.
This is relatively easy.
In the Browser, select the chamfer, right-click and select 'Edit Feature'.

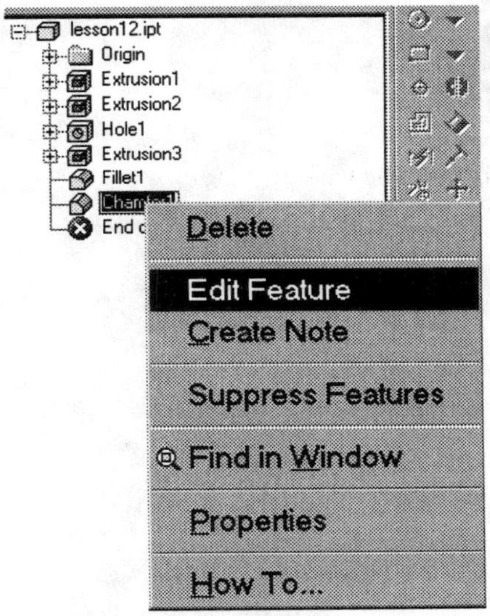

In the Chamfer Dialog box, edit the 2mm dimension and change it to 6 mm.
Press 'OK'.

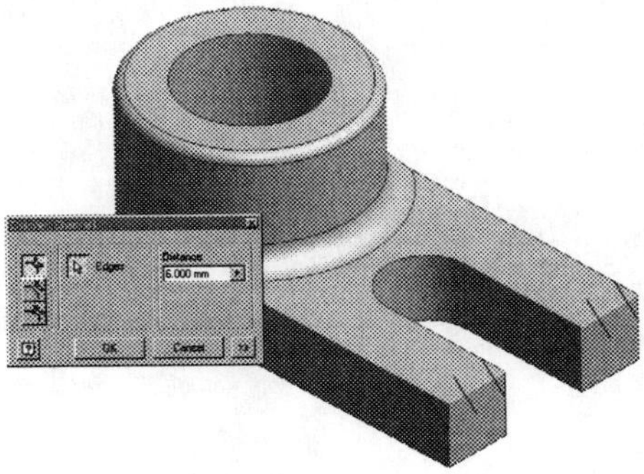

Note that the part automatically updates.

Variable fillet

Initiate the fillet tool again.

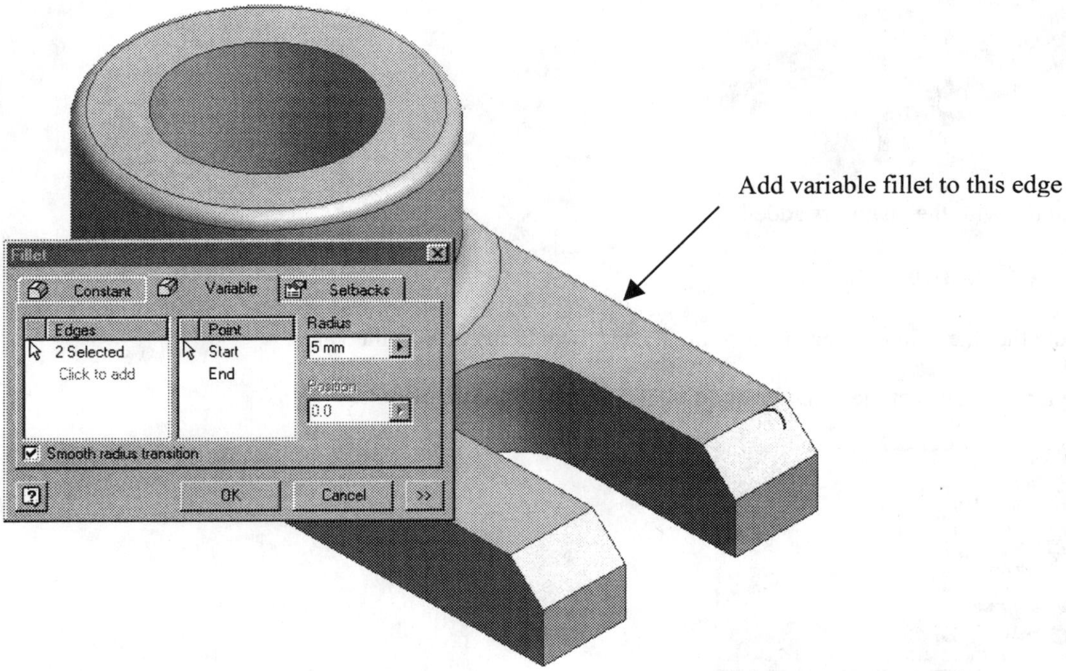

Select the Variable tab. Then pick the indicated edge.

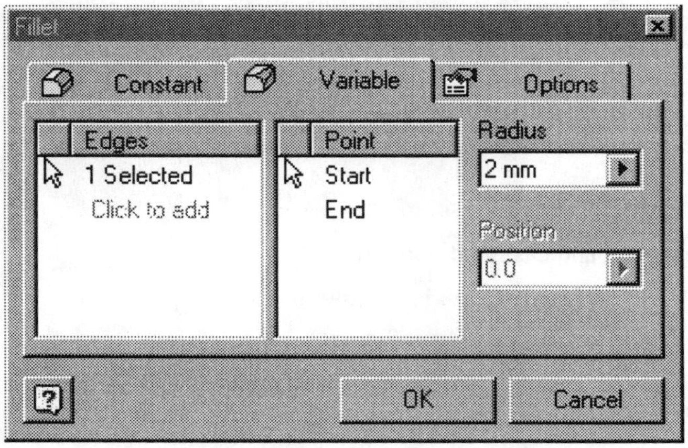

Notice that one edge is shown selected. The start point is highlighted in the graphics window and the radius is set at 2 mm.

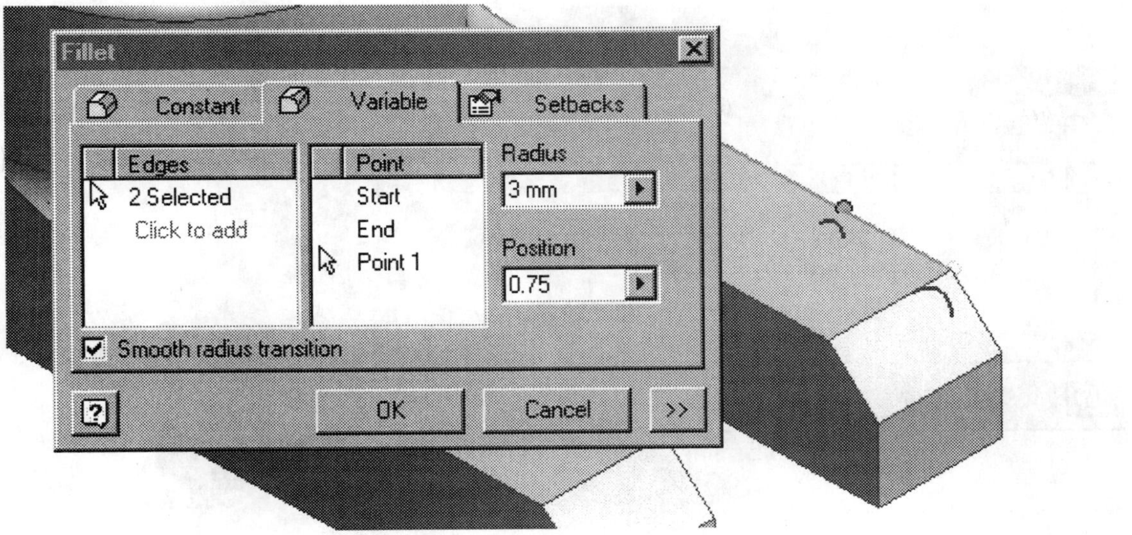

Pick a point on the edge. Set the position to 0.75. Notice the point will shift to the correct location. Set the radius to 3 mm.

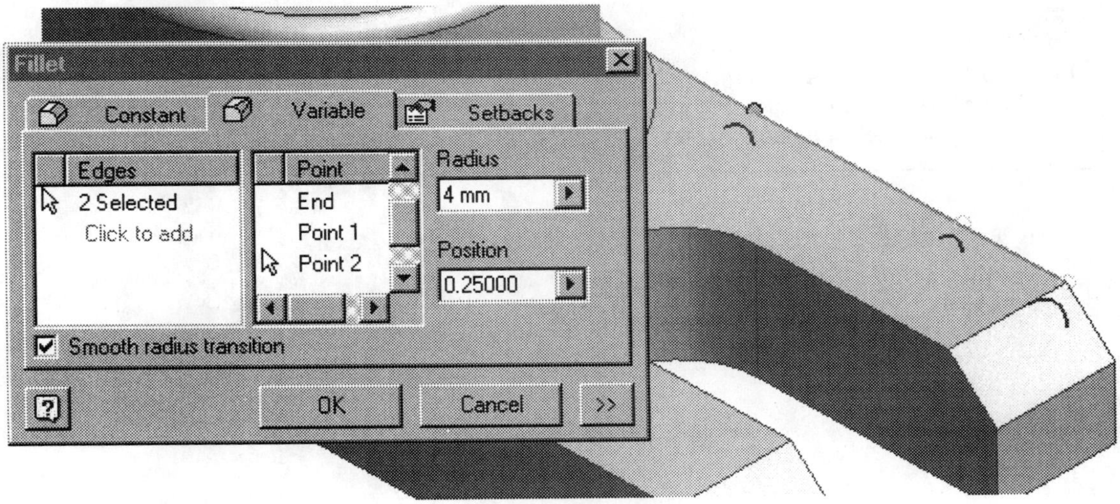

Pick a point on the edge. Set the position to 0.25. Notice the point will shift to the correct location. Set the radius to 4 mm.

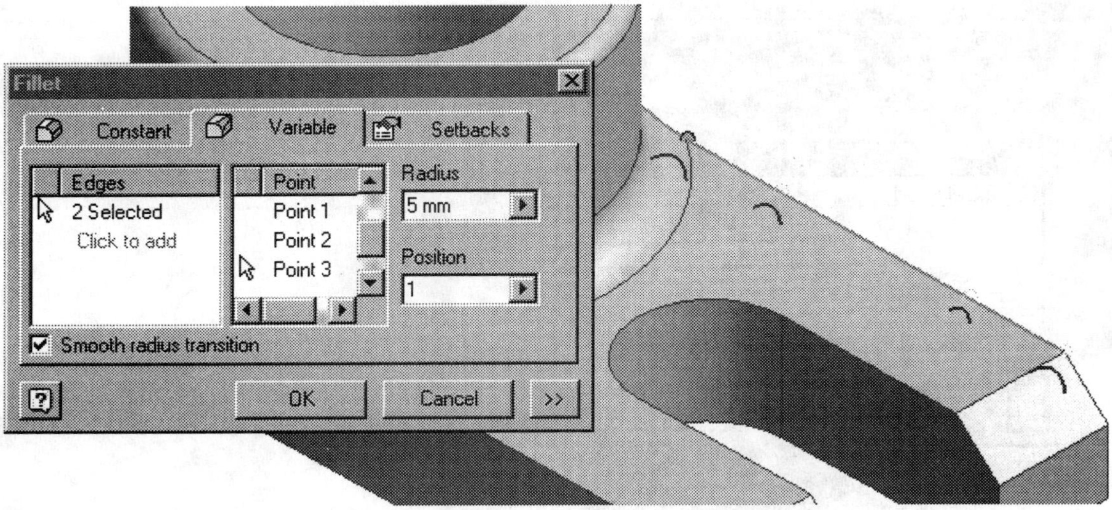

Pick a point on the edge. Set the position to 1. Notice the point will shift to the correct location. Set the radius to 5 mm.

TIP: Do NOT press 'OK' until you are done placing points. If you accidentally press 'OK', highlight the fillet in the browser or graphics window, right click and select 'Edit Feature' to add additional points. To delete a point, select it and press the 'Delete' key on the keyboard.

TIP: To modify or check any of the point values, highlight the point in the point dialog box and the radius and position for that point will be displayed. The values can be edited easily. Note: Once a point is added, it **CANNOT** be deleted. The user would have to delete the fillet and redefine.

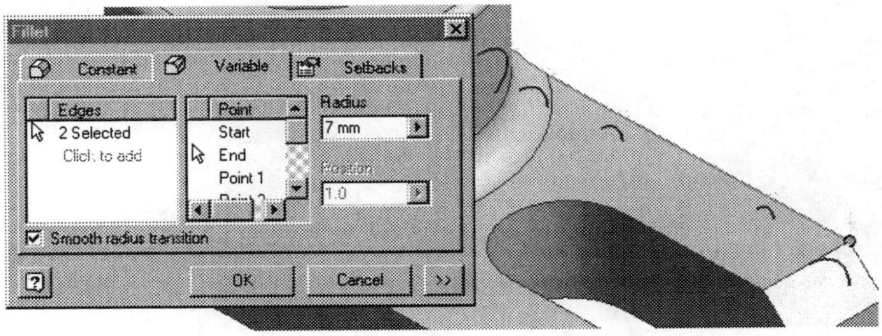

Highlight the End point in the point list and modify the radius to 7 mm.
Press 'OK'.

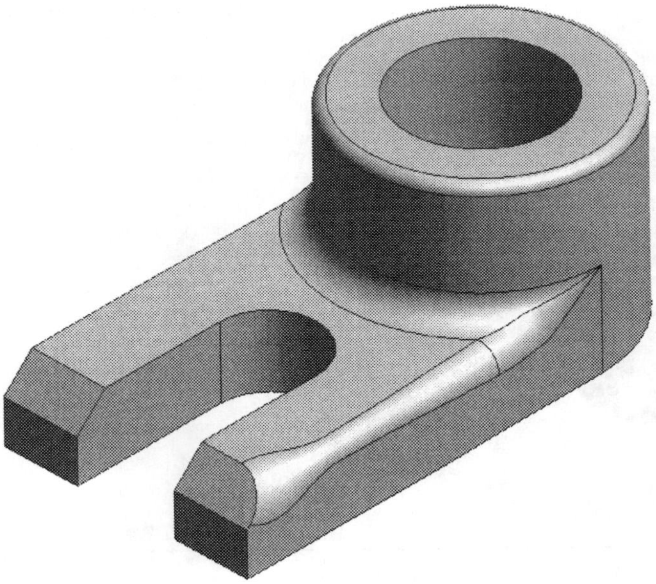

The variable fillet.

Experiment with different point positions and values to see how the fillet changes.

Chamfer Distance- Angle

Let's add a chamfer using Distance-Angle to the bottom hole.

Select the Chamfer tool.

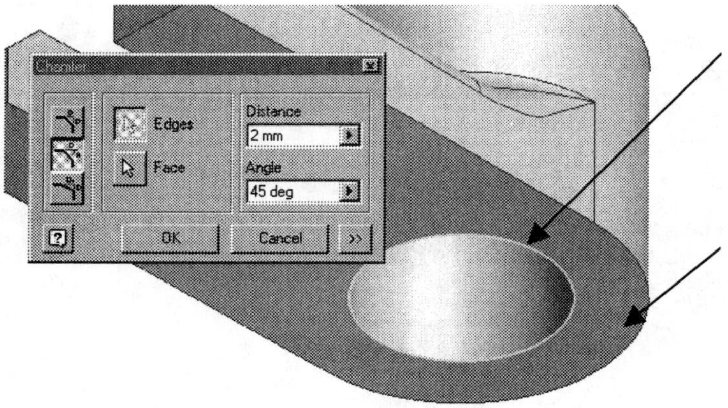

Set the distance to 2 mm and angle to 45 deg.

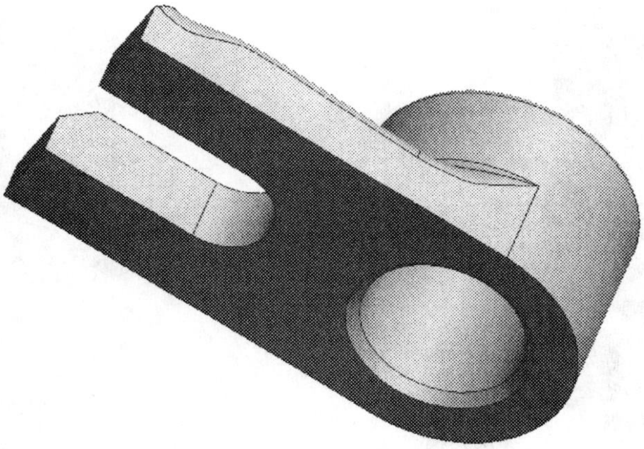

TIP: If you create a chamfer using one method, i.e. Equal Distance, you CAN use 'Edit Feature' to change it to a different method, i.e. Distance-Angle without having to delete the chamfer.

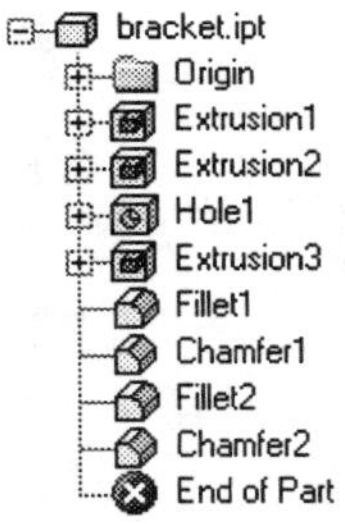

Notice that in the browser there is no distinction between a chamfer created using Equal Distance and a chamfer using Distance- Angle. A chamfer is a chamfer.

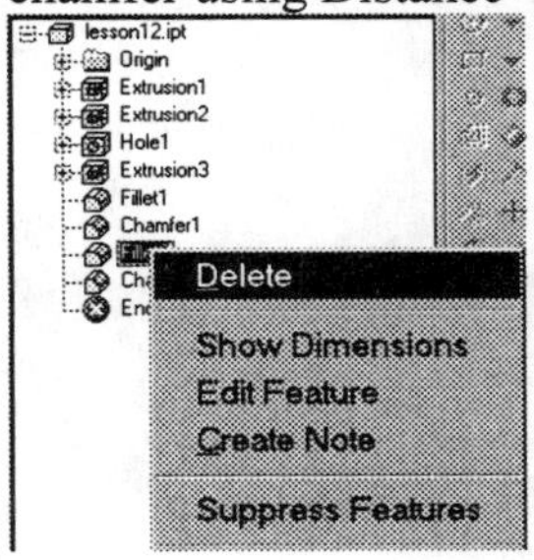

To delete fillets and chamfers

Highlight the fillet in the browser, right click and select ‘Delete’. Notice that the corresponding feature also highlights in the graphics window.

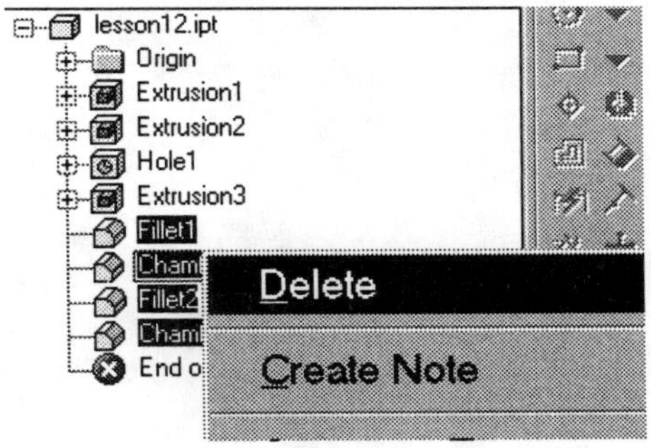

Delete all the fillets and chamfers. You can select and delete them all at one time by holding down the Control key to perform a multi-select.

To quickly add fillets

Select the fillet tool.

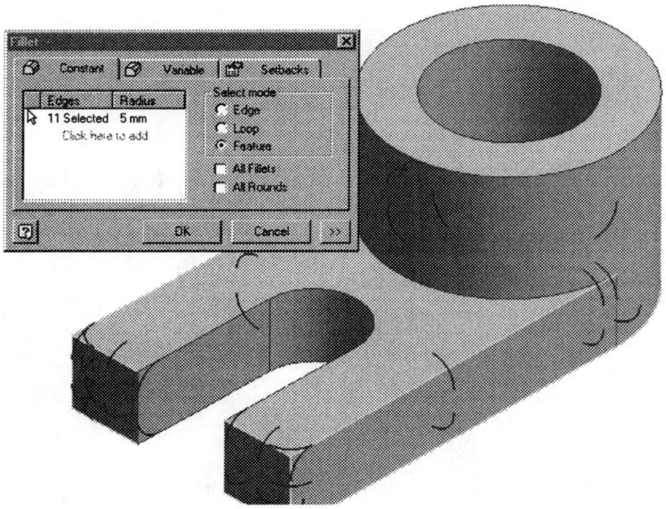

Enable the Feature select mode. Select the Extrusion1 in the browser.
Set the Radius to 5.
Press 'OK'.

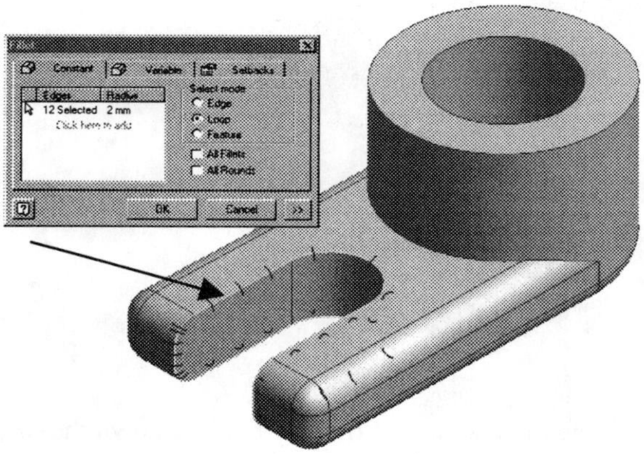

Select the fillet tool. Enable loop mode. Select the edge indicated. Set radius to 2 mm.
Select the next line in the Fillet dialog box.

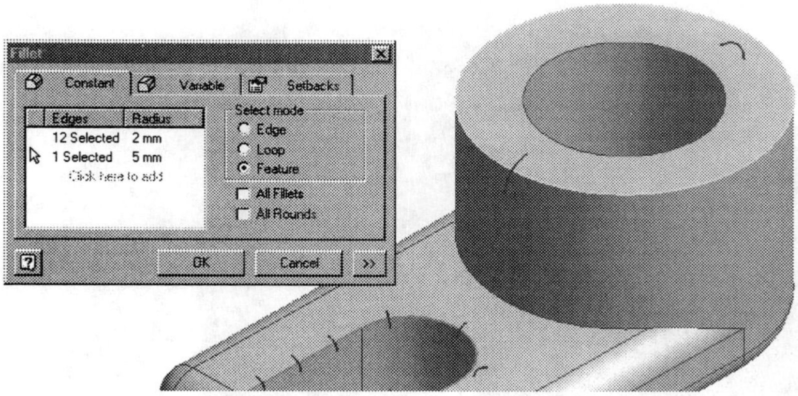

Enable the Feature select mode.
Select Extrusion2 in the browser.
Set the Radius to 5 mm.

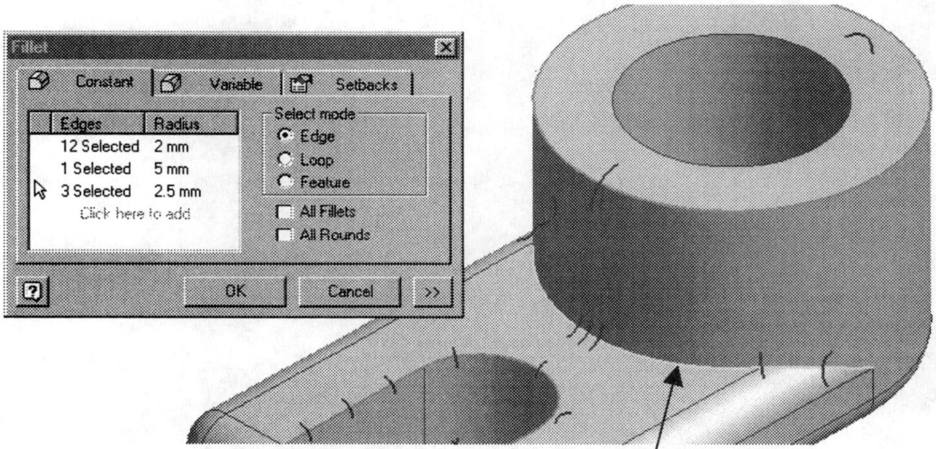

Select the next line in the Fillet dialog box.
Set the Select mode to Edge.
Select the bottom of the cylinder.
Set the radius to 2.5 mm.

Press ‘OK’.

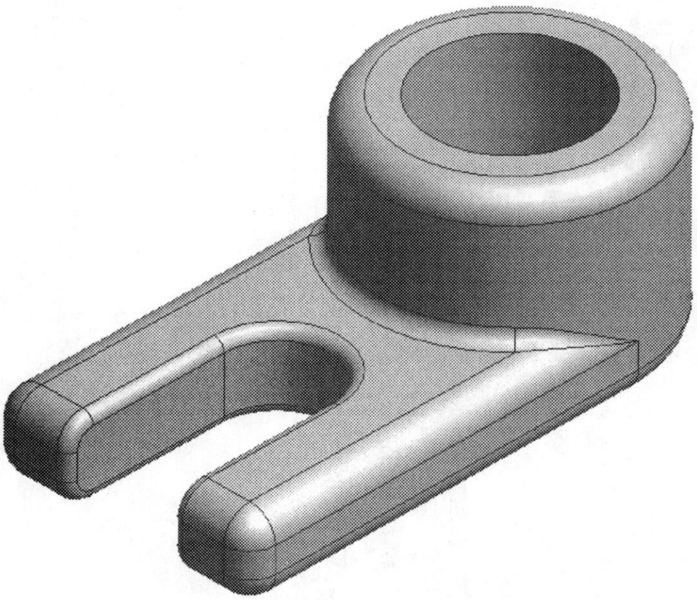

Zoom in to the corner where the fillets meet.

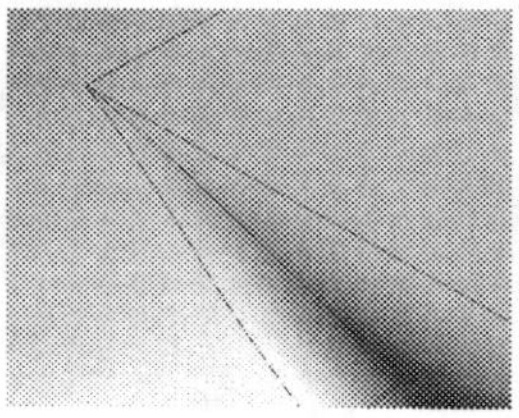

The method in which corners are created is set in the More area of the fillet dialog box.

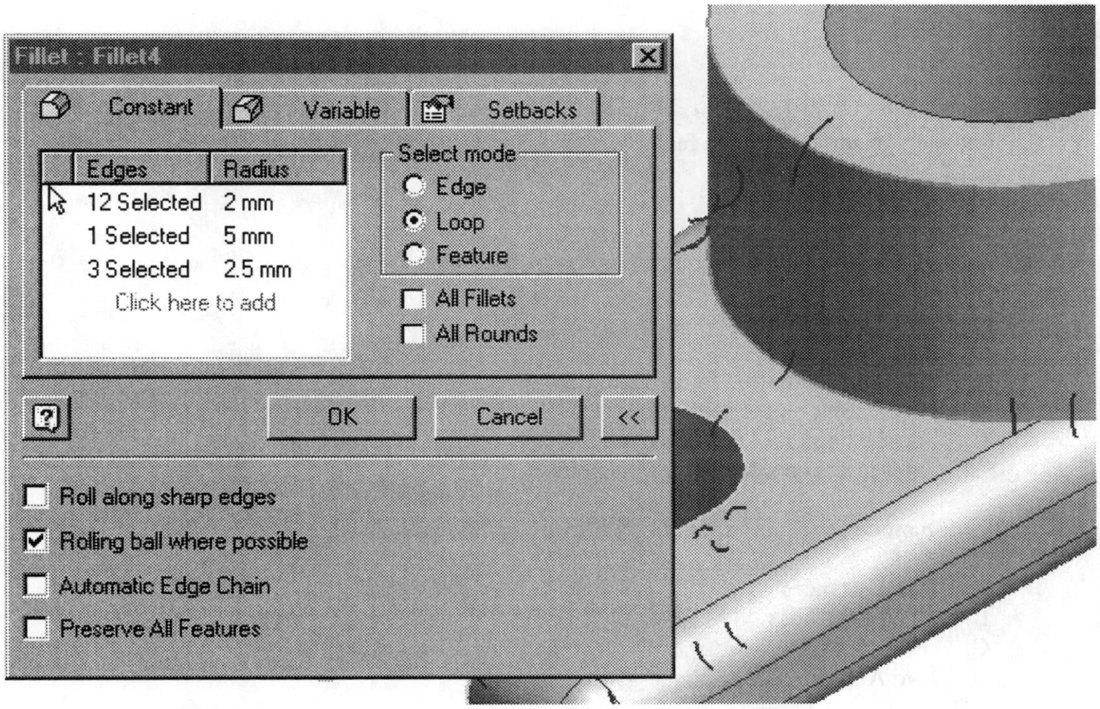

Select the fillet just created in the browser. Right click and select 'Edit Feature'.
Click the More button. Disable Automatic Edge Chain.
Press 'OK'.

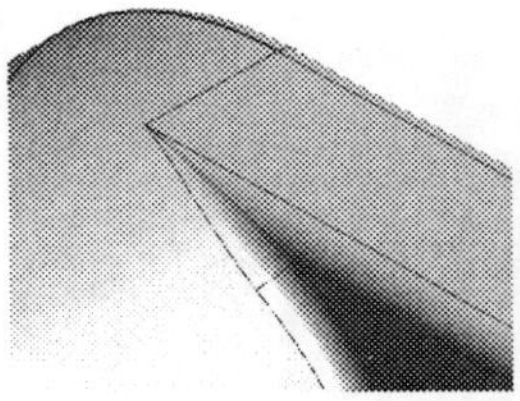

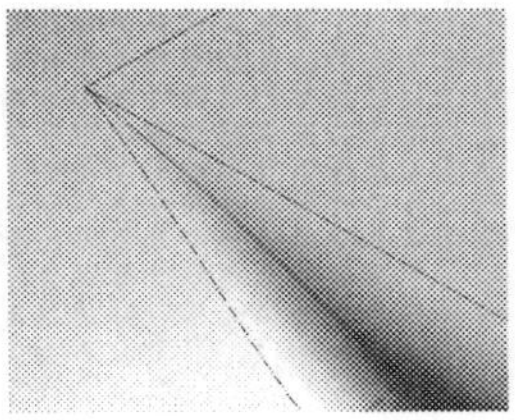

Blend Option Rolling Ball option

Compare the difference on corner preferences.

Review Questions

1. True- False

You cannot add a chamfer to a hole feature.

2. True- False

You cannot add a fillet to a hole feature.

3. When creating a variable fillet to add a point:

   A. Press the add button in the dialog box
   B. Pick a point on the selected edge
   C. Use the point tool on the sketch toolbar
   D. Enter in the coordinates for the point

4. The option mode for chamfer that is NOT available in Inventor is:

   A. Two Distances
   B. Equal Distances
   C. Distance-Angle
   D. Two Angles

5. The option mode for a constant fillet that is NOT available in Inventor is:

   A. Edge
   B. Loop
   C. Feature
   D. Plane

6. The tab on the fillet dialog box that is NOT available is:

   A. Settings
   B. Constant
   C. Variable
   D. Options

7. To delete a chamfer:

   A. Highlight the chamfer in the browser, right click and select 'Modify'.
   B. Highlight the chamfer in the browser, right click and select 'Delete'.
   C. Highlight the chamfer in the browser, right click and select 'Edit Feature'.
   D. Select the Erase tool and then select the chamfer.

8. True-False

Once you create a variable fillet, you cannot add points.

9. True-False

Once you create a variable fillet, you cannot delete points.

10. True-False

Once you create a chamfer using a method, you cannot modify the chamfer to use a different method.

ANSWER: 1) F; 2) F; 3) B; 4) D; 5) D; 6) A; 7) B; 8) F; 9) T; 10) F

NOTES:

Lesson 13

Patterns

Learning Objectives

At the conclusion of this lesson, the user will be familiar with:

- Creating Circular Patterns
- Creating Rectangular Patterns
- Modifying Patterns
- Managing Occurrences

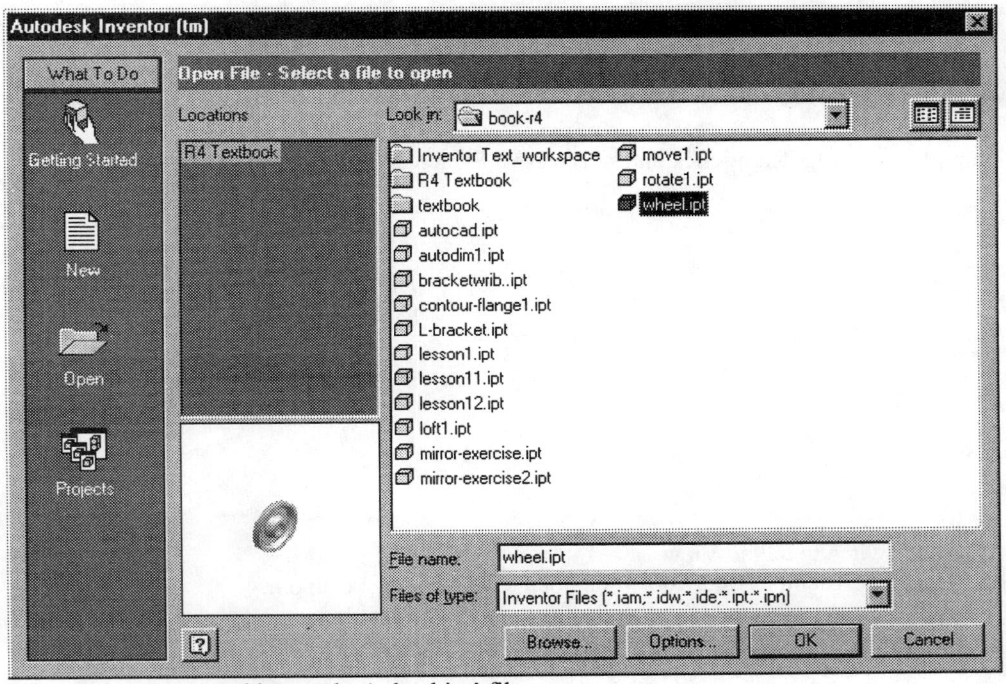

Select File->Open and locate the 'wheel.ipt' file.

In this lesson we will modify the 'wheel.ipt' and create a circular pattern of bolt holes.

Highlight the inner plane shown. Right-click and select 'New Sketch'.

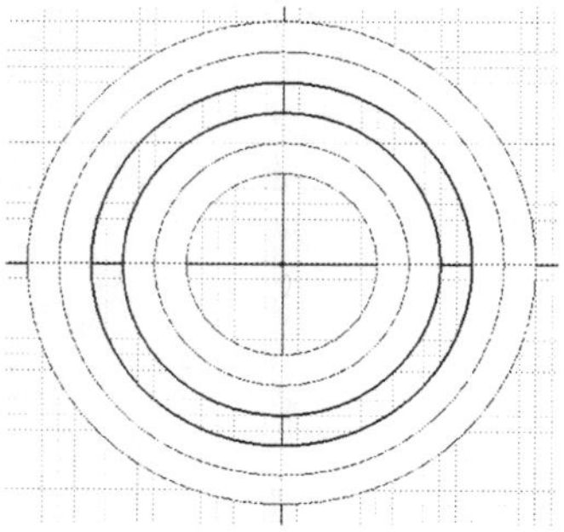

Use the Look At tool to switch to a Plan View.
In a part like this, it can be difficult to figure out which plane we want to sketch on.
Inventor assists us by darkening the lines of the object to reveal our target plane.

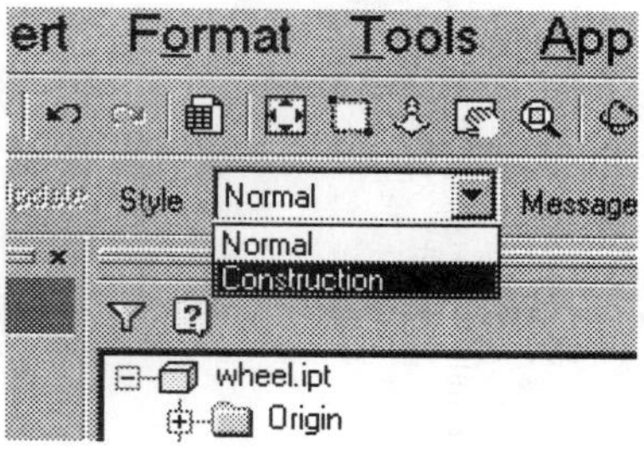

Select 'Construction' under Style and draw a horizontal and angled line as shown.

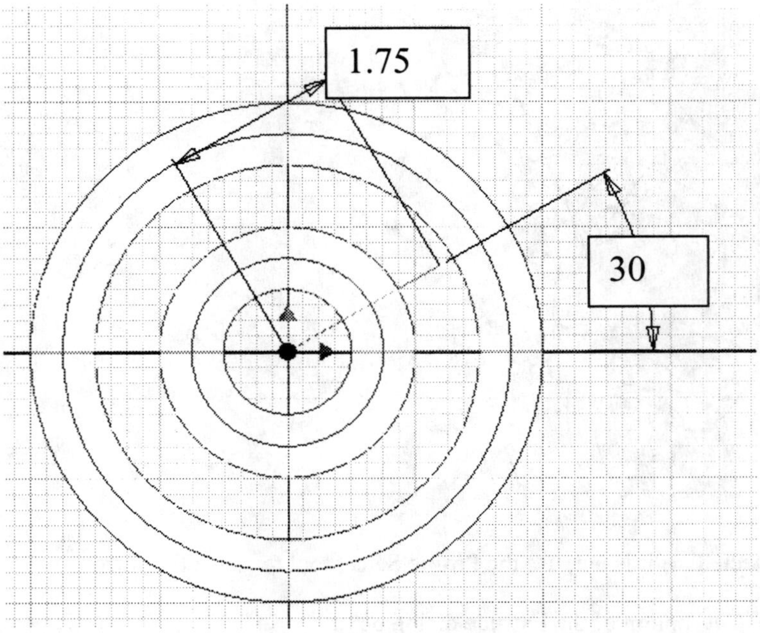

Project the center point onto the current sketch using the Project Geometry tool. Switch to 'Normal' Style and add a 0.25 diameter circle at the endpoint of the angled line.

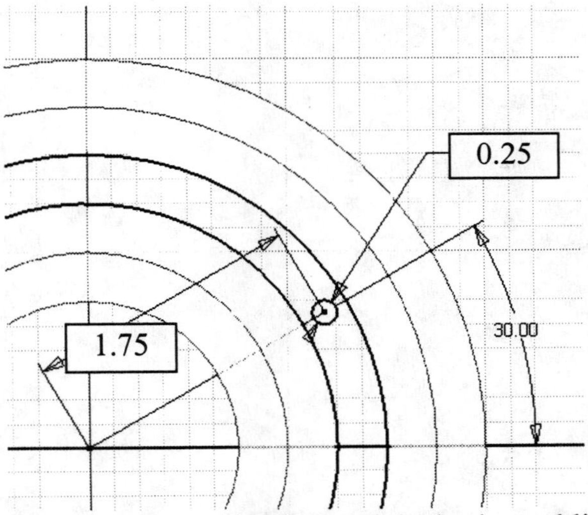

Note that the angled line and the horizontal line are both part of the sketch. These are used to locate the circle.

Right-click to select 'Done' and repeat to select 'Isometric View'.

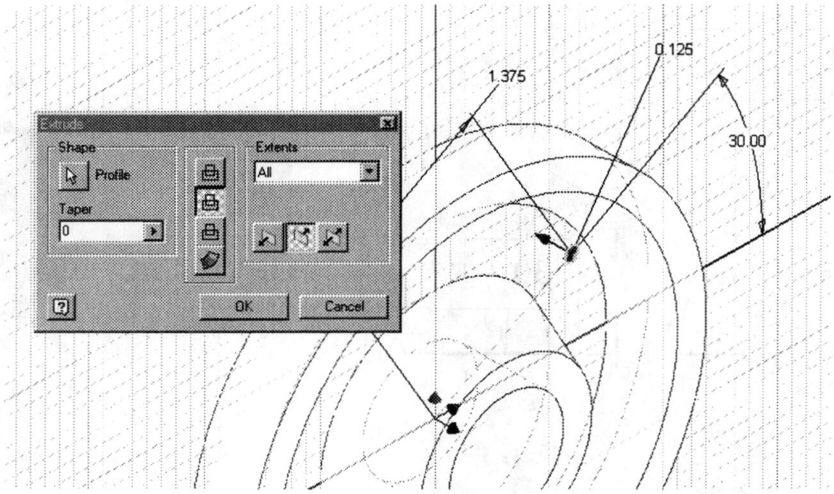

Select the 'Extrude' icon.
Verify that the circle is the profile selected. If it is not, use the Profile Select tool to select the correct profile.
Use the left mouse button to pick the 'Cut' option of the Extrude dialog box.
Set 'Extents' to All.
Once everything is set up properly, press 'OK'.

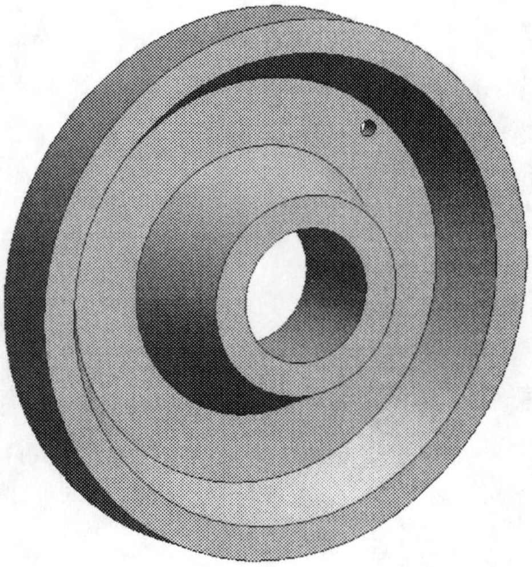

Our wheel with the hole correctly made.

Now we are ready to array the hole.

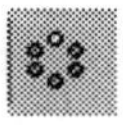

Circular Pattern

Select the Circular Pattern tool located in the Features toolbar.

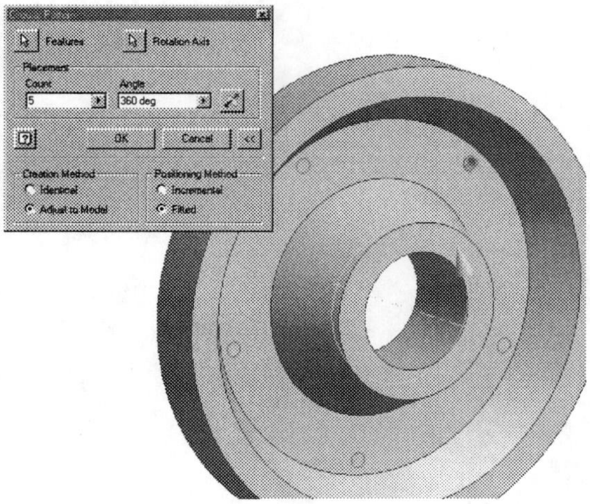

With the Features button depressed, select the hole we just made. The hole may be selected in the browser or in the graphics window. It will highlight to indicate it was selected properly.

We must now select a rotation axis. Depress the Rotation Axis button and select the center cylinder. It will highlight when selected.

Modify the dialog box to show a count of 5 and an angle of 360 as shown.
Note that we can change the direction of the array by pressing on the direction icon.

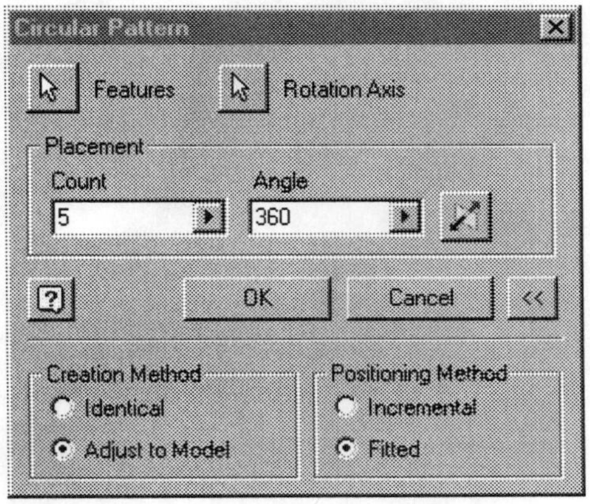

Pressing the double arrow button enlarges the dialog box to reveal some additional options.
Enable 'Fitted' and 'Adjust to Model'.

Then, press 'OK'.

TIP: To create a pattern by specifying an angle between entities, specify an angle in the angle edit box and enable the Incremental Positioning Method.

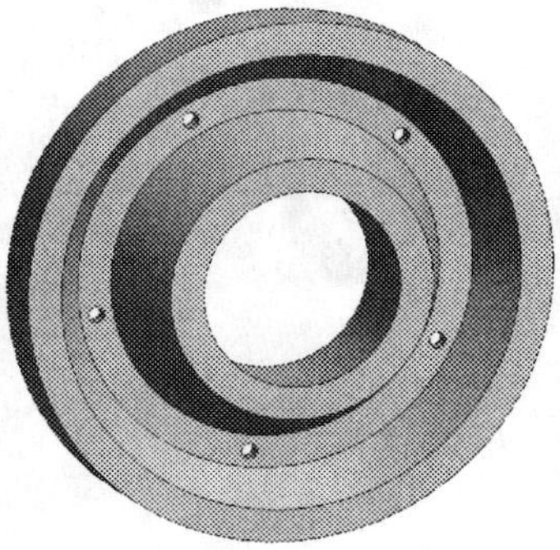

Use the Orbit tool to rotate our model so we can see the effects of the array.

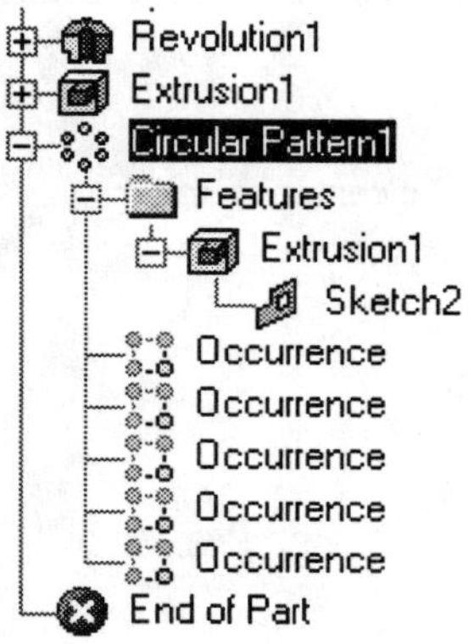

Note that the circular pattern is listed in the browser.

Modifying a circular pattern

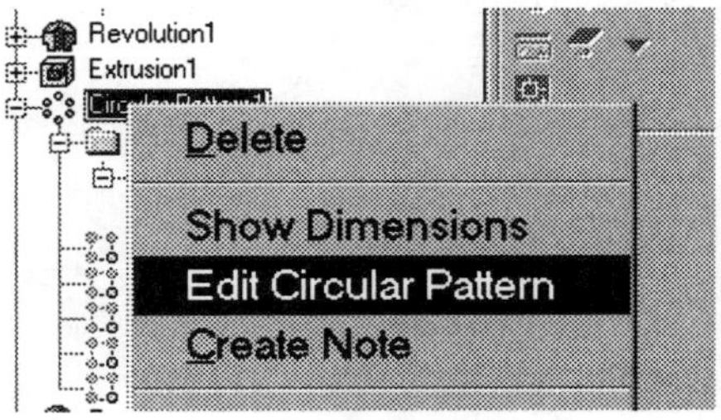

Highlight the circular pattern in the browser, right click and select 'Edit Circular Pattern.'

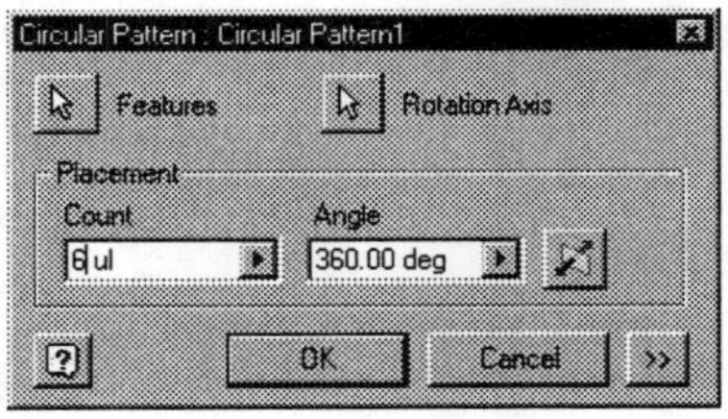

Change the count from 5 to 6. Press 'OK'
Note that the pattern automatically updates.

TIP: Inventor R3 allows you to suppress an occurrence individually. You can suppress all occurrences by suppressing the circular pattern.

Inventor R4 and below does not allow the user to transform individual occurrences into independent features.

Save Copy As 'Array1.ipt'.

Review Questions

1. Each individual member of a pattern is referred to as a(n):

   A. Member
   B. Occurrence
   C. Item
   D. Child

2. To make a pattern invisible:

   A. Locate it in the browser, right click and select 'Suppress'.
   B. Locate it in the browser, right click and select 'Delete'.
   C. Locate it in the graphics window, right click and select 'Suppress'.
   D. Locate it in the graphics window, right click and select 'Delete'.

3. When creating a circular pattern, the user must identify all of the items listed below EXCEPT:

   A. The feature to be patterned
   B. The angle between the features to be patterned
   C. An axis of rotation
   D. The total number of items in the pattern

4. To modify a pattern:

   A. Highlight the pattern in the browser or graphics window, right click and select 'Modify'
   B. Highlight the pattern in the browser or graphics window, right click and select 'Edit Feature'
   C. From the menu, select Modify->Pattern
   D. From the Features toolbar, select 'Pattern Edit'.

5. True or False

To specify a pattern using the angle between entities rather than a total angle, enable Incremental Positioning and specify an incremental angle.

6. True or False

Inventor R4 will not allow the user to make a member of a pattern into an independent feature.

7. True or False

If you suppress a circular pattern, all members of that pattern will also be suppressed.

ANSWERS: 1) B; 2) A; 3) B; 4) B; 5) T; 6) T; 7) T

Lesson 14

Lofting

Learning Objectives

When you have completed this lesson, you will have:

- Used the precise input toolbar to sketch profiles
- Created an Offset Work Plane
- Created a Simple Lofted Model

If you have a part that blends from one shape to another and it cannot be created by extruding or revolving, lofting is the best answer. A lofted solid blends two or more distinct shapes. Before creating a lofted solid, we must define the profiles or sketches to be blended.

Lofts follow these rules:

- A minimum of two profiles must be specified
- Each profile must be on it's own work plane
- Work planes may be offset or angled.
- Perpendicular Work Planes can not be used
- An existing planar face may be used for the start or end of a loft

We'll start a new file with standard part using inches.

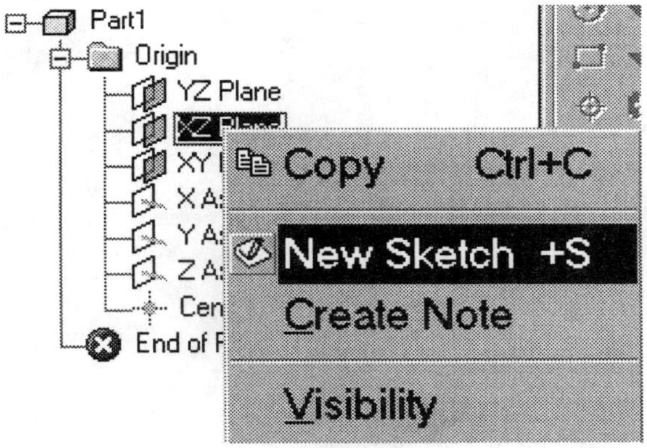

Exit out of the sketch that Inventor starts us in.
Delete that sketch.
We will create our loft using the Top or XZ plane.
Select the XZ plane in the browser.
Right click and select New Sketch.

The bottom of our part will be a circle with a diameter of 2 inches. We need to be able to line up our profiles. We can use the Precise Input toolbar to assist us.

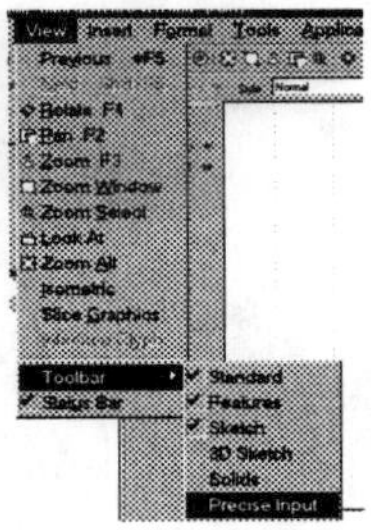

Go to View->Precise Input to enable the toolbar.

TIP: We can enable any toolbar by right clicking on the Standard Toolbar and selecting the desired toolbar.

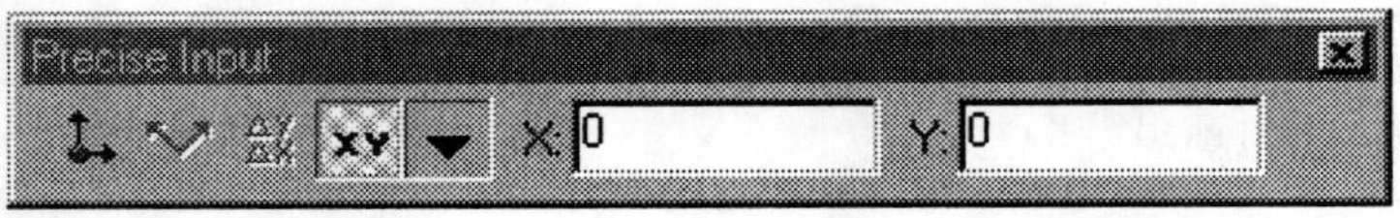

Select the circle tool from the Sketch panel bar. Notice that the X and Y edit windows are now available. Type 0 for X and 0 for Y to locate the circle exactly at 0,0.

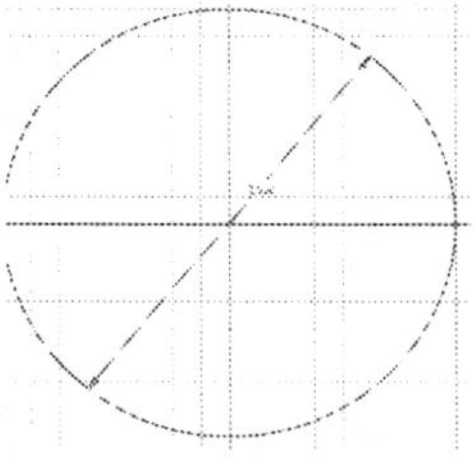

Dimension the circle with a diameter of 2.00.
Select Finish Sketch and switch to 'Isometric View'.

We need to create a workplane offset from the existing XZ plane where the circle sketch is located. Select the 'Workplane' icon located in the Features toolbar.

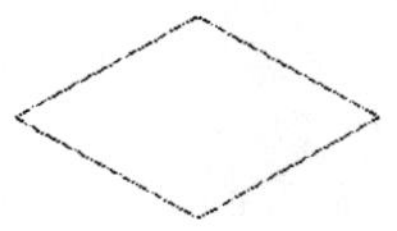

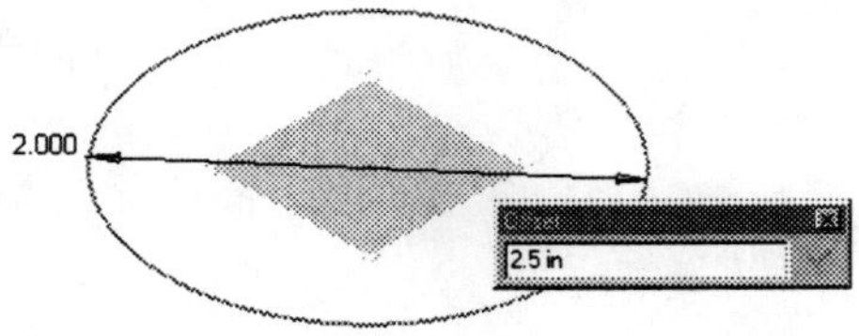

To locate the new workplane, highlight the XZ plane in the browser to make it visible then select one of the corners of the existing workplane. Hold down the left mouse button and drag the new workplane into position. An Offset text box will appear allowing us to enter in a value. Enter '2.5' and select the green check mark to okay.

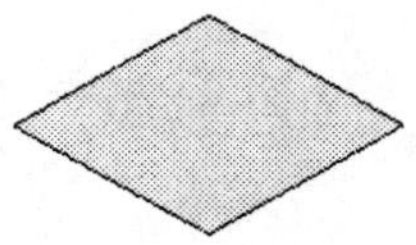

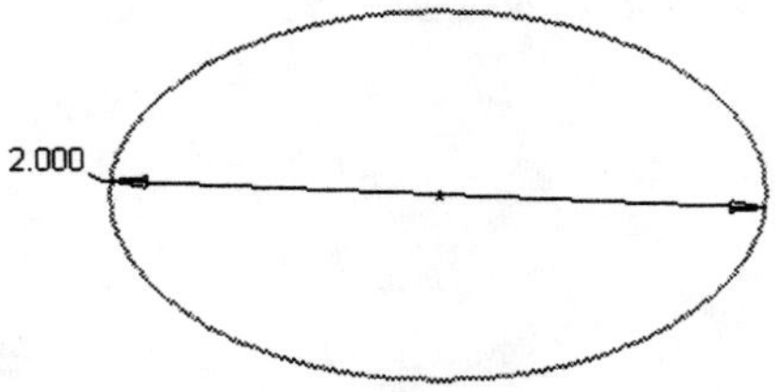

Our new workplane will appear in the Drawing Screen area.

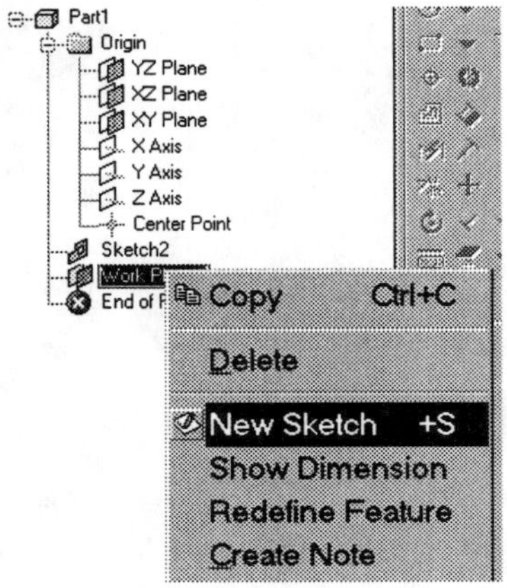

In the Browser, highlight the Workplane, right-click and select 'New Sketch'.

Select the rectangle tool. For the starting corner, type –1.25 for X and –1.25 for Y in the Precise Input toolbar.

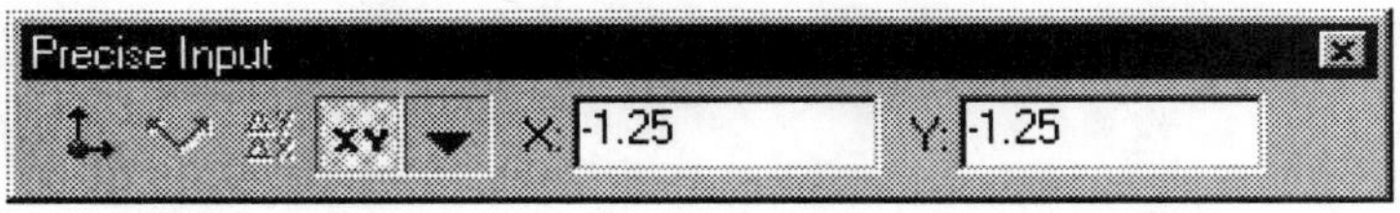

Press ENTER to accept the data entry.

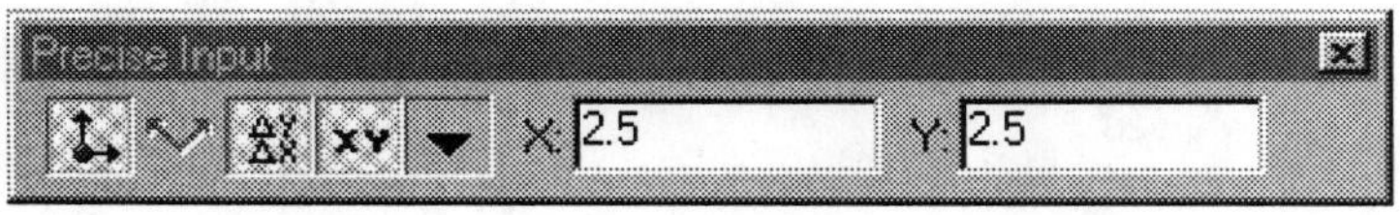

For the upper right corner, pick the delta x/delta y button and type 2.5 for X and 2.5 for Y.
This sets the rectangle to be 2.5 units wide by 2.5 units high.
ENTER to accept the data entry.

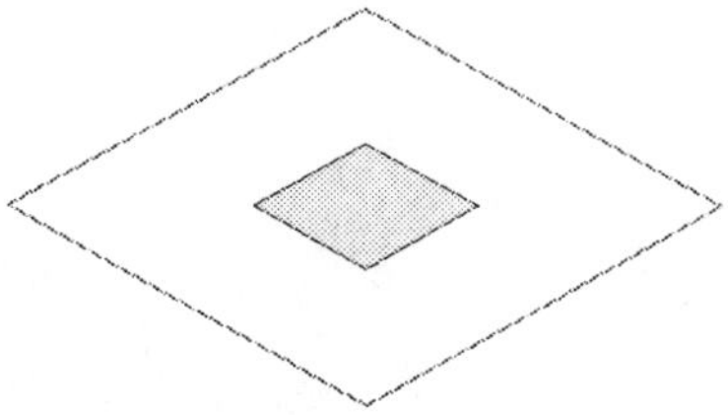

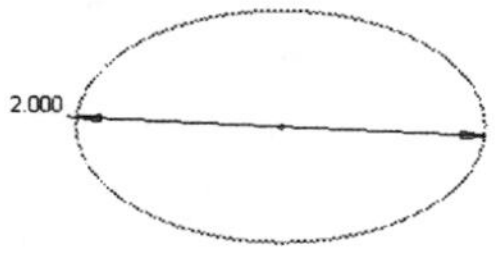

Finish the sketch and switch to 'Isometric View.'

Creating a Loft

Select the 'Loft' tool from the Features toolbar.

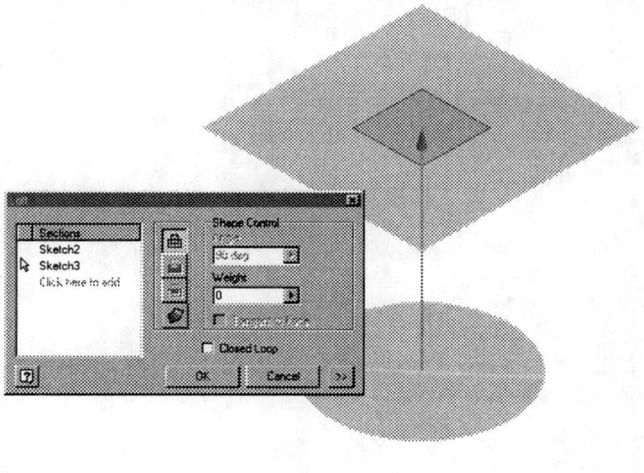

Left pick inside the Sections box of the Loft Dialog box.
Then select the circle first and then the rectangle. They should both be highlighted and we should see an arrow indicating the direction of the loft. The direction is based on the order in which the sketches are selected.

TIP: To add a sketch to the Sections window, the user can:

- Click in the Sections Window and then select the sketch.
- Pick the sketch in the graphics window and it will automatically be added to the Sections window.
- Pick the sketch in the browser and it will automatically be added to the Sections window.

Press 'OK'.

Turn off the Visibility of the Work Plane by selecting it in the browser, right click and disabling Visibility.

Use the Orbit tool to rotate the part, so we can see how the loft looks.

Modifying a Loft

Let's edit the 'Loft' feature.
Click on the Loft feature in the browser.

We see the two sketches that comprise the Loft.
If we pass our mouse over the Sketch, we see the circle and rectangle highlight.
Let's rename each sketch 'Circle' and 'Rectangle'.
Double-pick on each sketch and rename it appropriately.
(If you double pick quickly, you will open the sketch up for editing. Exit out and try again.)

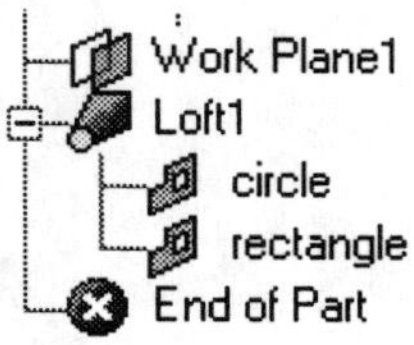

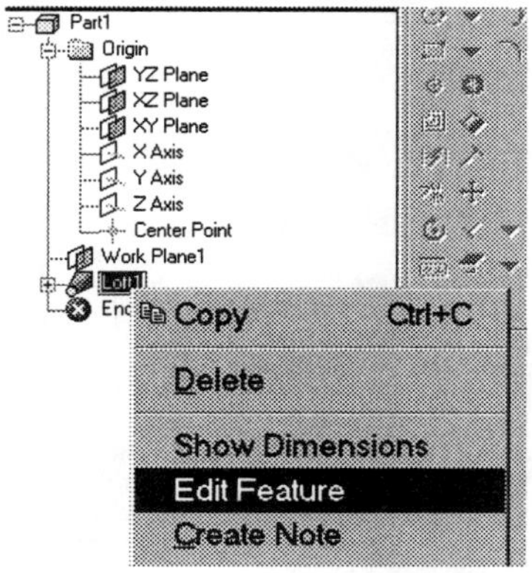

In the Browser, highlight the 'Loft'. Right-click and select 'Edit Feature'.

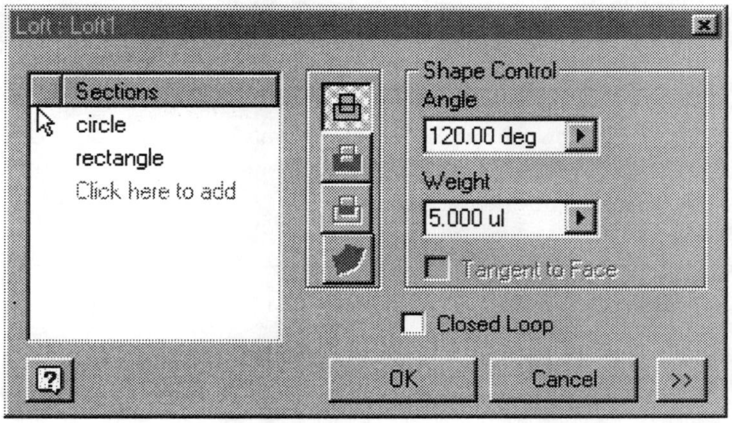

In the Loft dialog box, highlight the circle. In the 'Weight' edit box, type '5'.
In the Angle edit box, type '120'.

The Angle Edit Box will be greyed out until a value other than 0 is typed in the Weight edit box.

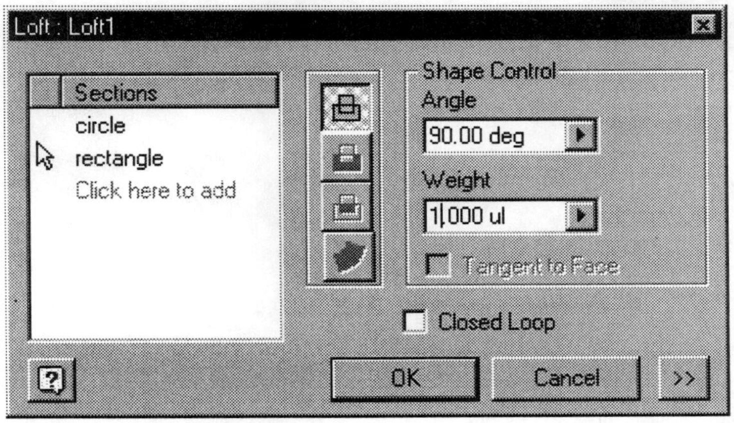

Next, select the rectangle. In the 'Weight' edit box, type '1'. In the Angle edit box, enter '90' as shown.
Press 'OK'.

The modified model.

TIP: The larger the weight applied to a loft the more gradual the transition. A small weight creates an abrupt transition. The weight value is a ratio based on the size of the model.

Use the Orbit tool to examine the model.
Experiment with different weights and angles to see how they affect the lofting process.

Save our part as 'loft2.ipt'.

TIP: If your loft shows too great a transition between profiles, you can either reduce the distance between the work planes or add additional profiles to the loft.

TIP: To delete a sketch to be used as a section, pick it with the left mouse button, so that it highlights in blue, then press the 'Delete' key on your keyboard.

Review Questions

1. Lofts require all of the following EXCEPT:

   A. Two or more profiles
   B. A Path
   C. Each profile to be on it's own work plane
   D. Work Planes can not be perpendicular

2. True or False

Lofts are used when the feature has an irregular profile.

3. True or False

Weight controls the amount of transition between profiles

4. True or False

You cannot use an existing face as the start or end of a loft.

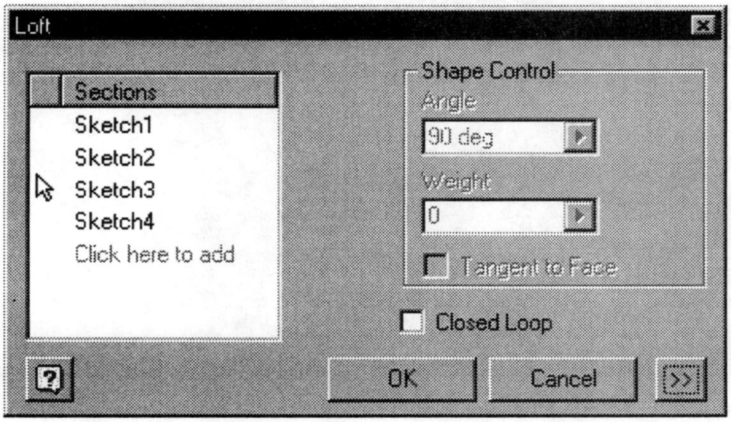

5. To eliminate a sketch from the Sections window:

   A. Highlight the sketch in the Sections window, right click and select 'Delete'.
   B. Highlight the sketch in the browse, right click and select 'Delete'.
   C. Highlight the sketch in the graphics window right click and select 'Delete'
   D. Highlight the sketch in the Sections window and press the 'Delete' key on your keyboard.

6. To add a sketch to the Sections window:

   A. Click in the Sections Window and then select the sketch.
   B. Pick the sketch in the graphics window and it will automatically be added to the Sections window.
   C. Pick the sketch in the browser and it will automatically be added to the Sections window.
   D. All of the above

7. The direction of the loft is based on:

   A. the size of the profiles with the start of the loft using the largest profile and the end being the smallest profile
   B. the weight of each profile
   C. the order in which the profiles are selected
   D. the angle between profiles

8. In order for a profile to be used in a loft, it must be:

   A. fully constrained
   B. on a different work plane than the other profile(s)
   C. extruded
   D. a circle or a rectangle

9. True or False

Once a profile has been added to a loft, it cannot be deleted.

10. True or False

Once a loft has been created, additional profiles cannot be added.

ANSWERS: 1) B; 2) T; 3) T; 4) F; 5) D; 6) D; 7) C; 8) B 9) F 10) F

Lesson 15

Creating a Base Sweep

Learning Objectives

In this lesson, we will gain mastery over the following tools:

- Sweep

The features of "real world" parts can most often be modeled using *Extrude* and *Revolve*. *Sweep* and *Loft* are powerful commands because of their capability to produce complex part geometry. In this exercise, we will create a cotter pin using a Sweep operation.

Sweeps are unique in that they require two profiles. A good practice is to create the path sketch and rename it as 'path' to make it easy to locate in the browser. Then create the profile sketch and rename it 'cross_section' in the browser.

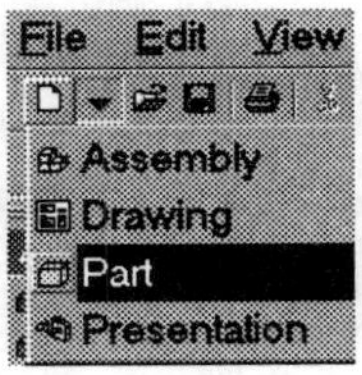

Start a new part using inches.

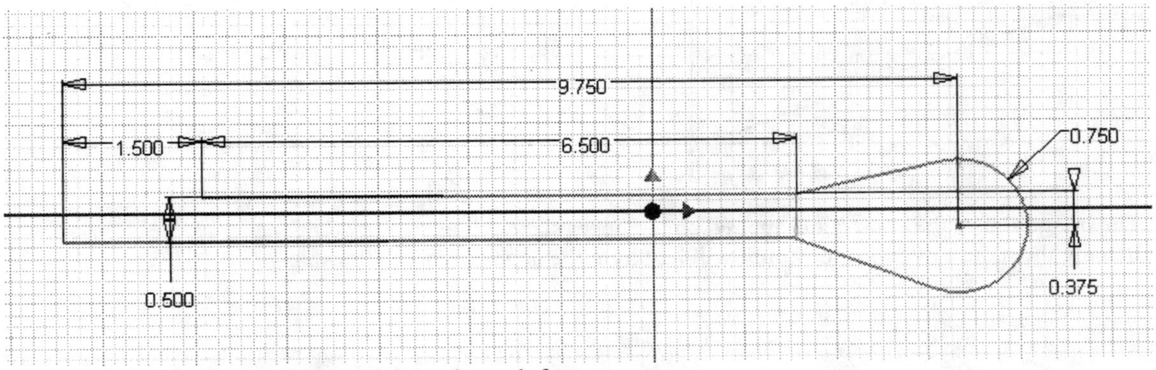

Create the sketch shown. This will form the path for our sweep.

Hints on sketch creation for the path:

Use constraints to help create the geometry.
The slanted lines connecting the horizontal lines to the arc should be constrained equal.
Add a tangent constraint between the slanted lines and the arc.

TIP: A path may consist of lines, splines, or arcs. It must be a 2D sketch and reside on a single work plane. It must be an open sketch and should not intersect itself.

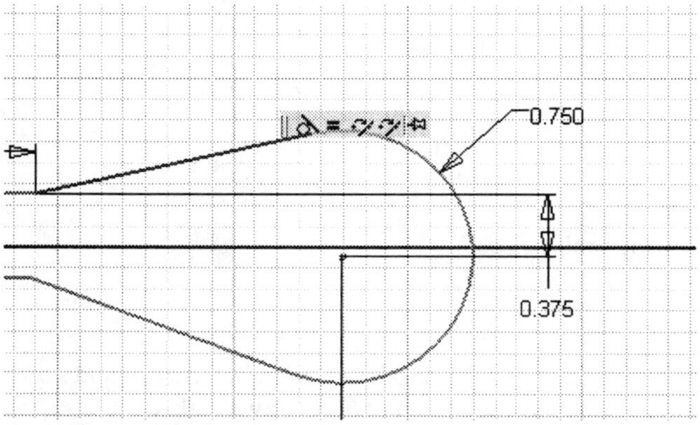

Use Show Constraints to see the constraints applied to the geometry.

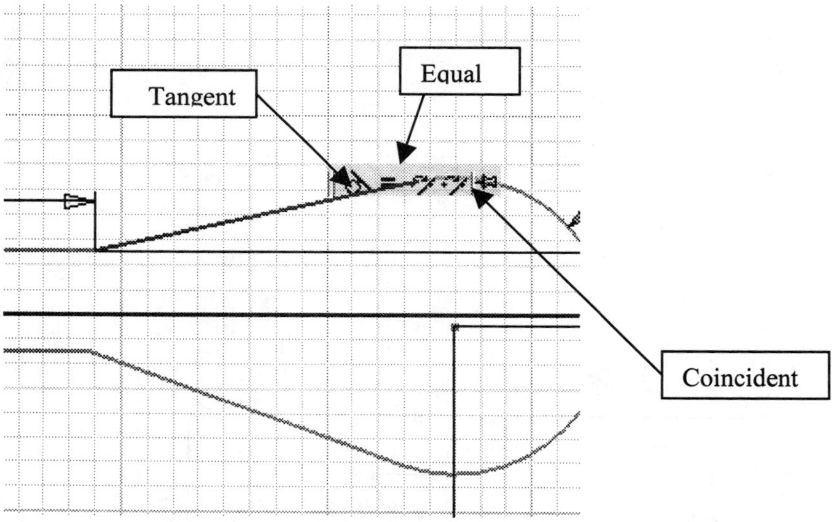

The image shows the constraints applied on the upper slanted line.
Placing the mouse over the constraint will highlight the geometrical relationship.

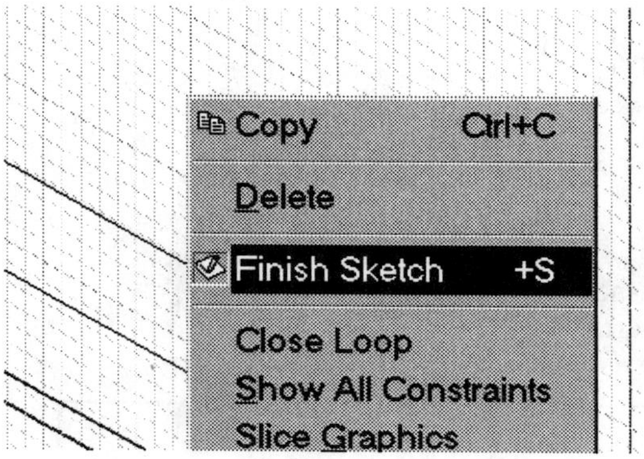

Right click and select 'Finish Sketch'.

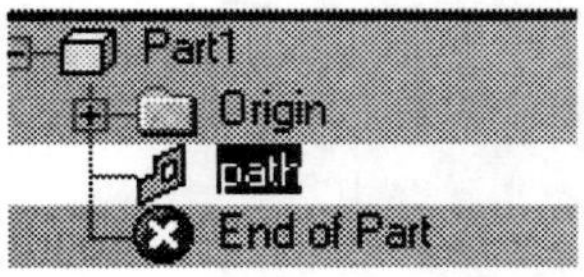

Locate the sketch in the browser and rename it ‘path’.

Paths

Paths must be on a plane that intersects with the sweep profile plane.

Create Work Plane

Select the work plane tool from the Features toolbar.

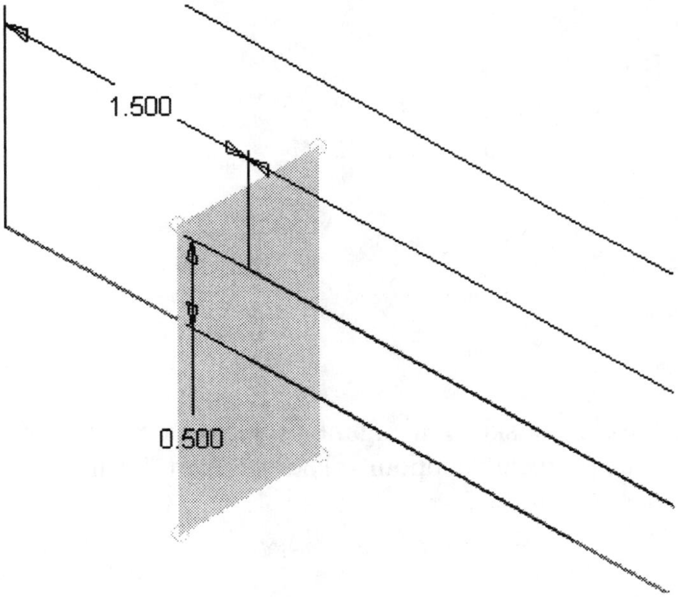

Select the endpoint of the bottom line and then the top line. A work plane will be placed normal to the line. It may take a few tries before you are able to place the work plane successfully.

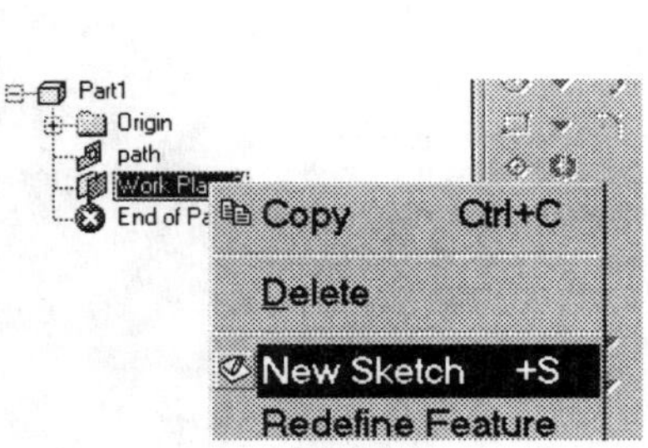

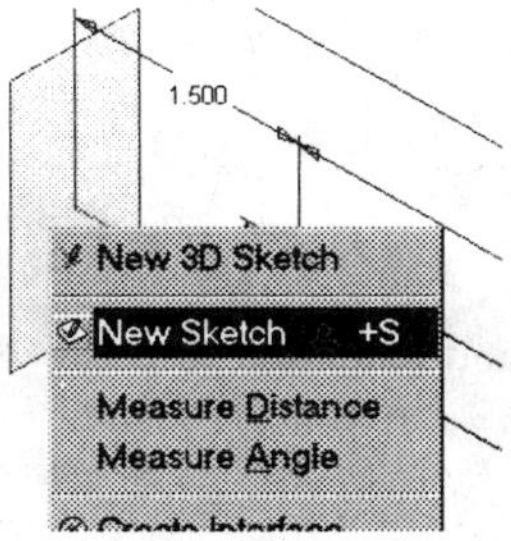

Select the plane just created in the browser or in the graphics window. Right click and select 'New Sketch'.

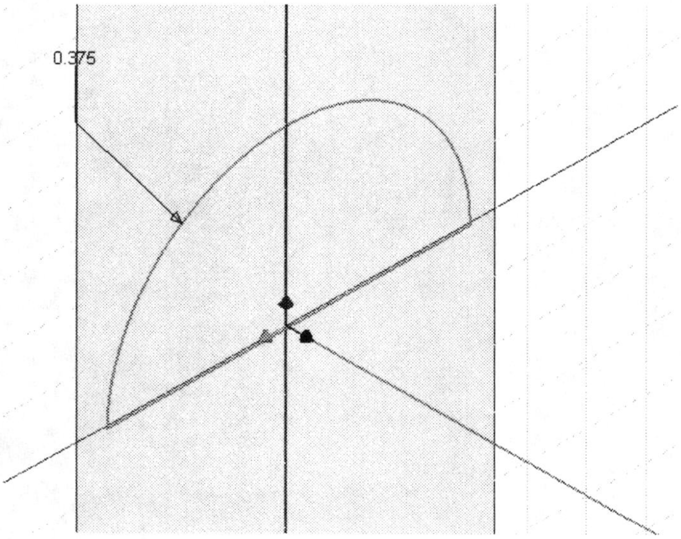

Project the end point of the line onto the current sketch using the Project Geometry tool. Then constrain the center of the arc to the projected endpoint. The radius of the arc is 0.375.

Right click to select 'Finish sketch'.

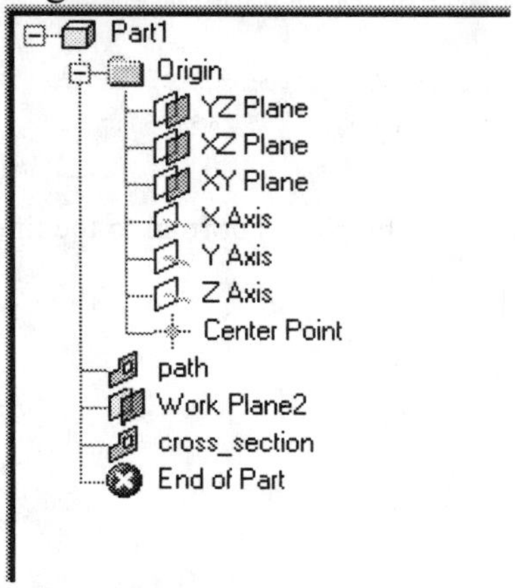

Rename the sketch 'cross_section'.

Time to create the sweep.

TIP: The user can specify more than one profile to sweep along a path.
Profiles may be nested but may not be intersecting.
To select more than one profile, press the Control key and select the desired profiles.
Profiles may reside on the same plane or different planes, but all profiles must be perpendicular to the path.

Creating a Sweep

Select the Sweep tool from the Features toolbar.

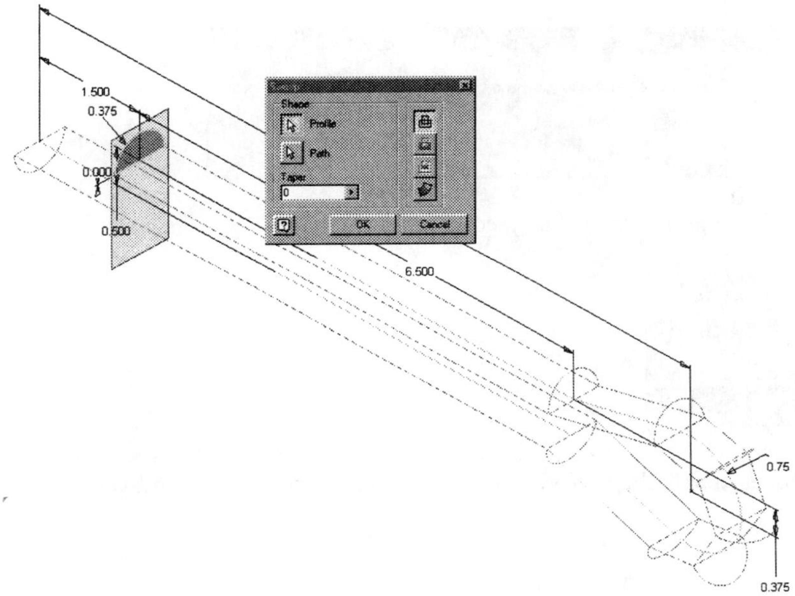

Inventor will make some assumptions on which profile is the path and which profile is to be used for the sweep. We use the preview to assist us in deciding if everything has been set up OK. We can always use the selection tools in the Sweep dialog box to make changes.

To use the selection tools, press the Profile button and then select the half-circle sketch. Then select the Path tool and select the path. You can select the cross_section and path from the browser or the graphics window. Notice that the default is the 'Join' button – the top button.
The preview in this case looks perfect, so we select 'OK'.

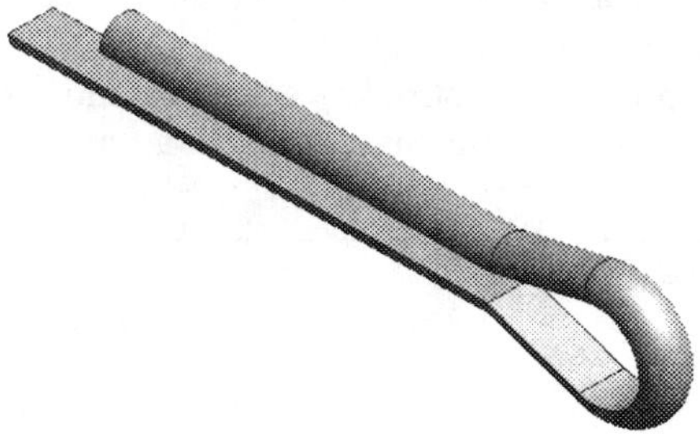

If the sweep gives an intersect error

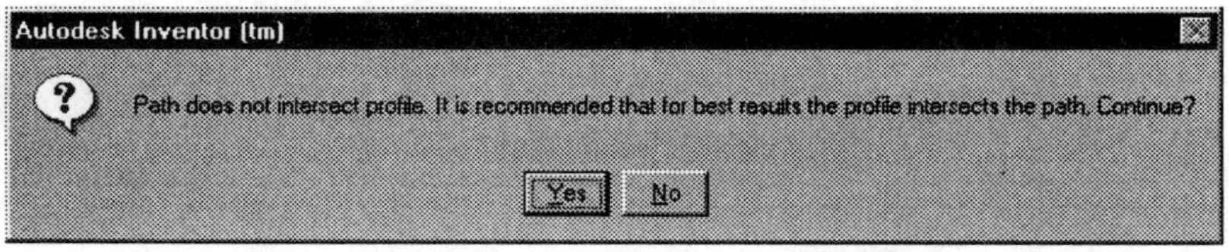

It means that your path and profile are not aligned.

Go to the cross section sketch in the browser. Select, right click and select 'Edit Sketch'.

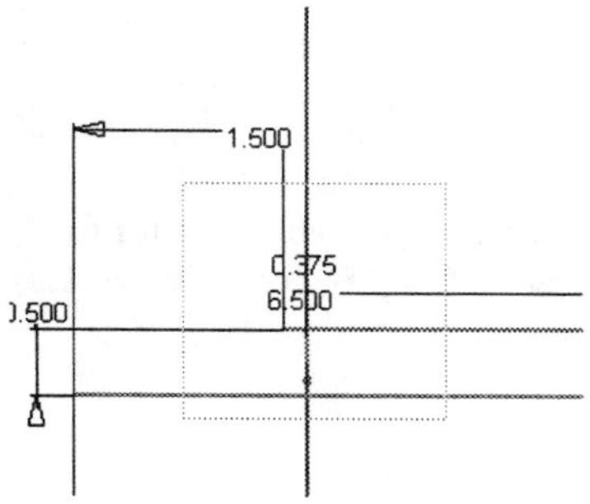

With your mouse, draw a window around the sketch.
The sketch will grey out. We can now move our sketch.

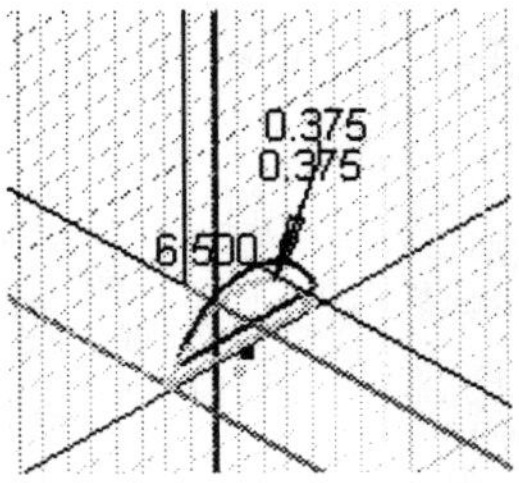

Hold the mouse down and drag the sketch into a new location.
Right click and select 'Finish Sketch'.
Try performing the sweep again.

The sweep feature appears in the browser.

Use Save to save our completed cotter pin. Name the file 'cotter-pin'.

Review Questions

1. The Sweep tool is located on this toolbar:

   A. Feature
   B. Sketch
   C. Drawing
   D. Sheet Metal

2. To perform a sweep, the user needs to create these two sketches:

   A. Profile and Sweep
   B. Top and Bottom
   C. Handle and Bristles
   D. Profile and Path

3. If an intersection will occur:

   A. Inventor will make the sweep any way
   B. Inventor shows a dialog box warning the user and asks if the user wishes to continue
   C. Inventor will lock up and cause a fatal error
   D. The Design Doctor will automatically pop up to correct the problem

4. To add a draft angle to a sweep, the user should add a value to this option in the Sweep dialog:

   A. Draft Angle
   B. Taper
   C. Angle
   D. Face Draft

5. When creating a sweep, all of the following are true EXCEPT:

   A. There can only be one path
   B. There can only be one profile
   C. There can only be one direction
   D. There can only be one draft angle

6. The dialog box for the Sweep command changes depending on:

   A. How many profiles are defined
   B. Whether the sweep is a base feature or not
   C. What type of path is defined
   D. Whether or not a draft angle is defined

ANSWERS: 1) A; 2) D; 3) B; 4) A; 5) B; 6) B

Lesson 16

Creating Sheet Metal Parts

Learning Objectives

In this lesson, the user will gain further mastery of the sheet metal environment and the following tools:

- Settings
- Face
- Hole
- Rectangular Pattern
- Corner Chamfer

We start by opening a sheet metal part using metric units. Select the metric tab of the dialog box.

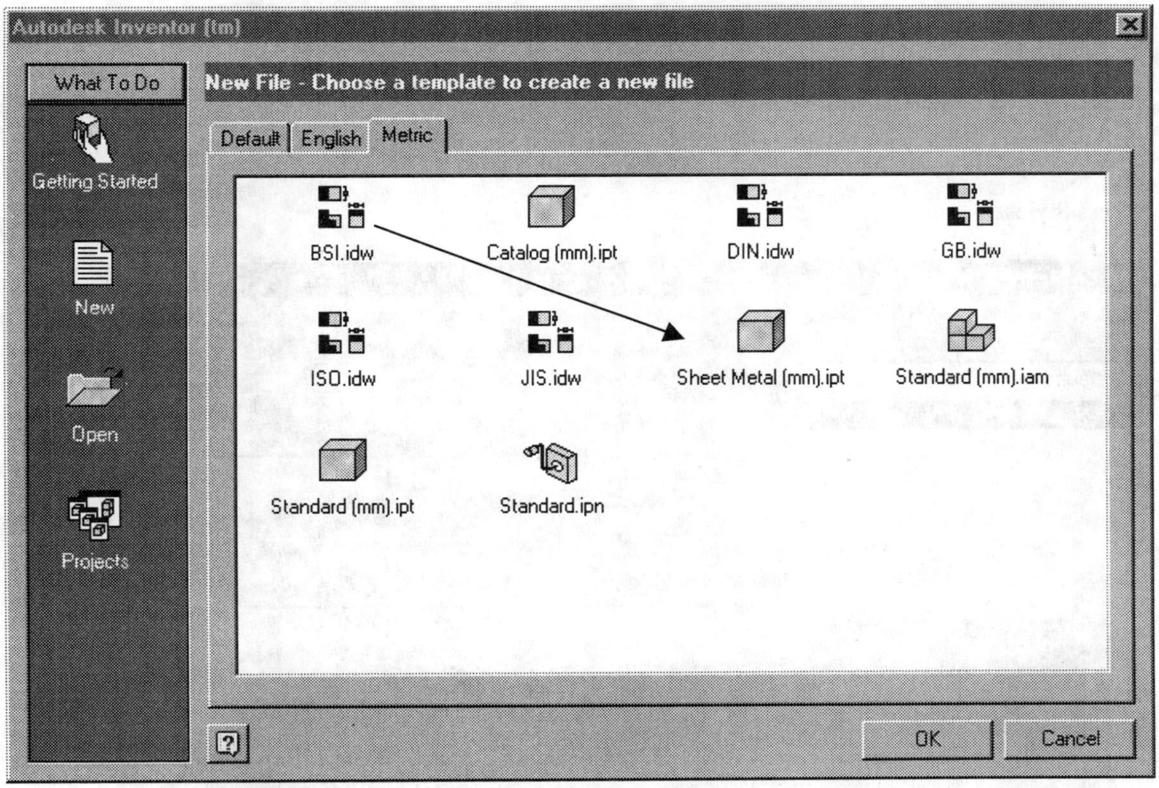

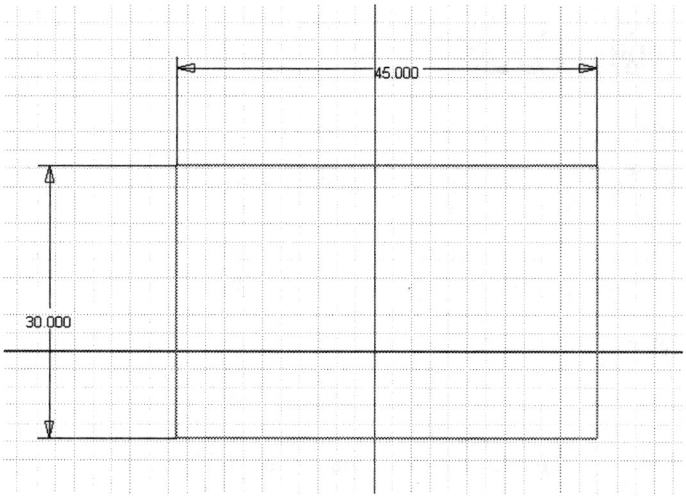

We create our first profile using the Rectangle tool and dimensioning 45 mm wide by 30 mm high.

Sheet Metal Styles

Access Styles.

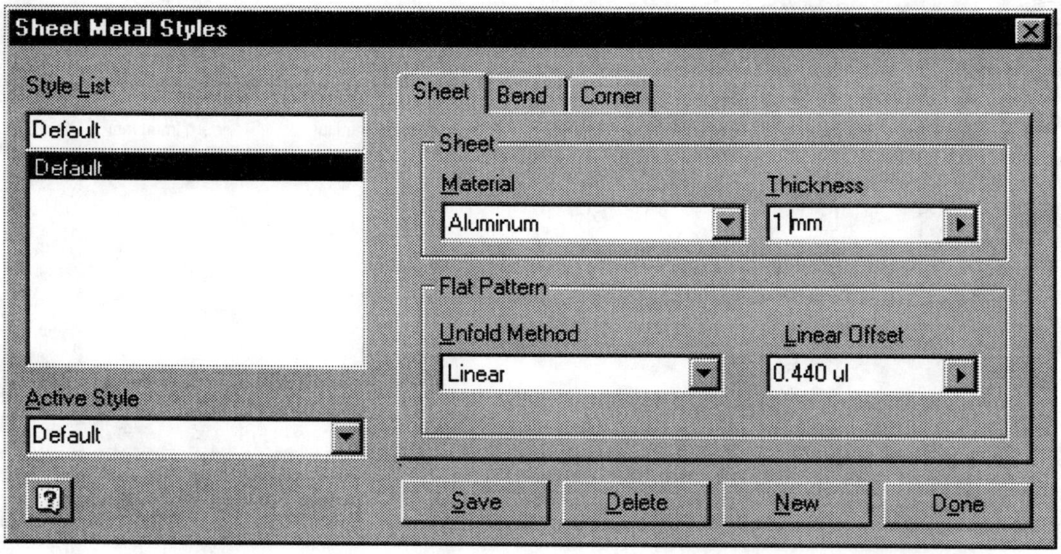

Set to Aluminum with a Thickness of 1 mm.
Press 'Done' and then 'OK'.

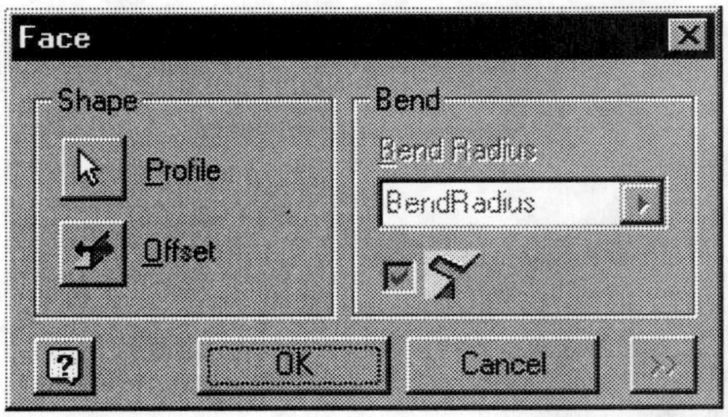

Creating a Face

Switch to an isometric view.

Select the Face tool. The profile we created in automatically selected. Press 'OK'.

TIP: The face tool works differently than the Extrude tool. We only need to select a profile and a direction. Inventor automatically uses the thickness defined in Settings.

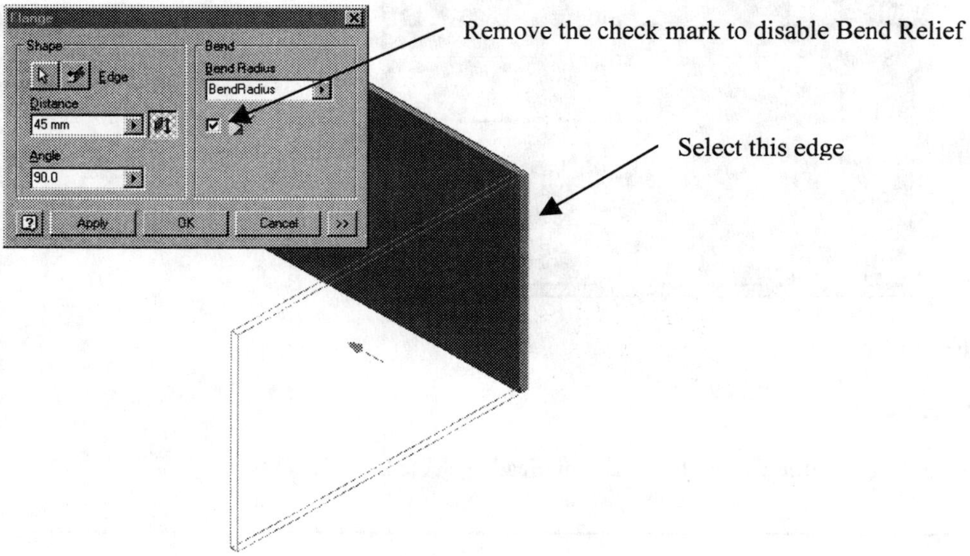

Creating a Flange

Select the Flange tool to add a Flange. Set the Distance to 45 mm. Disable the Bend Relief box. Press 'Apply'.

TIP: To add the flange, we only need to select the edge. We do not need to draw a profile.

Add a Flange to the opposite side using the same settings as shown.

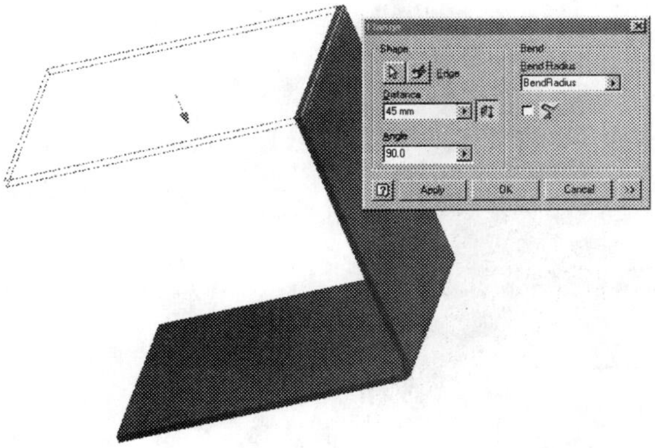

Press ‘Apply’ to add.

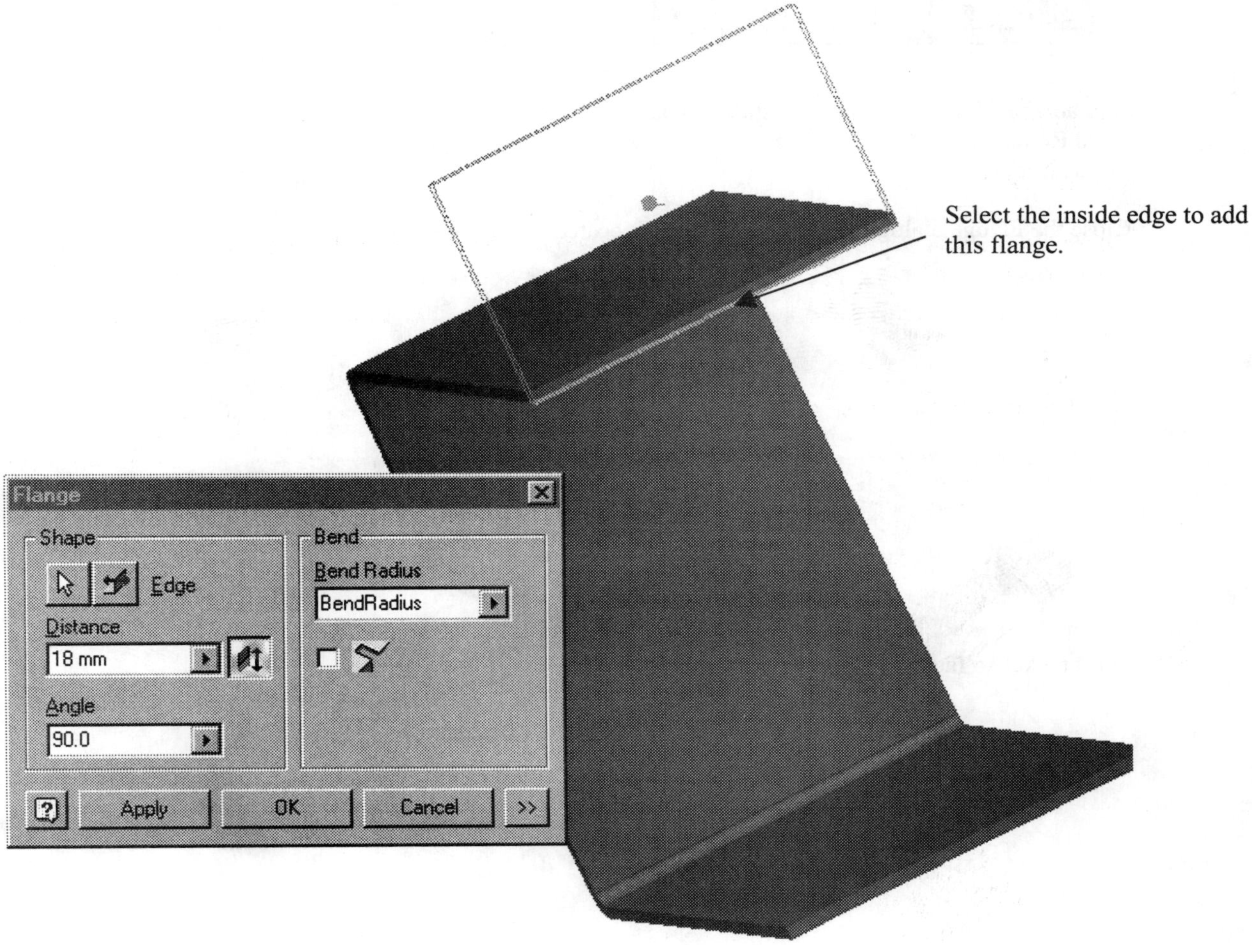

Add a flange as shown. Distance should be set to 18 mm. Bend Relief should NOT be checked. Press ‘Apply’.

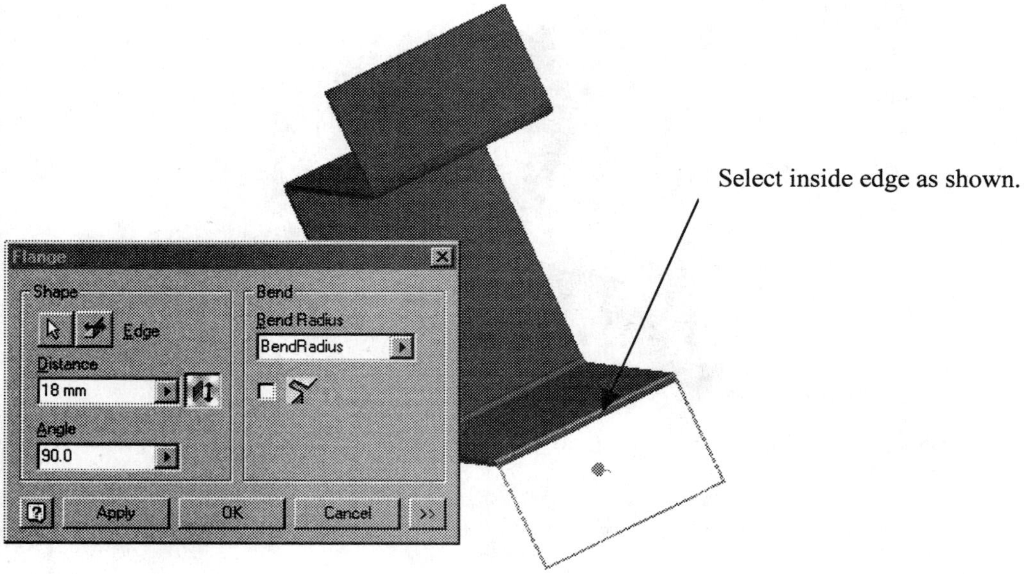

Add another flange as shown. Distance should be 18 mm.
Bend Relief should NOT be checked.
Press 'Apply'.

Close the Flange dialog box by pressing the X located in the upper right corner.

Our bracket so far.

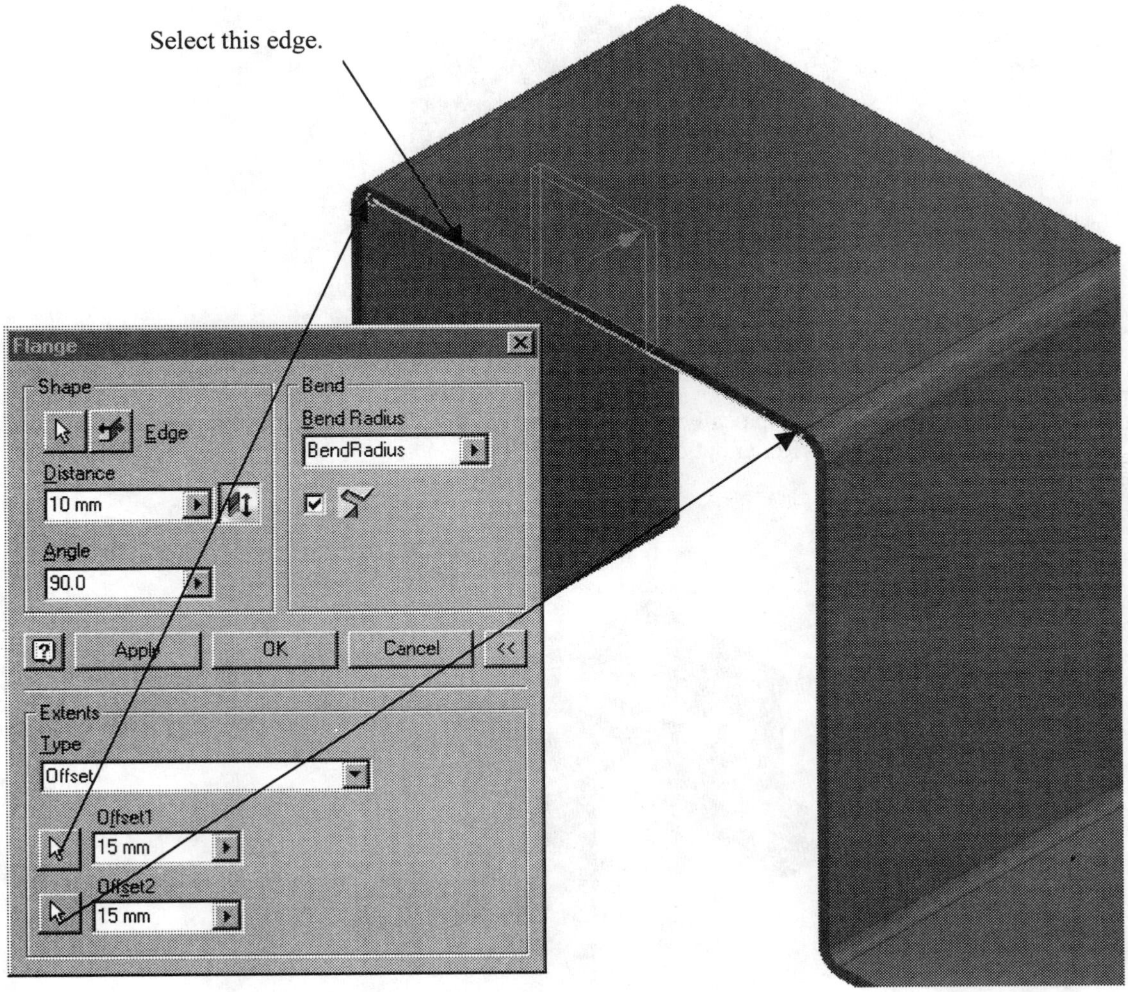

Select the Flange tool again.
Select the bottom edge as shown.
Set the distance to 10 mm.
Press the 'More' button.
Set Type to Offset.
Select the left point as shown.
Set the Offset to 15 mm.
Select the right point as shown.
Set the Offset to 15 mm.
Enable the Bend Radius as shown.
Press 'Apply'.

Our model so far.
Note that a bend relief was automatically added using the values in the Settings dialog box. This occurred because we enabled the Bend Relief option.

Adding a Hole Feature

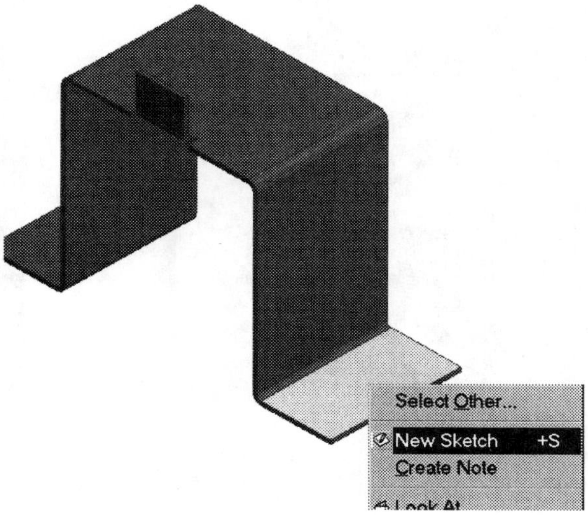

Select the foot as shown and 'New Sketch'.

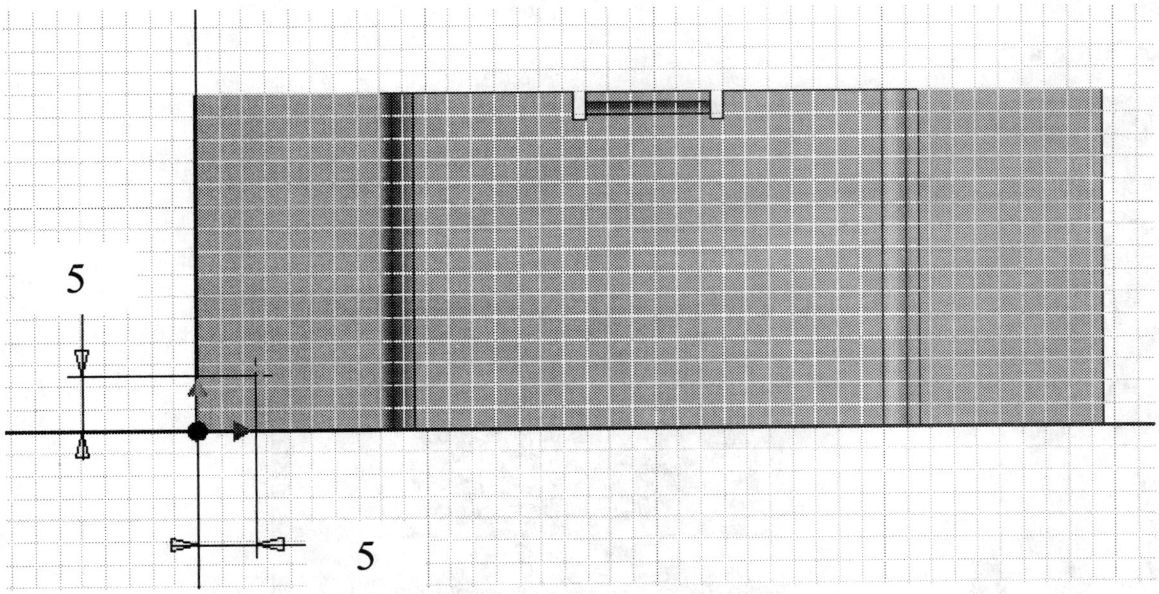

Place a Point, Hole Center as shown.

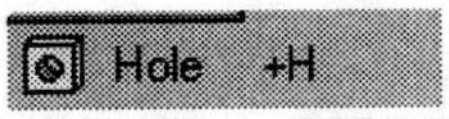

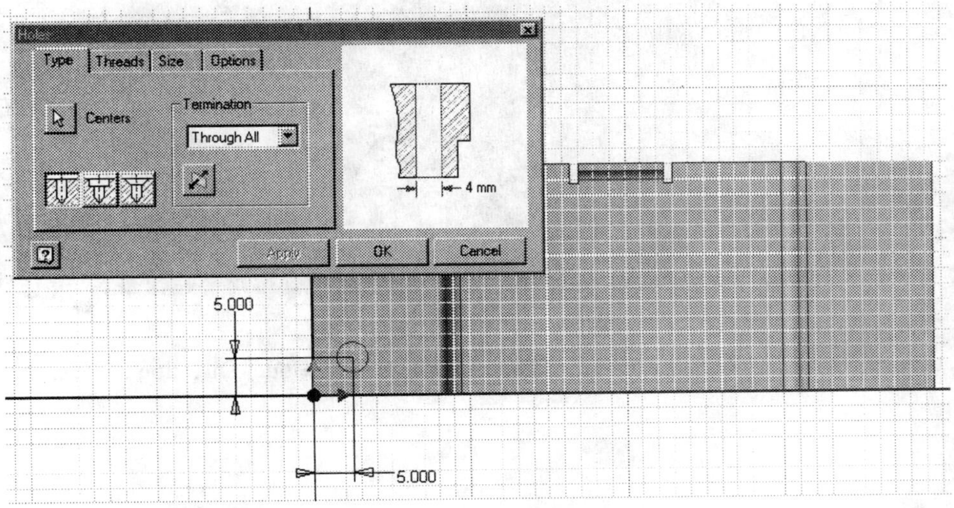

Create the hole as shown with Diameter of 4 mm and Termination of Through All.

Adding a Pattern

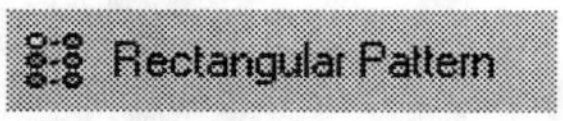

Select the Rectangular Pattern tool.
Select the hole from the browser to be patterned.

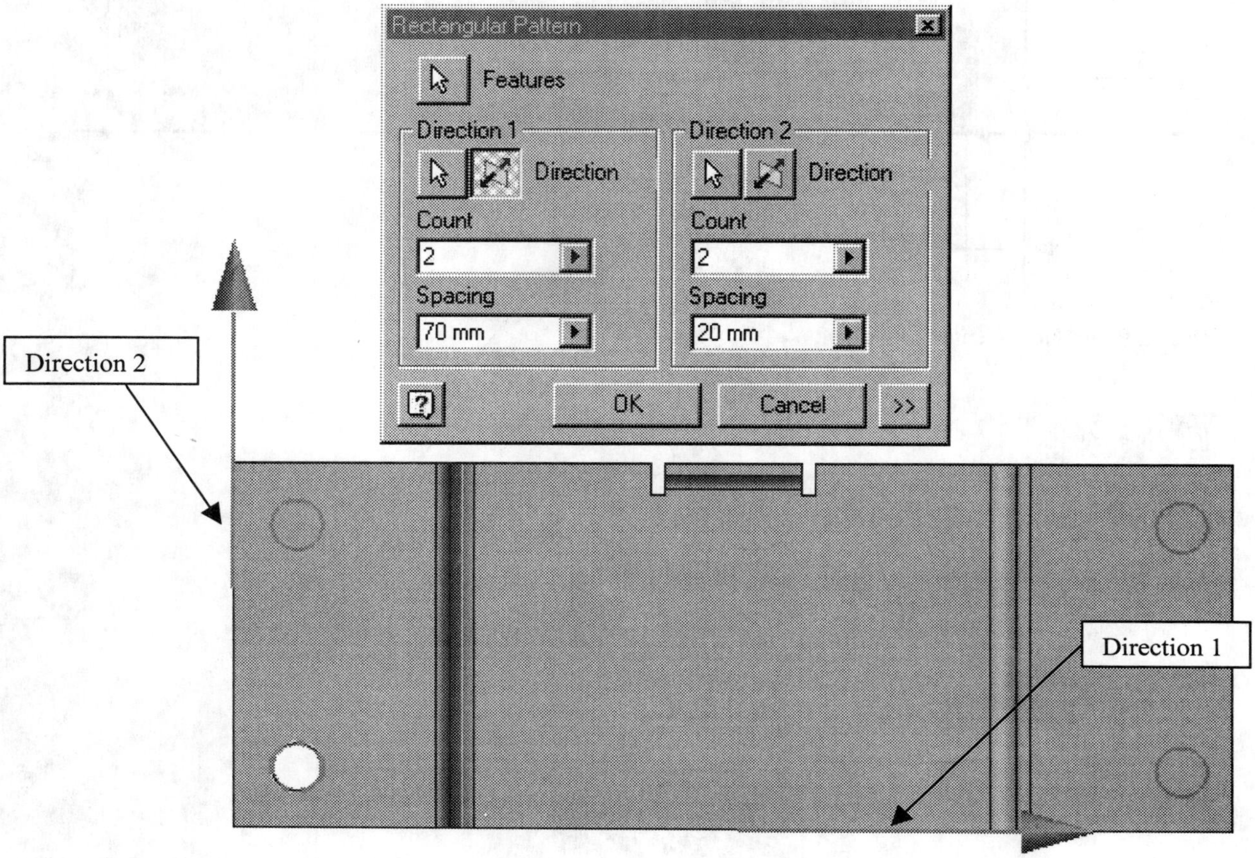

Set the pattern as shown. Under Direction 1, set Spacing of 70 mm. Under Direction 2, set spacing of 20 mm.

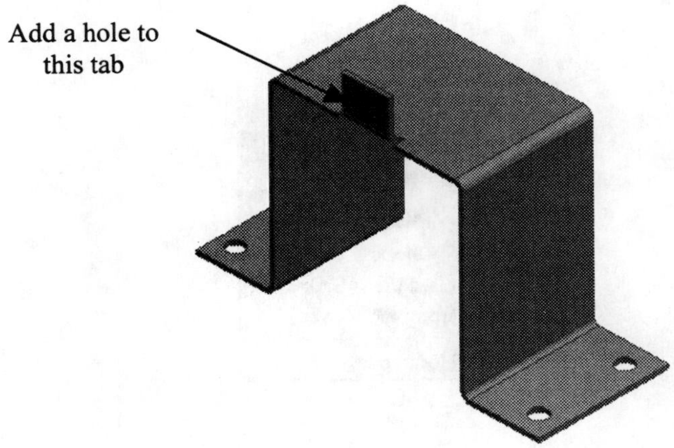

Add a hole to the small tab as shown.
Select the front plane of the tab.
Right click and select 'New Sketch'.
Place a point as shown.

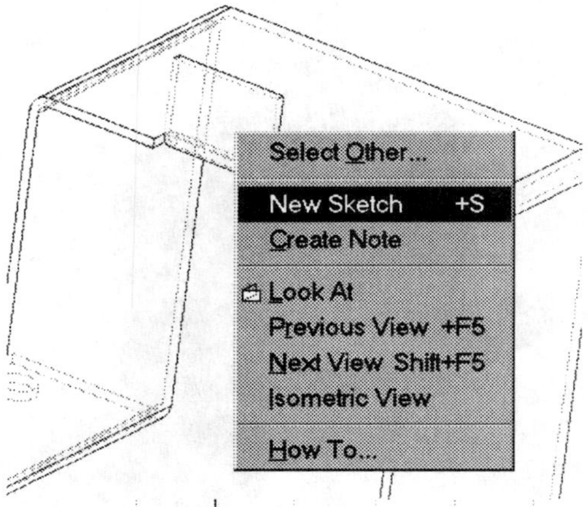

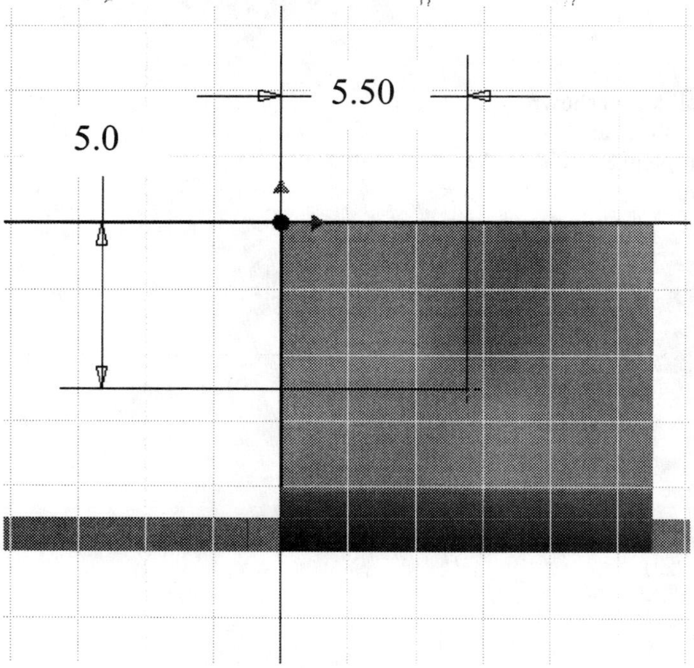

Set the hole to 3 mm in Diameter and Termination of Through All.

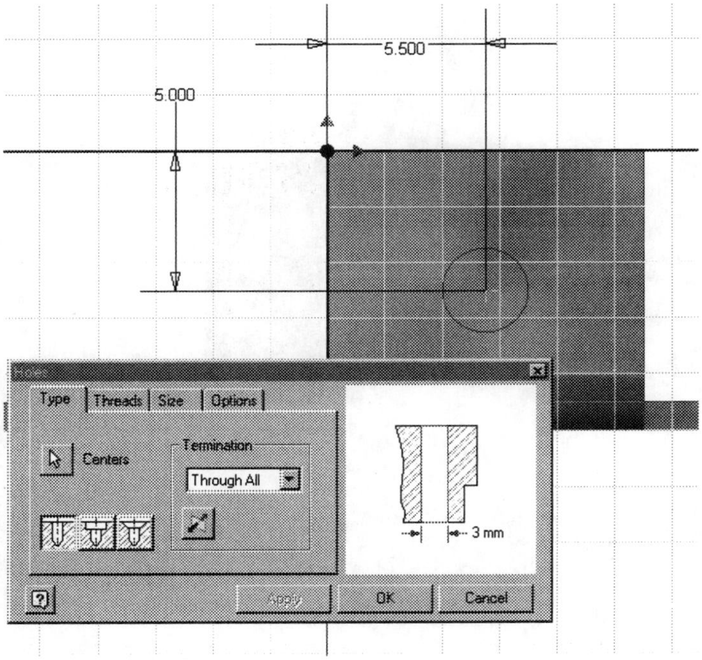

Adding Corner Chamfers

Add Corner Chamfers to the edges of the feet as shown.

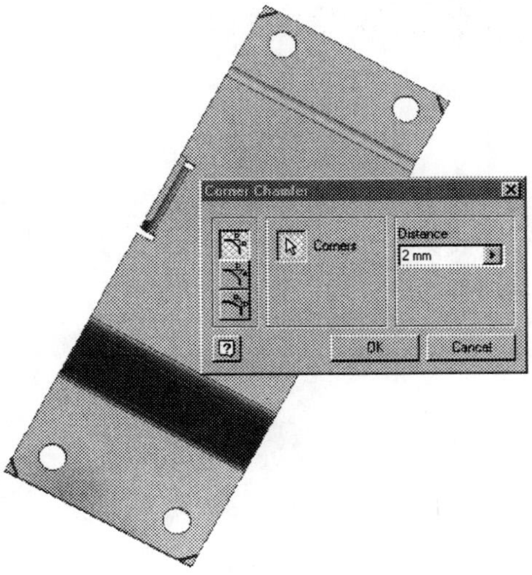

Use the Equal Distance option (top left button). Select all four corners as shown. (Use Rotate to aid in selection.) Set the Distance to 2 mm.
Press OK.

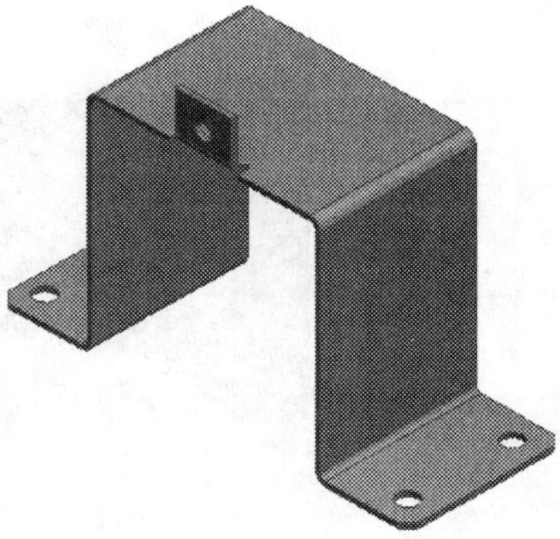

Creating a Flat Pattern

Select the Flat Pattern tool.

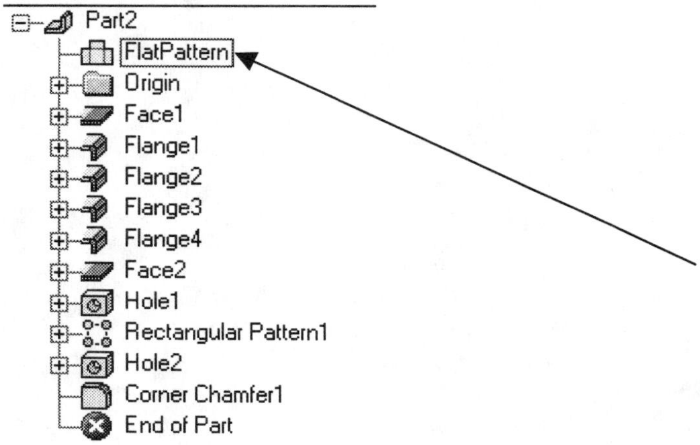

A Flat Pattern icon is automatically added to the Browser.

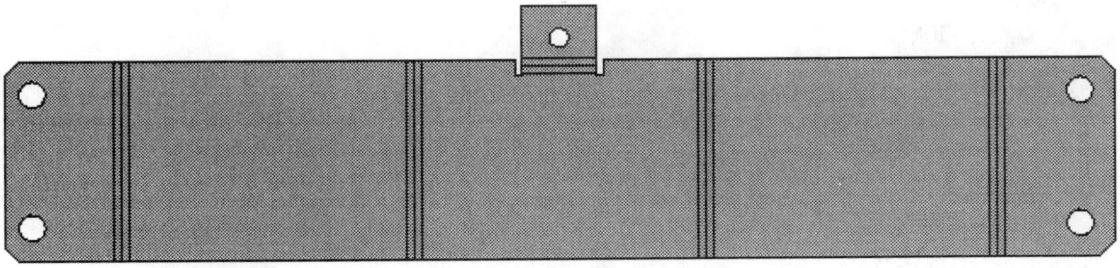

Our model is viewed as a Flat Pattern.

TIP: The Flat Pattern will automatically update with any changes we make to the model.

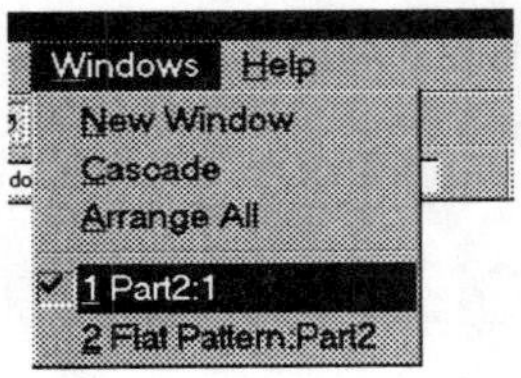

The Flat Pattern is actually viewed in a separate window that was instantly created when we selected the Flat Pattern tool. To switch back to our 3D model, go to Windows under the Menu and select our Part window.

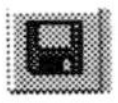

Save our file as 'sheet-metal.ipt'.

Review Questions

1. The first feature in a sheet metal part is created using:

   A. FACE
   B. FLANGE
   C. CORNER SEAM
   D. EXTRUDE

2. To create a face 90 degrees in relation to an existing face that is the same width, use this tool:

   A. FACE
   B. EXTRUDE
   C. FLANGE
   D. BEND

3. To select the type of material used in a sheet metal part, use:

   A. Options
   B. Styles
   C. Properties
   D. Physical

4. To automatically apply a bend relief when adding a flange or a face:

   A. Enable Bend Relief in the Settings Dialog box
   B. Enable Bend Relief in the Flange/Face dialog box
   C. Use the bend relief tool
   D. Enable Bend Relief in the Options dialog box.

5. When we use the Flat Pattern tool, this happens:

   A. A flat pattern view is created to be used as a drawing view
   B. The 3D model is transformed into a flat piece of sheet metal
   C. The 3D model is patterned in a single row
   D. A text file is created to be used by a CNC operator

6. When we first open up a sheet metal part file, this toolbar is active in the panel bar:

   A. Sheet Metal
   B. Solids
   C. Features
   D. Sketch

ANSWERS: 1) A; 2) C; 3) B; 4) B; 5) A; 6) D

Lesson 17

Creating a Basic Part

Learning Objectives

This lesson builds the user's modeling skills. The part created will also be used to practice creating auxiliary views and section views. Be sure to save this file for use in those lessons.

Upon completing this lesson, the user will have gained further mastery of the following tools:

- Extrude
- Work Planes
- Holes
- Fillet
- Insert Design Element
- Rectangular Pattern
- Rib

week 4
Chapter
17, 21, 22
Review
9-16
Date
2-4=2-8

Under the menu, select File->New.

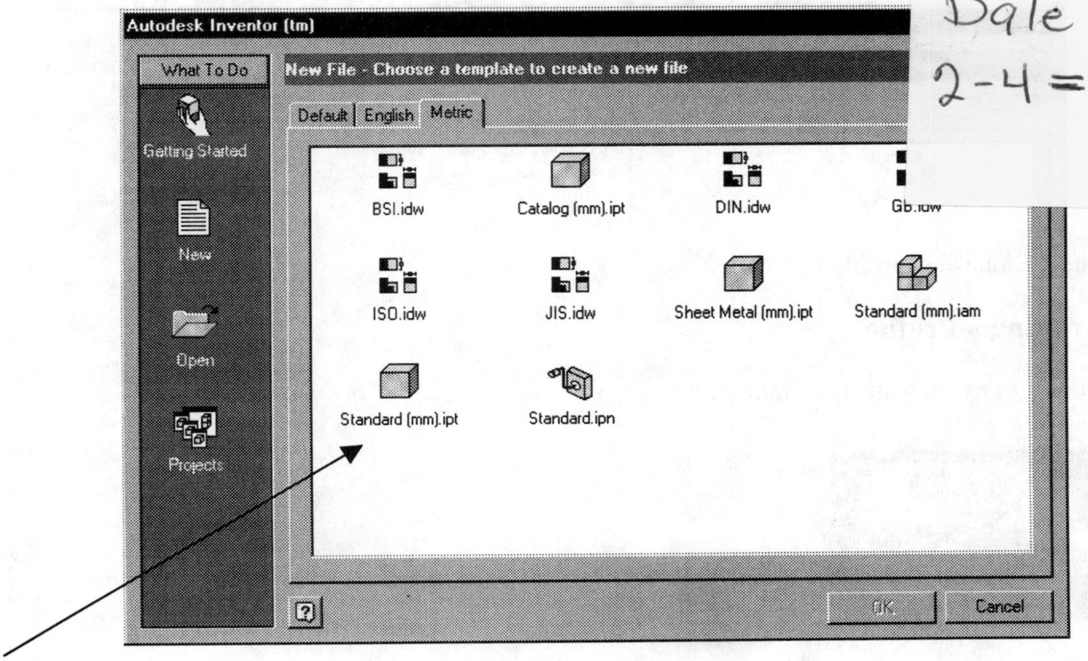

We start by opening a Metric Part file.

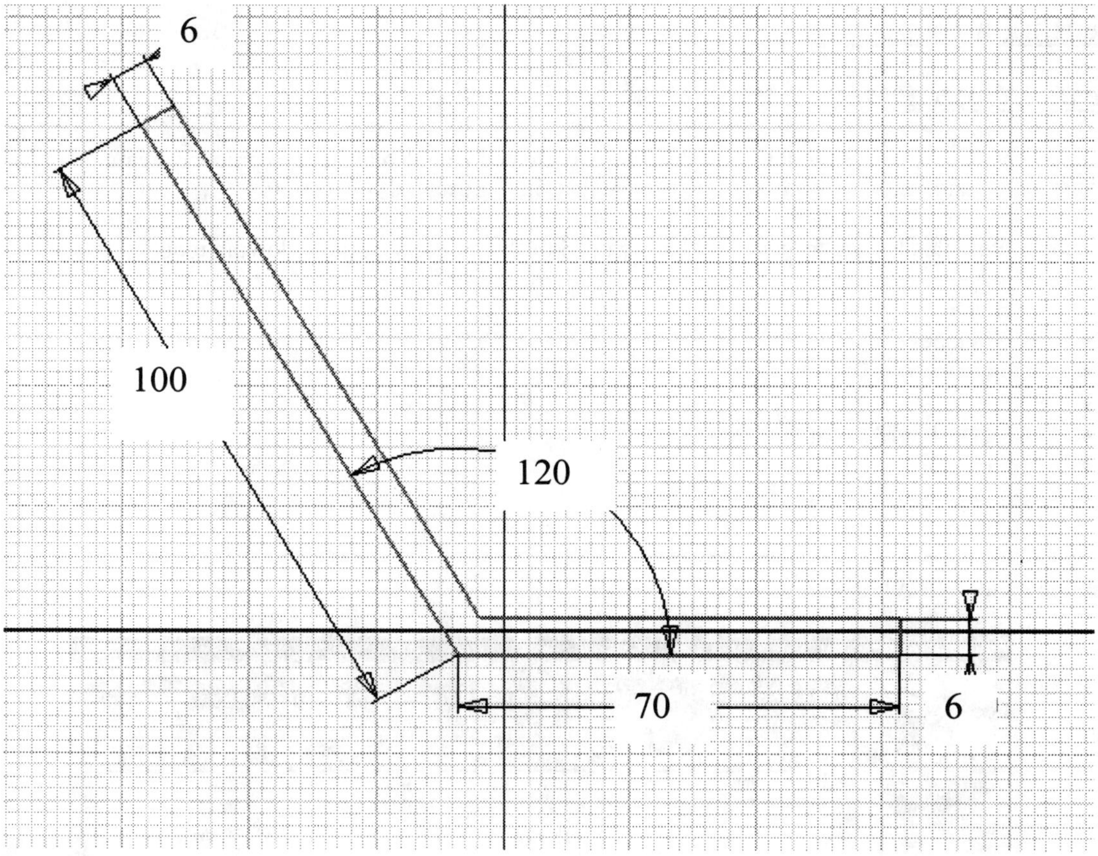

Create the following profile.

Extruding a Profile

Extrude it as a base feature 120 mm.

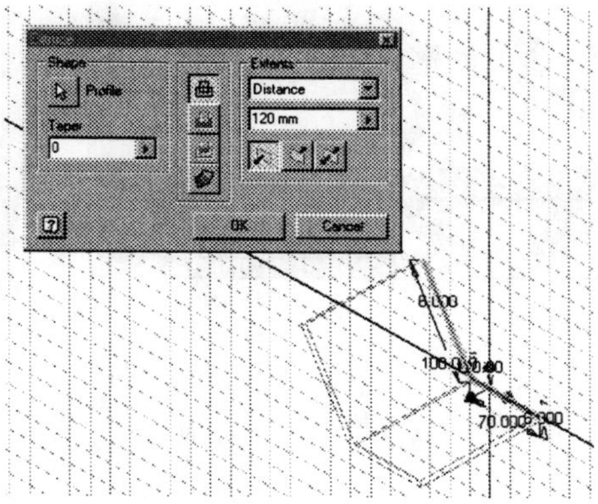

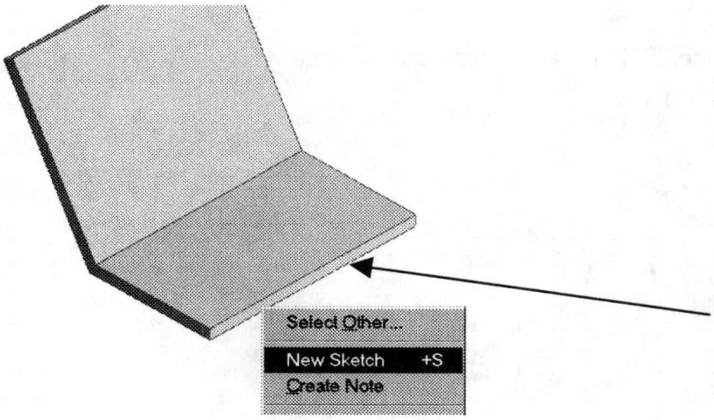

Select the face shown for a New Sketch.

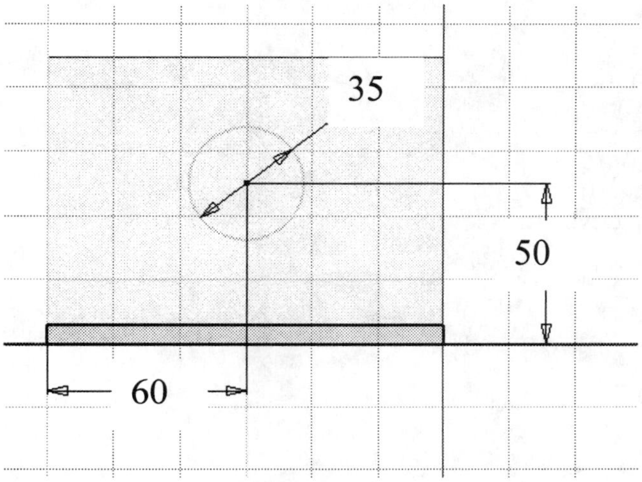

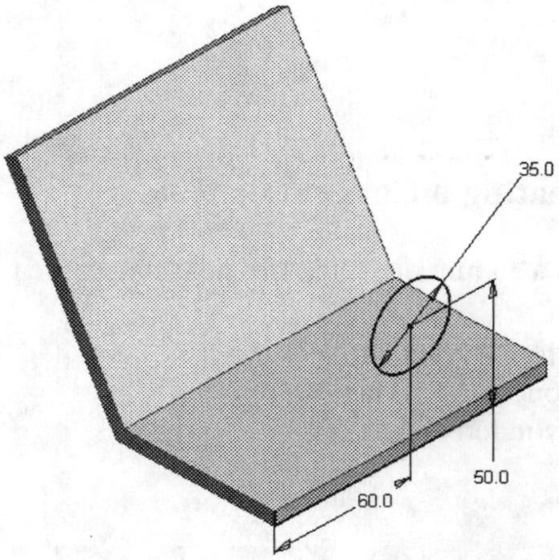

Draw a circle as shown.

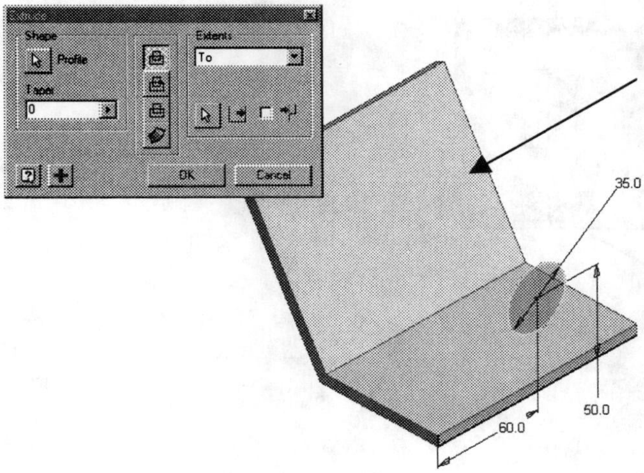

Select this face as the 'To' Plane

Extrude To a Plane

Use Extrude with a ‘To’ Extents. Select the inclined face as the terminating plane.

Creating a Concentric Hole

Add a 33 mm diameter thru hole concentric to the cylinder.

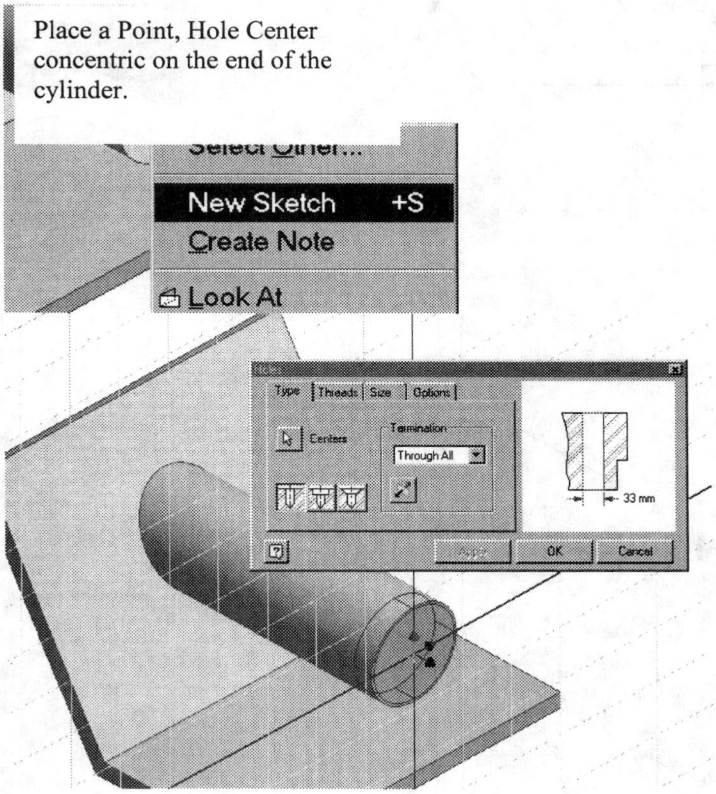

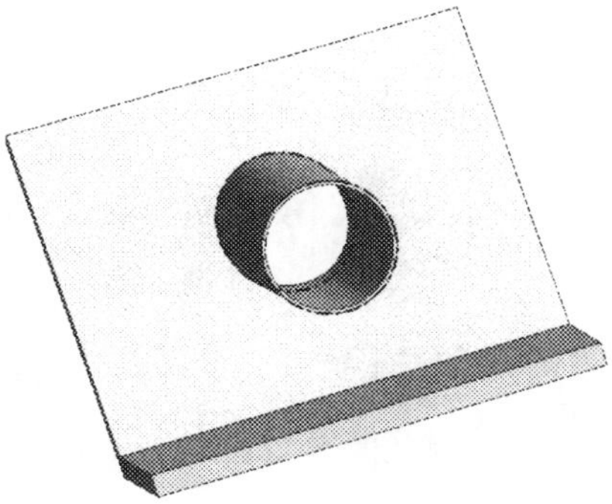

Adding Constant Fillets

Add an R11 fillet to the bend.

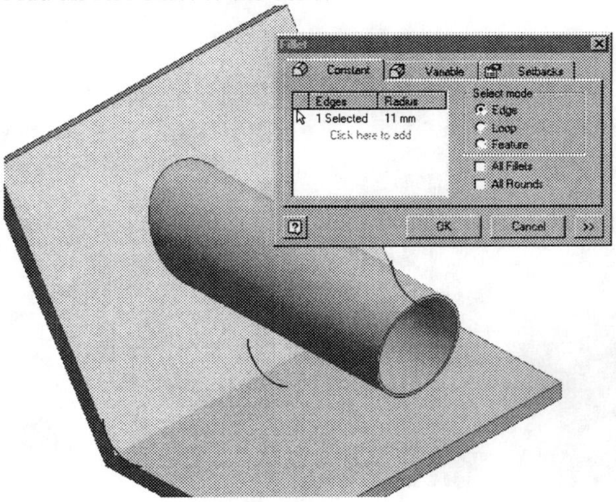

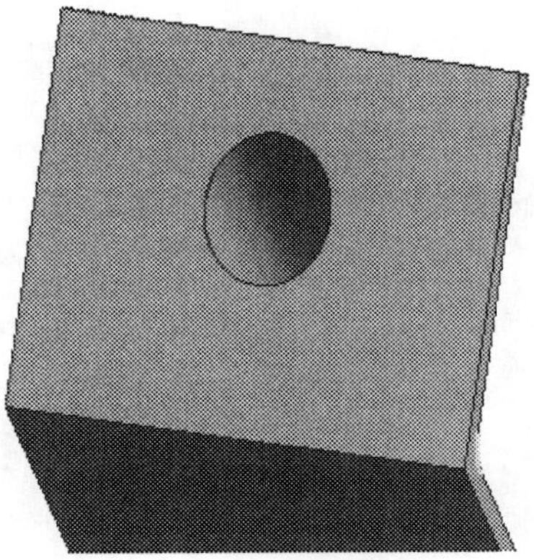

Rotate the part so that you see the back side.

Edit Fillet

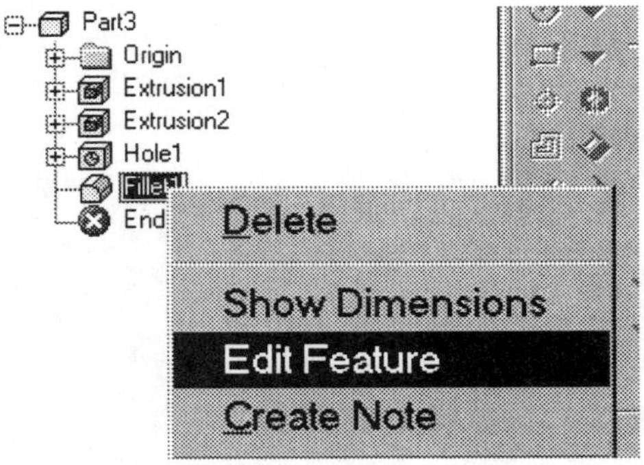

Locate the fillet in the browser.
Right click and select 'Edit Feature'.

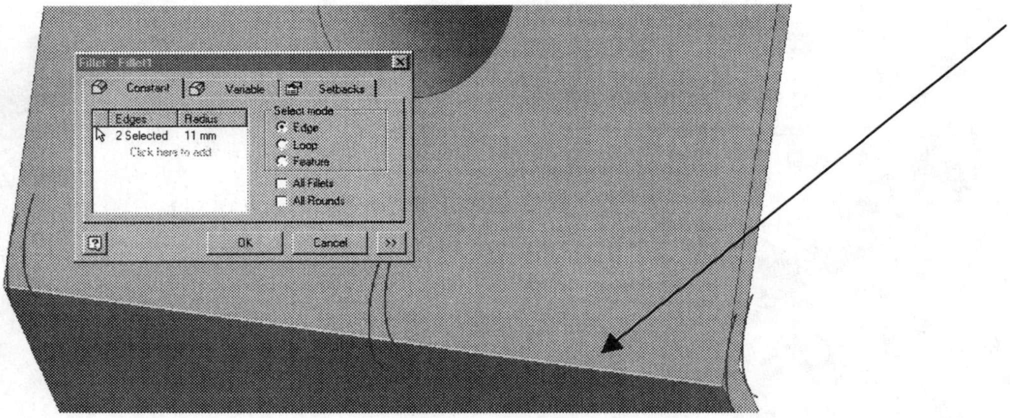

Select the back edge to add to the selection set.
Press 'OK'.

Switch back to an Isometric View.

Insert Design Element

Use the Insert Design Element to add a slot to the inclined plane as shown.

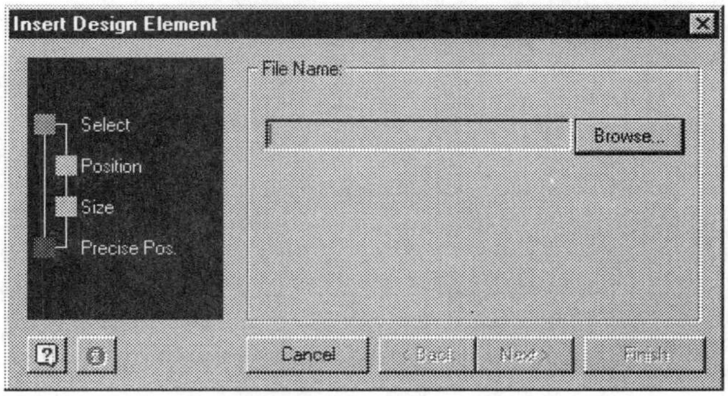

Press the 'Browse' button.

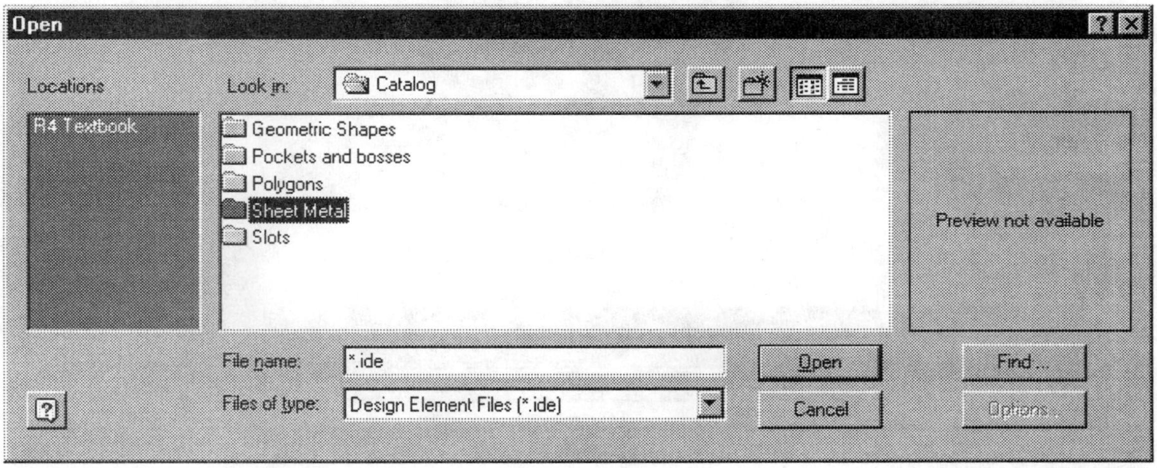

Select the Sheet Metal subdirectory.

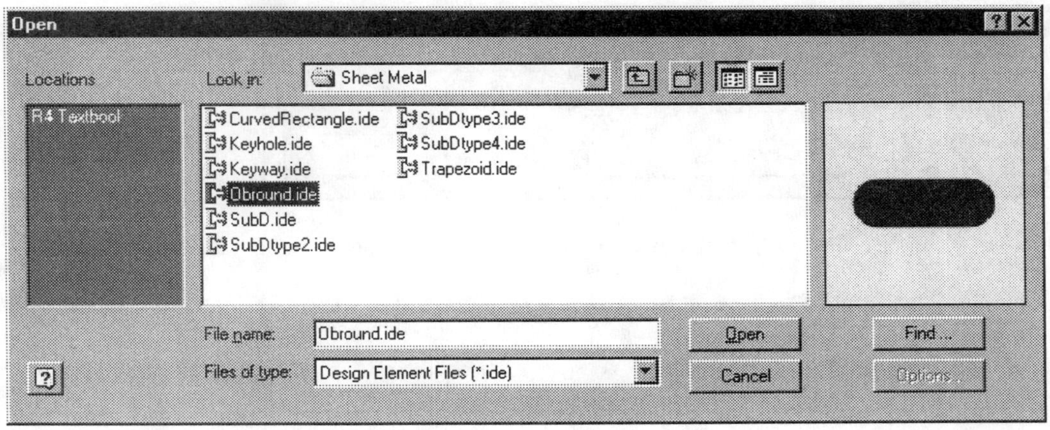

Locate the Obround.ide file under Sheet Metal.

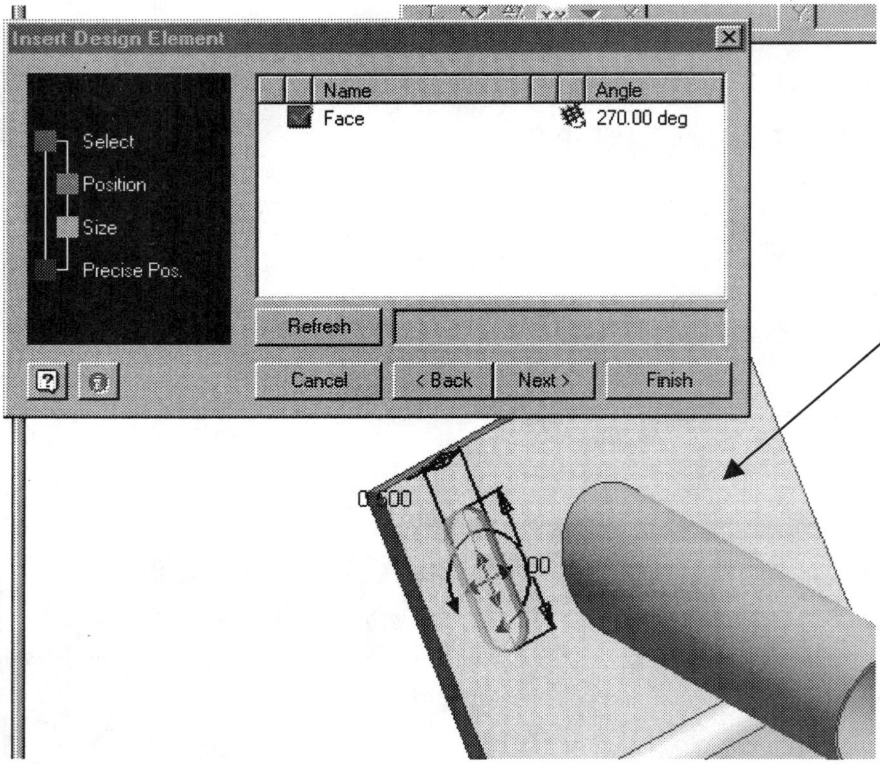

Select this face.

Locate the slot as shown.

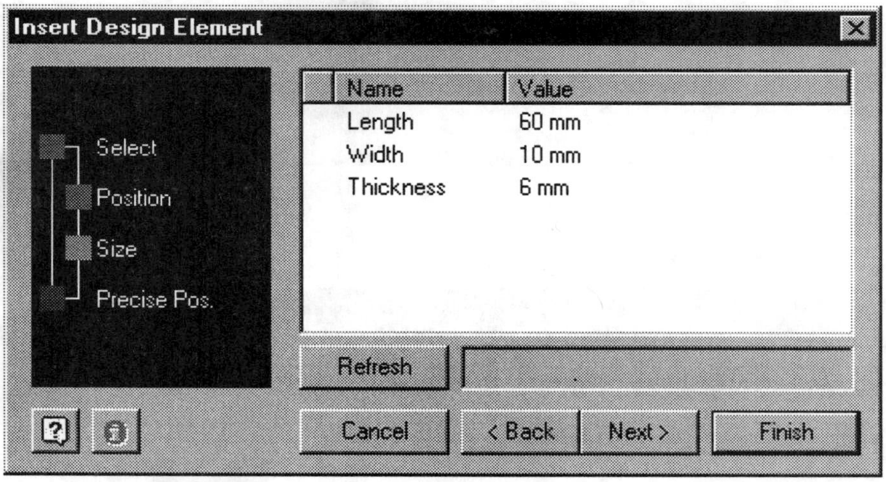

Modify the parameters as shown. Note that we can assign metric values even though the default is inches.

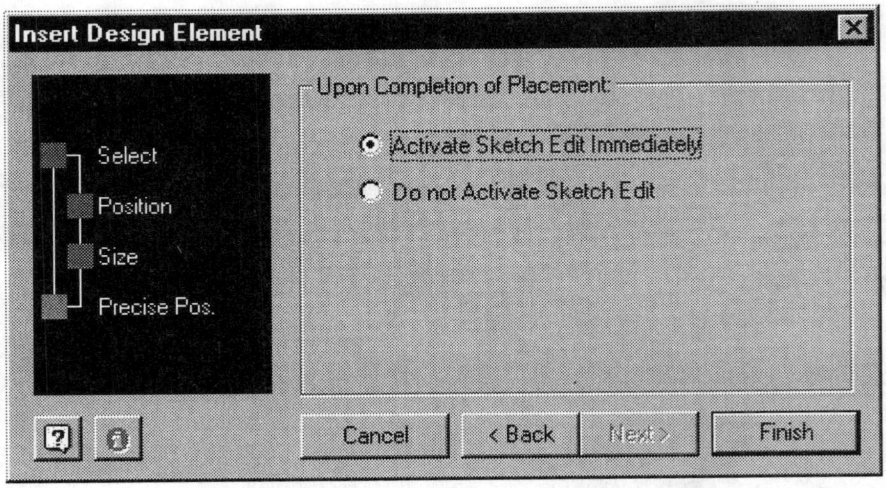

Activate Sketch Mode so we can locate the sketch properly.

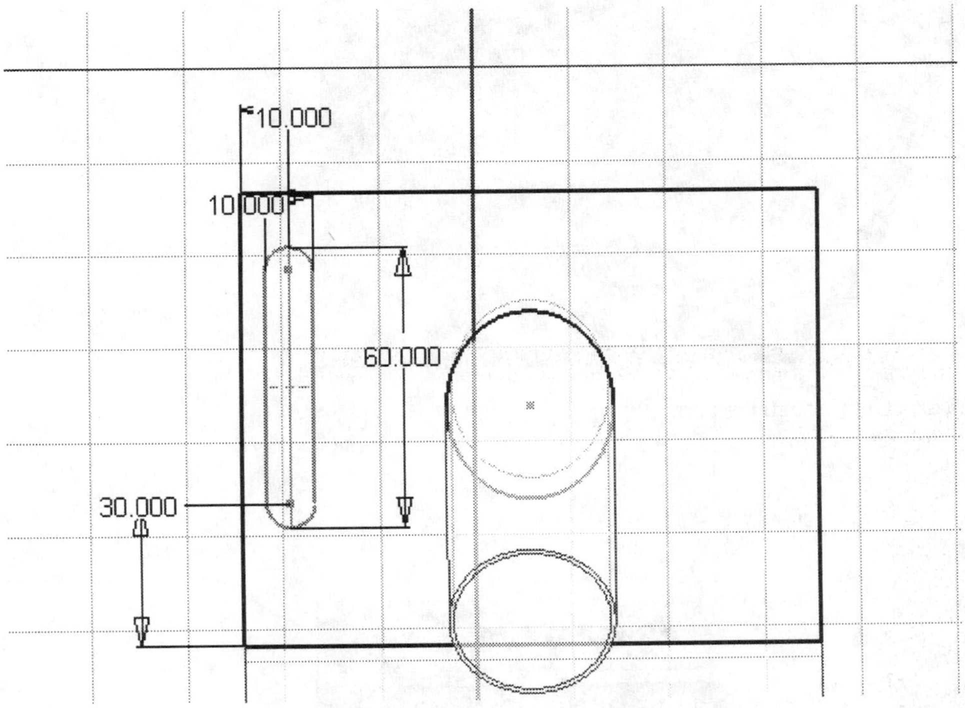

Locate the slot as shown.

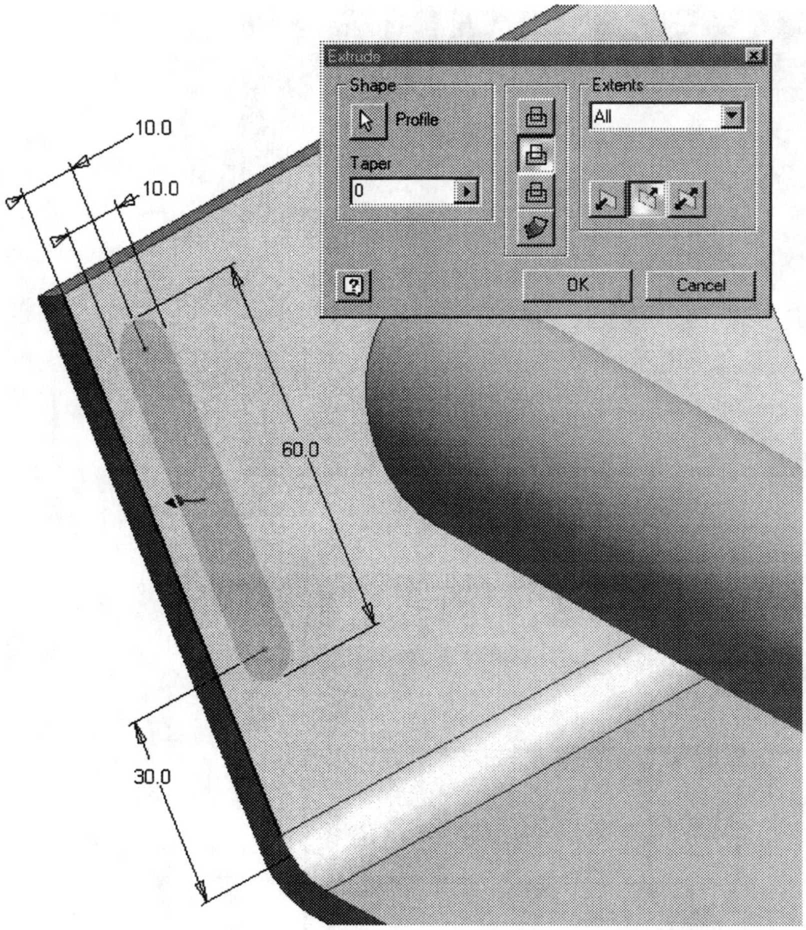

Extrude the sketch as a Cut through the part.

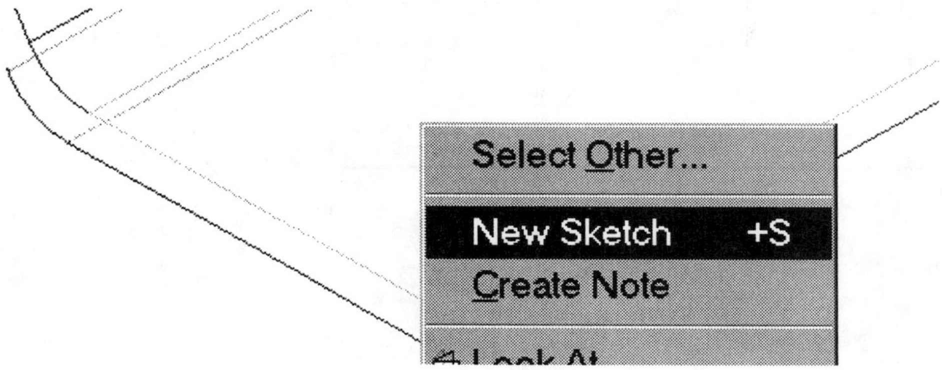

Select the bottom face for a New Sketch.

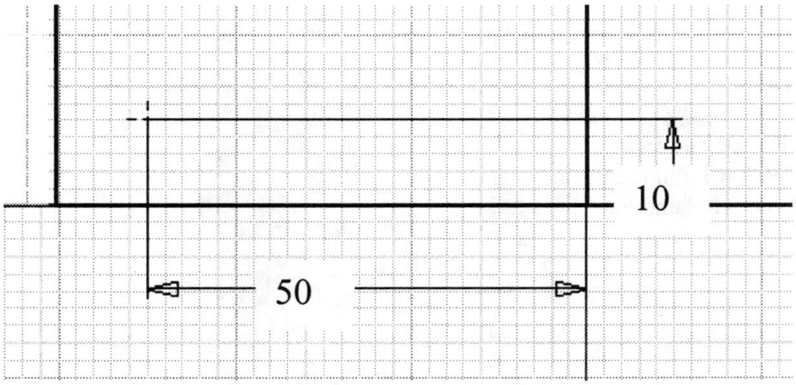

Place a Point, Hole Center as shown.

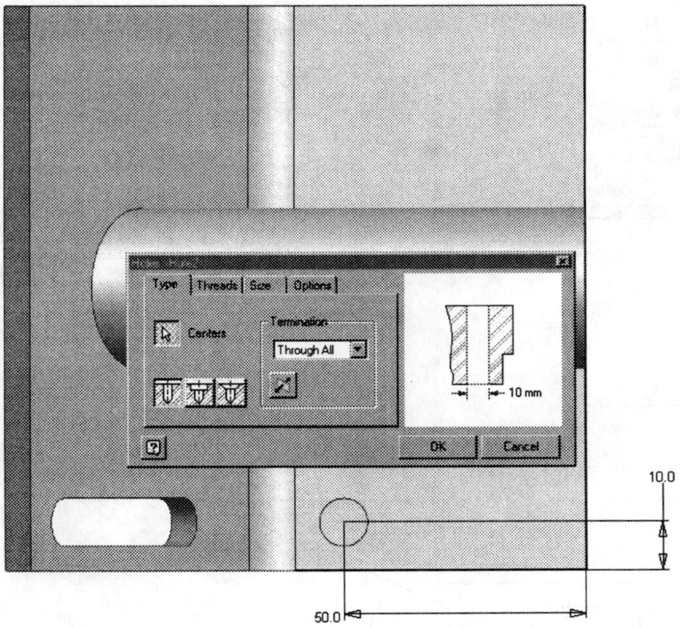

Place a 10 mm through hole as shown.

Create a Rectangular Pattern

Place a Rectangular Pattern of four holes as shown.
Set the Spacing to 40 mm for Direction 1 and the Count to 2.
Set the Spacing to 100 mm for Direction 2 and the Count to 2.

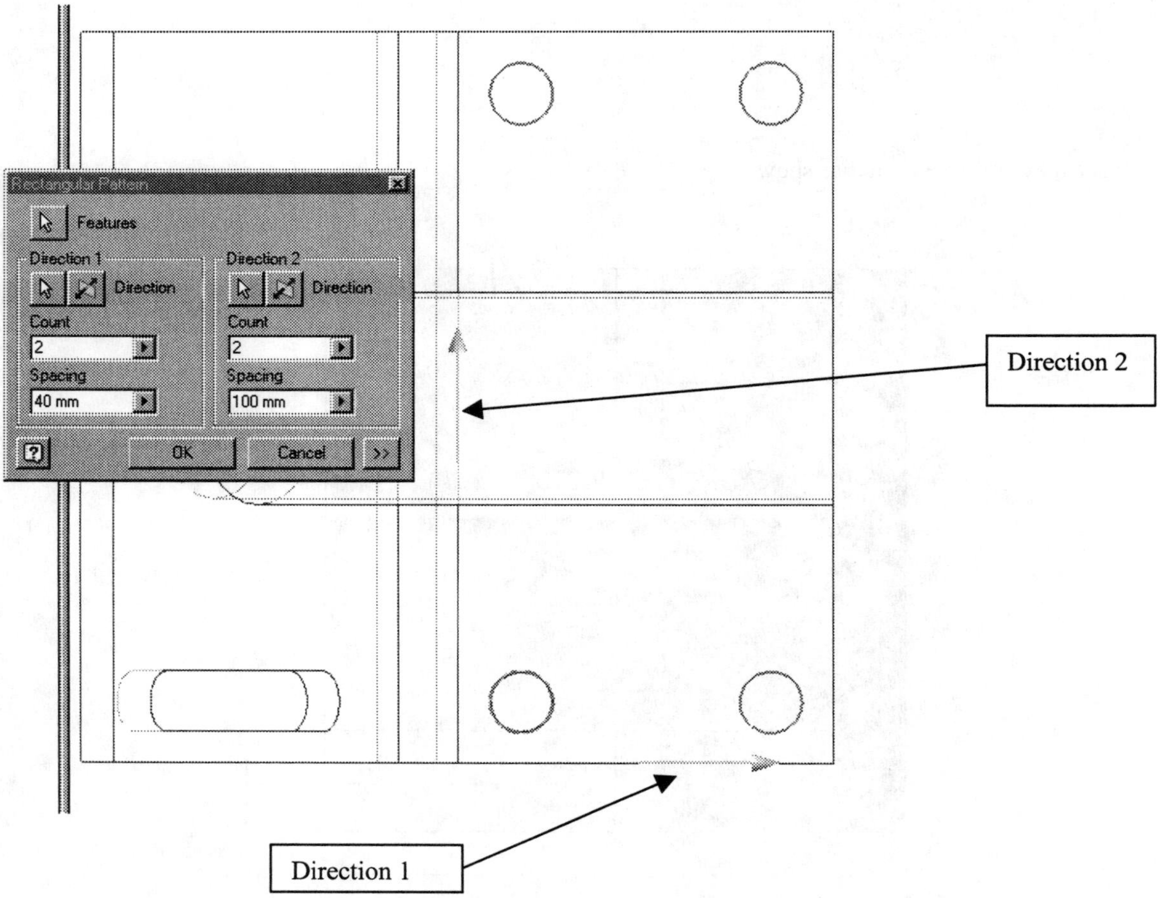

Creating a Rib

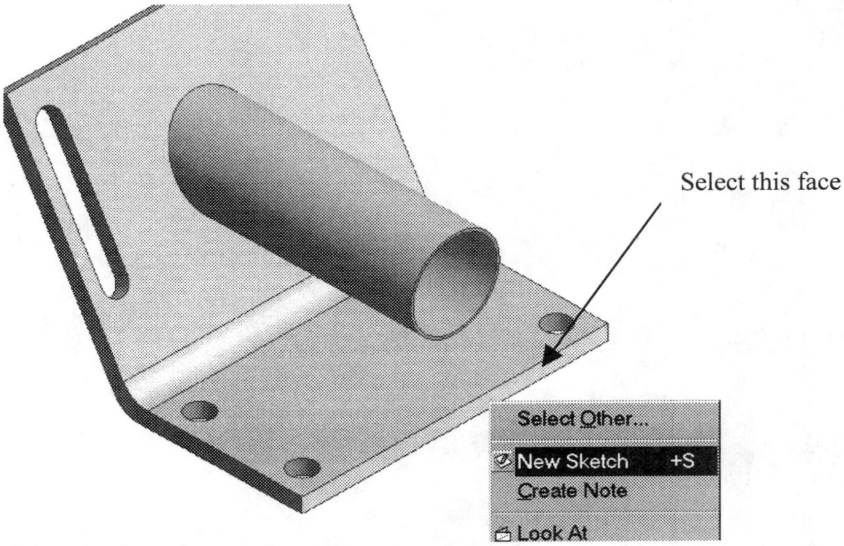

Select the front face as shown for a new sketch.

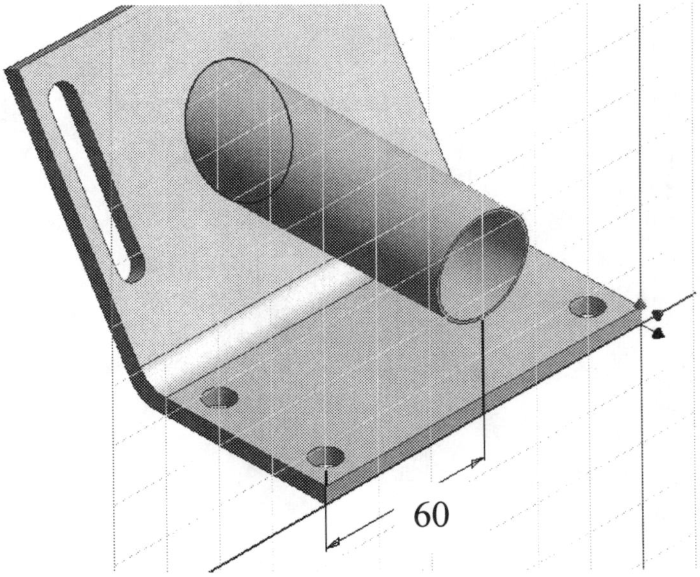

Draw a vertical line as shown.

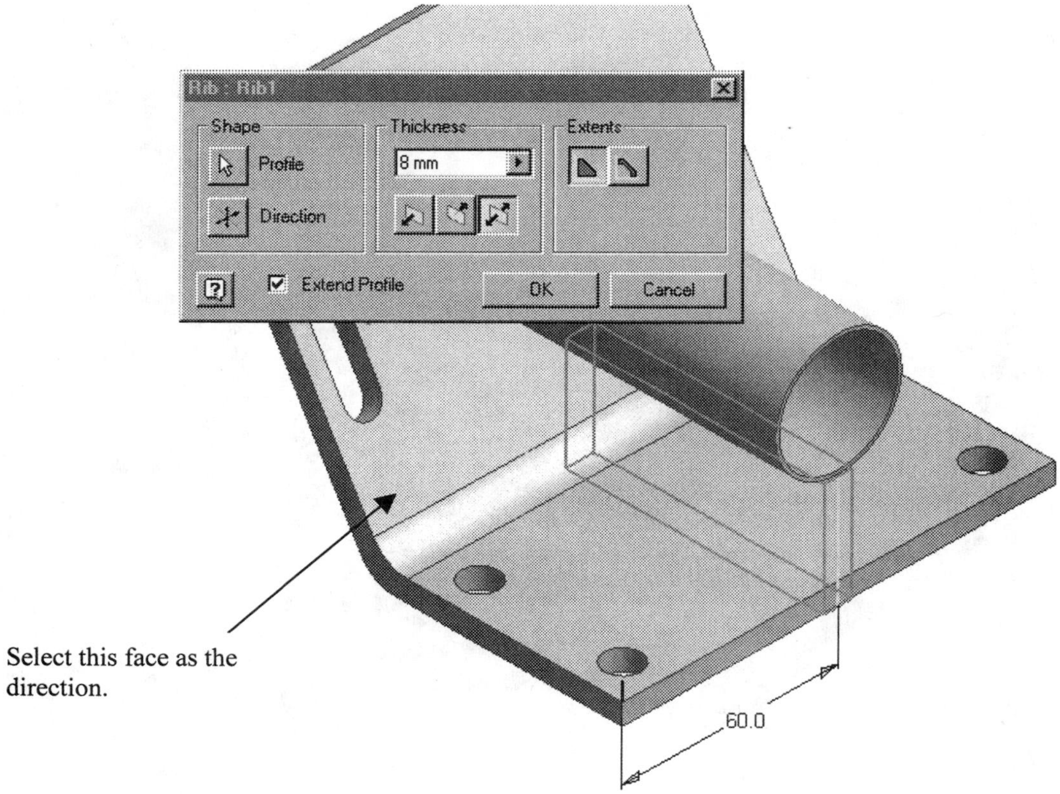

Select the Rib tool.
Select the inclined face for the direction.
Set the thickness to 8 mm.

Set the extrusion direction as Mid-Plane. 
Set the Extents as Next Face.
Press 'OK'.

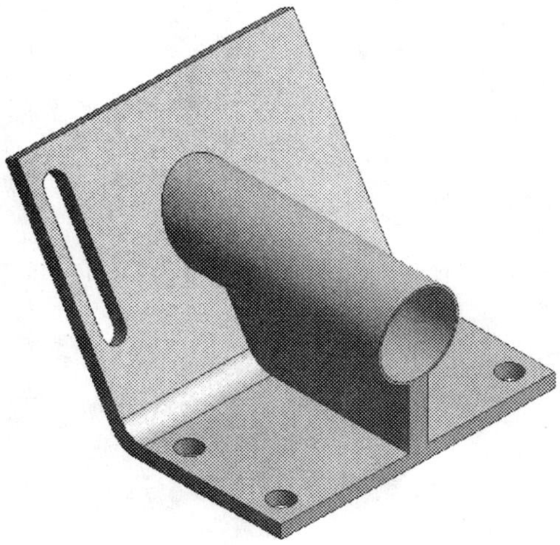

Adding Fillets to a Rib

Add R3 fillets along all the rib's edges.

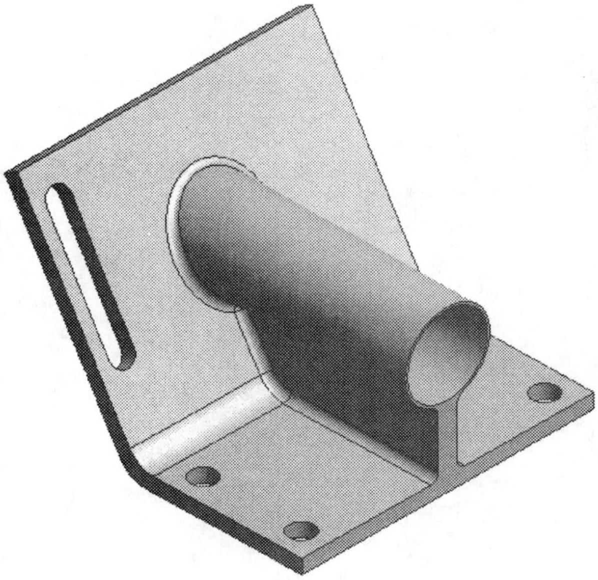

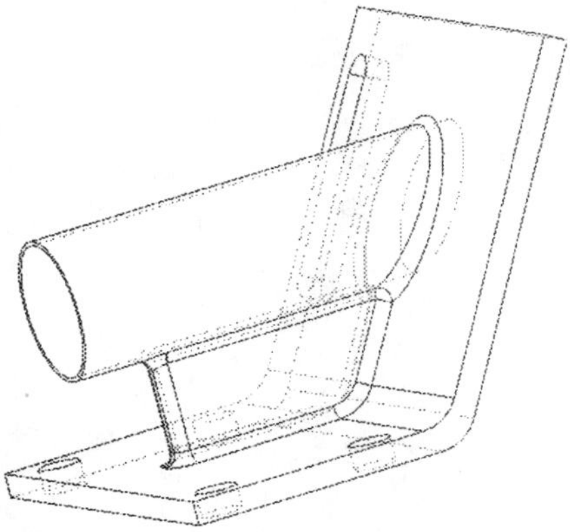

HINT: If you get an error message when adding the fillets. Try adding a few fillets at a time instead of all at one instance.

Add an R10 fillet to the four corners of the bracket.

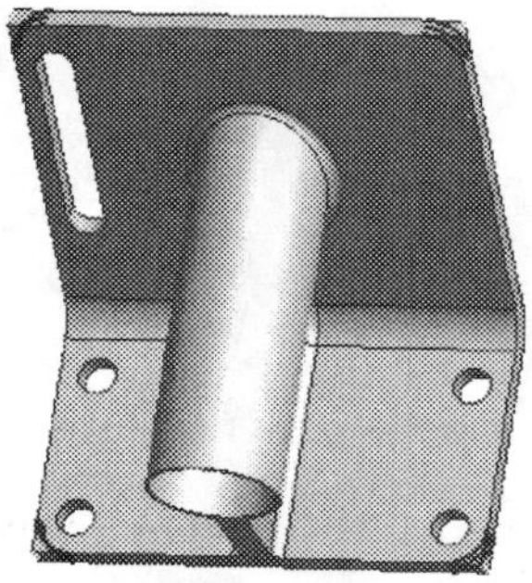

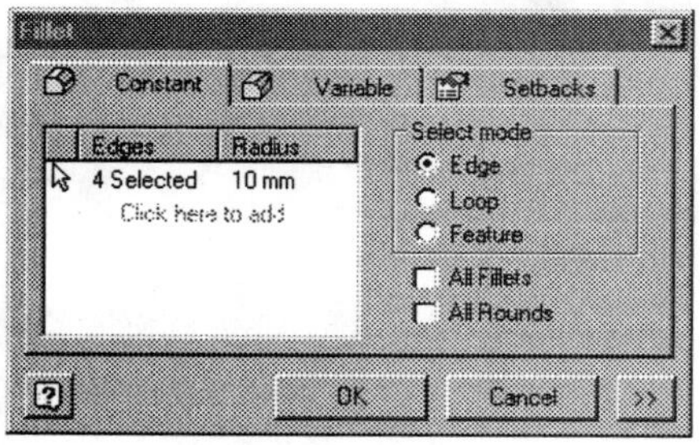

Save the completed bracket as ‘lesson17.ipt’.

Review Questions

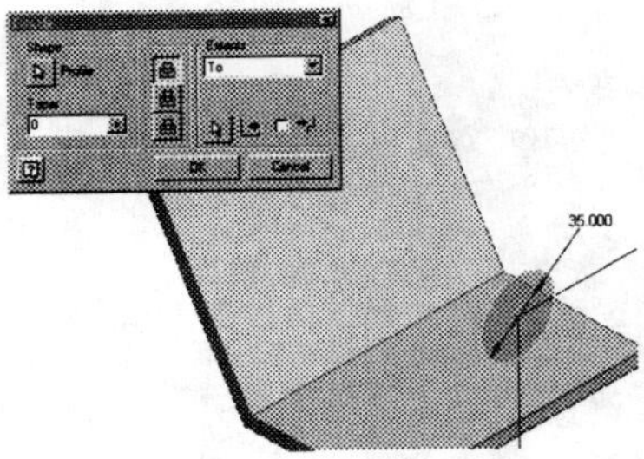

1. In this step, we selected the front edge as our sketch plane but drew our sketch above and away from the front edge. We were able to do this because:

   A. When we select the front edge, we are actually selecting a planar surface
   B. Inventor automatically created a work plane for our use
   C. It's magic
   D. None of the above

2. In the same step we selected the inclined plane as the 'To' Extents. Why did we do this and not specify a distance?

   A. Specifying a distance would require us to measure
   B. If we specified a distance the cylinder would not automatically create an angle when it intersects the inclined face.
   C. Specifying a distance is more work
   D. All of the above

3. When we inserted the Design Element, we were able to modify the parameters. The parameters for the Design Element were in inches even though we were creating a metric part. Why?

   A. Because most machine shops in the United States use standard units.
   B. Because when we set up Inventor we selected ANSI as our default units
   C. Because the design element is an ANSI part
   D. The units for the Design Element are determined when the Design Element is created and saved. The Design Element selected was created using inches.

Match the toolbar icons with their functions:

4. 

5. 

6. 

7. 

8. 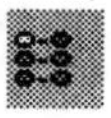

A. RECTANGULAR PATTERN
B. RIB
C. INSERT DESIGN ELEMENT
D. EXTRUDE
E. HOLE

ANSWERS: 1) A; 2) D; 3) D; 4) D; 5) E; 6) B; 7) C; 8) A

Lesson 18
Drawing Management

Learning Objectives:

Upon completion of this lesson, the user will be familiar with:

- Creating BaseViews
- Creating Orthographic Views
- Creating Auxiliary Views
- Creating Section Views
- Creating Detail Views
- Creating Sheets
- Creating Title Blocks
- Modifying Title Blocks
- Managing Views
- Managing Sheets

We do not see either the Drawing Management toolbar or the Drawing Annotation toolbar unless we are in the drawing layout environment.

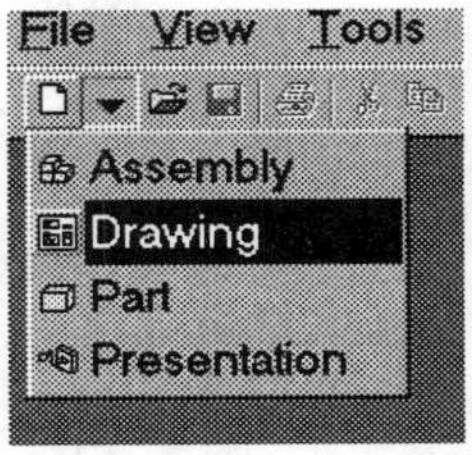

To get there, we select Drawing under the New File pull-down.

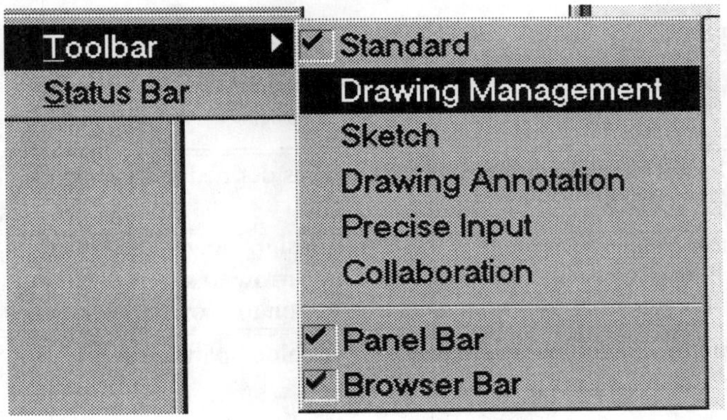

If we look under Toolbar, we see that we have two new drawing toolbars available, plus Sketch, Precise Input, and Collaboration.

The Drawing Management Toolbar

Create View

Create View creates and places a single view into a drawing, independent of any existing views. The dialog box remains open until you close it, enabling you to make changes to view setup before placing the view.

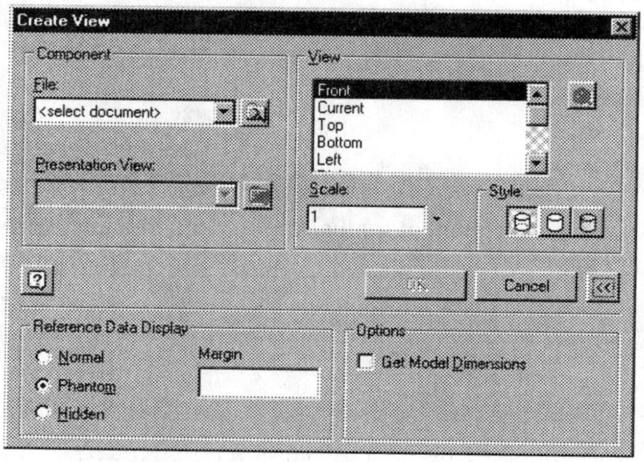

Setup Selects the model and view to document and sets the orientation of the view.	
File	Specifies the part, assembly, or presentation file to use for the drawing view. Specify the file name in one of the following ways. • Enter a file name in the box. • Click the arrow to select from the list of open files. • Click the Explore button to browse for the file.
Design View	This option is available if the selected file is an assembly that contains defined design views. Specifies the assembly design view to use. The name of the active design view is displayed in the box. To use another view in the active design view file, click the arrow to select from the list. To use a design view file that is not currently open, click the button to browse for the file.
Presentation	If the selected file is a sheet metal part, specifies whether to use the folded part or the flat pattern for the view. Click the arrow and select from the list. If the selected file is a presentation document, specifies the presentation view to use. The name of the active presentation view is displayed in the box. To use another view in the active presentation file, click the arrow to select from the list. This option is available only if the selected file is a sheet metal part or is a presentation file that contains several presentation views.
View	Sets the view orientation. Select one of the standard views from the list. If you are creating a view from a presentation view, the last item on item on the list is the saved camera view of the presentation.

Display Style sets the display style for the view. To change the display style, click a button.	
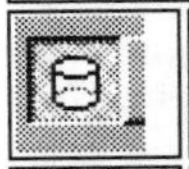	Sets the display to show hidden lines.
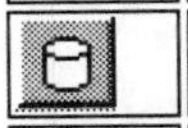	Sets the display to remove hidden lines.
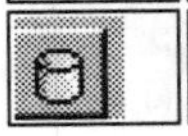	Sets the display to a shaded rendering.

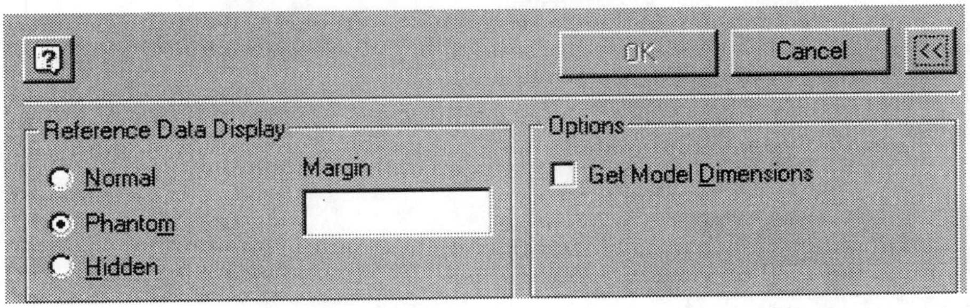

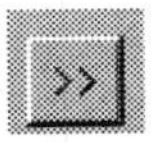

Pressing the More Button reveals more options:

Reference Data Display	
Normal Phantom Hidden	Linetype display for hidden/reference geometry
Margin	Sets the scale for the linetype used
Options	
Get Model Dimensions	Enabling this button automatically inserts model dimensions with the view. Only those dimensions that are planar to the view and have not been used in existing views on the sheet will display.

Scale sets the scale of the view, relative to the part or assembly. Enter the desired scale in the box or click the arrow to select from a list of commonly used scales.

Dimensions set the visibility of model dimensions in the view. Select the check box to display the model dimensions; clear the check box to hide model dimensions.

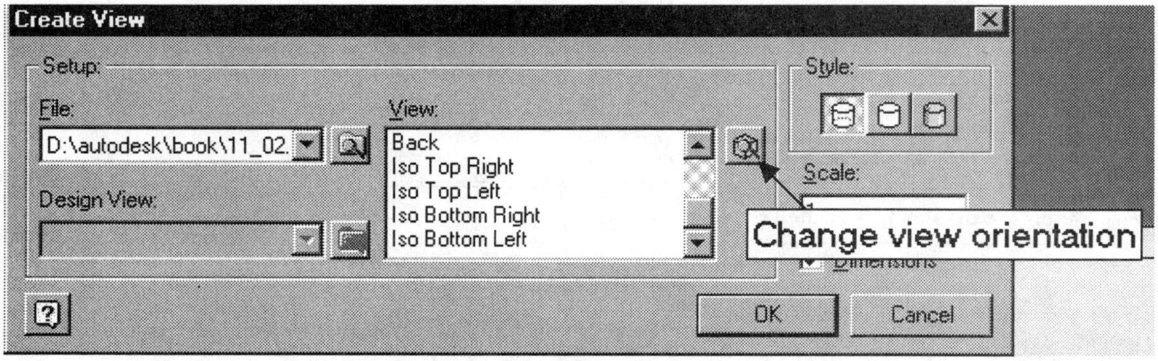

When creating a base view, if the user does not like any of the standard views set up by Inventor, he can select the Change View orientation button.

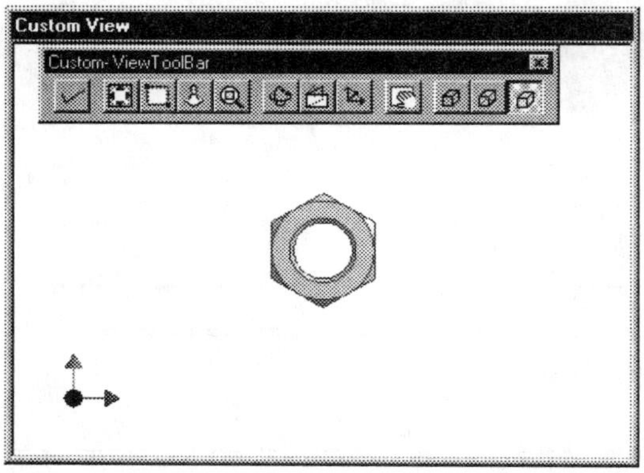

This brings up a special View window where the user can specify the orientation for the base view. Simply use the viewing tools to orient your part in the desired manner and press the check mark to set the base view.

Projected View

You can create a projected view with a first-angle or third-angle projection, depending on the drafting standard for the drawing. You must have a base view before you can create a projected view. Use the Projected View button on the Drawing Management toolbar.

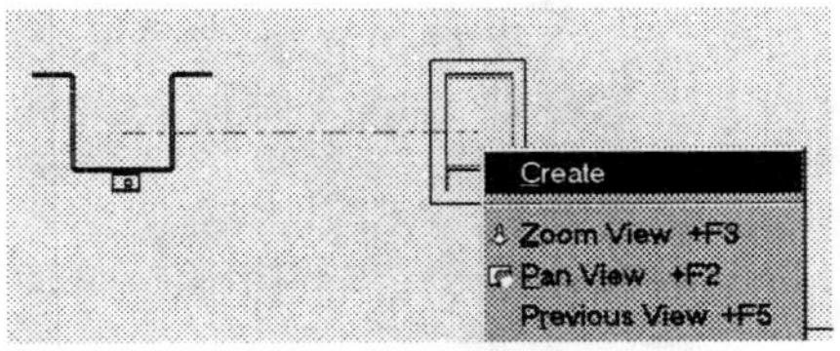

1. Click the Projected View button.
2. Select the base view for the projection.
3. Move the preview to the desired location and click to place the view. As you move the preview, the orientation of the projected view changes to reflect its relationship to the base view.
4. Continue placing projected views by moving the preview and clicking.
5. To quit placing projected views, right-click and select Create from the menu.

TIP: Orthographic projections are aligned to the base view and inherit its scale and display settings. Isometric projections are not aligned to the base view. They default to the scale of the base view but do not update if you change the scale of the base view.

Auxiliary View

Places an auxiliary view by projecting from an edge or line in a base view. The resulting view is aligned to the base view.

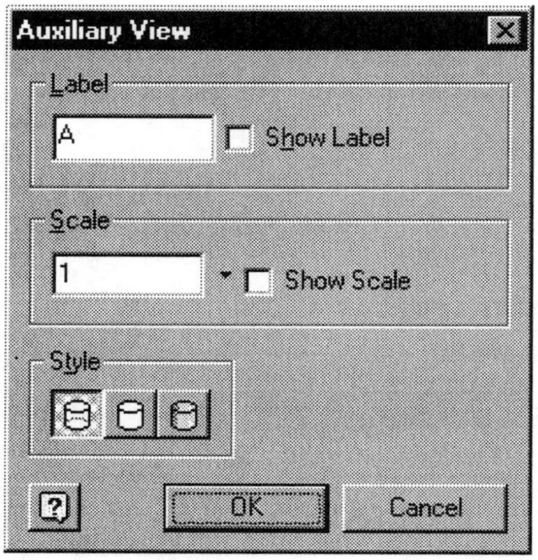

The Label specifies the view label determined by the active drawing standard. To change the label, select the label in the box and enter the new label.	
Show Label	Displays or hides the view label. Select the check box to display the label; clear the check box to hide the label.
Show Scale	Displays or hides the view scale. Select the check box to display the scale; clear the check box to hide the scale.
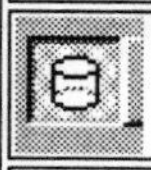	Sets the display to show hidden lines.
	Sets the display to remove hidden lines.
	Sets the display to a shaded rendering.

Section View

Creates a full, half, offset, or aligned section view from a specified base view. You can also use Section View to create a view projection line for an auxiliary or partial view. A section view is aligned to its base view.

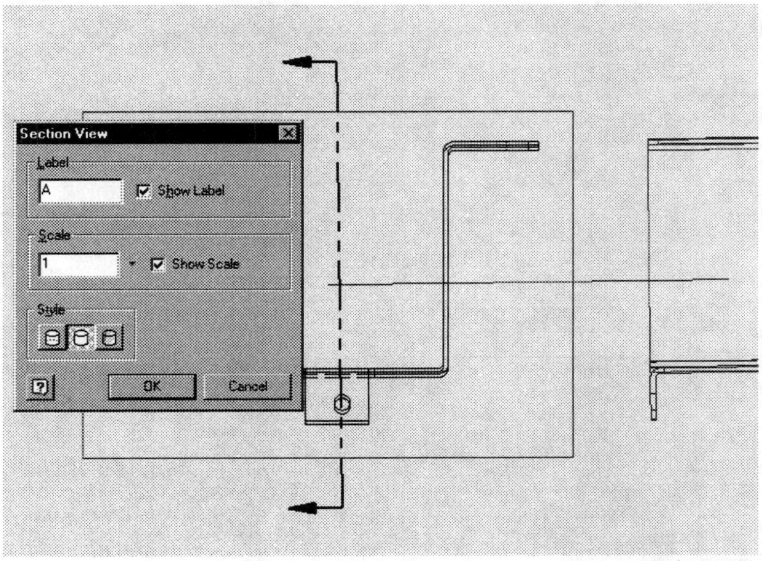

The Label specifies the view label determined by the active drawing standard. To change the label, select the label in the box and enter the new label.	
Show Label	Displays or hides the view label. Select the check box to display the label; clear the check box to hide the label.
Show Scale	Displays or hides the view scale. Select the check box to display the scale; clear the check box to hide the scale.
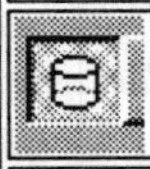	Sets the display to show hidden lines.
	Sets the display to remove hidden lines.
	Sets the display to a shaded rendering.

TIP: To place the view without alignment to the base view, press Ctrl as you move and place the preview.

Detail View

Creates and places a detail drawing view of a specified portion of a base view. The view is created without an alignment to the base view.

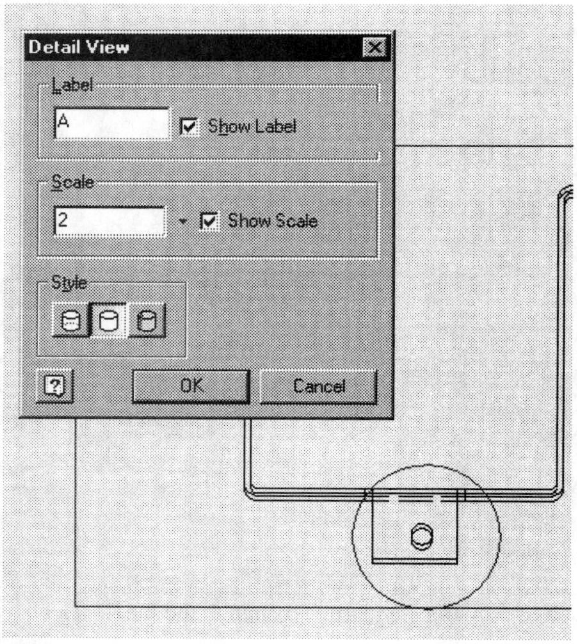

The Label specifies the view label determined by the active drawing standard. To change the label, select the label in the box and enter the new label.	
Show Label	Displays or hides the view label. Select the check box to display the label; clear the check box to hide the label.
Show Scale	Displays or hides the view scale. Select the check box to display the scale; clear the check box to hide the scale.
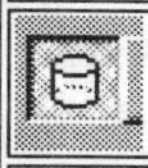	Sets the display to show hidden lines.
	Sets the display to remove hidden lines.
	Sets the display to a shaded rendering.

New Sheet

Adds an additional sheet or page to the drawing layout.

Draft View

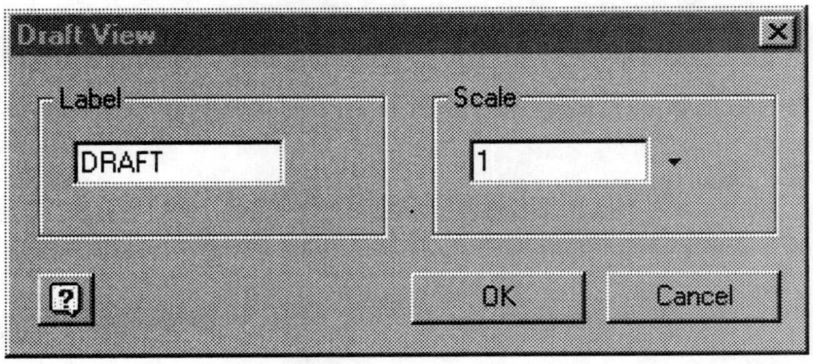

The Draft View is actually a layer that can be used to store redlines, notes, and additional geometry.
Users can use the Draft View to mark up drawings for engineering changes.
The Draft View automatically enables the Sketch Toolbar.

Edit Sheet

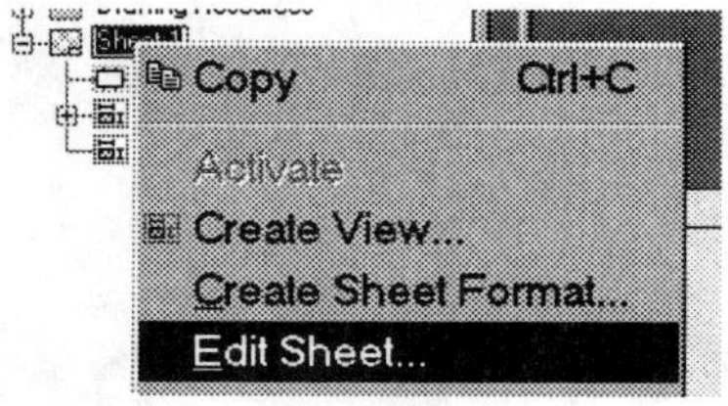

You can change the sheet size or settings by selecting the Sheet in the browser, right click and select 'Edit Sheet'.

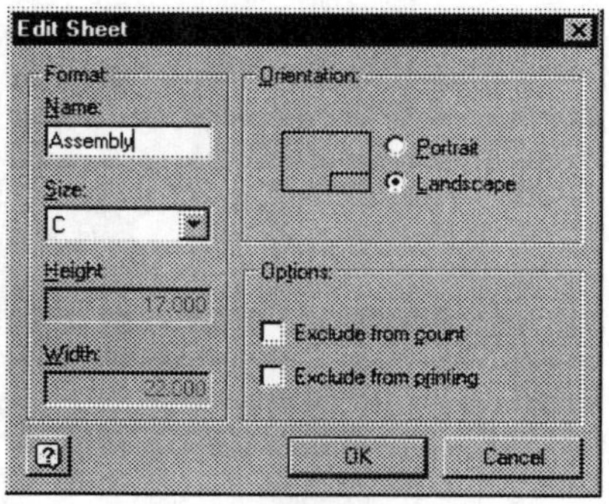

Size	Specifies a standard sheet size or format. Click the arrow and select the size or sheet format from the list. The standard sheet sizes are at the top of the list and current sheet formats are at the bottom of the list. Changing the sheet size changes the settings in the Height and Width boxes. Select Custom Size from the list to enter a different height and width.
Height	Sets the height of the sheet in drawing units. If you specify a standard size or sheet format in the Size box, this value is set automatically and the box is dimmed. To set a non-standard Height, select Custom Size and then enter a value in this box.
Width	Sets the width of the sheet in drawing units. If you specify a standard size or sheet format in the Size box, this value is set automatically and the box is dimmed. To set a non-standard Width, select Custom Size and then enter a value in this box.
Orientation	Sets the orientation of the page. Portrait sets the short edges of the paper at the top and bottom of the page. Landscape sets the long edges of the paper at the top and bottom of the page.
Options specify whether the page is to be counted and printed with the rest of the drawing.	
Exclude from count	Specifies whether to exclude the selected sheet in the count of sheets in the drawing. Select the check box to exclude the sheet from the count; clear the check box to include the sheet in the count.
Exclude from printing	Specifies whether to exclude the selected sheet when printing the drawing. Select the check box to exclude the sheet from printing; clear the check box to print the sheet with the drawing.

TIP: The name of the sheet can be changed by clicking in the Sheet Name edit box and typing in a new name.

Create a Sheet Format

You can define one or several sheet formats and add them to the Drawing Resources folder. Once you add a sheet format to a drawing, it can be used to add new sheets to that drawing.

1. Add a new sheet to the drawing, using either the default sheet or one of the existing sheet formats.
2. Set the size and orientation for the sheet.
3. Add the standard components to the sheet, including a border, title block, and standard views. Note: To be included in the format, views must be completely within the border of the sheet.

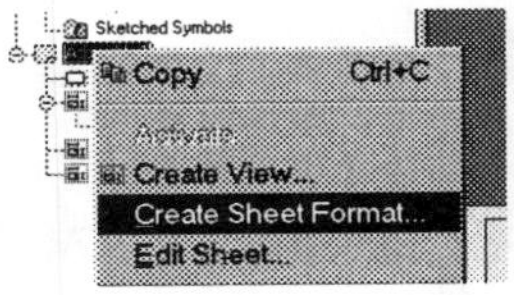

4. Right-click the sheet and select Create Sheet Format from the menu.

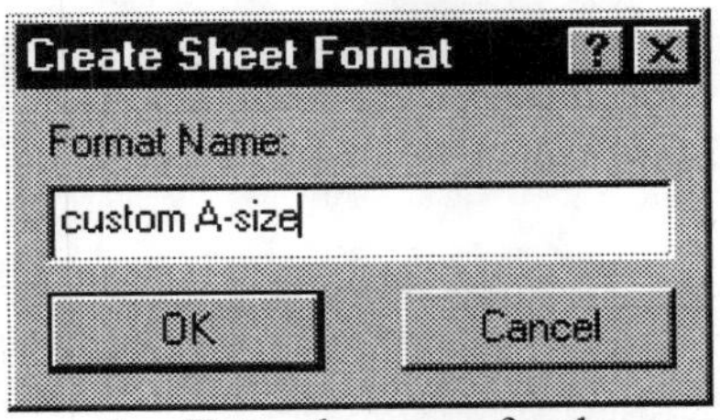

5. Enter the name for the new sheet format in the edit box.

Note: When you save the sheet format, it is added to the Drawing Resources folder in the browser. To add a sheet using the new format, expand Drawing Resources and Format, and then double-click the desired sheet.

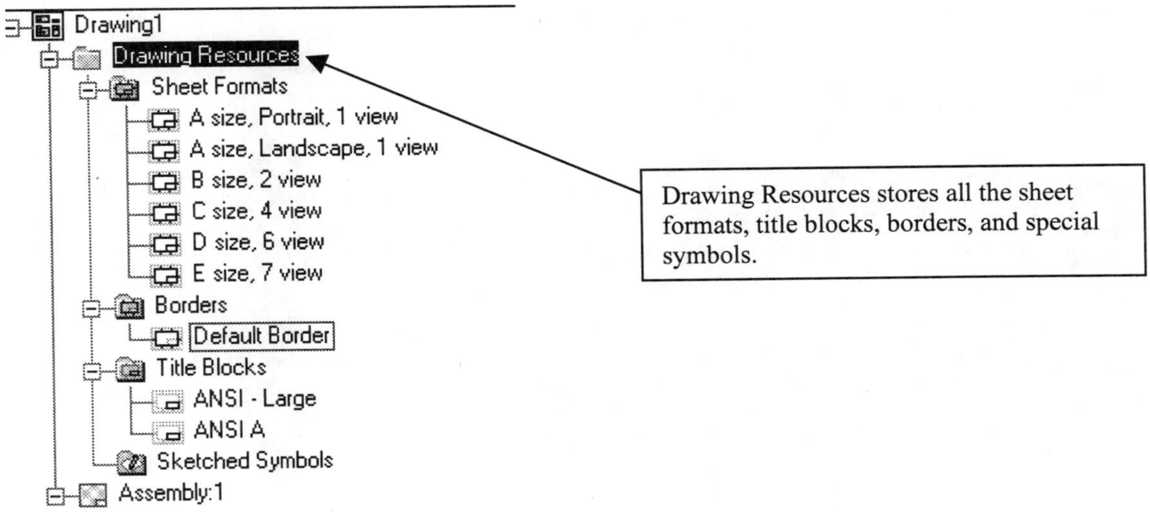

Define New Title Block

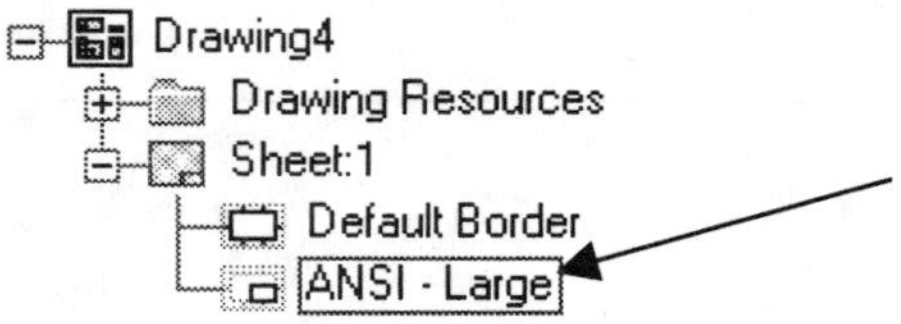

This is the default title block placed when a new drawing files is created.

Inventor automatically places a Border and a title block when we start a new drawing.

To remove the title block from the drawing, select in the browser, right click and select 'Delete'.

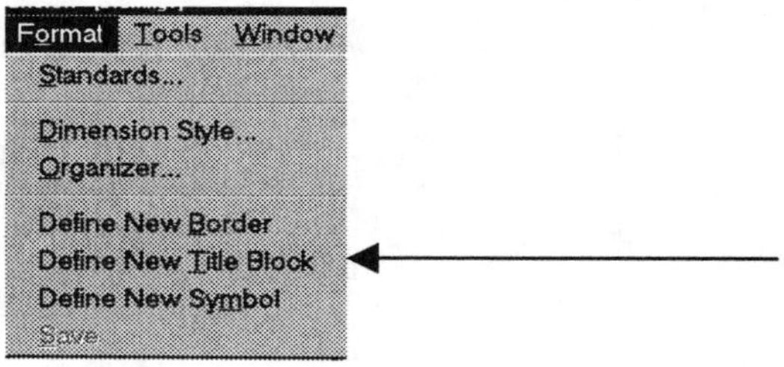

Format->Define New Title Block changes our graphics screen and panel tool bar to the Define New Title Block mode.

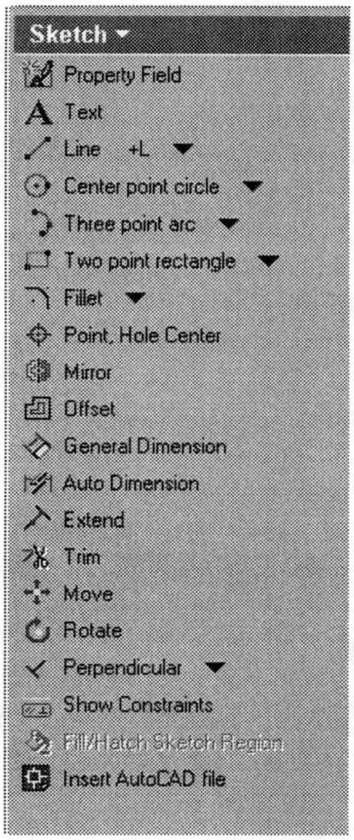

When we are in Define New Title Block mode, a special Sketch toolbar is available to us. The tool bar has all of the sketch tools we are familiar with, plus some new ones.

The unique Title Block sketch tools are:

- Property Field
- Fill Sketch Region

Property Field

To create an attribute for the title block, use the Create Property Field tool.

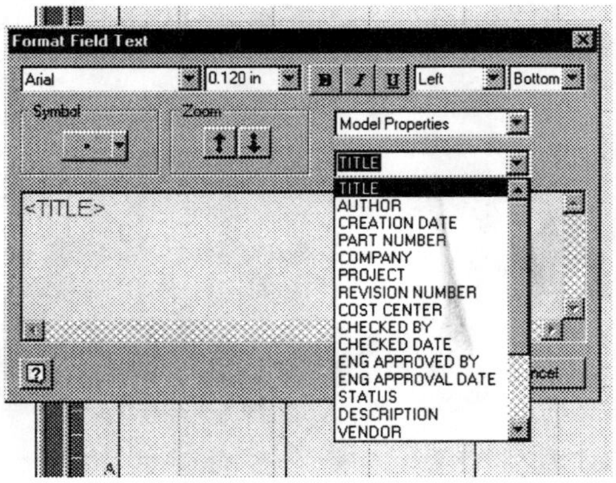

Inventor has many pre-defined fields available for use in a title block. The data assigned to the property fields is stored in the File Properties dialog box.

TIP: Adding text labels for the properties is a separate operation; use the Text button on the sketch toolbar.

Use the Property Field button on the Drawing Sketch toolbar to add part number, creation date, sheet number, and other properties to a title block format, border format, or sketched symbol. When you use property fields, information is automatically updated when in the drawing when changes are made to the file.

1. Create a new drawing resource or open an existing drawing resource to edit it.
2. Click the Property Field button on the Sketch toolbar.
3. In the graphics window, click to place the insertion point for the property.
4. In the Format Field Text dialog box, select the category and property to add.

The property name is displayed in the edit box as a placeholder for the property value. You can select it and use the options in the dialog box to change the text formatting. The formatting is applied to the property value when it is displayed in the drawing or printed.

Fill/Hatch Sketch Region

This tool allows the user to create special paint effects by adding color to any closed geometry, such as circles and rectangles. This tool is greyed out until a closed polygon is added to the Title Block.

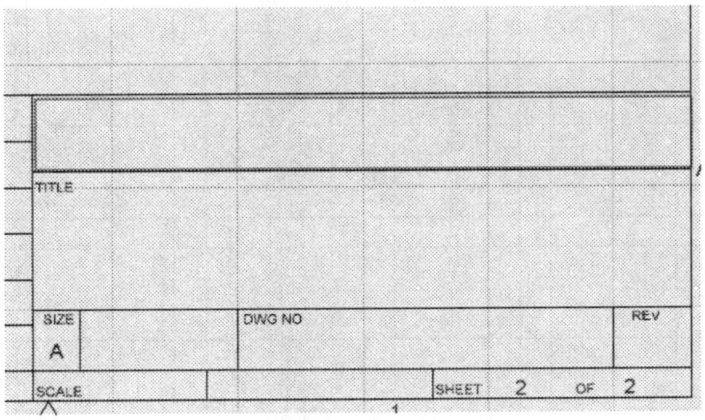

Draw a rectangle in the title block area.

Select the Fill/Hatch Sketch Region tool.
Select the rectangle or the profile you wish to fill with color.

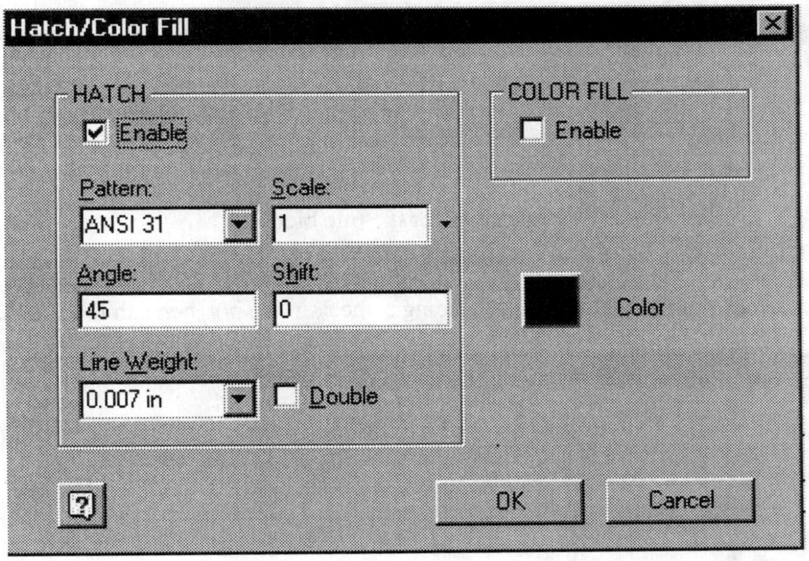

The Hatch/Color Fill dialog appears. Pick the Enable box to place a check mark.
Press the square next to the word Color.

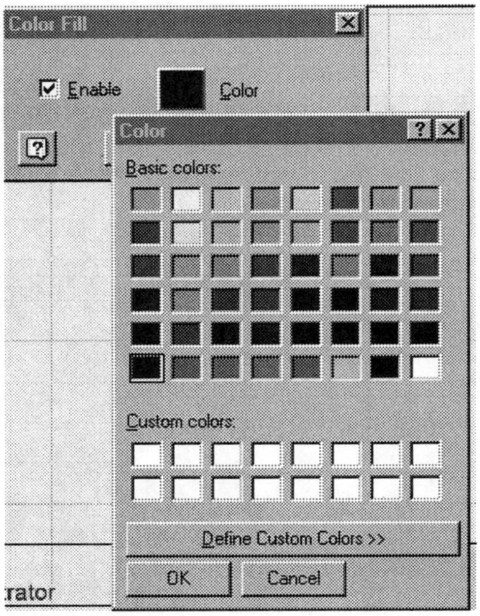

Select a color and press 'OK'.

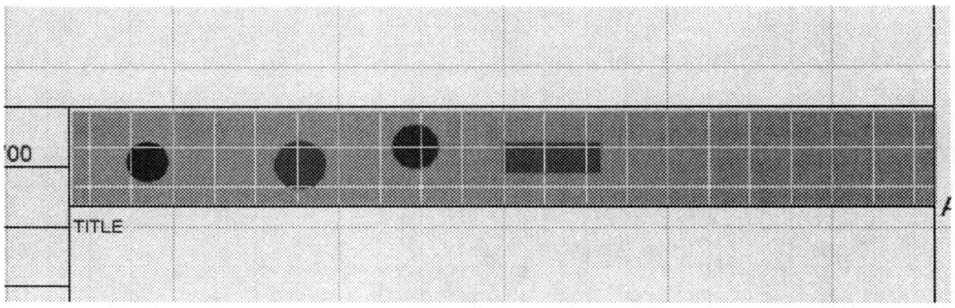

The user can use the sketch tools to create multi-colored graphics for the title block.
Simply create the desired shapes and then fill in the color.

In order to create a Hatch pattern, enable the Hatch pattern by placing a check in the box beneath the Hatch.

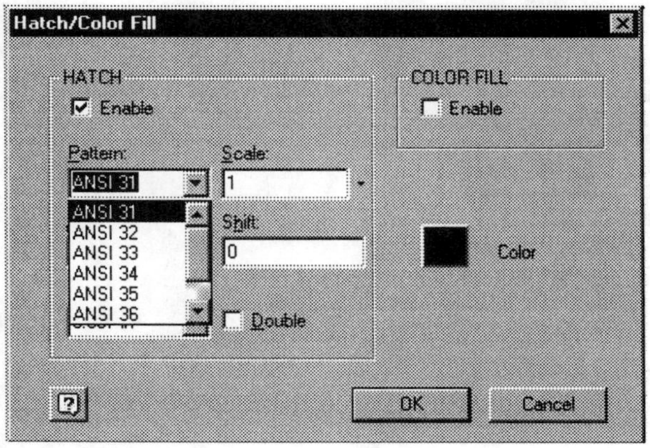

The Pattern dropdown contains a list of available hatch patterns.

To change a hatch pattern that has been placed, simply pick on the hatch pattern.

Creating a Custom Title Block

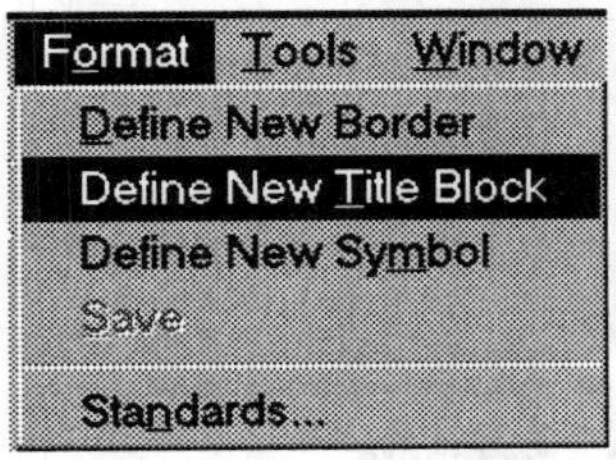

If we are not currently in the Define New Title Block mode, we switch to that mode by using Format->Define New Title Block.

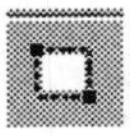
Use ZOOM WINDOW to zoom into the title block area.

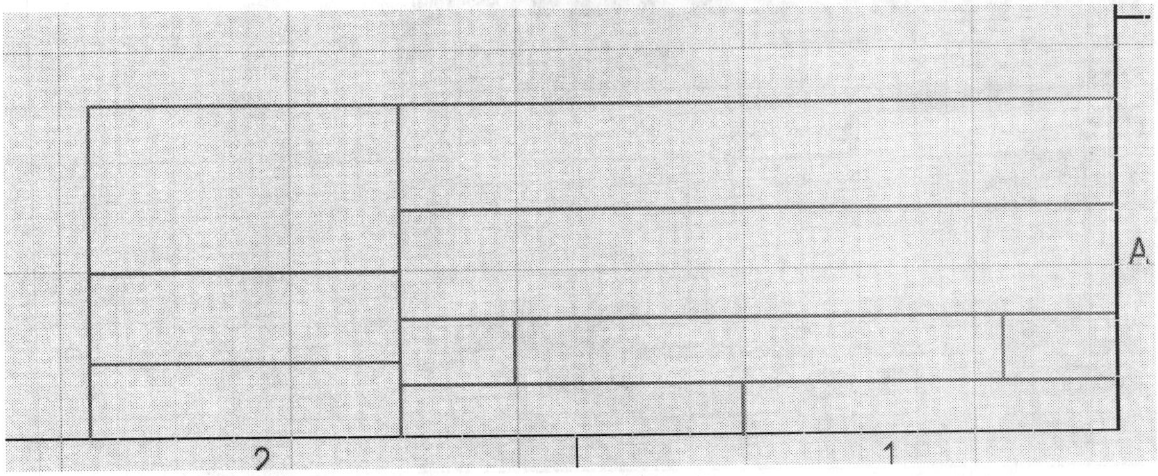

Draw the lines as shown using the Line tool.

TIP. When you use dimensions to set the size of elements in a title block or border, the dimensions are hidden when you finish editing

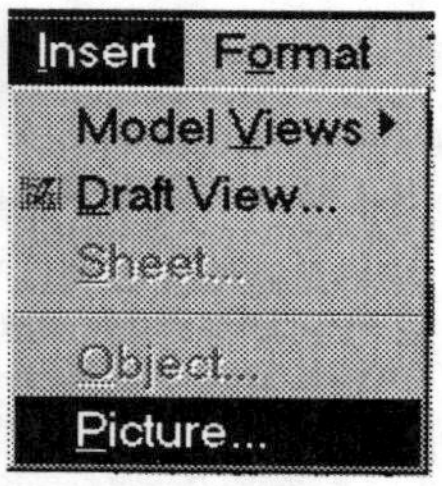

To insert a company logo, use Insert->Picture.

Next, indicate the area the picture is to be placed by picking two points to form a rectangle.

> **TIP:** Inventor R4 will only accept bitmaps for insertion, so your file must have a *.bmp extension.

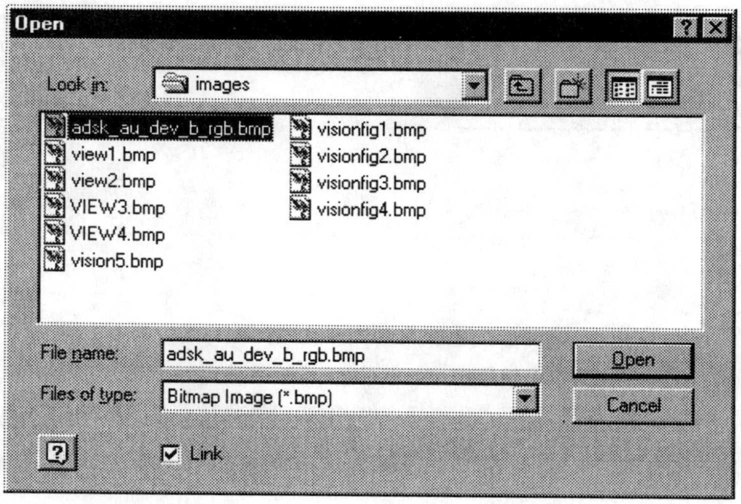

Locate the desired file and select 'Open'.

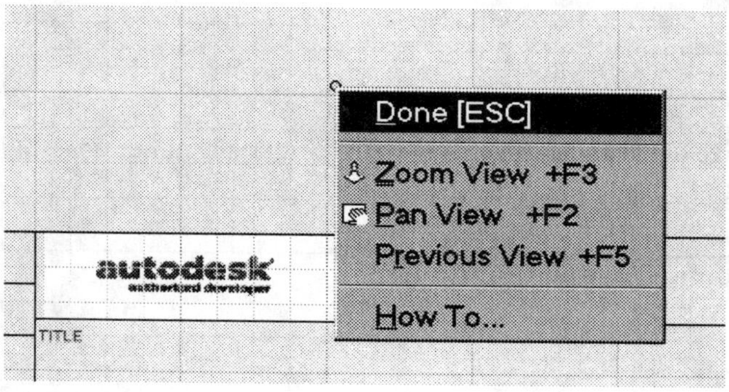

Right click and select 'Done'.

Select the Property Field tool. Draw a rectangle next to the logo to indicate the location for company information.

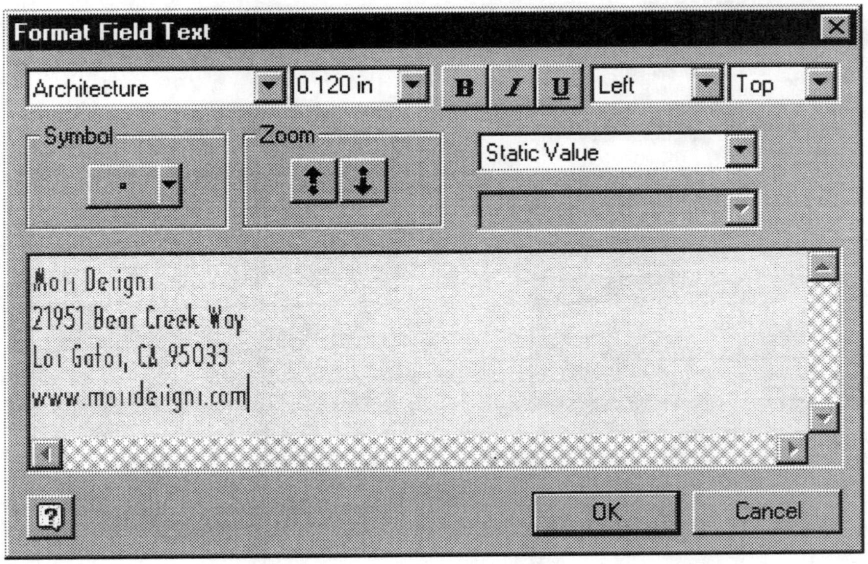

Select Static Value. Set the desired font and type in your company information. A Static Value means that the data entered will not be changed. This is similar to a constant attribute in AutoCAD.

Select 'OK'.

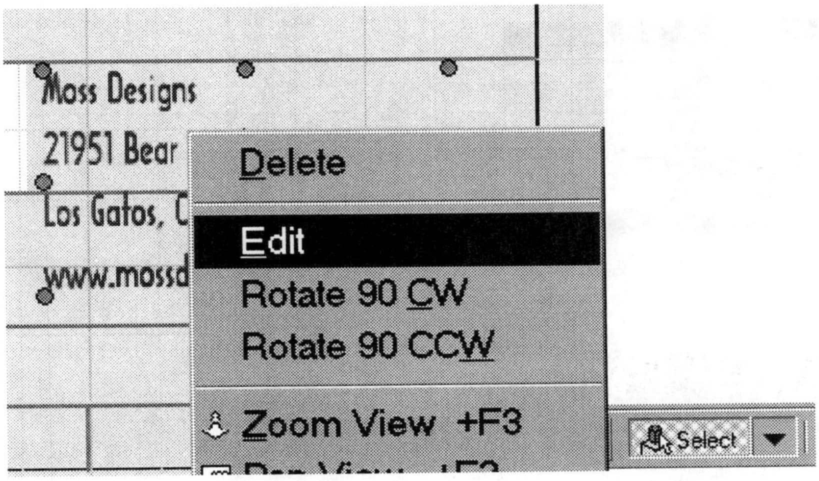

To modify a Property Field

If the results are not what we want, we simply activate the Select mode and click on the text. Right click to select 'Edit'.

To add a prompted entry (similar to an attribute), select the Property Field tool again.

Draw a rectangle to indicate where to place the text.

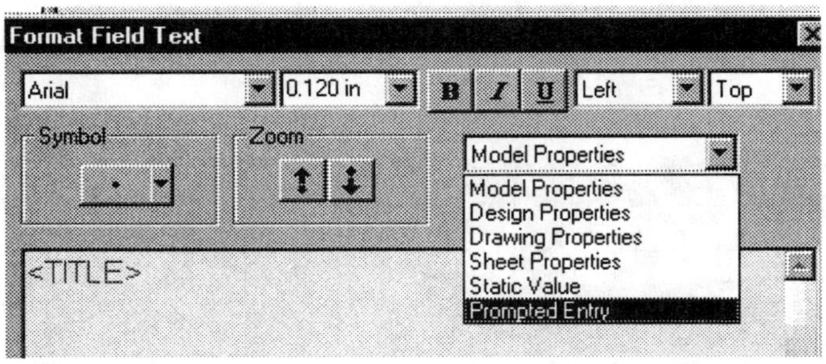

Select Prompted Entry.

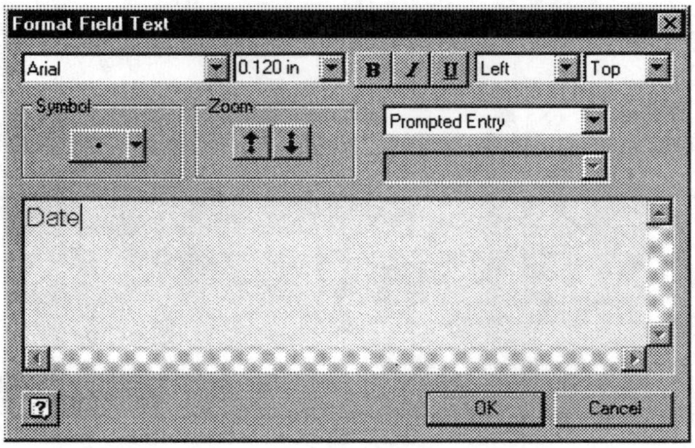

Type in the desired prompt.

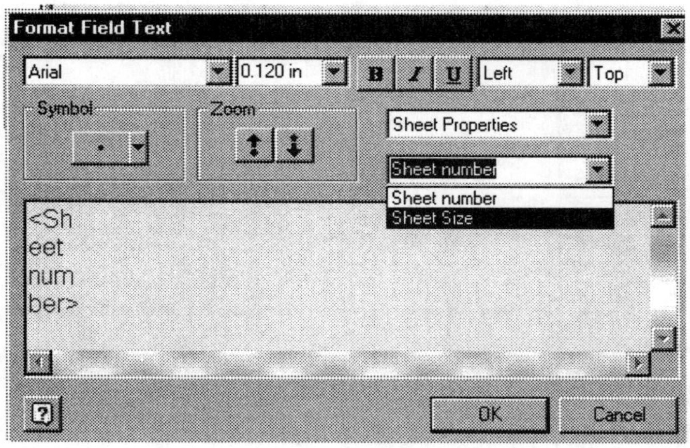

To add a field for sheet Size, select Sheet Properties and select Sheet Size.

TIP: By using Sheet Properties instead of using a Prompted Entry, the value will automatically update when the user redefines the sheet properties in the browser.

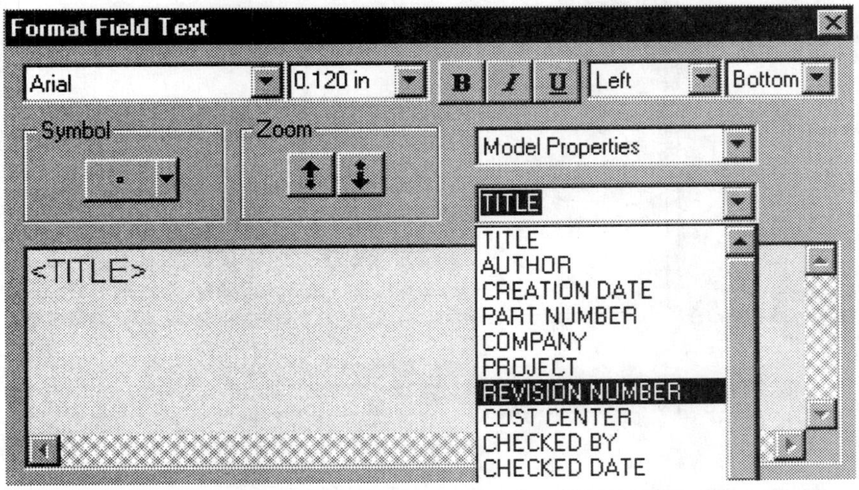

To add the revision field, use Model Properties->Revision Number.

This value is set under File->Properties. Here is where Inventor gets the information used to fill in the title block.

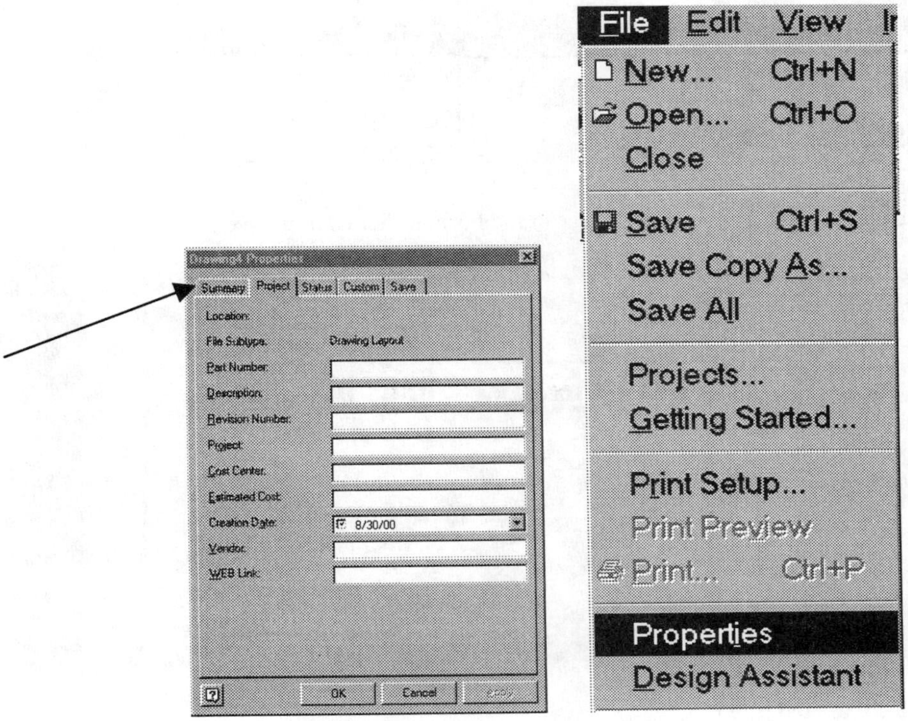

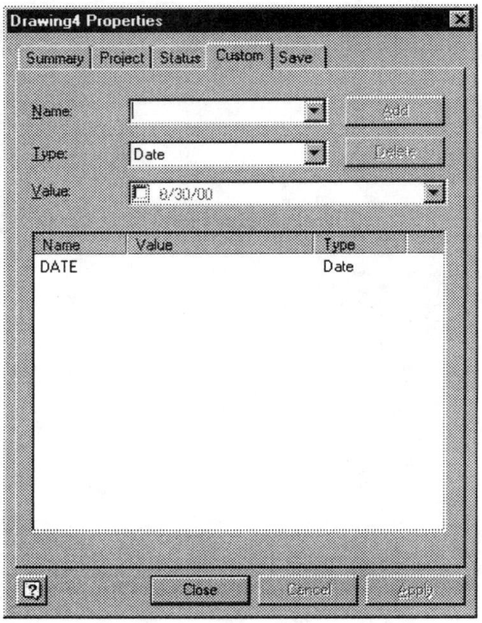

If you would like to add fields to be used in your title block, you can add custom fields under the Custom Tab in the Properties dialog box.

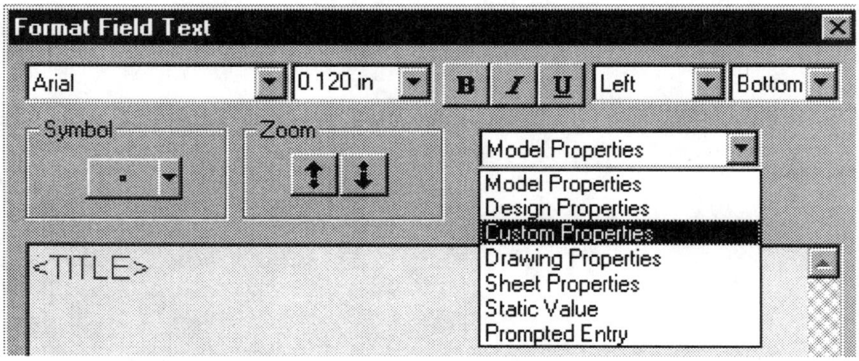

The Custom fields will then appear in the Format Field dialog box.

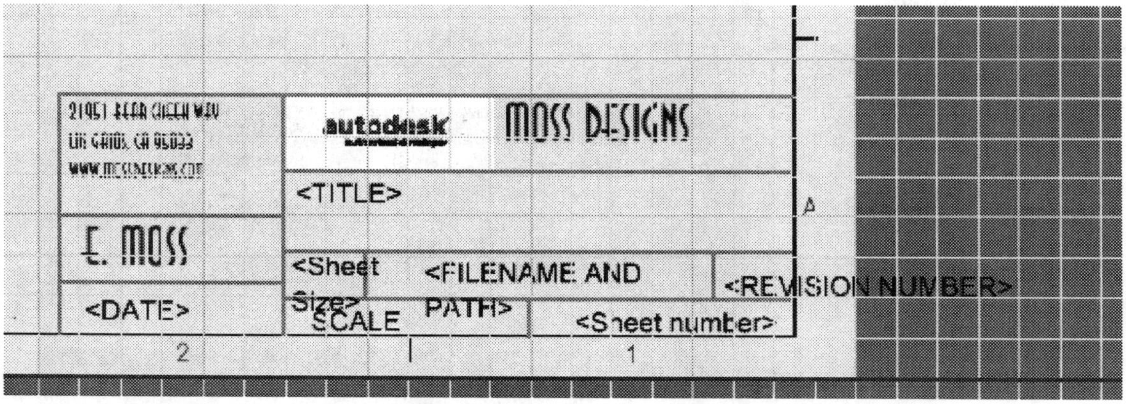

The completed title block.

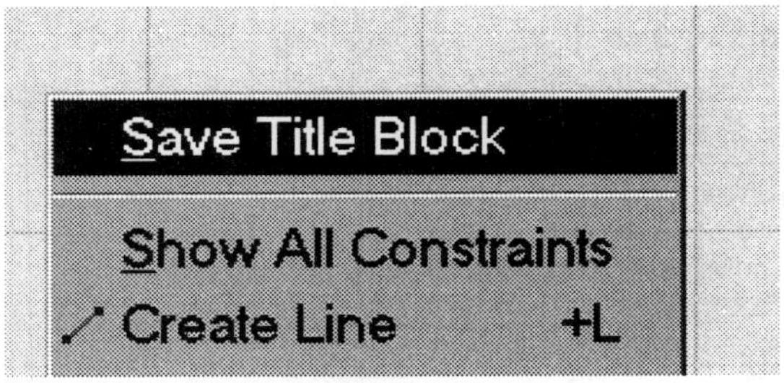

Once the title block is complete, right click and select 'Save Title Block'.

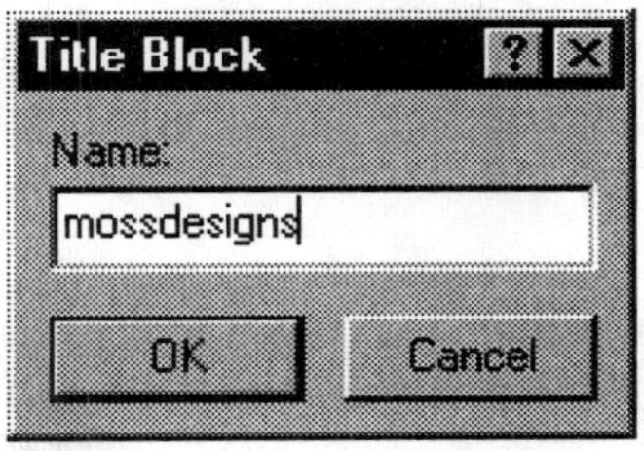

Assign a name to your title block. Do not use punctuation marks. Spaces are OK.

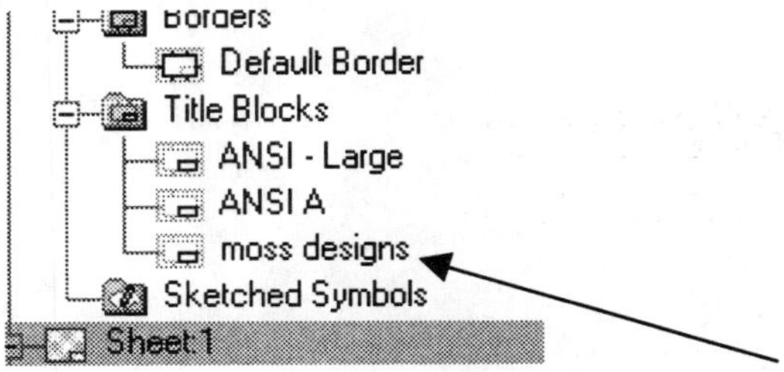

Your new title block name automatically appears in the browser.

To insert, select and double click.

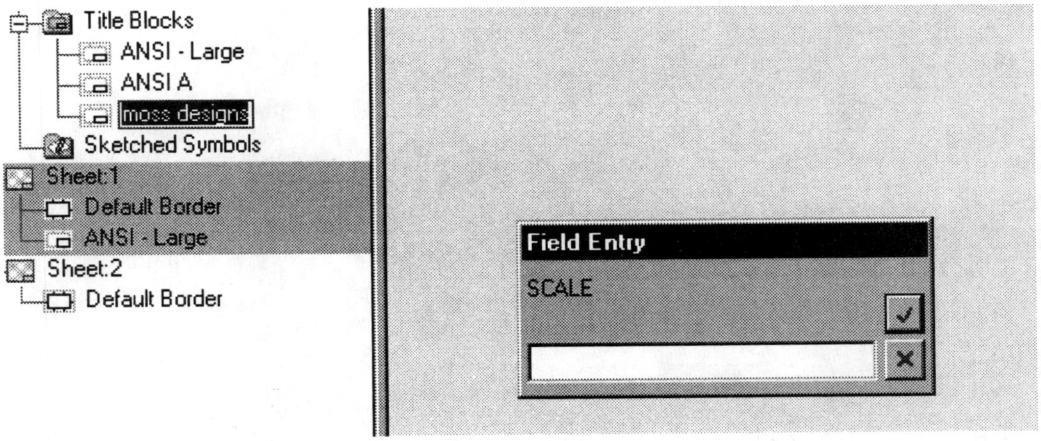

You will then be prompted for any prompted entry fields that were defined.

To copy a custom title block from one drawing to another

Open the source drawing that contains the desired title block and the destination drawing.

In the Source drawing, highlight the Title Blocks category. Right click and select 'Copy'.

Activate the destination drawing by picking on that drawing's title bar.

Highlight the Title Blocks category in the browser. Right click and select 'Paste'.

Managing Views

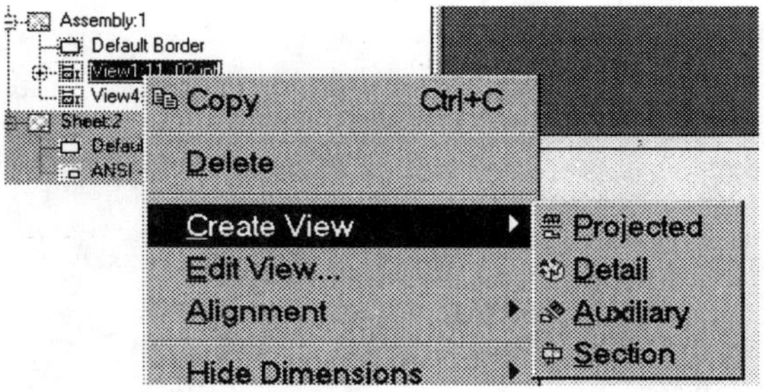

- To create a dependent view, select the view name, right-click and then select Create View.

Edit View

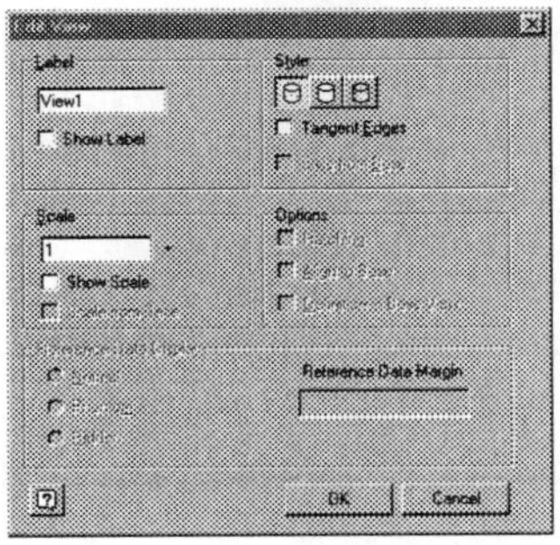

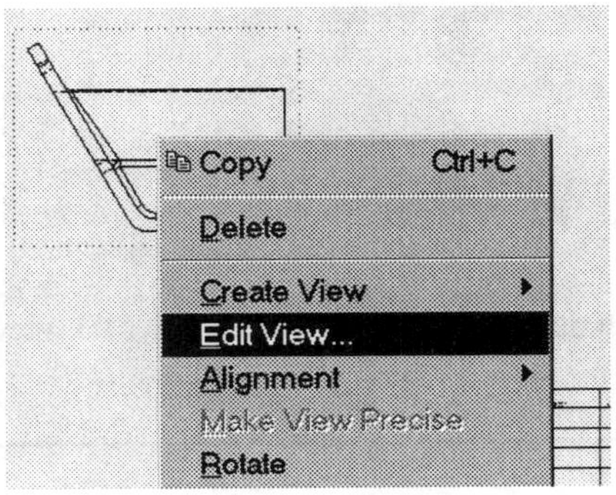

- To change the label, scale, or other attributes of a view, select the view name, right-click and then select Edit View or you can select the view in the graphics window, right click and then select Edit View

Label changes the label for the selected view. When you create a view, a default label is determined by the active drafting standard. To change the label, select the label in the box and enter the new label.	
Show Label	Displays or hides the view label. Select the check box to display the label; clear the check box to hide the label.
Sets the scale of the view, relative to the part or assembly. Enter the desired scale in the box or click the arrow to select from a list of commonly used scales. **Note: If Scale from Base is selected, you cannot change the scale of a dependent view**.	
Show Scale	Displays or hides the view scale. Select the check box to display the scale; clear the check box to hide the scale.
Scale from Base	Sets the scale of a dependent view to be the same as that of its base view. When selected, the dependent view maintains the same scale as its base view. To change the scale of a dependent view, clear the check box.
Tangent Edges	Sets the visibility of tangent edges in a selected view. Select the check box to display tangent edges; clear the check box to hide them.
Style from Base	Sets the display style of a dependent view to be the same as that of its base view. When the check box is selected, the dependent view uses the same display style as its base view. To change the display style, of a dependent view, clear the check box.
Options sets options for the view.	
Hatching	Sets the visibility of the hatch lines in the selected section view. Select the check box to display the hatch lines; clear the check box to hide them.
Align to Base	Removes the alignment constraint of the selected view to its base view. When the check box is selected, an alignment exists. Clear the check box to break the alignment. Note: You cannot use this option to add an alignment that does not exist. You must use the alignment options on the context menu for the view.
Definition in Base View	Displays or hides the view projection line for the view. Check the box to display the line, remove the check to hide the line.

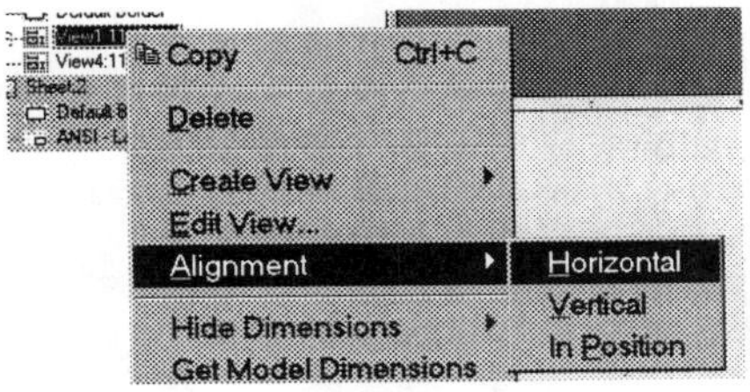

- To work with the view alignment, select the view name, right-click and then select Alignment.

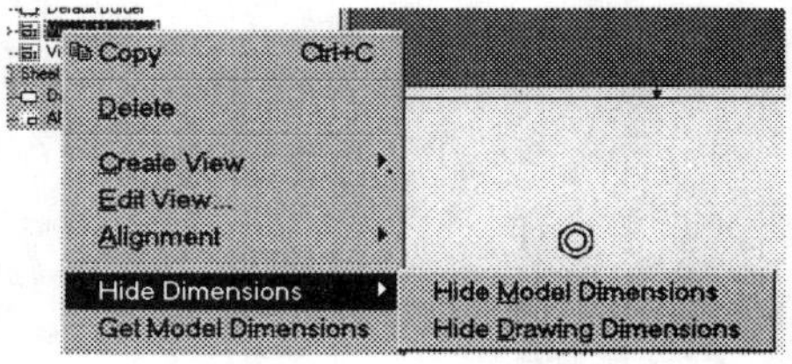

- To show or hide the dimensions in the view, select the view name, right-click and then select Hide Dimensions.

> **TIP:** A single model dimension cannot be used in multiple views on the same sheet.

Rotate View

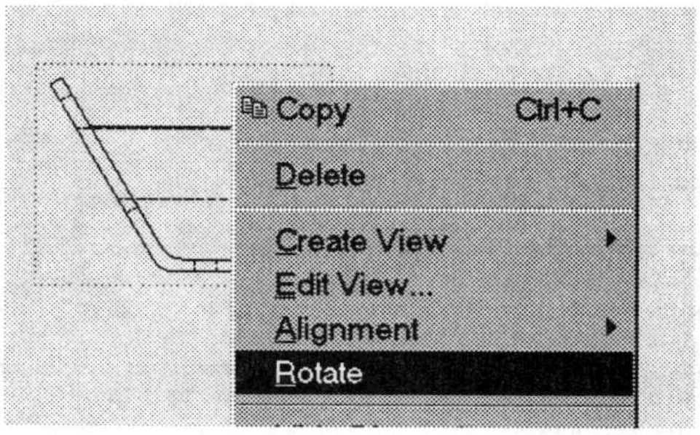

Inventor R4 also allows you to rotate a view. This comes in handy when a view is placed using the wrong orientation.

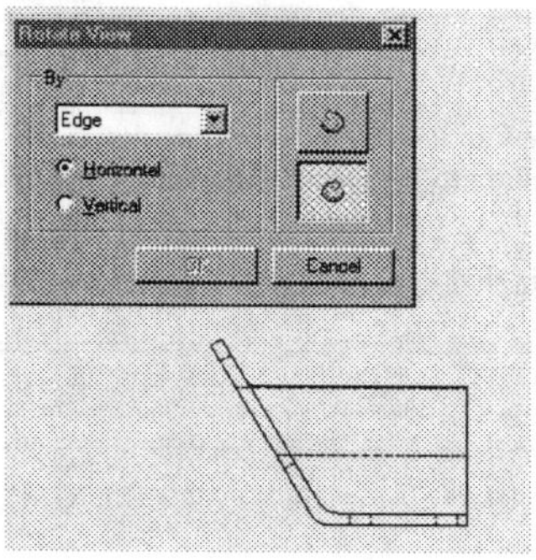

Select the edge of the drawing view to be used as the axis of rotation.

Press the rotation buttons to change the orientation.

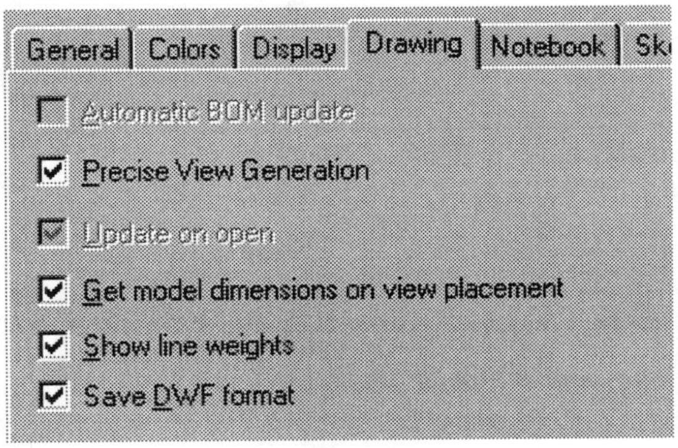

To automatically display dimensions when creating a view, go to Tools -> Application Options. Select the Drawing tab. Enable the 'Get Model dimensions on view placement.

Modifying Line Styles and Colors of Views

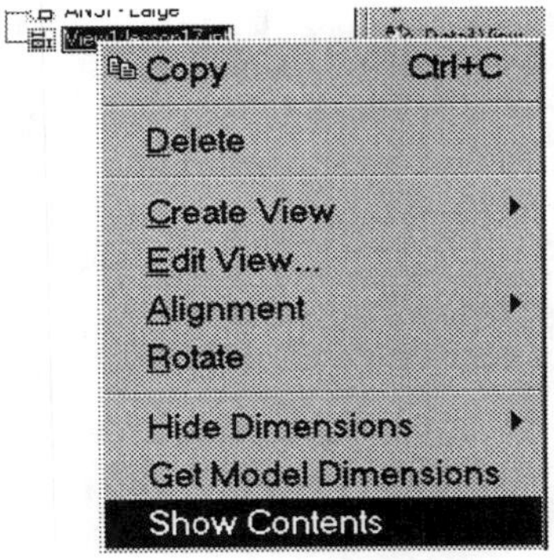

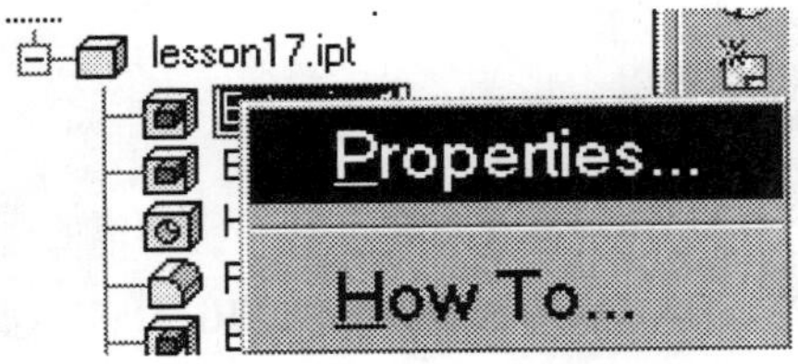

- To show the parts in a view, select the view name, right-click and then select Show Contents. You can expand the contents and right-click a part feature's properties to set its visibility options.

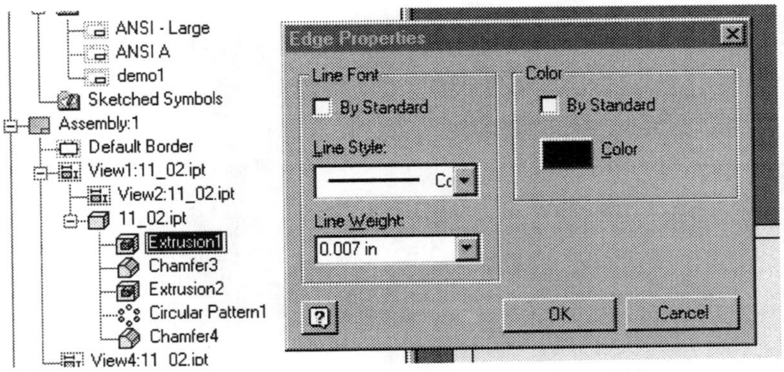

Highlight the feature. Deselect the By Standard boxes for Line Style and Color and then set the line styles and color to the user preference.

Change View Name

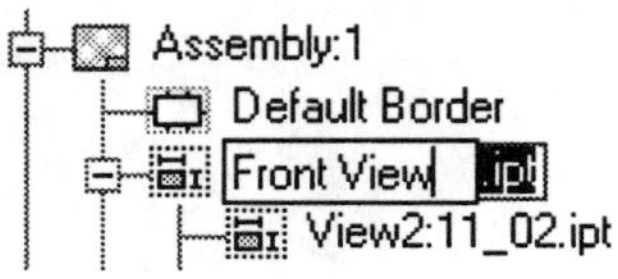

- To change the name of a view, select the sheet name, click at the end of the name and then enter the new name.

Copying Views from one Sheet to Another

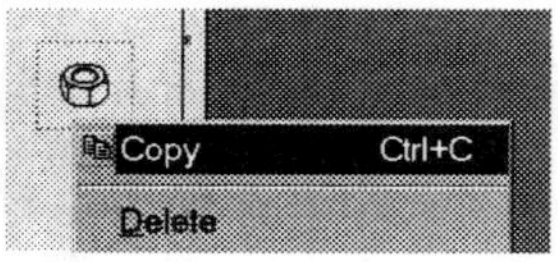

Activate the source sheet. Highlight the desired view in the graphics window or browser. Right click and select 'Copy'.

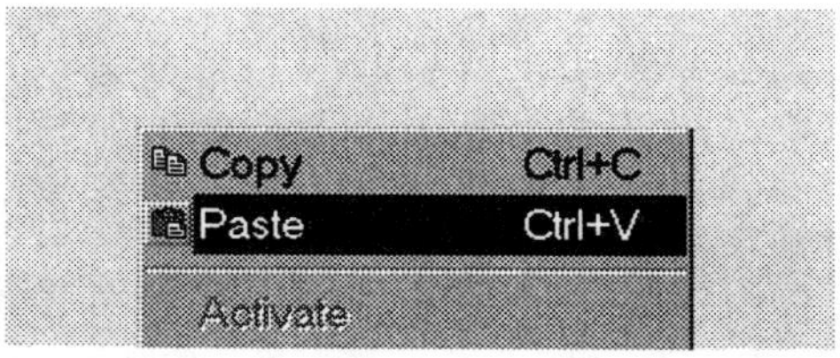

Activate the destination sheet. Pick anywhere on the sheet. Right click and select 'Paste'.

Deleting Views

To delete a view, select in the browser or the graphics window. Right click and select 'Delete'.

If the view selected is a base view (a view that has dependent views), you will get the following message:

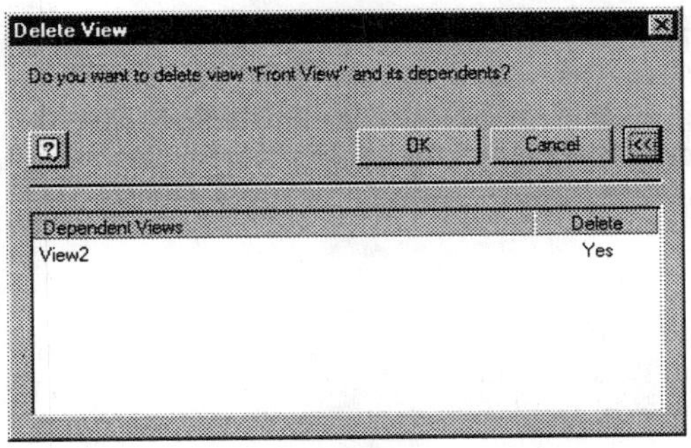

Pressing the More button will provide a list of the dependent views.

To retain a dependent view, pick in the column under the word Delete.

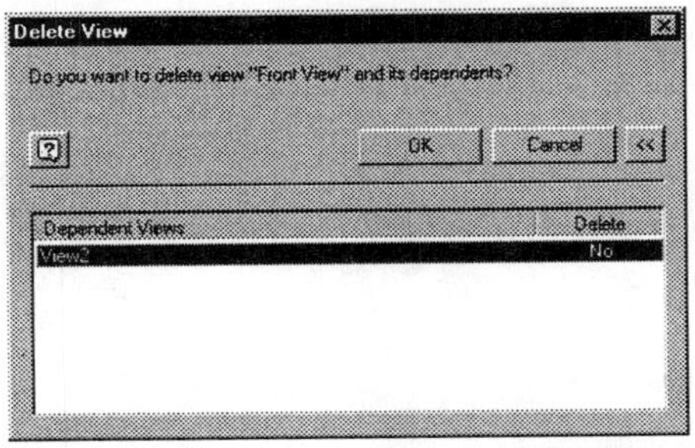

The word "Yes' will change to 'No'.

Sketch Overlay

You can add overlay sketches that are associated with the underlying sheet. A sketch can contain geometry, such as lines and arcs, or text. If a drawing view is selected when you activate the Sketch tools, the sketch is attached to the view. If you move the view, the sketch moves with it.
An overlay sketch cannot be saved as part of a drawing template, or copied between drawings. However, if you copy a view or sheet that has a sketch associated to it, the sketch is copied as well.
Use the tools on the Sketch toolbar to add sketched elements to a drawing. Sketches on a drawing sheet reside on overlays that are associated with the underlying sheet. If a drawing view is selected when you activate the sketch tool, the resulting sketch is associated with the selected view.

1. Click the Sketch button on the Command toolbar to activate the sketch.
2. Click the Grid button on the Sketch toolbar and set the grid spacing to the optimum distance for the sketch task.
3. Use the tools on the Sketch toolbar to create the sketch.
4. When the sketch is finished, click the Sketch button to deactivate the sketch overlay.

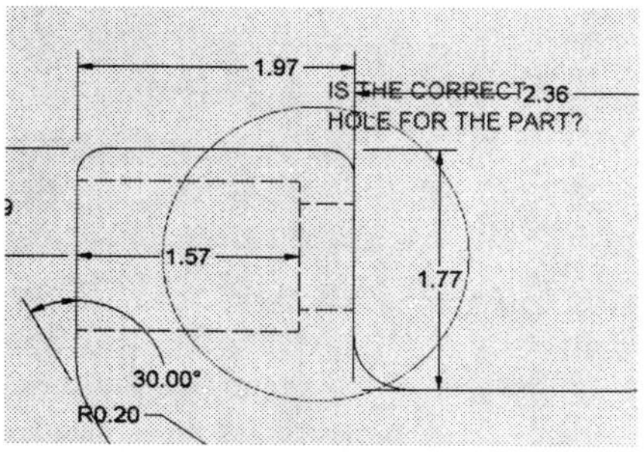

TIP: To edit a completed sketch, select a sketch element in the graphics window or browser, right-click, and select edit to reactivate the sketch.

- Use the Zoom Window button on the Standard toolbar to zoom in on the area where you are working.
- Set the grid to the spacing needed to quickly line up the sketch elements.
- Check the Snap to Grid setting to more easily place sketch elements.
- To select a group of sketch elements, activate the Select tool, then click in the graphics window and drag a box around the elements.
- Use the dimension tools to set the size of sketched geometry or to add dimensions between the geometry in a sketch and elements in the underlying drawing view.

Sketch overlays are a useful tool for redlining drawings without affecting views or drawing data.

Sketched Symbols

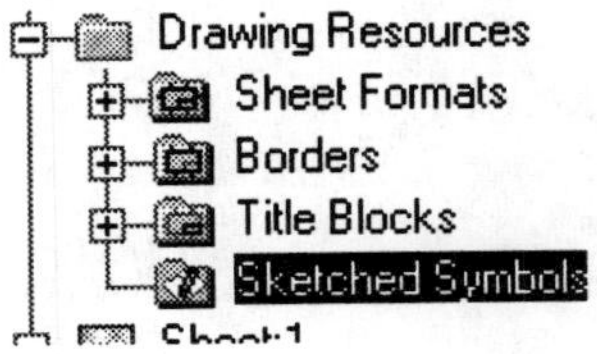

Sketched Symbols are one of the items listed under Drawing Resources

You can add a sketched symbol to the active sheet in the drawing. The symbol is associated to the sheet on which you place it. If you delete the sheet, the sketched symbol is deleted. If you copy the sheet, the sketched symbol is copied.

1. Activate the sheet on which to place the symbol.
2. Open the Drawing Resources>Sketched Symbols folder in the browser.
3. Right-click the symbol name, then select Insert from the menu.

TIP: Select and drag the symbol to move it to a new location after inserting it.

The browser for each drawing or drawing template contains a Sketched Symbols folder in the Drawing Resources folder. You can create custom sketches and add them to Sketched Symbols to use in the drawing.

Define New Symbol

The sketch can contain geometry, text, or imported bitmap images.

1. Open the drawing file or template that will contain the sketched symbol.

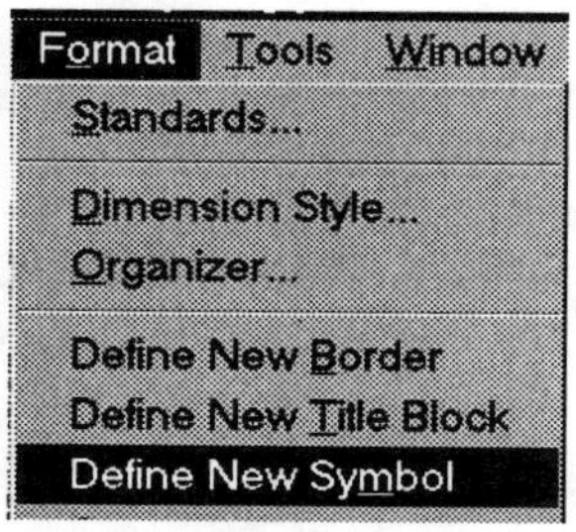

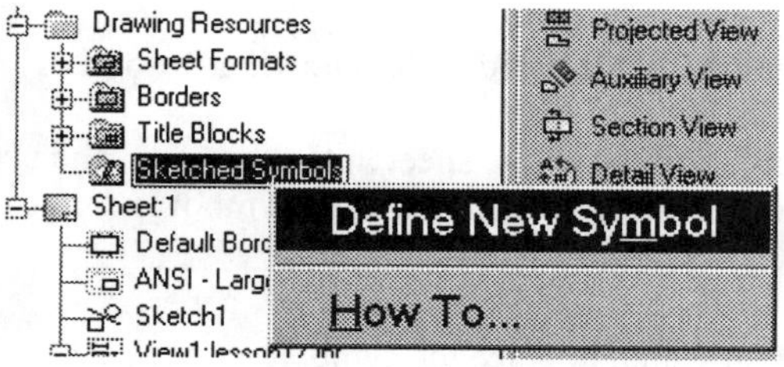

2. Select Format>Define New Symbol to open a sketch window.

Or Select on the Sketched Symbols in the browser, right click and select 'Define New Symbol'.

3. Use the tools on the Sketch toolbar to create the sketch.

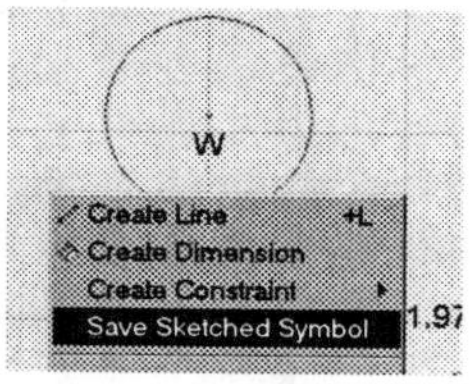

4. Select Format>Save Sketched Symbol to end the operation or right click and select 'Save Sketched Symbol.

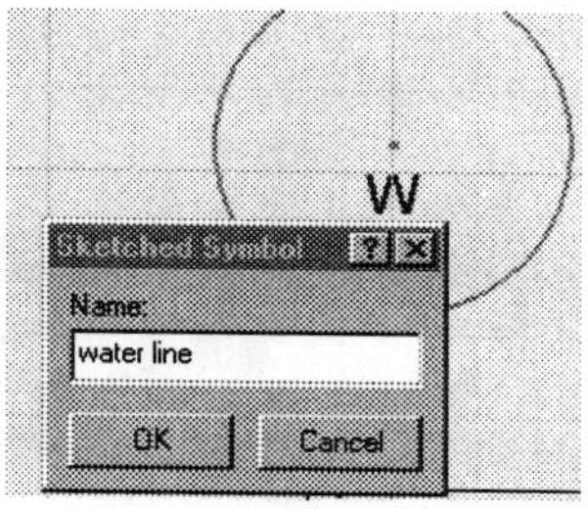

5. Enter the name for the new symbol in the dialog box.

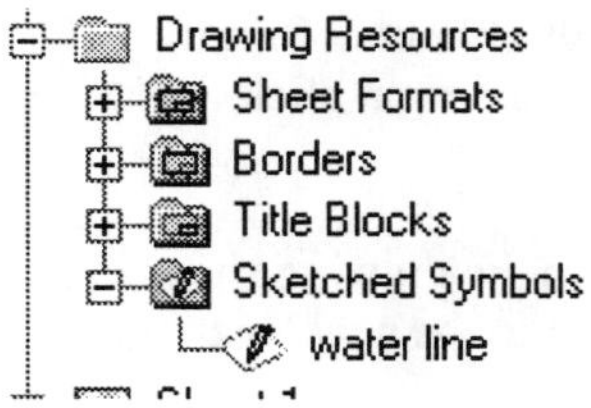

The new symbol is added to Drawing Resources in the drawing browser. To add a sketched symbol to a drawing, double-click the symbol name in the browser.

Sketched symbols are either associated with a sheet or with a view. If a sketched symbol is associated with a sheet, it is considered a symbol. If a sketched symbol is associated with a view, it is considered a callout.

You can add a sketched symbol to a drawing view as a callout. The symbol is associated to the view. If you delete the view, the sketched symbol is deleted. If you copy the view, the sketched symbol is copied.

1. Activate the sheet on which to place the symbol.
2. Open the Drawing Resources>Sketched Symbols folder in the browser.
3. Right-click the symbol name, then select Insert Callout from the menu.
4. In the graphics window, click to set the start point for the leader line.
5. Move the cursor and click to add a vertex to the leader line.
6. When the symbol indicator is in the desired position, right-click and select Continue to place the symbol.

Continue placing callout symbols. When you finish placing symbols, right-click and select Done from the menu to end the operation.

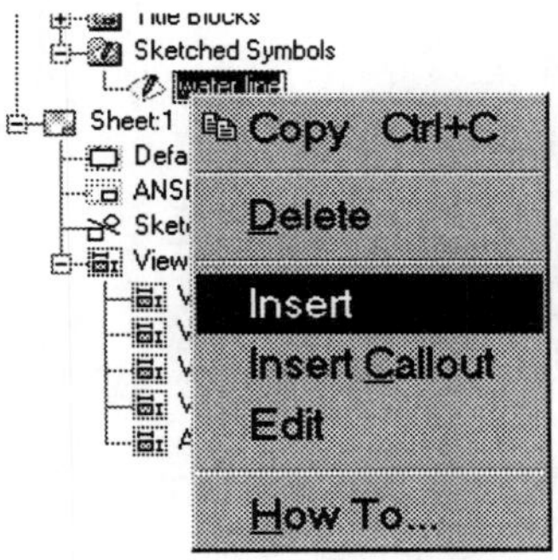

Selecting a sketched symbol in the browser and right clicking brings up the menu shown. The user can edit, delete, or insert the sketched symbol to associate it with a sheet or insert as a callout to associate it with a view.

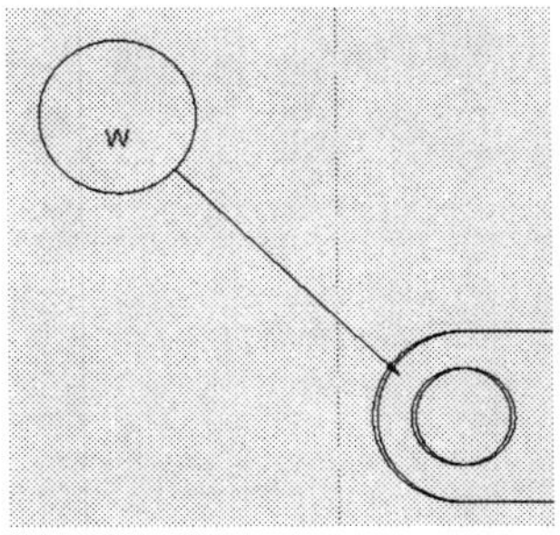

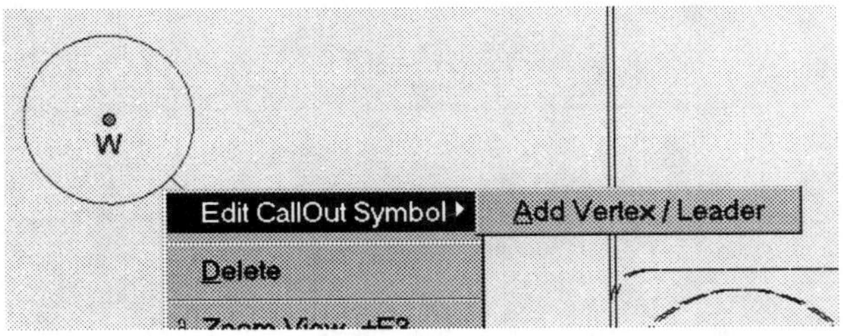

Inserting a sketched symbol as a callout, automatically adds a leader line to the symbol. Simply pick the start point of the leader and then pick location for the symbol. To edit, select and right click to get the edit menu.

Selecting the Insert option places the sketched symbol in a random location in the drawing sheet. To relocate the symbol, hold down the Control key and pick and drag the symbol to the new location.

Drawing Borders

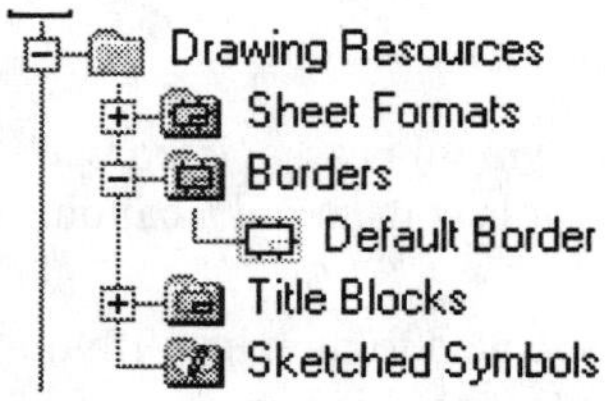

Drawing Borders are located under the Drawing Resources folder.
Your first drawing sheet automatically has a border applied.

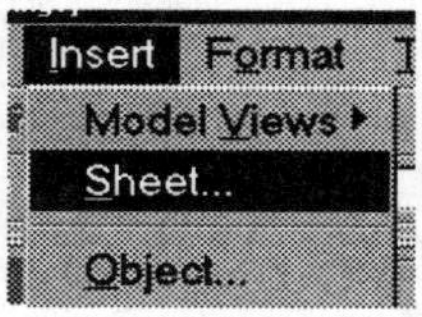

However, if you use Insert ->Sheet to add a new sheet to your drawing file, no border or title block is automatically placed. This is because many companies use a different format for sheets other than Sheet 1.

Insert Drawing Border

To add the Default Border, highlight it in the browser, right click and select 'Insert Drawing Border'.

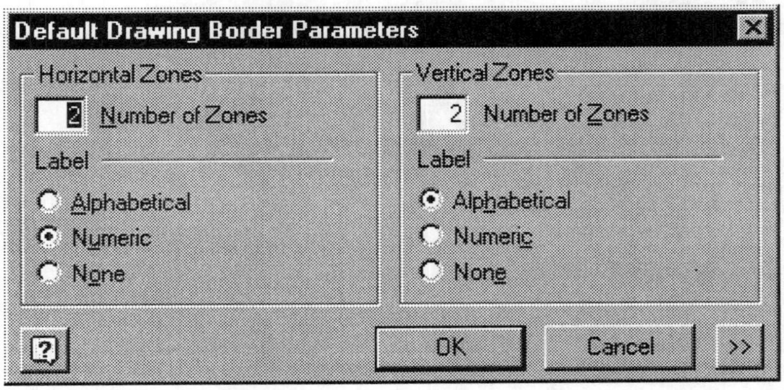

The Default Drawing Border Parameters dialog box appears.

Zones set the number and style for the zones that the border defines.	
Horizontal Zones	Sets the number and style for the horizontal zones. Number of Zones sets the number of horizontal zones. Enter the number in the box. Zone Labeling Sets the label style for horizontal zones. Click to select an option.
Vertical Zones	Sets the number and style for the vertical zones. Number of Zones sets the number of vertical zones. Enter the number in the box. Zone Labeling sets the label style for vertical zones. Click to select an option.

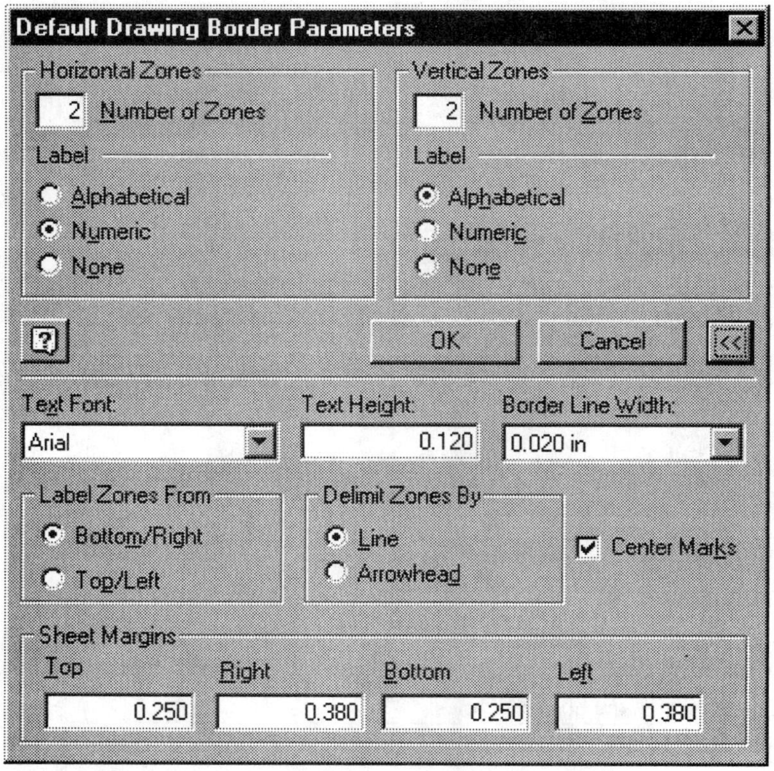

Selecting the More button  expands the dialog box so that you can set the text size and style, line width, zone properties, and page margins. Click to expand or collapse.

Text Font	Sets the typeface for the zone labels. Click the arrow and select the font from the list.
Text Height	Sets the font height for the zone labels. Enter the height in the box.
Border Line Width	Sets the line thickness for the border. Click the arrow and select the thickness from the list.
Center Marks	Specifies whether to a incorporate center marks into the border. Select the check box to add center marks; clear the check box to omit them.
Delimit Zones By	Specifies the mark used to show zone boundaries. Click to select an option. Line sets lines to indicate the boundaries. Arrowhead sets arrows to indicate the boundaries.
Label Zones From	Sets the starting point for zone labels. Click to select an option. Bottom/Right starts the labeling at the bottom, right corner of the page. Horizontal labels proceed from right to left and vertical labels proceed from bottom to top. Top/Left starts the labeling at the top, left corner of the page. Horizontal labels proceed from left to right and vertical labels proceed from top to bottom.
Sheet Margins	Sets the space between the edge of the page and the border line on each side of the sheet. Enter the size for each margin.

TIP: You cannot edit the default border after it is placed. To change the border, delete it and insert a new border with the desired properties.

Define New Border

You can also create your own border formats.

1. Open the drawing file or template that will contain the border format.
2. Select Format>Define New Border from the Autodesk Inventor menu to open a sketch window.
3. Use the tools on the Sketch toolbar to create the border.
4. Click Format>Save border to end the operation.
5. Enter the name of the new border in the dialog box.

The new border is added to Drawing Resources in the drawing browser.

Drawing Management Toolbar

Button	Tool	Function	Special Instructions
	Create View	Creates a view of a 3D model	The user must select the 3D model file to be used
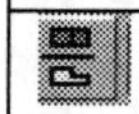	Projected Views	Creates an orthographic view	Requires a base view to have been defined
	Auxiliary View	Creates an auxiliary view	Select an edge to project a view
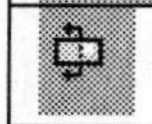	Section Views	Creates a section view	User must define a section line before the view can be created
	Detail View	Adds a detail view	
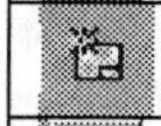	New Sheet	Adds a new layout sheet	
	Draft View	Adds a sketch overlay to a drawing	Used to mark up or redline a drawing
	Property Field	Creates text field	Select source for text Only available when in Define New Title block mode
	Fill Sketch Region	Adds color to profiles	Can be used to create logos or graphics Only available when in Define New Title block mode

Review Questions

1. True or False

Deleting a base view automatically deletes all dependent views.

2. True or False

A single model dimension cannot be used in multiple views on the same sheet.

3. True or False

Sketch overlays are used to clip or edit drawing views.

4. True or False

Drawing views cannot be copied from one sheet to another.

5. True or False

You can only create a view using the default orientations, i.e. Front, Top, Right.

6. 'Show Contents' is used to:

   A. List the views in a drawing
   B. List the features in the part
   C. List the format of a title block
   D. List the format of a sheet

7. The 'Fill Sketch Region' tool is used to:

   A. Add color to a profile in a title block
   B. Add color to a sketch overlay
   C. Add color to a view
   D. Add hatching to a section view

8. If you change the scale of the base view from 1:2 to 1:1, the scale of the isometric view:

   A. will change to 1:1
   B. will change to 3:4
   C. will remain 1:2
   D. will change to 4:3

9. The Section View tool creates all the section view types listed EXCEPT:

   A. Full
   B. Half
   C. Offset
   D. Revolved

ANSWERS: 1) F; 2) T; 3) F; 4) F; 5) F; 6) B; 7) A; 8) C; 9) D

NOTES:

Lesson 19

Drawing Annotation

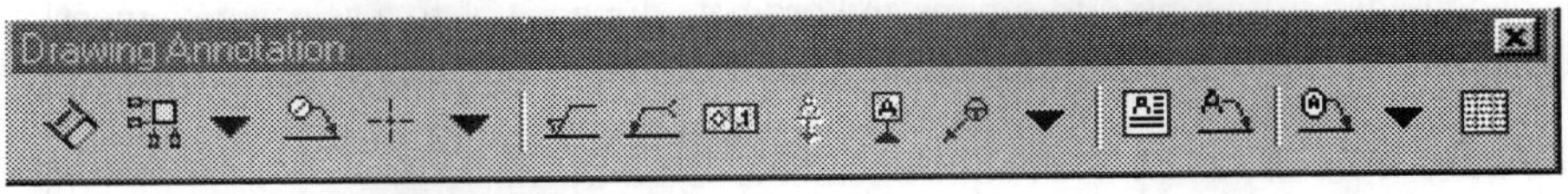

Drawing Annotation Toolbar

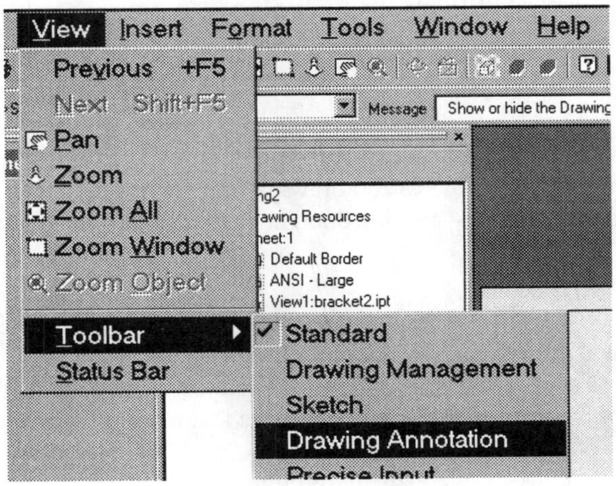

The Drawing Annotation Toolbar can be accessed through the View->Toolbar menu.

Pressing on the top of the Panel Bar and selecting it can also activate the Drawing Annotation toolbar. Using this method will retire the Drawing Management Panel bar.

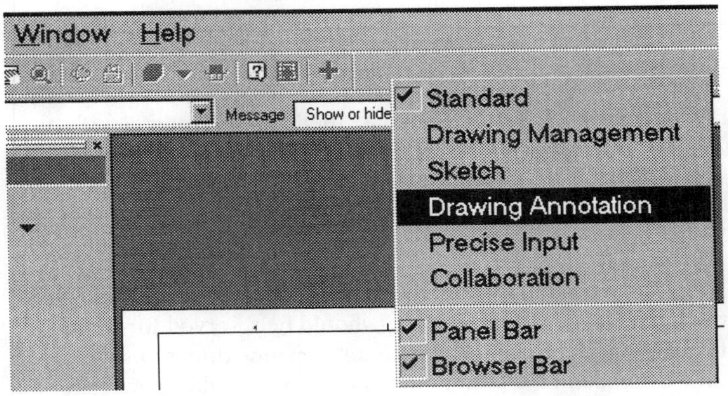

You can also access any toolbar by right clicking on the standard toolbar at the top of the screen.

This toolbar contains tools that add annotations to a drawing. It is divided into four sections: Dimension, Symbol, Text, and Parts List tools.

- Dimension tools add general drawing dimensions and ordinate dimensions to a selected element.
- The center mark tools add center marks, center lines, center line bisectors, and centered patterns to a drawing.
- The symbols tools add a variety of GDT and other symbols to a drawing.
- The text tools add notes to a drawing.
- Parts list and balloon tools add those annotations to a drawing.

General Dimension

Use the General Dimension button on the Drawing Annotation toolbar to add drawing dimensions to a view. Drawing dimensions do not affect the size of the part, but they provide documentation in the drawing.

1. Click the General Dimension button.
2. In the graphics window, select the geometry and drag to display the dimension.
   - To add a linear dimension for a line or edge, click to select the geometry.
   - To add a linear dimension between two points, two curves, or a curve and a point, click to select each point or curve.
   - To add a radial or diametric dimension, click to select an arc or circle.
   - To add an angular dimension, select two curves.
   - To add an implied intersection dimension, select two curves to define the intersection, right-click and select Intersection, then select the element to dimension.
3. Click to place the dimension in the desired location.

As you develop a drawing, you can use two types of dimensions to document your model. Model dimensions are the dimensions that control the feature size in the part. They were applied during the sketching or creation of the feature. In a drawing view, you can display model dimensions that are planar to the view.

Drawing dimensions are dimensions that you add to further document the model. Drawing dimensions do not change or control features or part size. You can add drawing dimensions as annotations to drawing views or geometry in drawing sketches.

Modifying a drawing dimension in the Drawing Layout WILL NOT update the Model. However, if you change the model dimension it will update in the Drawing Layout and in the Model.

If you set the option to edit model dimensions from a drawing when you installed Autodesk Inventor, you can change the model dimensions in the drawing. Changes in the drawing should be reserved for minor changes to individual dimensions. If significant changes or changes involving dependent features are required, it is strongly recommended that they be made in the part model. You cannot make changes to a part in an assembly view. To edit the model, you must open the part file (*.ipt) and make the changes. If you close your drawing file, your drawing views will automatically update after you save the part file when you re-open the file. If you keep your drawing file open while modifying the part file, your drawing views will not update until you save the part file and then use the Update button.

If you change the size of a part that has multiple occurrences in an assembly or is used in multiple assemblies, all occurrences of the part change.

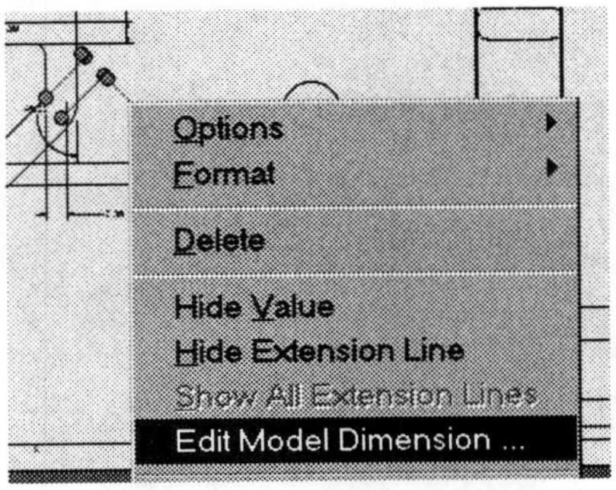

The 'Edit Model Dimension' will only be available on the menu if you selected that option when you installed Inventor.

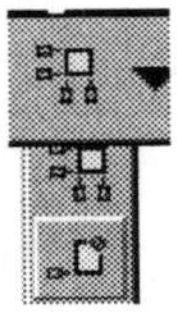

The Ordinate Dimension is actually a flyout with two options available: Ordinate Dimension Set and Ordinate Dimension.

Ordinate Dimension Set

Use the Ordinate Dimension button on the Drawing Annotation toolbar to add ordinate dimensions. This tool links all the dimensions placed as a group. The first point selected is automatically assumed to be the origin. You must place all the dimensions along one axis, right click and select 'Create'. Then repeat to place dimensions along the other axis.

The dimensions automatically align and adjust to avoid interference as you place them.

1. Click the Ordinate Dimension Set button.
2. In the graphics window, click to set the datum for the first dimension.
3. Position the cursor and click to place the first dimension value.
4. Continue selecting points and placing dimensions.
5. To change options for the dimension set, right-click at any time and select options.
6. To end the operation, right-click and select Create.

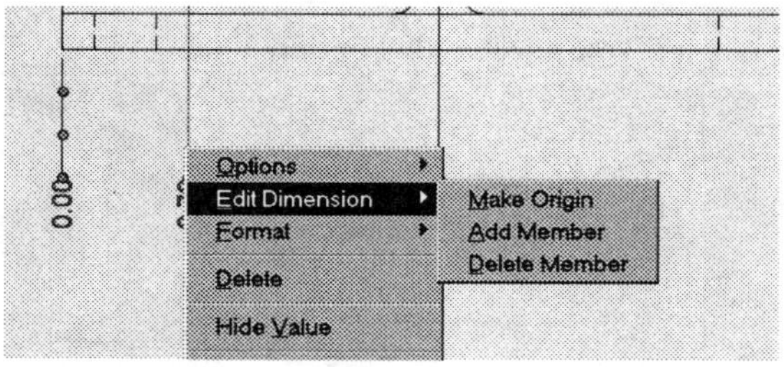

To modify ordinate dimensions, select the dimension set in the graphics window and right-click to display the menu. You have to option to reset the Origin, Add or Delete a dimension.

The first point picked when placing an ordinate dimension is automatically assigned the 0 value. Place all the dimensions desired for that axis (whether horizontal or vertical), then right click to select Create. Then place the dimensions for the other axis.

Pressing 'O' on the keyboard will also initiate the Ordinate dimension command.

Ordinate Dimension

The Ordinate Dimension Set tool places multiple ordinate dimensions along a single axis. The Ordinate Dimension tool allows the user to place one or more dimensions on one or more axis.

The other difference between the tools is that ordinate dimensions placed with the Ordinate Dimension Set are considered a group so if you delete one dimension in the set, you delete all the dimensions along the same axis in that set. Dimensions placed with the Ordinate Dimension tool are considered independent of all the other ordinate dimensions along the same axis.

The Ordinate Dimension tool also requires that the user identify the origin of the part before any ordinate dimensions are placed.

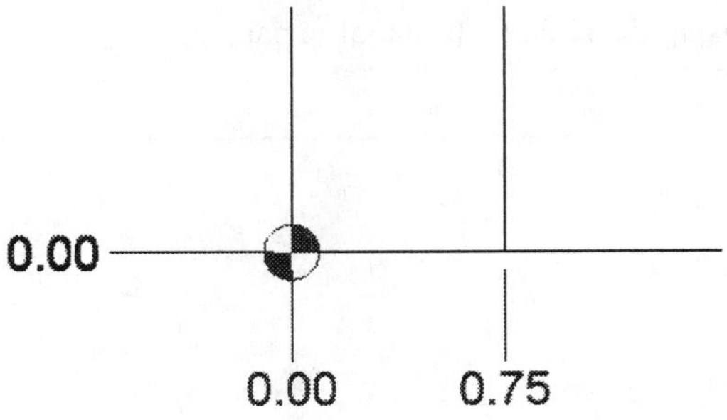

The tool places a marker at the origin point.

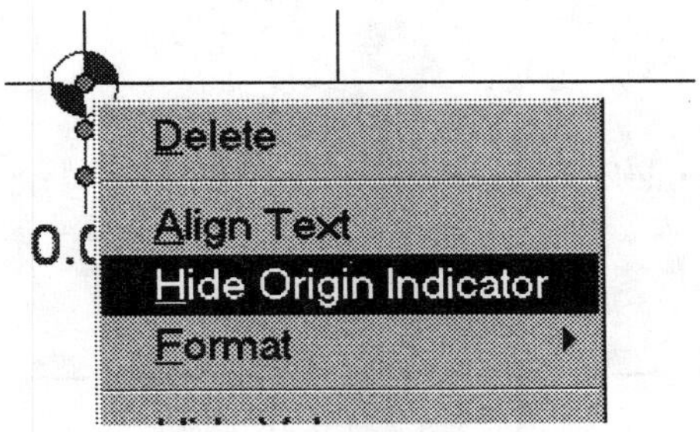

To hide the marker, select it, right click and select 'Hide Origin Indicator'.

Hole/Thread Notes

Use the Hole Notes button on the Drawing Annotation toolbar to add a hole or thread note with a leader line. The text, style, color, and line weight for the notes are determined by the active drafting standard.

1. Click the Hole Notes button.
2. In the graphics window, click to select the hole.
3. Move the cursor and click to place the note.
4. When you are finished placing hole notes, right-click and select Done.

Hole notes can be added only to hole features created using the Hole feature tool in parts.
To edit the Hole Note, select, right-click and select 'Text'.

Center Mark

There are four types of center markings that you can add to a drawing view; center marks, center line bisectors, center lines, and centered patterns. To choose a center marking option, click the arrow next to the active center marking button, and select from the pop-up menu.

1. Click the Center Mark button.
2. In the graphics window, click a feature to place a center mark.
3. Continue selecting features to place center marks.
4. Right-click and select Done to terminate the operation.

Pressing 'C' on the keyboard will also activate the Center Mark command.
This is a pull-down with other options available.

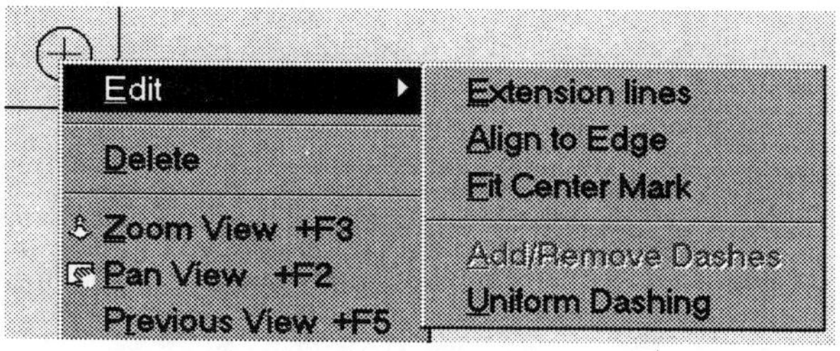

1. Select the center mark to edit.
2. Right-click and select Edit to display the submenu.
3. Select the desired option.

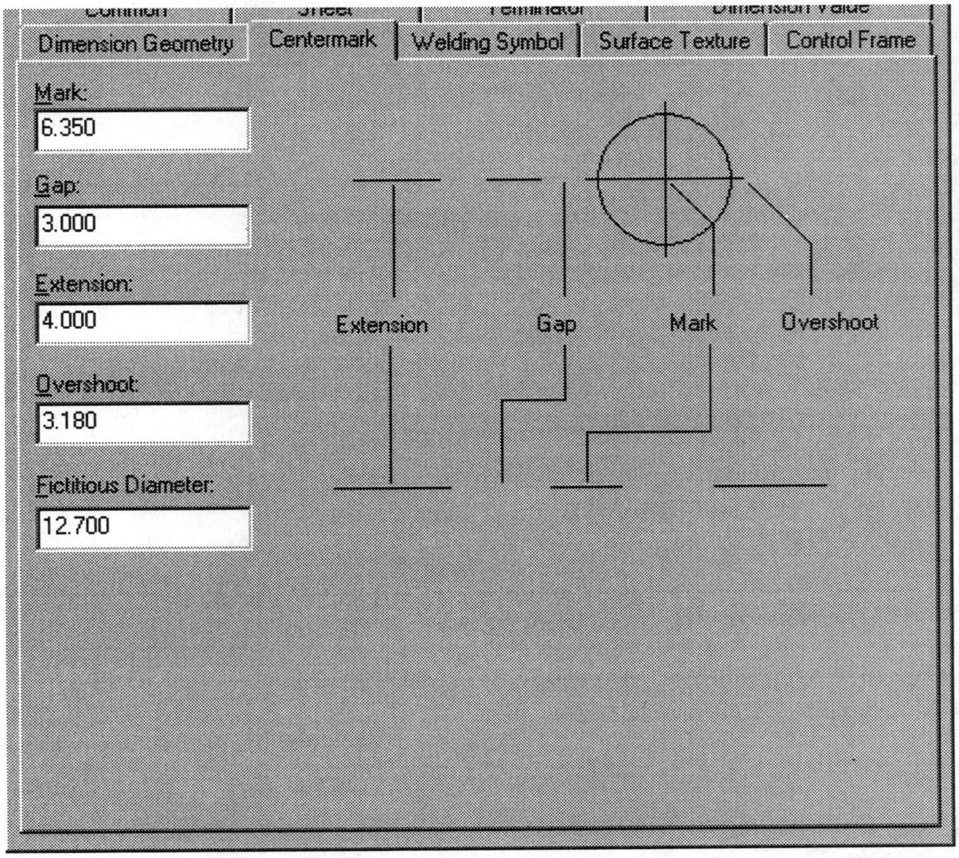

The Center Mark Standards are accessed under Format->Standards in the menu.

Mark	Sets the size of the center indicator mark.
Gap	Sets the gap distance between the center indicator and the extension line.
Extension	Sets the minimum length of center mark extension lines.
Overshoot	Sets the distance that center mark extension lines extend beyond the edges of the features that they define.
Fictitious Diameter	Sets the size of center marks for suppressed pattern features.

You can lengthen or shorten an extension line for any center line or center mark by dragging its endpoint. In addition, you can edit center marks in the several ways.

Center Line

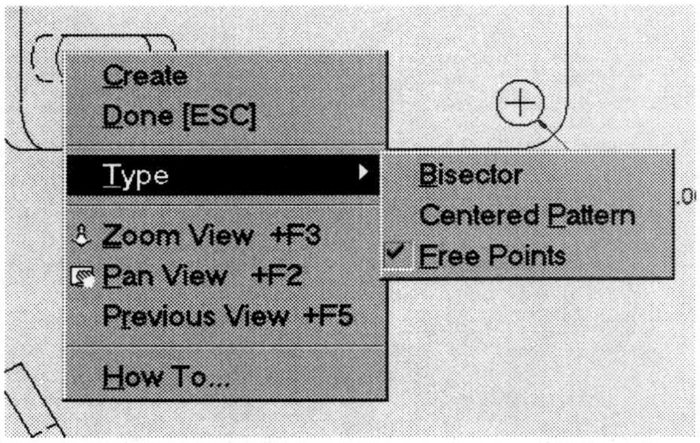

1. Click the Center Line button.
2. In the graphics window, click a feature to start the center line.
3. Click a second feature to add the center line.
4. Continue selecting features until all desired features are added.
5. Right-click and select Done to accept the displayed center line. The operation remains active so that you can add other center lines.

TIP: If the features form a circular pattern, the center mark for the pattern is automatically placed when you have selected all of the members.

Center Line Bisector

1. Click the Center Line Bisector button.
2. In the graphics window, click two lines to place the center line bisector between them.
3. Right-click and select Done to accept the displayed center line. The operation remains active so that you can add other center line bisectors.

Centered Pattern

1. Click the Centered Pattern button.
2. In the graphics window, click the defining feature for the pattern to place its center mark.
3. Click the first feature of the pattern.
4. Continue clicking features in a clockwise direction until all desired features are added.
5. Right-click and select Done to accept the displayed centered pattern. The operation remains active so that you can add other centered patterns.

TIP: No center line is added between the final feature in the pattern and the beginning feature. You can manually extend the line if needed.

Surface Texture Symbol

Specifies the content of a surface texture symbol. The options in the dialog box are determined by the active drafting standard

The symbols can be created as stand-alone objects, be placed directly on the geometry in a drawing view, or reside on top of a leader line which points to the geometry. Surface Texture Symbols may also be used in notes and in the tolerance block.	
Surface Type	Click a button to select the desired surface type. Basic Material removal required Material removal prohibited
Miscellaneous	Specifies the general attributes of the symbol. Click the button to add or remove each attribute. Force tail adds a tail to the symbol. Majority indicates that this symbol specifies the standard surface characteristics for the drawing. All-around adds the all-around indicator to the symbol.
Surface characteristics	Defines the values for the surface characteristics. Enter the appropriate values in the boxes. A specifies the roughness value, roughness value Ra minimum, minimum roughness value, or grade number. A' specifies the roughness value, roughness value Ra maximum, maximum roughness value, or grade number. Available only when A has an entered value. B specifies the production method, treatment, or coating. If the active drafting standard is based on ANSI, this box can be used to enter a note callout. B' specifies an additional tail for the production method if the drafting standard is based on ISO or DIN. This option is available only when B has an entered value. C for ANSI, specifies the roughness cutoff or sampling length for roughness average; for ISO or DIN, specifies the waviness height or sampling length; for JIS, specifies the cutoff value and evaluation length. C' for ANSI, specifies the roughness cutoff or sampling length for additional roughness value; for ISO or DIN, specifies the sampling length for additional roughness value; for JIS, specifies the reference length and evaluation length. D specifies the direction of lay. Click the arrow and choose the symbol from the list. This option is not available when the removal prohibited option is selected. E Not available when the Machining Removal Prohibited is selected. Specifies the machining allowance. F specifies the roughness value other than Ra or the parameter value other than Ra. For ANSI, can also specify the waviness height. F' specifies the surface waviness for JIS. This option is not used for ANSI, ISO, or DIN standards.

The user picks points to place the symbol. The first point selected indicates the location of the arrowhead. The user can then select any number of points to control the placement of the leader and symbol. When finished, right click and select ‘Continue’. Selecting ‘Done’ is equivalent to canceling out the command. Selecting ‘Back up’ allows the user to back up one selected point and select a new point. (similar to the Undo command in AutoCAD)

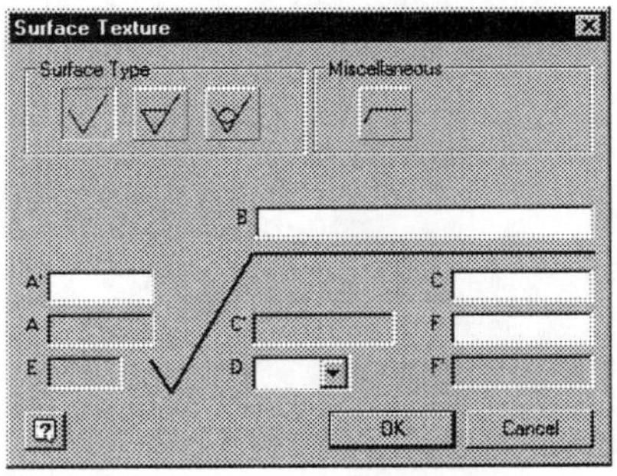

1. Click the Surface Texture Symbol button.
2. In the graphics window, click to set the start point for the leader line. When the symbol indicator is in the desired position, right-click and choose Continue to place the symbol and open the dialog box. Set the attributes and values for the symbol.

Continue placing surface texture symbols. When you finish placing symbols, right-click and select 'Done' from the menu to end the operation.

The Surface Texture Symbols are controlled in the Standards dialog box under the Surface Texture tab.

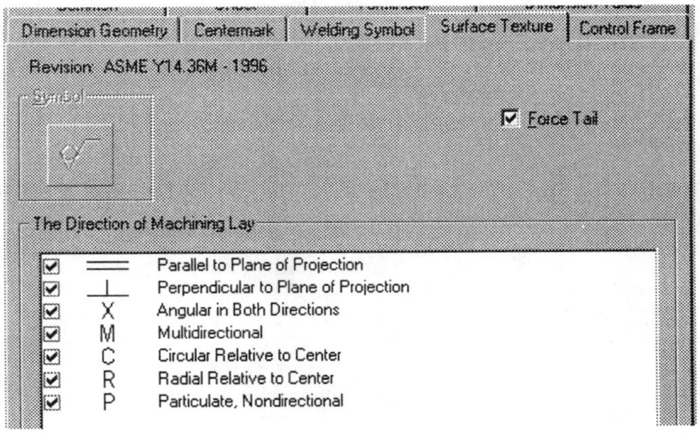

TIPS: To place a symbol without a leader, double-click to set the symbol location and open the dialog box.

The options in the dialog box are determined by the active drafting standard.

If you place the first point on a highlighted edge or point, the leader line is attached to the geometry.

If you turn off a symbol in the Standards dialog that is already used in a drawing, the existing symbols will continue to display, but the symbol will not be available when new symbols are added.

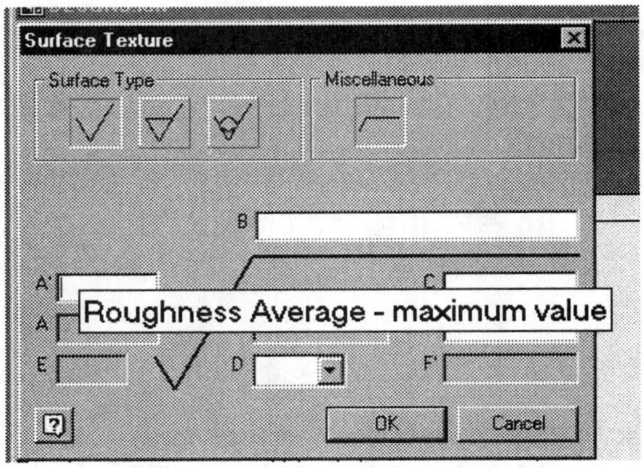

Moving your mouse over the dialog box will bring up a help tip to assist in filling out the dialog box.

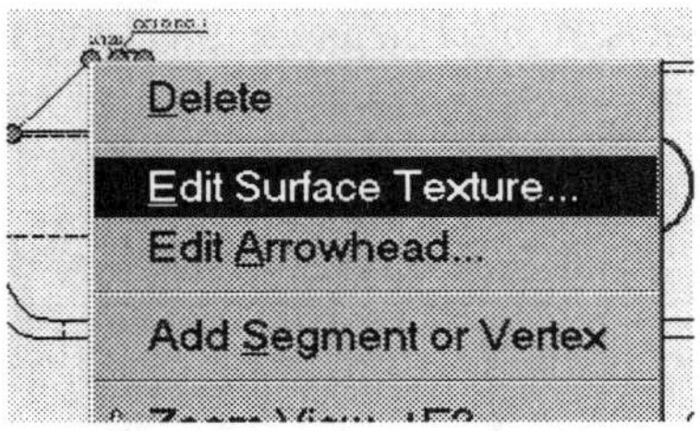

To edit an existing symbol:

1. Activate the select tool
2. Pick the symbol to edit.You should see green grips activate.Right click and select the editing mode desired.

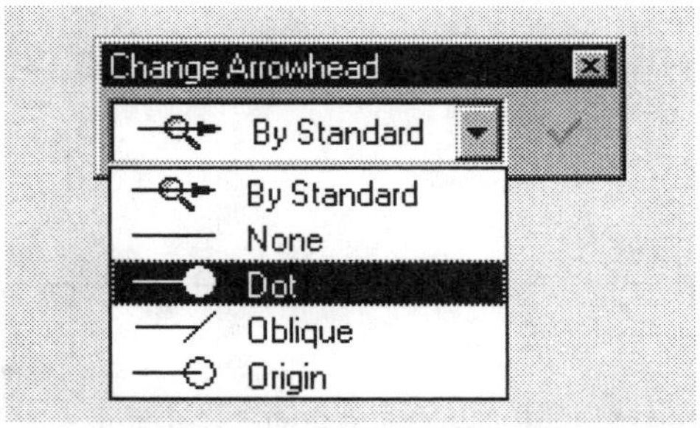

Selecting the Edit Arrowhead option will bring up a dialog where the user can select the current standard or a different arrowhead.

Selecting the 'Add Segment or Vertex option' activates the Grip mode and the user can use the mouse to stretch or modify the leader for the symbol.

Weld Symbol

Specifies the content of a welding symbol. The dialog box opens when you place a welding symbol. The options available are determined by the active drafting standard.

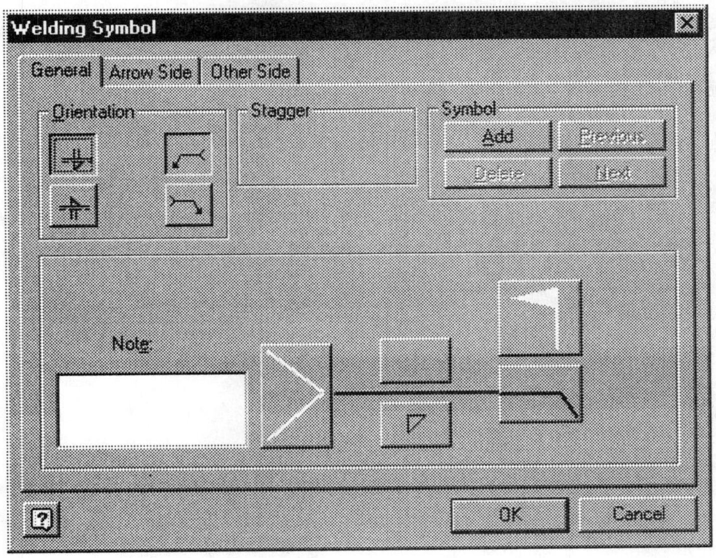

The General Tab sets the components and layout of the welding symbol.	
Orientation	Sets the orientation for the components of the welding symbol. Click the button to set the desired orientation for each component. ◆ Swap arrow side reverses the arrow side and other side for the selected reference line. ◆ Identification line Available for ISO and DIN only. Sets the location of the identification line to the arrow side or the other side for the selected reference line. ◆ Left/right orientation sets the location of the reference line relative to the leader line.
Stagger	Staggers the welding symbols for fillets. Available only if fillet welding symbols are set on both sides of the reference line.
Symbol	◆ Selects, adds, or deletes reference lines on the welding symbol. ◆ Add adds a reference line to the symbol. The selected reference line is moved toward the arrowhead and the new line is added further from the arrowhead than the selected reference line. You can set the orientation and other attributes for the new reference line. ◆ Delete removes the selected reference line from the symbol. ◆ Previous selects the next reference line away from the arrowhead. ◆ Next selects the next reference line toward the arrowhead.
Note	Adds text to the selected reference line. Enter the text in the box.
Arrow side	Opens the Arrow Side options so that you can set the symbol and values for the selected reference line.
Other side	Opens the Other Side options so that you can set the symbol and values for the selected reference line.
Flag	Specifies whether to add a flag indicating a field or site weld to the selected reference line. Click the button to turn the flag off or on.
All-around symbol	Specifies whether to use an all-around symbol on the selected reference line. Click the button to turn the symbol off or on.

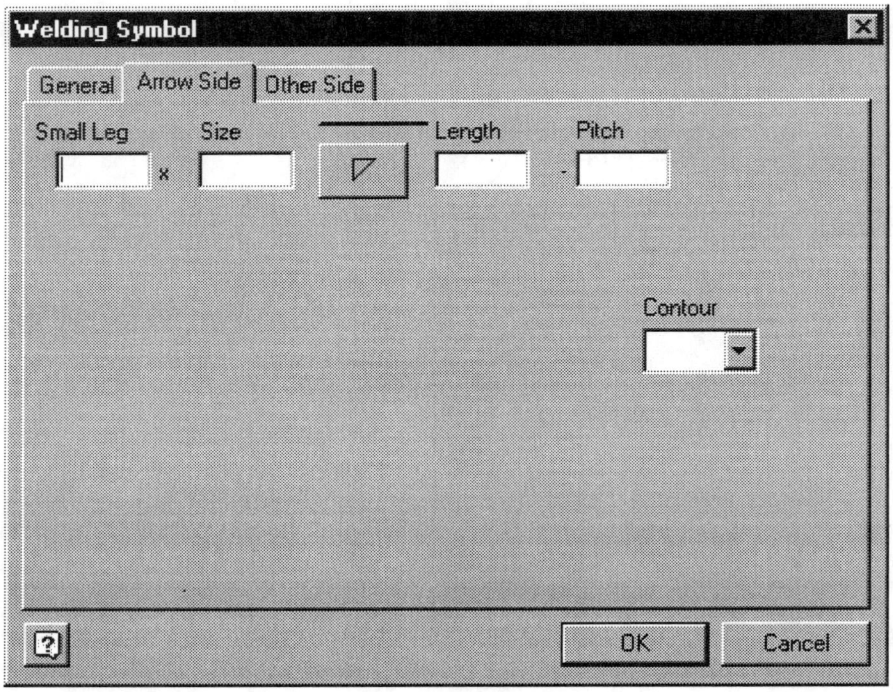

The Arrow Side tab sets the symbols and defines the values for each side of the welding symbol. The available options change, depending on the specified weld type and the active drafting standard. Choose the weld type and secondary fillet type, if applicable, then specify the corresponding attributes.

Secondary fillet type	Specifies the type of weld for secondary fillets. Click the button to display and choose from the palette of available weld types. This button is available only when the active drafting standard is based on ANSI.
Angle	Specifies the angle between weldments.
Brazing	Specifies whether the weld is brazed. Select or clear the check box to add or remove the brazing symbol.
Clearance	Specifies the clearance for the braze.
Contour	Specifies the contour finish for the weld. Click the arrow and choose the contour from the list.
Depth	Specifies the depth of the weld.
Diameter	Specifies the diameter of the weld.
Gap	Specifies the space between weldments.
Height	Specifies the height of the weld.
Length	Specifies the length of the weld.
Method	Specifies the finish method for the weld. Click the arrow and choose the method from the list.
Middle	Specifies the type of inspection to perform on the weld.
Number	Specifies the number of welds.
Pitch	Specifies the distance between welds.
Root	Specifies the root thickness of the weld.
Root gap	Specifies the gap for the weld.
Size	Specifies the size of the weld.
Small leg	Specifies the thickness of the weld.
Spacing	Specifies the space between welds.
Thickness	Specifies the thickness of the weld.

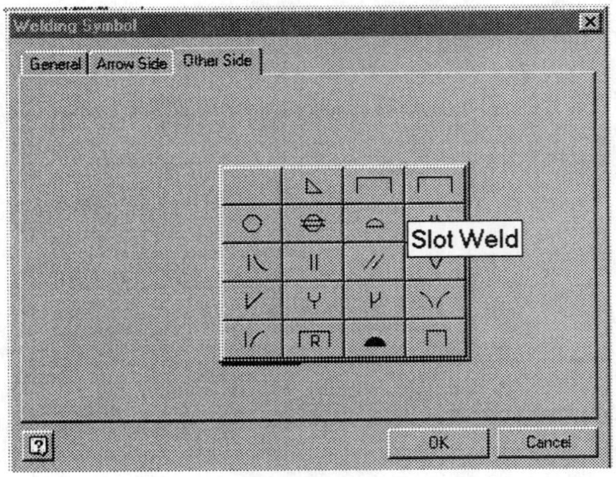

Weld type	Specifies the type of weld. Click the button to display and choose from the palette of available weld types. The weld types displayed on the palette are determined by the active drafting standard.

TIPS: Running your mouse over the buttons without clicking will reveal a help indicating what each symbol represents.

To add or remove symbols from the palette, customize the drafting standard.

To associate the welding symbol with geometry, move the cursor over the desired edge and click when the edge highlights. Symbols that are associated with geometry will move if you move the drawing view.

Move the cursor and click to add a vertex to the leader line.

The line type, line weight, color, and gap for the symbol are determined by the active drafting standard.

To place the symbol:

1. Click the Welding Symbol button.
2. In the graphics window, click to set the start point for the leader line.
3. When the symbol indicator is in the desired position, right-click and select Continue to place the symbol and open the Welding Symbol dialog box. The options in the dialog box are determined by the active drafting standard.
4. Set the attributes and values for the symbol.

Continue placing welding symbols. When you finish placing symbols, right-click and select 'Done' from the menu to end the operation.

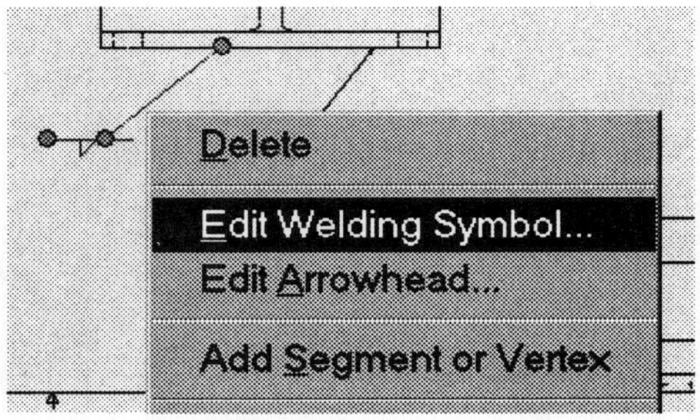

To edit an existing symbol:

1. Activate the select tool
2. Pick the symbol to edit. You should see green grips activate.Right click and select the editing mode desired.

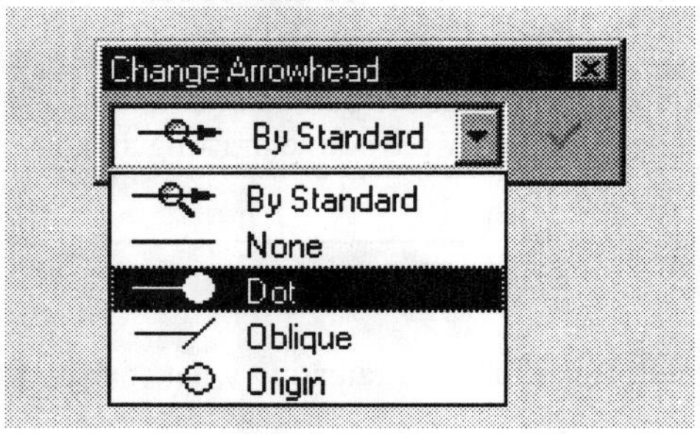

Selecting the Edit Arrowhead option will bring up a dialog where the user can select the current standard or a different arrowhead.

Selecting the 'Add Segment or Vertex option' activates the Grip mode and the user can use the mouse to stretch or modify the leader for the symbol.

Feature Control Frame

Specifies the content of a feature control frame. The options in the dialog box are determined by the active drafting standard.

Sym	Specifies the tolerance symbol. Click the button to open the symbol palette and select the desired symbol. The symbols on the palette are determined by the active drafting standard.
Tolerance	Sets the tolerance values. Tolerance 1 specifies the tolerance. Tolerance 2 specifies the lower tolerance (ANSI standard only).
Datum	Specifies the datums that affect the tolerance.
Insert modifier buttons	Adds modifier characters to the text at the insertion point. Click a button to add the desired character. The available characters are determined by the active drafting standard.
All Around	Adds an all-around character next to the feature control frame. Select the check box to add the character; clear the check box to remove it.

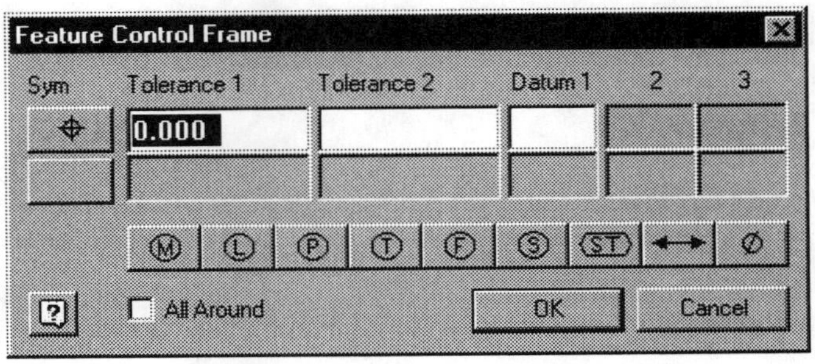

1. Click the Feature Control Frame button.
2. In the graphics window, click to set the start point for the leader line. If you place the point on a highlighted edge or point, the leader line is attached to the geometry. If you are creating a leader line, move the cursor and click to add a vertex to the leader line.
3. When the symbol indicator is in the desired position, right-click and select 'Continue' to place the symbol and open the dialog box. The options in the dialog box are determined by the active drafting standard.
4. Enter the information for the symbol and close the dialog box.

Continue placing feature control frames. When you finish placing symbols, right-click and choose 'Done' from the menu to end the operation.

TIPS:
The text boxes in the second row are available only if you select a tolerance-type symbol for the row. You can specify in the active drafting standard whether to merge corresponding fields when the information is the same.

You can create a feature control frame with a leader line or as a stand-alone symbol. The color and line weight of the symbol are determined by the active drafting standard.

To place a symbol without a leader, double-click to set the symbol location and open the dialog box.

Feature Identifier Symbol

NOTE: This tool is NOT available in ANSI standard mode. To access this symbol, go to Format-Standards and select ISO, DIN, or JIS.

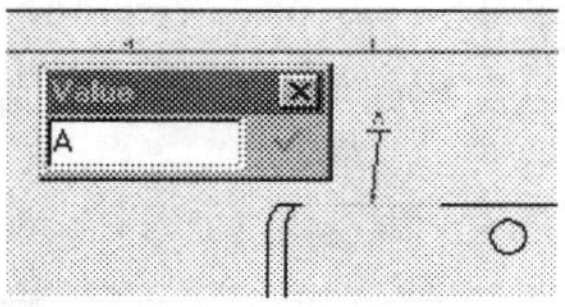

Use the Feature Identifier button on the Drawing Annotation toolbar to create a feature identifier symbol with a leader line. The color and line weight of the symbol are determined by the active drafting standard.

1. Click the Feature Identifier button.
2. In the graphics window, click to set the start point for the leader line.
3. Move the cursor and click to add a vertex to the leader line. You can only add one vertex.
4. When the symbol indicator is in the desired position, click to place the symbol and open the Value dialog box.
5. Enter the appropriate label for the symbol and then click the check mark to close the dialog box.

Continue placing feature identifier symbols. When you finish placing symbols, right-click and select Done from the menu to end the command.

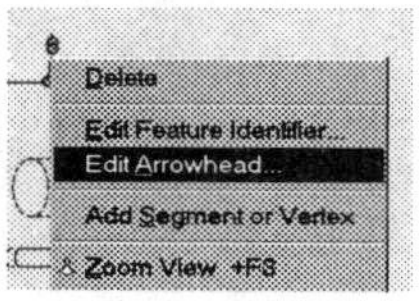

To edit an existing symbol:

1. Activate the select tool
2. Pick the symbol to edit. You should see green grips activate.Right click and select the editing mode desired.

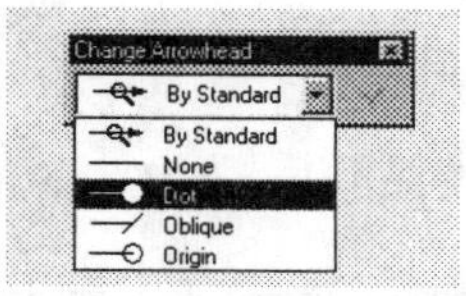

Selecting the Edit Arrowhead option will bring up a dialog where the user can select the current standard or a different arrowhead.

Selecting the 'Add Segment or Vertex option' activates the Grip mode and the user can use the mouse to stretch or modify the leader for the symbol.

Datum Identifier Symbol

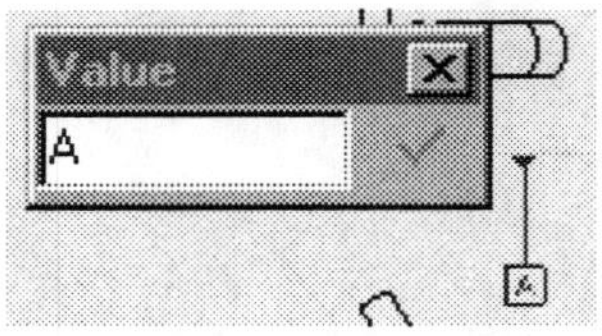

Use the Datum Identifier button on the Drawing Annotation toolbar to create one or more datum identifier symbols. You can create a datum identifier with a leader line or as a stand-alone symbol. The color and line weight of the symbol are determined by the active drafting standard.

1. Click the Datum Identifier button.
2. In the graphics window, click to indicate the start point for the leader line or double-click to place a symbol without a leader. If you place the point on a highlighted edge or point, the leader line is attached to the geometry.
3. If you are creating a leader line, move the cursor and click to add a vertex to the leader line. You can only add one vertex.
4. When the symbol indicator is in the desired position, click to place the symbol and open the Value dialog box.
5. Enter the appropriate label for the symbol and then click the check mark to close the dialog box.

Continue placing datum identifier symbols. When you finish placing symbols, right-click and choose 'Done' from the menu to end the operation.

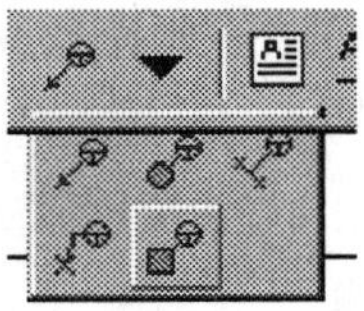

Datum Target

Click the arrow next to the Datum Target Symbol button and choose the datum target type from the pop-up menu.

Dimension	Specifies size of the target area. Enter the number.
Datum	Specifies the label for the target.

Target types are Leader, Line, Rectangle, Circle, and Point.

1. Click the arrow next to the Datum Target button.
2. Select the target style from the palette.
3. In the graphic window, click to set the start point for the datum.
    - Leader datum start point sets the terminator for the leader line.
    - Line datum start point sets one end of the datum line. Click to set the other end.
    - Rectangle datum start point sets the center of the rectangle. Click again to define the area.
    - Circle datum start point sets the center of the circle area. Click to again to define the area.
    - Point datum start point places the point indicator.
4. Move the cursor and click to add a vertex to the leader line.
5. When the symbol indicator is in the desired position, right-click and choose Continue to place the symbol and open the Datum Target dialog box.

Enter the appropriate dimension value and datum for the symbol

Continue placing datum target symbols. When you finish placing symbols, right-click and choose 'Done' from the menu to end the operation.

TIPS:
To stack datum targets, right-click an existing datum target and select Attach Balloon from the menu.

The color, target size, and line weight of the symbol are determined by the active drafting standard.

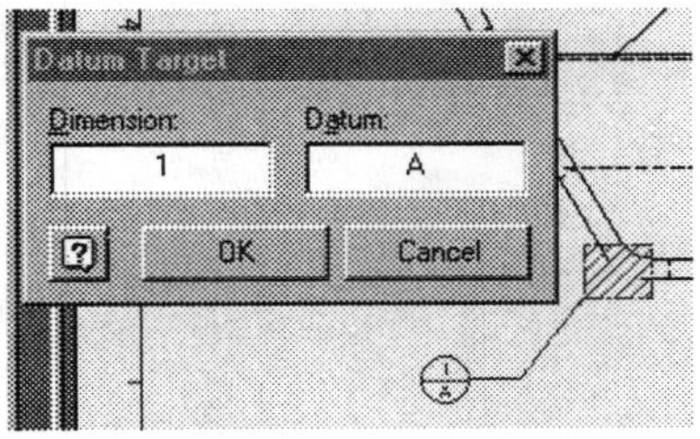

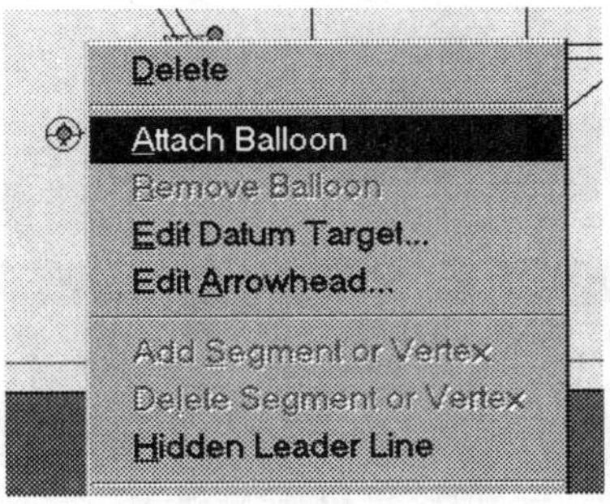

To edit an existing symbol:

1. Activate the select tool
2. Pick the symbol to edit.You should see green grips activate.4. Right click and select the editing mode desired.

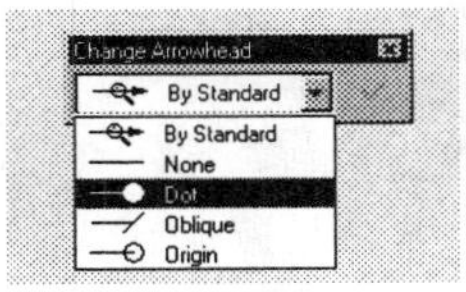

Selecting the Edit Arrowhead option will bring up a dialog where the user can select the current standard or a different arrowhead.

Selecting the 'Add Segment or Vertex option' activates the Grip mode and the user can use the mouse to stretch or modify the leader for the symbol.

To stack datum targets, select Attach Balloon from the menu.

Selecting 'Hidden Leader Line' changes the linetype of the leader to Hidden.

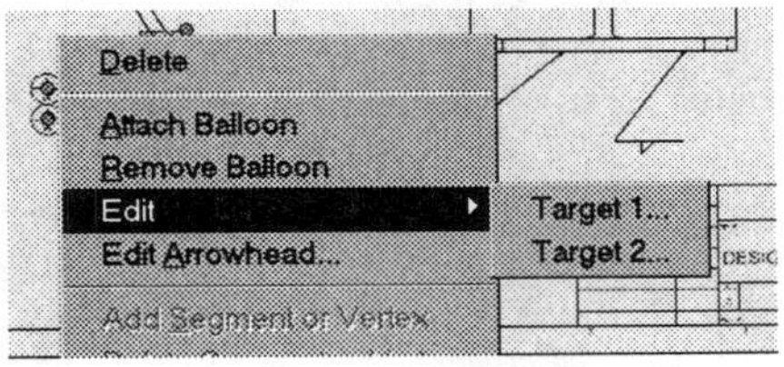

If you have stacked datum targets and need to make modifications, the right click menu adapts to give you the option of editing different targets.

Text

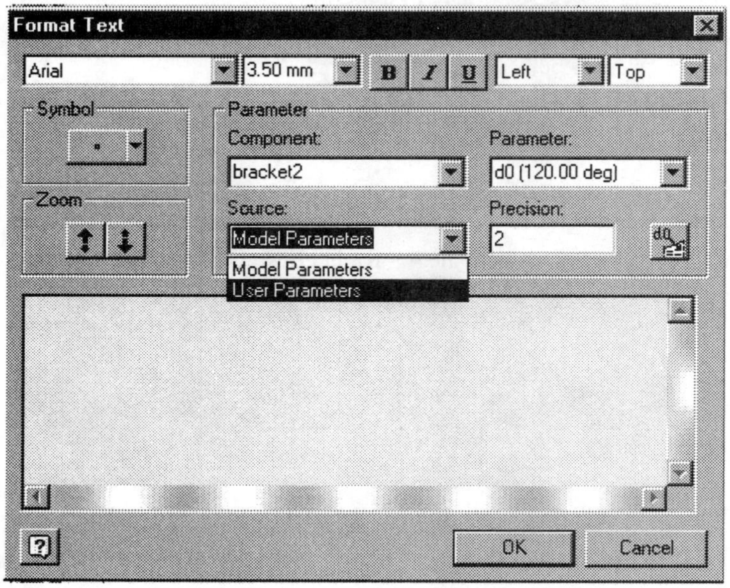

Use the Text button on the Drawing Annotation toolbar to add general notes to a drawing. General notes are not attached to a view, symbol, or other object in the drawing.

1. Click the Text button.
2. Use one of the following methods to define the text box:
    - Click to place the top-left corner of the text box. When you enter the note, the width of the box adjusts to the longest line of text.
    - Drag to define the area of the text box. When you enter the note, the text wraps within the defined width of the box.
3. Enter the text at the blinking insertion point. You can click to reposition the insertion point relative to previously entered text.
    - To add a symbol to the text, click the symbol button in the Text dialog box and select the symbol from the palette.
    - To add a named parameter from the model file to the text, specify the source and parameter name, then click the Add Parameter button.
    - To change the formatting, select the text then choose the formatting options.

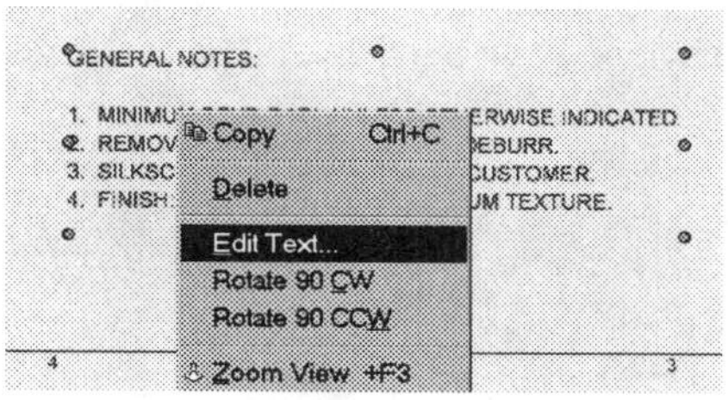

To modify a general note, select it in the graphics window, right-click, and select the operation from the menu.

- To copy the note, select copy. You can paste the text to another place on the drawing sheet, to a different sheet in the same drawing, or to a sheet in another drawing.
- To remove the note, select Delete.
- To edit or format the existing text, select Edit Text to open the Format Text dialog box.
- To rotate the note, select the desired rotate direction.

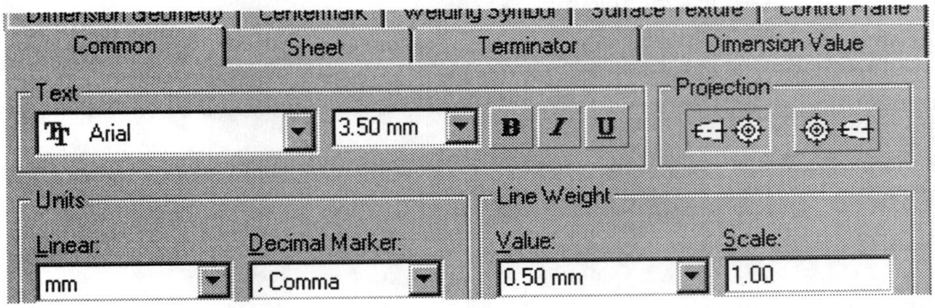

TIPS:
The default text format is controlled by the active drafting standard. To change the default text for a drawing or template, modify the drafting standard. Go to Format->Standards and select the Common tab.

Leader Text

Use the Leader Text button on the Drawing Annotation toolbar to add notes with leader lines to a drawing.

1. Click the Leader Text button.
2. In the graphics window, click to set the starting point for the leader line. If you place the point on a highlighted view, the leader line is attached to the view.
3. Use one of the following methods to define the text box:
    - Click to place the top-left corner of the text box. When you enter the note, the width of the box adjusts to the longest line of text.
    - Drag to define the area of the text box. When you enter the note, the text wraps within the defined width of the box.
4. Enter the text at the blinking insertion point. You can click to reposition the insertion point relative to previously entered text.
    - To add a symbol to the text, click the symbol button in the Text dialog box and select the symbol from the palette.
    - To add a named parameter from the model file to the text, specify the source and parameter name, then click the Add Parameter button.
    - To change the formatting, select the text then choose the formatting options.

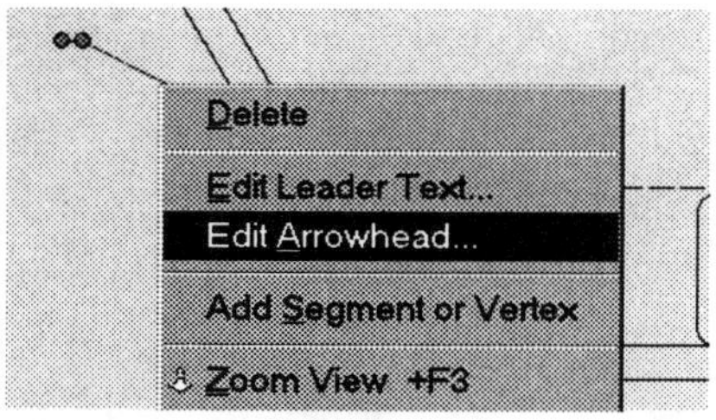

To modify a note, select it in the graphics window, right-click, and select the operation from the menu.

- To remove the note, select Delete.
- To edit or format the existing text, select Edit Text to open the Format Text dialog box.
- To change the arrowhead or other terminator, select Edit Arrowhead and select the new terminator from the dialog box.
- To add a point to the leader line, select Add Segment or Vertex, then click in the graphics window to place the point. You can drag the added point to redefine the leader line.

TIPS:

If you attach a note leader line to a view or to geometry within a view, the note is moved or deleted when the view is moved or deleted.

The active drafting standard controls the default text format. To change the default text for a drawing or template, modify the drafting standard. Go to Format->Standards and select the Common tab.

Balloon/ Balloon All

Use the desired Balloon button (Balloon/Balloon All) on the Drawing Annotation toolbar to add reference balloons to a drawing.

To add a balloon to an individual part (Balloon):

1. Click the Balloon button.
2. In the graphics window, select the part and then click to set the start point for the leader line.
3. Move the cursor and click to add a vertex.
4. When the symbol indicator is in the desired position, right-click and choose Continue to place the symbol. The symbol style is determined by the active drafting standard.

Continue placing balloons. When you finish placing balloons, right-click and select Done from the menu to end the operation.

To add balloons to all the parts in a view:

1. Click the arrow next to the Balloon button and select Balloon All.
2. In the graphics window, select the view.

Editing Balloons:

The default style for balloons is defined by the active drafting standard. After placing a balloon, you can change the arrowhead style, attach or remove additional balloons, or add segments to the leader line.

To remove a balloon from a stacked set, right-click the balloon and select 'Remove Balloon' from the menu. <u>If there are several attached balloons, the last balloon to be attached is removed first.</u>

A balloon can contain the item number of a first-level component in the assembly, or of an individual part, depending on the setting in the active drafting standard. You can change the level of the item number in a balloon.

To change the Level of a balloon reference, right-click the balloon and select Part to show the item number for the part to which the balloon is attached, or First-Level Component to show the item number for the subassembly that contains the part.

TIPS:

A first-level component can be either a subassembly or a part.

If you add balloons to a drawing before creating a parts list, the balloons will show the item numbers of first-level components. You can select a balloon and change it to show the item number of the part to which it is attached.

Typing 'B' will initiate the Balloon command.

Parts List

Adds a parts list for the components of the assembly in the selected view.

Sets the number of levels of components to include in the parts list. Select the desired level.	
First-Level Components	Creates a parts list that shows only the top level of components of the assembly in the selected view. Subassemblies and parts that are not part of a subassembly are shown, but not the parts in the subassemblies.
Only Parts	Creates a parts list that shows the parts of the assembly in the selected view. Subassemblies are not shown, but the parts in the subassemblies are shown.
Set the scope of parts list to include all or a range of components of the assembly in the selected view when the Level is set to Only Parts. Not available when First-Level Components is selected.	
All	Creates a parts list for all the components in the selected view.
Items	Creates a parts list for the specified range of parts. Select Items then enter the part numbers, separated by commas, or click the parts in the graphics window to include them in the list.

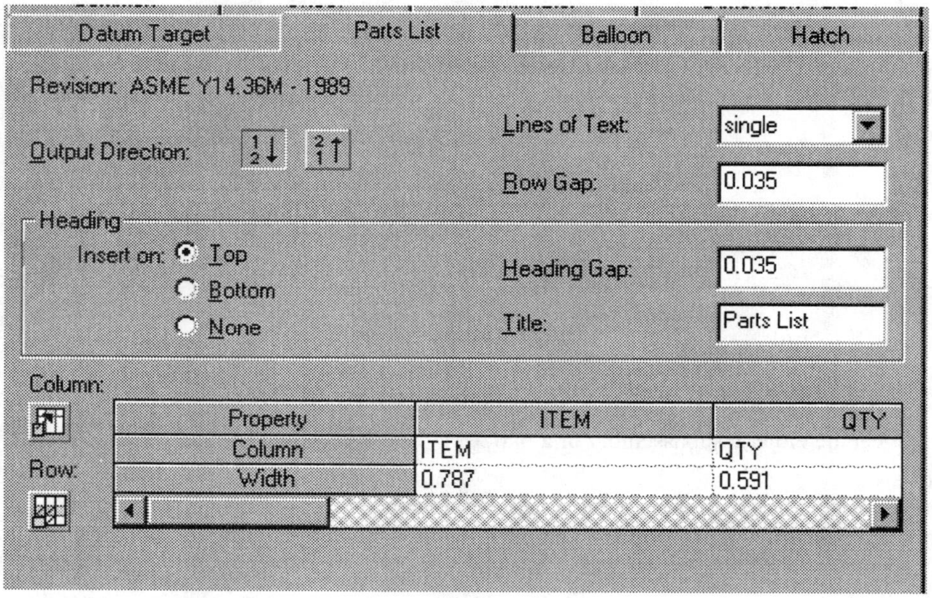

The Parts List format is set in the Drafting Standards dialog box. Access by selecting Format->Standards.

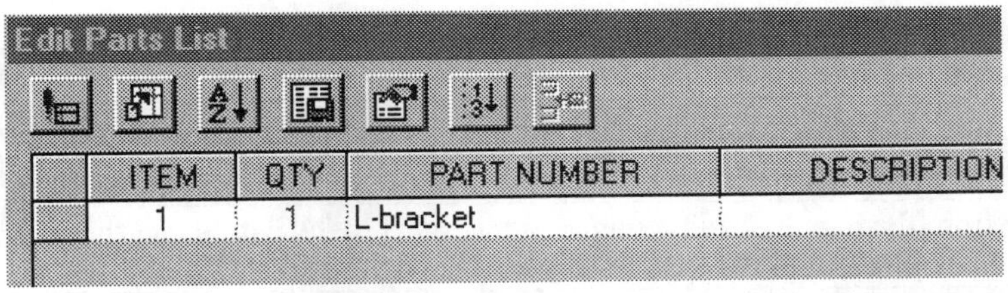

Parts List Operations performs operations on the selected parts list. Click the appropriate button to perform the operation.	
	Compare checks the values in the selected parts list against the current properties values for the parts. If the values differ, the corresponding cells in the spreadsheet are highlighted.
	Column Chooser opens the Column Chooser dialog box so that you can add, remove, or change the order of the columns for the selected parts list.
	Sort opens the Sort Parts List dialog box so that you can change the sort order for items in the select parts list.
	Export opens the Export Parts List dialog box so that you can save the selected parts list to an external file.
	Heading opens the Heading Parts List dialog box so that you can change the title text or heading location for the selected parts list.

TIPS:
To change the default heading location and title text for parts lists, use Format>Standards>Parts List to change the attributes of the active drafting standard.

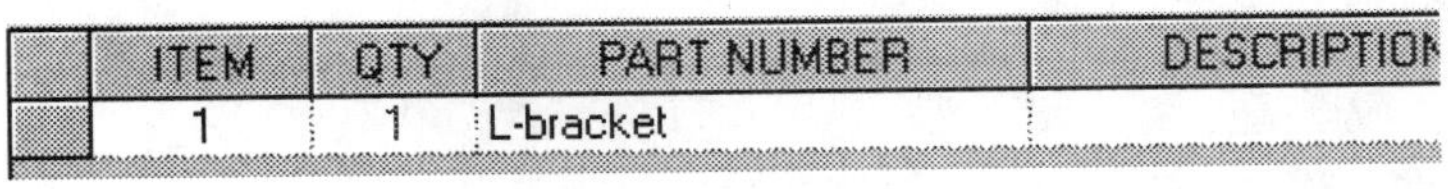

Spreadsheet displays the content and setup of the selected parts list. As you perform operations or change column properties, the changes are reflected in the spreadsheet. Items that have corresponding balloons are marked with a balloon symbol. If you compare the parts list to the current properties for the parts (click the Compare button), the values that are inconsistent are highlighted in the spreadsheet. To resolve, right-click a highlighted cell and select the desired resolution from the menu.	
Update Value	Changes the value in the selected cell to match the value in the part properties.
Update All	Changes the values for all the highlighted cells to match the values in the part properties.
Keep Value	Keeps the value in the selected cell, even though it diverges from the value in the part properties.
Keep All	Keeps the values of all the highlighted cells, even though they diverge from the values in the part properties

Custom Parts adds non-graphic parts such as adhesives and lubricants to the parts list.	
	Adds a row to the parts list and renumbers the items in the list. Click the Add button to add the row, then enter the part information.
	Removes a custom part row from the parts list and renumbers the items in the list. Select the row to remove, then click the Delete button.
Column Properties sets the width and alignment for the columns in the selected parts list.	
Name	Displays the name of the selected column.
Width	Sets the width of the selected column. Enter the width in the box.
Name Alignment	Sets the alignment for the column title. Click a button to select left, center, or right alignment.
Data Alignment	Sets the alignment for the data in the column. Click a button to select left, center, or right alignment.

When a parts list is placed, its setup is determined by the settings in the active drafting standard. You can modify the settings for a parts list after placing it.

1. Select the parts list in the graphics window or from the browser.
2. Right-click and select Edit Parts List from the menu.
3. Click the appropriate button in the dialog box to perform any of the following operations:
    - Compare parts list values with part properties
    - Change the columns that display in the parts list
    - Change the sort order of the parts list
    - Export parts list data to an external file
    - Change the title name or heading location for the parts list
    - Change the name of the column heading
    - Add custom parts to the parts list
4. Click the More button to display and change column properties.

Changing the Heading Location or Title of a Parts List

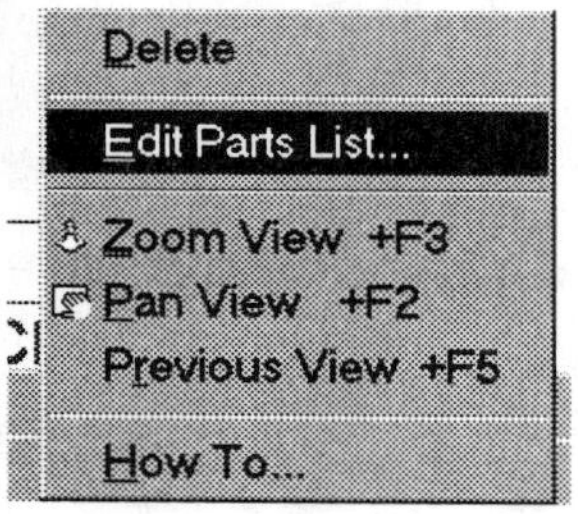

To change the location of the Parts List Heading, right click on the Parts List, and select 'Edit Parts List'.

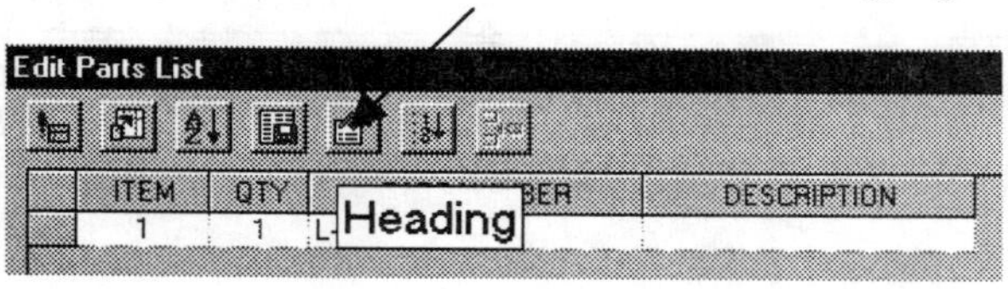

Select the Heading button in the dialog box.

This brings up another dialog where the user can set the location or change the title of the Parts List.

Drawing AnnotationTools

Button	Tool	Function	Special Instructions
	General Dimension	Creates a dimension between two points, lines, or curves.	Double click on a dimension to edit.
	Ordinate Dimension Set	Places a set of ordinate dimensions along an axis. The first dimension placed is automatically assumed to be the origin dimension.	To edit, select then right click to access the edit options
	Ordinate Dimension	Creates an ordinate dimension	Requires the user to select an Origin prior to placing the dimension
	Hole/Thread Notes	Adds a hole or thread note with leader	Hole notes can only be added to features created with the Hole tool.
	Center Mark	Creates a center mark	Style of center mark is set up in Drafting Standards under Format
	Center Line	Creates a center line	Right click to get assistance in placing the line
	Center line Bisector	Creates an angle bisector	Select two lines to bisect
	Centered Pattern	Creates a centerline for a circular pattern	
	Surface Texture Symbol	Creates a surface texture symbol	Some options not available in ANSI mode.
	Weld Symbol	Creates a weld symbol	Drafting Standards control the linetype, color, and gap
	Feature Control Frame	Creates a feature control symbol	Typing F can be used to initiate this command
	Feature Identifier Symbol	Creates a feature identifier symbol	NOT available in ANSI standard mode
	Datum Identifier Symbol	Creates a datum identifier symbol	
	Datum Targets	Datum Target with leader	
		Datum Target with circle	
		Datum Target with line	
		Datum Target with point	
		Datum Target with rectangle	
	Text	Creates a text block	Similar to MTEXT
	Leader text	Creates text with a leader attached.	
	Add balloon	Adds a reference balloon	Inventor assigns the reference numbers to parts automatically
	Balloon All	Adds balloons to all the parts in a view	
	Parts List	Creates a parts list	Customize the parts list using property fields

Review Questions

1. True or False

   You can select and delete only one ordinate dimension created using the Ordinate Dimension Set tool.

2. True or False

   When placing ordinate dimensions using the Ordinate Dimension Set tool, you can switch between the two axes – that is, place a dimension along the x-axis, place a dimension along the y-axis, then place a dimension along the x-axis.

3. True or False

   You can not hide the Origin Indicator placed with the Ordinate Dimension tool.

4. True or False

   Inventor only has one style of Datum Target.

5. To modify a linear dimension:
   - A. Select the dimension, right click and select 'Edit Dimension'
   - B. Select Edit from the Menu.
   - C. Double click on the dimension
   - D. Right click in the graphics window and select 'Edit Dimension'.

NOTES:

Lesson 20

Orthographic Views

Learning Objectives

At the conclusion of this lesson, the user will have gained mastery of the Drawing Management tools.

Open a new drawing file.

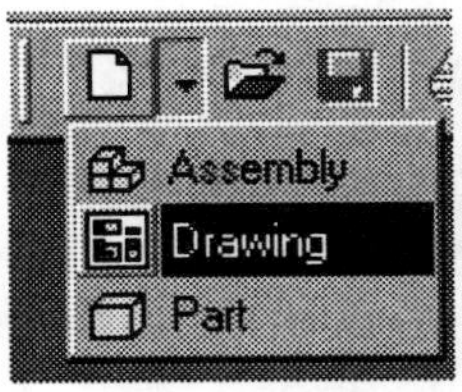

Create a Base View

Inventor automatically assumes that the first view placed on a drawing sheet is the Base or primary view. To create a base view, issue the 'Create View' command.

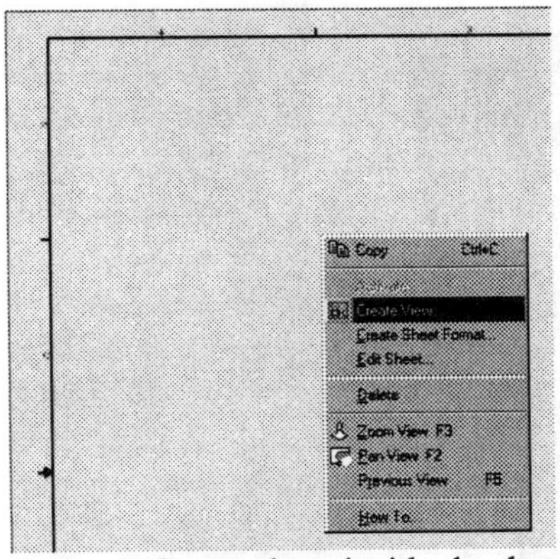

Right click anywhere inside the drawing sheet and select 'Create View'.

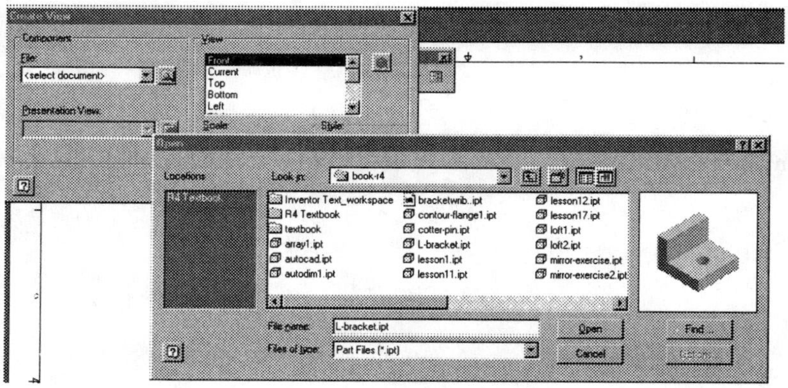

Verify that the 'Front' view is highlighted in the dialog box.
Select 'Hidden' as the style as shown.
Set the Scale to 1 as shown.
Enable Dimensions by placing a check in the box next to Dimensions in the lower right corner.
Click on the file browser button. Locate the file called 'L-bracket.ipt' and press 'Open'.

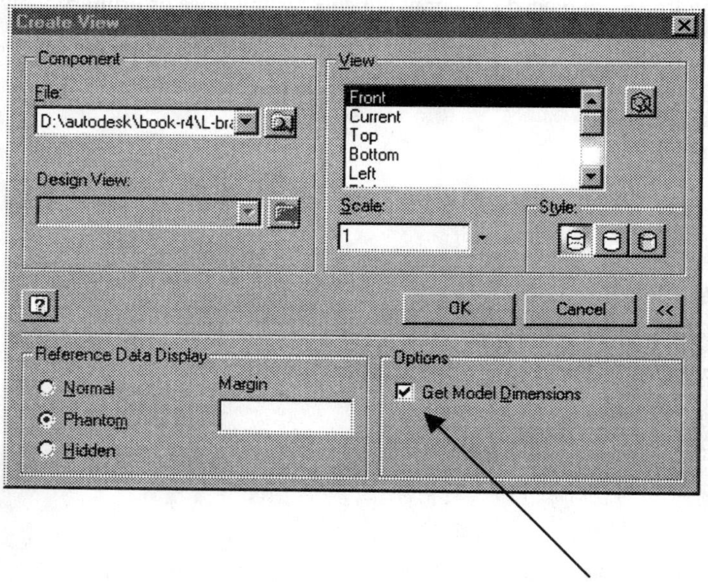

Make sure the 'Get Model Dimensions' is enabled.

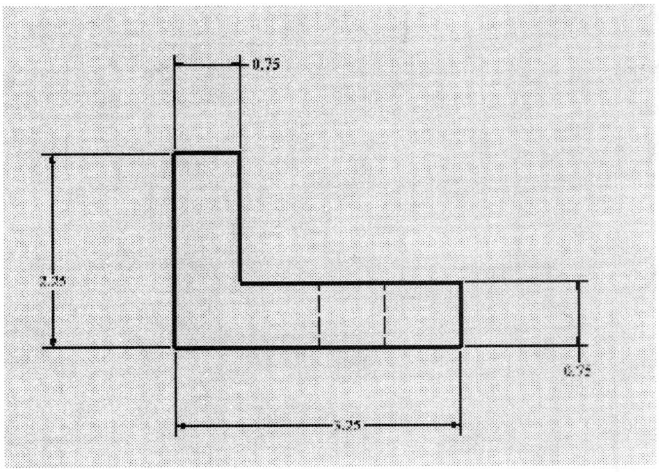

Place the view by picking in the lower left side of the drawing sheet.
Note that the dimensions appear with the view.

Create a Projected View

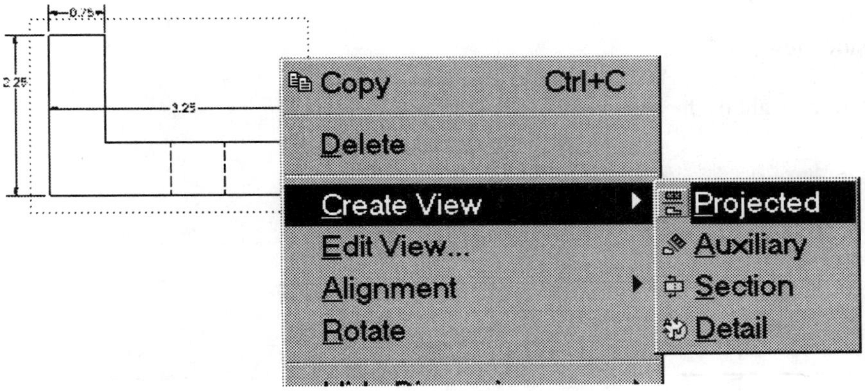

Highlight the base view by picking on it. (A red dotted rectangle should appear as shown)
Right click the mouse to bring up the menu. Select Create View->Projected.

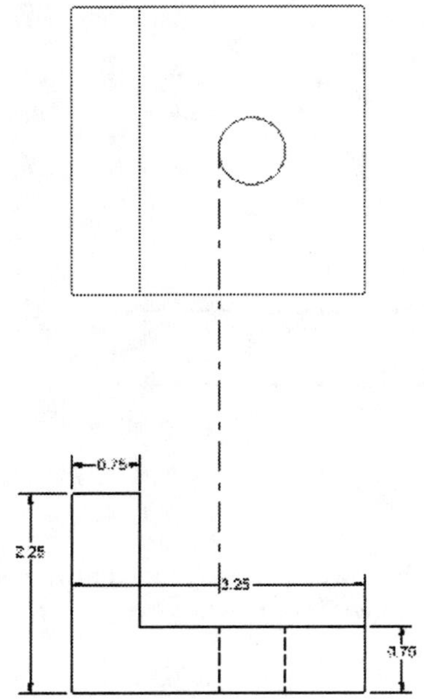

Pick the location for the top view.

Create the right side view

Move the mouse to the right of the base view.

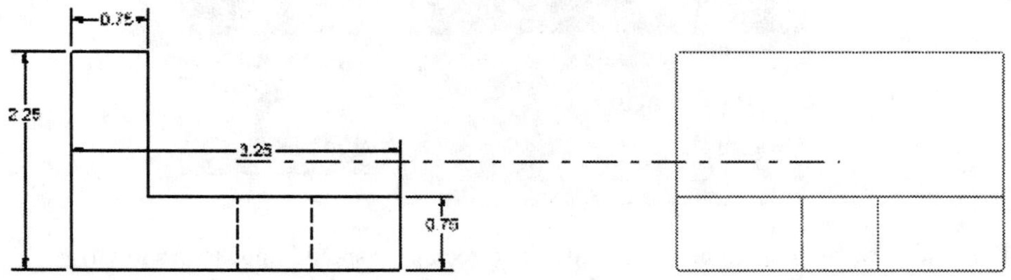

Pick to place the right side view.

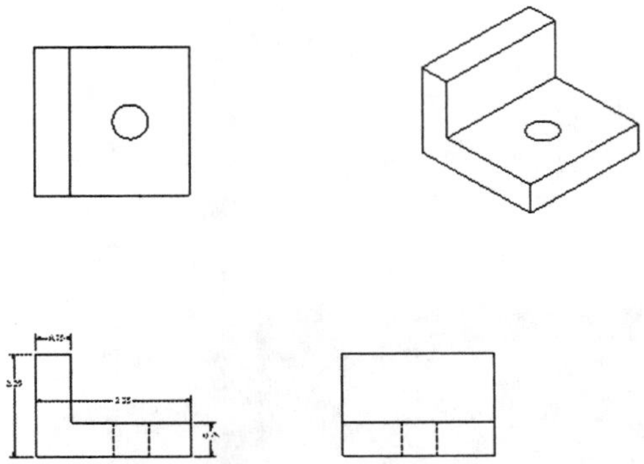

Place isometric view

Move the mouse above the right side view and pick to place the isometric view.

Right click the mouse and select 'Create' to set the views in place and finish.

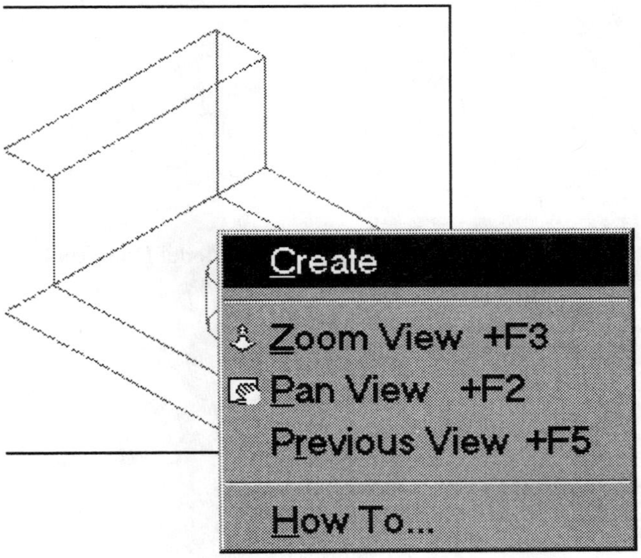

Bring up the Drawing Annotation toolbar.

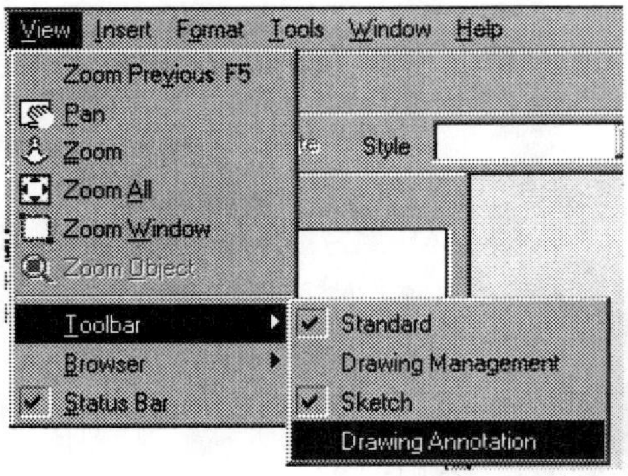

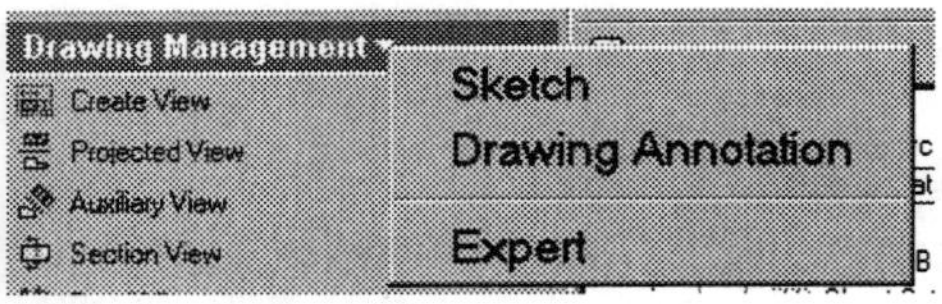

To activate the Drawing Annotation Toolbar:

- Go to View->Toolbar->Drawing Annotation and select.
- Left pick on the top bar of the panel bar toolbar and select Drawing Annotation

Add dimensions to a View

Use 'Zoom Window' to zoom into the top view.

Pick on the view so that it highlights. Right click the mouse and select 'Get Model Dimensions'.

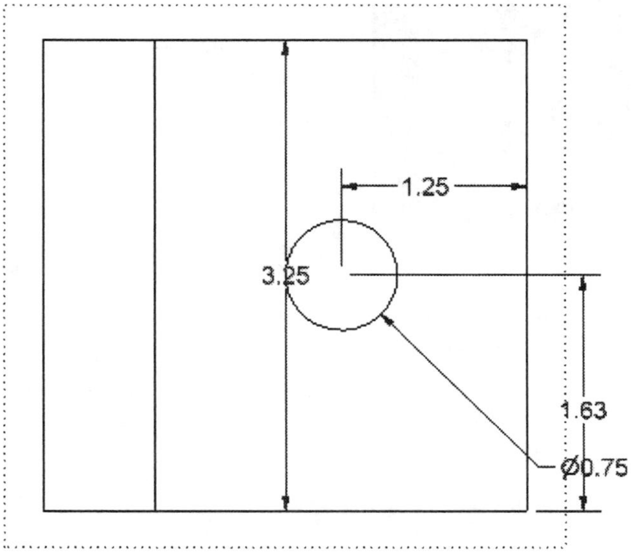

The dimensions will appear as shown.

Deleting Dimensions

Select the hole diameter dimension. Right click and select delete.

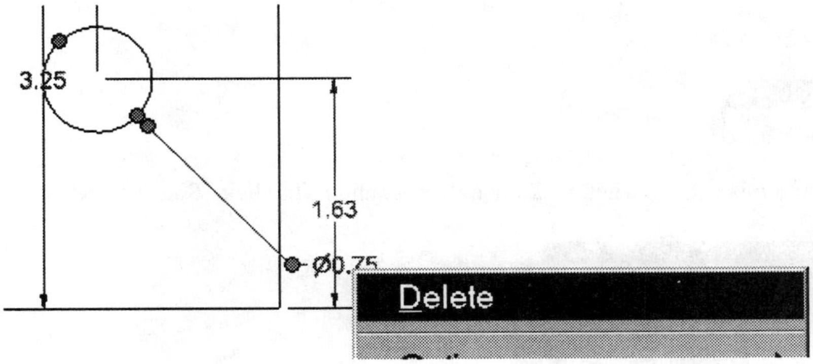

Create Hole/Thread Notes

Select the Hole/Thread Notes tool.

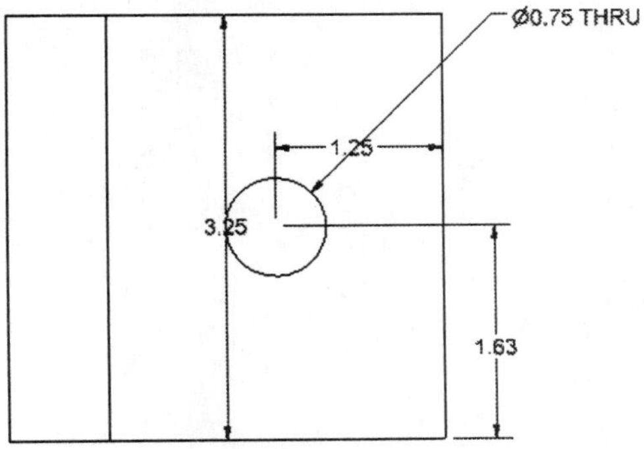

Pick the hole where you want to add the annotation. Then drag out to place the leader shoulder. The hole note is automatically created using the hole definition.
Right click and select 'Done' when the text is located correctly.

Editing A Hole Note

If for some reason, you don't like the appearance of a hole note, it can be modified.

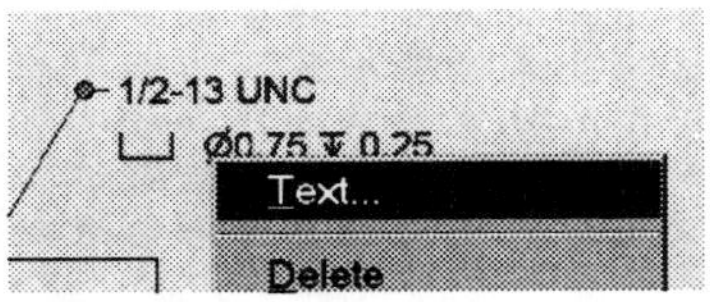

Make sure the Select button is active. Then pick the hole note and right click. Select 'Text'.

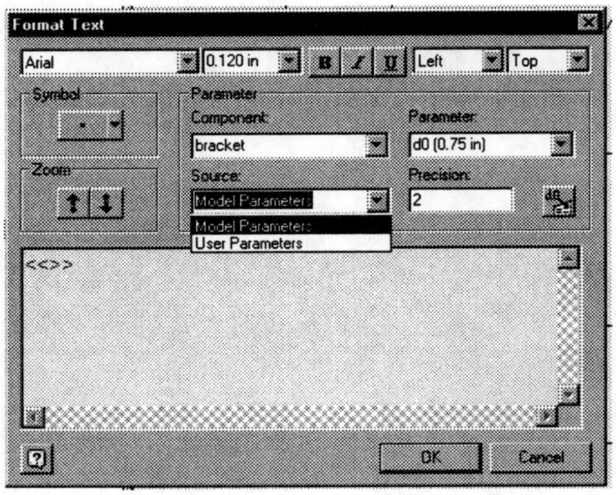

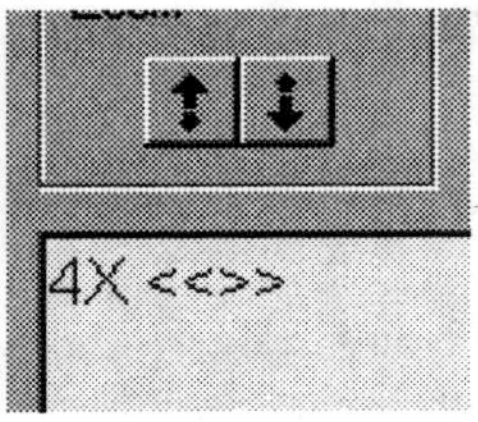

The <<>> in the edit box indicates the default value for the text. Simply delete the default and type in the desired note or add text.

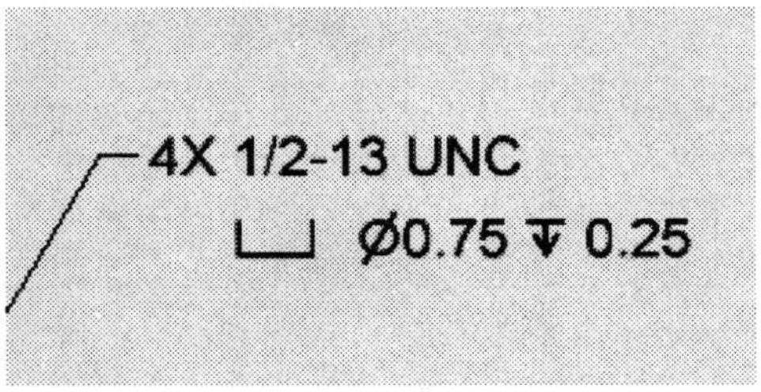

TIPS: If you accidentally delete the default value, simply type <<>> in the edit box and the default value will be restored.

Move Dimensions

To relocate a dimension, select it and grab one of the green dots. These act like grips. Drag the dimension to the desired location.

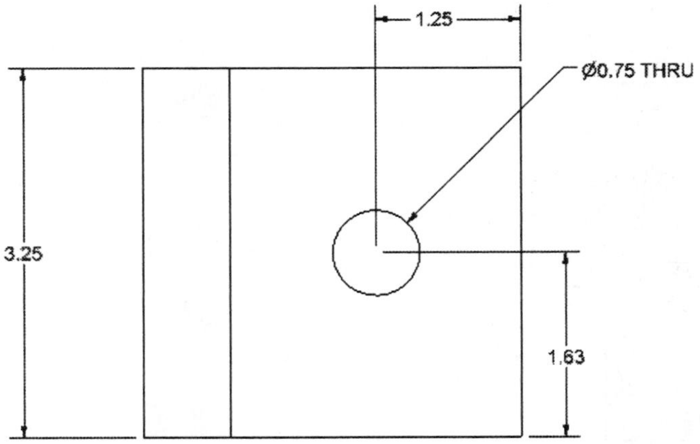

Dimension Standards

The format of dimensions, such as precision and font, is set in the Drafting Standards. To access, select Format->Standards from the menu.

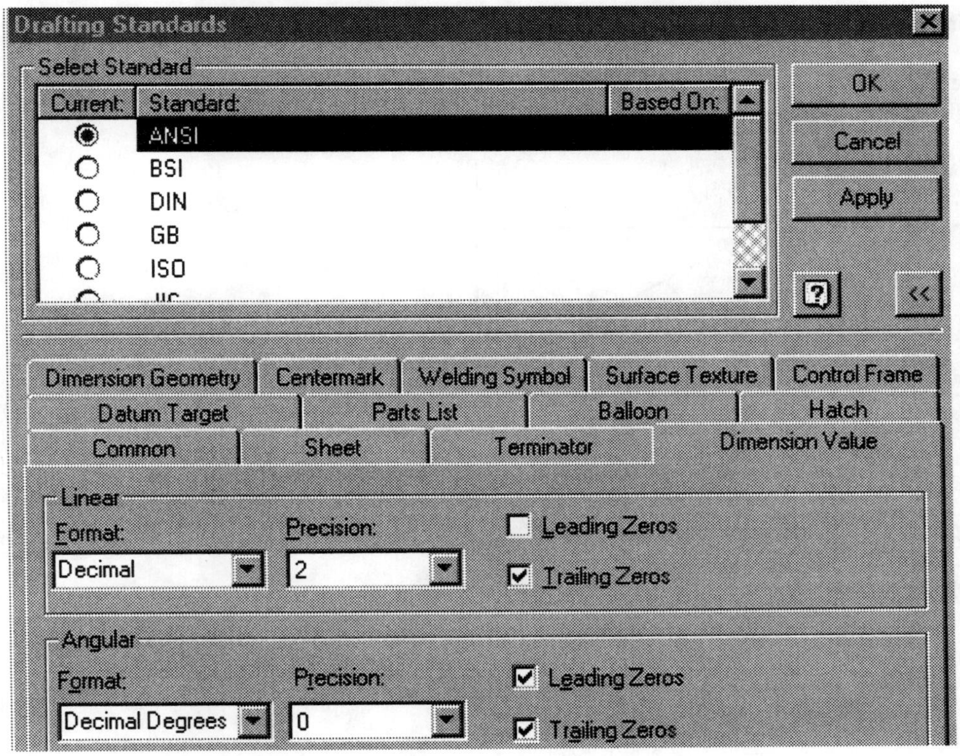

The Common tab controls the font of dimensions.

Create Center Mark

Add a center mark to the circle.

Select the Center Mark tool from the Drawing Annotation toolbar.
Then pick the circle.

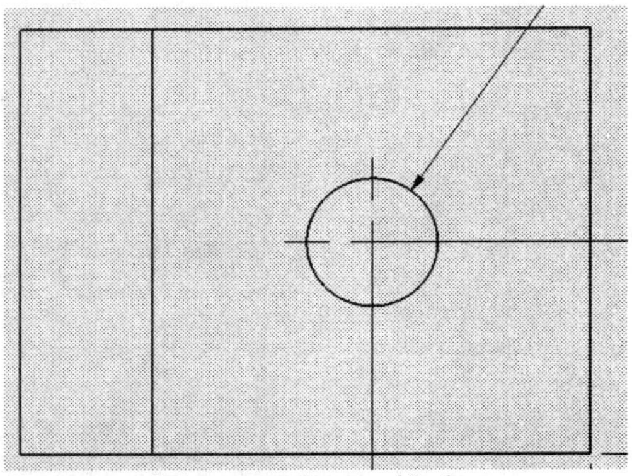

Center mark has now been added.

Create Centerline

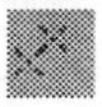

Let's create a centerline for the hole shown in the right side view.

The Centerline tool is located on the Drawing Annotation toolbar under the Center mark drop down.

Select the Centerline tool. Select the top horizontal line and then the bottom horizontal line of the bracket. Right click the mouse and select 'Create'.

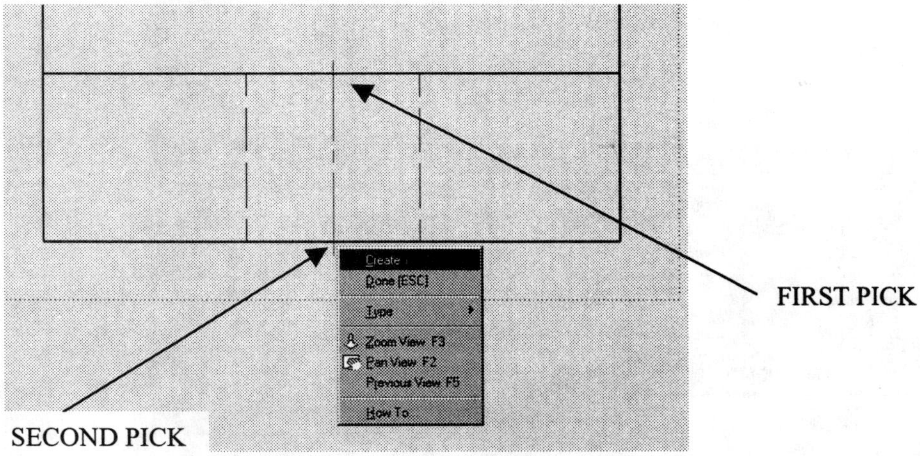

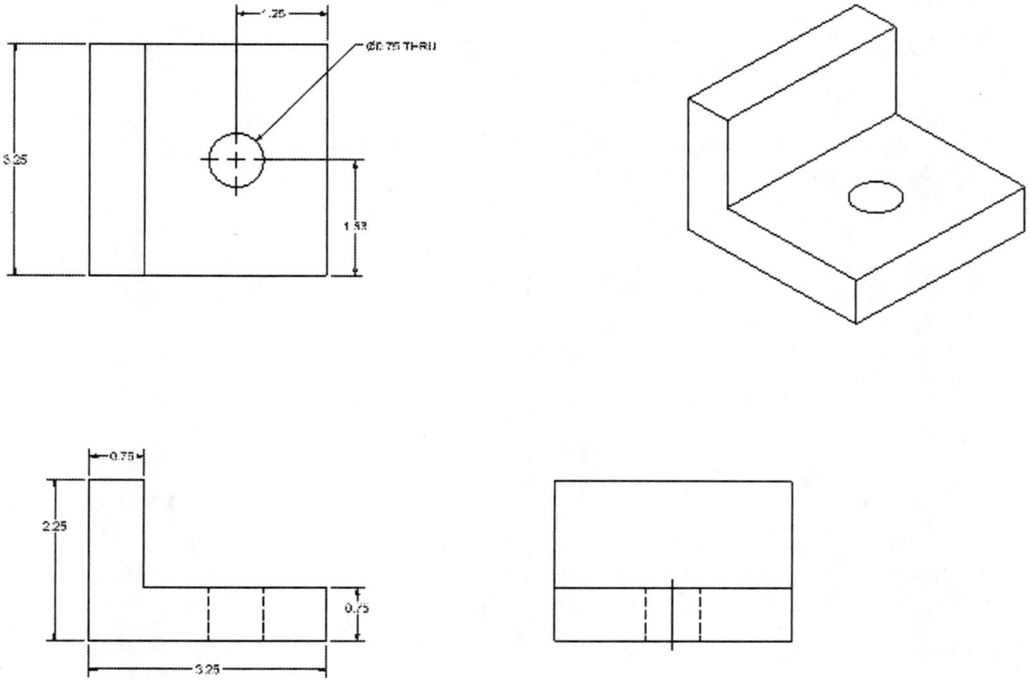

Our completed drawing.

Save the drawing as 'orthol.idw'.

Notes:

Lesson 21
Auxiliary Views

Learning Objectives

At the conclusion of this lesson, the user will be able to create and edit auxiliary views using parts with inclined planes.

We can use the part created in Lesson 17.

Open a new drawing file using the part. The file name is 'lesson17.ipt'.

Create the basic orthogonal views as shown.

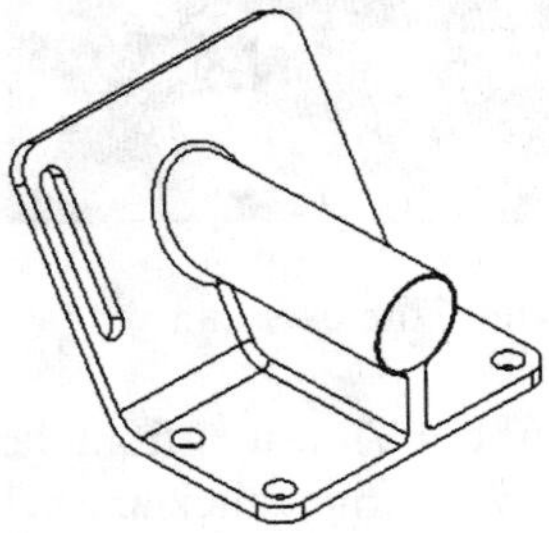

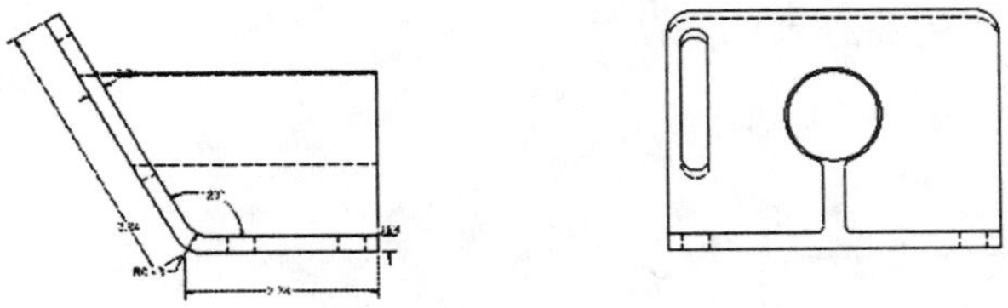

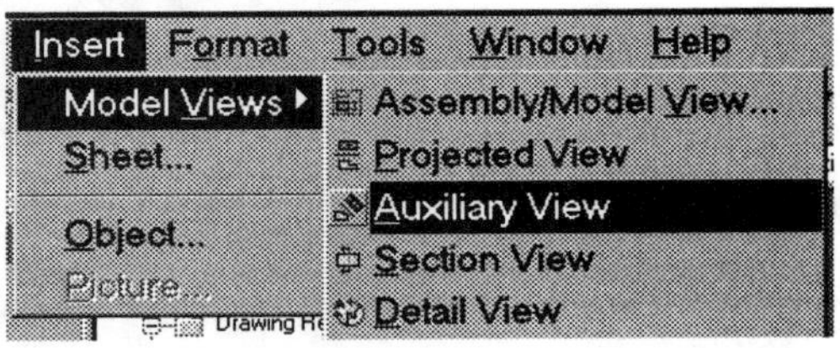

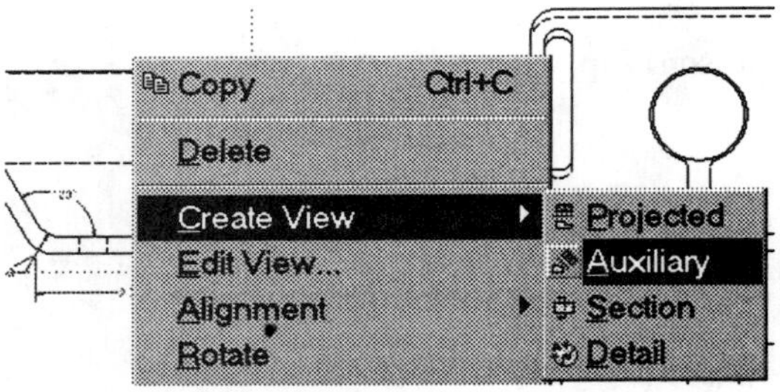

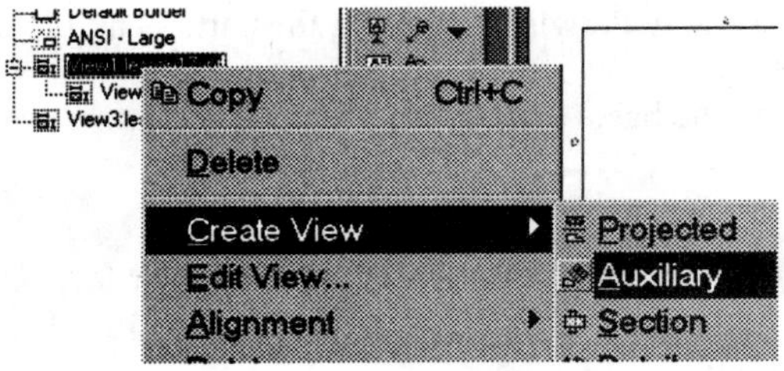

To create an auxiliary view, the user can:

- Select the Auxiliary View tool from the Drawing Management tools.
- Select the base view, right click and select Create View->Auxiliary
- Go to Insert->Model Views->Auxiliary View from the menu.
- Go to the browser, select the source view for the Auxiliary view, right click and select Create View-> Auxiliary View

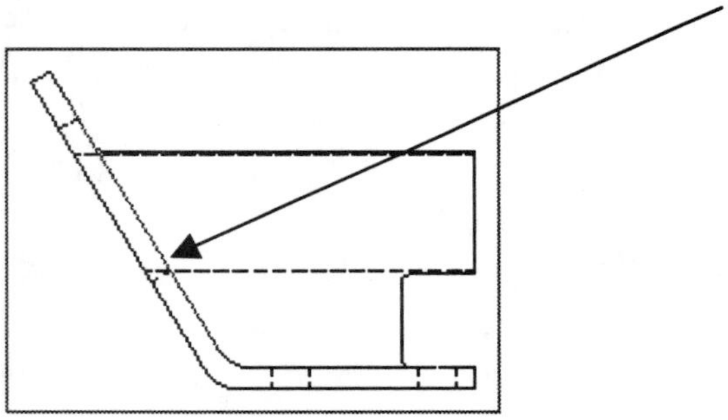

Select the line that the auxiliary view will use as the source plane.

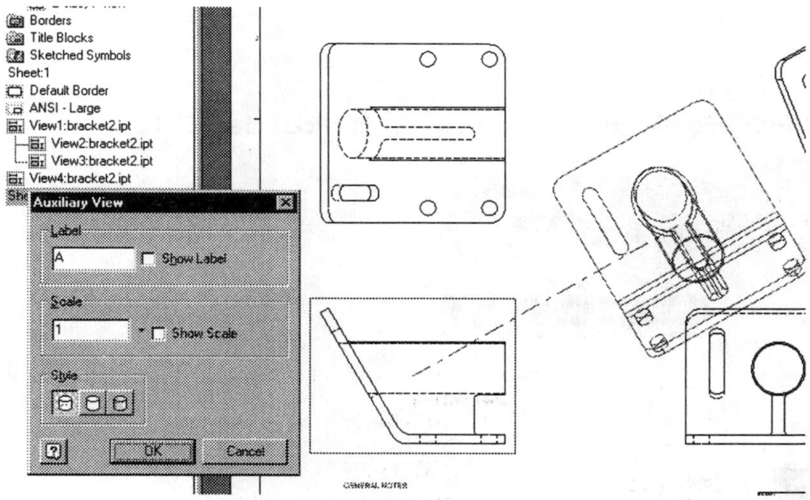

Drag the mouse to where you want to place the view. Pick to place the view.

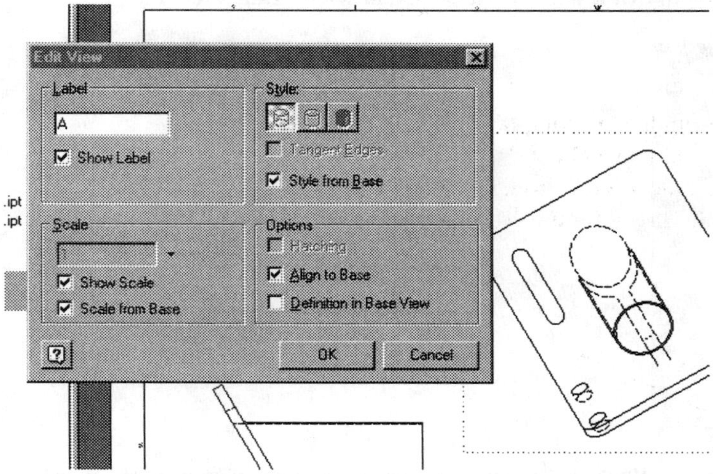

If you want the view to be labeled, place a check in the Show Label box.
If you wish the Scale to be shown, place a check in the Show Scale box.

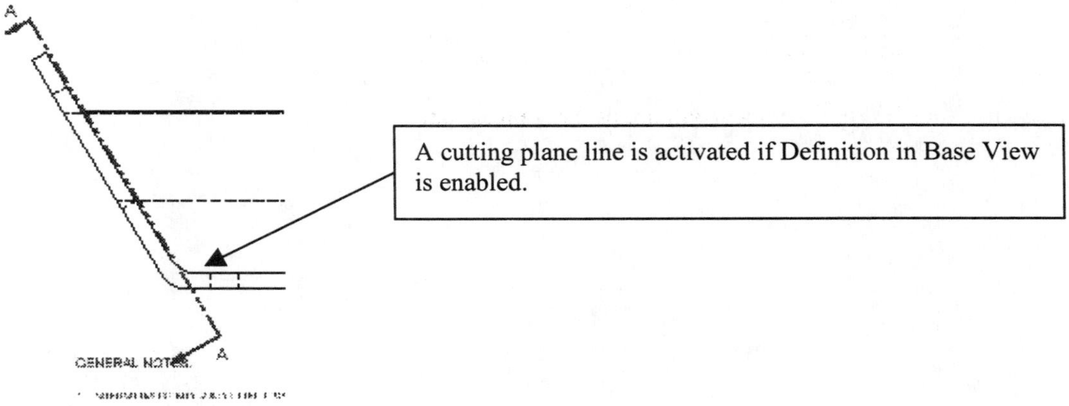

Edit Auxiliary View

To edit the settings of the Auxiliary View, select the Auxiliary View, right-click and select 'Edit'.

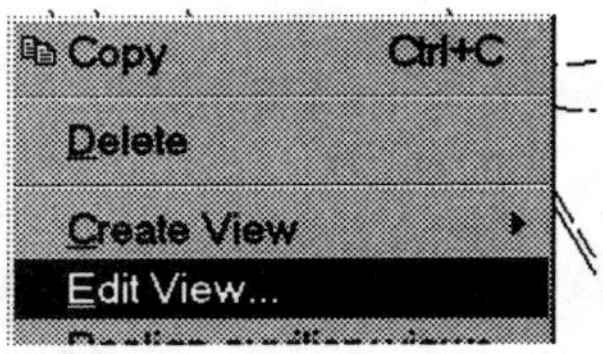

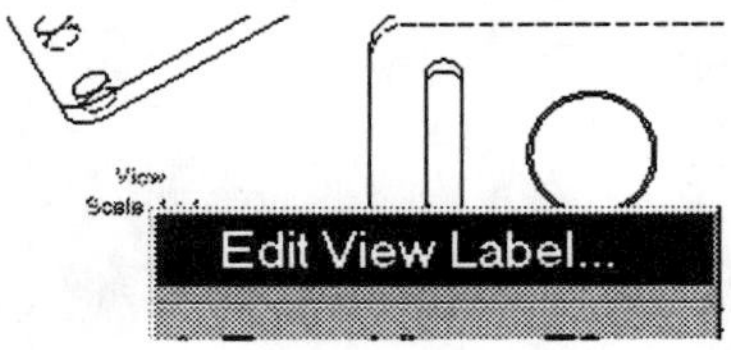

The View Label can be edited by selecting the view label, right-click and select 'Edit View Label'.

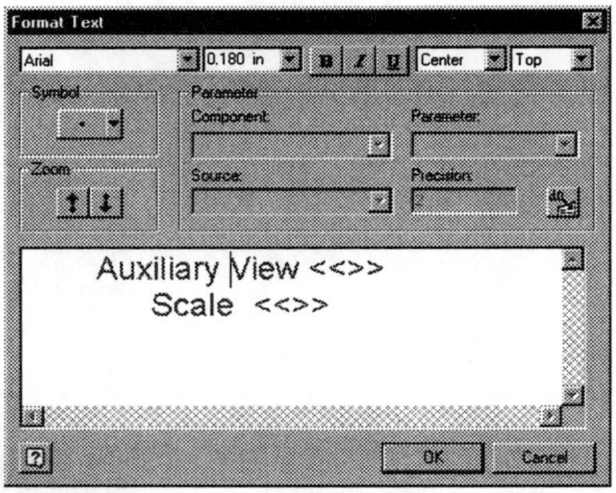

A dialog box comes up. To add the word Auxiliary as shown, just place the mouse in front of the word View and type 'Auxiliary'. Press 'OK'.

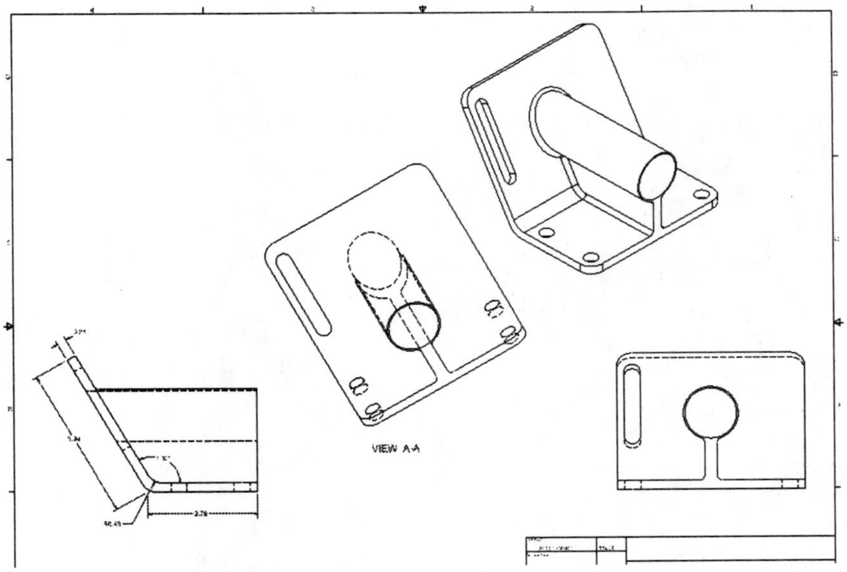

Our completed drawing.

Save the drawing as 'aux1.idw'.

Notes:

Lesson 22

<u>SectionViews</u>

<u>Learning Objective</u>

At the conclusion of this lesson, the user will be able to create section views.

We can use the bracket created in Lesson 17.

Open a new drawing file using the lesson17.ipt file. Create the basic orthogonal views as shown.

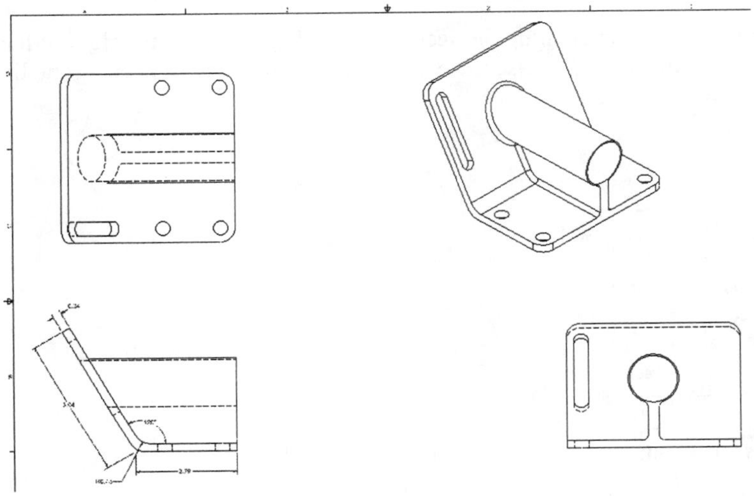

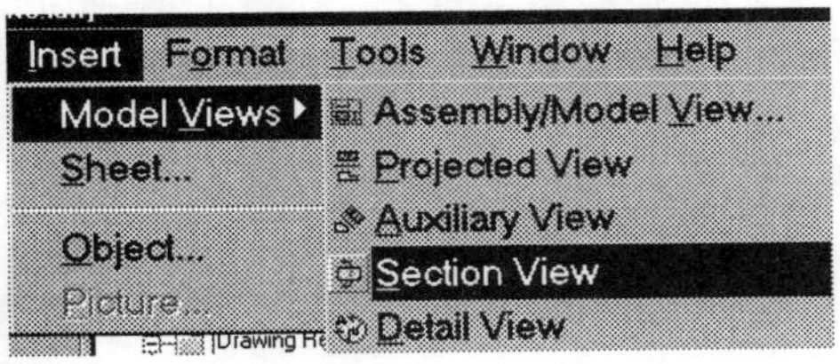

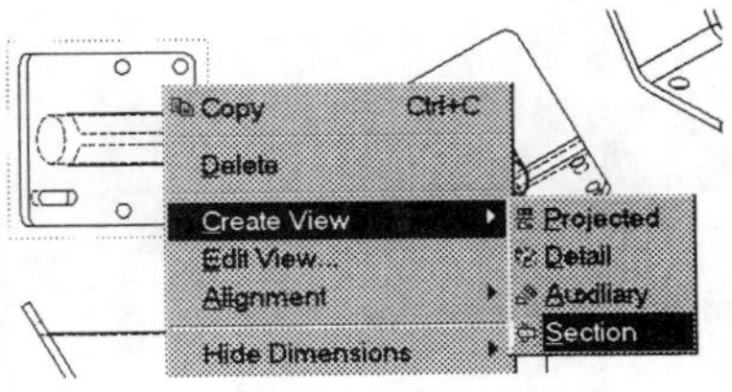

Creating a Section View

To create a section view, the user can:

- Select the SectionView tool from the Drawing Management tools.
- Select the view to be used for the section, right click and select Create View->Section
- Go to Insert->Model Views->Section View from the menu.

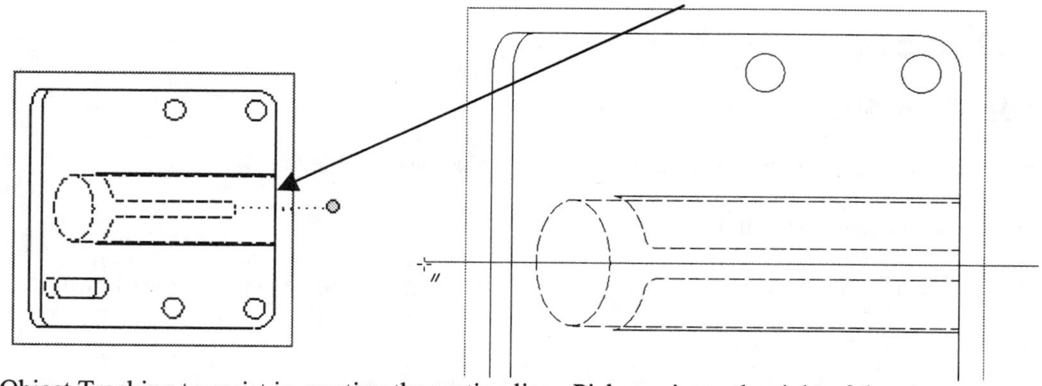

Use Object Tracking to assist in creating the section line. Pick a point to the right of the view. Then drag the mouse to the left side. Use the cursor cues to assist you in keeping the line straight. Pick a point to the left of the view.

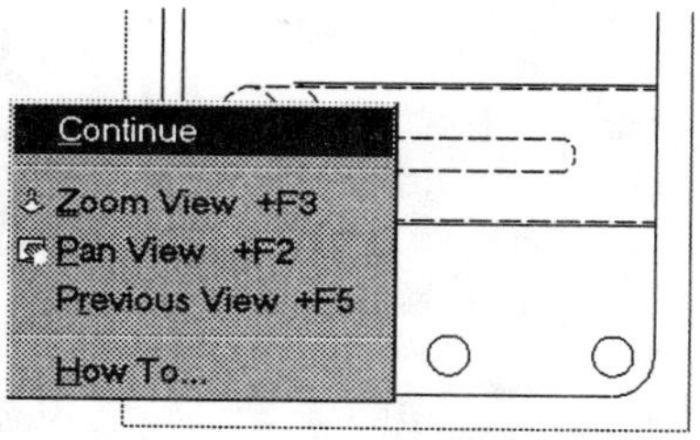

Right click and select 'Continue'.

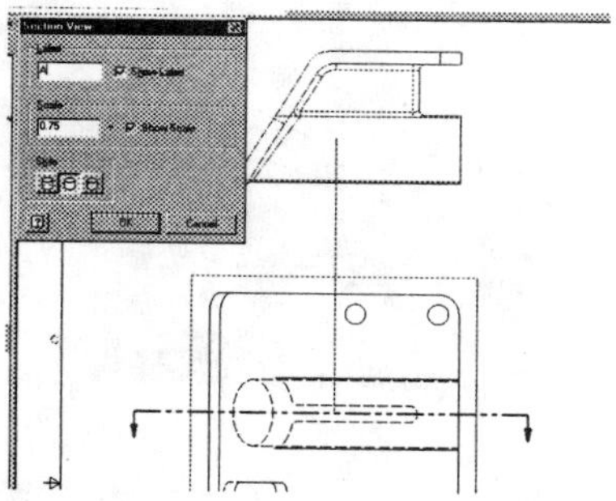

Drag the mouse to where you want to place the view. Pick to place the view.

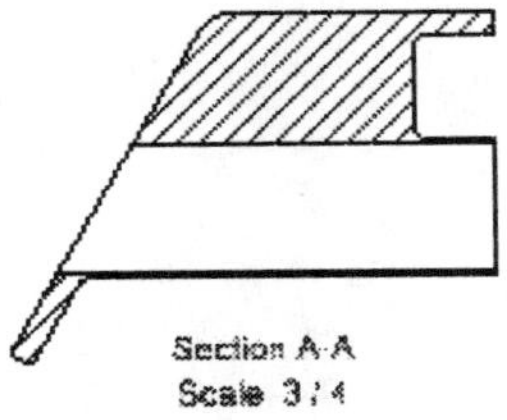

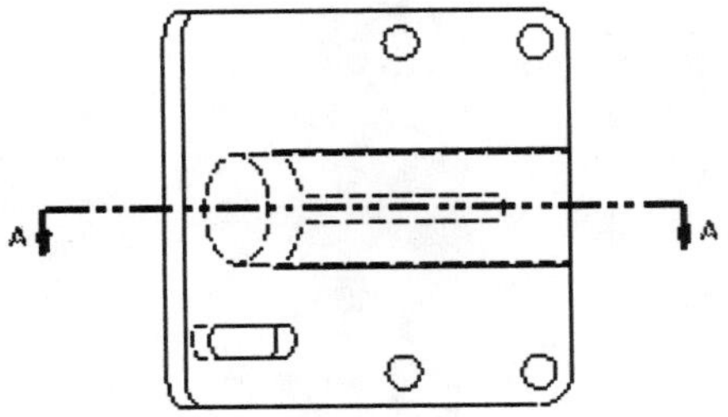

TIP: To get a straight line as shown, just draw a straight line using the object tracking. Inventor will add the shoulders, arrowheads and labels automatically.

To move the View Label, select with the mouse and then drag and place with the mouse.

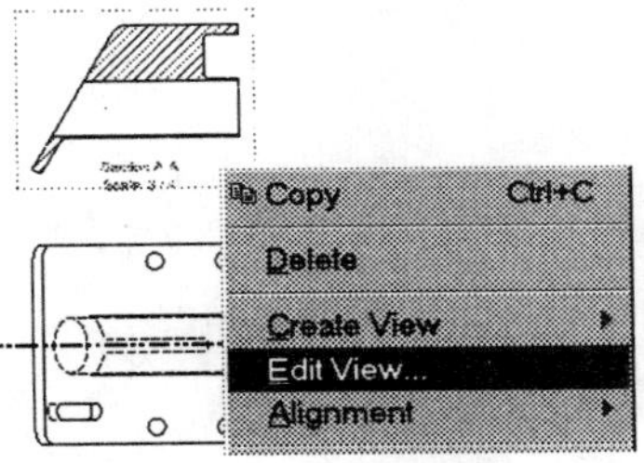

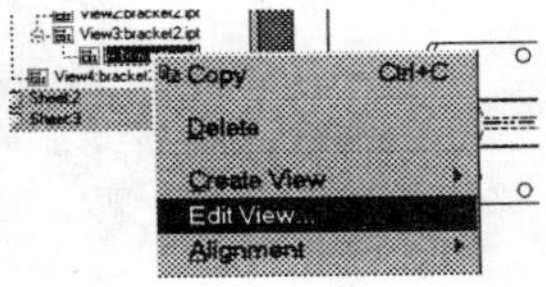

Editing a Section View

To edit the view:

- Select the view, right click and select 'Edit View'
- Select the view in the browser, right click and select 'Edit View'

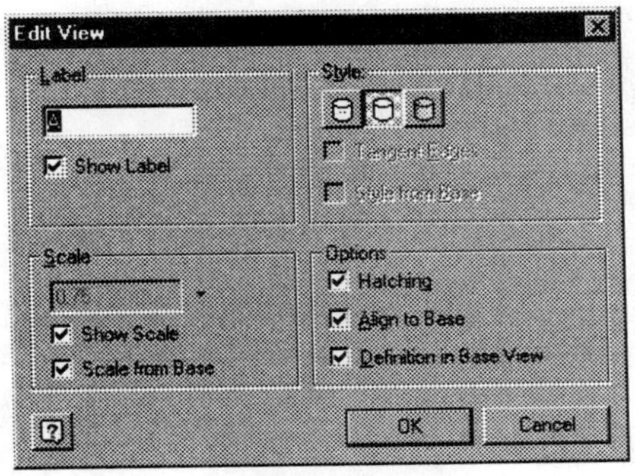

The Edit View dialog box appears.

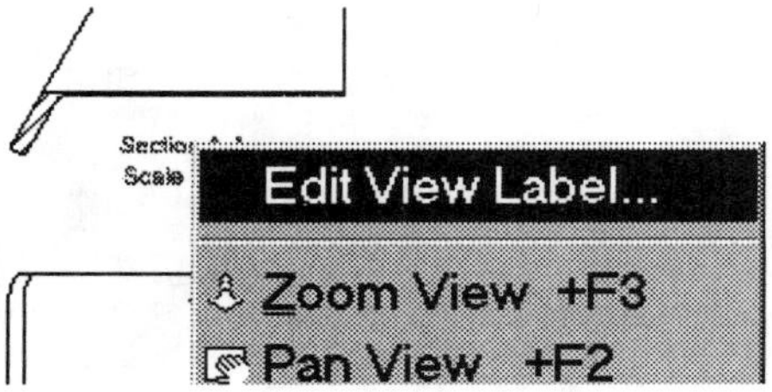

To edit the View Label, select, right-click and select 'Edit View Label'.

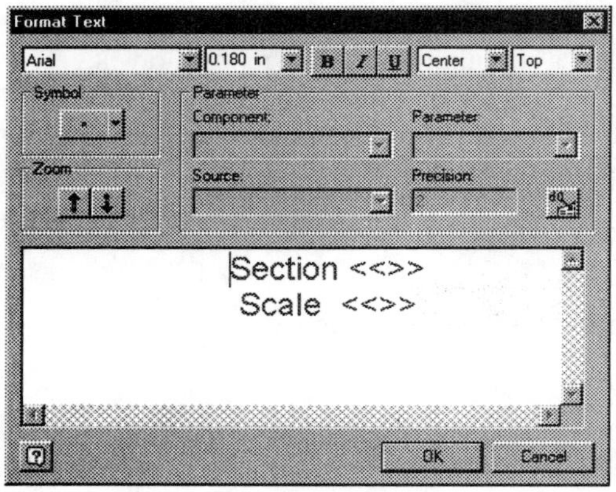

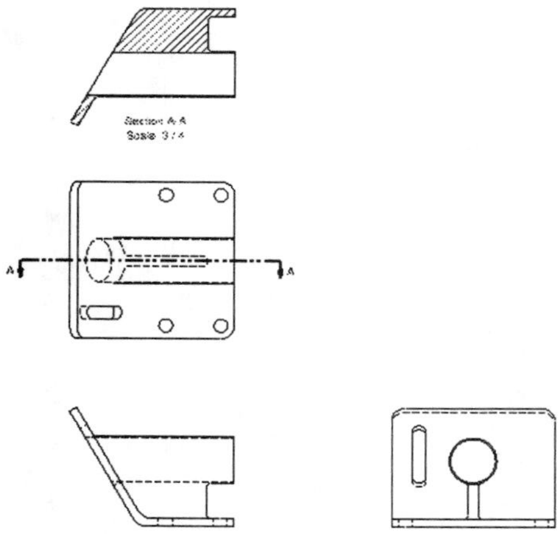

Our completed drawing.
Save the drawing as 'section1.idw'.

Lesson 23

Creating Detail Views

Learning Objective

By the conclusion of this lesson, the user will be able to create detail views.

Using the basic auxiliary drawing we created, we will add a detail view.

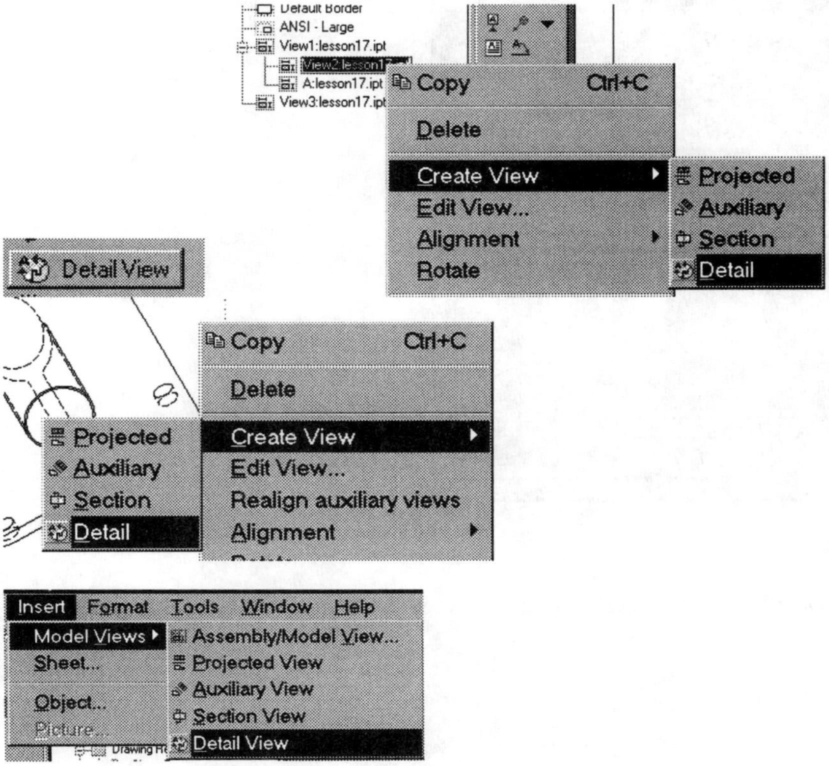

Creating a Detail View

To add a Detail View, the user can:

- Select the Detail View tool from the Drawing Management tools.
- Select the view where the detail is to be added, right click and select Create View->Detail
- Go to Insert->Model Views->Detail View from the menu.
- Go to the browser, select the source view for the detail view, right click and select Create View->Detail

> **TIP:** To set a different fence shape, right-click and select the fence shape from the menu before clicking to indicate the outer boundary.

1. Click the Detail View button.
2. Select an existing view as the base
3. In the dialog box, set the label, scale, and display style for the view. If you do not change these settings, the default settings will be assigned.
4. In the graphics window, click to indicate the center of the desired detail, then move the cursor and click to indicate the outer boundary of the detail.
5. Move the preview to the desired location and click to place the view.

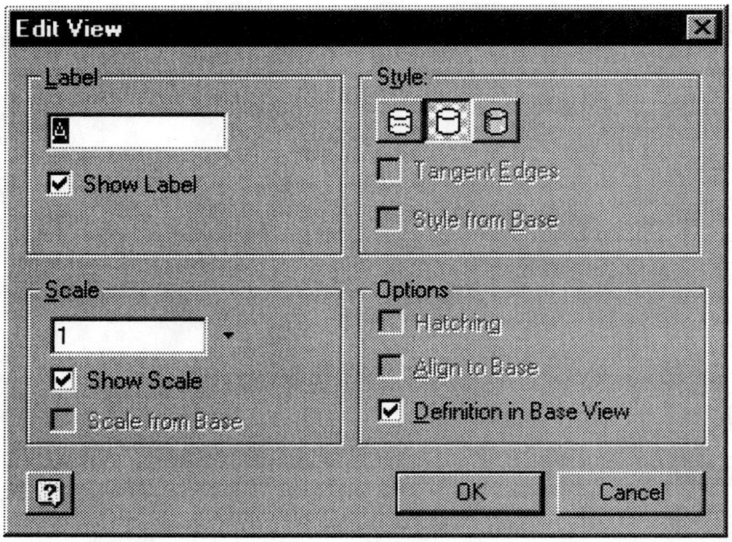

Fill in the dialog box as shown.

Pick to place the circle for the Detail View and then drag and select with the mouse to place the Detail View.

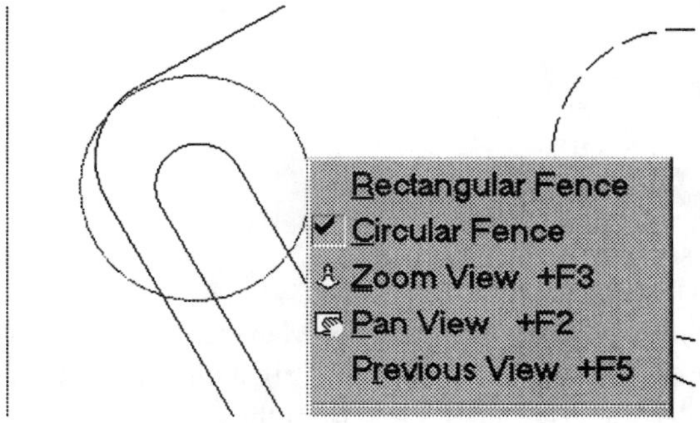

To change from a Circular Fence to a Rectangular Fence, right click and select the desired mode after picking the center point for the detail view.

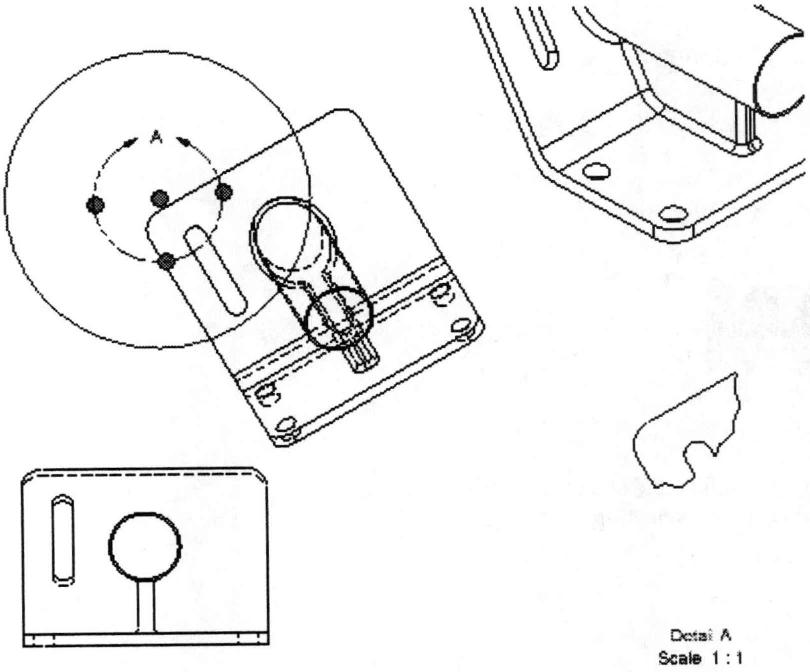

Using the select tool, the user can select the detail circle and stretch it to enlarge it or shrink it. The Detail View will automatically update.

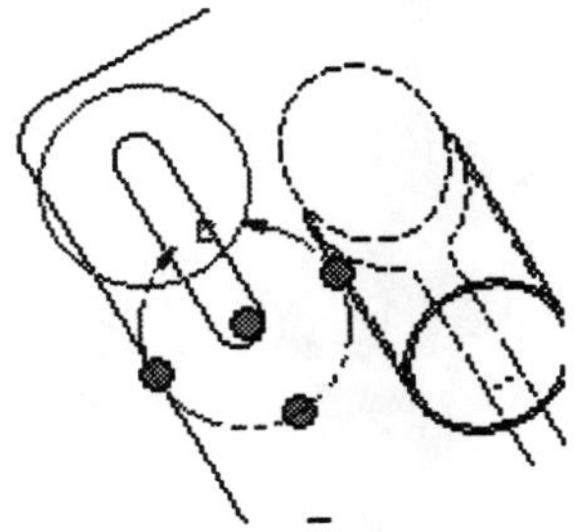

The user can also move a detail view. Simply select the center of the circle, hold down the mouse and drag to the new location. The detail view will automatically update.

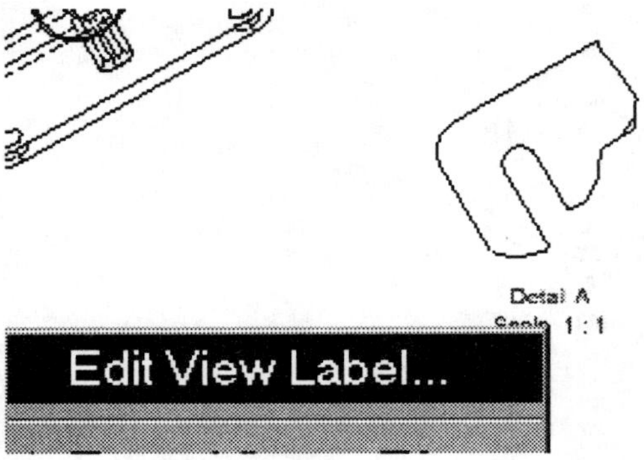

Modifying a View Label

To edit the View Label, select, right-click and select 'Edit View Label'.
The View Label can be moved easily by selecting with a mouse and dragging it to a new position.

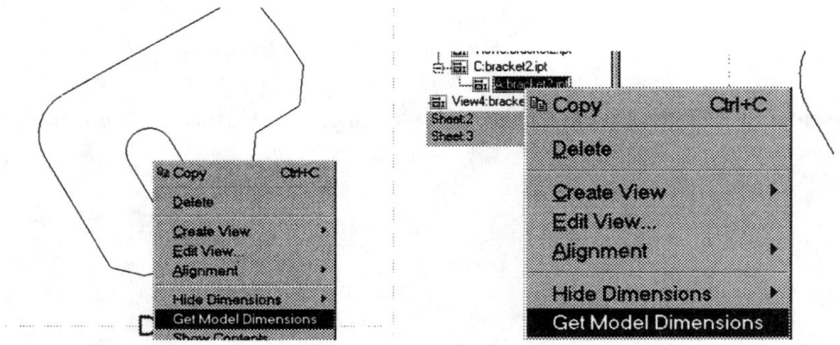

Dimensioning a Detail View

To dimension the Detail View, the user can:

- Select the view in the drawing area, right click and select 'Get Model Dimensions'
- Select the view in the browser, right click and select 'Get Model Dimensions'

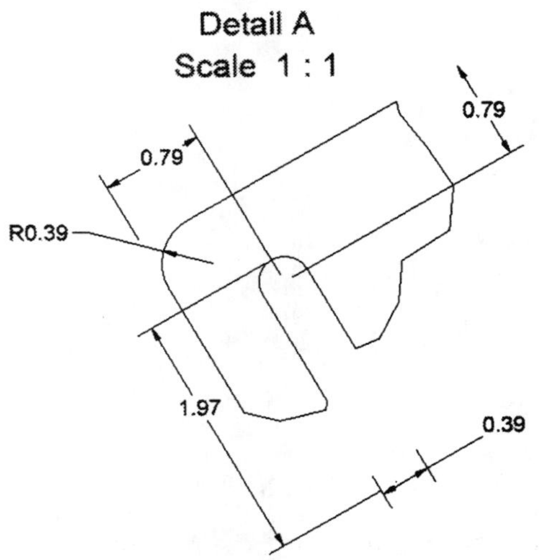

Use the standard methods to arrange and edit the dimensions.

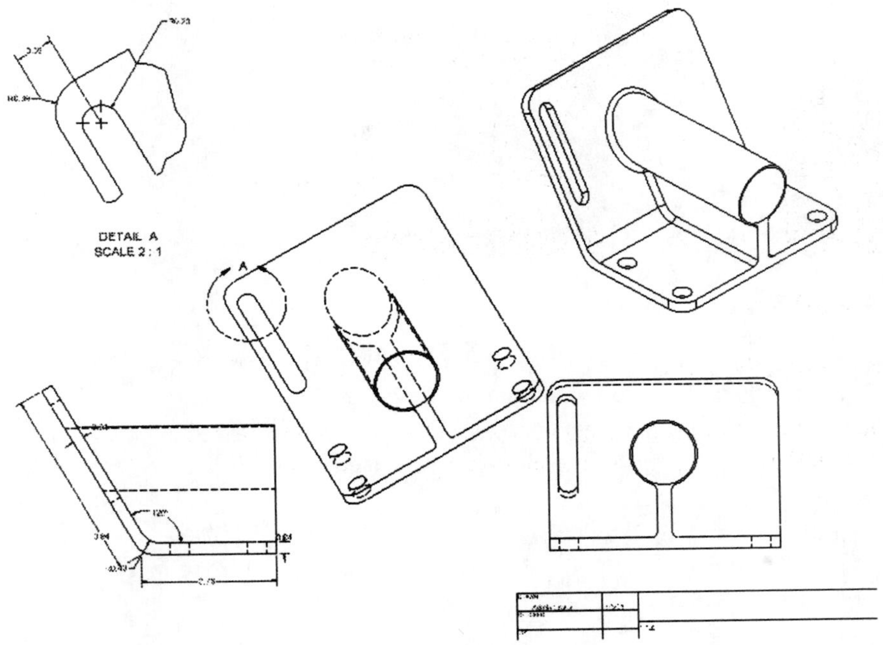

Our detailed drawing.
Save the drawing as 'detail1.idw'.

Notes:

Lesson 24

Drafting Standards

Learning Objectives

At the conclusion of this lesson, the user will be able to:

- Create templates defining custom drafting standards
- Copy one drafting standard to another
- Modify drafting standards

Drafting Standards allow the user to set up standards for parts, assemblies and drawings. Standards control linetype, units, colors, etc.

The Standards are set up under the Format Menu.

The Drafting Standards set up the drafting standards for the active drawing or template. You can apply a drafting standard to the drawing, modify an existing standard, or create a custom standard based on an existing standard.

TIP: The Drafting Standards apply to the active drawing only. If you have several drawing files open simultaneously, each file can have a different standard in effect.

When you create a new drawing, it is automatically assigned an active drafting standard that controls the format for dimensions, text, line weights, terminators, and other elements that are dictated. You can use the default standard, select from another named standard (ANSI, BSI, DIN, GT, ISO, or JIS), or customize a standard to meet your own requirements.

In an Autodesk Inventor drawing, drafting standard settings also include elements that are not part of the named standard, such as naming conventions for sheets and views, display color for elements on the drawing sheet, format for the parts list, and selection of the special characters and symbols for annotations.

You can change any of the elements controlled by the drafting standard. By customizing an existing standard or developing your own standard, you can enforce company conventions or optimize your working environment.

When you customize the drafting standard in a drawing, the changes apply only to that drawing. To make customized standards available in all new drawing files, make the changes in the template that you use to create new drawings. Set the customized standard as the active standard in the template, so that it is automatically set as the active standard in all new drawings.

If you use several drafting standards, you can customize all of them in a single template file and select the active standard when you create a new drawing. As an alternative, you can create different template files, customizing a single standard in each one.

TIP: The best method to manage Drafting Standards is to create template files with the desired standards defined and use these templates when starting a new drawing.

The active drafting standard controls many attributes of a drawing. You can create a custom drafting standard based on an existing drafting standard.

1. Open a drawing or template file.
2. Select Format>Standards to open the Drafting Standards dialog box.
3. Click the prompt at the end of the list of standards.
4. In the New Standard dialog box, enter the name of the custom standard and select the base standard.
5. In the Drafting Standards dialog box, click the More button to open and change specific attributes of the custom standard.

The active drafting standard in a drawing or template file controls many defaults and options. In addition to the elements that are dictated by ANSI, DIN, ISO, and JIS standards, the Drafting Standards dialog box contains many default values an options that you can change.

- Display color for sheets, lines, and other elements.
- Naming conventions for views and sheets.
- Formats for dimension values
- Symbols and options available for drawing annotations.
- Default format for parts lists.
- Default balloon style

Creating a Part Template

To create a part template:

All new part files are created with a template. You can create your own templates and add them to the templates provided by Autodesk Inventor.

1. Create a new part, using an existing template.

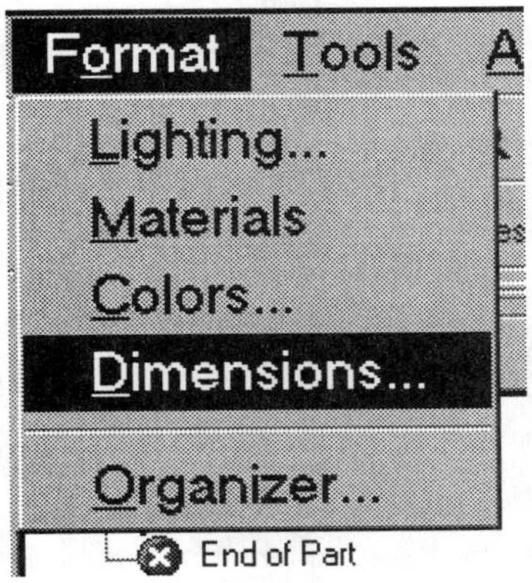

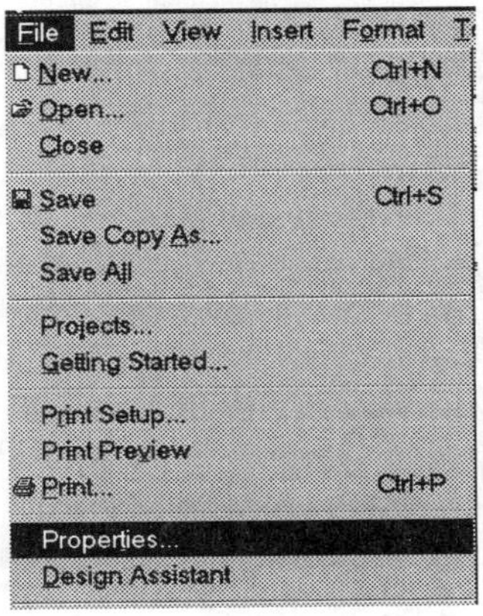

2. Set the default units of measurement. Go to Format->Dimensions or use File->Properties.

These both bring up the same dialog box.

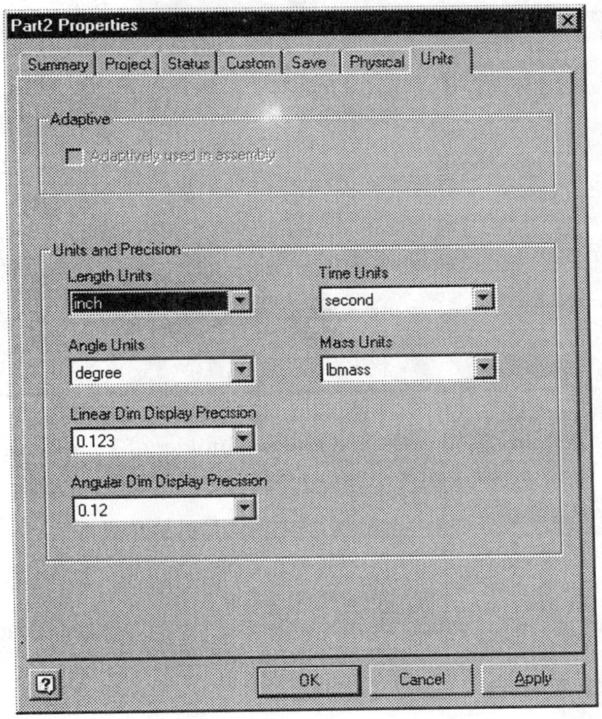

Go through each tab and set it up to the defaults you would like for most parts you work on.

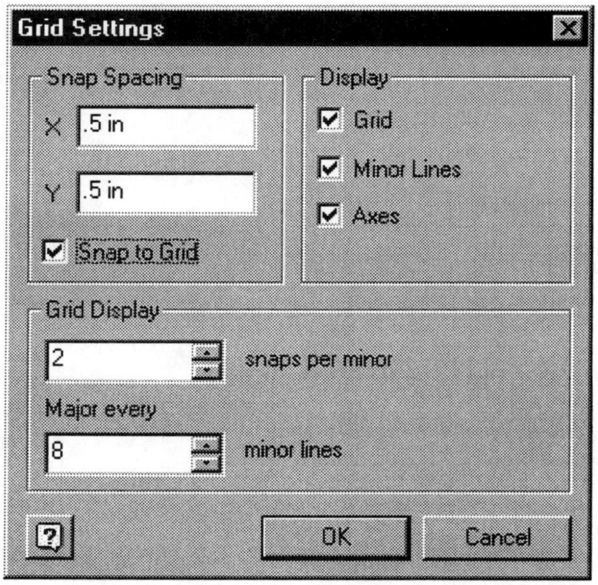

3. If needed, change the grid setting and the sizes of the origin work planes to better accommodate the average part size.
4. Create any work features, sketches, or geometry that will be included in every new part file.
5. Define commonly used parameters or link to a spreadsheet of parameters.

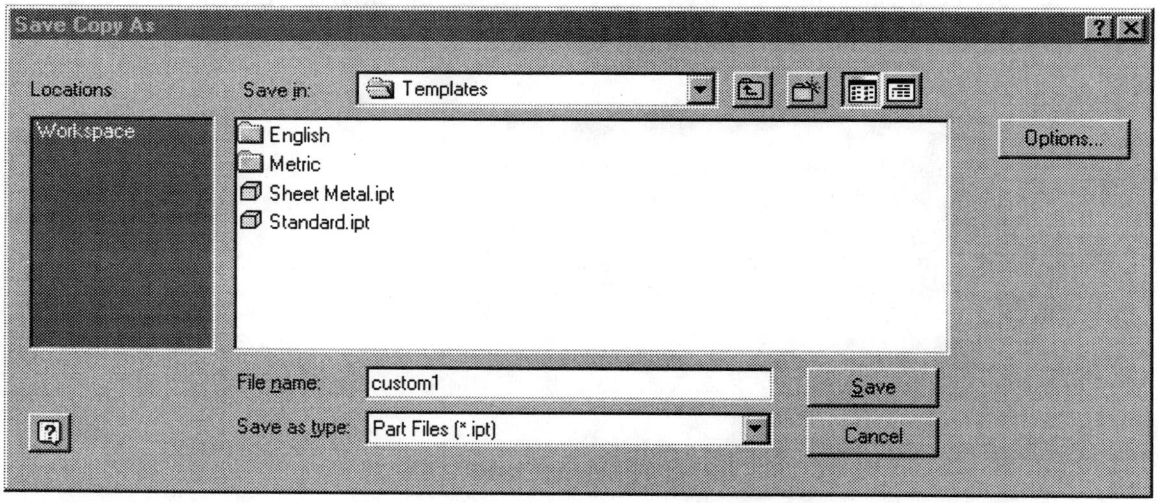

6. Save the file in the Autodesk\Inventor<*version*>\Templates folder or a subfolder of Templates. A part file automatically becomes a template when it is saved to the Templates folder.

TIP: The file *standard.ipt* in the Templates folder is the default part template. To replace the default template, remove *standard.ipt* and replace it with a template that has the same name.

Then the next time you use File->New, you can access your custom part template.

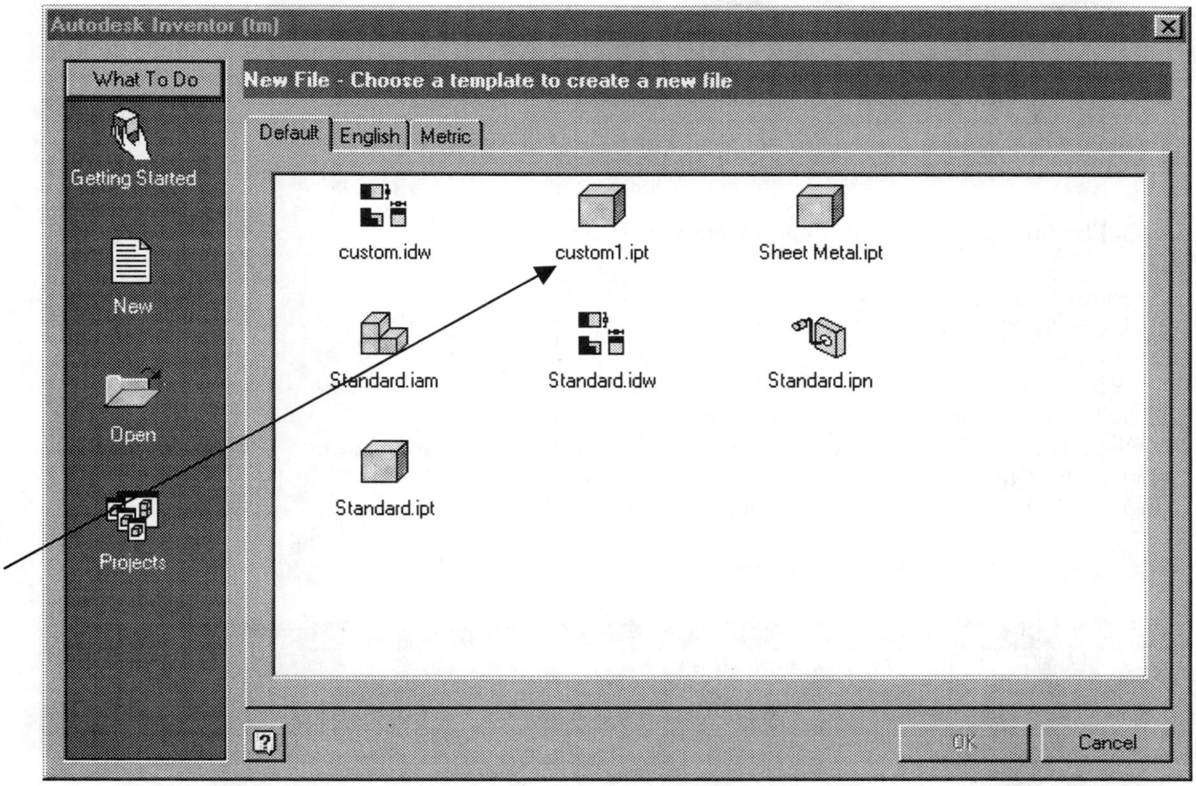

TIP: You can only access templates (and the start-up dialog) using the File->New menu. If you bypass the start-up dialog by using the pull-down tool, the new file uses the templates that begin with *standard*. If you wish to by-pass the start-up dialog, but use custom settings, save your templates as *standard.ipt*, *standard.idw* or *standard.ipn* in the templates directory. It is a good idea to save the original standard.* files in a back-up directory in case you are unhappy with the results.

TIP: To add tabs to the New dialog box, create new subfolders in the Templates folder and add template files to them. The New dialog displays a tab for each subfolder in the Templates folder.

Creating a Drawing File Template

To create a drawing file template, open a standard drawing file. Set up your sheets, borders, and title blocks. Be sure to include multiple sheets in the event your drawing will have more than one page. Use Tools->Options->Common to set the font to be used in dimensions. Use Format->Standards to set the units and Dimension Values. Use File->Properties to set any defaults for property fields to be used in the Title Block.

Check List for Creating a Custom Drawing Template:

Title Block for Sheet 1
Title Block for Sheet 2
Border for Sheet 1
Border for Sheet 2
Special Symbols defined under Sketched Symbols
File Properties set for Drawing (File->Properties) ; set Author, Company Name, etc.
Colors set for Drawing (Format->Standards->Common)
Dimension Values set for Drawing (Format->Standards->Dimension Value)

Once you have the drawing file set up to your specifications, select File->Save Copy As.

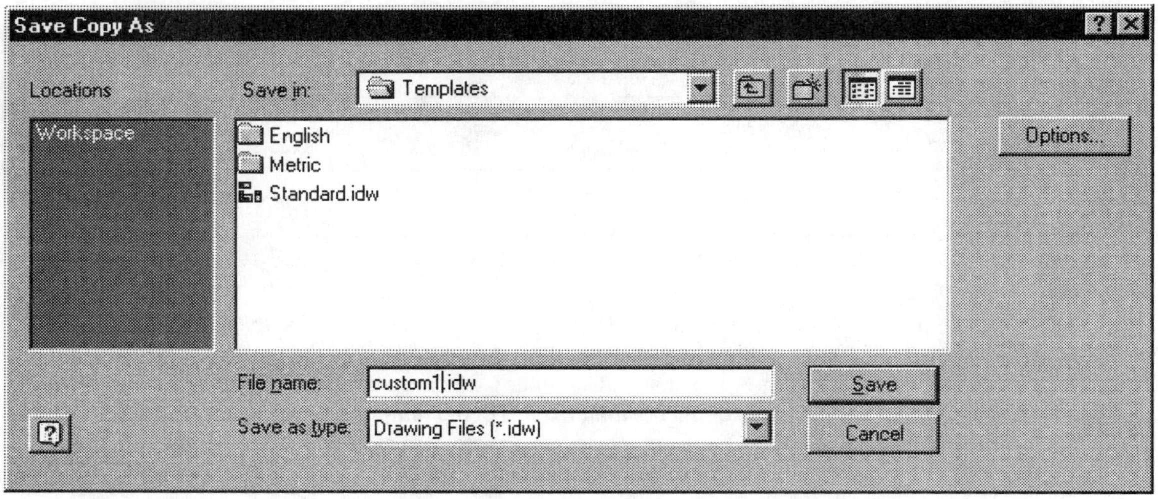

You can set any template to be the default template for creating new drawings. To make a template the default, save it in the Templates folder with the file name *standard.idw*. To avoid overwriting the existing default template, move or rename the existing standard template before saving the new template.

Files that reside in the Templates folder appear on the Default tab of the New dialog box when you create new files. Files that reside in a subfolder of the Templates folder appear as other tabs in the New dialog box.

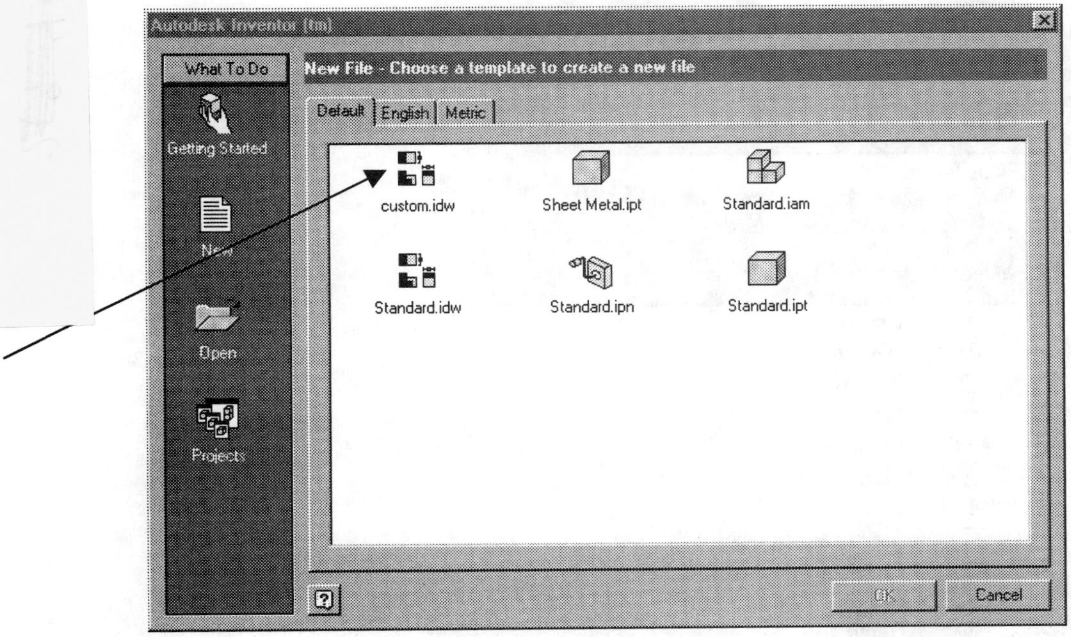

Your custom drawing template now appears in the Start Up dialog.

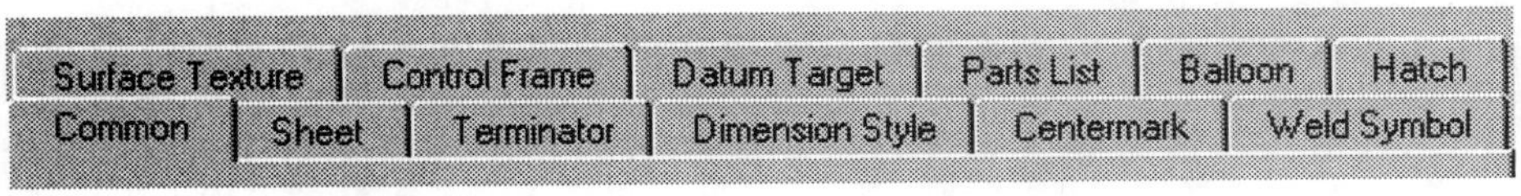

Drafting Standards can only be accessed inside of drawing files, not part files.

The Drafting Standards dialog has the following tabs:

- Common
- Sheet
- Terminator
- Dimension Style
- Centermark
- Weld Symbol
- Surface Texture
- Control Frame
- Datum Target
- Hatch
- Balloon
- Parts List

Dimension Style

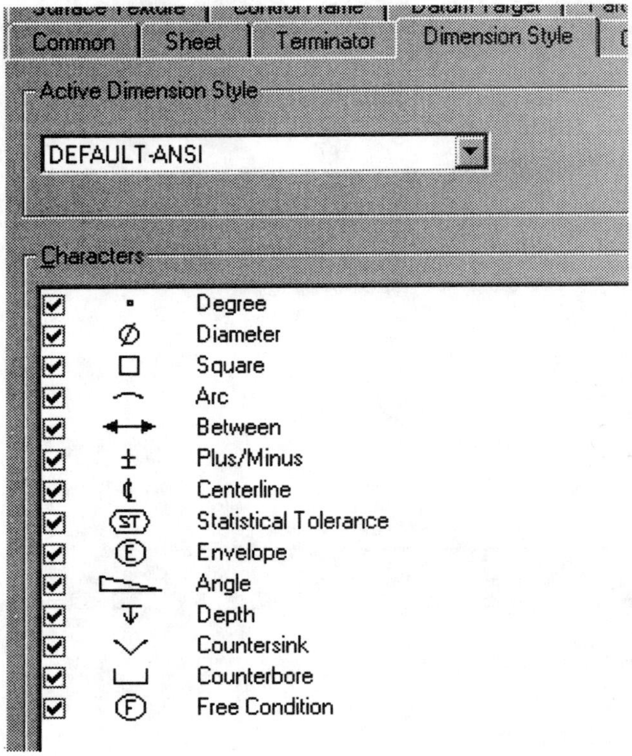

Sets the default display characteristics for dimension and tolerance values and defines which characters will be available to use in dimension text

Common

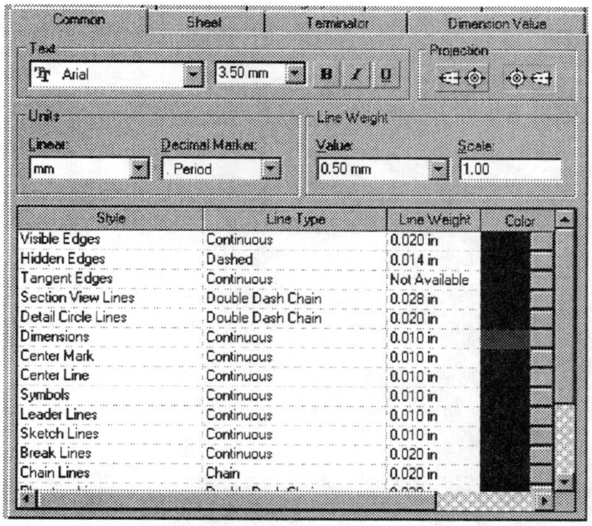

The default text attributes and line styles in a drawing are defined by the active drafting standard.

Text	Sets the default text. Select the type face and size from the drop-down lists. Click to apply bold, italic, or underline to the default text, if desired.
Projection	Sets the projection angle for drawing views. Click the appropriate button to choose first-angle or third-angle projection.
Units	Sets the measurement options for the drawing or template. Linear Sets the units of measurement. Click the arrow and select from the list. Decimal Marker Specifies the character to use as a decimal. Click the arrow and select from the list.
Line Weight	Sets line weights and scale that are available in the drawing or template file. Value Specifies the line weights that are available to assign to the various line styles in the selected drafting standard. Click the arrow to view a list of the existing weights. To add a line weight, enter the value. Scale Sets the scale of all line styles in the drawing or template file.
Styles	Sets the line weight and other attributes for the lines in the drawing. Style Selects a line style to edit. Click to select a style. Line Type sets the line type for the selected line style. Click the arrow and choose from the list. Line Weight sets the weight of the selected line style. Click the arrow and choose the weight from the list. To add a line weight to the list, enter it in the Line Weight Value edit box. Color Sets the color for the selected line style. Click the color button and choose the desired color from the Color dialog box.

On the Common tab, set the text format, define the line weight, and assign the line type and color for each line style. To change the color, pick the button on the far right next to the scroll bar. A color dialog will appear that allows the user to select a new color.

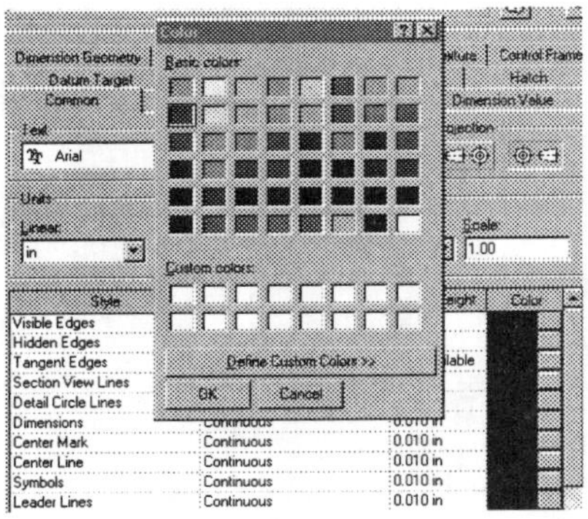

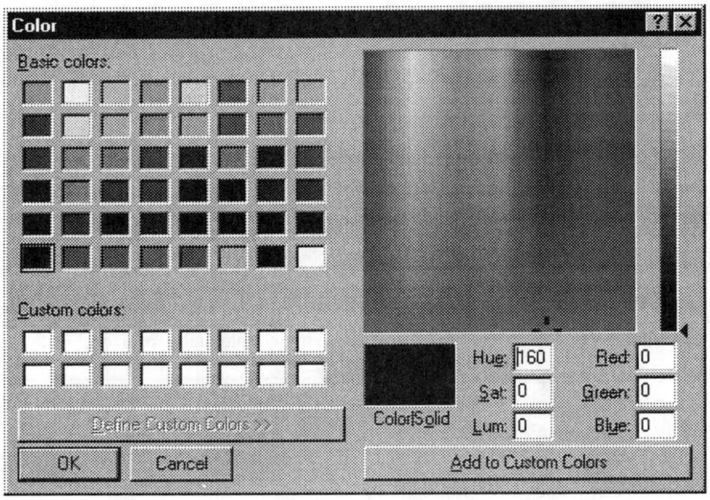

Pressing the Define Custom Colors buttons expands the color dialog box so that the user can create his own colors to be assigned to various geometries.

Style	Line Type	Line Weight	Color
Tangent Edges	Continuous	Not Available	
Section View Lines	Double Dash Chain	0.028 in	
Detail Circle Lines	Double Dash Chain	0.020 in	
Dimensions	Continuous	0.010 in	
Center Mark	Continuous	0.010 in	
Center Line	Continuous	0.010 in	
Symbols	Continuous	0.010 in	
Leader Lines	Continuous	0.010 in	
Sketch Lines	Continuous	0.010 in	
Break Lines	Continuous	0.020 in	
Chain Lines	Chain	0.020 in	
Phantom Lines	Double Dash Chain	0.028 in	
Stitch 1 Lines	Dashed Space	0.010 in	

The user can assign any desired color to various lines and geometries.

Centermark

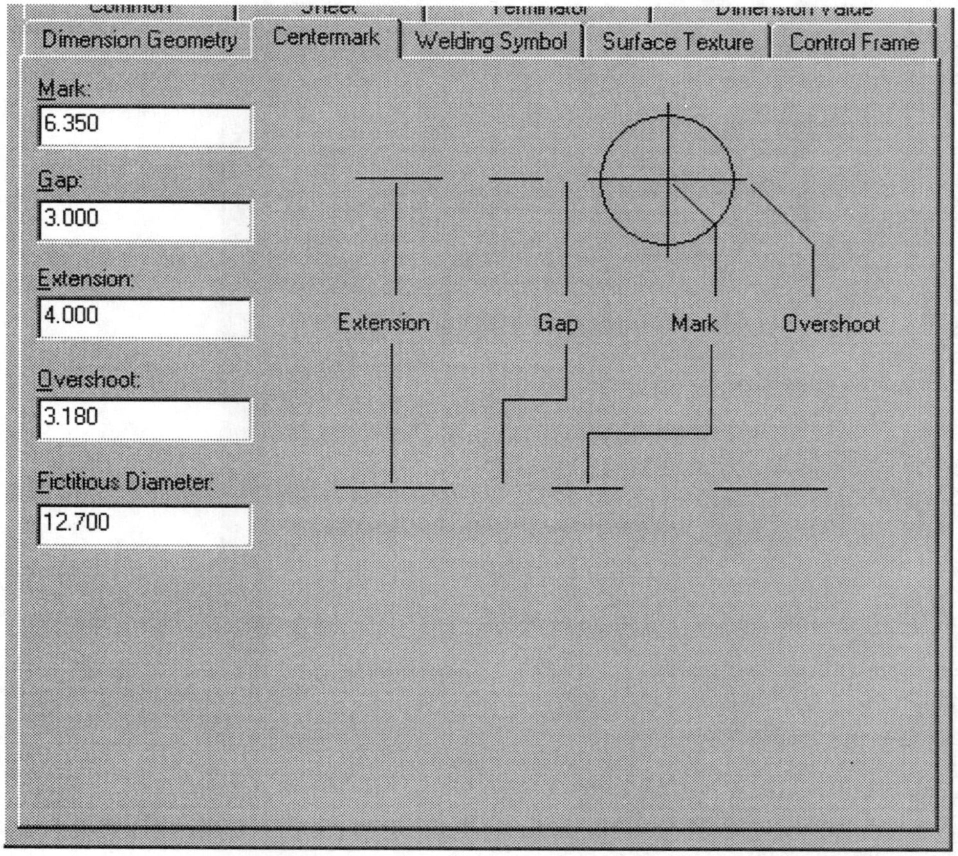

Mark	Sets the size of the center indicator mark.
Gap	Sets the gap distance between the center indicator and the extension line.
Extension	Sets the minimum length of center mark extension lines.
Overshoot	Sets the distance that center mark extension lines extend beyond the edges of the features that they define.
Fictitious Diameter	Sets the size of center marks for suppressed pattern features.

Surface Texture

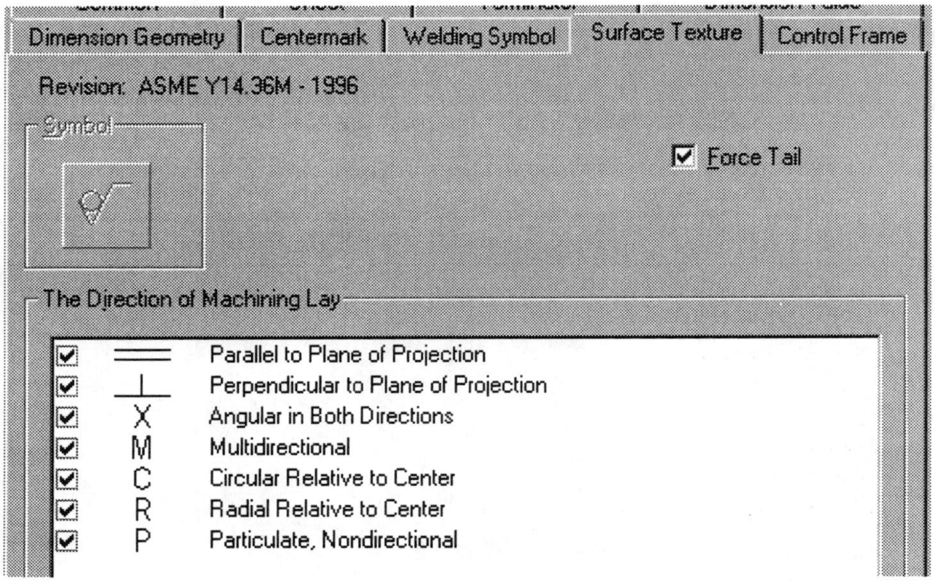

Sets the display characteristics for surface texture symbols and the options in the Surface Texture Symbol dialog box.

Symbol	Available only when creating or editing a custom standard. Sets the size of the machining-prohibited symbol. Click the button to switch between the options.
All Around	Available only when creating or editing a custom standard based on DIN, ISO, or JIS. Adds the All Around symbol button to the Surface Texture Symbol dialog box. Select the box to add the button to the dialog box; clear the check box to remove the button from the dialog box.
Multiline	Available only when creating or editing a custom standard based on DIN or ISO. Sets the symbol to accommodate two line of notes. Select the check box to use two lines; clear the check box to use one line.
Force Tail	Sets the default for the Force Tail option in the Surface Texture Symbol dialog box. Select the check box to set the default to On; clear the check box set the default to Off.
Direction of Machining Lay	The selection box specifies the machining lay options that will be available in the Surface Texture Symbol dialog box. Select a check box to use a symbol; clear the check box to make a symbol unavailable.

TIP: If you turn off a symbol that is already used in a drawing, the existing symbols will continue to display, but the symbol will not be available when new symbols are added.

Weld Symbols

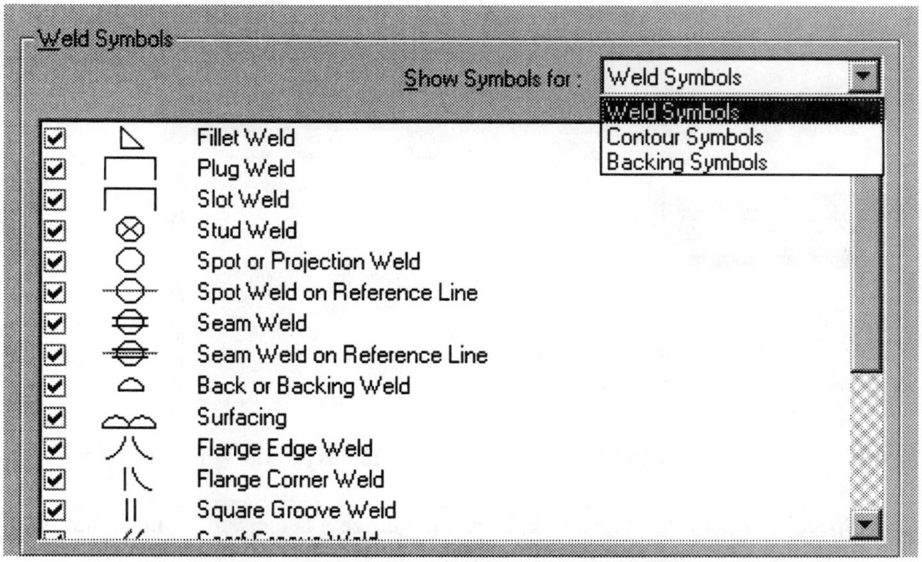

Sets the display characteristics for welding symbols and defines which welding symbols will be available to use in the drawing or template.

Identification Line	Sets the format for displaying a welding symbol identification line. If the selected standard is based on ANSI or JIS, this option is not available. Line Type sets the line style, such as dashed, dotted, or continuous. Click the arrow and select the style from the list. Gap sets the distance between the line and the welding symbol. Enter the distance.
Weld Symbols	Specifies which symbols will be available to use in the drawing. Show Symbols For selects the symbol set that is listed in the selection box below. Click the arrow and select a symbol set from the list. The selection box specifies the symbols that will be available in the Welding Symbols dialog box. Select a check box to use a symbol; clear the check box to make a symbol unavailable.

TIP: If you turn off a symbol that is already used in a drawing, the existing symbols will continue to display, but the symbol will not be available when new symbols are added.

Control Frame

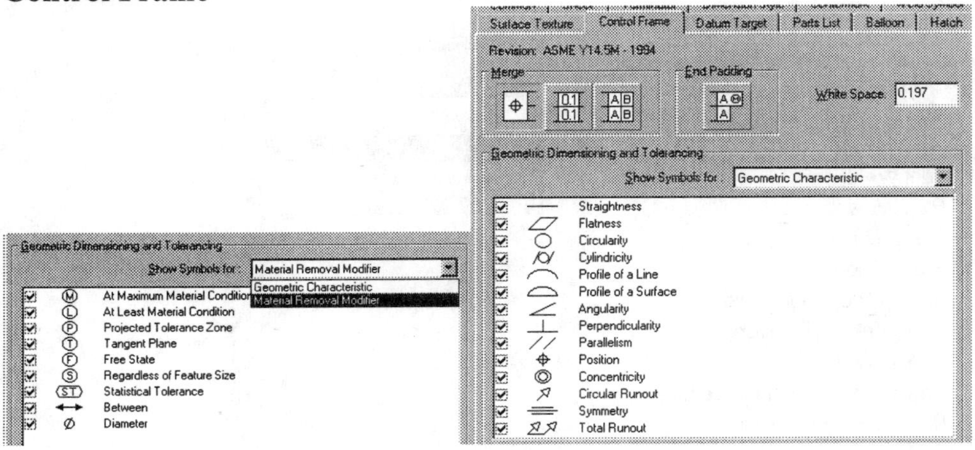

Sets the display characteristics for feature control frames and defines which symbols will be available to use in the drawing or template.

Merge	Specifies whether to combine cells when their data is the same. Click a button to alternate between merging and separating the cells. Symbol combines the cells if they contain the same symbol. Tolerance combines cells if they contain the same tolerance. Datum combines the cells if they reference the same datum.
End Padding	Adds space to short cells so that pairs of cells align vertically.
White Space	Sets the space before and after text in the tolerance and datum cells. Enter the amount of white space in the box. Click the button to alternate between padding and no padding.
Geometric Dimensioning and Tolerancing	Specifies which symbols will be available in the Feature Control Frame dialog box. Show Symbols For selects the symbol set that is listed in the selection box. Click the arrow and select a symbol set from the list. The selection box specifies the symbols that will be available in the Feature Control Frame dialog box. Select a check box to use a symbol; clear the check box to make a symbol unavailable.

TIP: If you turn off a symbol that is already used in a drawing, the existing symbols will continue to display, but the symbol will not be available when new symbols are added.

Balloons

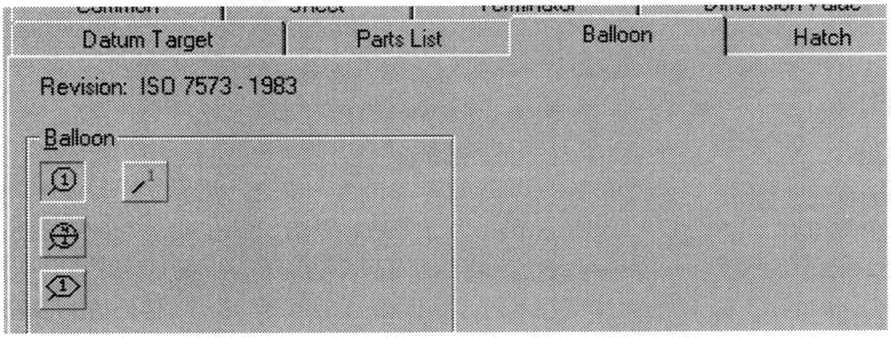

Use the Balloon tab in the Drafting Standards dialog box to set the style for the balloons you will add to a drawing, and the level of components to include when using automatic ballooning.

Balloon	Specifies the default balloon style for the drawing or template. Click to select the desired style.
Level	Sets the default number of levels of components to include when automatically adding balloons to a view. Select the desired level. First-Level Components Creates balloons for only the top level of components of the assembly in the selected view. Balloons are added for subassemblies and parts that are not part of a subassembly, but not for the parts in the subassemblies. Only Parts Creates balloons for all parts of the assembly in the selected view. Balloons are not created for the subassemblies, but are created for the parts in the subassemblies.

1. Select Format>Standards to open the Drafting Standards dialog box.
2. Select the drafting standard to change.
3. Click the More button to expand the dialog box and then click the Balloon tab.
4. Click the balloon style to use.
5. Set the level of components to include when automatically ballooning all of the components in a drawing view.

Parts List

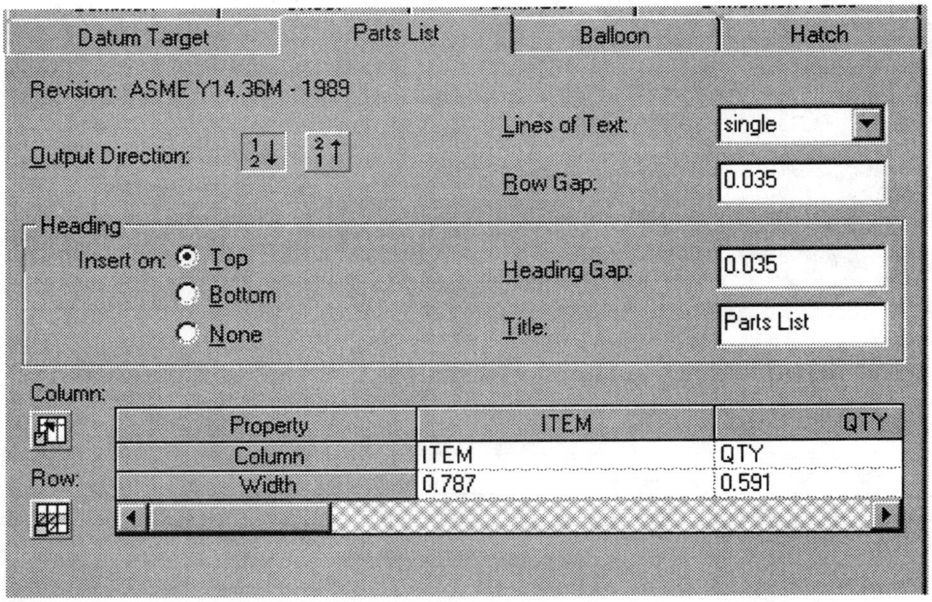

Use the Parts List tab in the Drafting Standards dialog box to set up the format for the parts lists you will add to a drawing.

1. Select Format>Standards to open the Drafting Standards dialog box.
2. Select the drafting standard to change.
3. Click the More button; button to expand the dialog box and then click the Parts List tab.
4. Set the sort order, title, heading, and other attributes of the parts list.
5. Click the Column Chooser button to open a dialog box and define the columns for the parts list.

Output Direction		Specifies the default display direction for the parts list. Click the appropriate button to display the list from the bottom up or the top down.
Lines of Text		Sets the line spacing for each row in the parts list. Click the arrow and select the desired height.
Row Gap		Sets the vertical space between the text and the cell frame. Enter the desired space in the box.
Heading		Specifies the format for the parts list heading. Insert On sets the location of the column headings. Click to choose Top, Bottom, or None. Heading Gap sets the vertical spacing between the heading text and the cell frame. Enter the desired space in the box. Title specifies the title for the parts list. Enter the title in the box. If the box is empty, the parts list will not have a title.
Column		Specifies the format and content of the columns.
		Opens the Column Chooser dialog box so that you can select the columns to include in the parts list.
		Opens the Row Keys dialog box so that you can select properties other than the part number to display a part as a separate item in the parts list.
	Property	Displays the properties included in the parts list. To add or remove properties, or to change the order of columns, Click the Column Chooser.
	Column	Displays the heading names for the columns in parts lists. To change a name, select the current heading and enter the new name.
	Width	Sets the default width for each column. To change the width of a column, select the cell and enter the new width.

Sheet

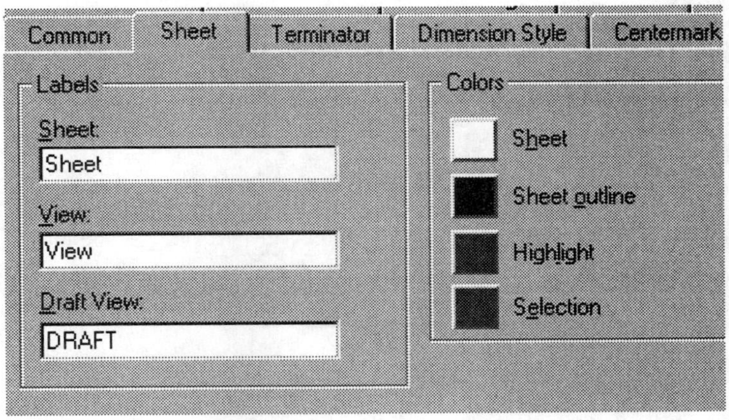

Sets the default labels for sheets and views, and sets the colors for elements on sheets in a drawing or template.

Labels	Sets the default labels assigned to new sheets and views in the drawing browser. As a new sheet or view is added, the label is used with an incremented number (for example, Sheet1, Sheet 2, Sheet3). Click in the box and enter the label.
Colors	Sets the display colors for elements of the sheet. Click a color button to open the Color dialog box and select the color for the associated element.
Sheet Color	Sets the background color for the sheet. The color of views, symbols, and other elements does not change; so set a background color that will provide good contrast.
Sheet Outline Color	Sets the outline color for the sheet.
Highlight Color	Sets the color of highlighted elements (when the cursor passes over them).
Selection Color	Sets the color of selected elements.

Datum Target

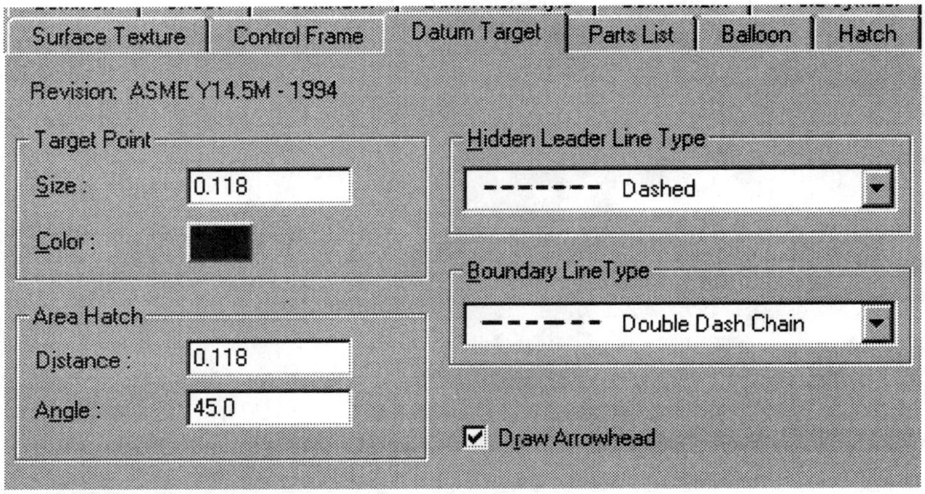

Sets the display characteristics for datum target symbols.

Target Point	Sets the characteristics of datum target points. Size sets the size of the target points. Enter the desired size in the box. Color specifies the color of the target points. Click the color button to display the Color dialog box and choose the color.
Area Hatch	Sets the characteristics of the datum target hatch pattern. Distance sets the spacing between hatch lines. Enter the distance in the box. Angle sets the angle of the hatch for rectangular and circular datum target symbols. Enter the angle in the box.
Hidden Leader Line Type	Sets the line style for hidden leader lines. Click the arrow and select a line type from the list.
Boundary Line Type	Sets the line style for boundary lines. Click the arrow and select a line type from the list.
Draw Arrowhead	Specifies the default termination for datum target symbols. Select the check box to use an arrowhead for datum targets; clear the check box to create datum target symbols without an arrowhead.

Hatch

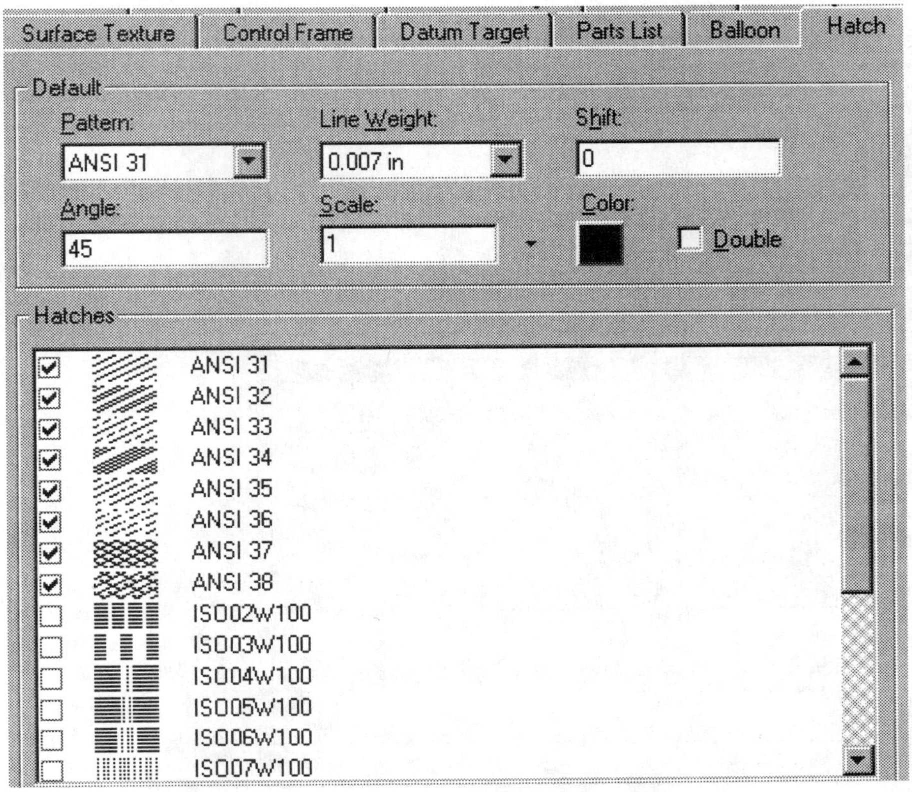

Sets the default attributes for section view hatch patterns.

Pattern	Specifies the basic pattern for the hatching. Click the arrow and choose the desired hatch pattern from the list.
Line Weight	Sets the thickness of the hatch lines. Click the arrow and choose the thickness from the list.
Shift	Shifts the hatch pattern to offset it slightly from the hatch pattern on a different part. Enter the distance for the shift.
Angle	Sets the angle for the hatch, relative to the view projection line. Enter the desired angle.
Scale	Sets the distance between lines in the hatch. A scale of 1 uses the distance specified in the drafting standard, a scale of 1:2 will result in line spacing that is one half that specified in the drafting standard.
Color	Left picking on the color rectangle brings up a color dialog where the user can set the color for hatch patterns.
Double	Creates a copy of the specified hatch pattern perpendicular to the first hatch pattern to a create crosshatch. Select the check box to create the crosshatch; clear the check box to use only the hatch pattern.
Hatches	Specifies the hatch patterns that will be available when modifying the hatch in a section view. Select a pattern to make it available; clear the check mark to make it unavailable.

Dimension Style

To create a Dimension Style, go to Format->Dimension Style.

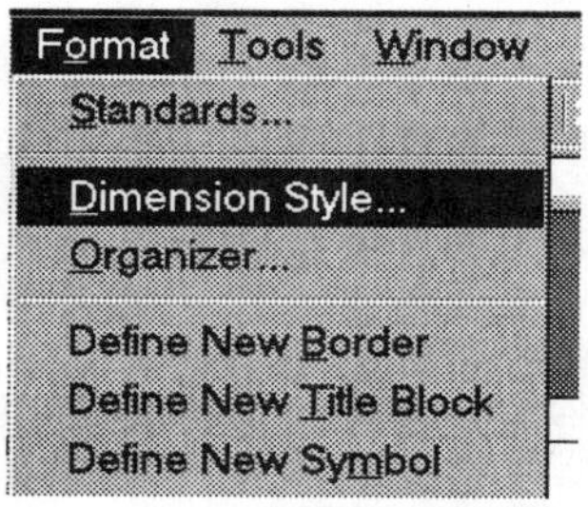

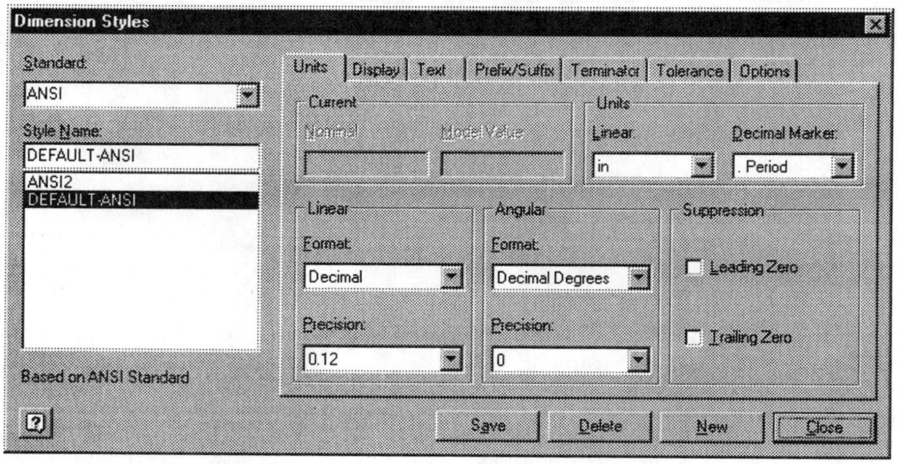

Linear	Sets the style for linear dimension values. Format sets the dimension format to either decimal or fraction. Click the arrow and select from the list. Precision sets the number of decimal places. Dimensions are truncated and rounded to the specified precision. Enter the number of decimal places. Leading Zeros adds a zero in front of dimension values less than 1 (for example 0.125). Select the check box to use leading zeros; clear the check box to suppress leading zeros. Trailing Zeros adds trailing zeros when needed to achieve the number of decimal places set in Precision (for example 1.000). Select the check box to use trailing zeros; clear the check box to suppress trailing zeros.
Angular	Sets the format for angular dimension values. Format sets the dimension format to Decimal Degrees or Deg-Min-Sec. Precision sets the number of decimal places. Dimensions are truncated and rounded to the specified precision. Enter the number of decimal places. Leading Zeros adds a zero in front of dimension values less than 1 (for example 0.125). Select the check box to use leading zeros; clear the check box to suppress leading zeros. Trailing Zeros adds trailing zeros when needed to achieve the number of decimal places set in Precision (for example 1.000). Select the check box to use trailing zeros; clear the check box to suppress trailing zeros.
Characters	The selection box specifies the special characters that will be available to use in the Text Format dialog box. Select a check box to use a character; clear the check box to make a character unavailable.

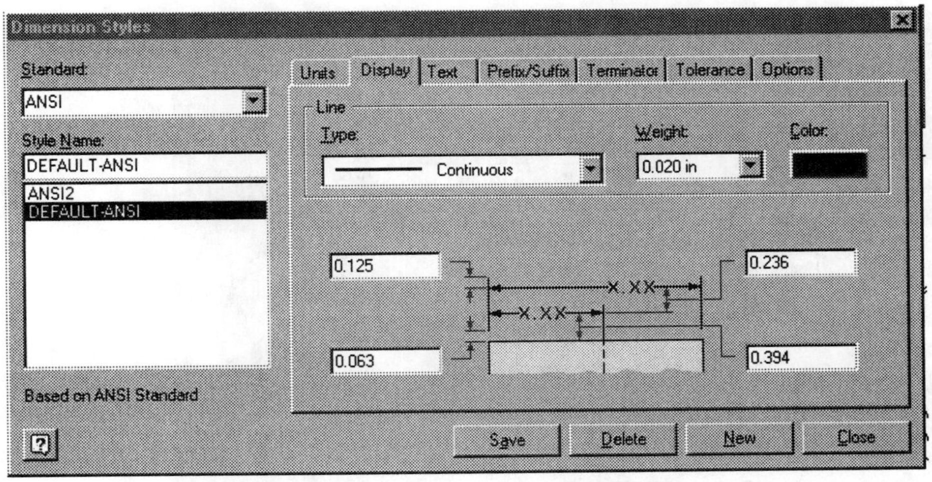

Display

Sets the display characteristics for dimension lines.	
Dimension Line	Sets the optimum offset and spacing for dimension lines. Enter the desired lengths in the boxes. Part Offset specifies the distance from an edge or point to the point where the placement indicator displays as you place dimensions. Spacing specifies the distance between the points where the placement indicator displays as you place dimensions.
Extension Line	Sets the gap and length for extension lines. Enter the values in the boxes. Origin Offset sets the size of the gap between the edge of the object being dimensioned and the beginning of the extension line. Extension sets the distance that the extension line extends past the dimension line.

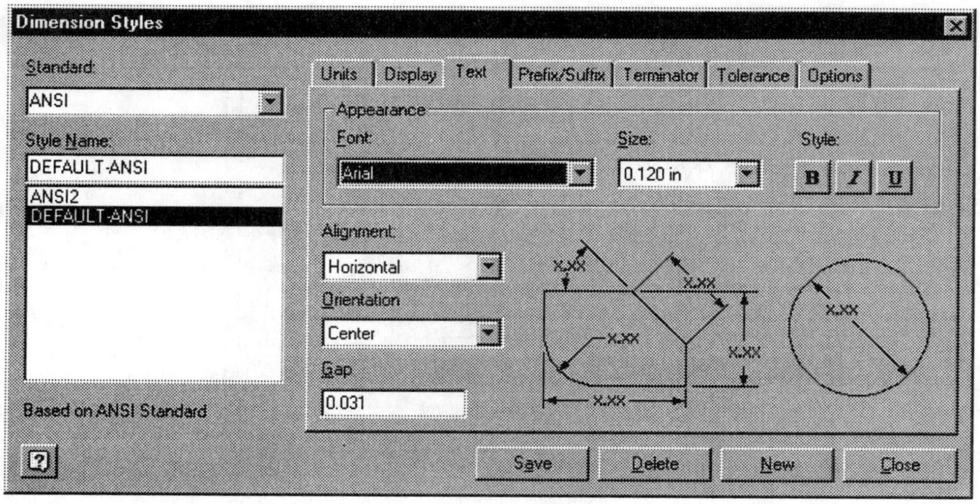

Text

Appearance	Sets the font, size and style for dimension text.
Text Position	Sets the position for dimension text. Orientation sets the vertical placement of the text relative to the dimension line. Click the arrow and choose the placement from the list. Gap sets the distance between the dimension line and the text. Enter the distance in the box.

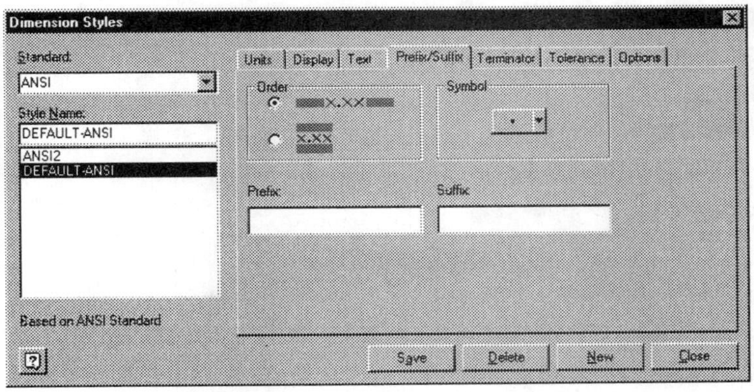

Prefix/Suffix

Assigns a value that will appear either before/above and after/below the dimension.

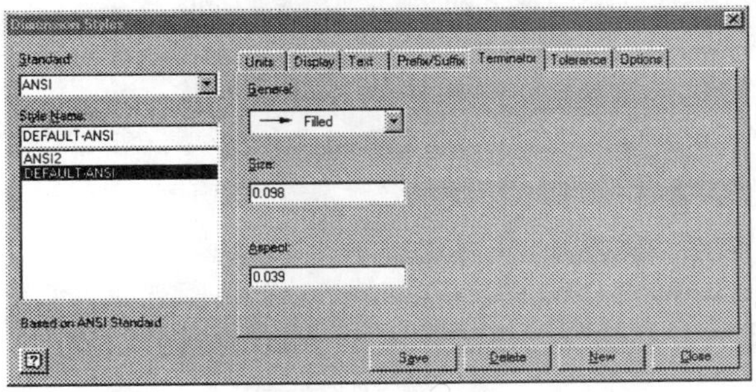

Terminator

The Terminator tab controls arrowhead styles to be used.

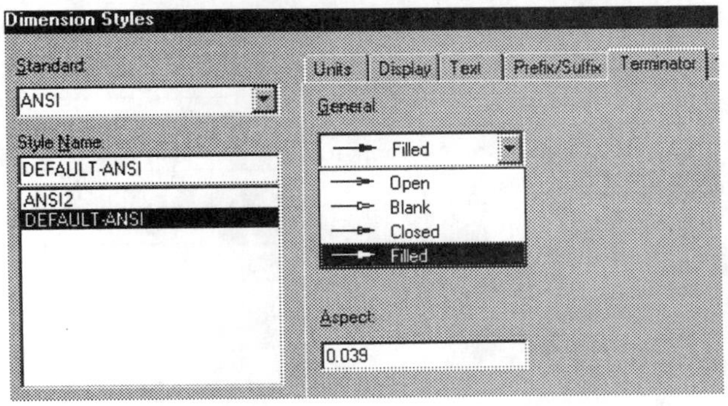

Defines the arrowheads used in the drawing or template.

General	Sets the default arrowhead style for the drafting standard. Click the arrow and select the desired style from the list.
Aspect	Sets the aspect ratio or angle of the arrowhead relative to the associated line. Enter the desired value.

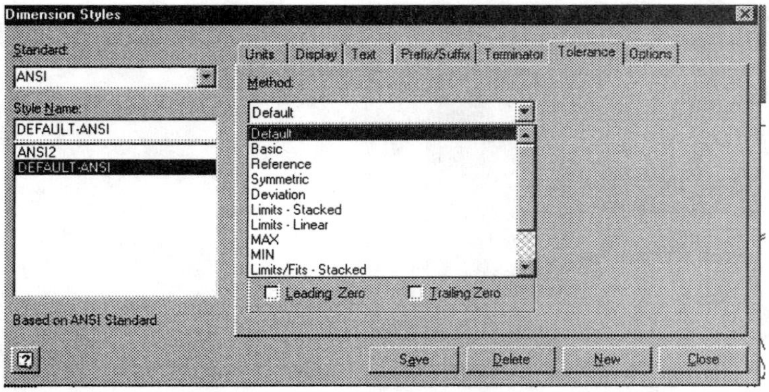

Tolerance

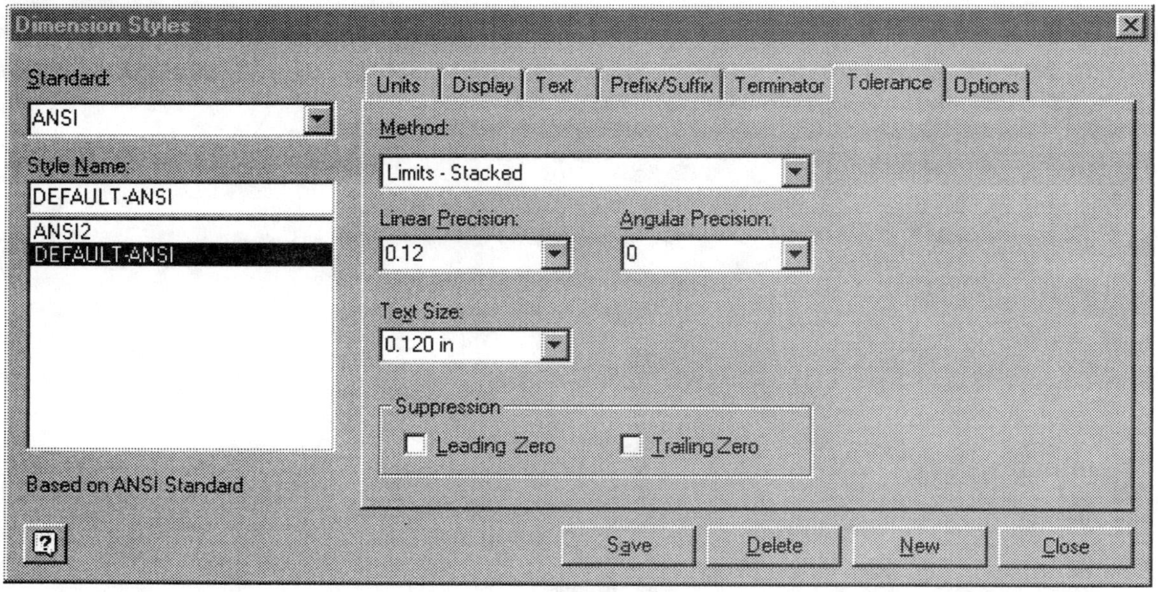

Method	Sets the tolerance style
Linear Precision	Sets the decimal places for the tolerance linear dimension.
Angular Precision	Sets the decimal places for the tolerance angular dimension.
Text Size	Sets the text size of the tolerance text
Suppression	Enables/disables leading and/or trailing zeros.

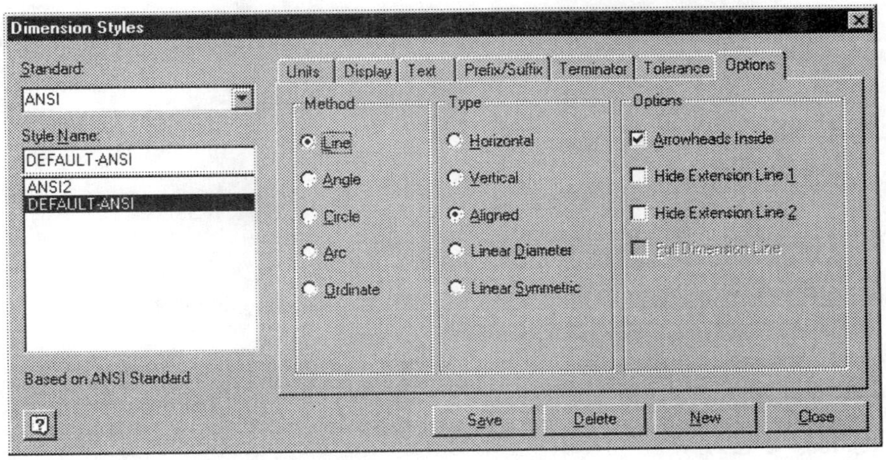

Options

Method	Sets the default appearance for extension lines
Type	Sets the default dimension to be applied
Options	Sets the default appearance for arrowheads.

Review Questions

1. True or False

Drafting Standards set up standards for parts, assemblies and drawings.

2. True or False

If you have more than one file open at a time, they all must use the same Drafting Standard.

3. To set up the background color for a drawing sheet:

   A. File->Properties->Custom
   B. Tools->Options->Drawing
   C. Format->Standards->Sheet
   D. Sheet->Edit

4. To set up the number of decimals to be used in dimensions:

   A. File->Properties->Units
   B. Tools->Options->Design Elements
   C. Format->Standards->Dimension Value
   D. Format->Dimension Style->Units

5. To set up the color of dimension text to be used in drawings:

   A. File->Properties->Units
   B. Tools->Options->Colors
   C. Format->Standards->Dimension Value
   D. Format->Dimension Style->Display

6. Custom templates must be saved in this directory:

   A. Support
   B. Projects
   C. Templates
   D. Root

ANSWERS: 1) T; 2) F; 3) C; 4) D; 5) D; 6) C

Lesson 25
Assembly Tools

Learning Objective

At the conclusion of this lesson, the user will have a good overall understanding of the tools used in constraining and managing assemblies.

The Assembly tool bar is divided into four sections: Component, Assembly Constraints, Component Management, and Component Viewing.

Assembly components can be individual parts or subassemblies that behave as a single unit. For example, a single-part base plate and a multi-part air cylinder subassembly are both components when placed in an assembly.

To make sure that they are always available when you open the assembly, add the paths for all components to the project file for the assembly.

The behavior and characteristics of a component depend on its origin.

A Mechanical Desktop part placed as a component in an Autodesk Inventor assembly acts much like any assembly component. You can add assembly constraints, set its visibility, and perform other assembly operations. However, you cannot edit the part in Autodesk Inventor.

Each Mechanical Desktop part is linked to the assembly through a special file called a proxy file. The proxy file contains the linking information so that the assembly component updates when you edit the part in Mechanical Desktop.

TIP: If you make extensive changes to any component in an assembly, some assembly constraints may not compute correctly when the Autodesk Inventor assembly file is updated. These constraints must be recreated.

Parts or subassemblies created using another CAD system can be inserted as components in the active assembly. You cannot change the size or shape of external components, but you can customize them by adding features.

Adaptive parts can change size and shape to satisfy assembly design requirements. When an adaptive part is constrained to other assembly components, underconstrained geometry in the adaptive part resizes.

When a part is first placed in an assembly, it is not defined as adaptive in the assembly context. You can create fixed-size geometry, and then place the part in an assembly. Select one occurrence in the assembly and designate it as adaptive.

Most assemblies contain a combination of existing components and components (parts and subassemblies) created in the assembly environment.

When you create components in place, you can use geometry from other parts (such as edges and hole centers) in feature sketches. Parts based on existing geometry are sized and positioned in relation to that geometry. Parts created in place have an automatic mate constraint applied between the part XY sketch plane and the part face you sketch on. You can define a part created in place as adaptive so that its size and shape can adjust as assembly requirements change.

Any part in an assembly may have all of its degrees of freedom removed and be fixed in position, relative to the assembly coordinate system. The origin of a grounded part will not move when you place assembly constraints, but a grounded part can still be designated as adaptive. The features on a grounded, adaptive part can change size or shape although its position is fixed.

TIP: The first component placed in an assembly is automatically grounded, so that subsequent parts may be placed and constrained in relation to it. If necessary, you can remove the grounded status of a part.

Placing the First Component

The first component placed in an assembly should be a fundamental part or subassembly, such as a frame or base plate, on which the rest of the assembly is built.

The first component in an assembly file sets the orientation of all subsequent parts and subassemblies. The part origin is coincident with the origin of the assembly coordinates and the part is grounded (all degrees of freedom are removed).

If necessary, you can restore degrees of freedom to the grounded part (the base component) and reposition it. Any components you have constrained to it will also move.

TIP: It is a good idea to place parts and subassemblies in the order in which they would be assembled in manufacturing.

Although there is no distinction in an assembly between components, you can think of the first component you place as the base component because it is usually a fundamental component to which others are constrained. If you place a first component and then want to change to a different base component, you can place a new component, specify it as grounded, and then reconstrain any components you placed earlier, including the first component. Right-click on the first component, clear the Grounded check box, and then constrain it to the new base component.

There is no limit to how many components can be grounded, but most assemblies have only one grounded component. Grounded components are appropriate for fixed objects in assemblies because their position is absolute (relative to the assembly coordinate origin) and all degrees of freedom are removed. Grounded components have no dependencies on other components.

You can use the Move button on the Assembly toolbar to relocate the grounded component. You can drag the component to its new position. The component is grounded in the new location.

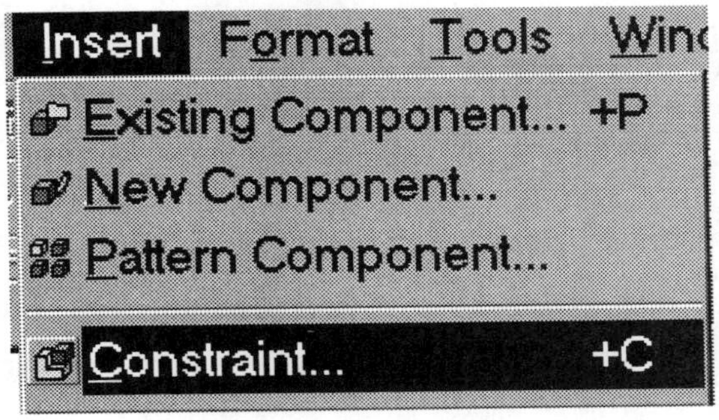

Assemblies can also be managed from the Menu. You can place an Existing Component, Create a New Component, Pattern a Component, or Add a Constraint under the Insert Menu.

Place Component

The first component in an assembly is automatically positioned with its origin coincident with the assembly coordinate origin. Additional components are positioned with the cursor, attached at the component center of gravity.

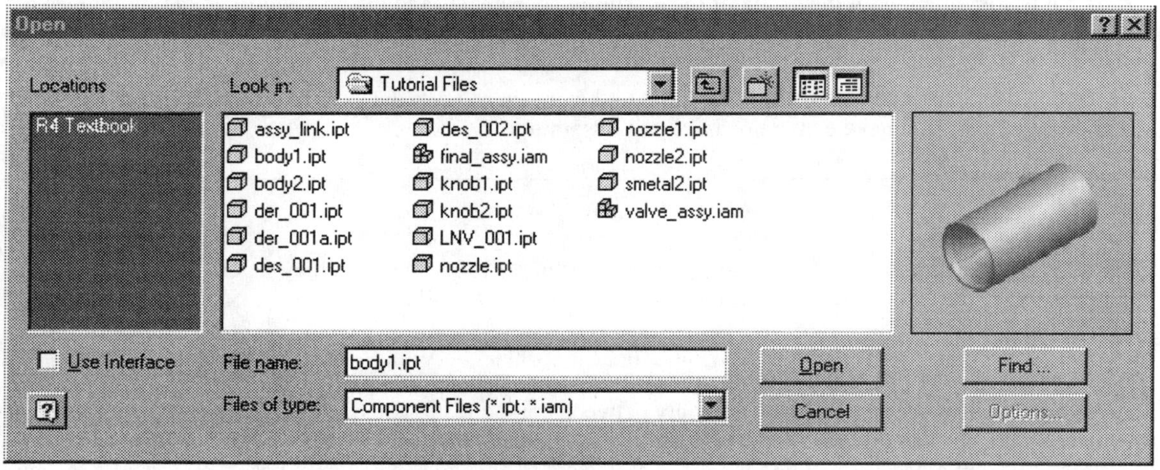

1. Click the Place Component button to choose a component to place.
2. Go to the folder that contains the component, select the component, and click Open.
3. The selected component is placed in the graphics window, attached to the cursor. Select a location and click to place an occurrence of the component.
4. Move the cursor to a different location and click to place a second occurrence, continuing until all occurrences are placed.
5. To quit, right-click and select 'Done'.

TIP: You can drag and drop a component from Windows Explorer or a browser window, but the component includes undisplayed default work planes that may offset the part from the cursor. Drag and drop places a single instance, unlike multiple occurrences as described above. Whether you place components through the dialog box or drag and drop, use assembly constraints to position components and remove degrees of freedom.

Typing a 'P' will initiate the Place Component command.

Create Component

You can create a new part in the context of an assembly file. Creating an in-place part has the same result as opening a part file, with the additional option of sketching on the face of an assembly component or an assembly work plane. To allow the size of the new part to change with assembly requirements, you can designate the part as adaptive and constrain it to fixed geometry in the assembly.

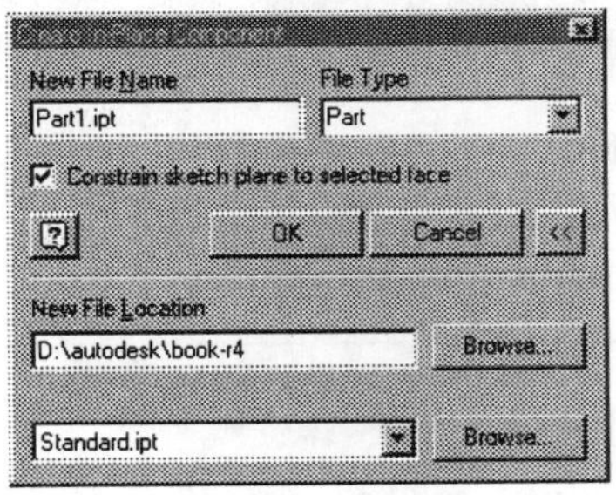

New File Name	Name of the file for the new component
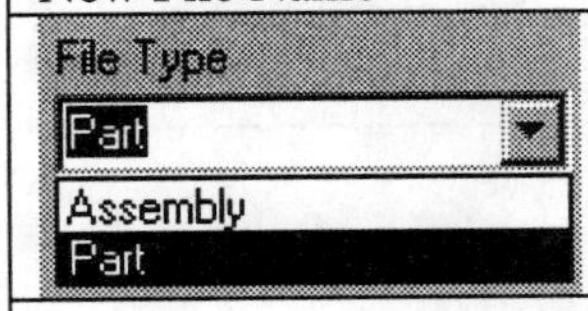	Part – defines part as a single component Assembly – defines part as a subassembly
	Constrain sketch plane to selected face Enabling will automatically add a mate constraint for the new part/subassembly Disabling means that the part will be "free-floating" and will need to be constrained later
New File Location	Set the subdirectory where the file is to be saved.
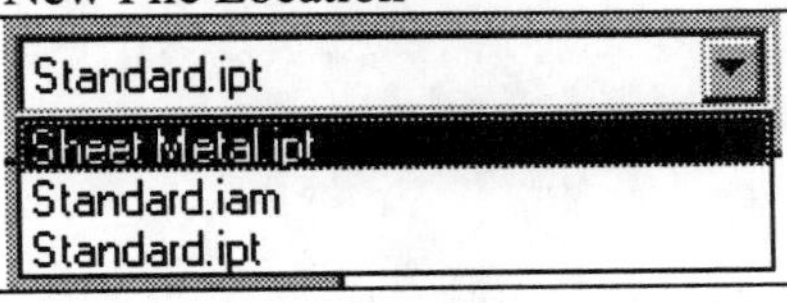	Sets the file extension to be defined to the new file.

Extruded features can start and end on faces of other parts. By default, extruded features with From To or To extents are adaptive.

1. Click the Create Component button.
2. In the dialog box, enter a name for the part and click OK.
3. Select a component face or work plane on which to sketch.
4. If you want to reorient the view to the sketch, click the Look At button.
5. Use the tools on the Sketch toolbar to create a sketch on a selected plane.
6. Select Extrude, Revolve, Loft, or Sweep to create a feature using the new sketch.
7. Continue to select faces on which to sketch and add new features as needed.

When the part is complete, double-click the top-level assembly in the browser to reactivate the assembly environment.

TIP: A mate constraint is automatically placed between the new sketch and the face or work plane. To omit this constraint, clear the check box in the Create Part In-Place dialog box when you create the part file. You can set options on the Adaptive tab of the Options dialog box to control feature termination.

Pattern Component

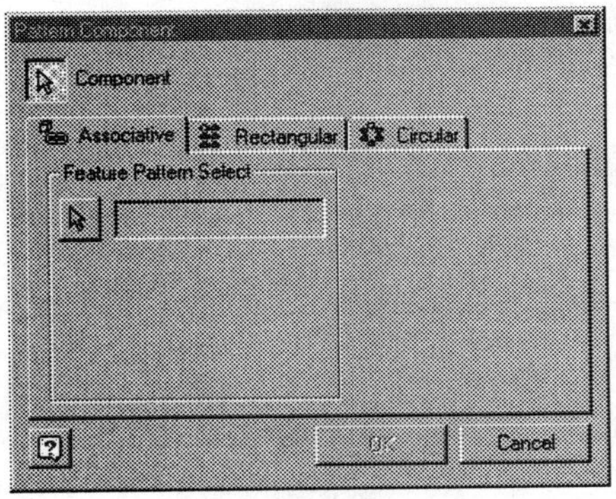

Arranging assembly components in a pattern saves time, increases your productivity, and captures design intent. For example, you may need to place multiple bolts to fasten one component to another or place multiple subassemblies into a complex assembly.

You can create a circular pattern by specifying the number of components and the angle between then. You can create a rectangular pattern by specifying column and row spacing. You can create both circular and rectangular patterns by matching features patterned on a part.

Usually, you pattern components at several points in the assembly design process. After you place a component in an assembly. When you place a component:

- You position it using an existing part feature pattern.
- You select the component and copy it into a pattern.

Individual occurrences are listed in the browser as individual parts. Individual or all occurrences can have visibility turned on or off.

You can arrange components in a circular or arc pattern by specifying the number, angle spacing, and rotation axis or by matching the spacing of features a part.

To pattern by specifying the number, angle spacing, and rotation axis:

1. Click the Pattern Component button then click the Circular tab, if necessary.
2. In the browser or graphics window, select one or more components to pattern.
3. In Circular Placement, click an edge or work axis to indicate the Rotation Axis. Click Flip to change the axis direction, if desired.
4. Enter the count (number of features) for the arc or circle and the angular spacing between features.

Apply assembly constraints to position individual components as needed.

To pattern by matching the spacing of features a part:

1. Click the Pattern Component button then click the Circular tab, if necessary.
2. In the browser or the graphics window, select one or more components to pattern.
3. In Circular Placement, click an occurrence of a feature in a pattern.

Components are copied in the placement and spacing of the feature pattern. Apply assembly constraints to position individual components as needed.

TIP: In the graphics window, you can select a part feature to pattern, but you must select an occurrence of the feature, not the original feature.

Place Constraint

Assembly constraints determine how components in the assembly fit together. As you apply constraints, you remove degrees of freedom, restricting the ways components can move.

To help you position components correctly, you can preview the effects of a constraint before it is applied. After you select the constraint type, the two components, and set the angle or offset, the components move into the constrained position. You can make adjustments in settings as needed, then apply it.

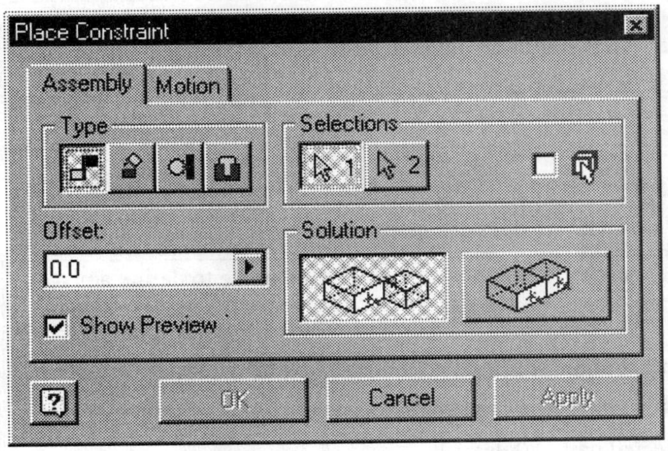

The Place Constraints dialog box creates constraints to control position and animation. Motion constraints do not affect position constraints.

The Assembly tab has constraints to control position:

- A **mate** constraint positions selected faces normal to one another, with faces coincident or aligns parts adjacent to one another with faces flush. The faces may be offset from one another.
- An **angle** constraint positions linear or planar faces on two components at a specified angle.
- A **tangent** constraint between planes, cylinders, spheres, and cones causes geometry to contact at the point of tangency. Tangency may be inside or outside a curve.
- An **insert** constraint positions cylindrical features with planar faces perpendicular to the cylinder axis.

To create a complex assembly, create several small assemblies and save each one as a separate file. Combine them in larger assemblies, constraining them to other subassemblies and parts as a single unit.

Group parts in subassemblies if you want to use them in more than one assembly. Modify small subassemblies or regroup parts to change assembly configuration.

The four types of assembly constraints are: Mate, Tangent, Angle, and Insert.

Mate Constraint

Mate constraint positions components face-to-face or adjacent to one another with faces flush. Removes one degree of linear translation and two degrees of angular rotation between planar surfaces.	
	Mate constraint positions selected faces normal to one another, with faces coincident.
	Flush constraint aligns components adjacent to one another with faces flush. Positions selected faces, curves, or points so that they are aligned with surface normals pointing in the same direction.

Angle Constraint

Angle constraint positions edges or planar faces on two components at a specified angle to define a pivot point. Removes one degree of angular rotation.	
	As selected positions components at the specified angle, based on the geometry selected.
	Flip Part 1 rotates the first selected part 180 degrees.
	Flip Part 2 rotates the second selected part 180 degrees.
	Flip both parts rotates both selected parts 180 degrees.

Tangent Constraint

Tangent constraint causes faces, planes, cylinders, spheres, and cones to contact at the point of tangency. Tangency may be inside or outside a curve, depending on the direction of the selected surface normal. A tangent constraint removes one degree of linear translation.	
	Inside Positions the first selected part inside the second selected part at the tangent point.
	Outside Positions the first selected part outside the second selected part at the tangent point. Outside tangency is the default solution.

Insert Constraint

Insert constraint is a combination of a face-to-face mate constraint between planar faces and a mate constraint between the axes of the two components. The Insert constraint is used to position a bolt shank in a hole, for example, with the shank aligned with the hole and the bottom of the bolt head mated with the planar face. A rotational degree of freedom remains open.	
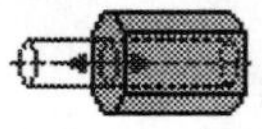	Opposed reverses the mate direction of the first selected component.
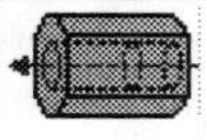	Aligned reverses the mate direction of the second selected component.

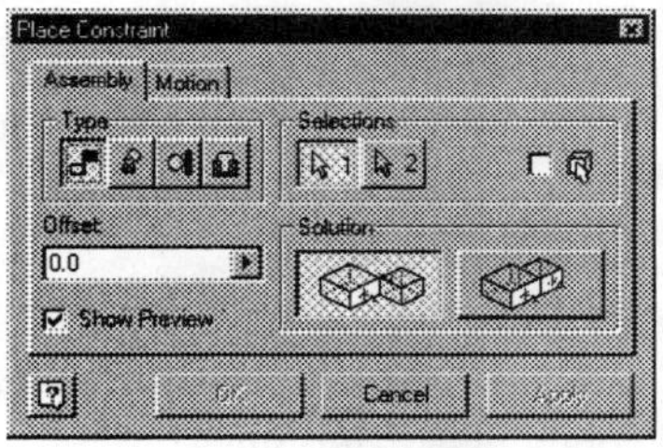

Selections select geometry on two components to constrain together. You can specify one or more curves, planes, or points to define how features fit together.	
	First Selection Selects curves, planes or points on the first component. To end the first selection, click the Second Selection button.
	Second Selection Selects curves, planes, or points on the second component. To select different geometry on the first component, click the First Selection tool and reselect.
	Pick Part First Limits the selectable geometry to a single component. Use when components are in close proximity or partially obscure one another. Clear the check box to restore selection mode.

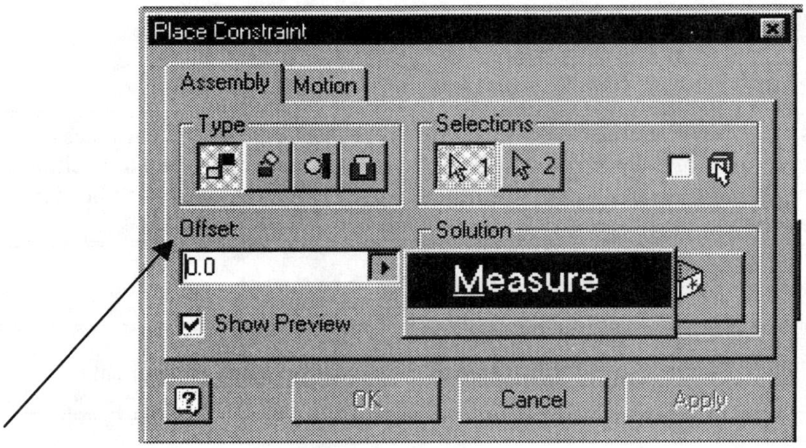

The Offset text box specifies distance by which constrained components are offset from one another.

Use to enter a value equal to a distance or angle that exists in the assembly, but when you do not know the offset or angle. Click the down arrow to measure the angle or distance between components, show dimensions of selected component, or enter a recently used value.

Specify positive or negative values. Default setting is zero. The first picked component determines the positive direction. Enter a negative number to reverse the offset or angle direction.

The Show Preview shows the effect of the constraint on the selected geometry. After both selections are made, underconstrained objects automatically move into constrained positions. Default setting is on. Clear the check box to turn preview off.

Motion Constraints

Motion constraints specify the intended motion between assembly components. Because they operate only on open degrees of freedom, they do not conflict with positional constraints, resize adaptive parts, or move grounded components.

Motion constraints are shown in the browser. When clicked or the cursor hovers over the browser entry, constrained components are highlighted in the graphics window.

Drive constraints are not available for motion constraints. However, parts that are constrained using motion constraints will drive according to the direction and ratio specified.

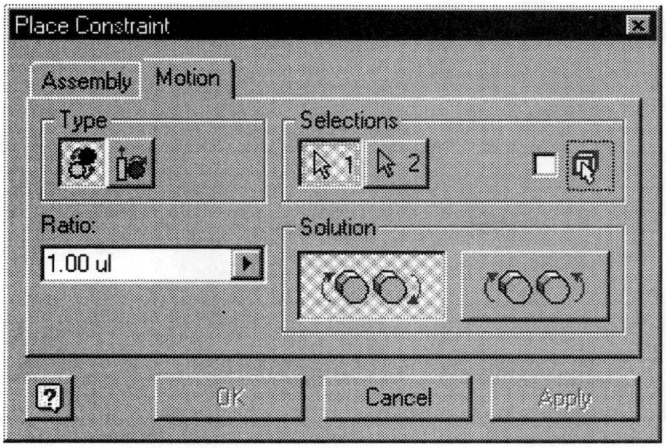

The Motion tab has constraints to specify intended motion ratios between assembly components:

- A **rotation** constraint specifies rotation of one part relative to another part using a specified ratio.
- A **rotation-translation** constraint specifies rotation of one part relative to translation of a second part.

The first part in an assembly is grounded. Its position is fixed, with the part origin coincident with the assembly origin.

When the next part is placed and constrained to the grounded part, it moves to the grounded part and fits together according to the type of constraint applied.

As you add parts, you can add constraints to position the new parts relative to the other assembled parts.

After constraints are positioned, you can use motion constraints to control rotation and translation in the remaining degrees of freedom. You specify a ratio to set movement between two components.

Drive constraints do not control motion between components, but simulate mechanical motion by driving a constraint through a sequence of steps for a single component. You can, however, animate two components by using the Equation tool to create algebraic relationships between components. A drive constraint operation is a temporary animation.

Motion constraints specify motion ratios between components, either by rotation or by rotation and translation. Such constraints are useful for specifying motion of gears and pulleys, a rack and pinion, or specifying motion between third-party components such as a gearbox and input and output shafts. Use work geometry and assembly constraints to limit the range of motion.

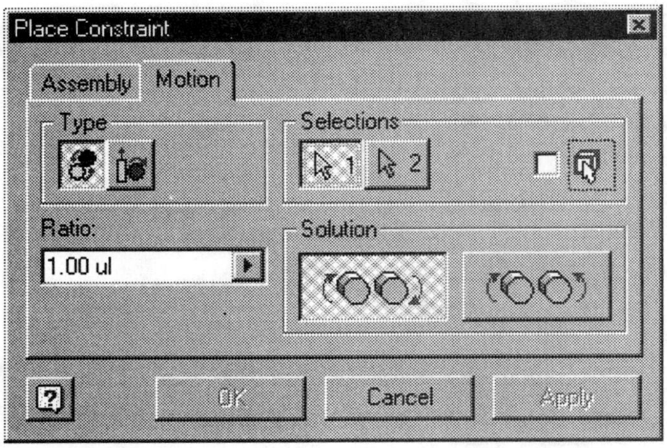

Type specifies the constraint type and illustrates the solution that shows the intended motion between selected components. May be applied between linear, planar, cylindrical, and conical elements. You can change constraint type when the dialog box is open during constraint placement or editing. When the cursor hovers over a component, an arrow shows the direction of the constraint. Click Forward or Reverse to change solution.	
	Rotation constraint specifies that the first selected part rotates in relation to another part using a specified ratio. Typically used for gears and pulleys.
	Rotation-Translation constraint specifies that the first selected part rotates in relation to translation of another part using a specified distance. Typically used to show planar motion, such as a rack and pinions.
Selections select geometry on two components to constrain together. You can specify one or more curves, planes, or points to define how features fit together.	
	First Selection Selects curves, planes or points on the first component. To end the first selection, click the Second Selection button.
	Second Selection Selects curves, planes, or points on the second component. To select different geometry on the first component, click the First Selection tool and reselect.
	Pick Part First Limits the selectable geometry to a single component. Use when components are in close proximity or partially obscure one another. Clear the check box to restore selection mode.

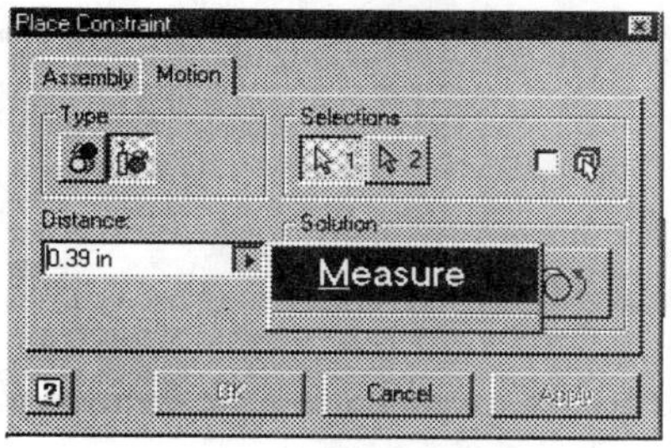

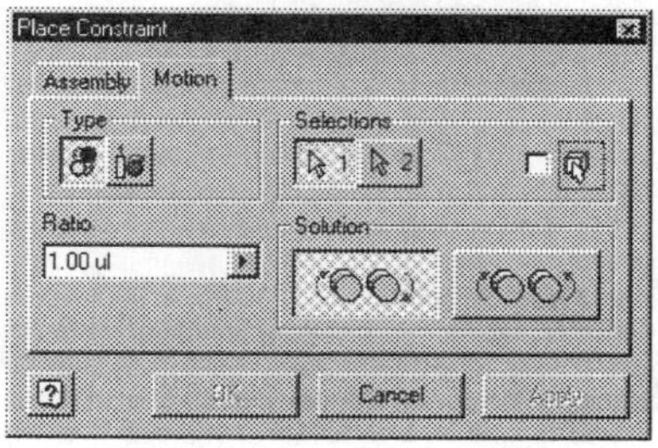

Ratio/Distance specifies the movement of the first selected component relative to the second selected component.

Ratio	For Rotation constraints, the ratio specifies how much the second selection rotates when the first selection rotates. For example, a value of 4.0 (4:1) rotates the second selection four units for every unit the first selection rotates. A value of 0.25 (1:4) rotates the second selection one unit for every four units the first selection rotates. The default value is 1.0 (1:1). If two cylindrical surfaces are selected, Autodesk Inventor computes and displays a default ratio that is relative to the radii of the two selections.
Distance	For Rotation-Translation constraints, the distance specifies how much the second selection moves relative to one rotation of the first selection. For example, a value of 4.0 mm moves the second selection 4.0 mm for every complete rotation of the first selection. If the first selection is a cylindrical surface, Autodesk Inventor computes and displays a default distance that is the circumference of the first selection.

TIP:
If you select a Rotation Type, then you must indicate Ratio.

If you select Rotation-Translation Type, then you must indicate Distance.

Although the ratio and distance parameters are used to specify of amount of movement for the second selection with respect to the first selection, the constraint is bi-directional so that if the second selection is moved, the first selection will move by an inverse amount of either the ratio or distance as appropriate to the constraint type.

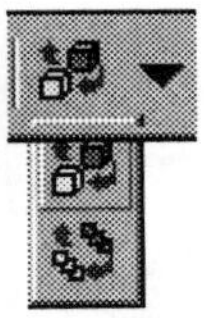

Replace Component/Replace All

The next tool in the Assembly toolbar is a flyout with two options: Replace Component and Replace All.

Replace Component

In the design process, you often need to replace one or more components in an assembly. You may design a placeholder component that you eventually replace with a standard purchased component, or replace one vendor's component with another.

You can select a part to replace an existing assembly component regardless of its location in the directory structure. In a networked environment, you need write permission to replace a component in the open assembly.

The new component is placed in the same location as the original component. The origin of the replacement component is coincident with the origin of the replaced component. Constraints can re-map. Mate and Flush constraints will usually be retained, but Angle and Insert constraints are often lost.

You can replace one assembly component with another component, but existing assembly constraints may be deleted.

1. Click the Replace Component tool, then click a component to replace.
2. In the Open dialog, go to the folder that contains the component, select the component, and click Open.

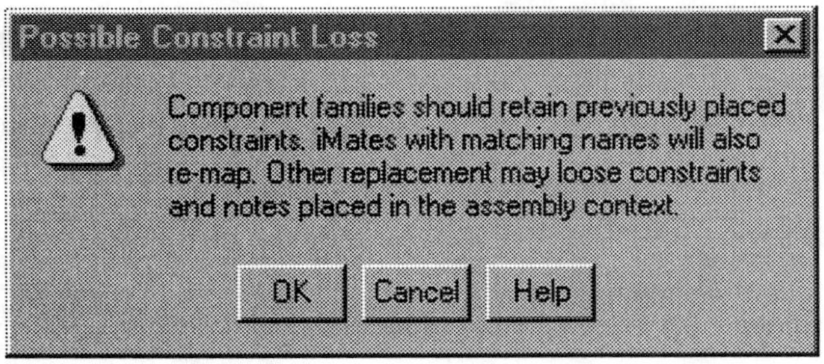

3. A warning message notifies you that constraints may be deleted. Click OK to continue or Cancel to discontinue replacing a component.

The new component is placed in the same location as the original component. The origin of the replacement component is coincident with the origin of the replaced component. Apply assembly constraints as needed to remove degrees of freedom.

TIP: You can select the component to be replaced either in the browser or by picking a part in the drawing window.

Replace All

The Replace All tool will replace all the occurrences of a component with another component.

1. Click the Replace Component tool, then click a component to replace.
2. In the Open dialog, go to the folder that contains the component, select the component, and click Open.

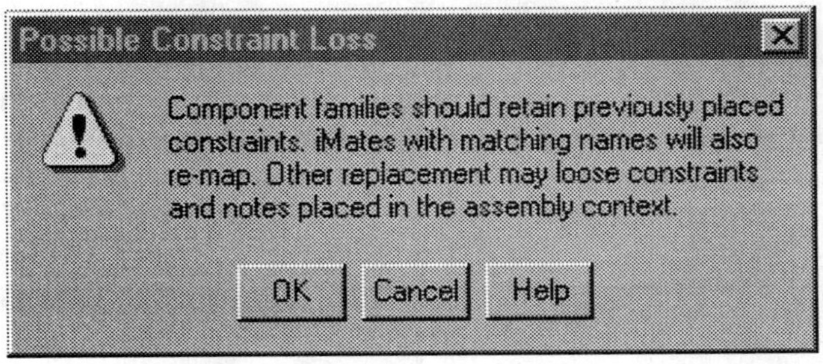

3. A warning message notifies you that constraints may be deleted. Click OK to continue or Cancel to discontinue replacing a component.

Move Component

When you constrain assembly components to one another, you control their position. To move a component, either temporarily or permanently, use one of these methods:

You can move a component to get a better view of its features. An unconstrained move is simply a temporary "get out of the way" move. You might want to move components to:

- See a face or feature on the selected component.
- See a face or feature on a part that is obscured by the selected component.
- Facilitate selection of a face or feature on a component by moving it to an uncluttered area of the screen.

An unconstrained move is convenient but it is temporary. The part remains in the moved location but snaps back to its constrained position when you apply a new constraint or update or refresh the assembly.

To see how a constrained component moves, you can drag it (and all components constrained to it). A constrained move honors previously applied constraints. That is, the selected component and parts constrained move together in their constrained positions.

A grounded component remains grounded at the new location. Components constrained to the grounded component remain in their constrained positions at the new location.

You can click any component in the edit target (the file that contains edits) and drag it to a new location. If you select a component that is not a child of the edit target (a part in a subassembly), the component acts as a handle and drags the whole subassembly.

You can simulate mechanical motion by driving a constraint through a sequence of steps. After you have constrained a component, you can use the Drive Constraint tool to animate it by incrementally changing the value of the constraint. For example, you can rotate a component by driving an angular constraint from zero to 360 degrees. The Drive Constraint tool is limited to one constraint, but you can drive additional constraints by using the Equations tool to create algebraic relationships between constraints.

Rotate Component

The Rotate tool on the Standard toolbar rotates the entire assembly. When you want to rotate a single component, use the Rotate Component tool on the Assembly toolbar. Operation of both Rotate tools is the same.

Keep the following behaviors in mind when you rotate components:

- You can rotate a constrained component.
- When you update the assembly, the components constrained to the rotated component snap into their constrained positions. The rotated component determines the viewing orientation of the components.
- Unconstrained components remain in their rotated positions when you update the assembly.
- Rotating a grounded component overrides the grounded position. The component is still grounded but its position is rotated.

If you require precise positioning of grounded components or other constrained components, use an assembly constraint to reorient a rotated component to the correct position relative to other components.

1. Click the component to rotate.
2. Drag to the desired view of the component.
   - For free rotation, click inside the 3D rotate symbol and drag in the desired direction.
   - To rotate about the horizontal axis, click the top or bottom handle of the 3D rotate symbol and drag vertically.
   - To rotate about the vertical axis, click the left or right handle of the 3D rotate symbol and drag horizontally.
   - To rotate planar to the screen, hover over the rim until the symbol changes to a circle, click the rim, and drag in a circular direction.
   - To change the center of rotation, click inside or outside the rim to set the new center.
3. Release mouse button to drop component in rotated position.

When you click Update, a constrained component snaps back to its constrained position. An unconstrained or grounded component relocates to the new position. Any components constrained to a grounded component snap into their constrained positions in the new location.

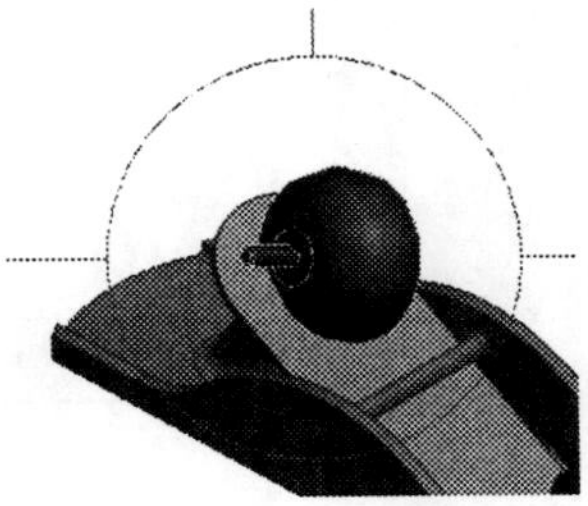

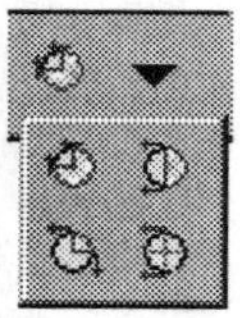

Section Views of Assemblies

You create a section view to visualize portions of an assembly within chambers or that are obscured by components. While the assembly is sectioned, you use part and assembly tools to create or modify parts-in-place.

To begin, open an assembly file containing one or more components.

1. Set visibility for components. Select the component in the graphics window or the browser, then:
    - To hide components, right-click and clear the check mark beside Visibility.
    - To show components in wireframe for context, right-click and clear the check mark beside Enabled.
2. Click one of the Section View tools on the Assembly toolbar, then select any planar or work plane to define the cutting plane.
3. Right-click and select Flip, if necessary to display the desired view of the section.
4. Click the Create Component tool on the Assembly toolbar. When prompted to select a sketch plane, select the plane used to define the section.
5. If desired, use the Project Cut Edges tool on the Sketch toolbar to project edges of a part cut by the section plane onto the sketch plane.
6. Use sketch and feature tools to create new geometry.

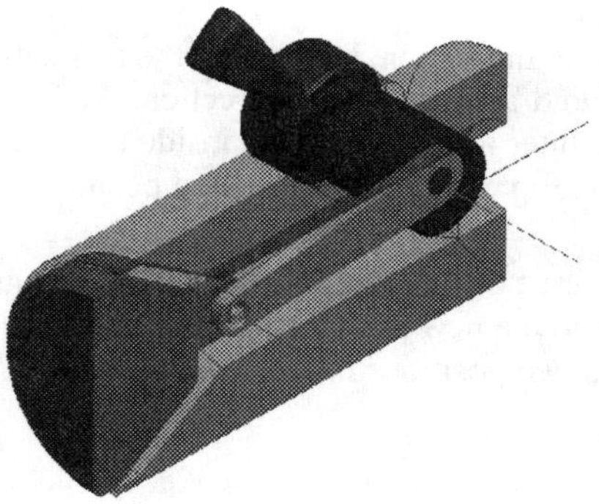

TIP: From Quarter section and Three-quarter section views, you can right-click and select the opposite view.

Component Visibility

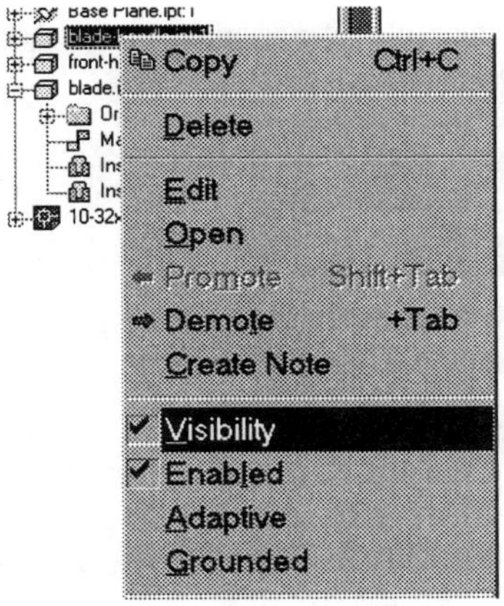

Visible and enabled components can be selected.
Visible but not enabled components cannot be selected. They are displayed in background style (wireframe).
Invisible and not enabled components cannot be selected and are not visible in the graphics window. Select an invisible and disabled components from the browser, then right-click to change its visibility status.
Invisible and enabled components can be selected in the browser but are not visible in the graphics window. The icon shown in the browser looks the same as that for components that are visible and not enabled. Select an invisible and enabled component from the browser, then right-click to change its status.

TIP: It is possible to turn off component visibility, but have the component still be enabled. This may be useful for quickly removing a needed component from view. Enabled components are fully loaded in an assembly file, while only the graphic portion of not enabled components are loaded. The assembly calculates faster because the data structure of not enabled components is not present, but its graphics are useful for a frame of reference.

Occurrence Properties

Occurrence properties control characteristics for an individual occurrence of a component in an assembly.

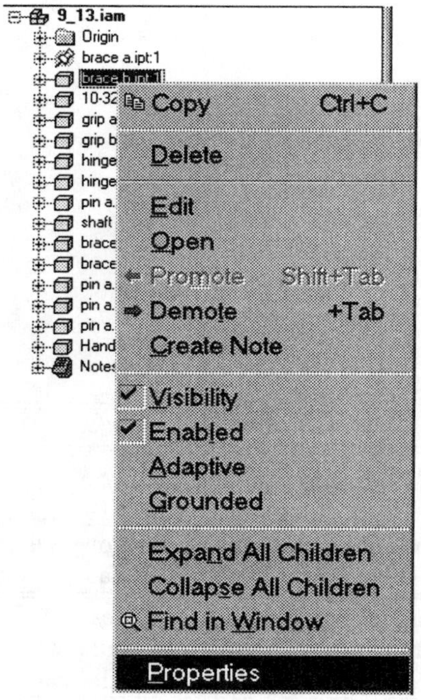

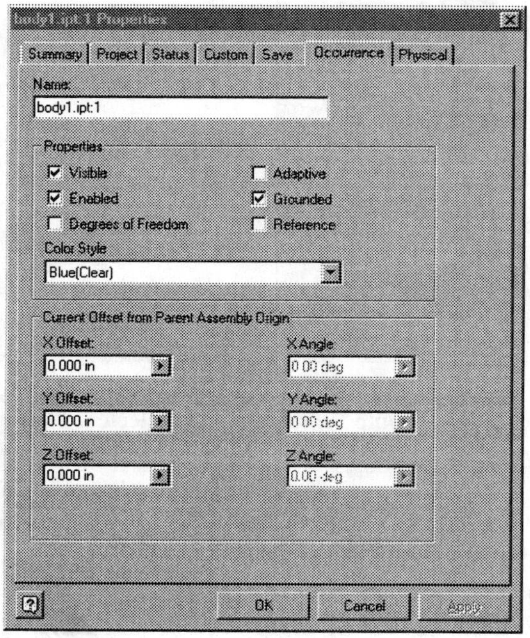

Click the occurrence in the browser, then right-click and select Properties. Click the Occurrence tab.

1. If desired, enter a descriptive name to replace the default name.
2. Select Visible to make the occurrence visible in the graphics window. Clear the check mark to make it invisible.
3. Select Enabled to make the occurrence selectable in the graphics window. Clear the check mark to change it to Not Enabled.
4. Select Adaptive to allow features in the occurrence to change shape and size when you apply constraints. Clear the check mark to make the occurrence a rigid body.

TIP: The adaptive status of an occurrence controls all occurrences in the assembly. When an adaptive part resizes, all occurrences of the part in other assemblies also resize.

5. Select Grounded to remove all degrees of freedom from the occurrence. Clear the check mark to to restore degrees of freedom.
6. In Color Style, click the down arrow and select from the list.
7. If desired, specify the precise position of the occurrence origin relative to the assembly origin. Enter an offset value or an angle for *x, y,* and *z* coordinates.

   Position values are temporary if the occurrence is not grounded. The values are reset when an ungrounded occurrence is moved, rotated, or constrained to a grounded component.

TIP: Except for the current Offset from Parent Assembly Origin, Color Style, or Name, you can set occurrence properties from the context menu. In the browser, right-click the occurrence to view the context menu. A check mark beside the property indicates it is On. Clear the check mark to switch the property Off.

Week 5
Chapter 26,2
Review
17, 21, 22
Date
02-10 = 2-16

Assembly Tools

Button	Tool	Function
	Place Component	Places a link to an existing part of subassembly i A change to any instance updates all other instan component.
	Create Component	Creates a new part or subassembly in an assembl
	Pattern Component	Creates copies of a component in a rectangular o pattern
	Place Constraint	Places an assembly constraint between two parts
	Replace Component	Replaces a component in an assembly with anotl
	Replace All	Replaces all occurrences of a component in an a
	Move Component	Enables a temporary translation of a constrained component. A constrained component returns to proper position when the user clicks Update. Enables permanent translation of a grounded component. A grounded component will remain in the placed position when Update is clicked.
	Rotate Component	Enables a temporary rotation of a constrained component. A constrained component returns to proper position when the user clicks Update. Enables permanent rotation of a grounded component. A grounded component will remain in the placed position when Update is clicked.
	Section Views	Displays a quarter section view of a model defined by hiding portions of components on one side of a defined cutting edge
		Displays a three quarter section view
		Displays a half section view
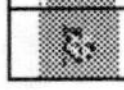		Displays an unsectioned view of the model

Lesson 26

Bottom Up Assemblies – Plane

Learning Objective

In this lesson, we will create a wood plane consisting of five parts in a bottom up assembly. A bottom up assembly consists of creating each part separately in it's own file. In many real world situations, project managers may divide components between several designers or drafters. Each person would get one or two parts to create and then the parts would be assembled into an assembly drawing. A bottom up assembly method may also be used by companies that promote modular designs; i.e. the reuse of parts in more than one assembly. Designers should be familiar with both bottom up and top down assembly methods.

Part 1 - Base

The first part to be created is the Base. We begin by starting a new part file called Base.ipt.

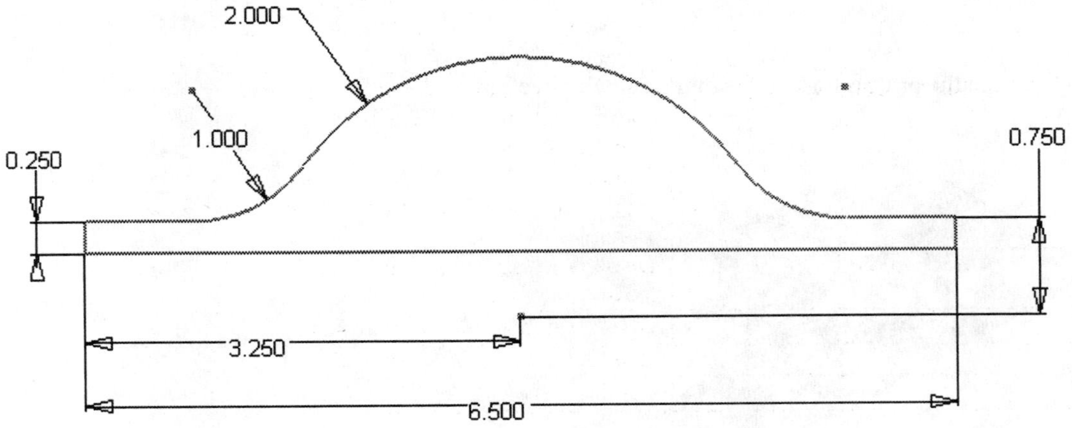

Sketch the geometry as shown. There should be tangent constraints between the arcs and top horizontal lines. Assume part symmetry.

Change to an isometric view.

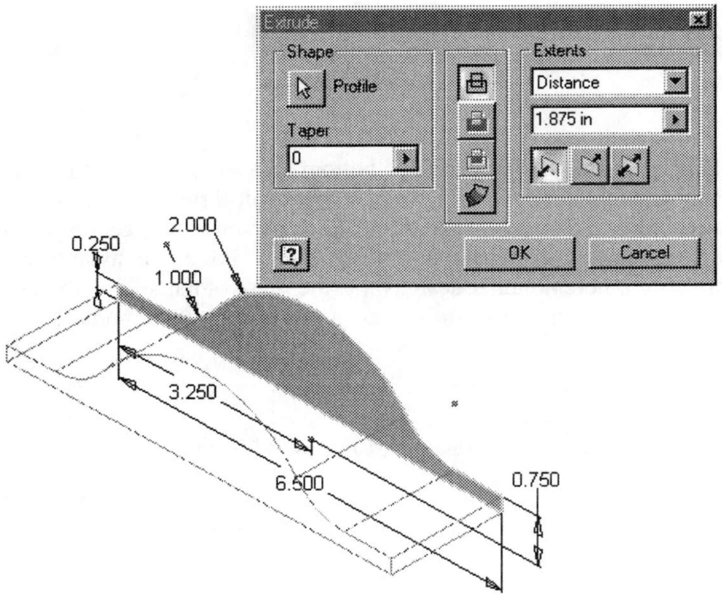

Extrude the profile 1.875 units in the default direction.

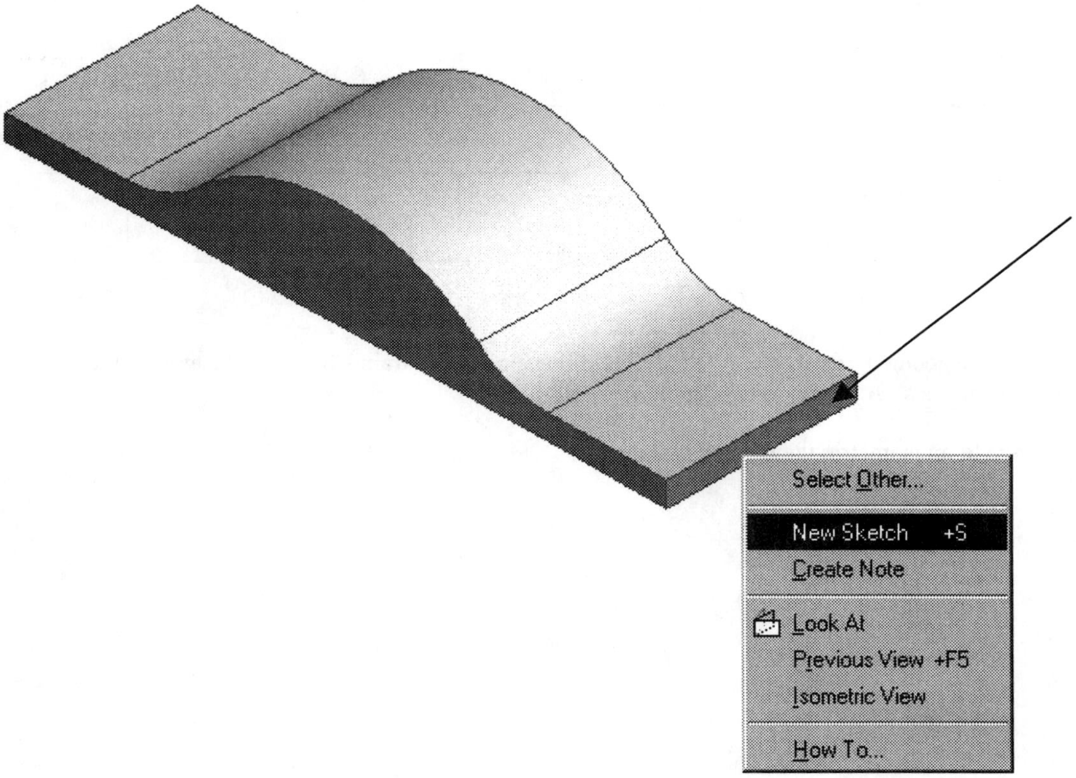

Select one end of the base as the sketch plane as shown.

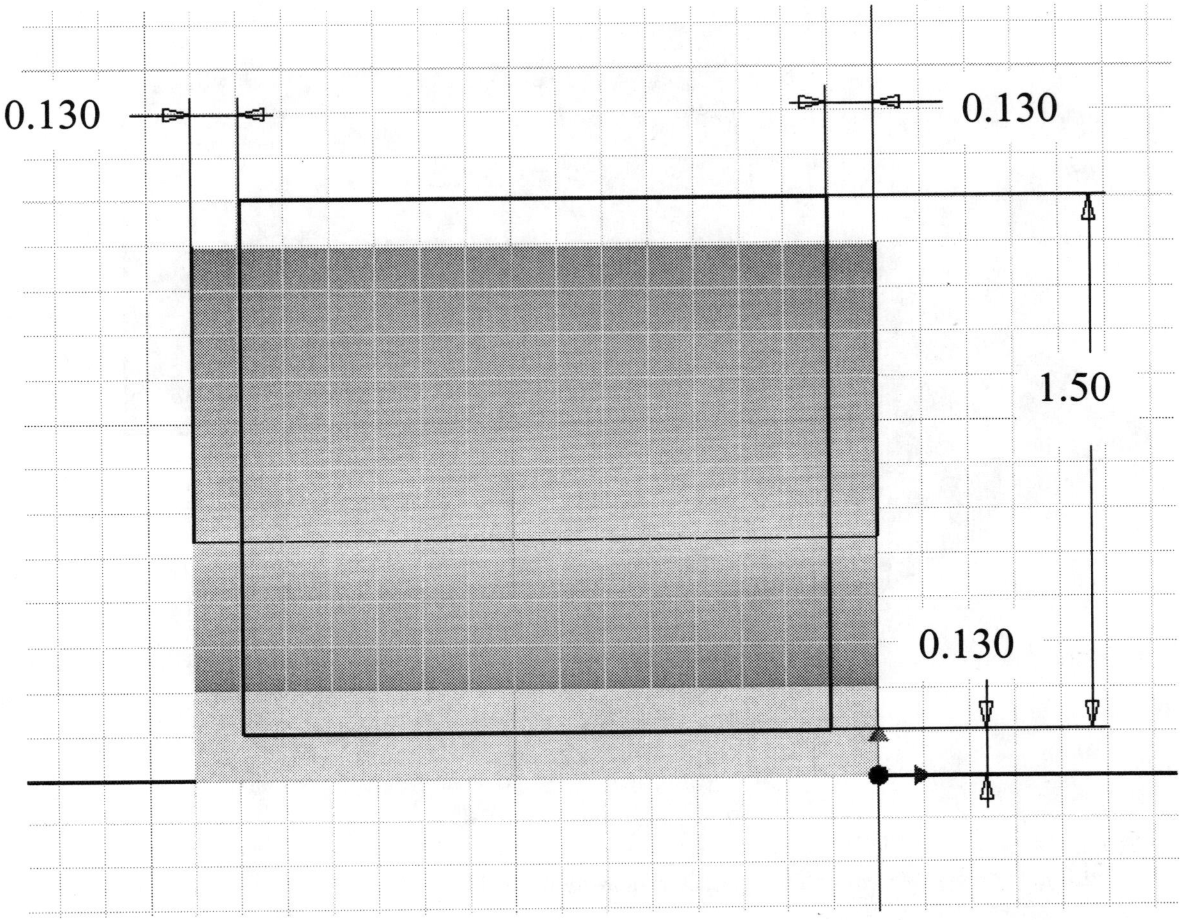

Sketch a rectangle as shown.

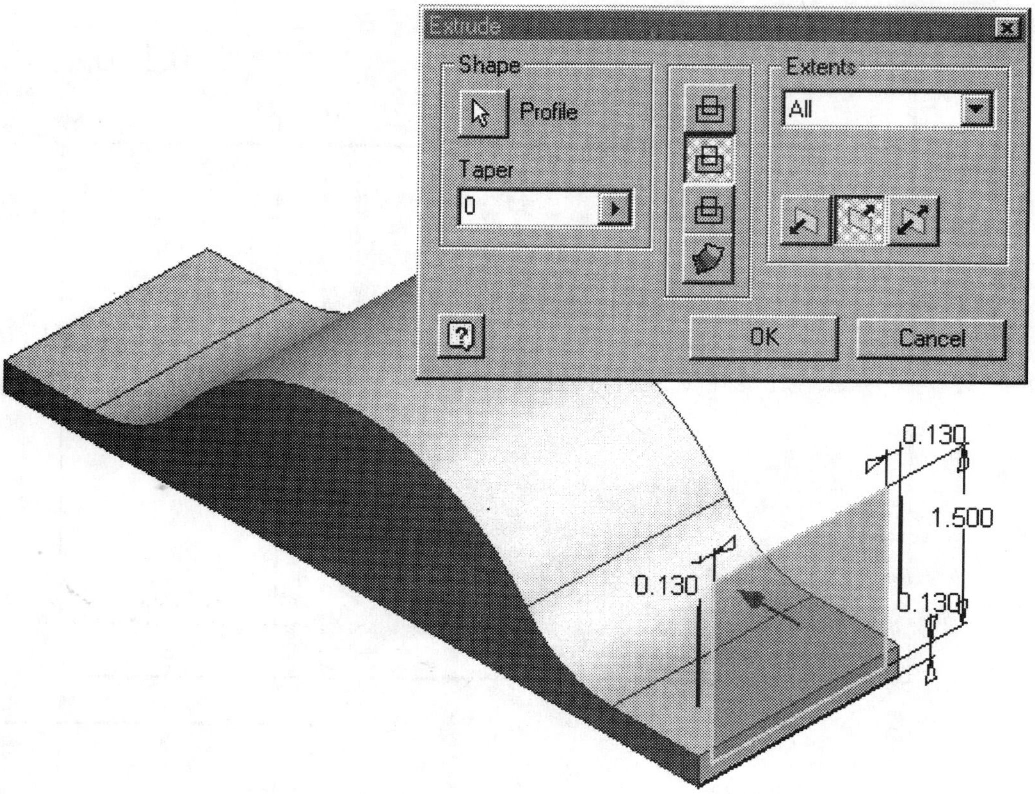

Extrude the rectangle through the part, cutting away the inside.

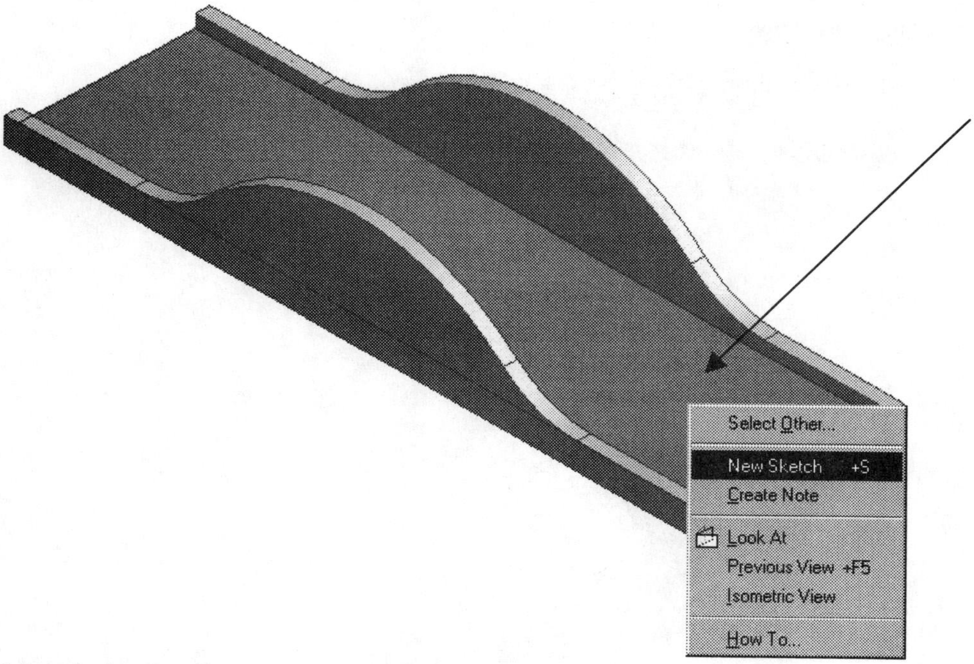

Select the bottom plane as the New Sketch Plane as shown.

Switch to a plan view by using the 'Look At' tool and selecting the bottom plane. 

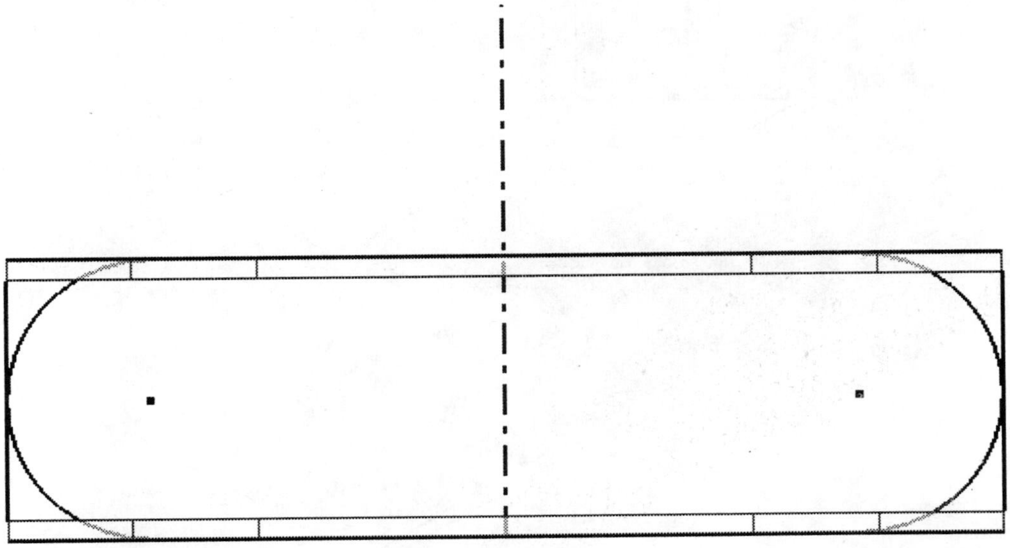

Sketch and create the profile shown.

Create a center line and use the Mirror tool to mirror the arcs.

Add a collinear constraint to the horizontal lines.

Add tangent constraints for each arc at the left and right ends.

When the sketch is fully constrained, it will change color to black.

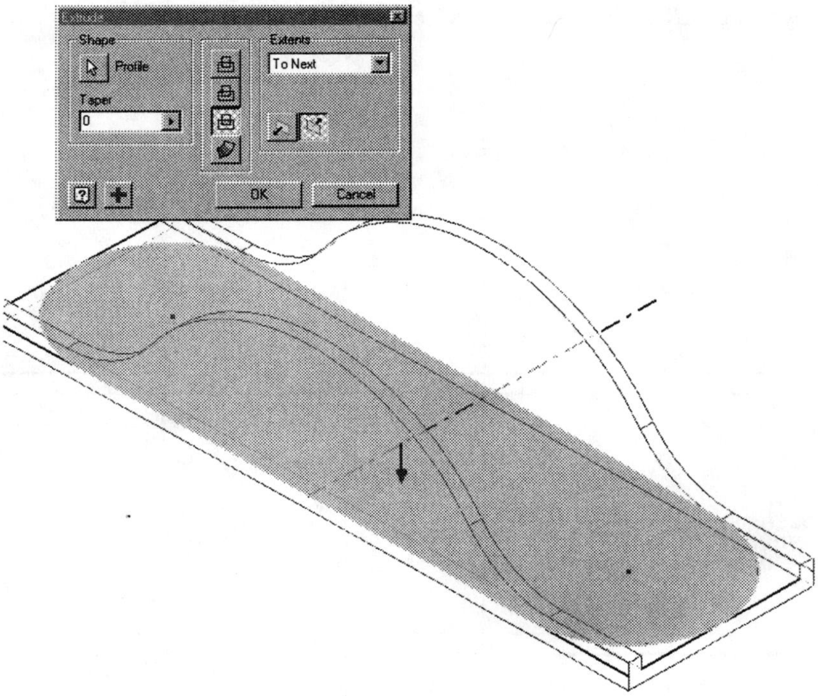

Switch to an isometric view. Extrude the profile using Intersect and the From To option. Select the top horizontal plane for the 'From' plane and the bottom of the part for the 'To' plane.

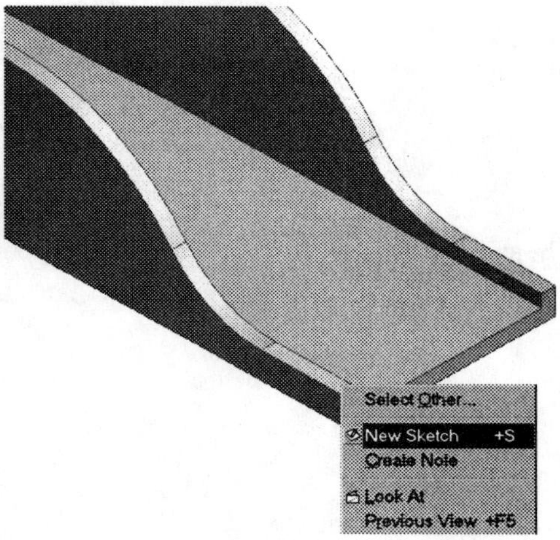

Select the top plane of the flange for a new sketch plane.

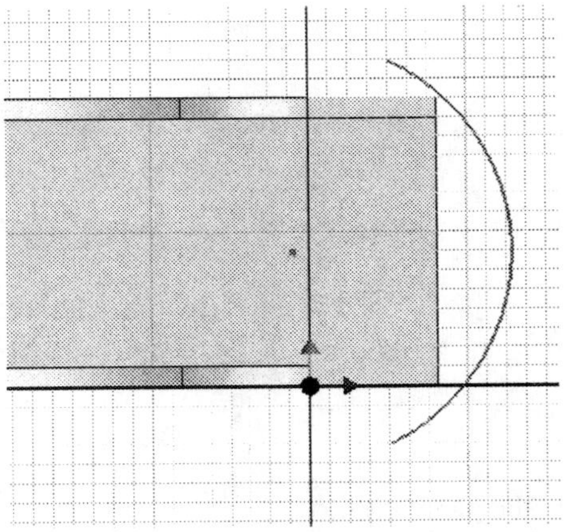

Draw a 3pt arc as shown.

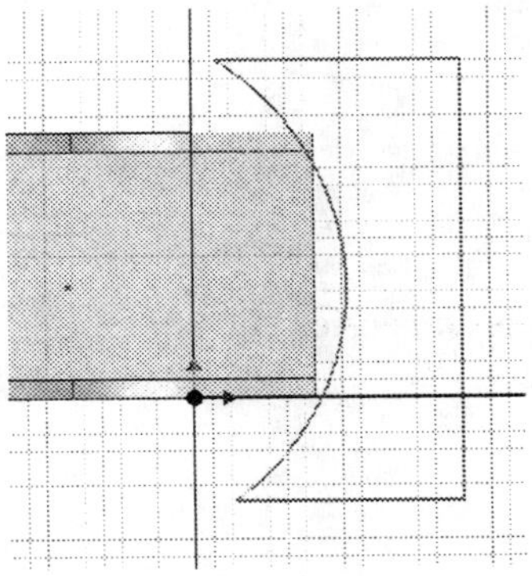

Draw three lines as shown.

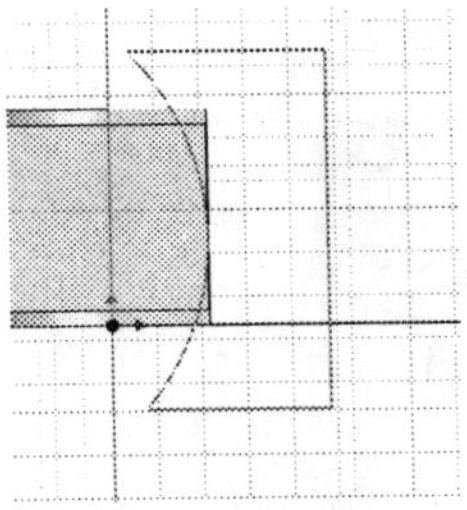

Add a tangent constraint between the arc and the vertical edge of the part.

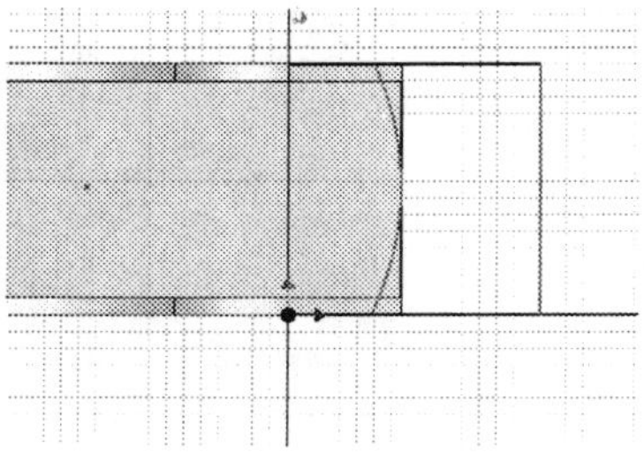

Add a collinear constraint between the horizontal lines and the part edges.

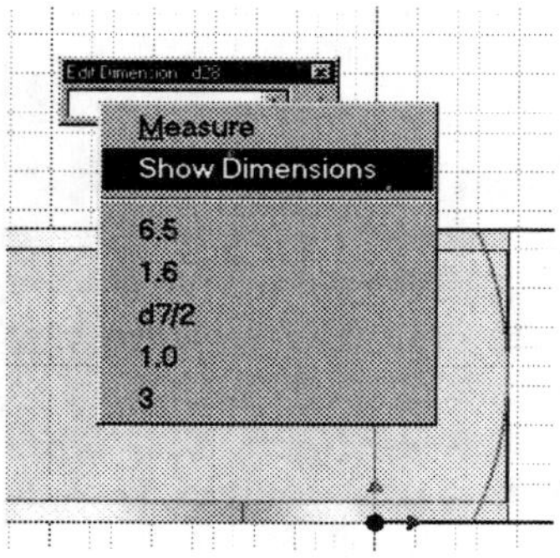

Position the arc so it is centered on the part.
Place the dimension and then use the 'Show Dimensions' option in the Dimension edit box.

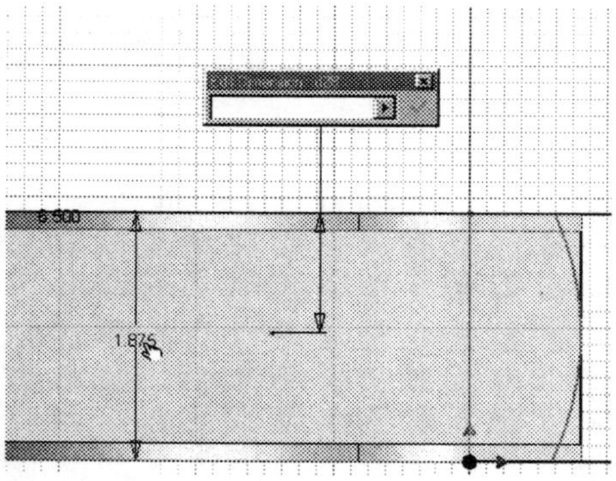

Select the base extrusion to display it's dimensions.
Select the vertical dimension of the base shown.

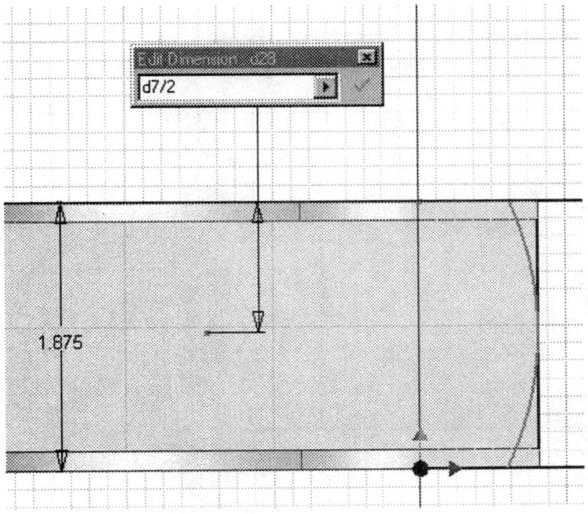

Create an equation by adding '/2' in the Edit Dimension box.
Select the green check mark to place the dimension.

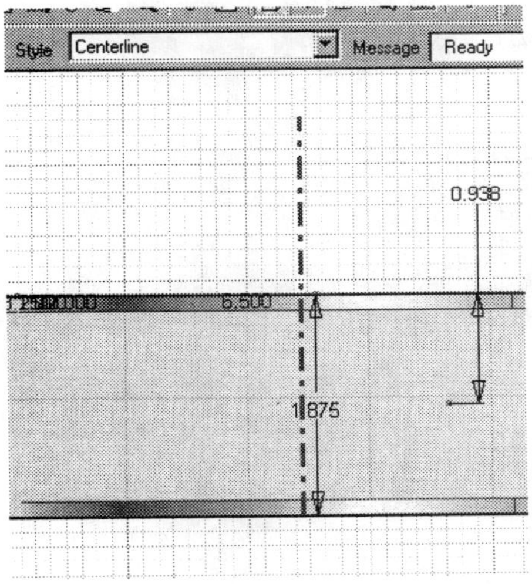

Add a centerline.
Draw a vertical line.
Select the line and then choose Centerline from the Style.

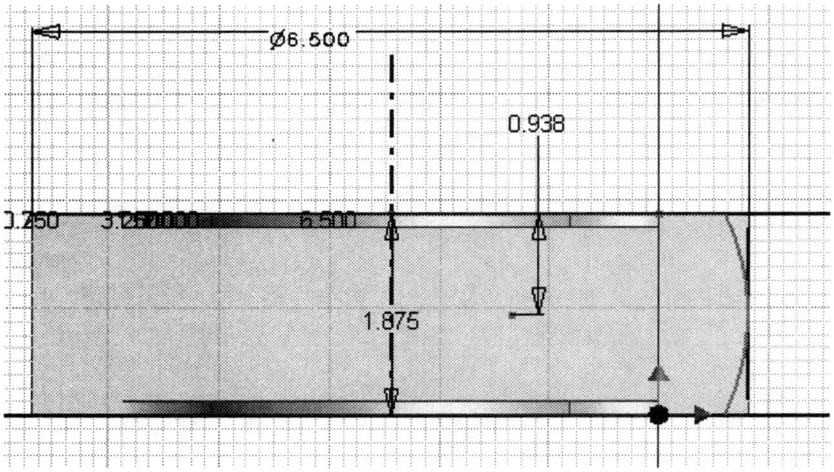

Dimension the centerline by selecting the 6.5 dimension value.

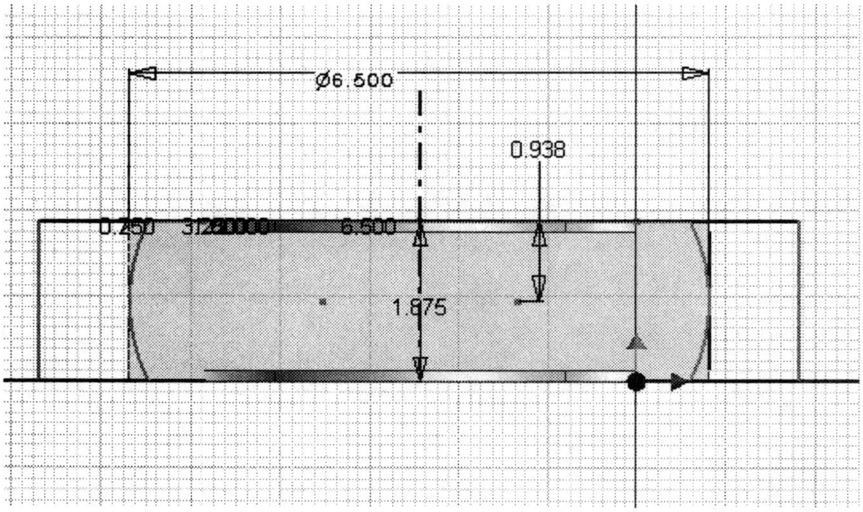

Select the mirror tool.
Select the sketch and centerline.

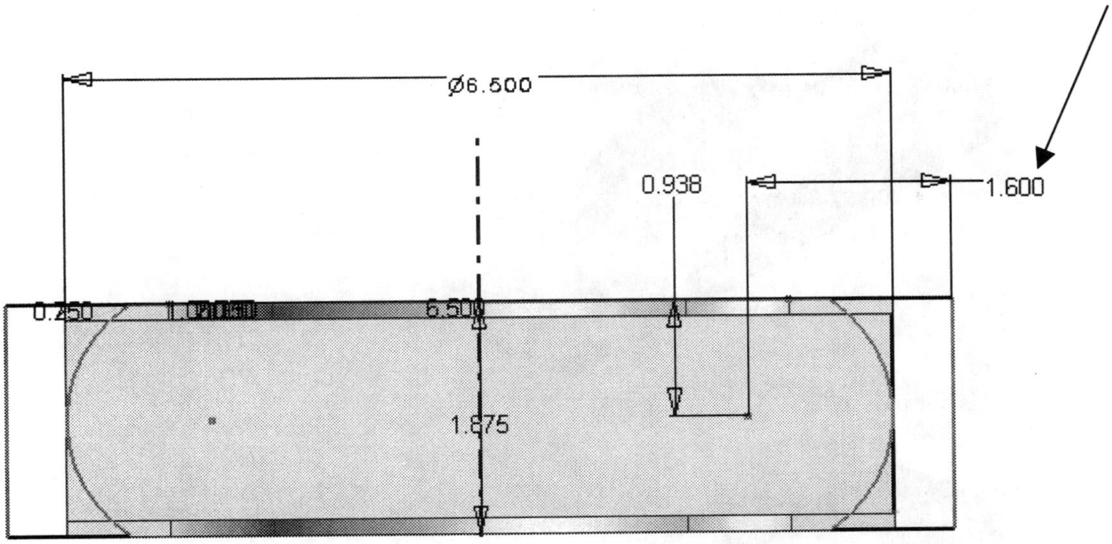

Add a horizontal dimension to constrain the width of the sketch.

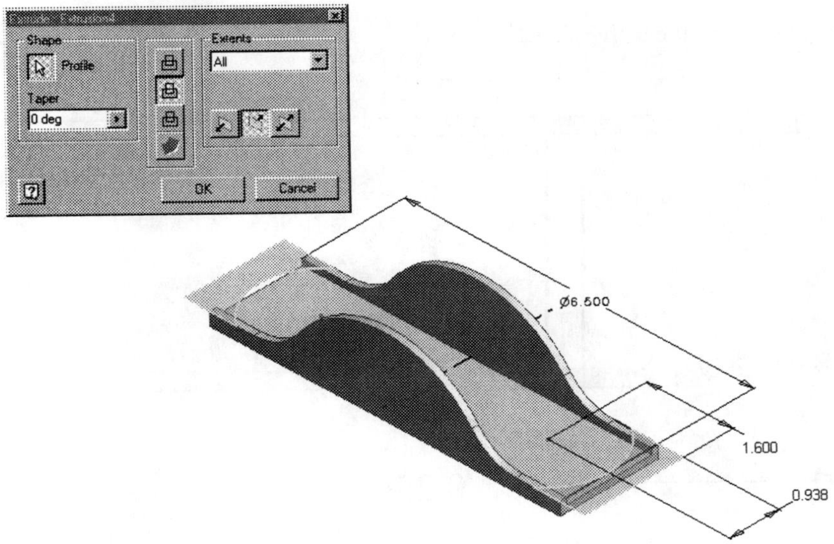

Select the Extrude tool.
Select both profiles.
Select the Cut option
Set Extents to All.
Press OK.

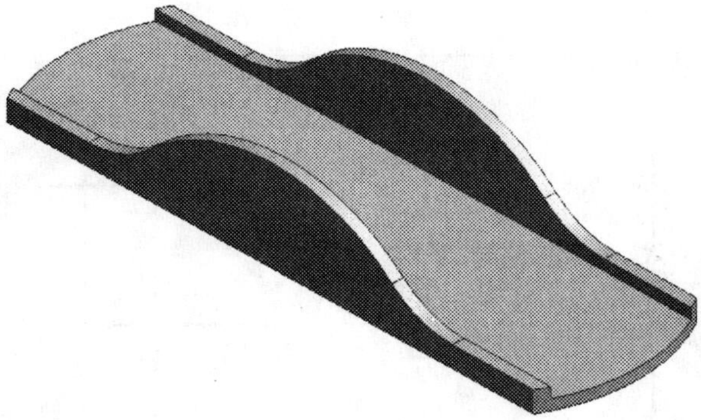

This is our part so far.

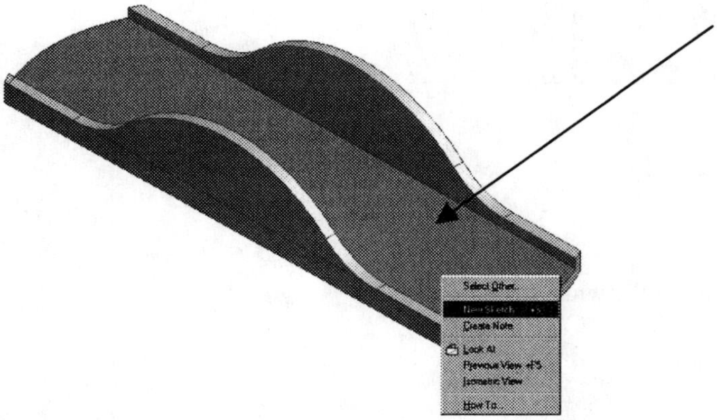

Select the inside bottom plane as the active sketch plane.

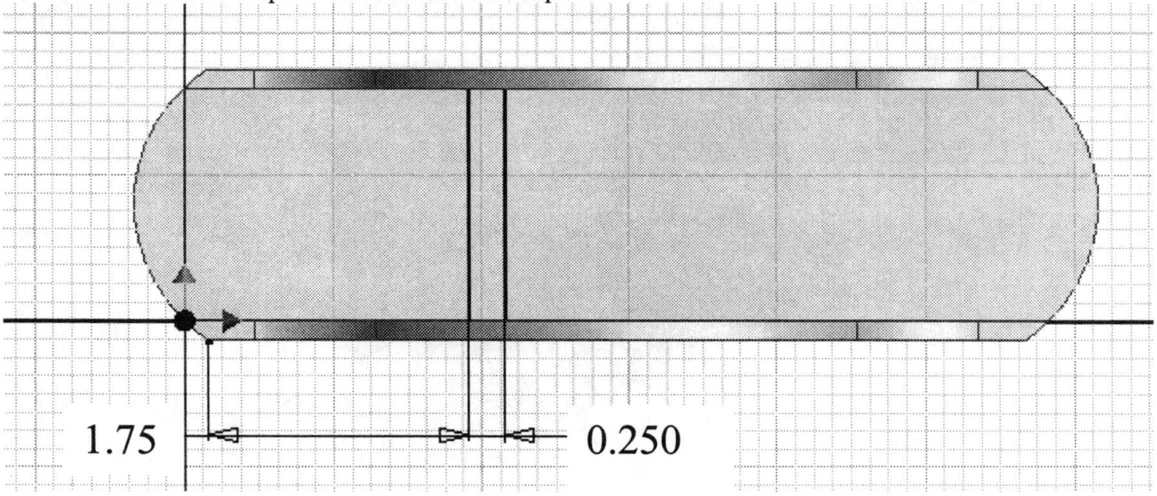

Sketch a rectangle. Add collinear constraints to the inside horizontal lines. Add dimensions shown.

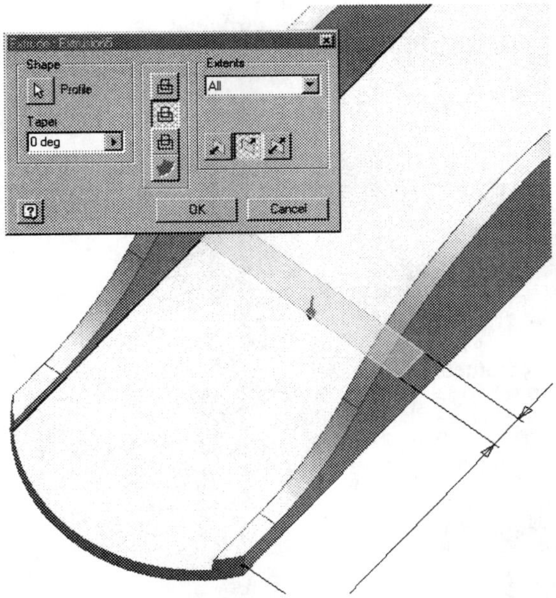

Extrude the profile using ‘Cut’.
Set Extents to ‘All’.

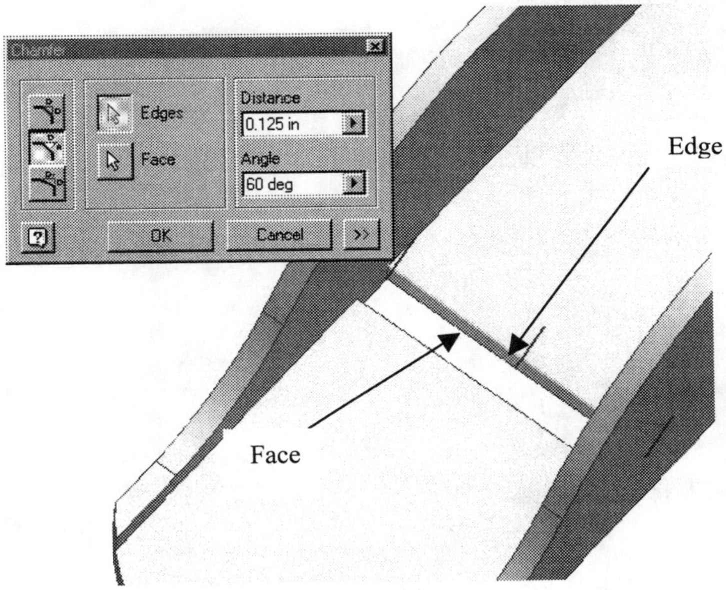

Add a chamfer using Distance of .125 and Angle of 60. Select the edge as shown.

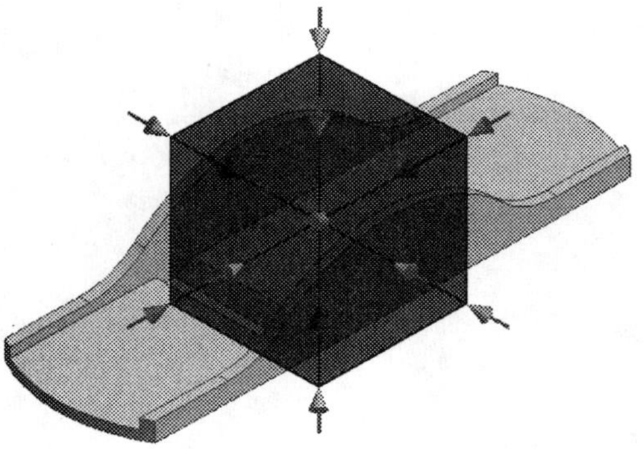

Use the Free Rotate tool to orient the part to the back isometric view.

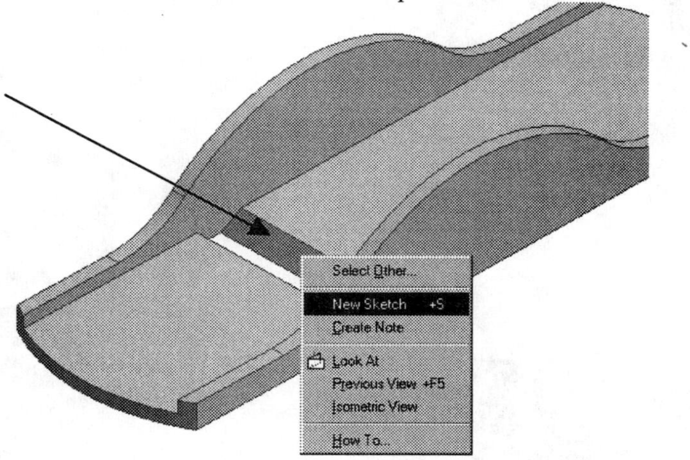

Select the chamfered face to be used as a New Sketch plane.

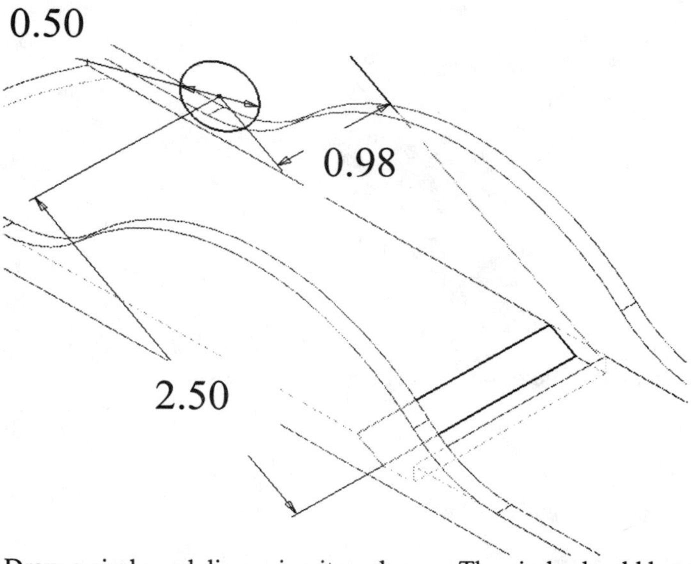

Draw a circle and dimension it as shown. The circle should be centered as shown.

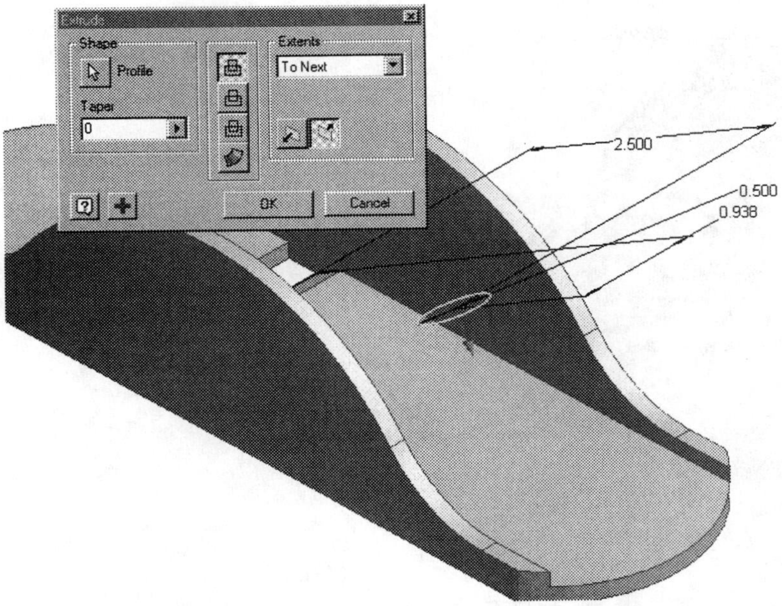

Extrude the profile using 'Join' and the 'To Next' option.
The preview should show a green arrow indicating the direction of the extrude.

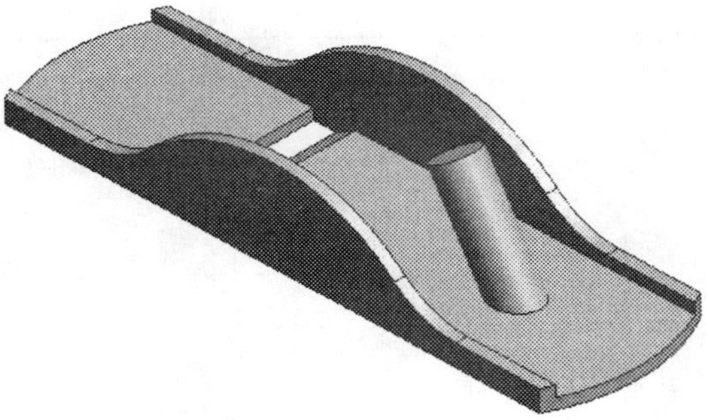

This is our part so far.

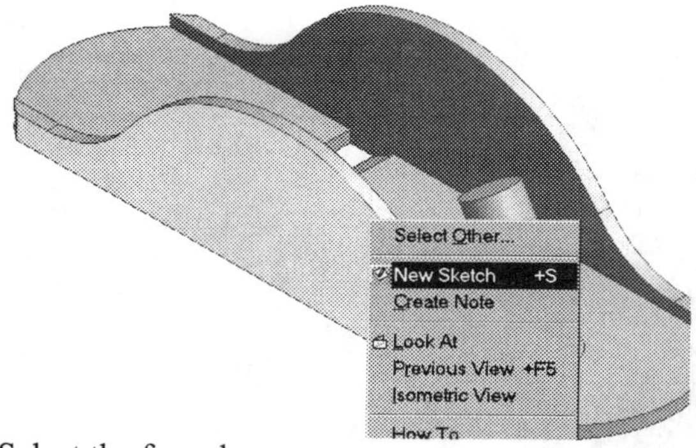

Select the face shown.
Right click and select 'New Sketch'.

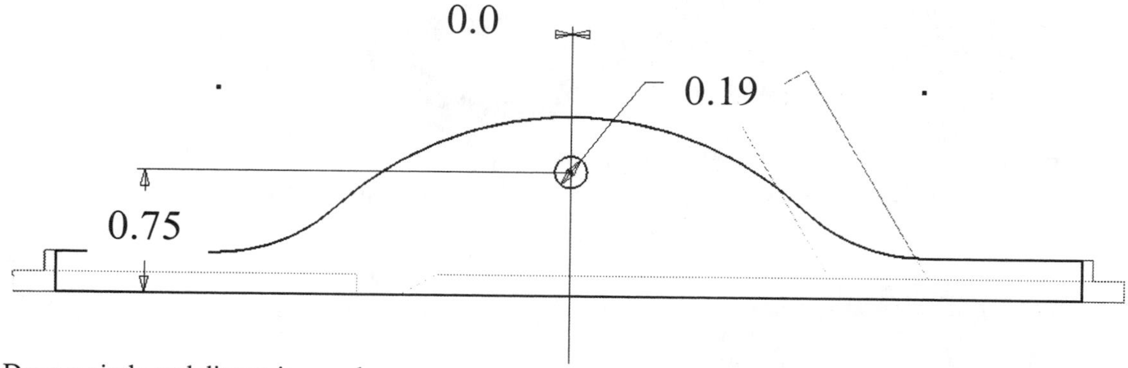

Draw a circle and dimension as shown.

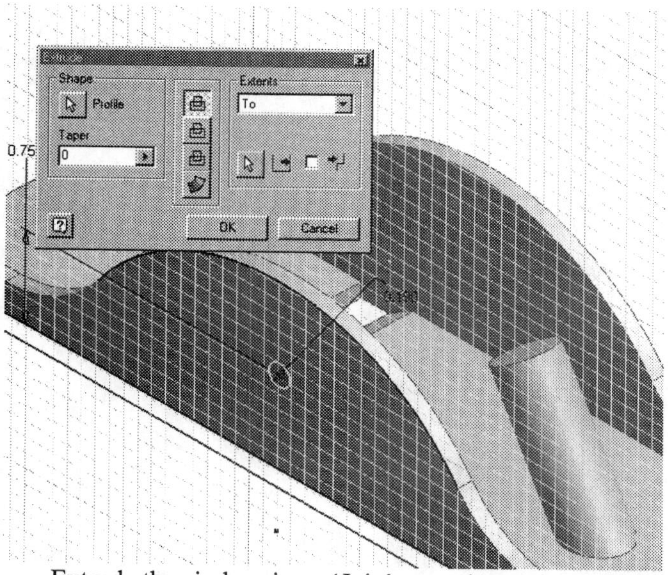

Extrude the circle using a 'Join' operation and 'To' the opposite face as shown.

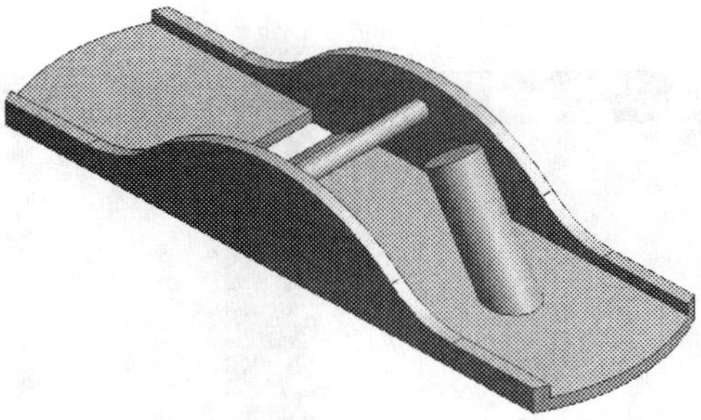

This is our part so far.

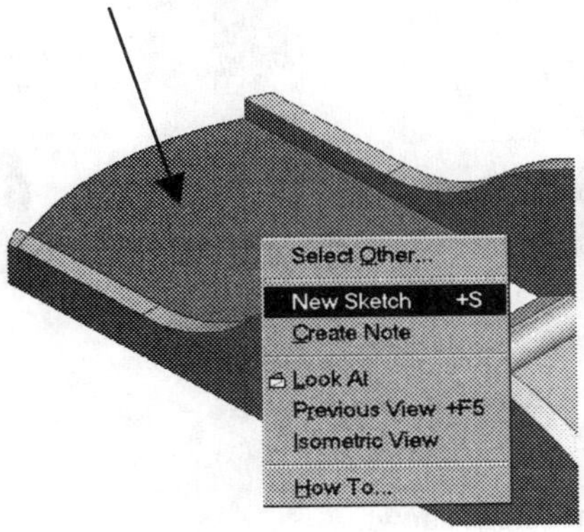

Select the plane shown as a New Sketch plane.

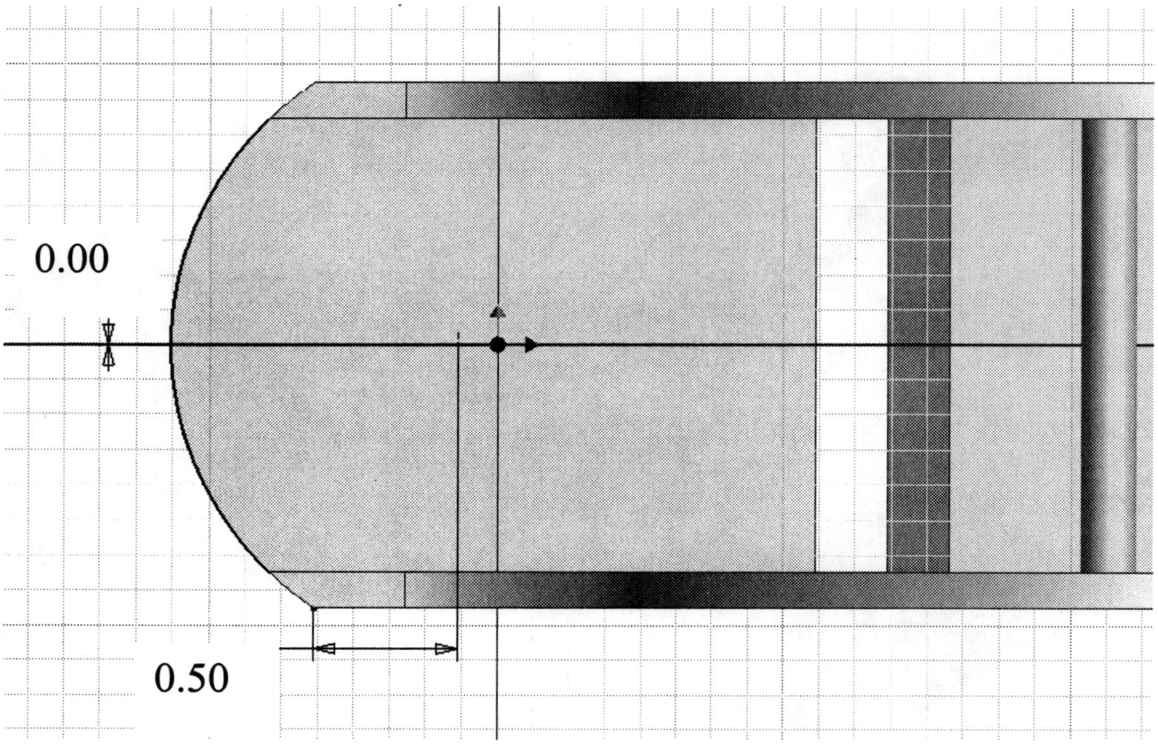

Place a Point, Hole Center on the sketch plane using the dimensions shown.

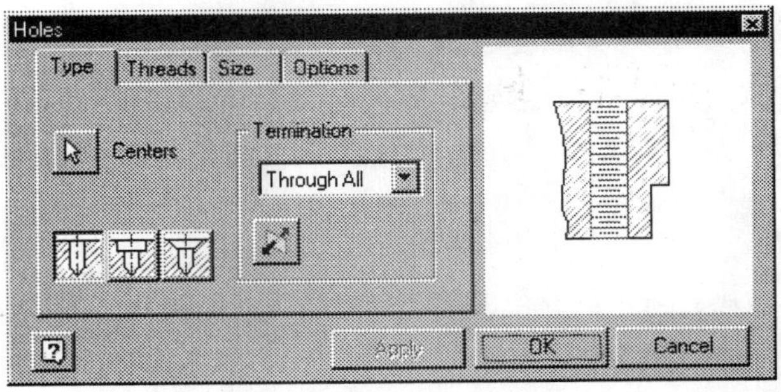

Select the Type tab and set the Termination to 'Through All'.

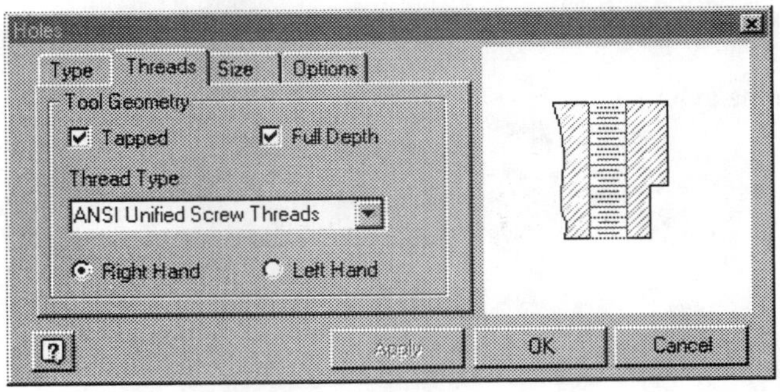

Select the Threads tab.
Enable 'Tapped' and 'Full Depth'.
Set the Thread Type to 'ANSI Unified Screw Threads'.
Enable Right Hand.

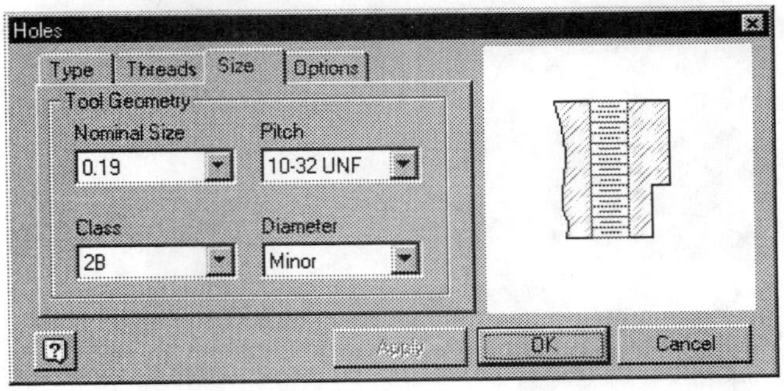

Select the Size tab.
Set the Nominal Size to 0.19.
Set the Pitch to 10-32 UNF.
Set the Class to 2B.
Set the Diameter to Minor.
Press 'OK'.

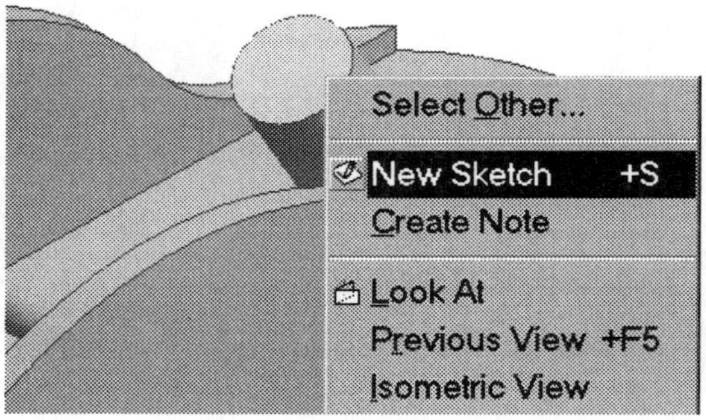

Select the top of the angled cylinder for a New Sketch.

Place a Point, Hole Center and concentric to the cylinder.

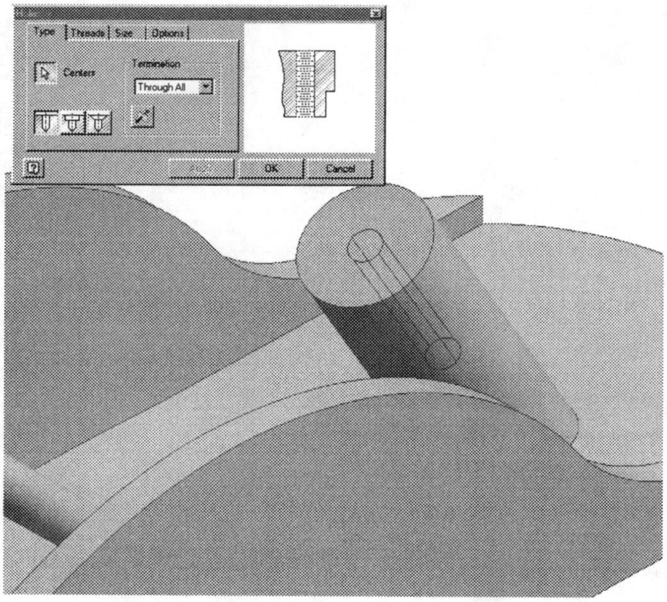

Select the Type tab.
Set the Termination to 'Through All'.

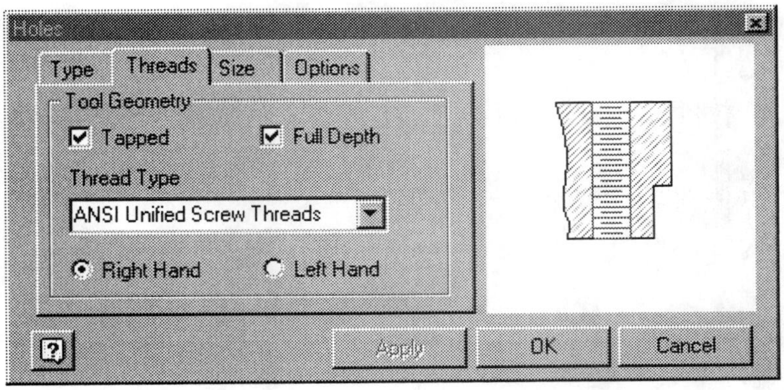

Enable Tapped.
Enable Full Depth.
Set the Thread Type to 'ANSI Unified Screw Threads'.
Enable Right Hand.

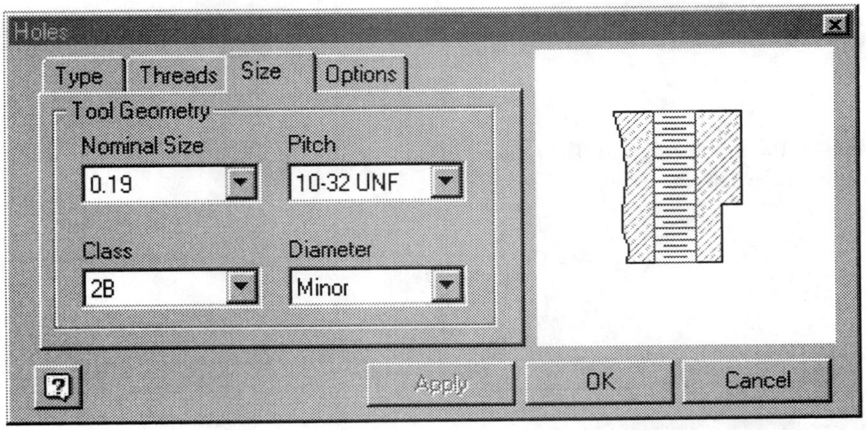

Select the Size tab.
Set the Nominal Size to 0.19.
Set the Pitch to 10-32 UNF.
Set the Class to 2B.
Set the Diameter to Minor.
Press 'OK'.

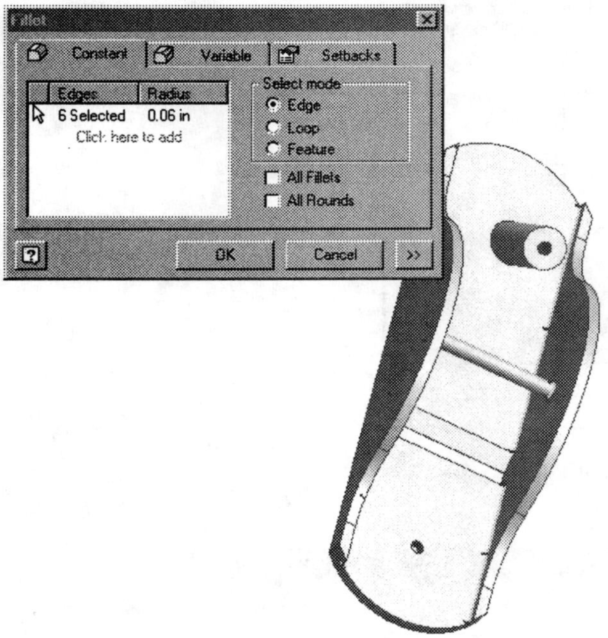

Add six .06 constant fillets to the inside edges of the plane and each end of the circular cross bar. We will need to rotate the part to select all the edges.

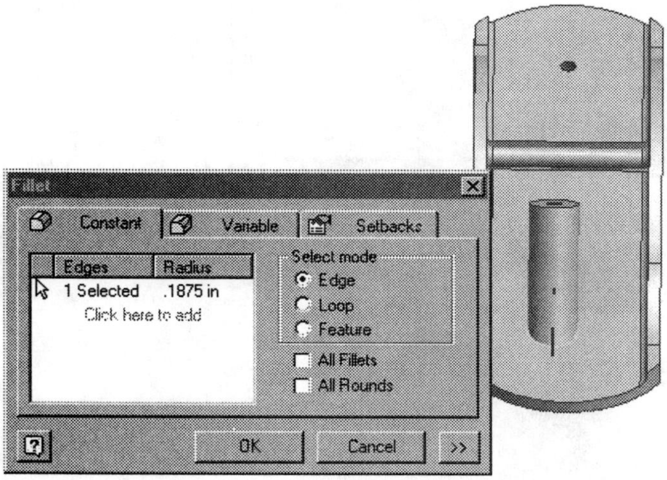

Add a .1875 fillet to the bottom of the angled extrusion.

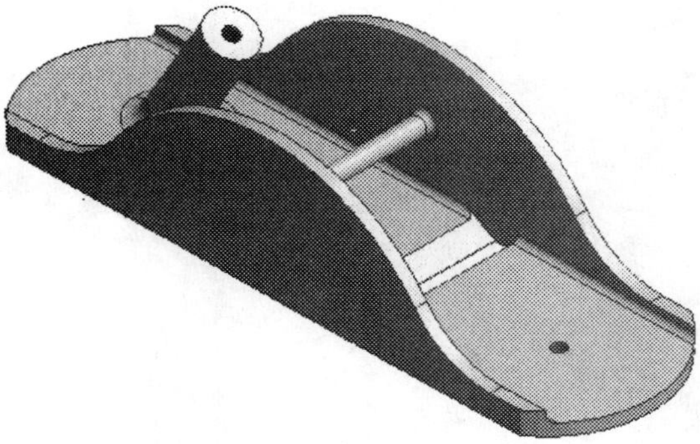

Our completed part. Save the part as 'Plane Base.ipt'

Part 2 – Blade

We will now start our second part in this assembly.

Start a New Part File for the blade of the wood plane.

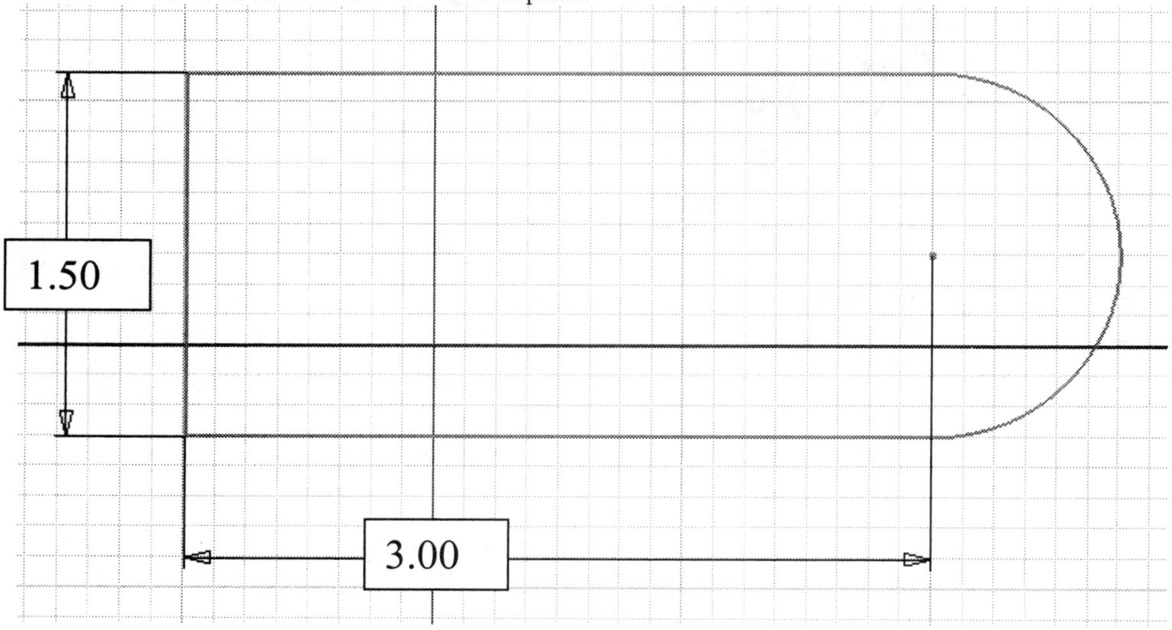

Create the sketch as shown.

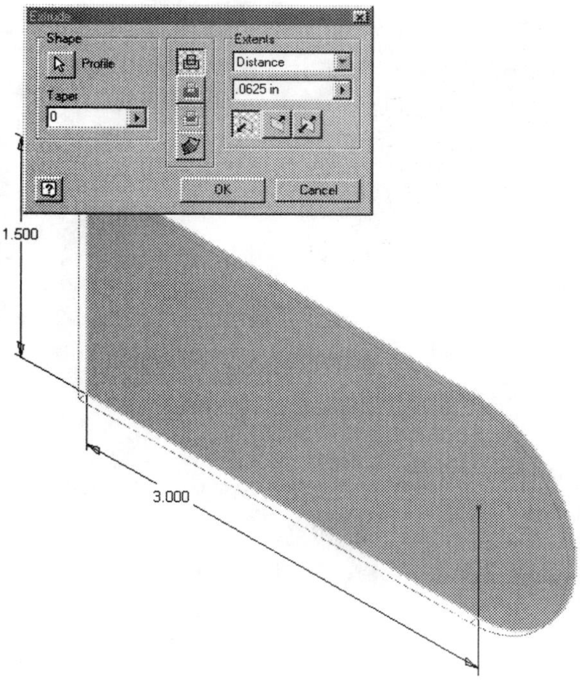

Switch to an isometric view and extrude the profile .0625.

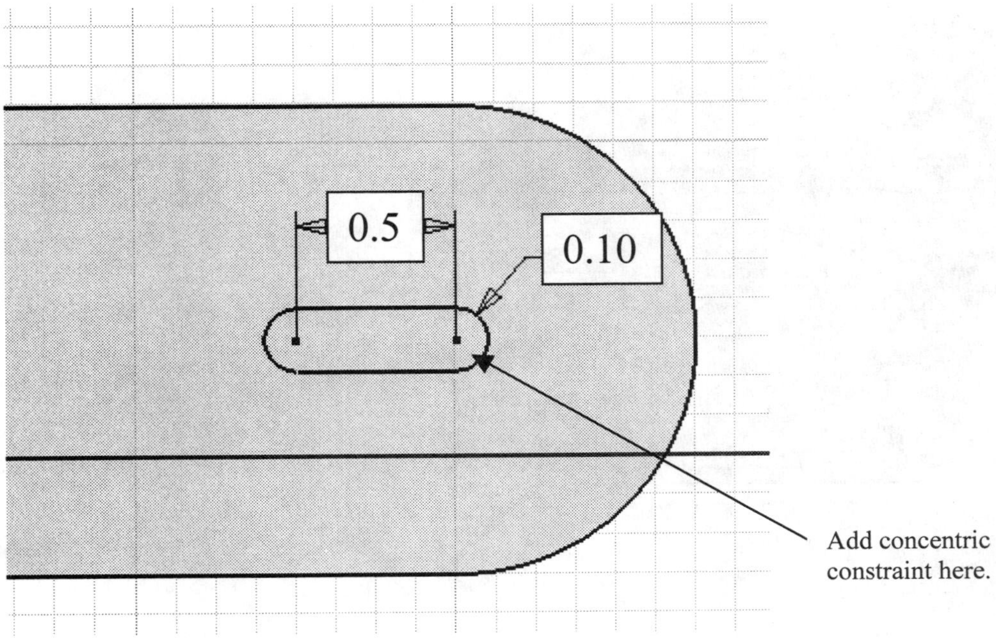

Create the slot sketch as shown. Add a concentric constraint between the arc on the front of the slot and the arc on the blade.

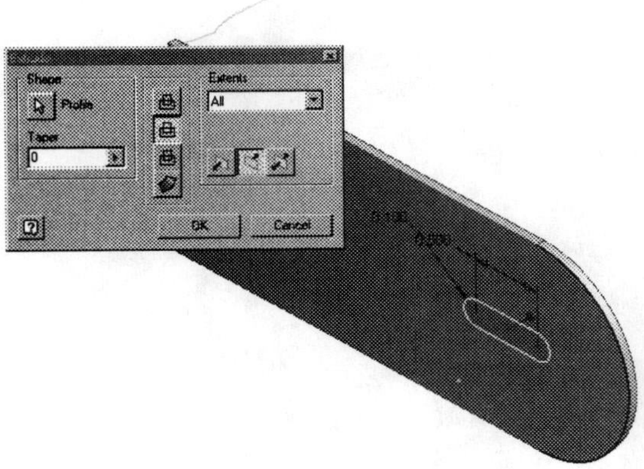

Extrude a Cut

Extrude the profile with a Cut operation and All as the termination.

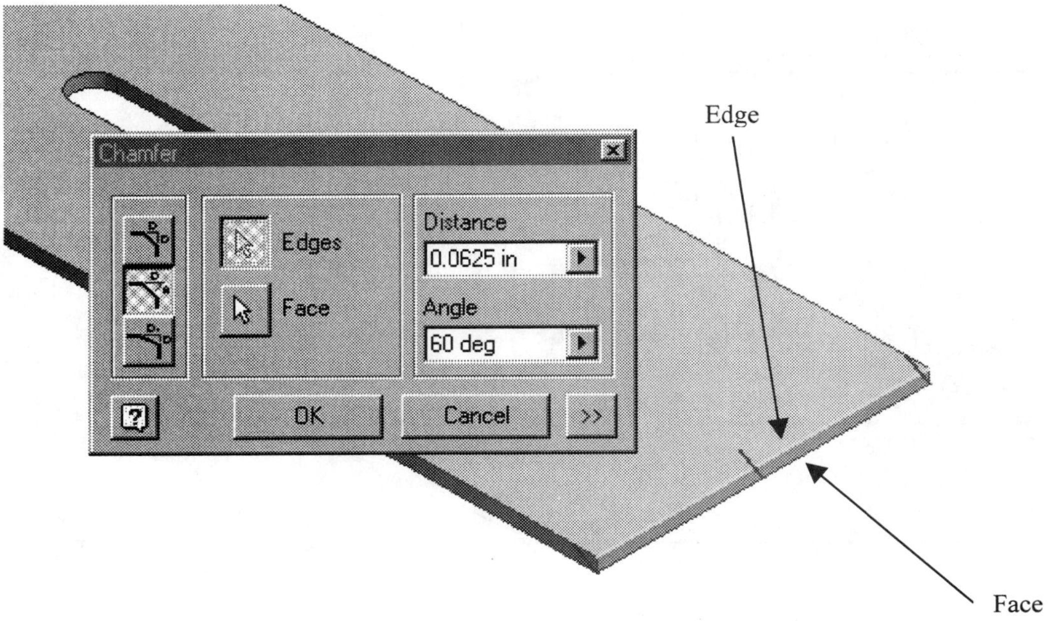

Add a Chamfer

Add a chamfer. Set the distance to .0625 and the angle to 60 degrees

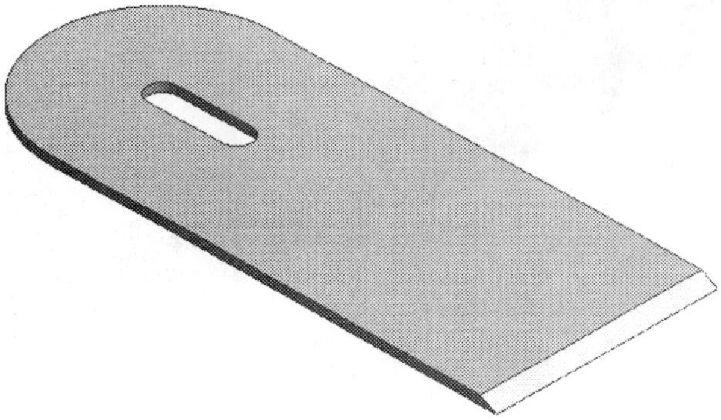

Save the file as 'blade.ipt'.

Part 3 – Front Handle

Start a new part file for the front handle.

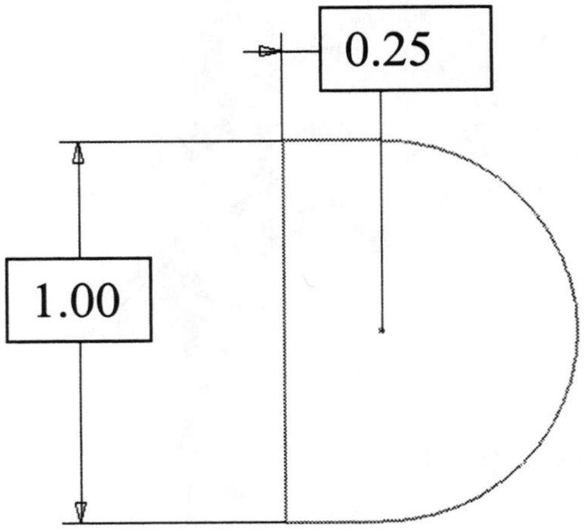

Create and dimension the profile shown.

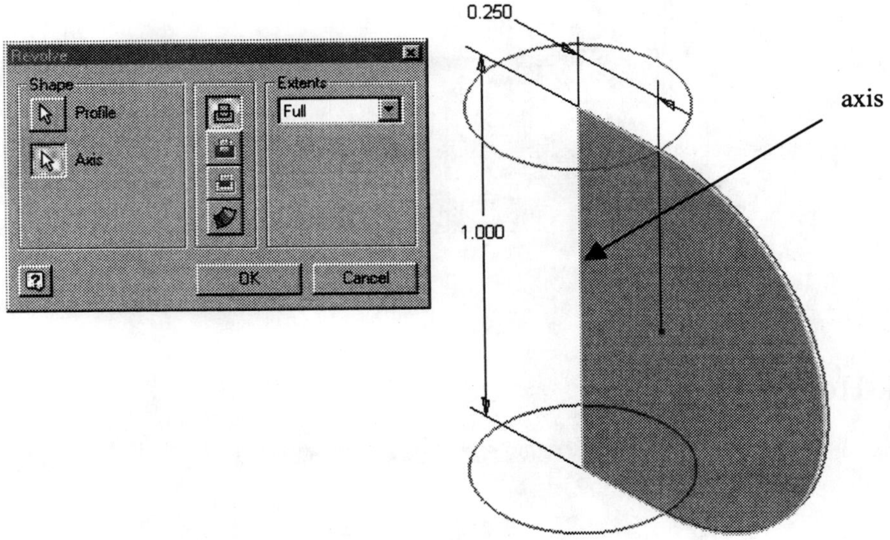

Create a Revolve

Revolve the profile 360 degrees around the vertical line.

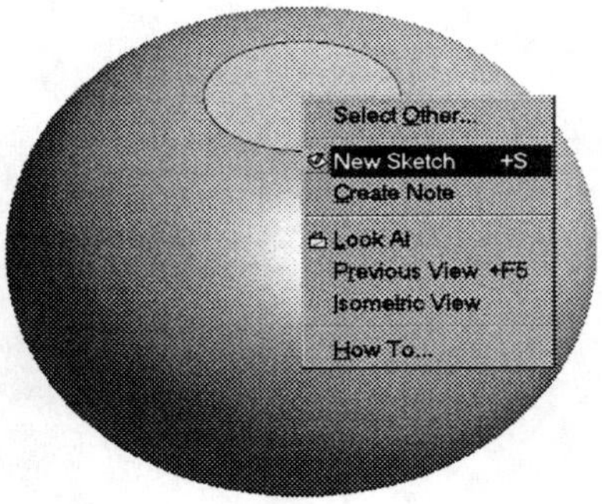

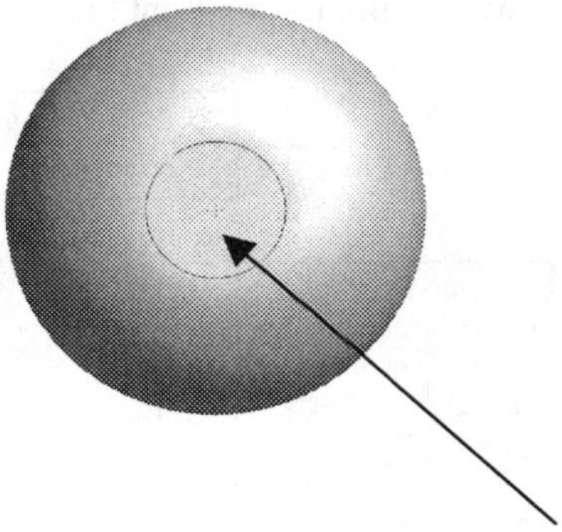

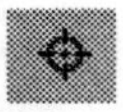

Point, Hole Center

Place a Point, Hole Center on one end concentric to the top of the handle.

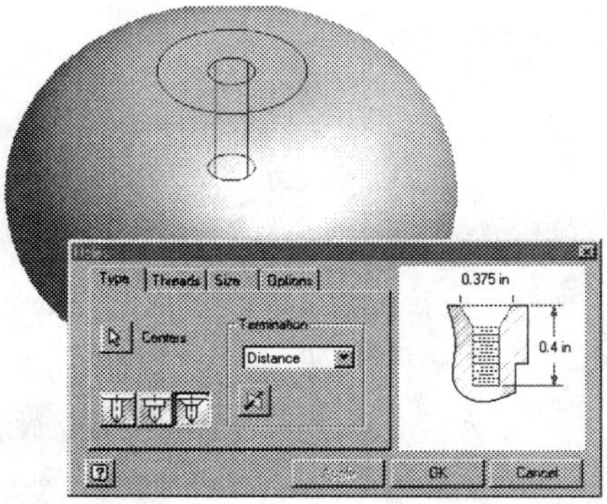

Countersunk Hole

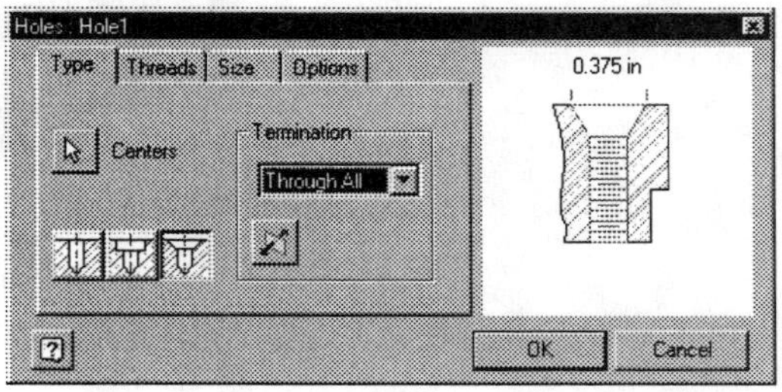

In the Type tab, set the Termination to 'Through All'.
Set the Hole Type to Countersunk.

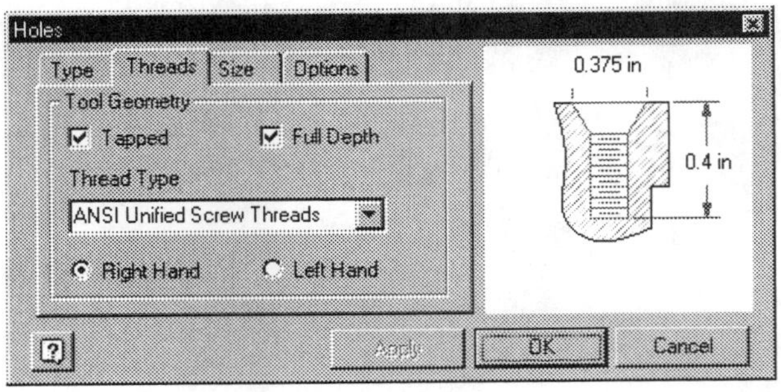

Select the Threads tab.
Enable Tapped and Full Depth.
Set the Thread Type to ANSI.
Enable Right Hand.

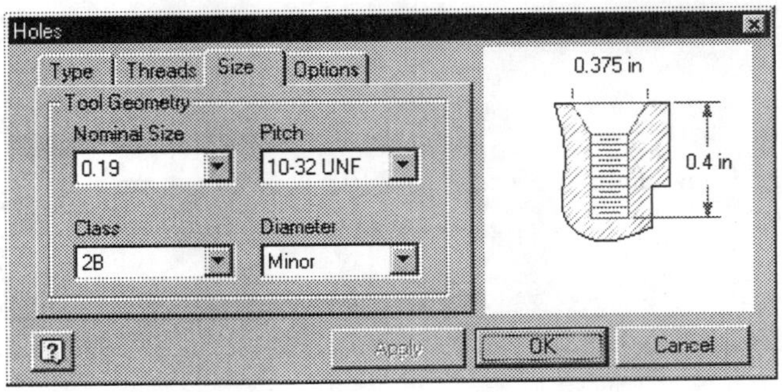

Select the Size tab.
Set the Nominal Size to 0.19.
Set the Pitch to 10-32 UNF.
Set the Class to 2B.
Set the Diameter to Minor.

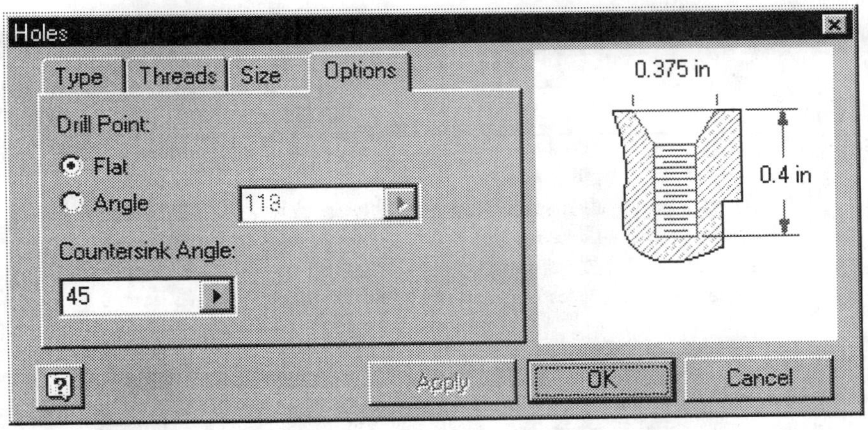

Select the Options tab.
Set the Drill Point to Flat.
Set the Countersink Angle to 45.
Press 'OK'.

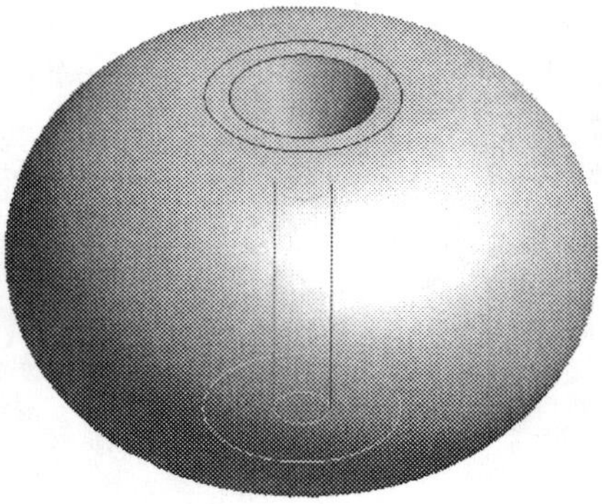

Save the file as 'front-handle.ipt'.

Part 4 – Blade Handle

To create the blade handle, we'll use the front handle file as our base file and make some modifications.

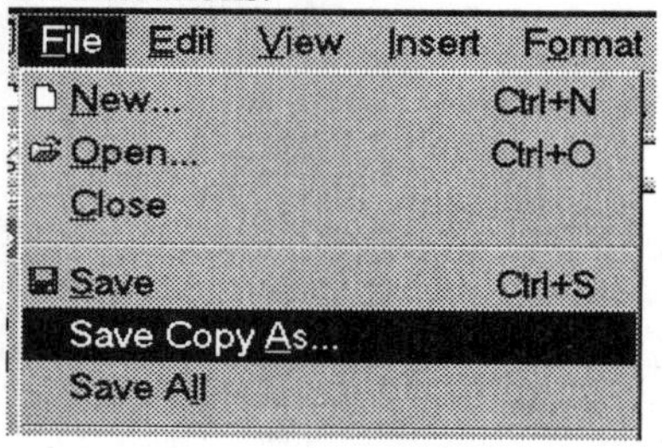

With the front-handle.ipt file open and active, perform a 'Save Copy As' under the File menu.

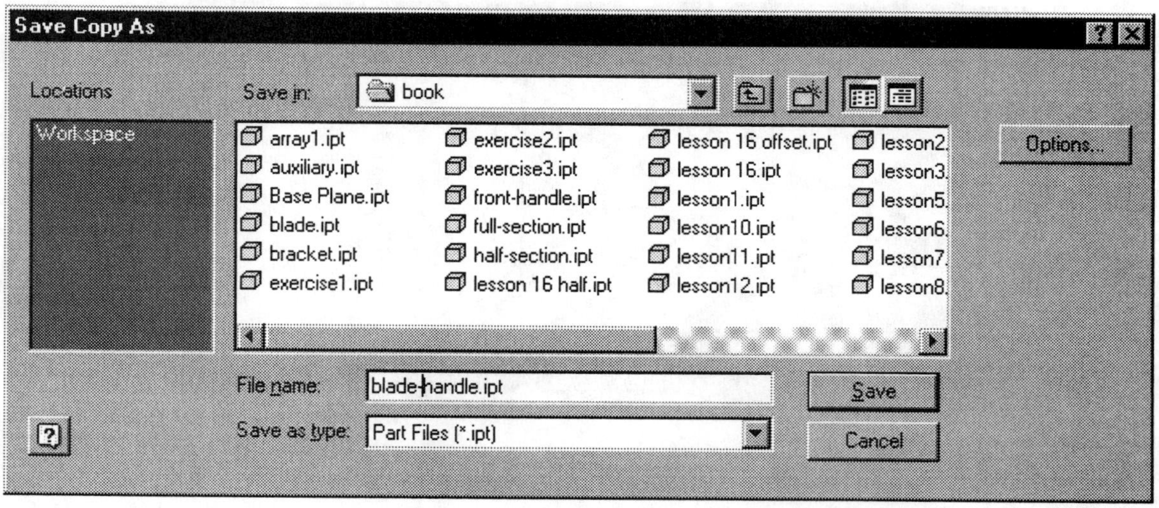

Save the file as 'blade-handle.ipt'.

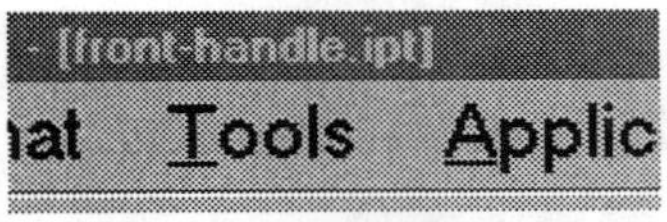

NOTE: Unlike AutoCAD or Word, this did not automatically switch us to the new file. We need to close the front-handle.ipt file and then open the blade-handle.ipt file we just created before we can proceed. Check the top of the menu to verify the file name you are working on.

Open the file we just created called 'blade-handle'.

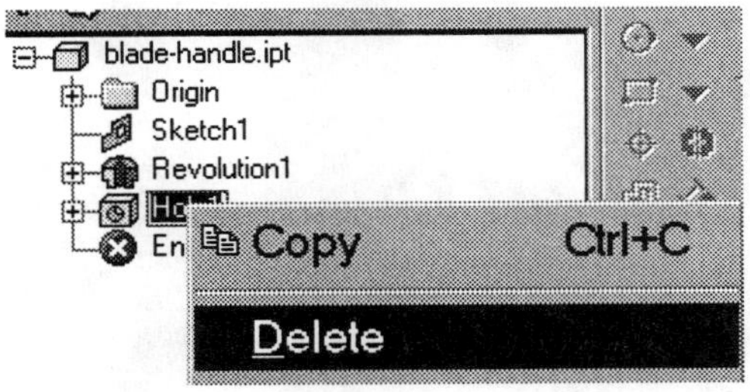

Highlight the countersunk hole in the Browser. Right-click and select 'Delete'.

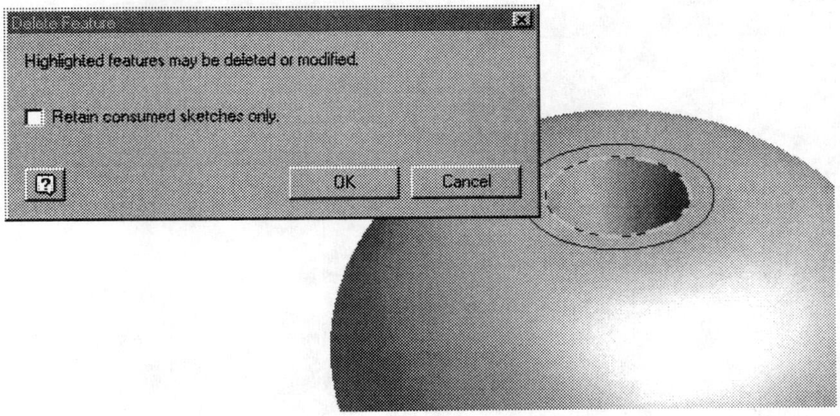

Enabling the Retain consumed sketches only allows the user to retain the sketch while deleting the feature only. Make sure this box is DISABLED. We want to delete both the sketch and the feature.

An alert box appears indicating the hole will be deleted.
Press 'OK'.

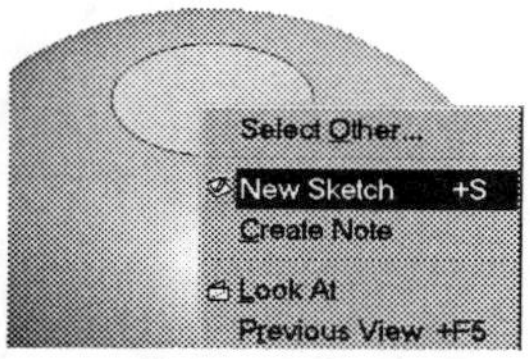

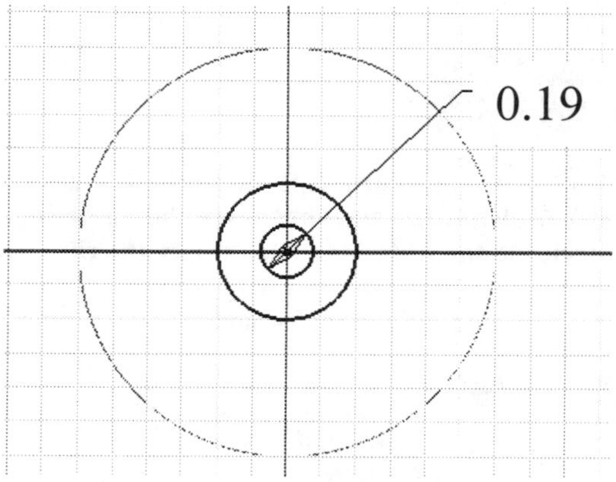

Select one end of the knob as the sketch plane. Draw a concentric circle with diameter of .19 as shown.

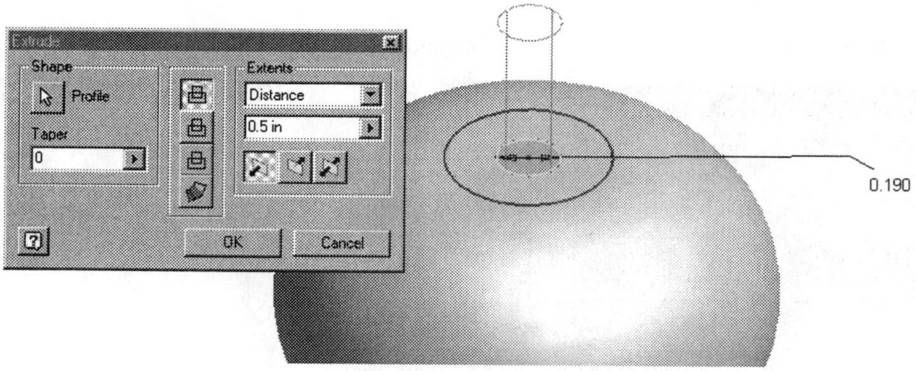

Extrude the profile .5 as shown.

Equal Distance Chamfer

Add a .03 equal distance chamfer to the front circular edge of the cylinder.

Our completed blade handle part.

Assembling the Model

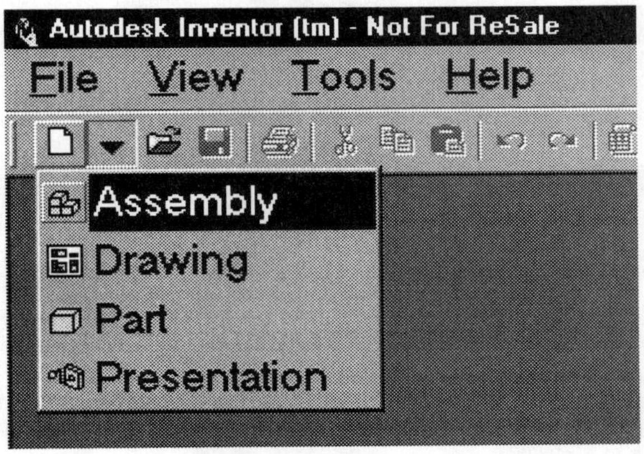

Go to File –Assembly to create a new assembly drawing.

We need to place all the components for our assembly in the file.
We could use the Place Component tool, but it is faster to use the Windows Explorer.
Open Windows Explorer and locate the subdirectory where our parts files are located.

Hold down the Control key to simultaneously select all four files we just created.
Locate and select:

Blade.ipt
Blade-handle.ipt
Front-handle.ipt
Plane Base.ipt

Drag and drop the file names into the assembly graphics window.

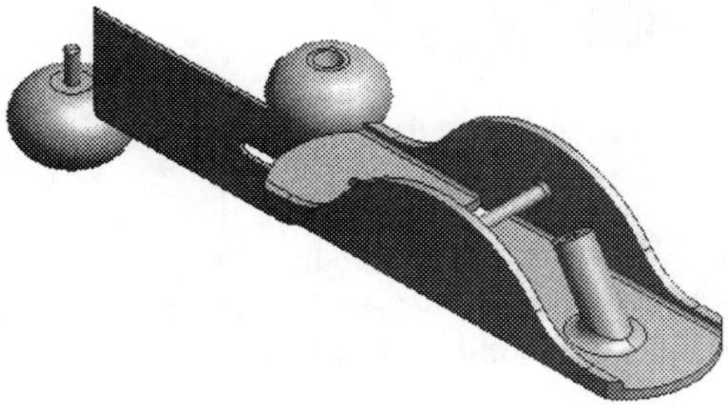

We have placed all four parts in one step.

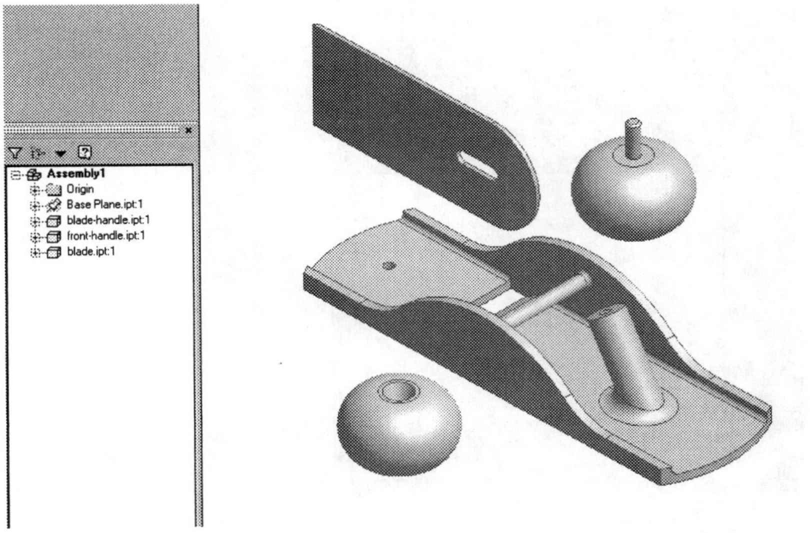

Our assembly with all the parts we created inserted.

We have all the parts we need except for one – the 10-32 x 1 countersunk screw.

You can select and place fasteners in Autodesk Inventor files. Use the Fastener Library Online Help topics to assist you in selecting and placing the fasteners.

TIP: In order to properly install the Fastener Library. Close Inventor during the installation. Reboot your computer following the installation. Open Inventor but do not open or start any files. Go to Tools->Fasteners Setup and set up the library path. If you have any files open, you will not be able to set up your library path.

Fastener Library

Fasteners are included on the Autodesk Inventor installation CD. Browse to the Bonus folder, and then double-click on Setup.exe to install fasteners.

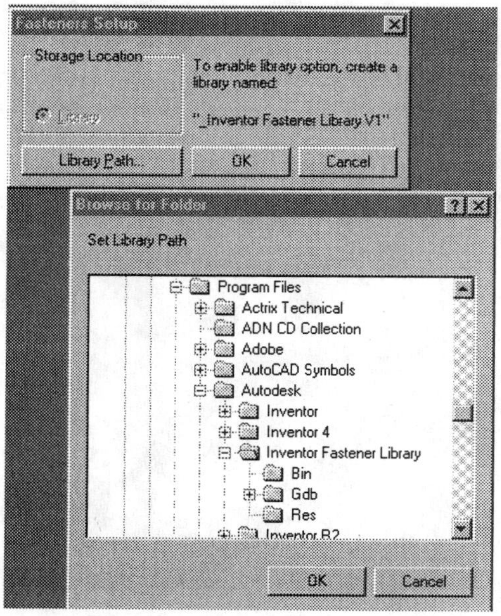

Following are instructions for installing the Fastener Library:

1. Double-click the setup.exe file in the Bonus folder on the installation CD. The Autodesk Inventor Release 4 Fastener Library setup will run and will be completed after approximately 5 to 10 minutes.
2. Start Autodesk Inventor Release 4 and close any open documents.
3. From the Tools menu, choose Fasteners > Fasteners Setup.
4. In the Fasteners Setup dialog box, choose Library Path to select the folder location to store the fasteners.

Note: When you select a folder in step 4, a new library search path is created in the active path file. The library path is created with the proper naming convention, for example:

[Library Search Paths]

_Inventor Fastener Library V1=E:\Inventor Files\Fastener Library

If no path file is defined, the search path is added to the Library Search Path section of the File Locations dialog box, which you can access by choosing Options from the Tools menu, then selecting the File Locations tab in the Options dialog box.

The Autodesk Inventor R4 Fastener Library provides a set of the most commonly used fastening hardware in five international standards. It is a library of non-parametric, non-editable, standards based parts commonly used in machine design. It is an Autodesk Inventor add-in/bonus application.
The library parts can be inserted into Autodesk Inventor assembly models and appear in the assembly browser with their description as the name. The fasteners also contain bill of material (BOM) property information. Important information regarding the BOM properties is below.

The five standards included are ANSI (USA), JIS (Japanese), ISO (International), GB (Chinese), and DIN (German). The types of fastener components included in the library are screws, threaded bolts, nuts, washers, and pins.

TIP: The fasteners in the Inventor R4 Fastener Library are non-parametric and non-editable. However, there are third-party developers who have created parametric fastener libraries for use with Inventor. A good source is Cad Management Group at http://www.cadmanagementgroup.com.

By default, a Bill of Materials or Parts List in Autodesk Inventor will display part description information. Examples of part description information are "Hexagon Socket Head Cap Screw" and "Hex-Head Bolt". Each of the Fastener Library parts contains this information. In addition to the basic description, each part also contains important standards information, which specifies the part and the international standard that it is based on. Examples of standards information are "ANSI B18.3 - 7/8 - 9 - 6 1/2" and "DIN 931-1 - M12 x 80". Together, the description and standards information fully specify the fastener.

You can configure the standards information in your BOMs on a per assembly basis. Alternatively, you can configure the default assembly template file that you use to include the standards information for all assemblies that you create based on that template. Detailed online help information is available in Autodesk Inventor to help you configure the information that is displayed in the BOM as well as how to setup and use templates.

If you are familiar with configuring the Bill of Materials, follow these instructions to include the standards information in your BOMs.

To display the "Standard" information of a fastener in the BOM:

Add the "Standard" property to the "Selected Properties" in the "Bill of Material Column Chooser".

To display the "Standard" property of a fastener in the Parts List:

Add the "Standard" property to the "Selected Properties" in the "Parts List Column Chooser".

To display the "Description" property of a fastener in the "Design Assistant":

Add the "Description" to the "Selected Properties" in the "Select Properties to View" dialog of the Design Assistant.

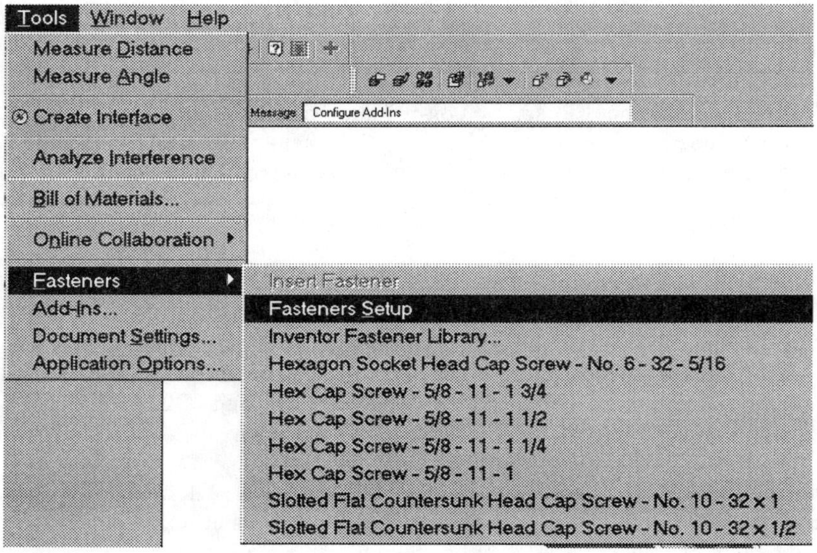

Go to Tools->Fasteners.
If you have just installed the fastener library, you need to do the Fasteners Setup.
To perform the Fasteners Setup, close all files.
Then go to Tools->Fasteners Setup.
Locate the path where you installed the Fasteners Library.
Press 'OK'.

Now re-open the assembly file and continue.

Insert Fastener

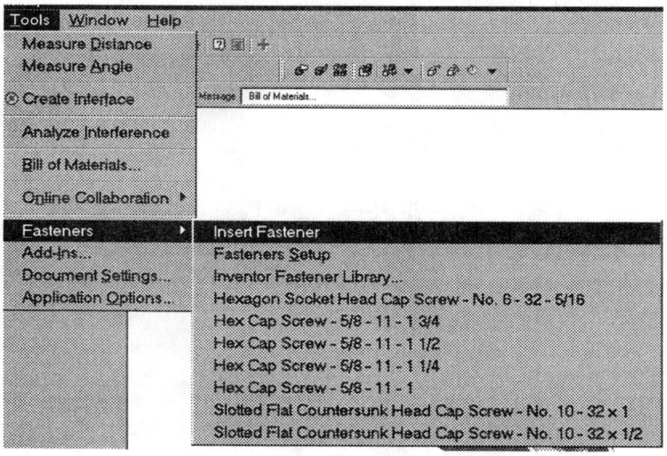

Go to Tools->Fasteners->Insert Fastener.

TIP: Inventor keeps track of your favorite fasteners in the menu. This saves time in selecting and placing fasteners. Use this short cut tool to quickly select a fastener.

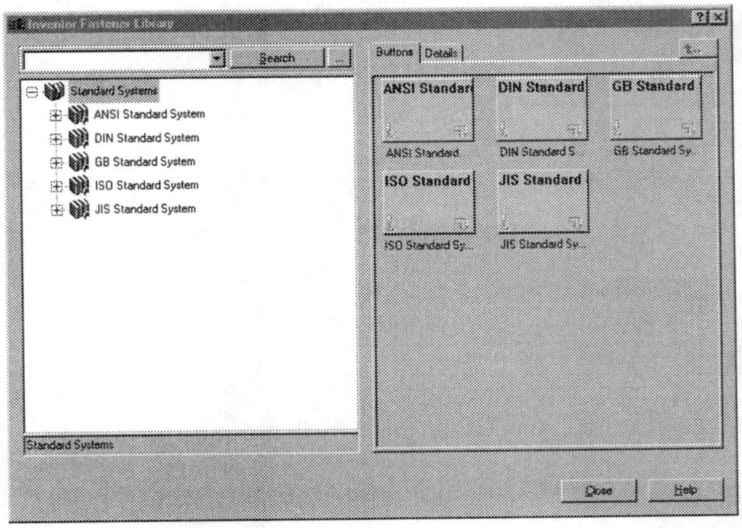

The Inventor Fastener Library dialog will appear.

We wish to insert a 10-32 countersunk screw.

We can locate the desired screw by using the browser on the left. As we go down the browser tree, the buttons on the right update. Passing our mouse over each button provides a help tip about the parts located under that button.

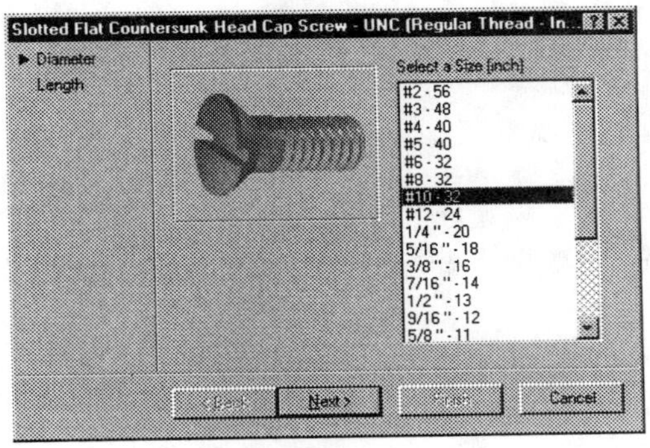

We select a Slotted Flat Countersunk Head Cap Screw- UNC. We highlight #10-32 and press 'Next'.

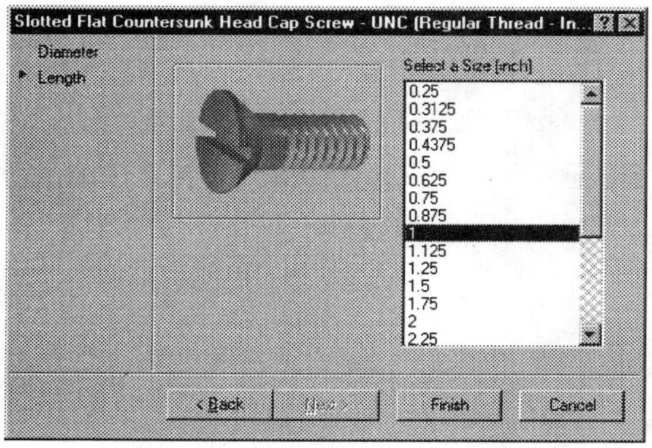

For a length, we select 1. Then we press 'Finish'.

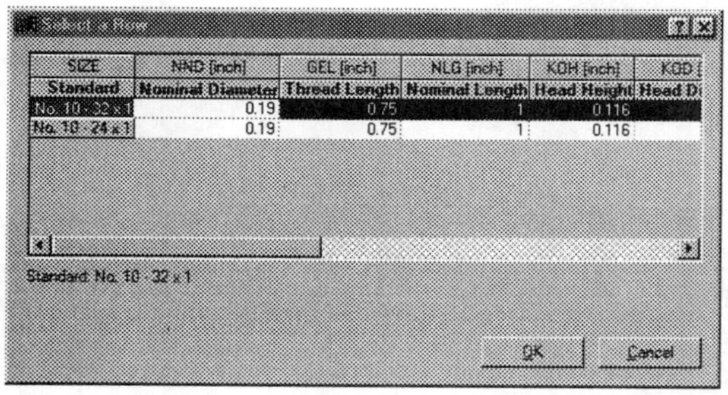

Inventor informs us there are two standard fasteners that meet our requirements. We select the 10-32 x 1. Next, we press 'OK'.

We only need one screw so once one instance appears in the browser and in the drawing window, we pick to place the screw and then right click and select 'Done'.

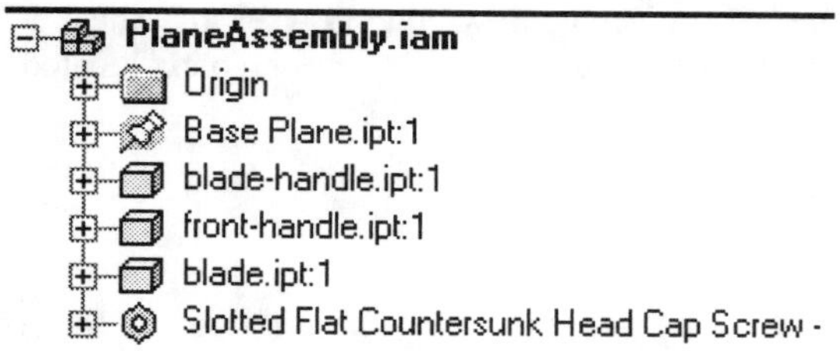

Notice how the Browser lists the fastener part. At this point, we have all the parts we need to build our assembly.

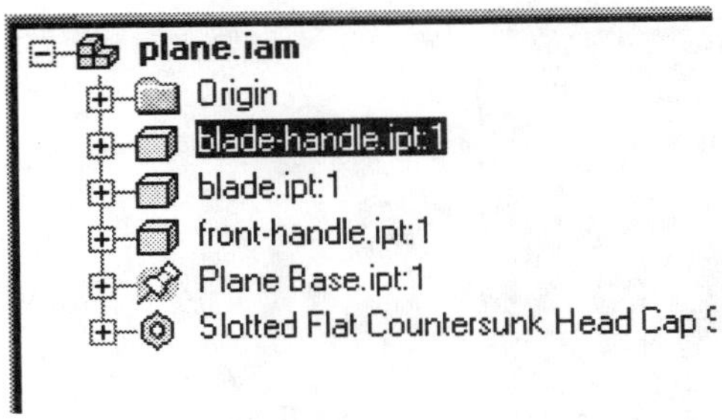

Set the Plane Base as Grounded.
Set all the other parts as Floating.

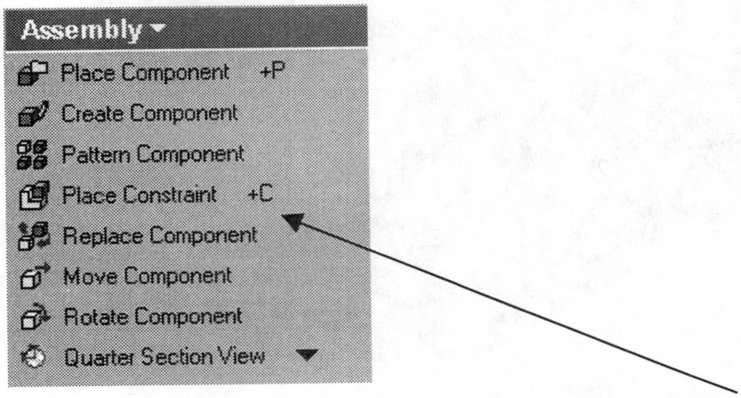

We use the 'Place Constraint' tool to create an Insert constraint between the front handle and the front hole. Rotate the front handle so we can see its bottom. Select 'Place Constraint'.

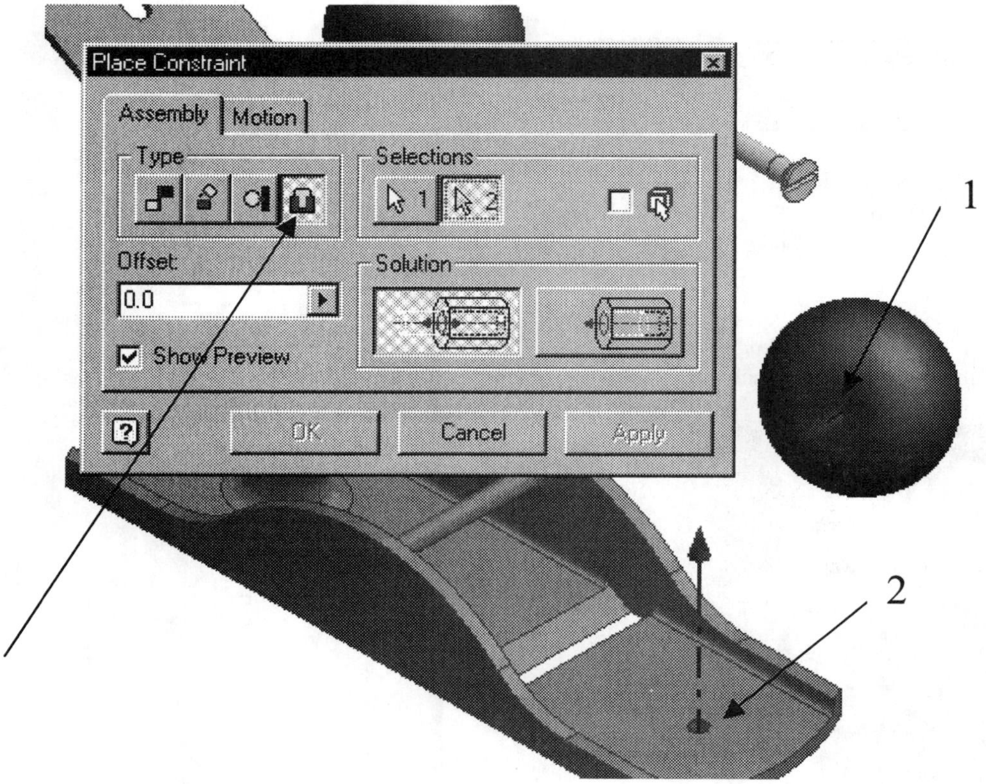

Make sure that the 'Insert' option is selected. Select the bottom of the front handle for 1 and the front hole for 2. Press 'Apply' and then close the dialog box.

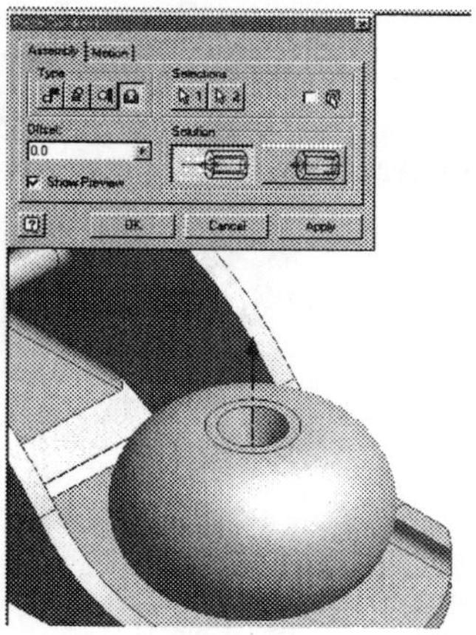

We should see a preview indicating that the constraint is placed correctly.
Press 'Apply'.

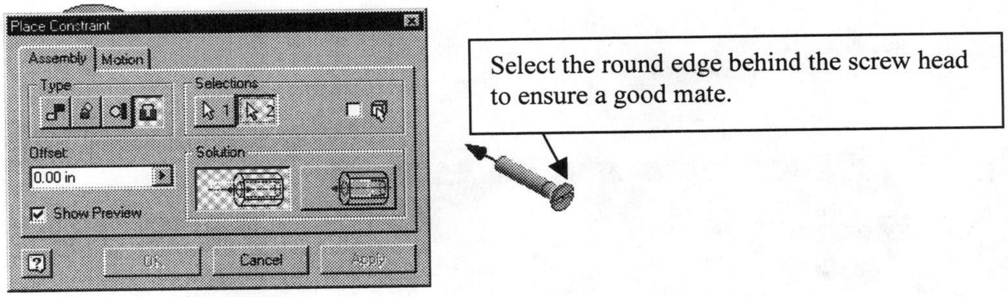

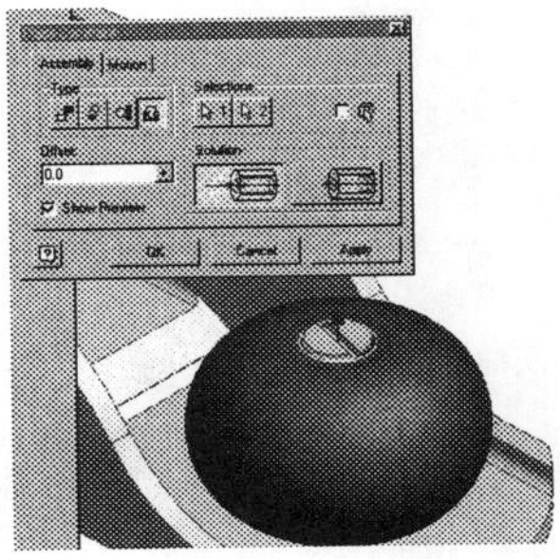

Use the 'Insert' Constraint to place the countersunk screw into the front handle. Notice that we have selected the top of the screw for our insertion point to ensure a good mating. Press 'Apply' and close the dialog box.

Our assembly so far.

Position the blade using a Mate Constraint with an offset of 0 as shown.

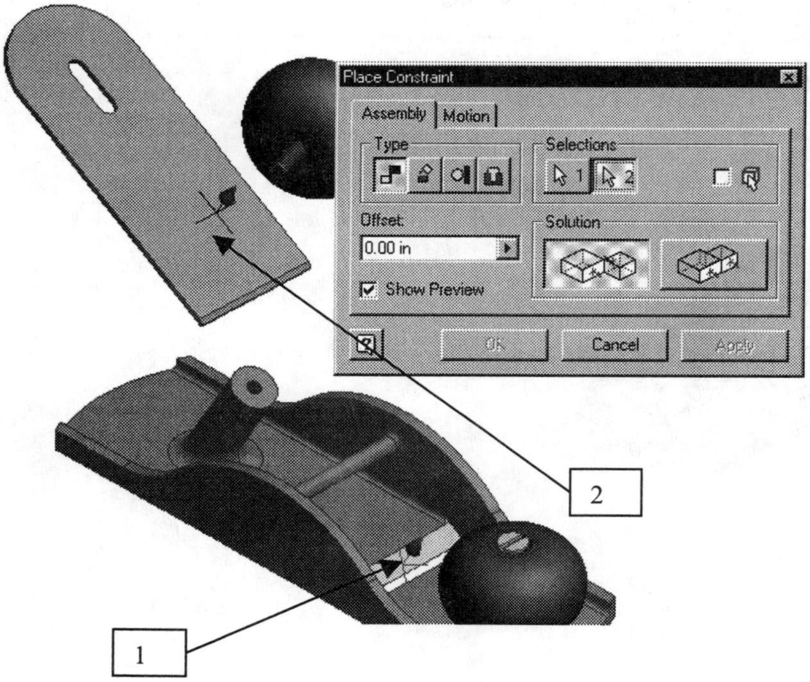

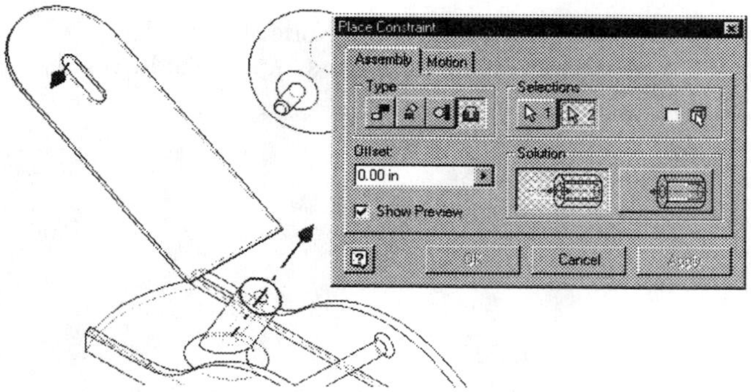

To get the blade aligned properly, add an Insert constraint of 0 between the bottom side of the slot and the tapped hole on the angled extrusion.

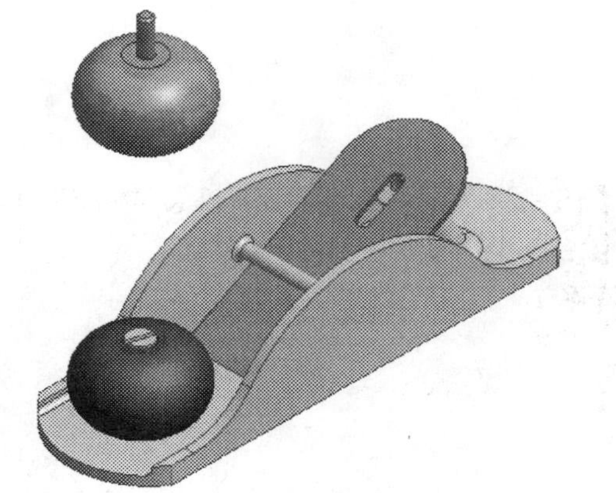

Finally, we add an Insert constraint between the blade knob and slot with an offset of 0.

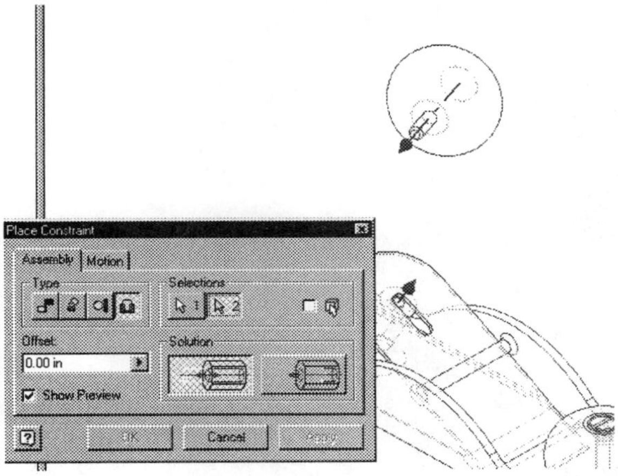

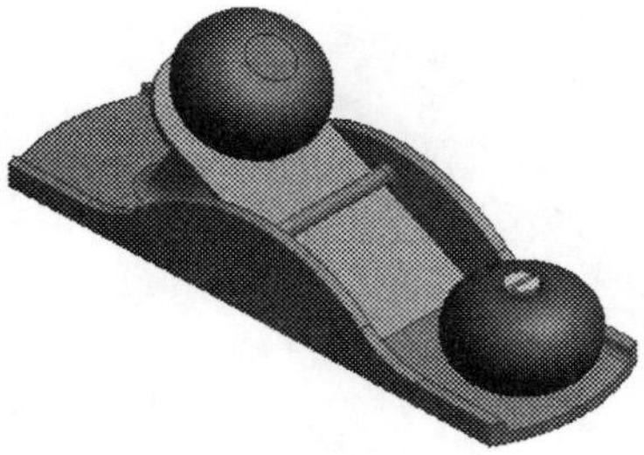

Our completed assembly.

Rotate the part around to make sure that everything has been placed properly.

Save the file as PlaneAssembly.iam.

This assembly will be used to create a Presentation file.

NOTES:

Lesson 27

Top- Down Assembly

Learning Objective

In this lesson, the user will create a top-down assembly. A top-down assembly means that all the parts are created in the same file. A top-down approach allows the designer to check for interference and make changes quickly on the fly.

When you first open Inventor, it gives you four choices...to build an assembly, to create a drawing, create a presentation or to build a part.

Inventor provides users the flexibility to create an assembly using the top down approach or the bottom up approach.

Let's create a hinge assembly using the top down approach and open an assembly drawing. We start by opening an assembly file.

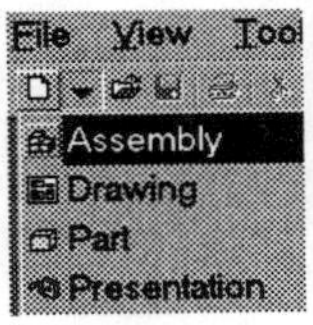

Inventor opens with a blank screen.

Part 1- Hinge Bracket

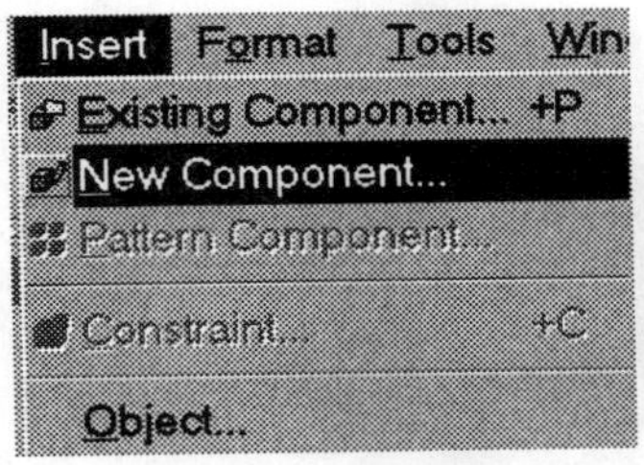

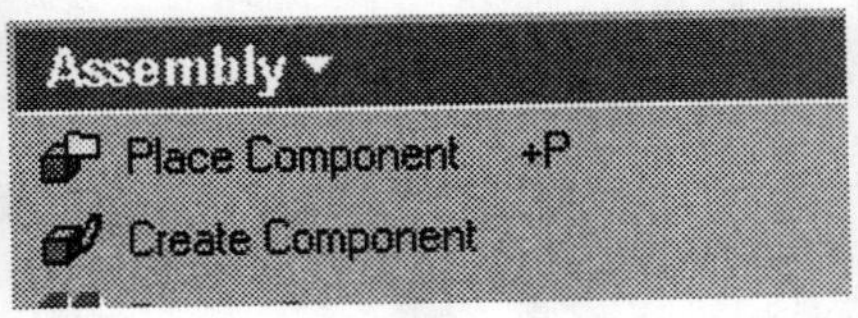

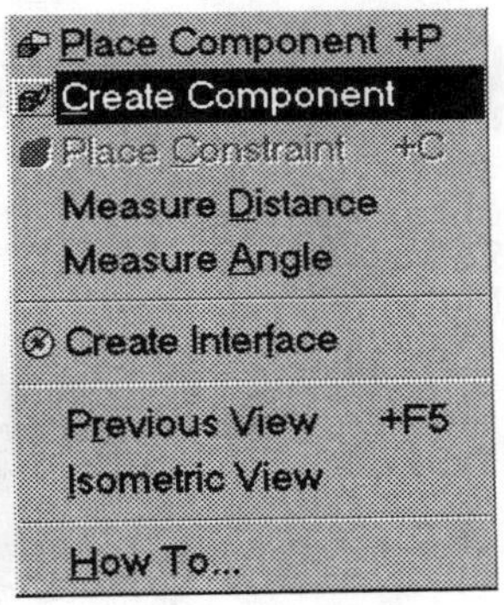

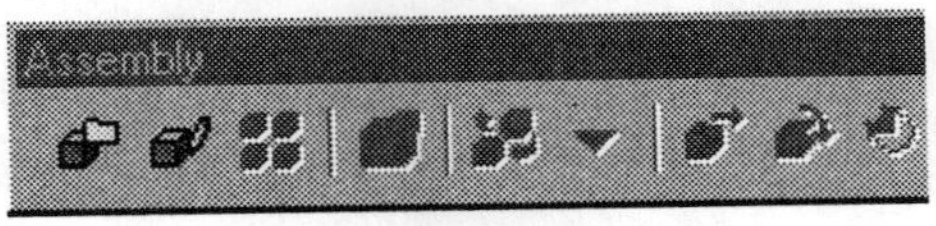

We can create a New Component using four methods:

- Go to the Menu and select Insert-> New Component
- From the Panel Bar select -> Create Component
- From the Assembly toolbar->Create Component
- Right click in the graphics window and select 'Create Component'

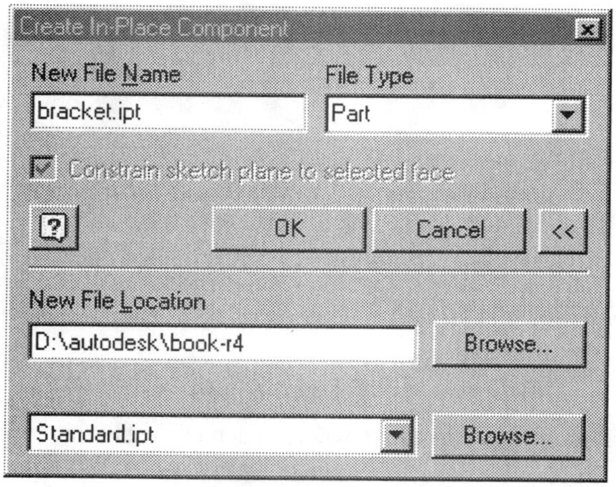

Now a new dialog box comes up. We name our component 'bracket' and note it will automatically create the external drawing file so the part can be re-used in future assemblies.

At this point, we have named our drawing file, defined it as a part, selected a standard template, and located it in our working directory, we can move on.

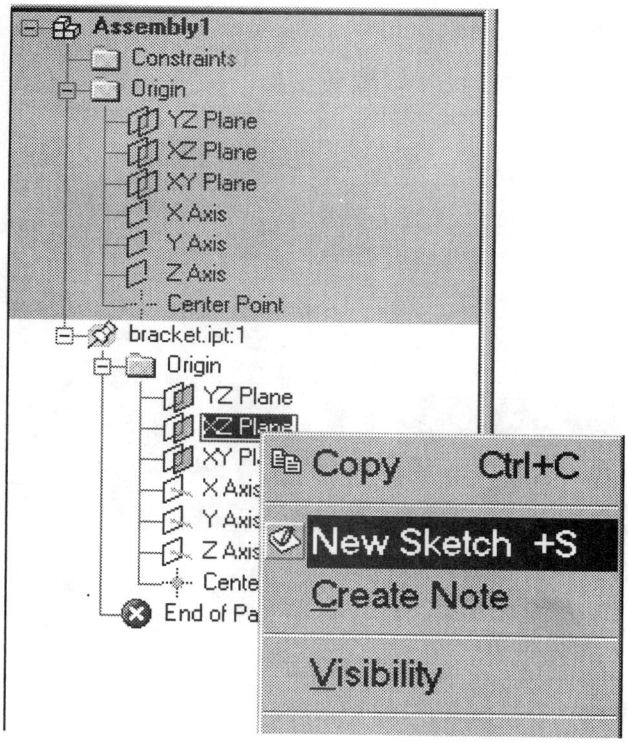

Note that the Assembly has it's own origin, axes and planes. Each part is assigned an origin, plane and axes as well.

Exit from the sketch.
Select the XZ Plane and start a New Sketch.

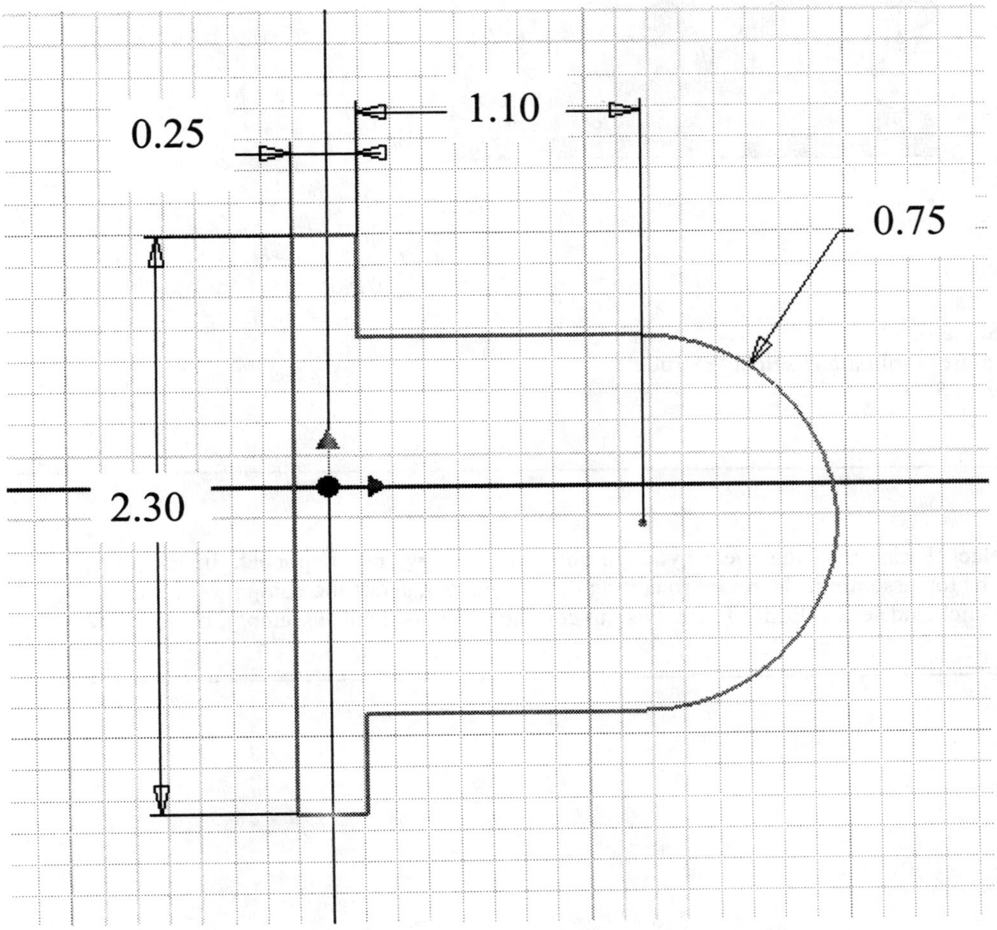

Create the sketch shown. Add geometric constraints as needed.

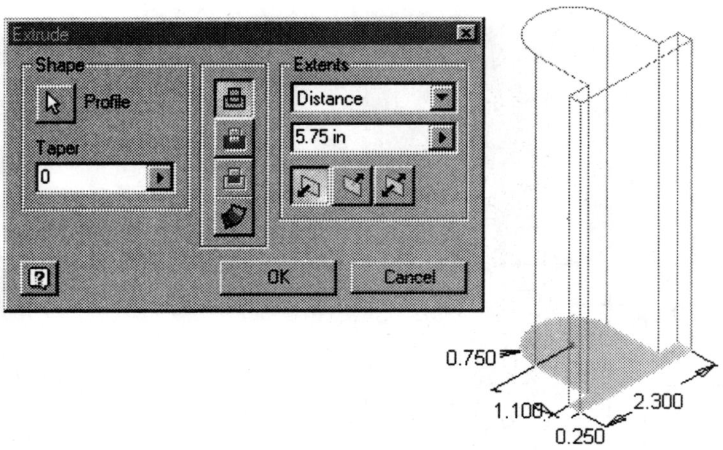

Select ‘Finish Sketch’.
Activate the Features toolbar and select ‘Extrude’.
Set the Distance to 5.75.
Press ‘OK’.

> **TIP:** If you select ‘Finish Edit’ that means you are finished creating your component. Inventor to returns you to the top assembly. To return to editing the component, select the component in the browser , right click and select ‘Edit’. If you wish to edit the part outside the assembly, right click and select ‘Open’.

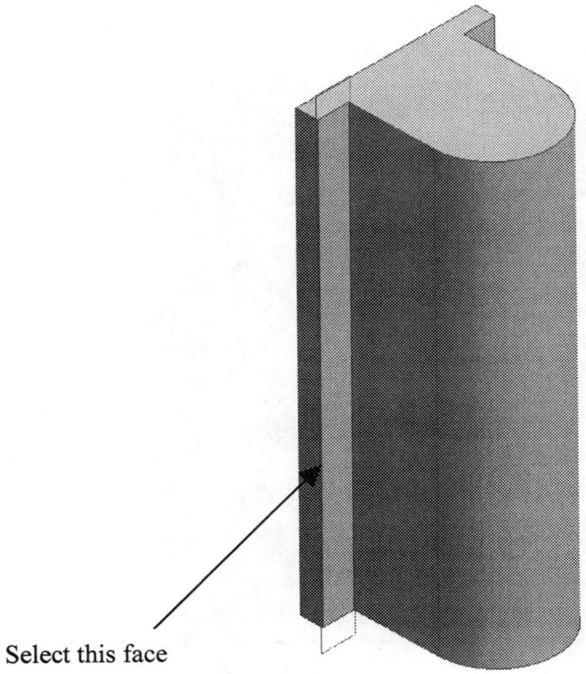

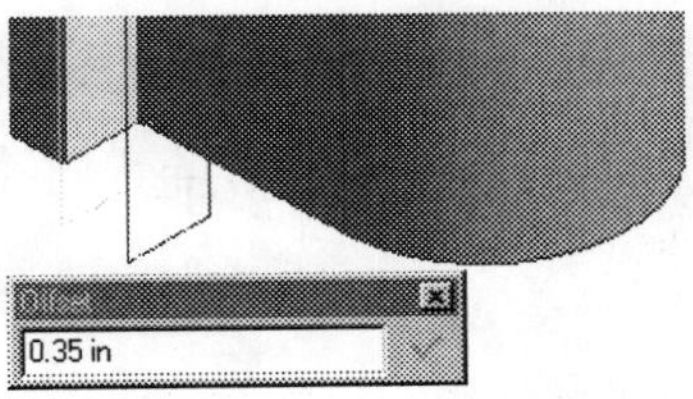

Create Offset Plane

Select the Work Plane tool from the Features toolbar.
Select the face indicated.
Drag the plane forward and enter a value into the text box of .35

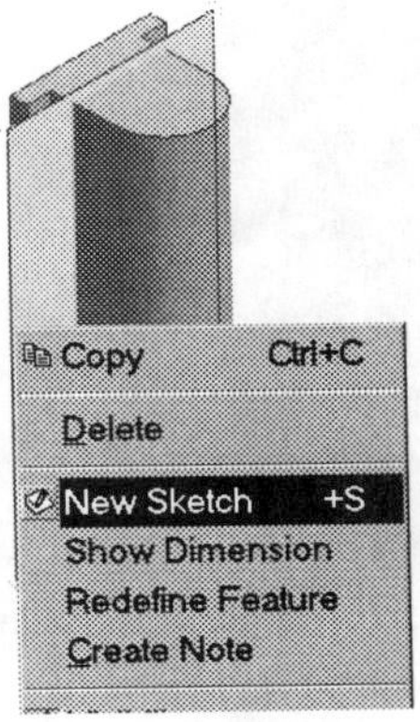

Select the New Work Plane.
Right click and select 'New Sketch'.

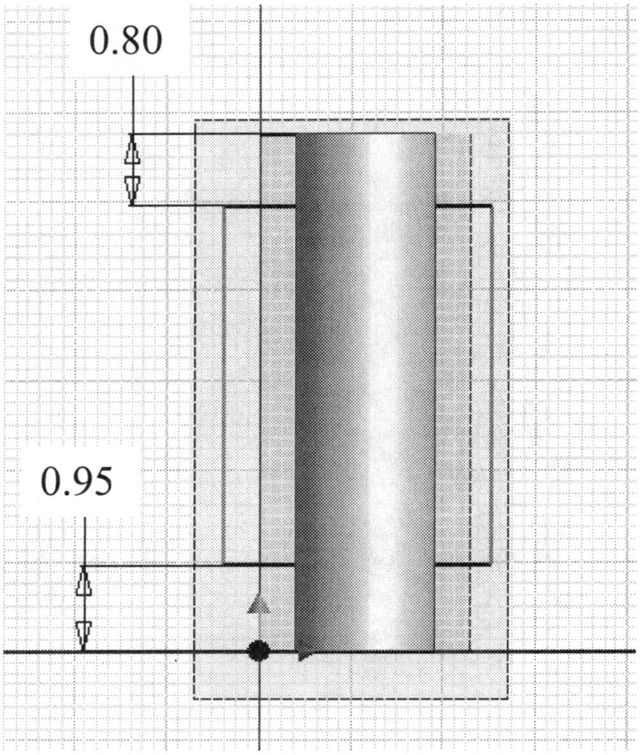

Draw a rectangle and dimension as shown.

Switch to an isometric view.

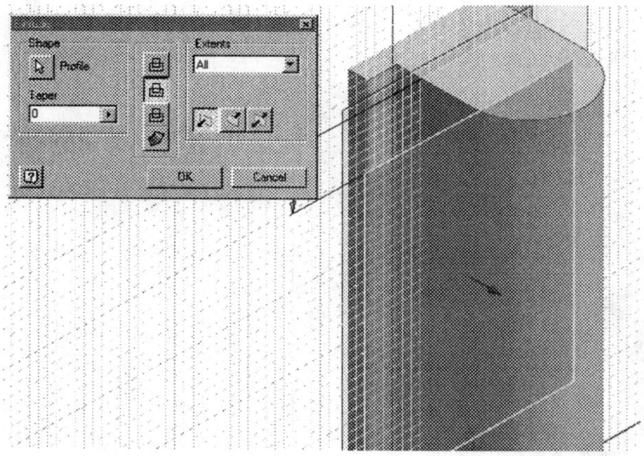

To make a cut, select the second button in the middle column on the 'Extrude' dialog box. The top button is a 'Join', the second button is a 'Cut', the third button is 'Intersect', and the fourth/bottom button is 'Surface'. Pass the mouse near these buttons and they will show the commands. The arrow color changes depending on the mode selected. A 'Cut' will preview as red. A 'Join' will preview as green. An 'Intersect' will preview as blue.

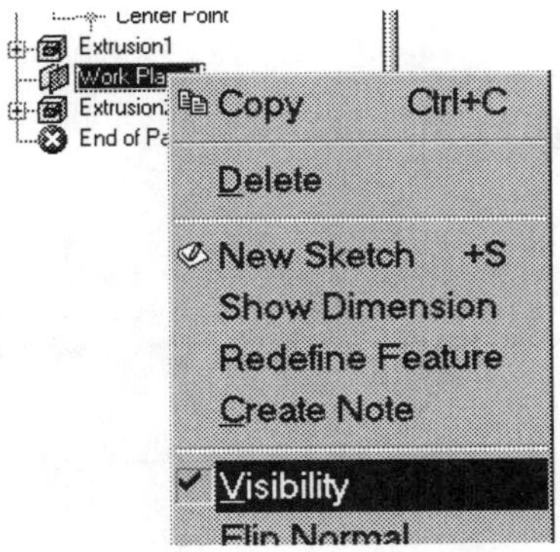

Turn off visibility on the Work Plane.
Select the Work Plane in the browser.
Right click and select 'Visibility'.

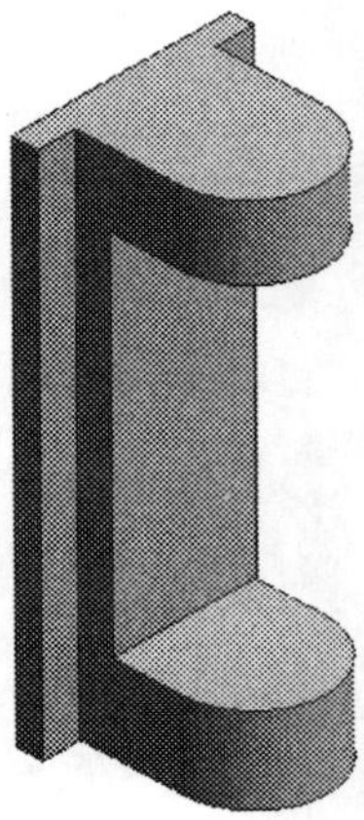

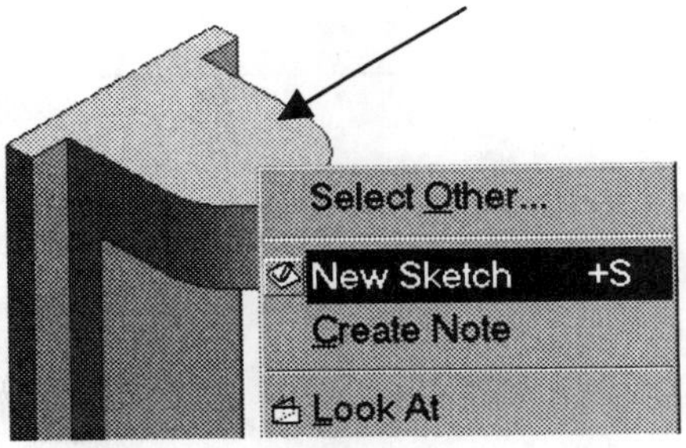

Select the top plane as shown.
Right click and select 'New Sketch' or enter Sketch mode by selecting the Sketch button on the Command toolbar.

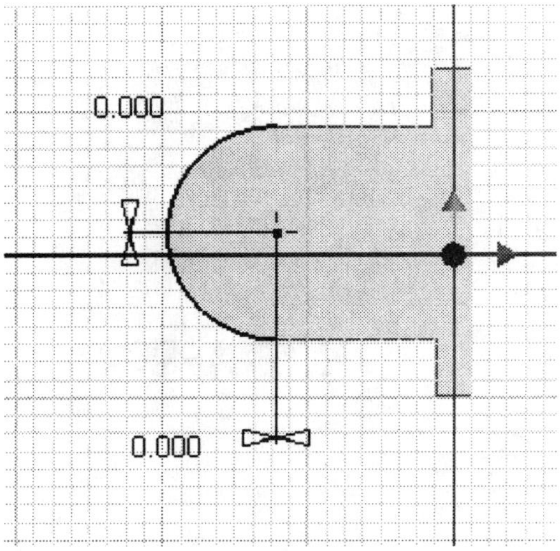

Place a Point, Hole Center so it is located concentric to the arc.

Select the Hole tool from the Features toolbar.

TIP: Setting the Termination to Through All will cause the hole to go through the top AND bottom of the part.

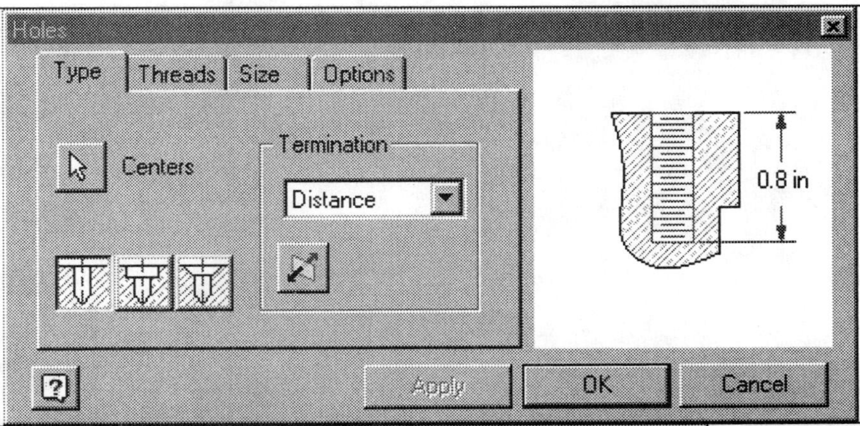

Set the Distance to 0.8
Set the Type to Drill/Ream.

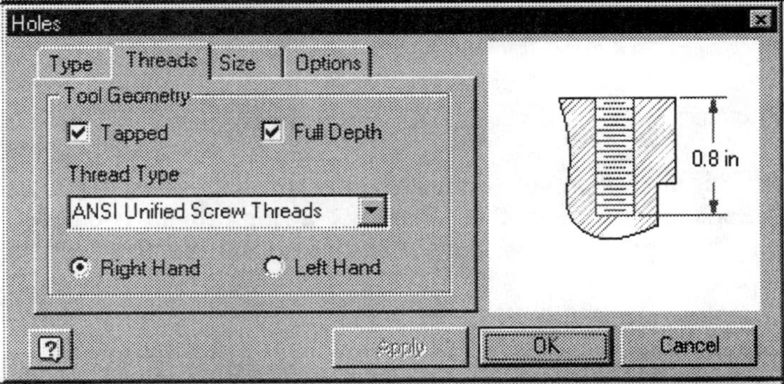

Select the Threads tab.
Enable Tapped and Full Depth.
Set Thread Type to ANSI.
Enable Right Hand.

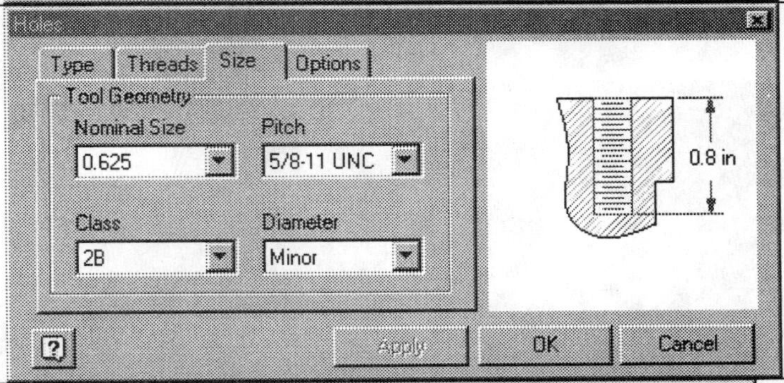

Select the Size tab.
Set the Nominal Size to 0.625.
Set the Pitch to 5/8-11 UNC.
Set the Class to 2B and the Diameter to Minor.

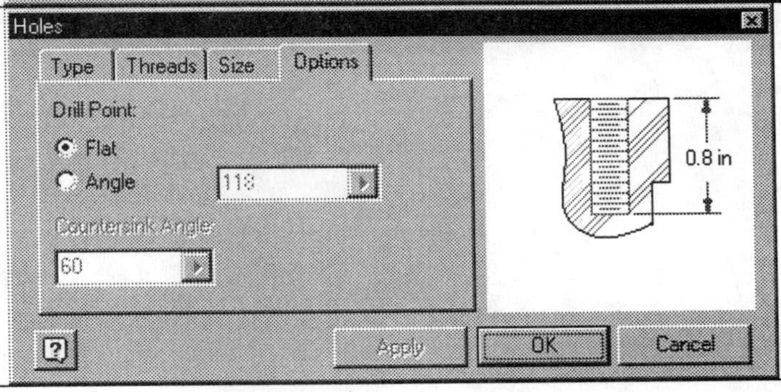

Select the Options tab.
Enable Flat Drill Point.

Press 'OK'.

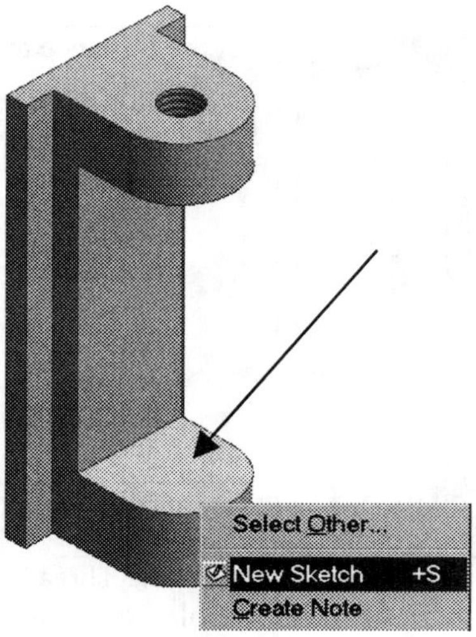

Select the Face indicated and start a new sketch.

We want to add a pin to the bottom flange. This pin is a press-fit part, so if we were really going to play mechanical designer, we would show a hole and then create another assembly drawing with the two parts (pin & bracket), but in the interest of keeping it simple, we'll just create it as an assembly and handle it as a note in the detailed drawing of the bracket part.

Select the bottom flange as shown by picking on it. A double-left pick will highlight it in green and then right click to bring up the pop-up menu.
Select 'New Sketch'.

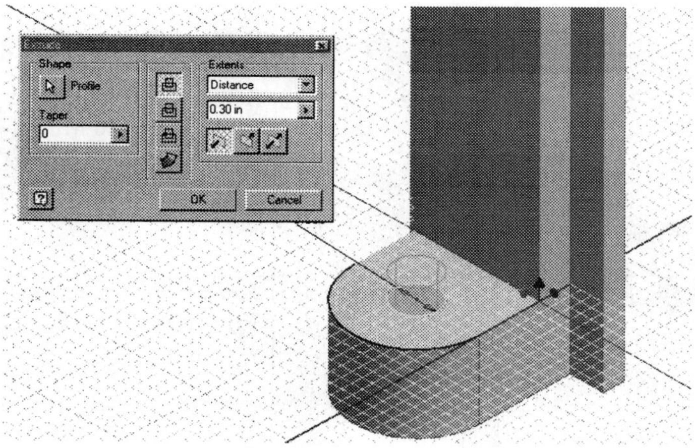

Draw a circle with a diameter of 0.5.
Locate it so that it is concentric to the arc.
Extrude as a 'Join'. Set the Distance to 0.3.

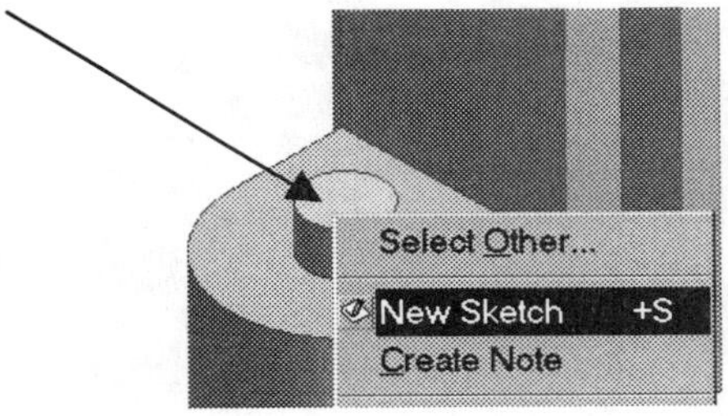

Select the face indicated and start a 'New Sketch'.

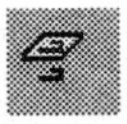

Project Geometry

Use the existing edge to create a new sketch.
Select the Project Geometry tool from the Sketch toolbar.
Then select the top edge of the cylinder.

TIP: In your Application Options under the Sketch tab, you can enable 'Automatic reference edges for new sketch. This will automatically project any geometry collinear to the new sketch plane. The default is for this to be enabled.

There is no need to dimension or constrain projected geometry as it is dimensioned and constrained by its source sketch.

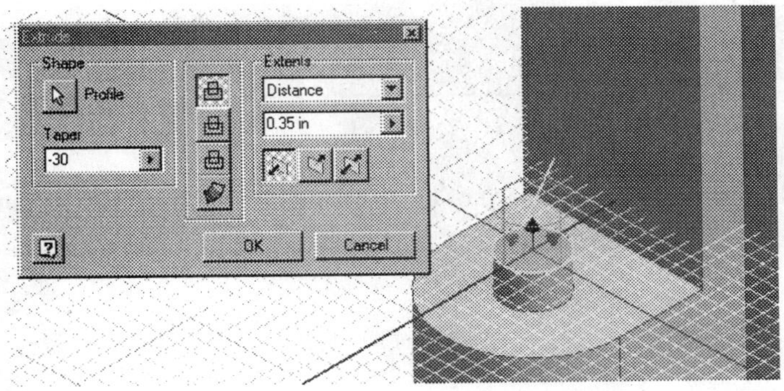

Extrude using Join.
Set the Taper to –30.
Set the Distance to 0.35.

Note that the preview shows you the taper direction. If you want the taper to go in, make it a negative number. If you want the taper to go out, make it a positive number. Set the distance to .35 as shown.

Press 'OK'.

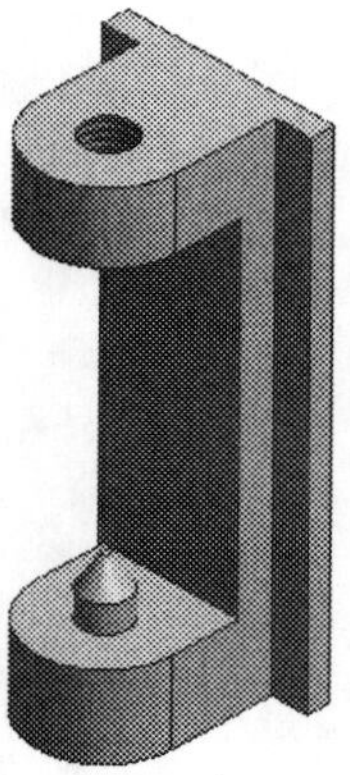

Our completed bracket.
Save the file.

Pressing the 'Return' button on our Command toolbar will return us to the Assembly environment.

Part 2- Hinge

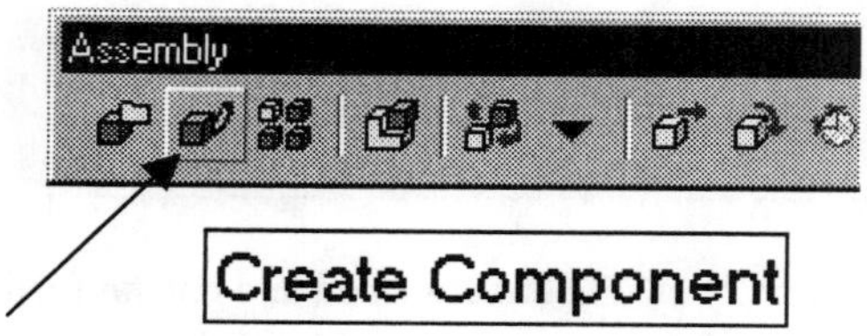

Select the 'Create Component' tool to start the next file.

TIP: In an assembly file, any planar surface of any part can be used as a sketch plane.

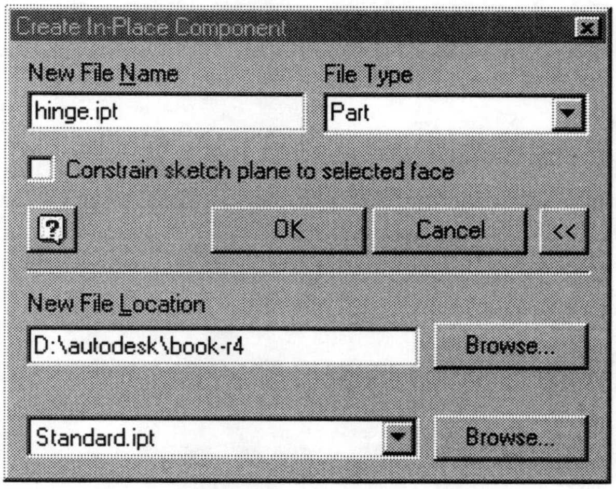

Fill out the dialog box as shown:

New File Name	Hinge.ipt
File Type	Part
Constrain sketch plane to selected face	Disabled

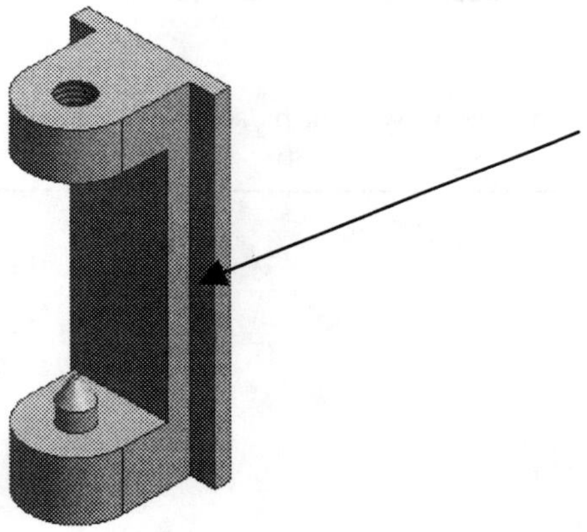

Select the face indicated to be used as the initial sketch plane.

You can change your viewpoint by selecting the Look at option in your View toolbar and then selecting your sketch plane.

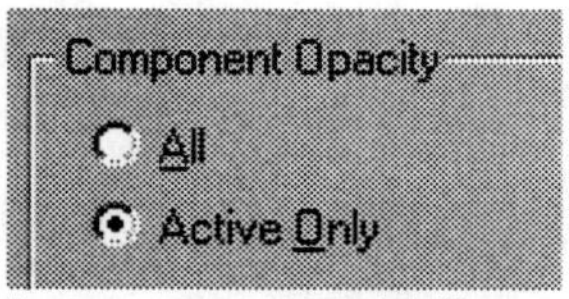

Inventor automatically turns all components other than the one currently being edited 'Opaque'. This option is set in Application Options under the Assembly tab. Enabling 'All' will turn off Opacity and make all parts appear according to the current View setting.

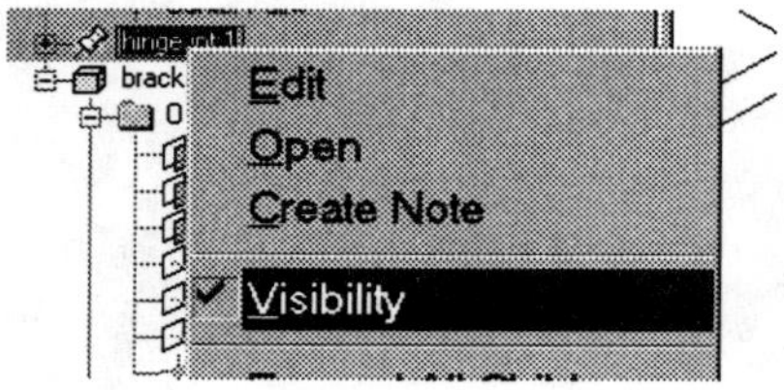

To assist creating the hinge, we can turn the bracket visibility to OFF. Get out of 'Edit Mode' by clicking on each part, right-clicking and selecting 'Finish Edit'. Then pick on the bracket or select it in the browser and highlight, right click and disable the visibility option.

TIP: We can control visibility of parts by selecting the part in the browser or by selecting the part in the drawing window.

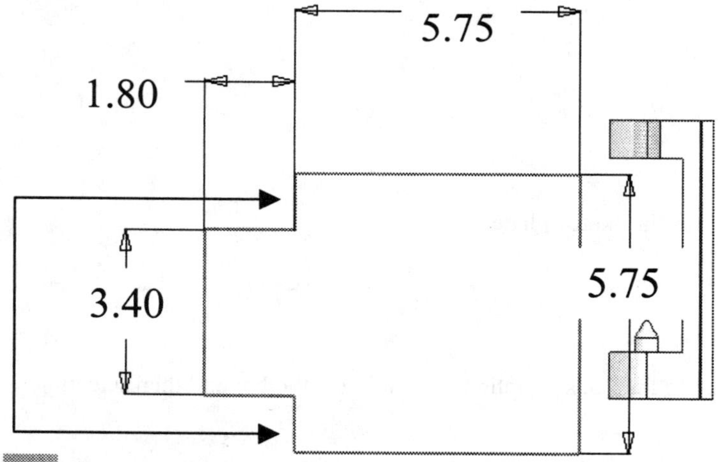

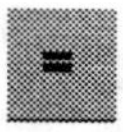

Create the sketch shown.
Add Equal Constraints to the lines indicated.

Right click and select 'Finish Sketch'.
Switch to an isometric view.

Select the Extrude tool.

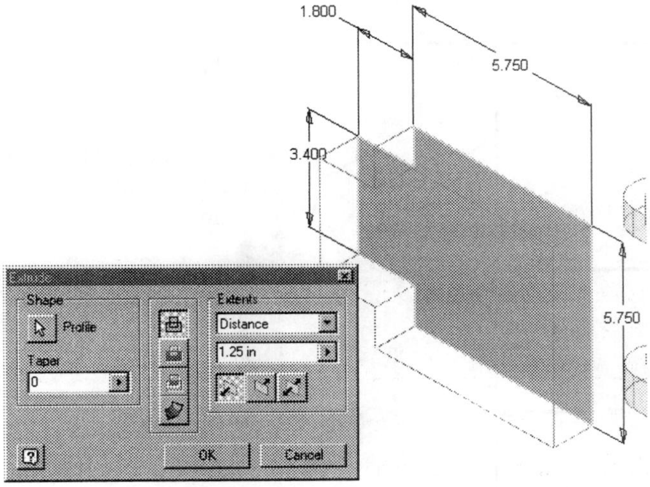

Modify the distance and enter a value of 1.25. Then press 'OK'.

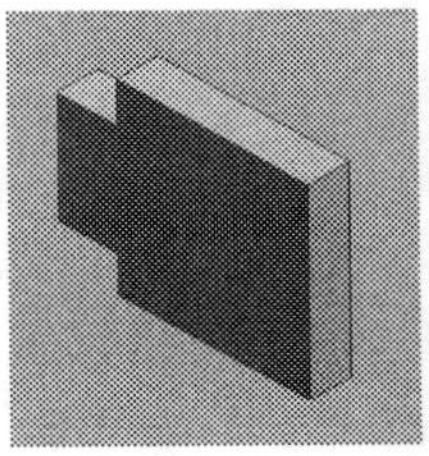

Your extruded part should look like the figure shown

Select the top plane as shown so that we can add a hole.

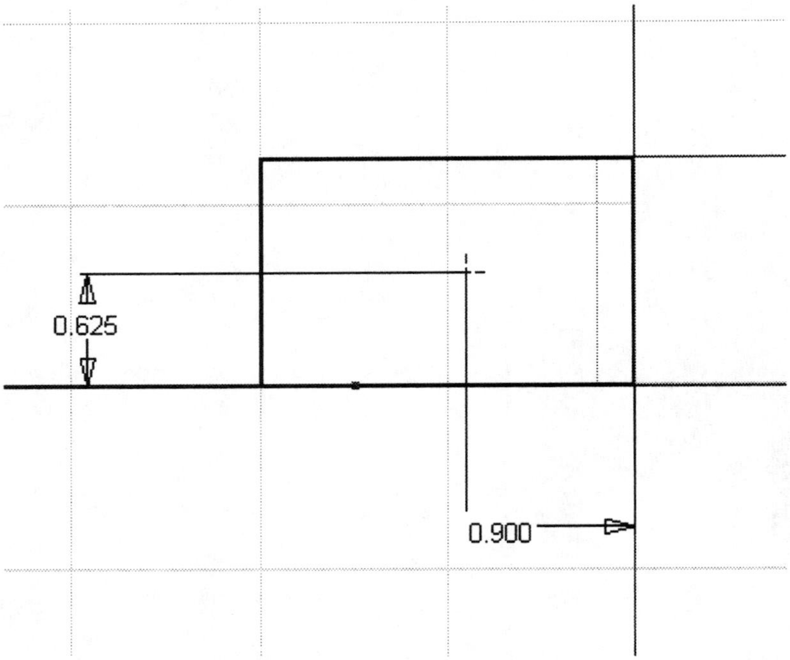

Select the Point, Hole, Center Tool on the left hand toolbar and locate your hole as shown.

Now, select the Hole tool located in the upper left of the screen.

TIP: See if you can use the 'Show Dimensions' option of the Edit Dimension box to add the dimensions.

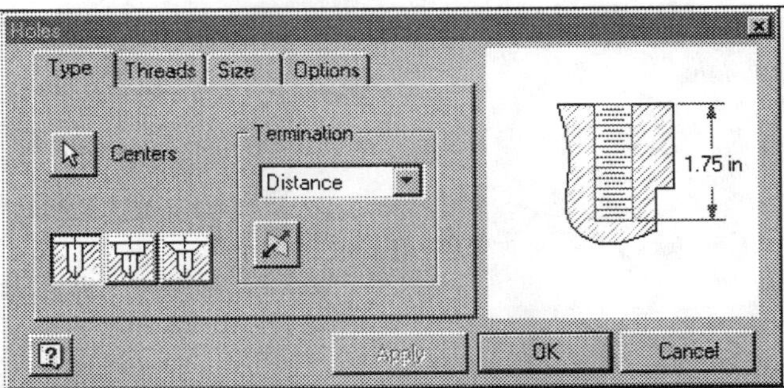

Set the Distance to 1.75.
Set the Type to Drill/Ream.

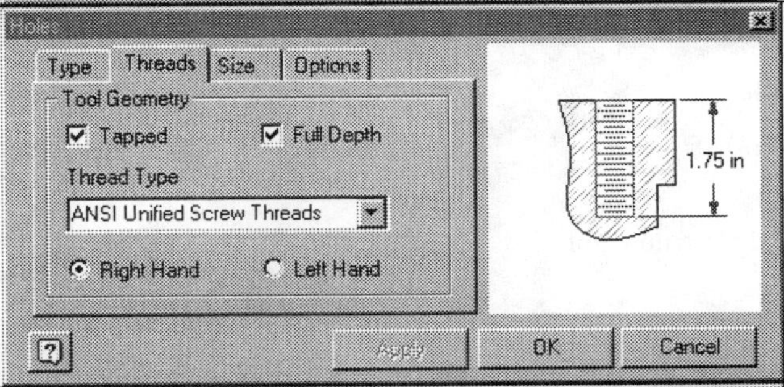

Select the Threads tab.
Enable Tapped and Full Depth.
Set Thread Type to ANSI.
Enable Right Hand.

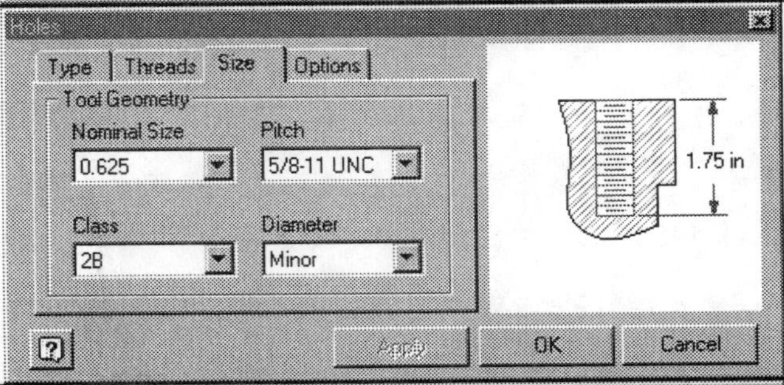

Select the Size tab.
Set the Nominal Size to 0.625.
Set the Pitch to 5/8-11 UNC.
Set the Class to 2B and the Diameter to Minor.

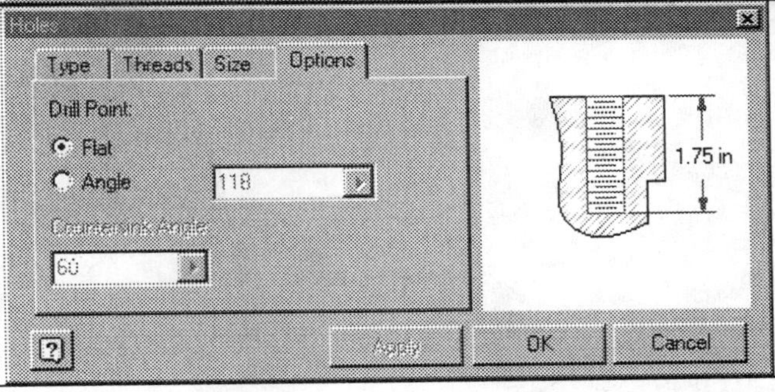

Select the Options tab.
Enable Flat Drill Point.

Press 'OK'.

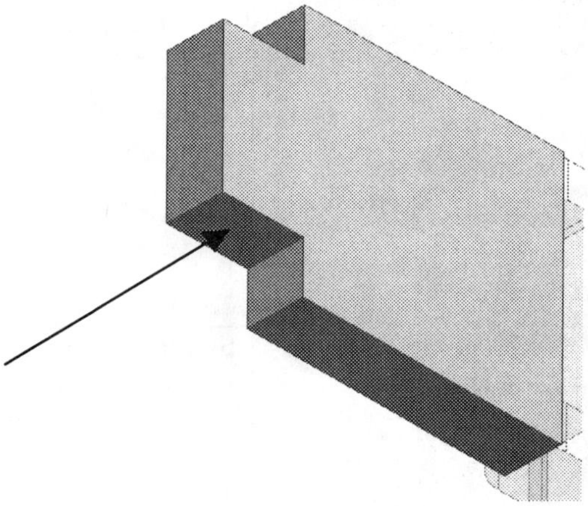

Rotate the part so we can select the face indicated for a new hole.

Copy Feature

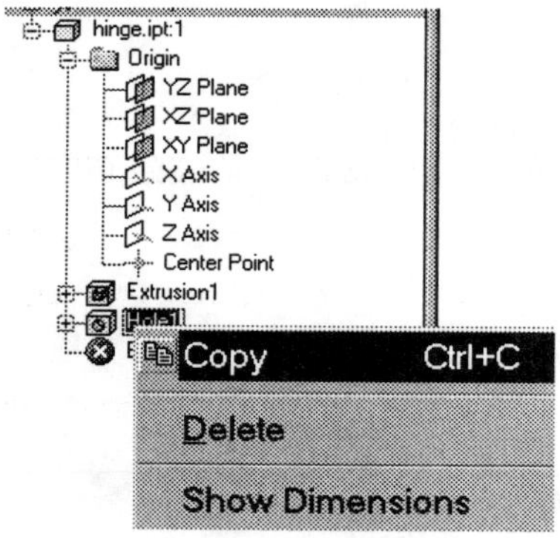

Locate the hole just created in the browser.
Right click and select 'Copy'.

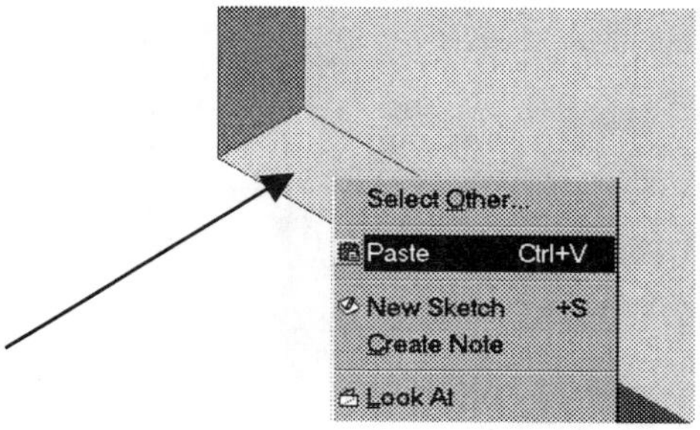

Select the face indicated.
Right click and select 'Paste'.

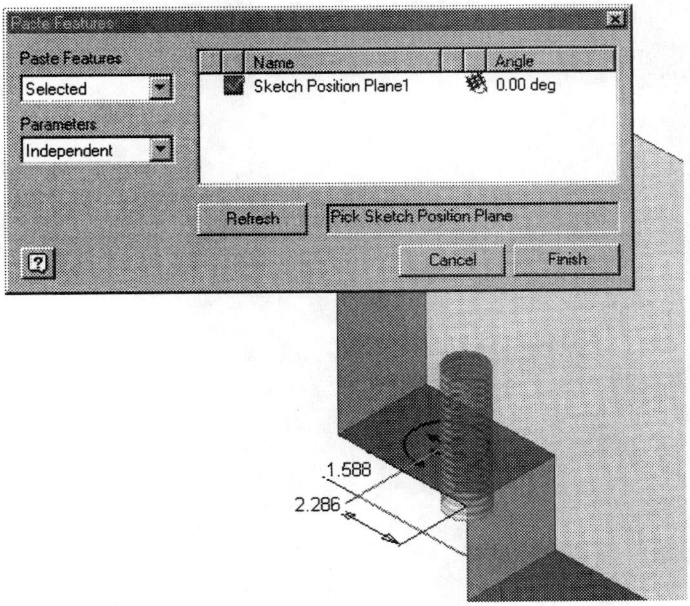

The Paste Features dialog box appears.
Press 'Finish'.

TIP: When you copy a feature you can make it Independent or Dependent. Dependent features get their dimension values from the source feature.

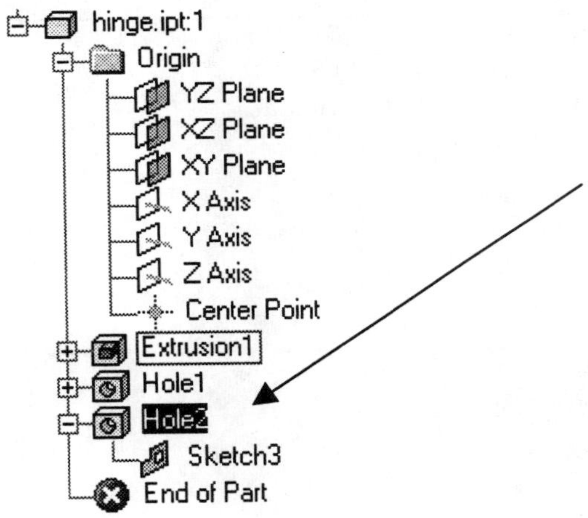

The second hole is placed, but it is not constrained.

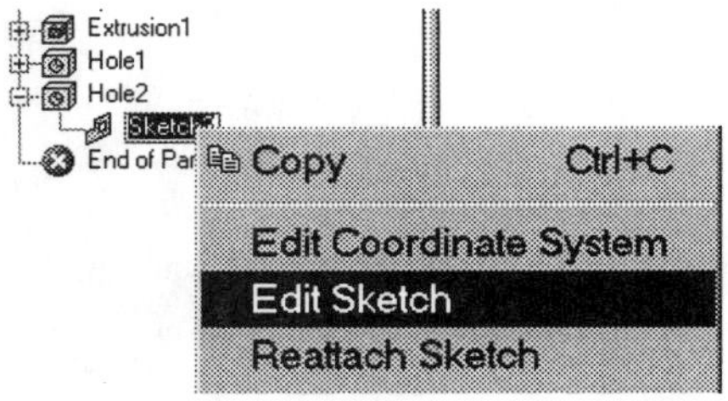

Select the sketch in the browser.
Right click and select 'Edit Sketch'.

Relocate the Point, Hole Center correctly.
Exit the sketch.

Edit Hole

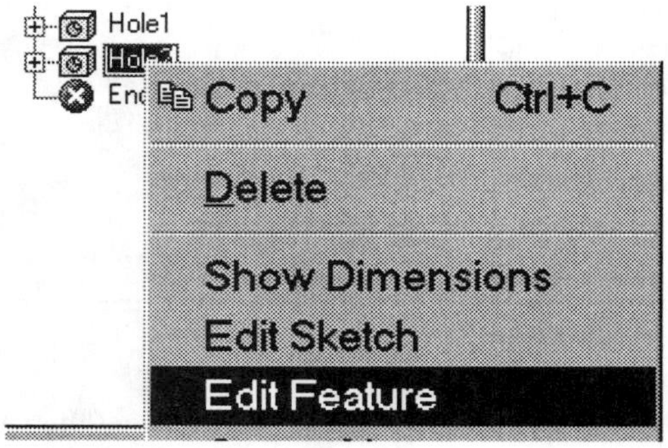

Locate the second hole in the browser.
Right click and select 'Edit Feature'.

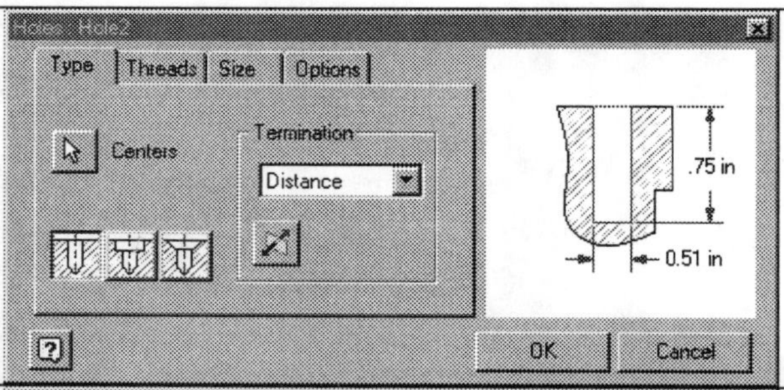	Set the Distance to .75. Set the diameter to 0.51. Set the Type to Drill/Ream.
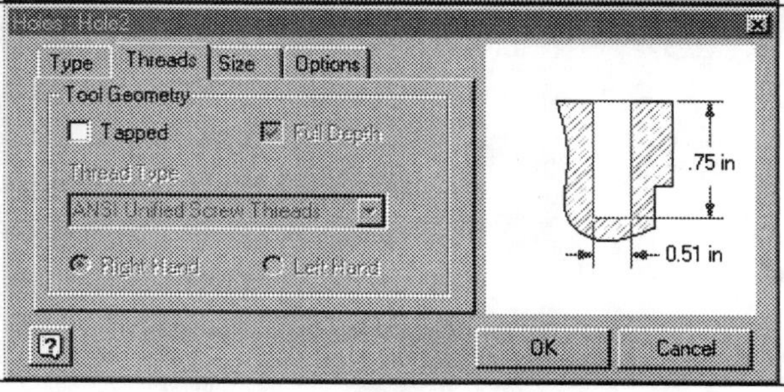	Disable the Tapped.

Press 'OK'.

Shell

Click the Shell tool.

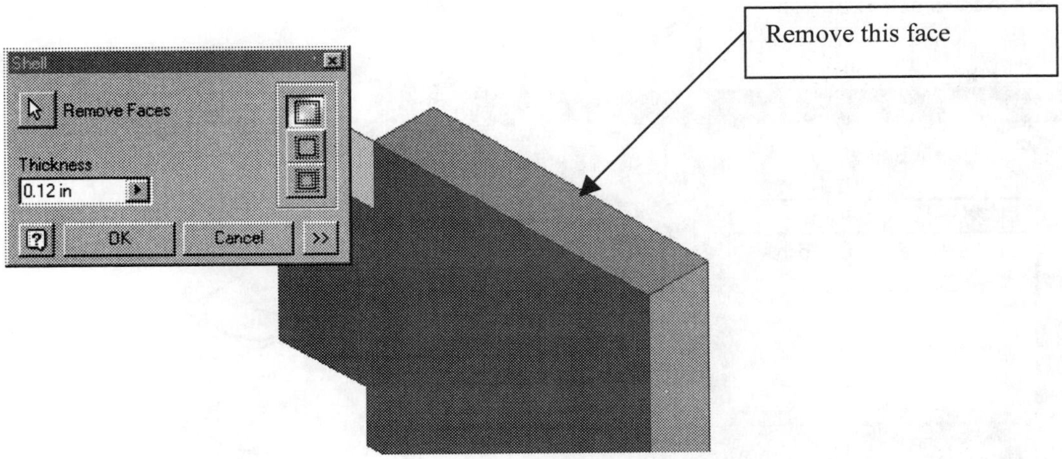

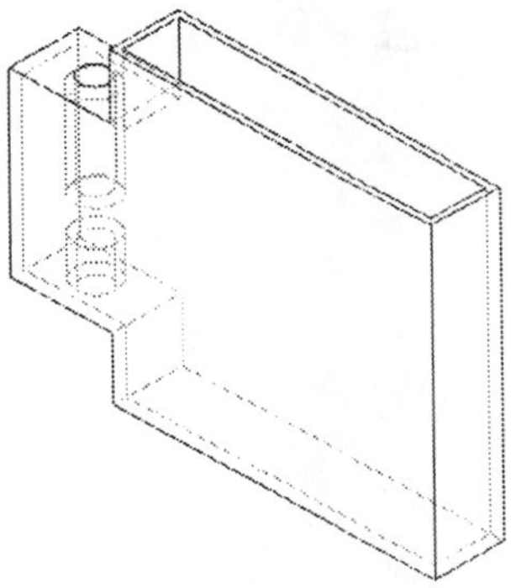

Change the View to Wire Frame for easier selection.

Add Fillet

Add fillets to the small extrusion.

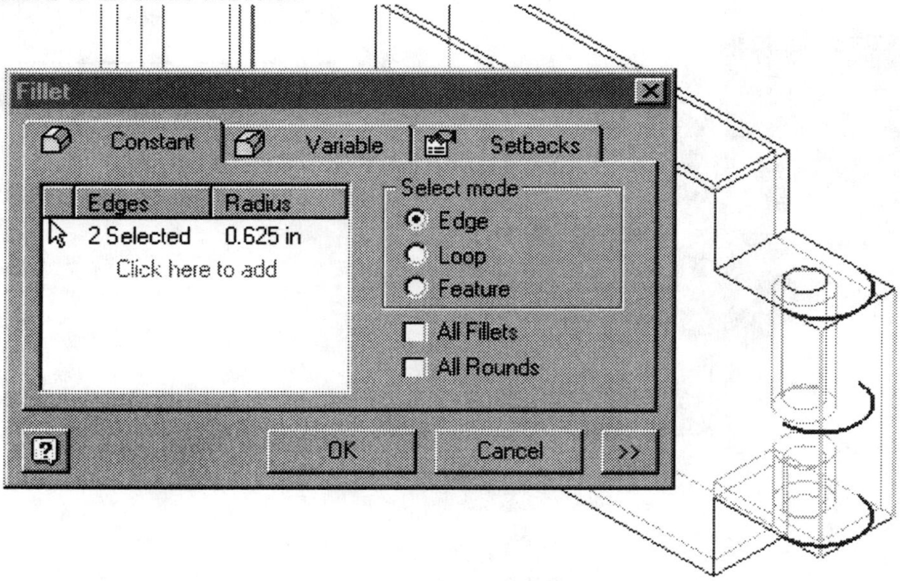

Set the fillet radius to 0.625 for the outer edges.

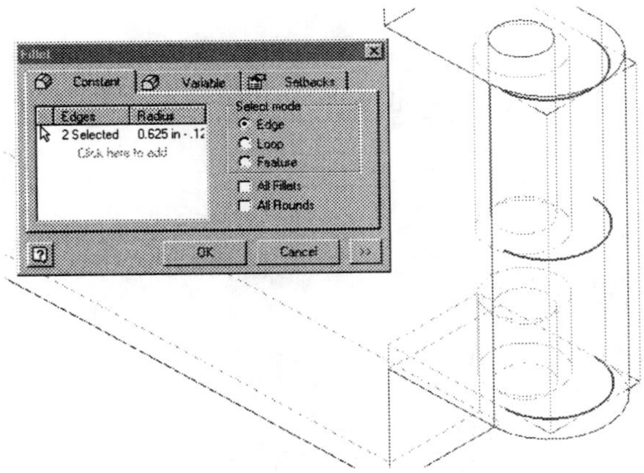

The inner fillet can use a formula. Type 0.625 – 0.120 in for the radius.

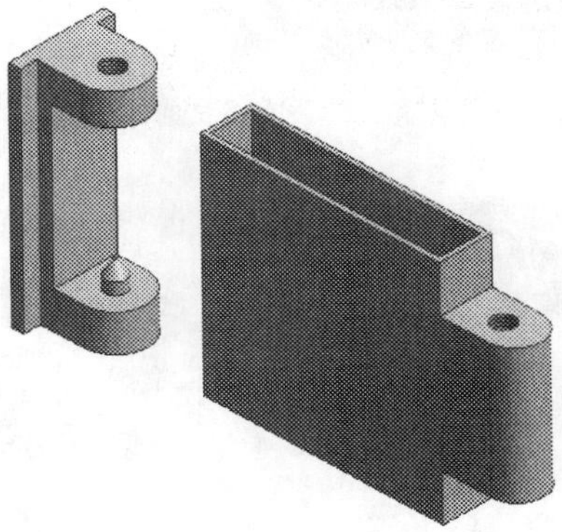

Our assembly so far.

Press the Return button or double-click on the assembly name in the browser to return to Assembly mode.

Part 3 – Bolt

Time for the third part, the bolt that will fasten the hinge and bracket together

We can use the Fastener Library to insert a bolt.

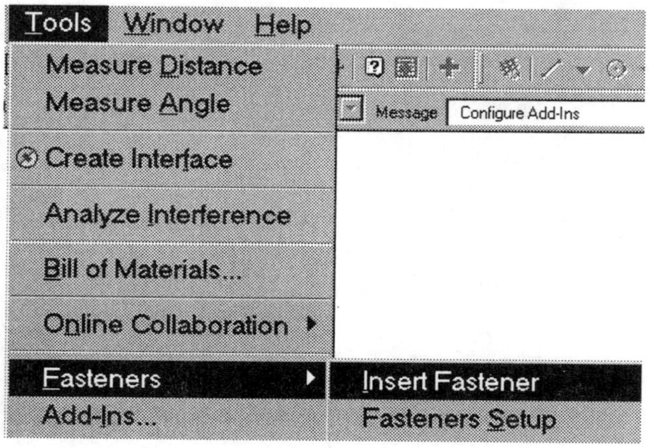

Go to Tools->Fasteners->Insert Fastener.

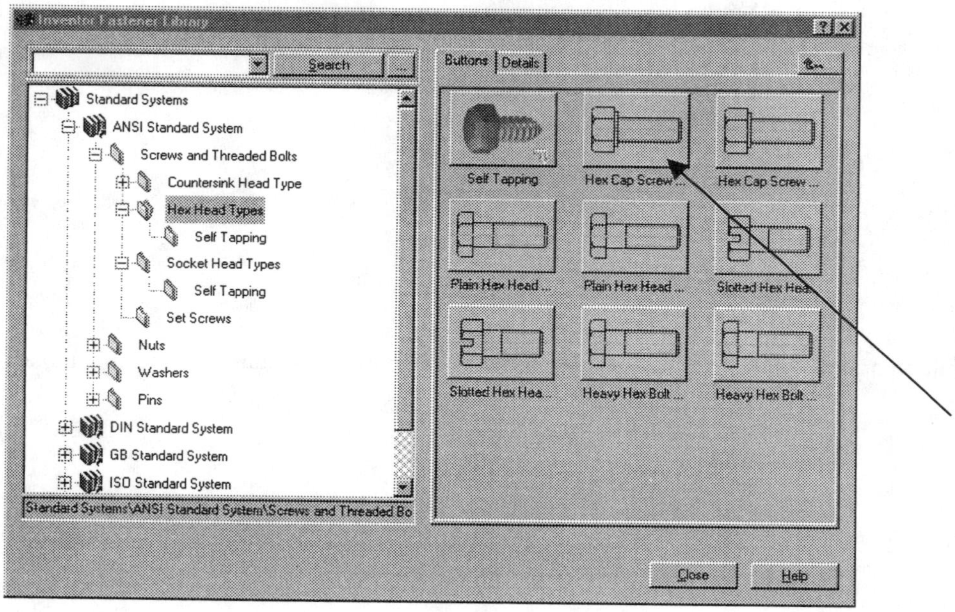

Go to ANSI->Screws and Threaded Bolts->Hex Head Types.
Select Hex Cap Screw- UNC.

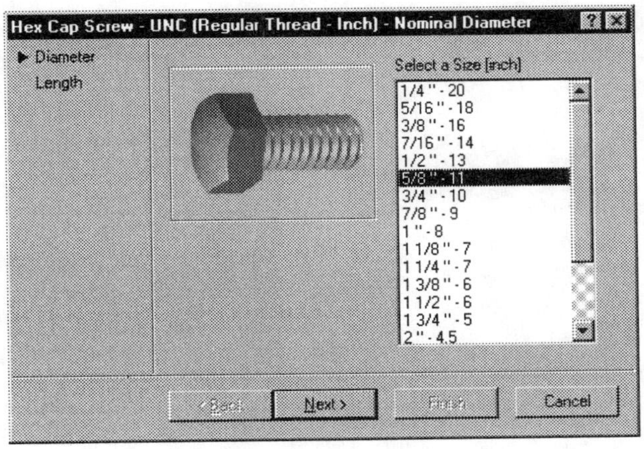

Select 5/8"-11 for size.
Then press 'Next'.

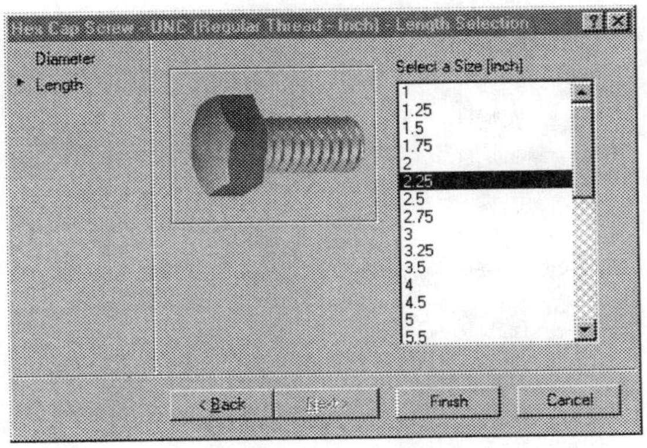

Select a length of 2.25 inch.
Then press 'Finish'.
To place in our assembly, pick a point in the drawing window. Then right click and select 'Done'.

Grounding Parts

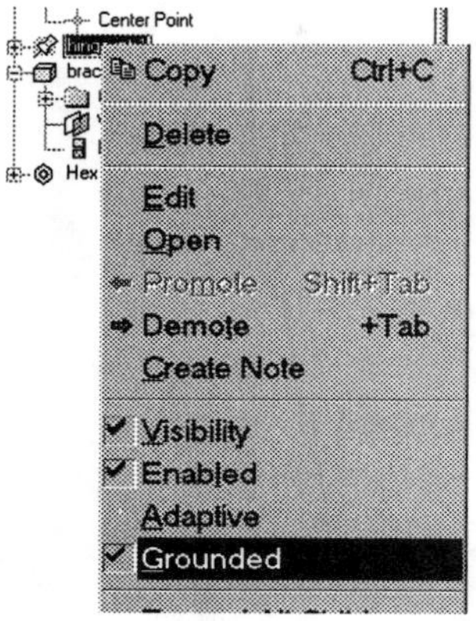

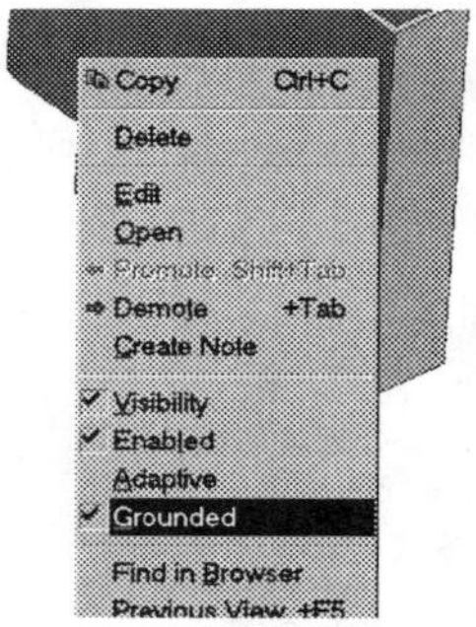

We can disable/enable the grounding by selecting the part in the browser or picking the part in the drawing window. Then right click and enable/disable Grounded.

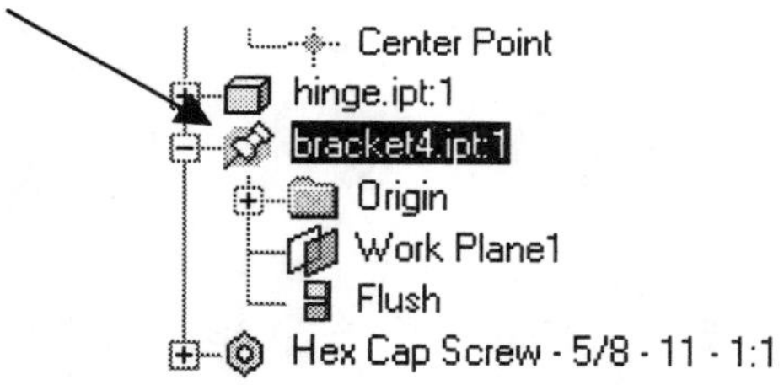

So we should see a pin next to the bracket.

Assembling the model

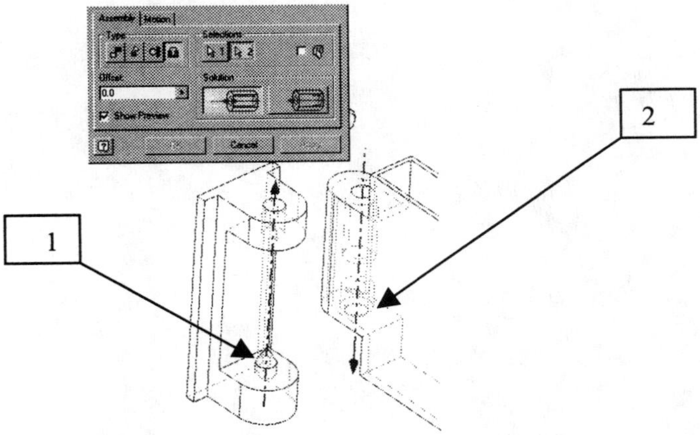

Add the constraint for the hinge and the bracket by using 'Insert' and selecting the parts.

Add an insert constraint between the bolt and the bracket.

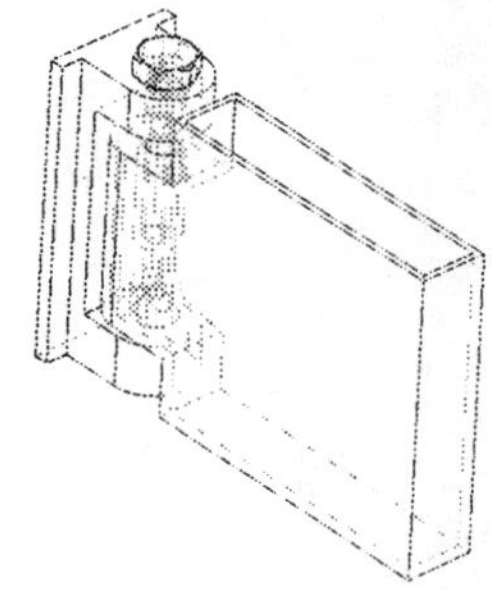

Our assembled hinge.

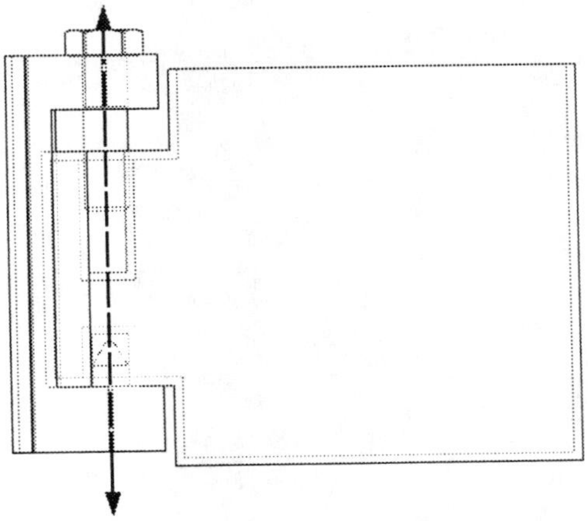

A side view shows us that the parts do not fit together properly.

Modifying a Constraint

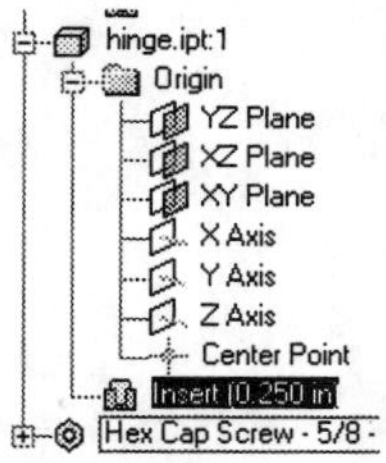

We start by editing the insert constraint between the bottom of the bracket and the bottom of the hinge.
Locate the Insert Constraint in the browser and highlight.
A small edit box appears on the left bottom of the browser.
Change the Offset to 0.250.
Press 'ENTER'.

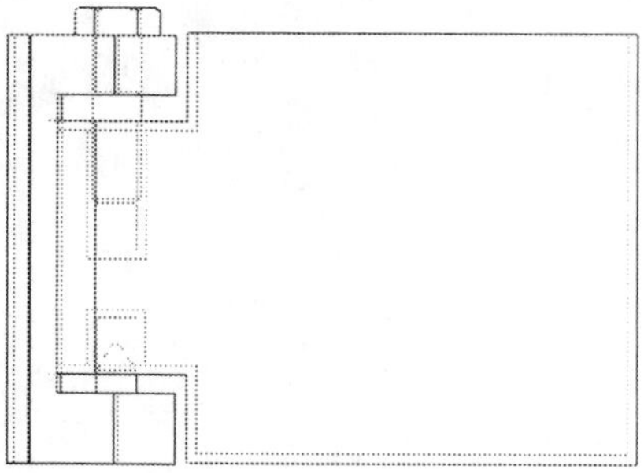

The bottom of the bracket is now flush with the bottom of the hinge.

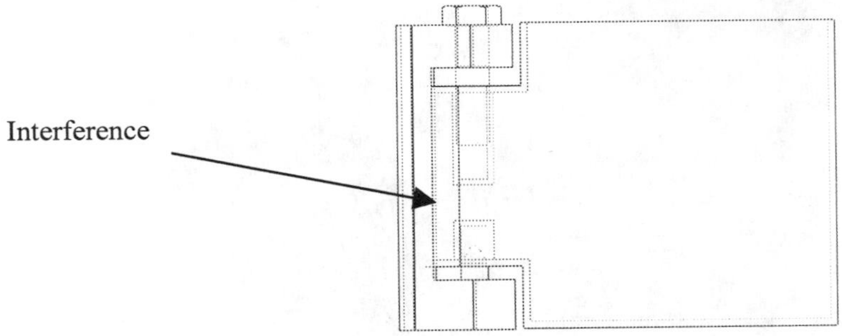

Our hinge is now situated properly in the vertical direction. We still have some interference between the hinge and the bracket.

Interference Checking

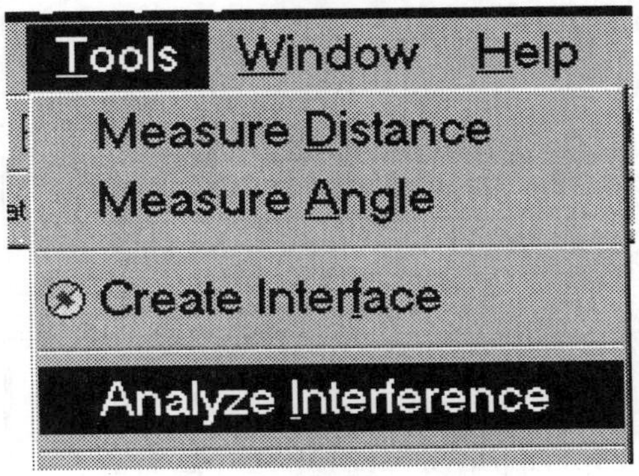

Go to Tools->Analyze Interference.

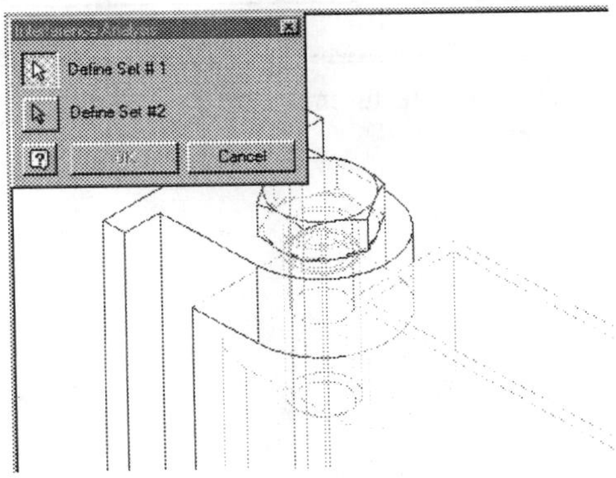

Select the hinge as Set #1. Select the Bracket as Set #2. Then press 'OK'.

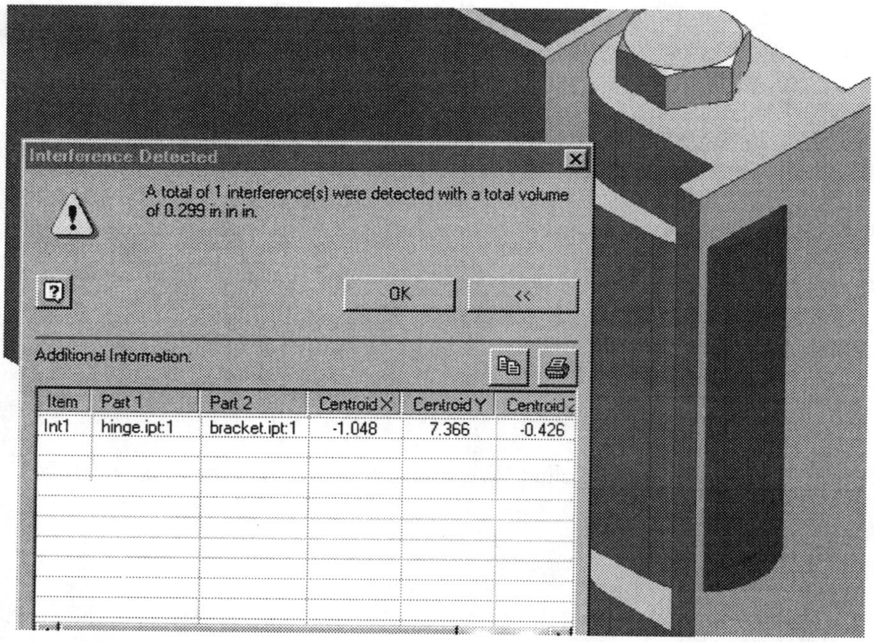

A window will come up reporting the interference issue.

When analysis is complete, the number of instances of interference and their combined volumes, if applicable, display in a message. Click OK to dismiss the dialog box or click the More button to show the analysis report in table form. To adjust width, drag column margins.	
Item	Lists the interference volume in numerical order, according to the browser order.
Part 1	Lists the file name of the part in Set #1 that interferes with a part in Set #2. If the part is a member of a subassembly, shows both the file name and the part number.
Part 2	Lists the file name of the part in Set #2 that interferes with a part in Set #1. If the part is a member of a subassembly, shows both the file name and part number.
Centroid	Lists the XYZ coordinates, relative to the assembly origin, of the interference centroid.
Volume	Lists the volume of the interference found.

You can modify parts to eliminate the interference. You can either print the interference report or copy it to the clipboard and open it in a text editor or spreadsheet.

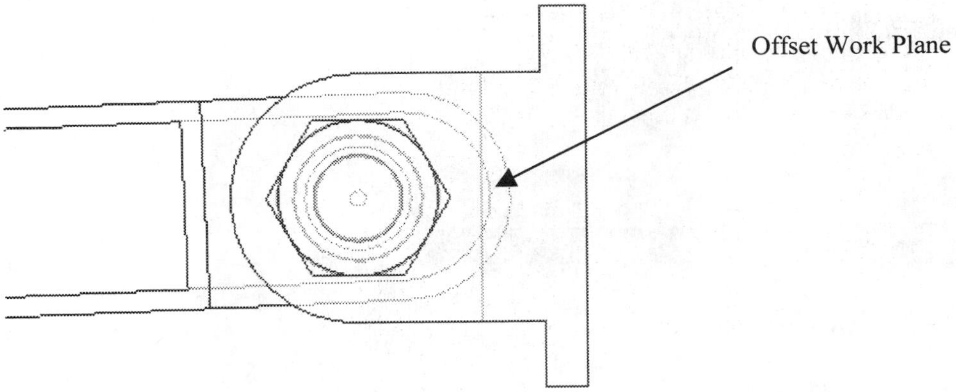

We see that the interference is due to the offset plane being too far forward.

Editing Parts in an Assembly

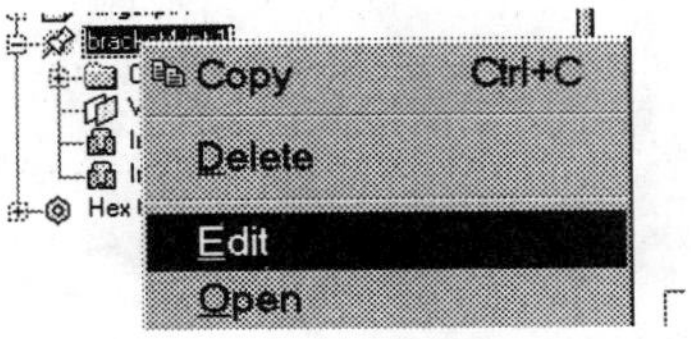

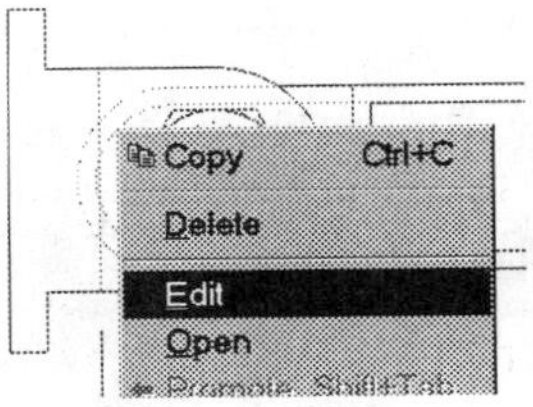

In order to correct this, we need to edit the bracket.

The user can edit a part inside of an assembly by:

- Highlighting the part in the browser, right click and select 'Edit'.
- Pick on the part in the drawing window, right click and select 'Edit'.

All the other parts automatically grey out to allow us to concentrate on the part being modified.

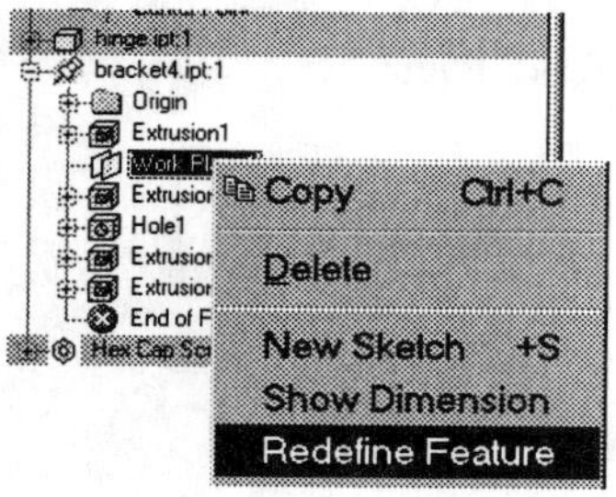

Modifying a Work Plane

To modify the work plane offset value:

- Highlighting the work plane in the browser, right click and select 'Redefine Feature'.
- Pick on the work plane in the drawing window, right click and select 'Redefine Feature'.

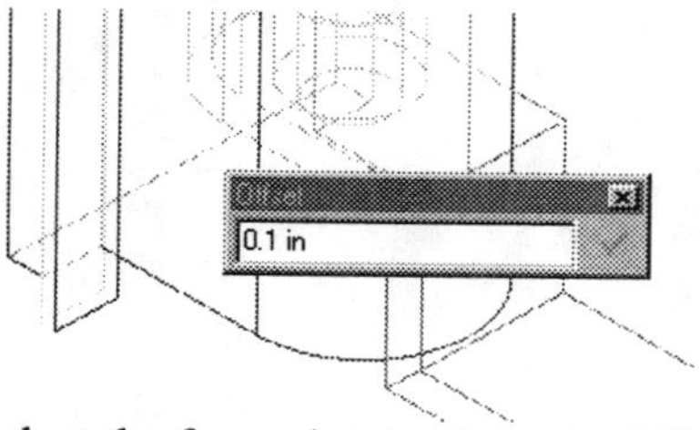

Select the front plane and set the Offset to 0.10 in.

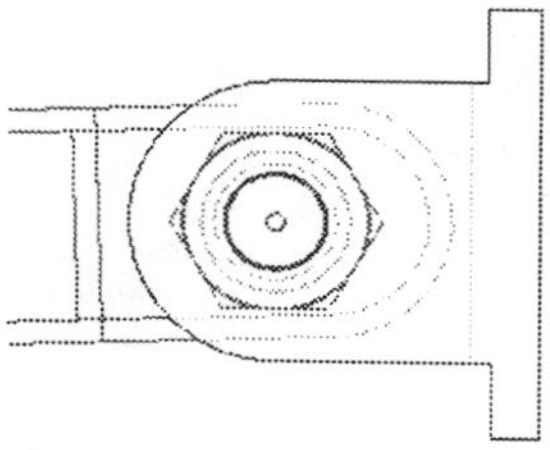

It now looks like our assembly has a decent fit with no interference.

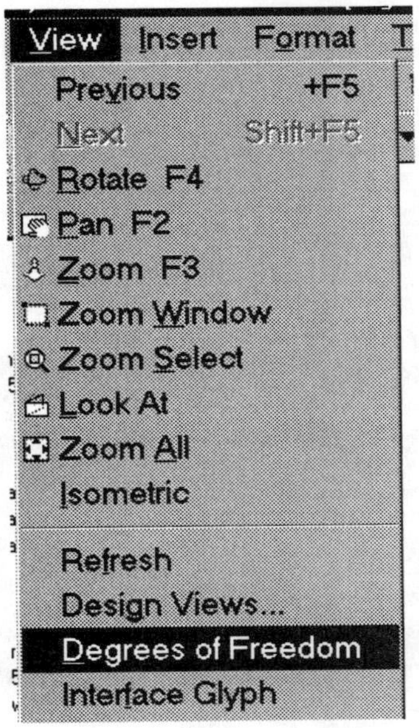

Degrees of Freedom

We can use the Degrees of Freedom tool to see if our assembly is constrained properly. Go to View->Degrees of Freedom.

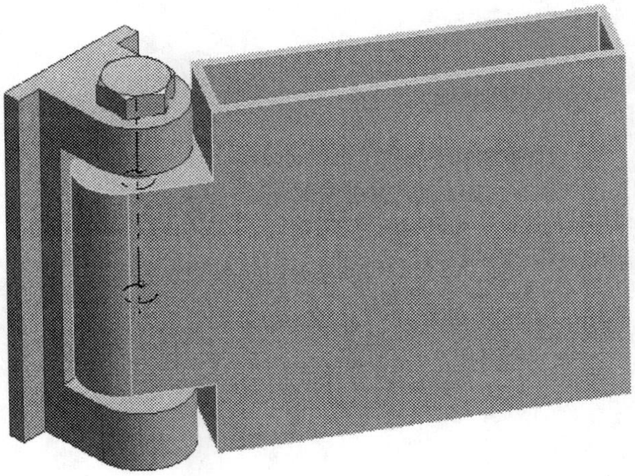

We see a rotation axis indicated.

Moving an Assembly

Switch to an isometric view. Change the view to solid.
Place the mouse on top of the hinge. Hold the left mouse button down and move the mouse.
You should see the hinge swing back and forth.

You'll notice that the hinge can rotate into and through the bracket.

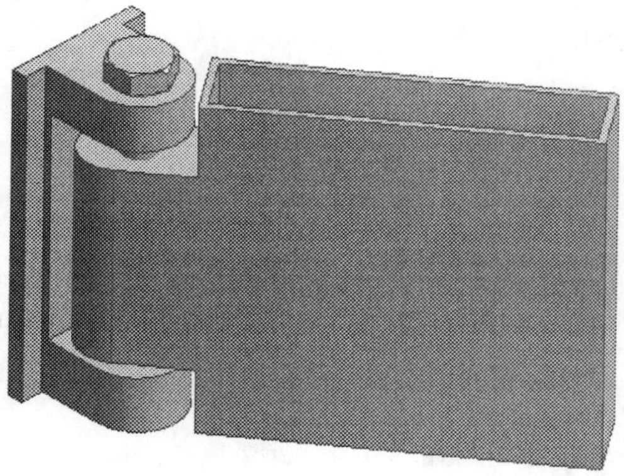

Save the assembly as 'hinge-assy.iam'.

Lesson 28

Presentations

Learning Objective

The user will learn how to create a Presentation File.

In this lesson, we'll be creating a presentation of the plane assembly.

You can develop exploded views and other stylized views of an assembly and use them to create drawing views that document your design. The stylized views are saved in a separate file called a presentation file. Each presentation file can contain as many presentation views as needed for a specified assembly. For example, we can turn off the visibility of some parts in a complex assembly and save a design view that shows only certain components.

You can automatically explode the view when creating a new presentation view. Assembly constraints will be used to determine the direction that the components will move to create the view.

After placing the view, you can manually tweak individual components in the view to create the optimum view of the components.

TIP: Presentation views do not recognize assembly constraints for any purpose other than creating the first automatic explosion. You can manually tweak a component along any specified vector.

Presentation views are used to:

- Develop a series of views that can be used for assembly instructions.
- Develop a series of views that show the relationship between moving parts of an assembly at different points in a cycle.
- Turn off the visibility of some parts in a complex assembly and save design views that show only certain components

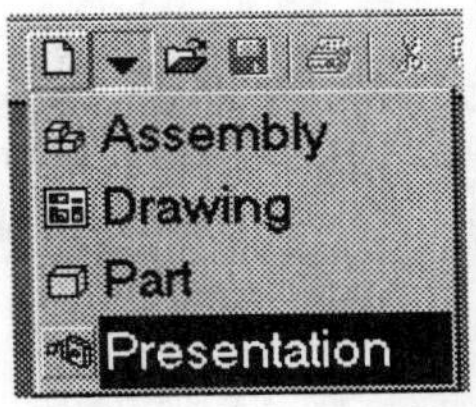

We start by selecting Presentation from the file drop down.

Presentation View Management Tools

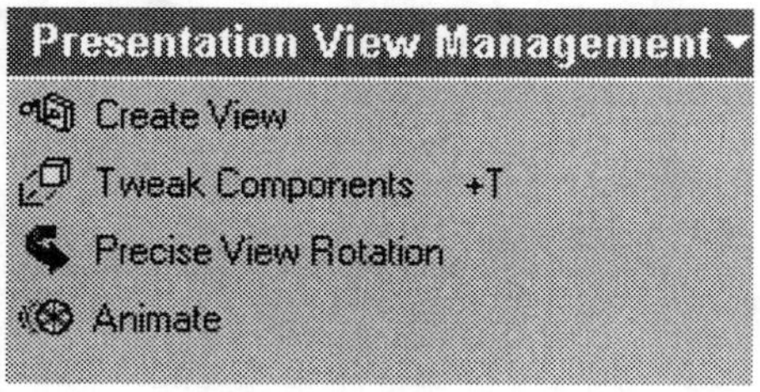

We have four tools available to us:

- Create View
- Tweak Components
- Precise View Rotation
- Animate

TIP: The first view that you add associates the presentation file to a model. You can add as many presentation views as needed of that model. All measurements in the presentation assume the default units specified in the model.

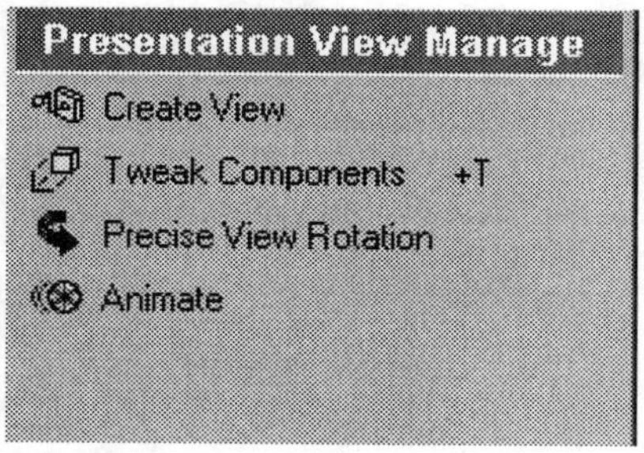

Create Presentation View

As you develop a presentation file, you can add as many presentation views as necessary for creating specialized drawing views. Use the Create Presentation View button on the Presentation View Management toolbar.
To automatically create an exploded view, select Automatic as the Explosion Method, and set the distance and trail options.

You can set a standard tweak distance for all components when you create a presentation view. Use the Create Presentation View button on the Presentation View Management toolbar.

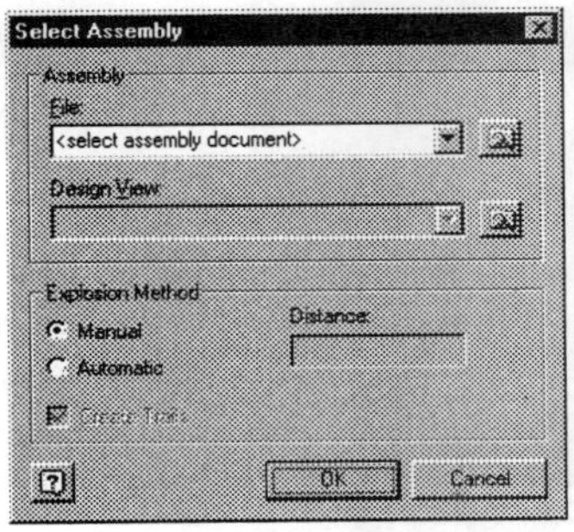

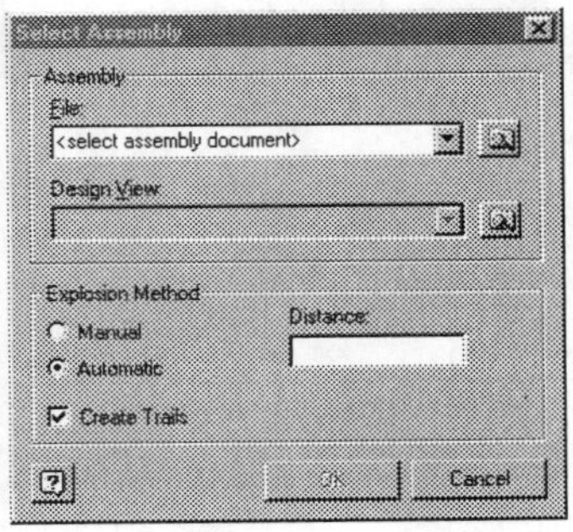

The Select Assembly dialog box selects the model and view to document and sets the orientation of the view.

File	Specifies the part, assembly, or presentation file to use for the drawing view. Specify the file name in one of the following ways. • Enter a file name in the box. • Click the arrow to select from the list of open files. • Click the Explore button to browse for the file.
Design View	This option is available if the selected file is an assembly that contains defined design views. Specifies the assembly design view to use. The name of the active design view is displayed in the box. To use another view in the active design view file, click the arrow to select from the list. To use a design view file that is not currently open, click the button to browse for the file.
Explosion Method	Manual - Creates the presentation view without creating an exploded view. You can manually add tweaks to create an exploded view later. Automatic - Sets the tweak distance and other options to automatically create an exploded view from the presentation view.
Distance	Specifies the standard tweak distance for each component when creating an exploded view. Enter the desired distance. Available only when Automatic is selected.
Create Trails	Displays the trails for each tweaked component when creating an exploded view. Available only when Automatic is selected.

TIP: To create several presentation views from the same design view, add the first view then use Copy and Paste to add copies of it. Each of the views can be modified without affecting the others.

Tweak Components

A tweak is when a component is moved out of its proper assembled position in order to view the assembly. The 'Tweak Components' tool specifies the tweak distance, direction, and other settings for a selected component or group of components when creating an exploded presentation view. Components can be moved and/or rotated.

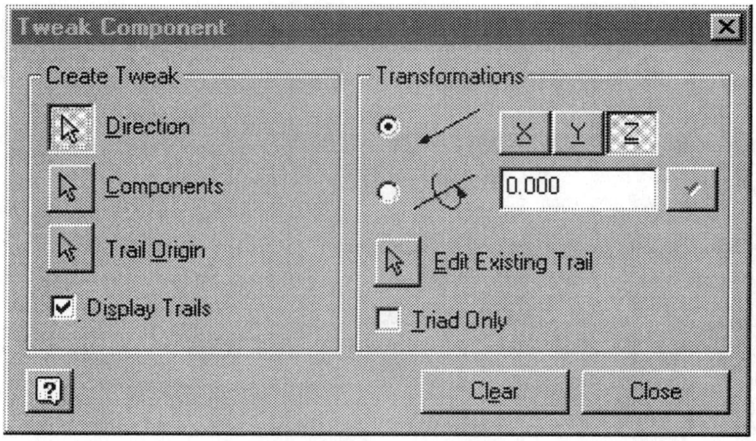

The Selections area of the dialog box allows the user to choose the components to tweak and sets the direction and origin of the tweak.	
Direction	Specifies the direction or axis of rotation for the tweak. Click the Direction button, then select an edge, face, or feature of any component in the graphics window to display the direction triad for the tweak.
Components	Selects the components to tweak. Click the Components button, then select the components in the graphics window or browser.
Trail Origin	Sets the origin for the trail. Click the Trail Origin button, then click in the graphics window to set the origin point.
Display Trails	Sets the display of trails when tweaking the components in an exploded view. Select the box to display the tweak trails for the selected components; clear the check box to hide the trails.
Clear	Clears the Component and Direction selections so that you can set up another tweak.

TIP: Click the open space in the browser to clear only the component selection.

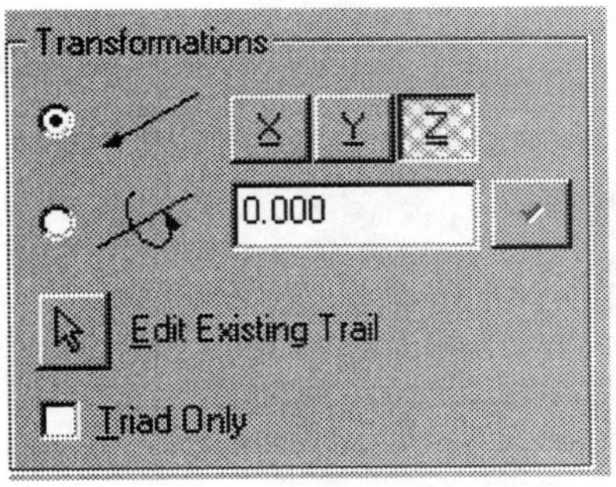

The Transformations section of the dialog box sets the distance and type of tweak for the selected components in an exploded view. After specifying the desired settings, click Apply to add the tweak to the view.	
Translate	Sets the distance and axis for the tweak. Select Translate, click X, Y, or Z to indicate the vector (as indicated by the direction triad), then enter the distance for the tweak in the box. When the desired tweak is set, click Apply to implement it.
Rotate	Changes the angle of the tweak triad. Select Rotate, click X, Y, or Z to indicate the axis, then enter the angle or rotation.
Edit Existing Trail	Allows the user to select an existing trail and modify it.
Triad Only	Specifies whether to rotate the selected components when the tweak triad is rotated. Select the option to include the components in the rotation, clear the box to rotate only the tweak triad.

Precise View Rotation

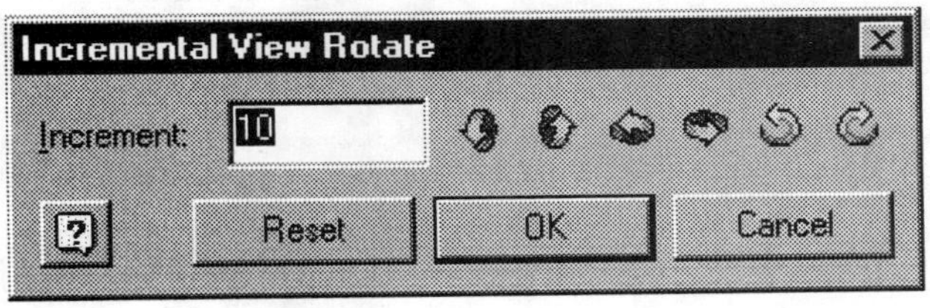

The Precise View Rotation tool rotates the assembly presentation view by specified increment.

Increment	Sets the distance, in degrees, the view will rotate with each click.
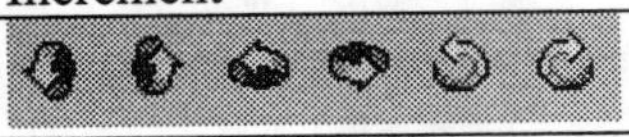	Rotates the view by the specified increment distance. Click an arrow to rotate the view in the desired direction.

Animation Tool

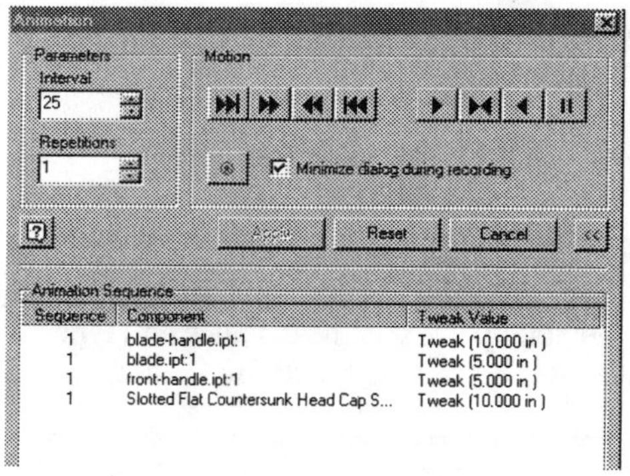

Sets up an animation of the active exploded view and records the animation to a file that you can replay.

Parameters specify the speed and number of repetitions for the animation.	
Interval	Sets the playback speed for the animation. The higher the number, the greater the time delay between frames. Enter the desired playback speed or use the up or down arrow to select the speed.
Repetitions	Sets the number of times to repeat the playback. Enter the desired number of repetitions or use the up or down arrow to select the number.
Plays the specified animation of the active exploded view.	
	Steps the animation forward one tweak at a time.
	Steps the animation forward one interval at a time. Click the button to move forward one interval.
	Steps the animation in reverse one interval at a time. Click the button to move back one interval.
	Steps the animation in reverse one tweak at a time.
	Plays the animation forward for the specified number of repetitions. Before each repetition the view is set back to its starting position.
	Plays the animation for the specified number of repetitions. Each repetition plays start to finish, then in reverse.
	Plays the animation in reverse for the specified number of repetitions. Before each repetition the view is set back to its ending position.
	Pauses the animation playback.
	Records the specified animation to a file so that you can play it back later.
Minimize during record	Minimizes the dialog box while the animation is being recorded. Select the box to minimize the dialog box; clear the check box to leave the dialog box active.

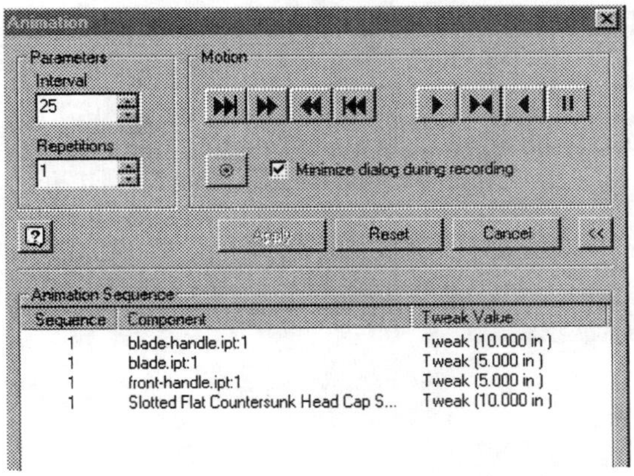

The Animation Sequence located under the More button changes the animation sequence of tweaks. Select the tweak, and then click the button for the desired operation.	
Move Up	Moves the selected tweak up one place in the list.
Move Down	Moves the selected tweak down on place in the list.
Group	Groups the selected tweaks to keep them together as you change the sequence. When tweaks are grouped, the group assumes the sequence order of the lowest tweak number.
Ungroup	Ungroups the selected tweaks so that they can be moved individually in the list. The first tweak in the group assumes a number one higher than the group. The remaining tweaks are numbered sequentially following the first.

TIP: You can pause the animation, stop the record and save it, then start a new recording from the pause point.

Creating a Presentation View

Select 'Create View' from the Tool list.

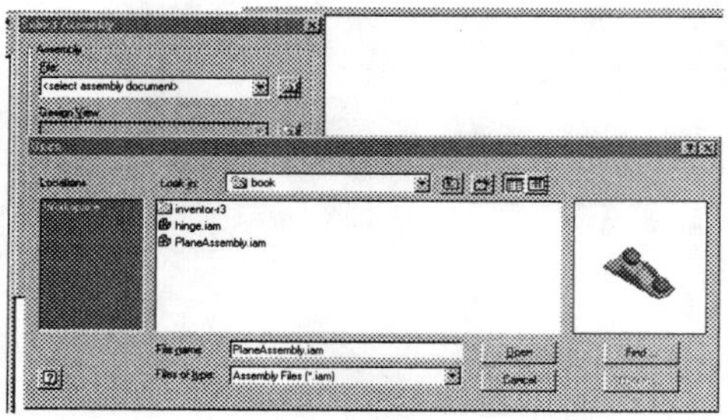

Use the 'Browse' button to locate our assembly file.

NOTE: Inventor will not work properly unless all the files being used are in the proper path. Files need to be located in the directory path workspaces/Project. If they are not located there, either add the correct path using 'Tools' or copy the files over.

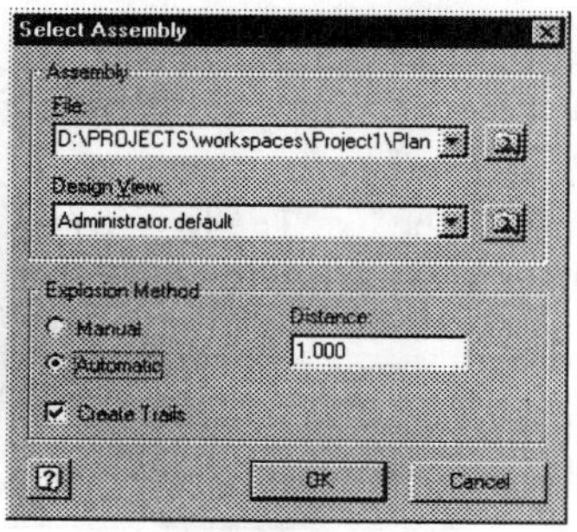

Set the 'Explosion Method' to Automatic. 'Distance' to 1. Enable 'Create Trails' as shown.
Press 'OK'.

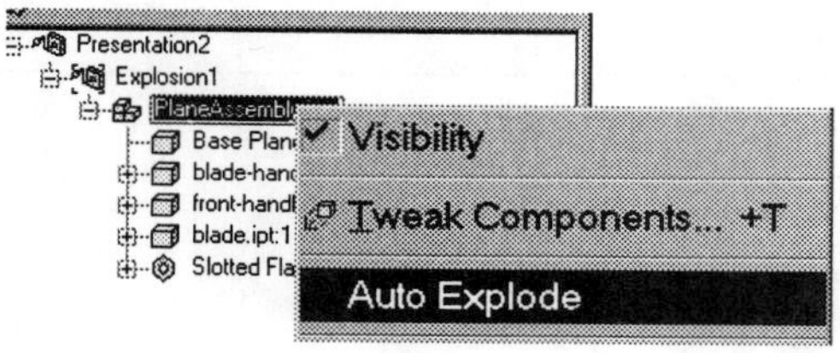

You can add a standard explosion distance to the components in the selected assembly or subassembly.

1. Right-click the assembly name in the browser and select Auto Explode from the menu.
2. In the dialog box, enter the standard tweak distance.
3. To display the trails for the automatic tweaks, make sure that Display Trails is selected.
4. Click the preview button to check the effect of your entries before clicking OK to accept them.

TIP: The specified distance will be added to any existing tweaks in the view.

Adding a Tweak

To add a tweak to a component:

- Highlight it in the Browser, right-click and select 'Tweak Components'
- Select it in the graphics window, right-click and select 'Tweak Components'
- Select the 'Tweak Component' tool and then select the component(s) to tweak
- Type 'T' on the keyboard

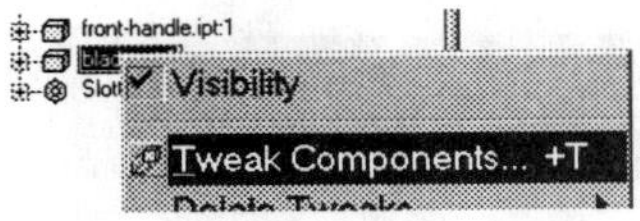

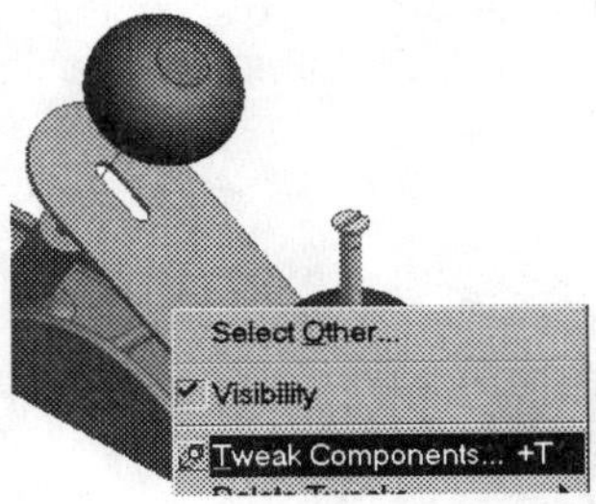

TIP: If a component is selected when you select the Tweak Components', it is automatically included in the components. Click the Clear button to clear the selections.

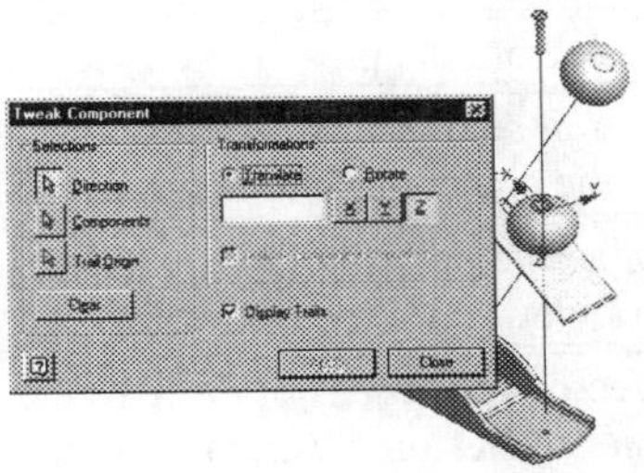

You can add tweaks to a component or group of components in an existing view. Use the Tweak Components button on the Presentation View Management toolbar.

1. Click the Tweak Components button.
2. In the graphics window, click a face, feature, or edge in the view to set the direction triad.
3. Select the components to tweak.
4. Click and drag an arrowhead on the direction vector to create a tweak in the direction of the arrow.
5. When the desired result is previewed in the graphics window, click Apply to implement the changes.

To add other tweaks, click the Clear button to reset the selections and repeat the previous steps.

TIP: You can also enter the tweak distance and set the direction vector using the settings in the dialog box.

Delete a Tweak

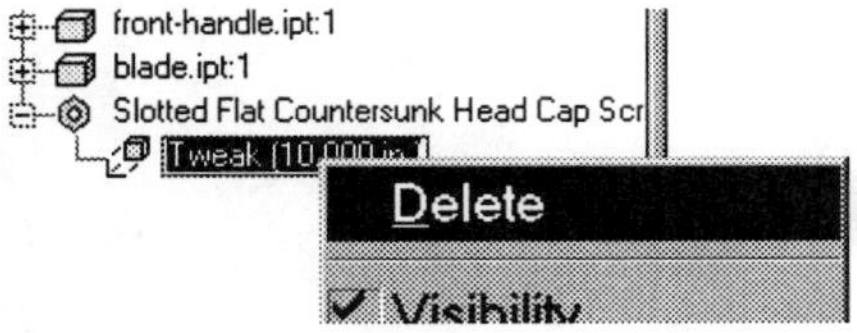

To delete a tweak, expand the browser to show the tweak on the component. Select, right click and select 'Delete'.

Tweak Options

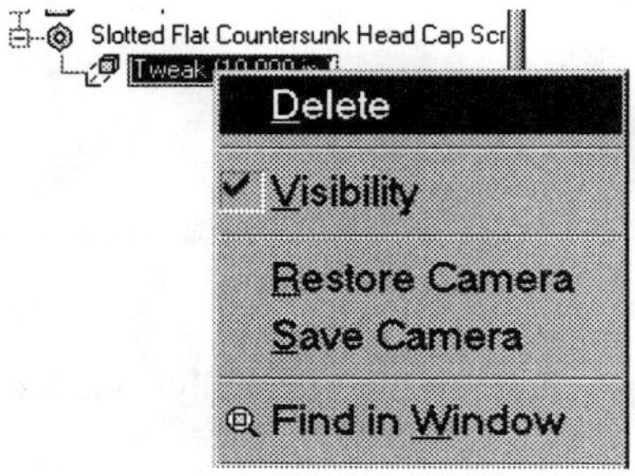

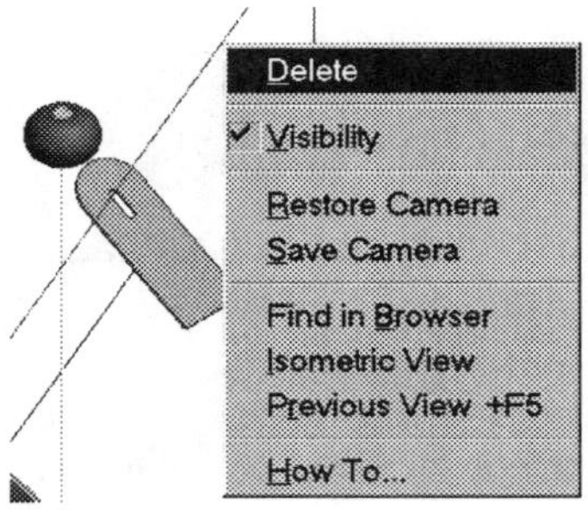

When a tweak is selected, the context menu may contain the following options.

Delete	Deletes the selected tweak from the presentation view.
Visibility	Sets the visibility of the trail segment. Select visibility to display the trail segment in the presentation view; clear the check mark to hide the trail segment.
Restore Camera	Restores the view of the active presentation to the last saved camera view. Available only if you have saved a camera view and then made changes to the view.
Save Camera	Sets the current view (vector and zoom) of the active presentation as the default view. After saving the view, you can use Restore Camera to return to that view at any time.
Find in window	Highlights the selected tweak and zooms the view to center it in the graphics window.

TIP: If the trails for the component are hidden, you cannot display a trail segment by turning on its visibility. Show the trails, then set the visibility of the trail segments.

Modifying a Trail

Trails in an exploded presentation view initially show the path used as components were moved to create the view. When you automatically explode a view, or add manual tweaks for individual components, you can choose whether to show the trails or hide them as the components are tweaked to create the view.

After creating tweaks, you can show or hide trails or move end points or segments of a trail. You can also add trails to existing tweaks to further clarify relationships between components in an exploded view.

You can set the visibility of trails in an exploded view.

- To hide the trails for a component, select the component in the graphics view or browser, right-click, and select Hide Trails.
- To turn off the visibility of an entire trail, select the trail in the graphics window, right-click, and select Visibility to clear the check mark.
- To turn off the visibility of a trail segment, select the tweak in the browser, right-click, and select Visibility to clear the check mark.

After a trail is created you can move its start point and end point. For some multiple segment trails you can also change the trail by moving one or more of its segments Trail segments that can be moved are displayed in a different color than those that are static.

1. In the graphics window, move the cursor over the start point, end point, or trail segment to display the degrees of freedom arrows.
2. Drag the point or trail segment in any of the indicated directions.

Add a Trail

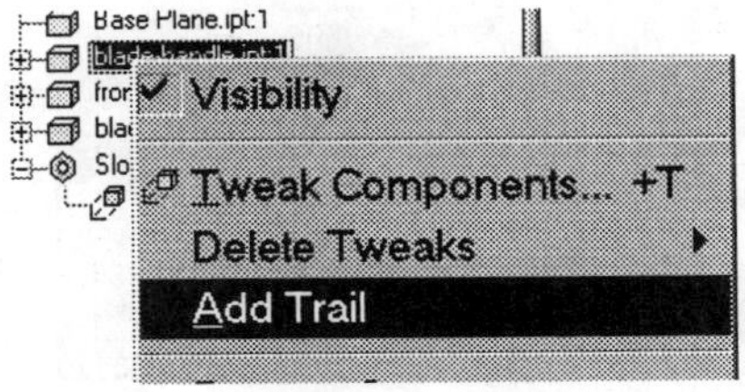

You can add a trail to an existing tweak to clarify relationships between components. For example, you may want to add trails between corresponding features on the components.

1. Select the component in the browser or the graphics window.
2. Right-click and select Add Trail from the menu.
3. Click in the graphics window to set the start point of the trail.
4. Right-click and select Done to place the trail.

TIP: New trails are generated using the values of the tweak. If the original trail has been moved, the trails may not match.

Changing a trail does not change the path of the tweak.

Copying an Exploded View

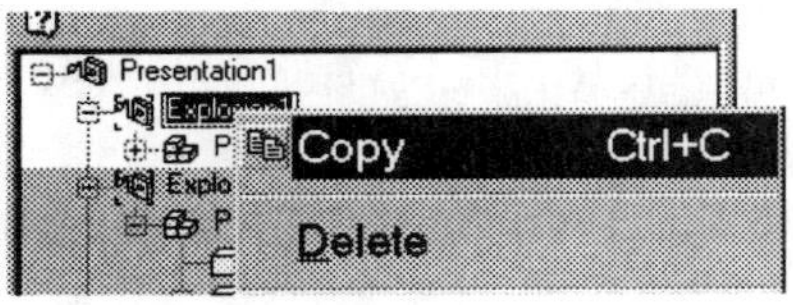

To copy an exploded view, highlight it in the browser, right click and select 'Copy'.

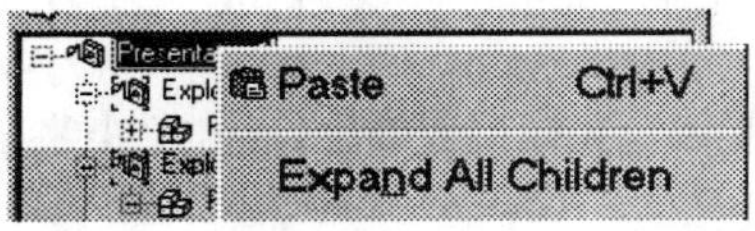

To paste it to the same presentation file, select the top of the browser list where it says Presentation, right click and select 'Paste'. We can now modify the copy to create a different version of the exploded view.

Creating an Animation

1. Select the 'Animate' tool under Presentation View Manager.

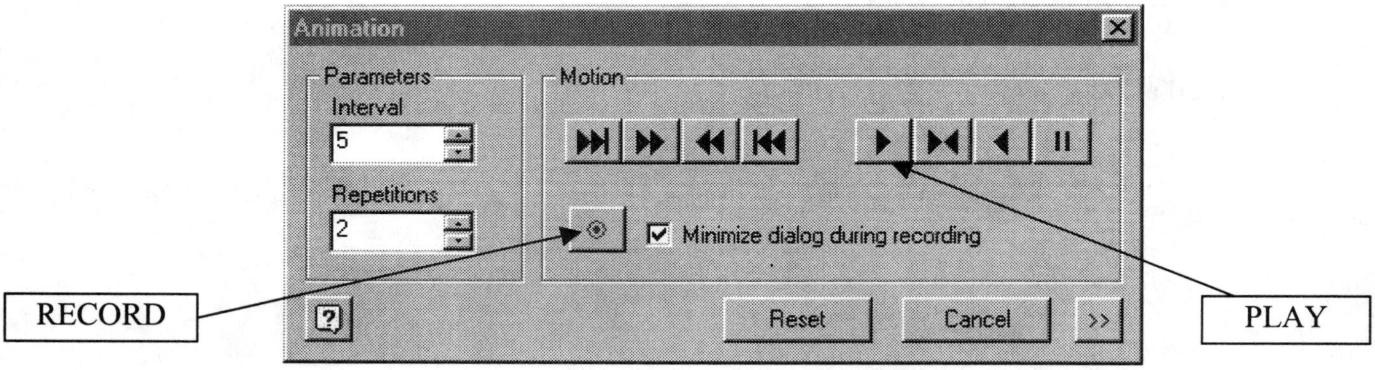

2. The Animation dialog box comes up. Set the Interval to 5 and the Repetitions to 2. Make sure the Minimize dialog is enabled. Press the 'Play' button.

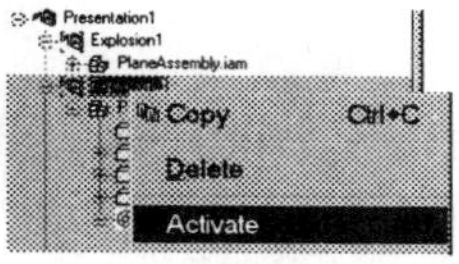

3. To restore the assembly to an exploded view, highlight the desired view, right click and select 'Activate'. Verify that the exploded view appears the way you want.

4. Press the Record button.

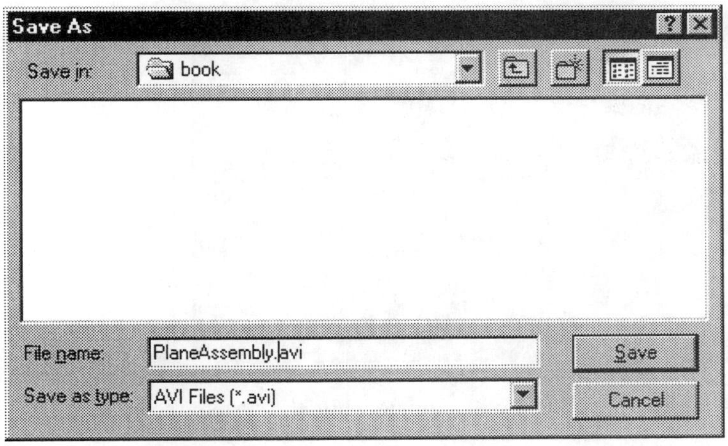

5. A dialog box comes up asking for the location and file name for the avi. Set the file name to PlaneAssembly.

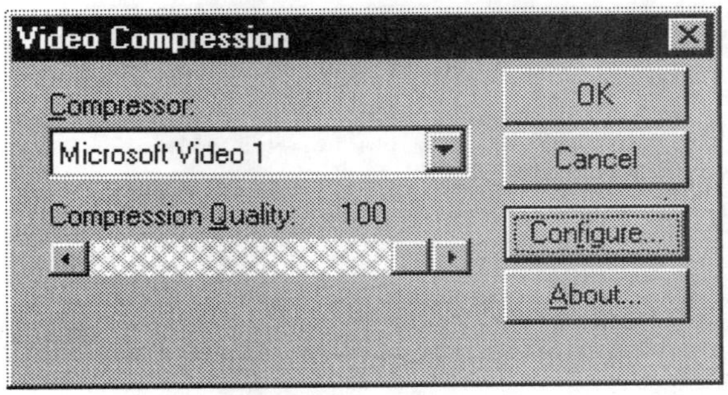

7. The Video Compression dialog box comes up. Set it to Microsoft Video 1 to make the file Microsoft compatible. Set the Compression Quality to 100.

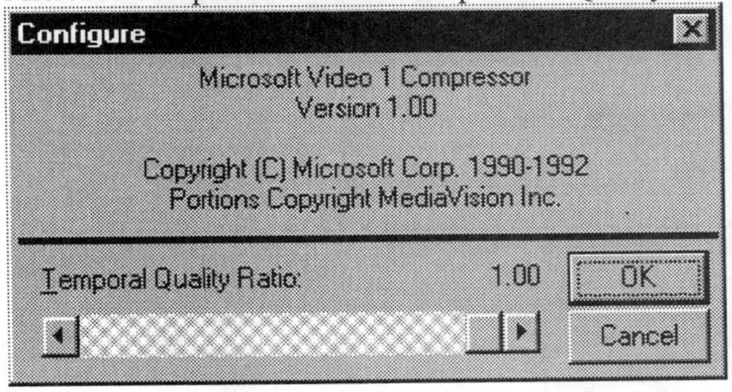

Press 'OK' twice to close all the dialog boxes.

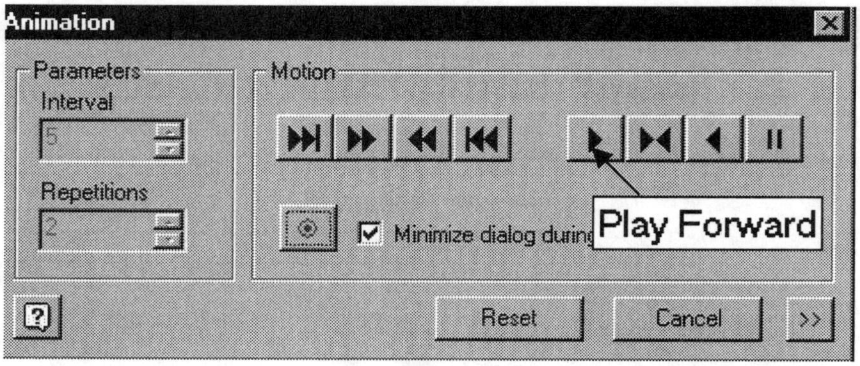

8. Press the 'Play Forward' button. The model will animate while the system records the avi.

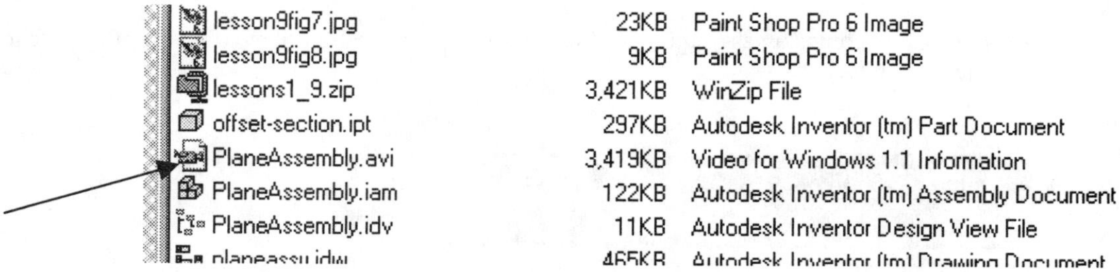

9. Use Windows Explorer to locate the avi file we just created.

10. Double click on the file to play it.

We have created an animation that can be loaded to a website or shown to a client.

Save our file as 'Explode1.ipn'.

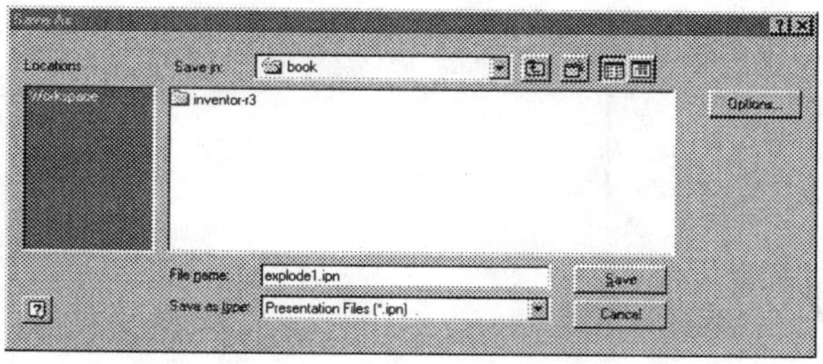

Presentation Tools

Button	Tool	Function
	Create Presentation View	Creates a new presentation view of an assembly
	Tweak Component	Moves components to create exploded views.
	Precise View Rotation	Rotates the view vector around the X/Y/Z axis in increments
	Animate	Animates the tweaks. Creates avi files.

Review Questions

1. True or False

Presentation files are used to create exploded views for drawing files.

2. True or False

Presentation files are used to create animation files.

3. True or False

A presentation files can contain more than one exploded view.

4. True or False

You can use the Visibility option to turn off the visibility of parts to develop a series of views to illustrate assembly instructions.

5. True or False

All measurements in a presentation file assume the default units used in the part or assembly file.

6. True or False

To create an exploded view, the user must manually move each component into position.

7. True or False

When creating an exploded view, trails can not be added automatically.

8. True or False

If you modify a copy of an exploded view, the source view will also change.

9. A tweak is:

   A. When you modify a component's size
   B. When you modify a component's location in an exploded view
   C. When you draw a line between components in an exploded view
   D. When you rotate an entire assembly

10. The Precise View Rotation

   A. Adds a rotation tweak
   B. Rotates an entire assembly
   C. Rotates only selected components
   D. Rotates the active view

ANSWERS: 1) T; 2) T; 3) T; 4) T; 5) T; 6) F; 7) F; 8) F; 9) B; 10) D

Lesson 29

Assembly Drawings

Learning Objective

At the conclusion of this lesson, the user will gain further mastery of:

- Balloons
- Parts Lists
- Exploded Assembly Views

To create an Exploded Assembly Drawing, follow these steps:

- Open a Drawing
- Create Views using a Presentation File
- Add Balloons
- Add Parts List

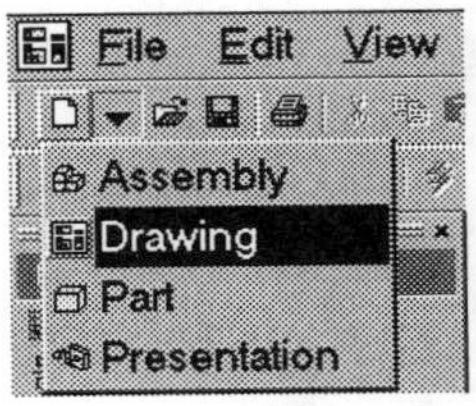

We start by opening a new Drawing file.

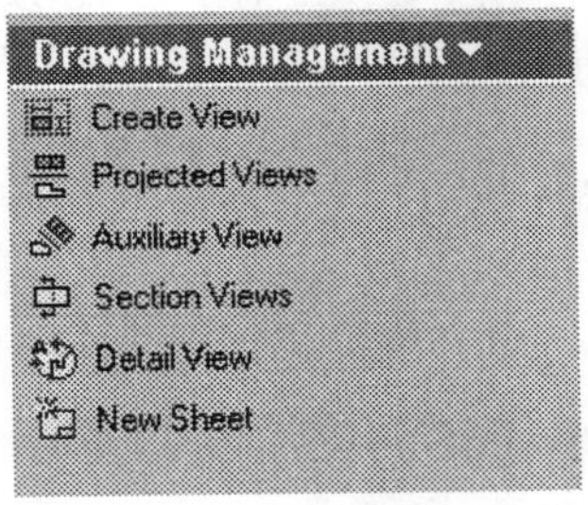

Select the Create View tool.

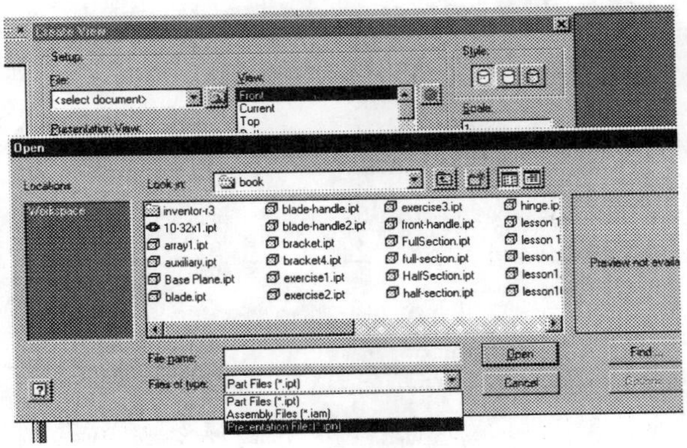

Select the browse button in the first window. Set the files of type to Presentation files.

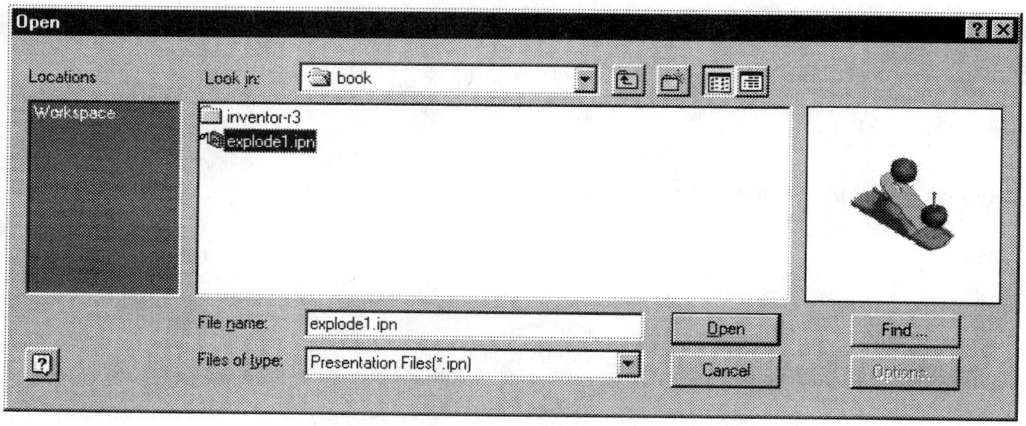

Locate the file called 'PlaneAssy.ipn'. This is the file that was created in Lesson 28.

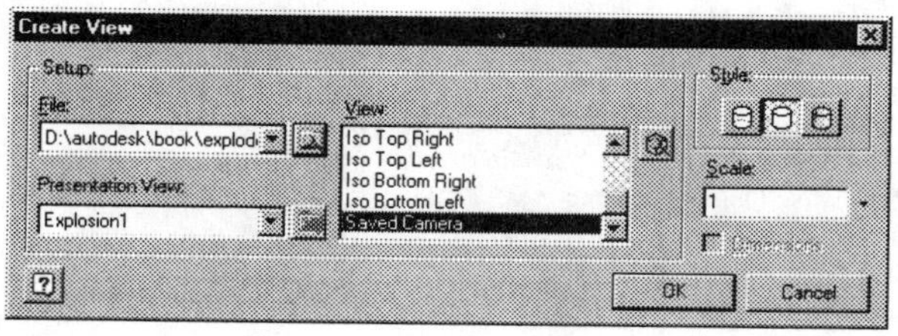

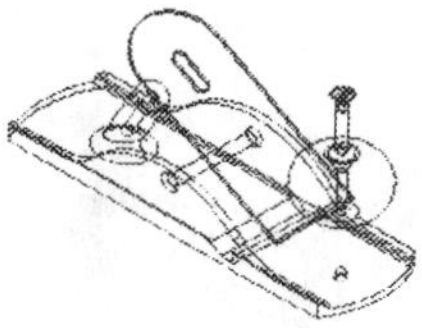

Select the Saved Camera View and place the view on the sheet.

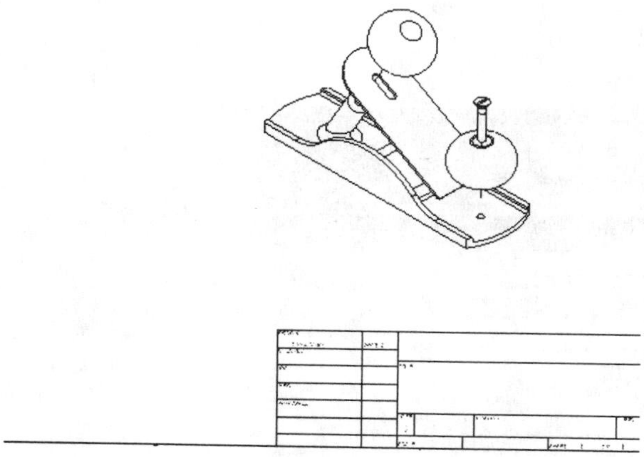

Select ' Create View' again to create a front view.

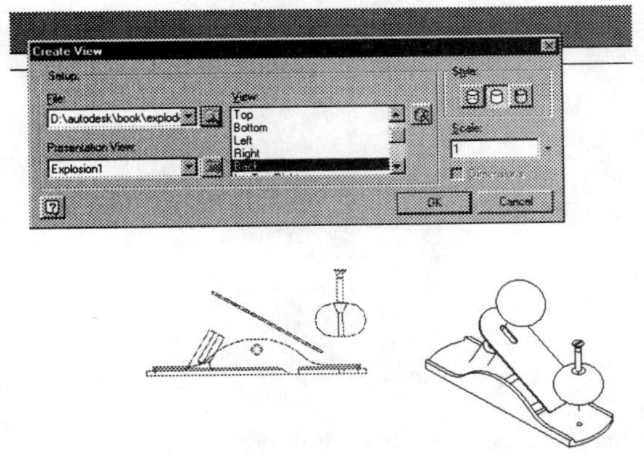

We locate the explode1.ipn file once again and select the Back View. We then place the view in our sheet as shown.

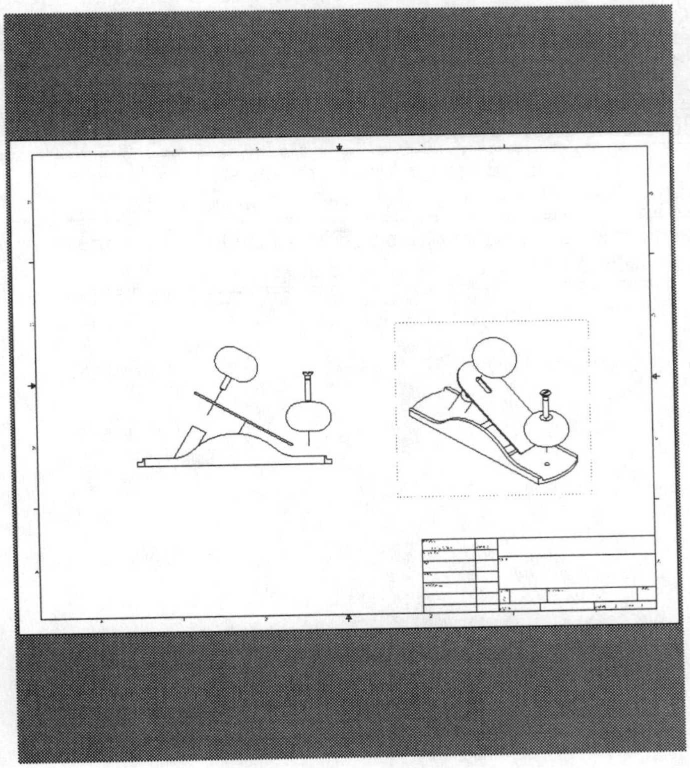

Trail Properties

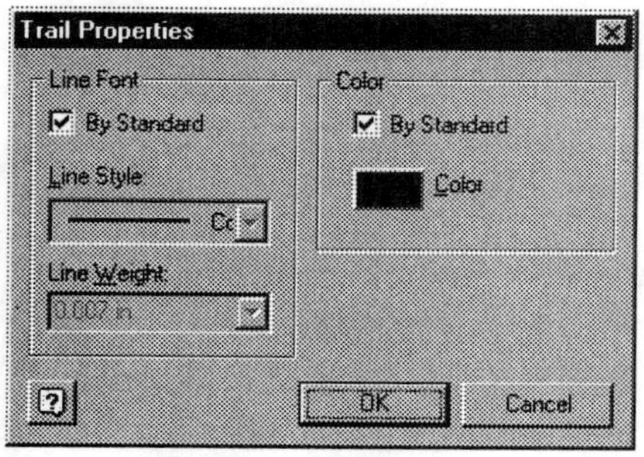

Trail Properties changes the line style, line weight, and color for selected trails in drawing views.

Line Font sets the line style and weight for the selected edge.	
By Standard	Sets the line style and weight to conform to the active drafting standard. Select the check box to set the line to the drafting standard; clear the check box to change the line style and weight.
Line Style	This option is not available if By Standard is selected. Changes the line style of the selected line. Click the arrow and select from the list.
Line Weight	This option is not available if By Standard is selected. Changes the thickness of the selected line. Click the arrow and select from the list.
Color sets the line color for the selected edge.	
By Standard	Sets the line color to conform to the active drafting standard. Select the check box to set the line to the drafting standard, clear the check box to change the line color.
Color	This option is not available if By Standard is selected. Changes the color of the selected line. Click the arrow and select from the Color dialog box.

Modifying Trails

In our drawing views, we notice that the trails are solid lines. Many users prefer trails to be a specific color and linetype.

To modify the trails, zoom in using Zoom Window and select the trail(s) we wish to modify. To select more than one trail, hold down the control key.

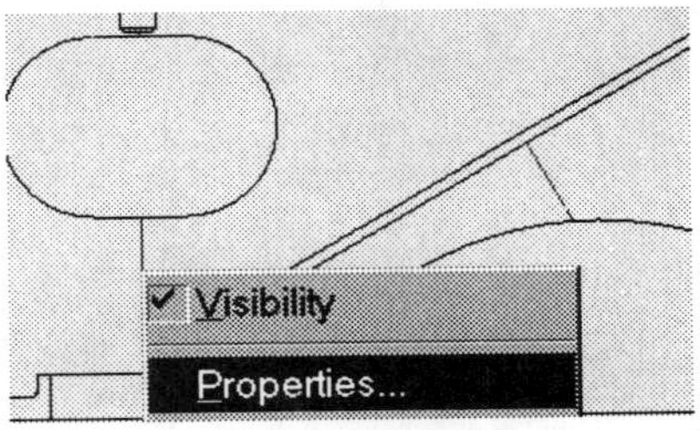

Right click and select 'Properties'.

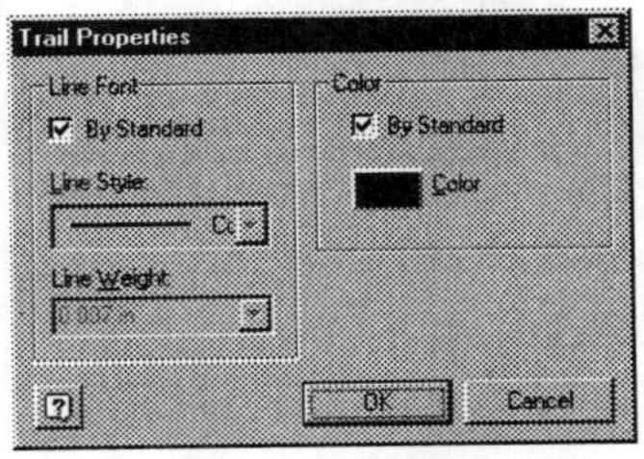

Disable By Standard for the Line Font and Color.

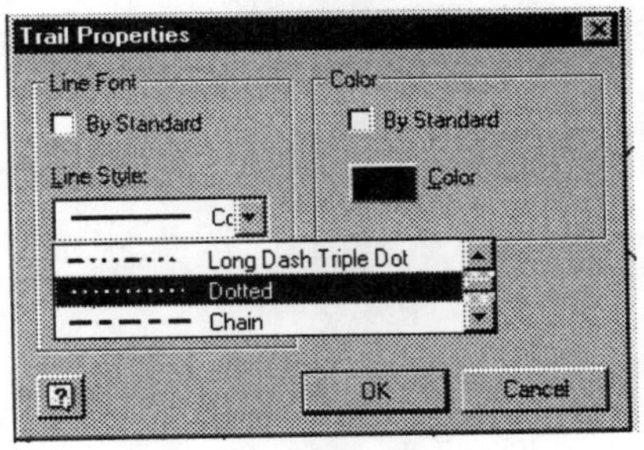

Using the pull down menu, locate and select 'Dotted' for the line style.

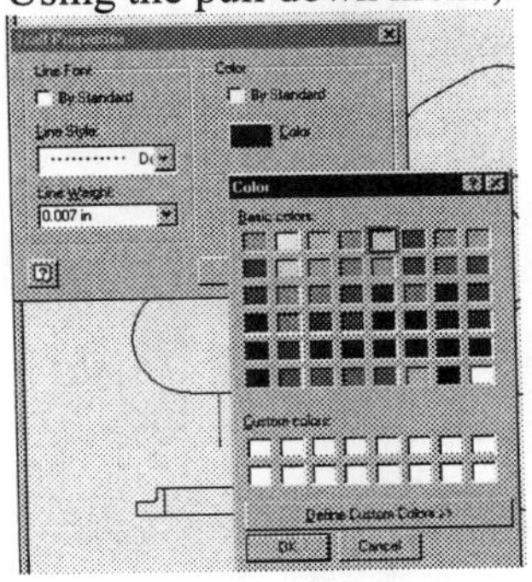

Press the Color button and select Cyan for the color.

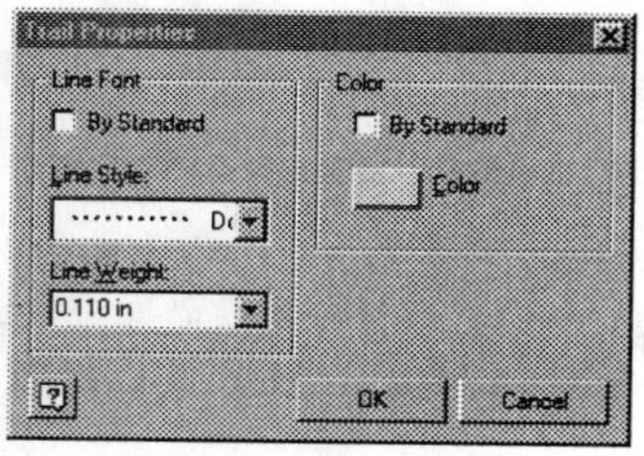

Change the Line Weight to 0.110.

Press ‘OK’.

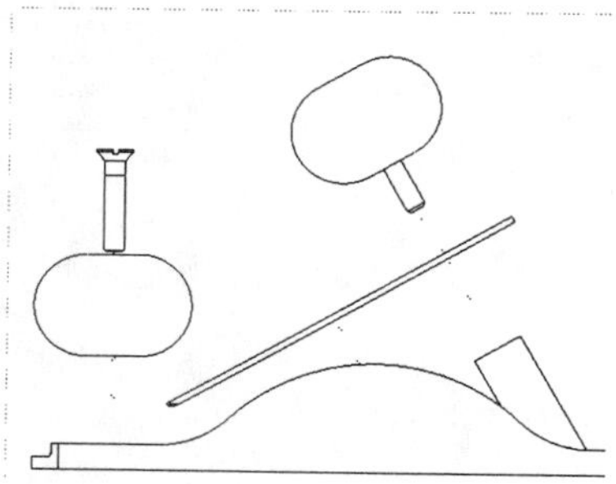

Note how the trails have changed.

Drawing Annotation Toolbar

Activate the Drawing Annotation toolbar.

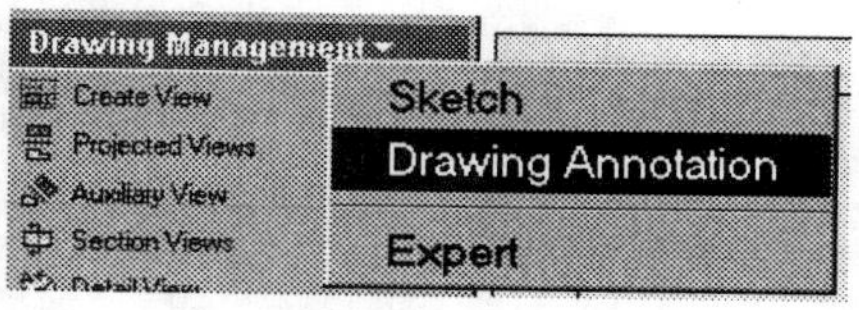

Right click anywhere inside the Drawing Management panel toolbar and select ‘Drawing Annotation’.

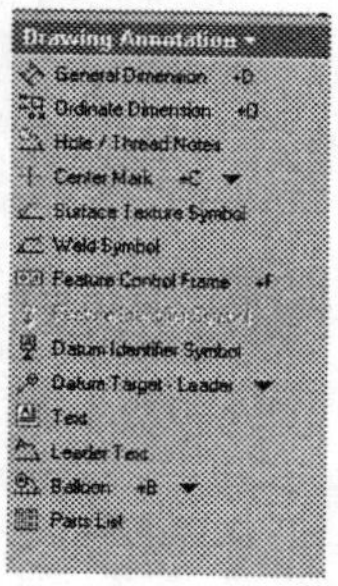

A Drawing Annotation toolbar will appear to replace the Drawing Management toolbar.

At the bottom of the menu we see ‘Balloon’ and ‘Parts List’.

Add Balloons

Click on the 'Balloon' button drop down arrow. There are two selections: placing individual balloons and Balloon All. Select 'Balloon All' and then select the Front Exploded View.

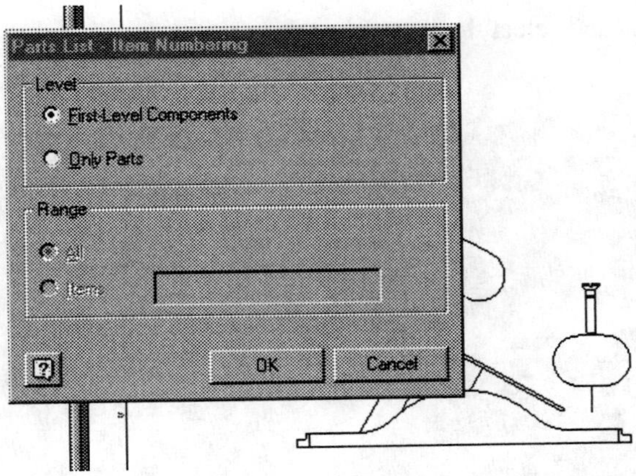

A dialog box appears allowing the user to select First-Level Components or Only Parts. Enable First-Level Components and select 'OK'.

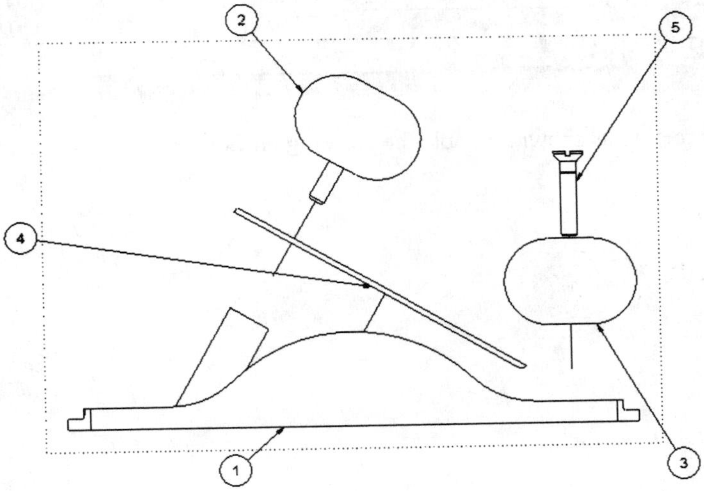

The balloons are automatically placed in the view. To move a balloon pick on it, hold down the green dot with the left mouse and place the balloon in the desired position.

TIP: The way the balloon looks is set in Drafting Standards. To modify the balloon appearance, go to Format->Standards. Balloon colors can be set under the Common tab under Symbol.

Go to Format->Standards and select the Parts List tab.

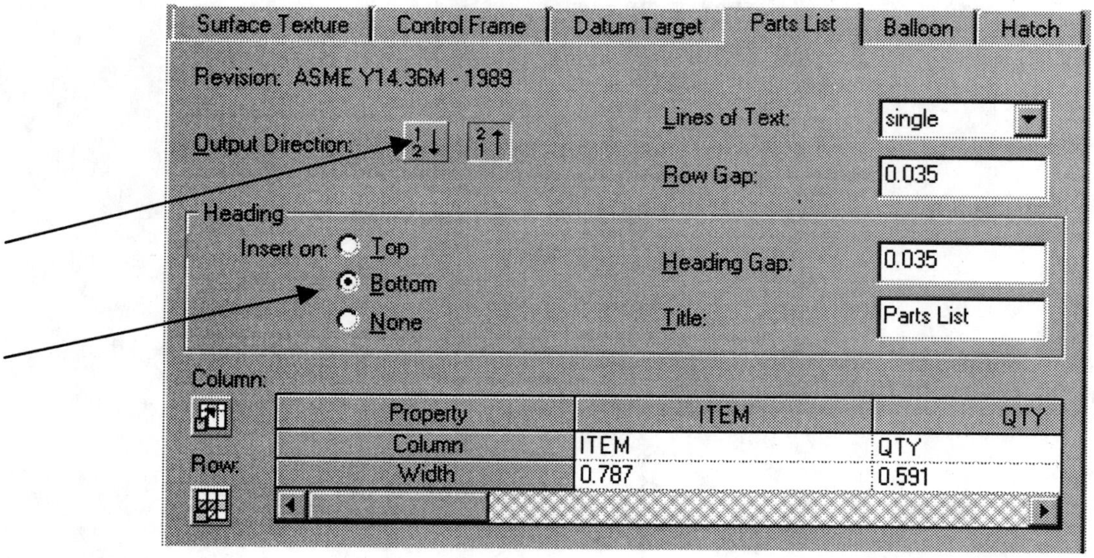

Set the Output Direction as shown. Enable the Heading on Bottom.

Insert Parts List

To create the Bill of Materials, press down the 'Parts List' tool then select the exploded view where the balloons were just placed.

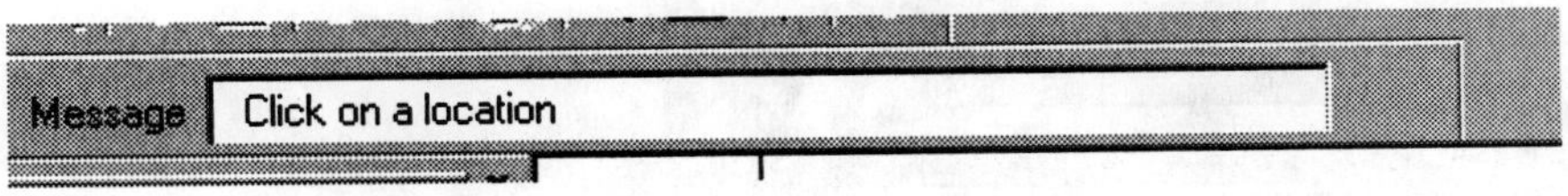

In the Message box, we see a prompt telling us to select a location for our Parts List. Place the Parts list in the lower left corner of the drawing.

5	1	ANSI B18.6.2 - No. 10 - 32 x 1	Slotted Flat Countersunk Head Cap Screw
4	1	blade	
3	1	front-handle	
2	1	blade-handle	
1	1	Base Plane	
ITEM	QTY	PART NUMBER	DESCRIPTION
Parts List			

The Part Number and Description information is taken from the Properties dialog for each file.

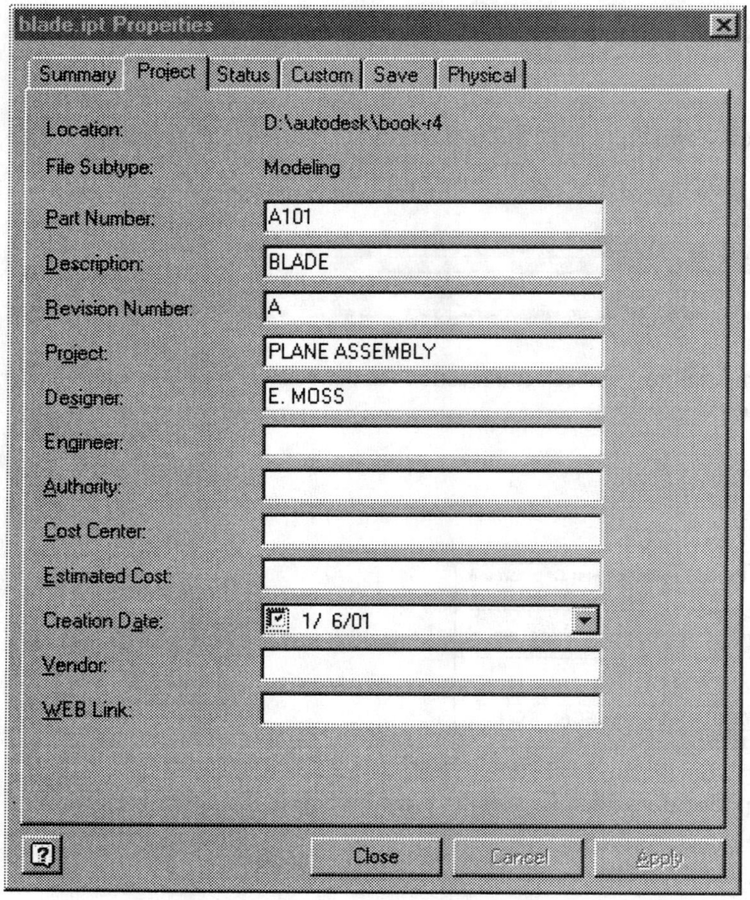

We should go back to each of our files and update the Properties so that our Parts List is automated.

Or we can edit the Parts List.

Edit Parts List

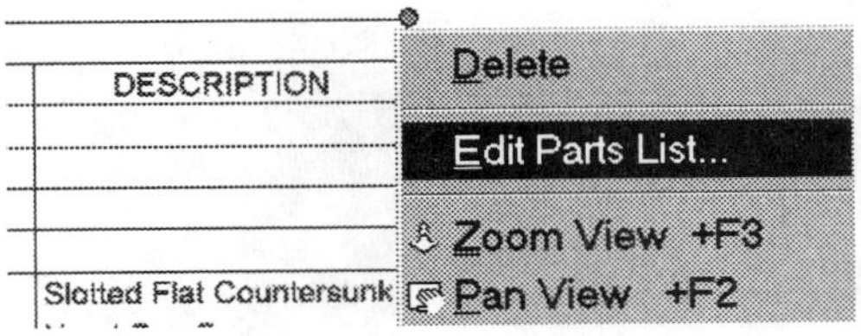

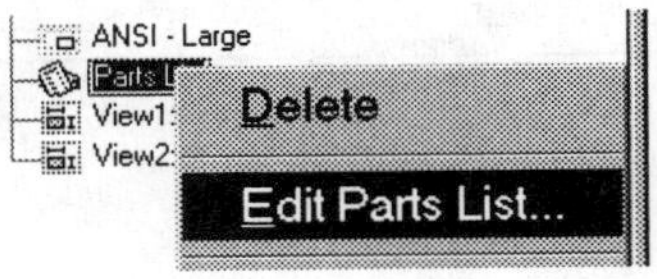

To edit the parts list, the user can:

- Select the Parts List in the drawing window, Right Click and select the 'Edit Parts List' option.
- Select the parts list in the browser, Right Click and select the 'Edit Parts List' option.

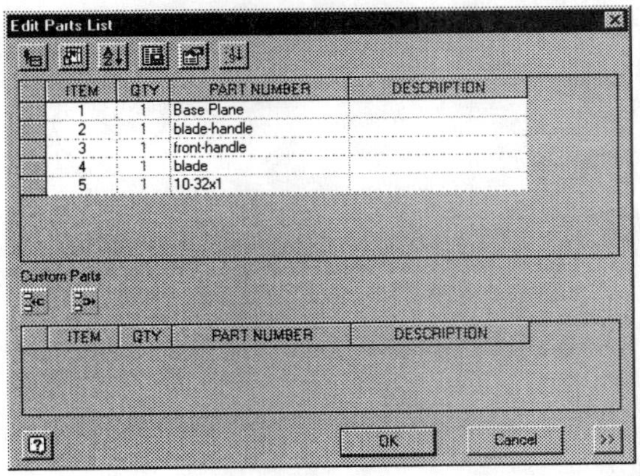

The Edit Parts List Dialog comes up.

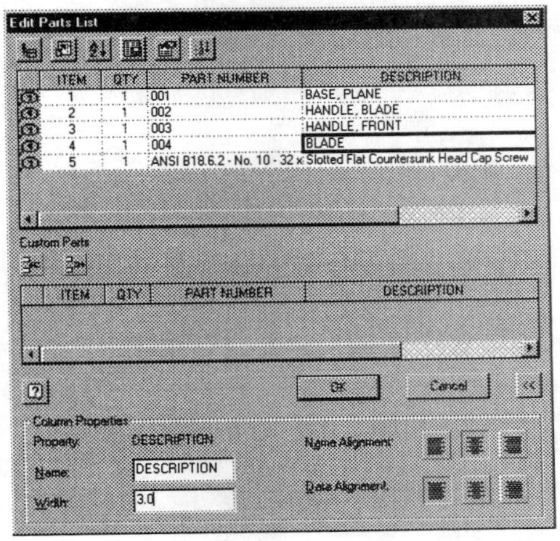

Modify the Parts List as shown. Set the width for the Description Field to 3.5
Press 'OK' to exit the Edit Parts List dialog box.

ITEM	QTY	PART NUMBER	DESCRIPTION
5	1	ANSI B18.6.2 - No. 10 - 32 x 1	Slotted Flat Countersunk Head Cap Screw
4	1	004	BLADE
3	1	003	HANDLE, FRONT
2	1	002	HANDLE, BLADE
1	1	001	BASE, PLANE

Parts List

Our updated Parts List appears.

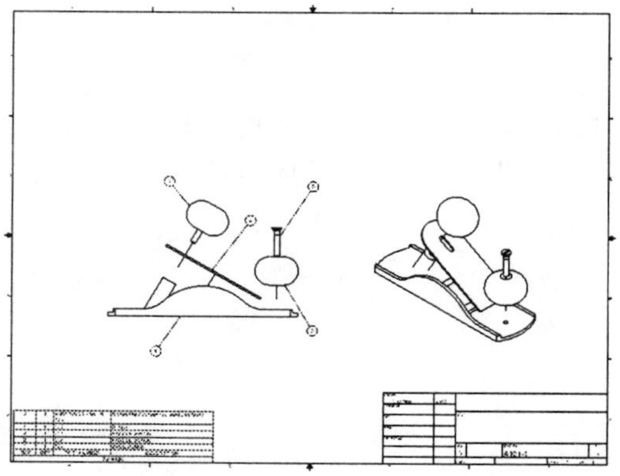

Our assembly drawing.

Save the drawing as PlaneAssembly.idw.

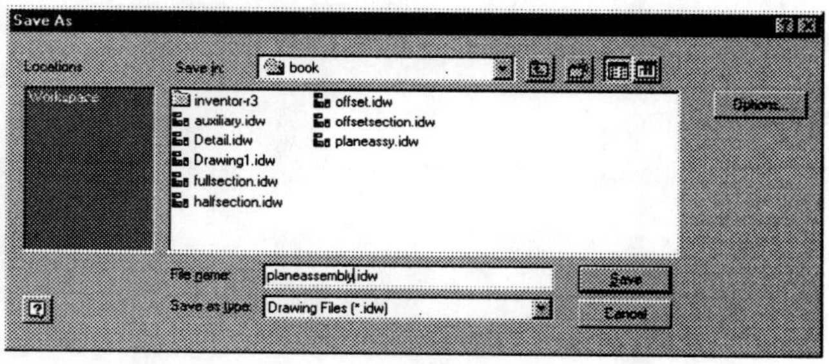

Review Questions

1. Assembly drawings use exploded views. The exploded views are created in:

    A. Assembly files
    B. Part files
    C. Presentation files
    D. Drawing files

2. To change the appearance of Trails:

    A. Select the trail, right click and select 'Properties'
    B. Use the Modify Trail tool
    C. Go to Format->Standards->Color
    D. Go to Tools->Options->Presentation

3. To select more than one trail at a time to modify, hold down this key:

    A. Shift
    B. Tab
    C. Control
    D. Space

4. To activate the Drawing Annotation toolbar in the Panel Bar:

    A. Go to View->Toolbars
    B. Right click in the Panel Bar area
    C. Right Click in the Graphics window
    D. Right Click in the browser

5. To change the format of a Parts List:

    A. Select the Parts List in the browser or graphics window, right click and select 'Properties'
    B. Go to Format->Standards->Parts List
    C. Go to Tools->Options->Parts List
    D. Go to File->Properties

ANSWERS: 1) C; 2) A; 3) C; 4) B; 5) B

NOTES:

Exercise 1: Plate

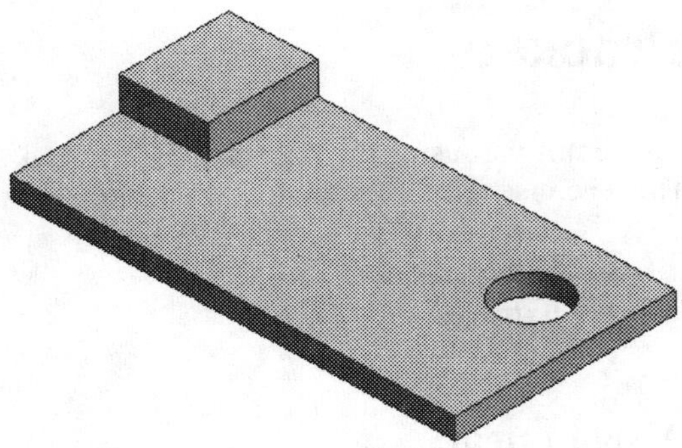

Create this part using the information provided. This exercise reinforces the following skills:

- Sketching
- Extrudes
- Cuts

Design Intent:

- The part is not symmetrical.
- The cut hole is a through hole.
- This is a metric part.

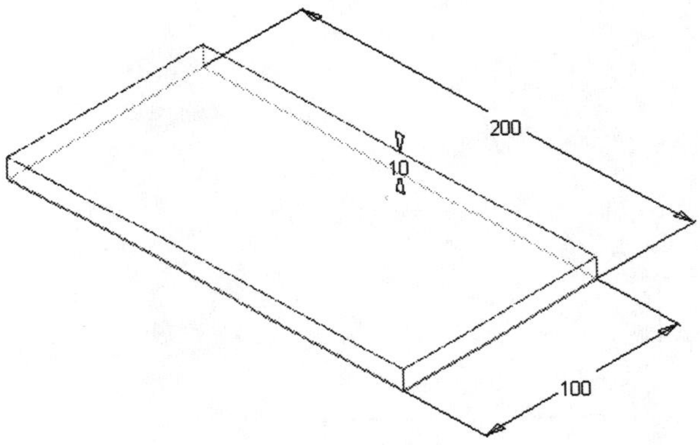

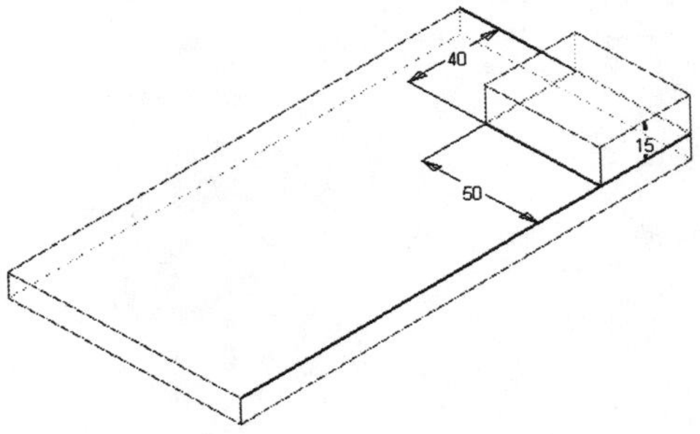

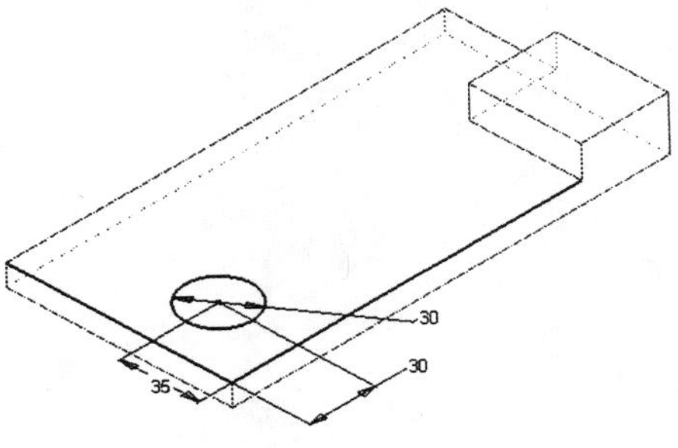

Exercise 2:

Bracket

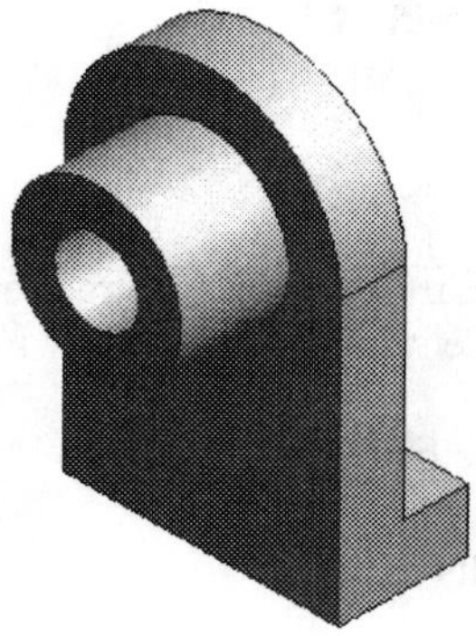

Create this part using the information provided.
This exercise reinforces the following skills:

- Sketching
- Extrudes
- Cuts

Design Intent:

- The part is symmetrical.
- The cut hole is a through hole and is concentric to the boss
- This is a metric part.

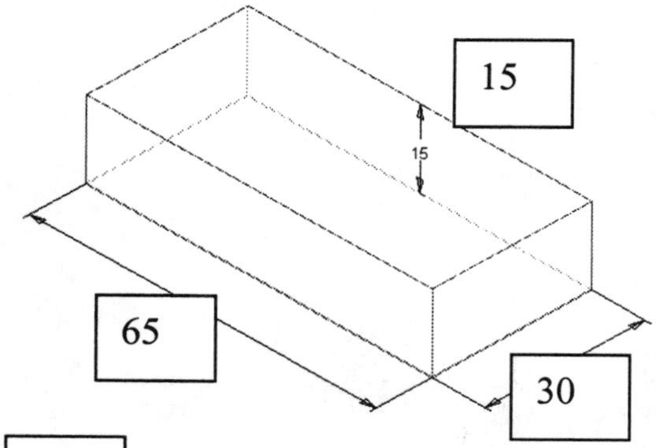

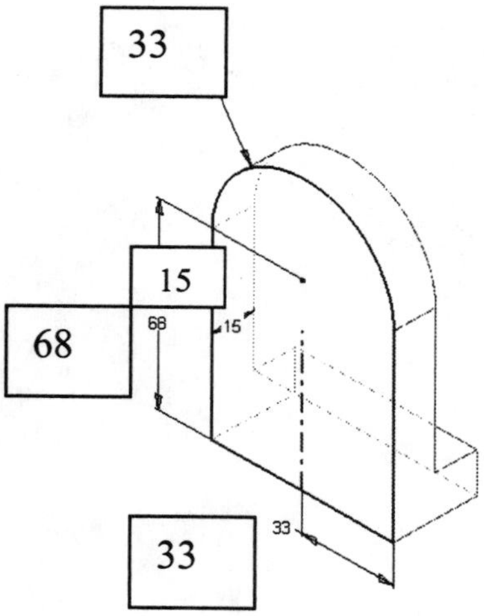

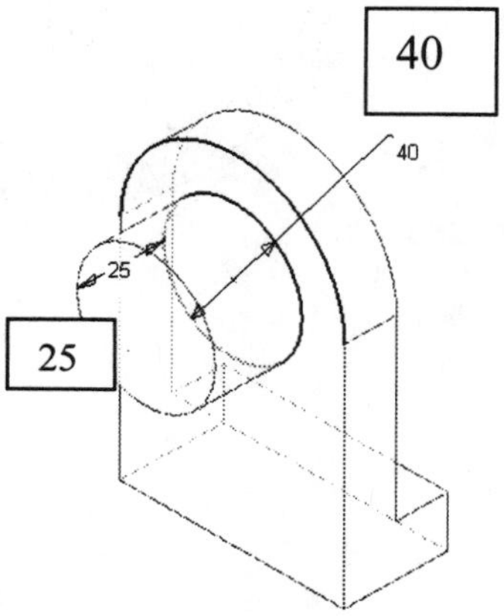

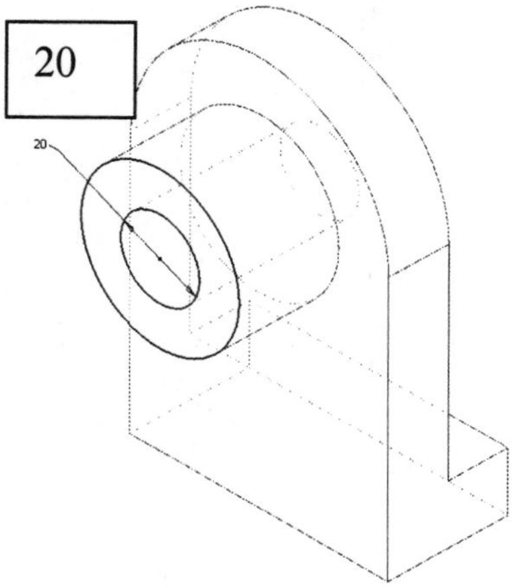

Exercise 3:

Flange

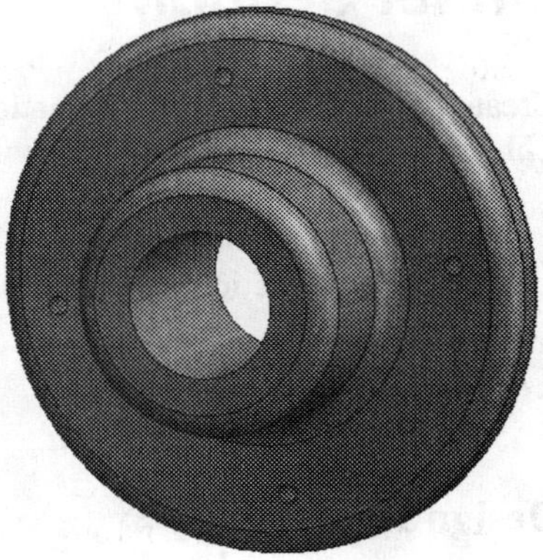

Create this part using the information provided.
This exercise reinforces the following skills:

- Revolves
- Circular Patterns
- Holes

Design Intent:

- The part is symmetrical.
- The four holes are ¼-20 patterned on a 4.25 diameter.
- Holes are tapped through, ANSI, Right Hand
- This is a standard part.
- All fillets are equal and are R.25 in.

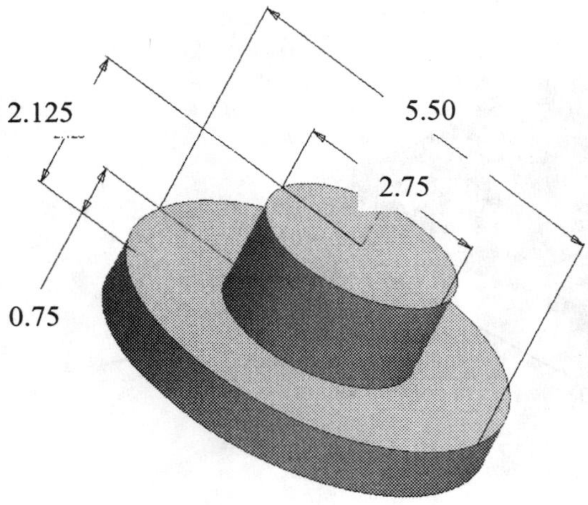

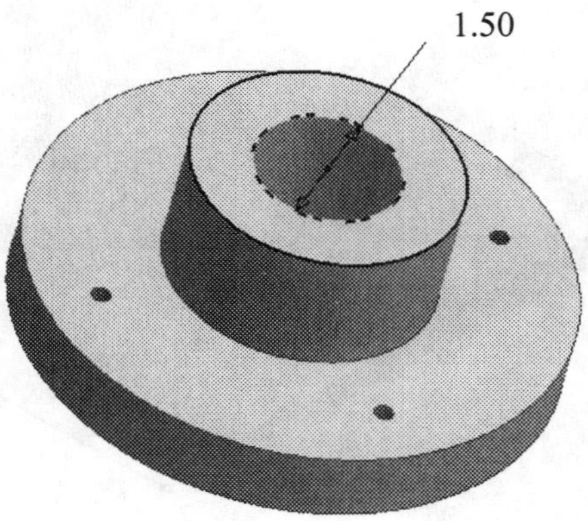

When creating a drawing, create a full section view.

Exercise 4:

Offset Section

Create this part using the information provided.
This exercise reinforces the following skills:

- Copy Sketch
- Offset Section
- Holes
- Cutaway view
- Sketch Doctor

Design Intent:

- The part is NOT symmetrical.
- The vertical holes are through all.
- This is a metric part.
- All fillets are equal and are 3 mm.

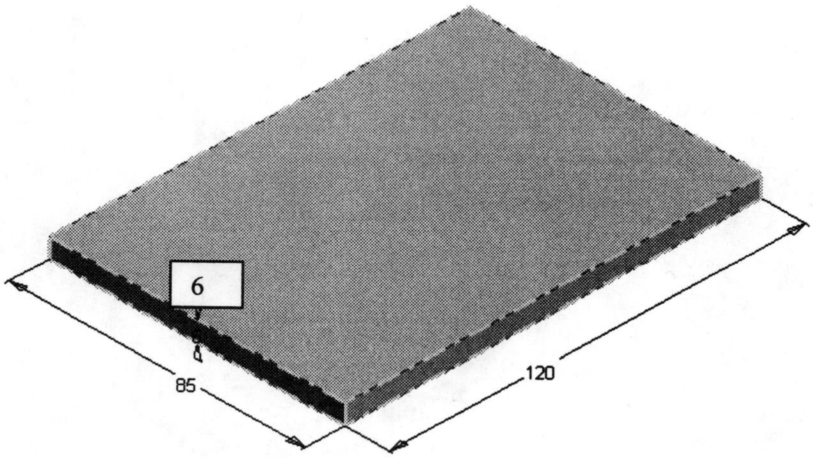

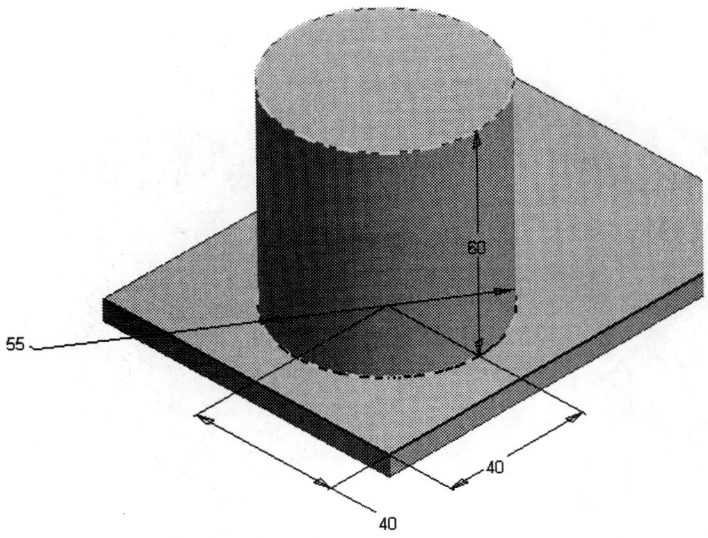
60
55
40
40

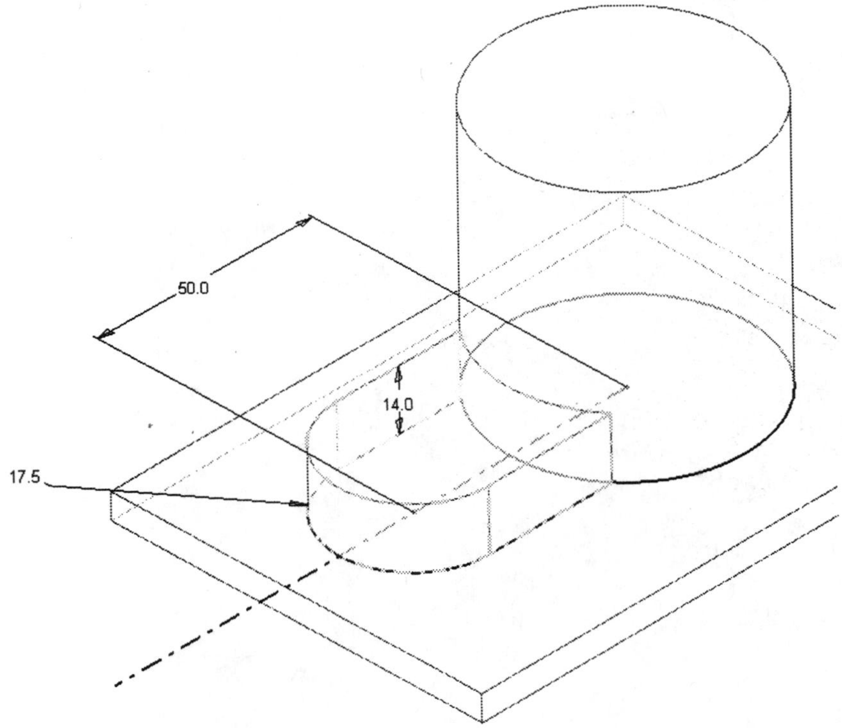
50.0
14.0
17.5

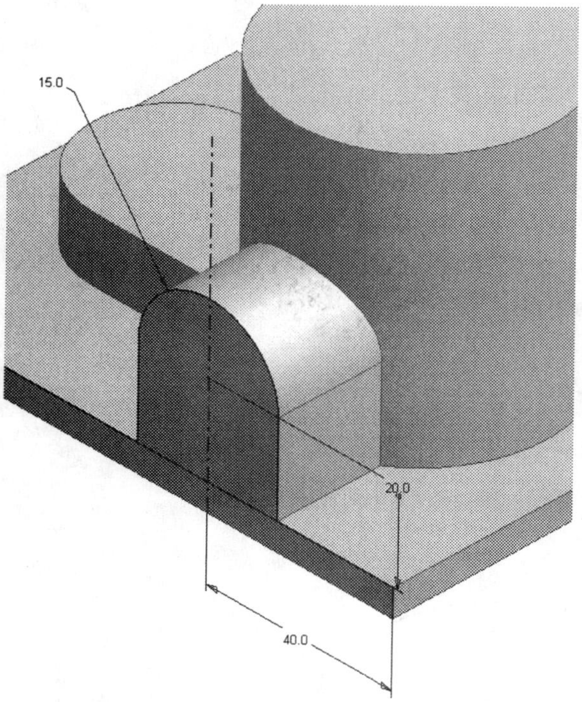
15.0
20.0
40.0

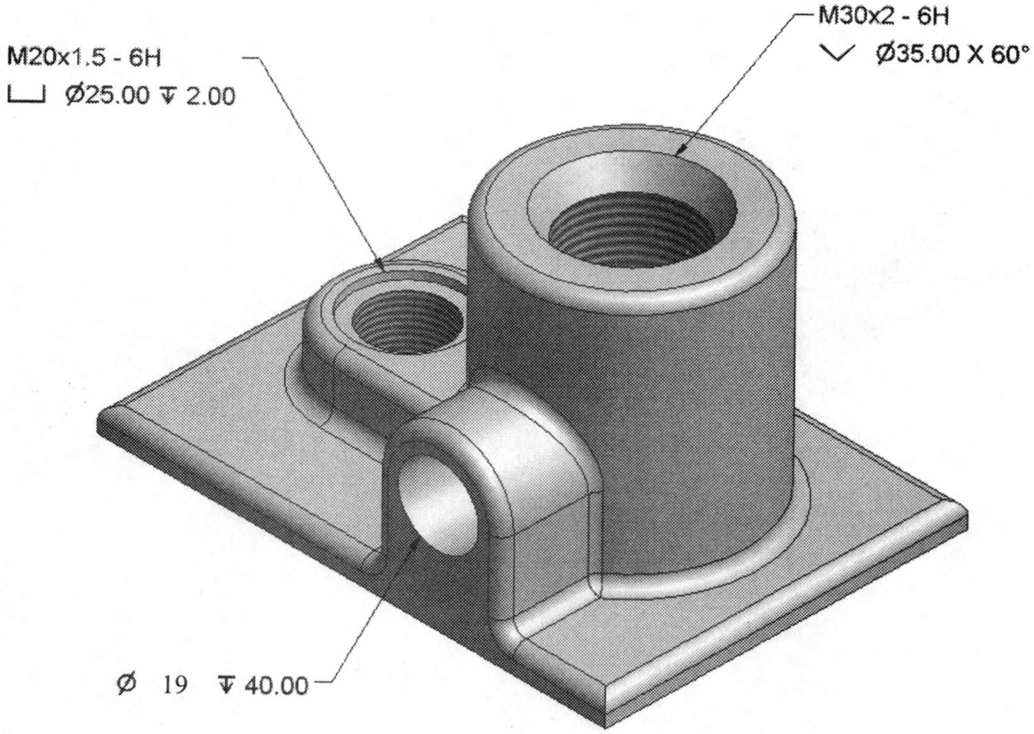
M30x2 - 6H
⌵ Ø35.00 X 60°
M20x1.5 - 6H
⌴ Ø25.00 ↧ 2.00
Ø 19 ↧ 40.00

Exercise 5:

Sweep Bracket

Create this part using the information provided.
This exercise reinforces the following skills:

- Sweep
- Rectangular Pattern
- Circular Pattern
- Holes
- Design Catalog
- Create Work Plane

Design Intent:

- The part is NOT symmetrical.
- The vertical holes are through all.
- This is a standard part.
- All fillets are equal and are 0.125 in.
- The counterbore holes have a counterbore diameter of 1.0, a through diameter of .640 and a counterbore depth of .641

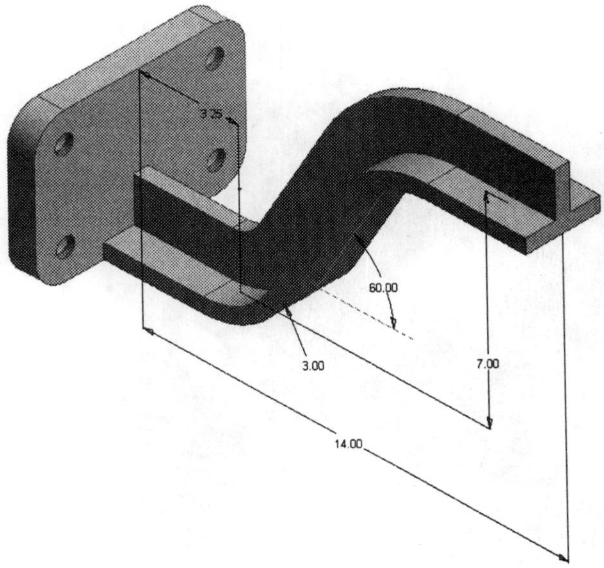

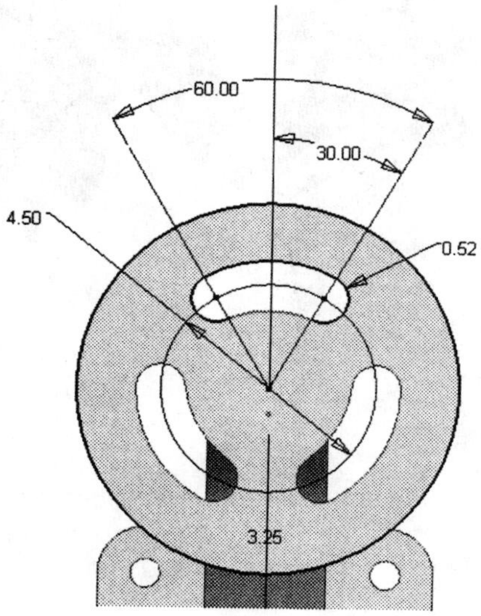
60.00
30.00
4.50
0.52
3.25

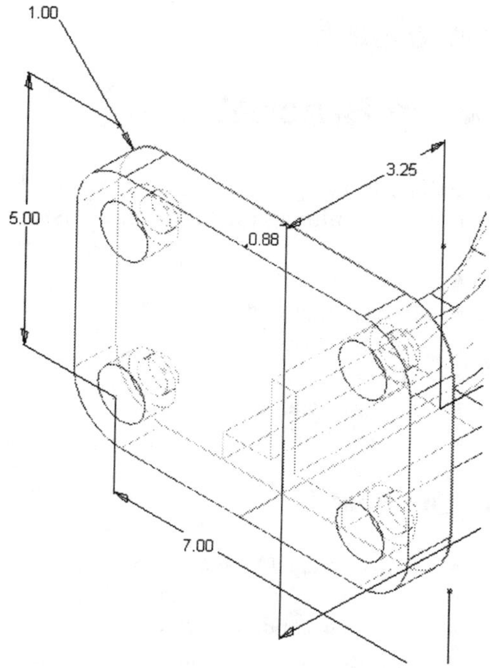
1.00
3.25
5.00
0.88
7.00

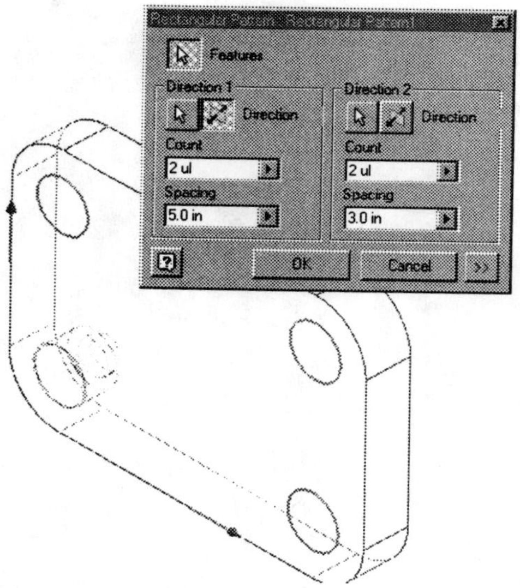
Features
Direction 1
Direction
Count
2 ul
Spacing
5.0 in
Direction 2
Direction
Count
2 ul
Spacing
3.0 in
OK
Cancel
>>

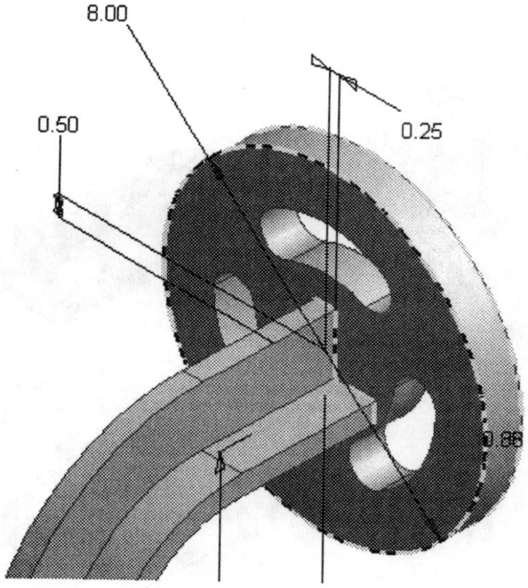
8.00
0.50
0.25

Exercise 6:

Sheet Metal Bends

Create this part using the information provided.
This exercise reinforces the following skills:

- Sheet Metal
- Chamfers
- Flanges
- Cut
- Hole

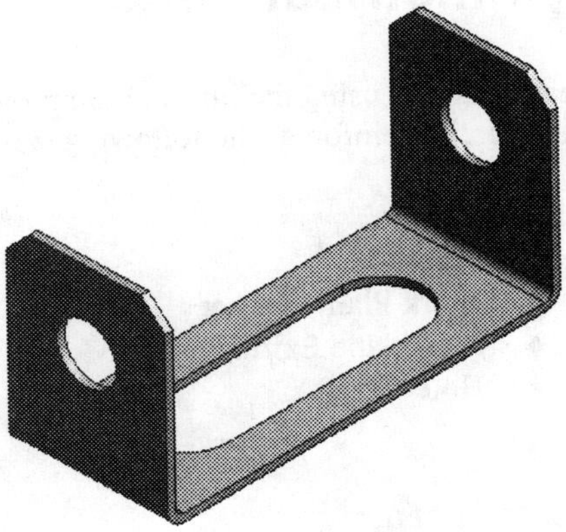

Design Intent:

- The part is symmetrical.
- All holes are diameter are 15 mm and through all.
- All chamfers are Distance 5 mm and Angle 45 degrees
- This is a metric part.
- Material thickness is constant 2 mm
- Bend radius is 2 mm

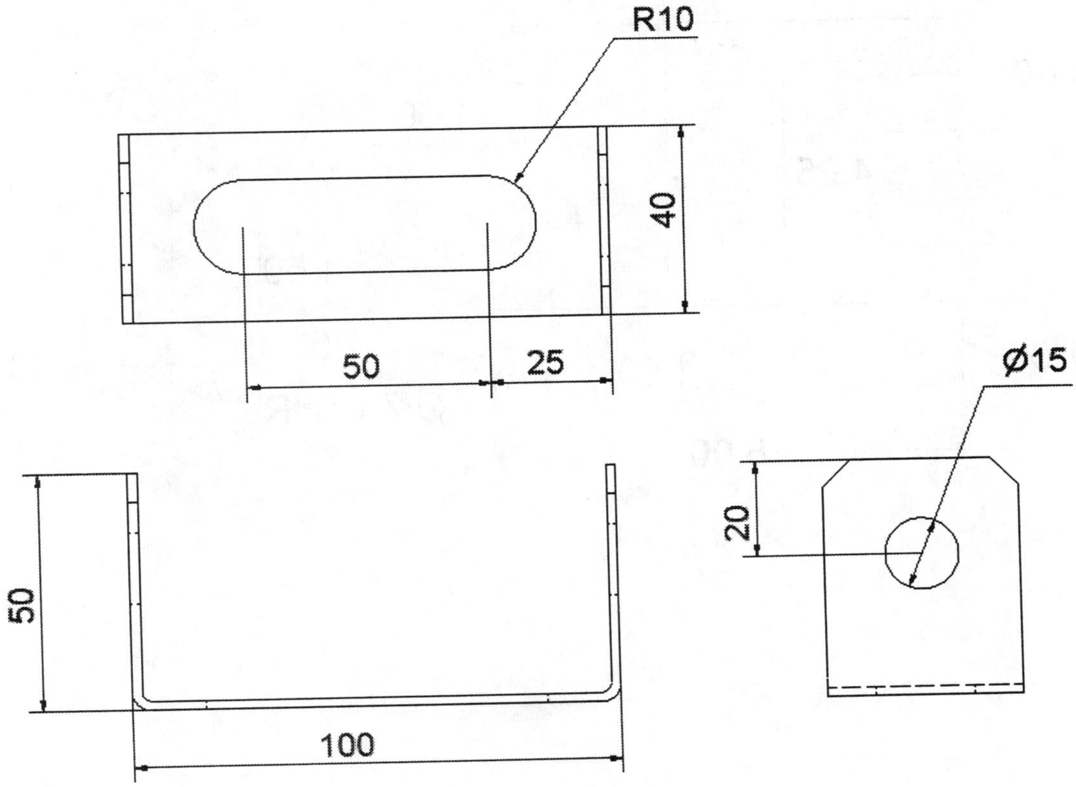

Exercise 7:

Symmetrical Plate

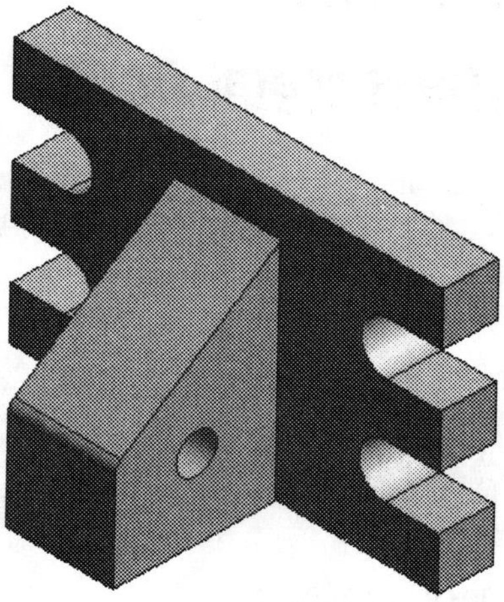

Create this part using the information provided.
This exercise reinforces the following skills:

- Mirror
- Fillet
- Work Plane- Offset
- Mid-Plane Extrusion
- Hole

Design Intent:

- The part is symmetrical.
- All holes are diameter are 0.75 and through all.
- All fillets are R.25.
- This is a standard part.

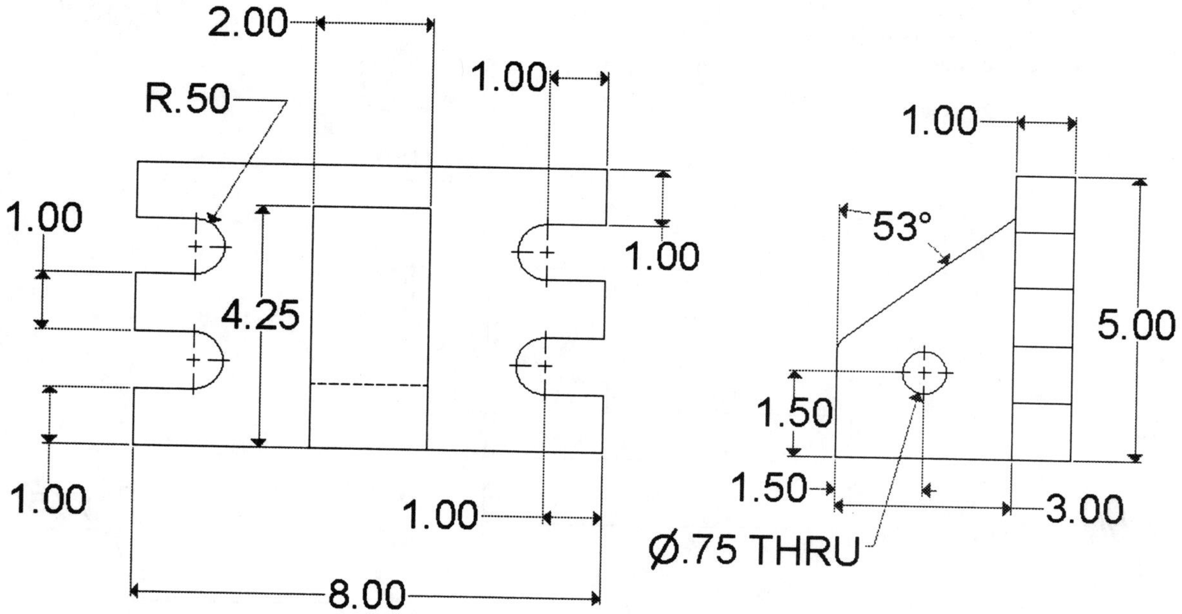

Exercise 8:

Sheet Metal Part

Create this part using the information provided.
This exercise reinforces the following skills:

- Flange
- Fillet
- Pattern
- Chamfer
- Hole

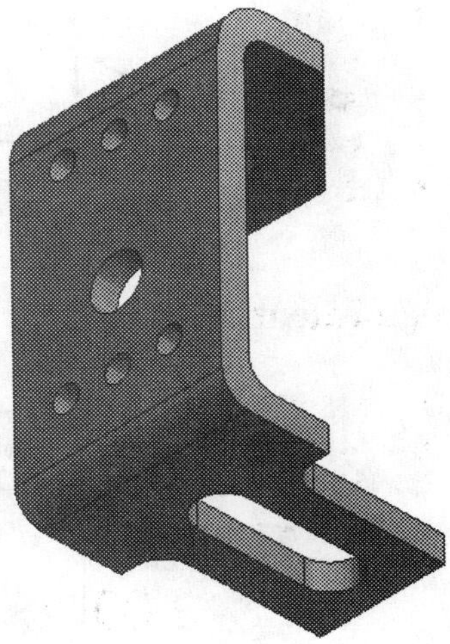

Design Intent:

- The part is NOT symmetrical.
- The six small holes are diameter 0.20 and through all.
- This is a stainless steel part with thickness of .25
- Create slot using Design Catalog slot
- This is a standard part.

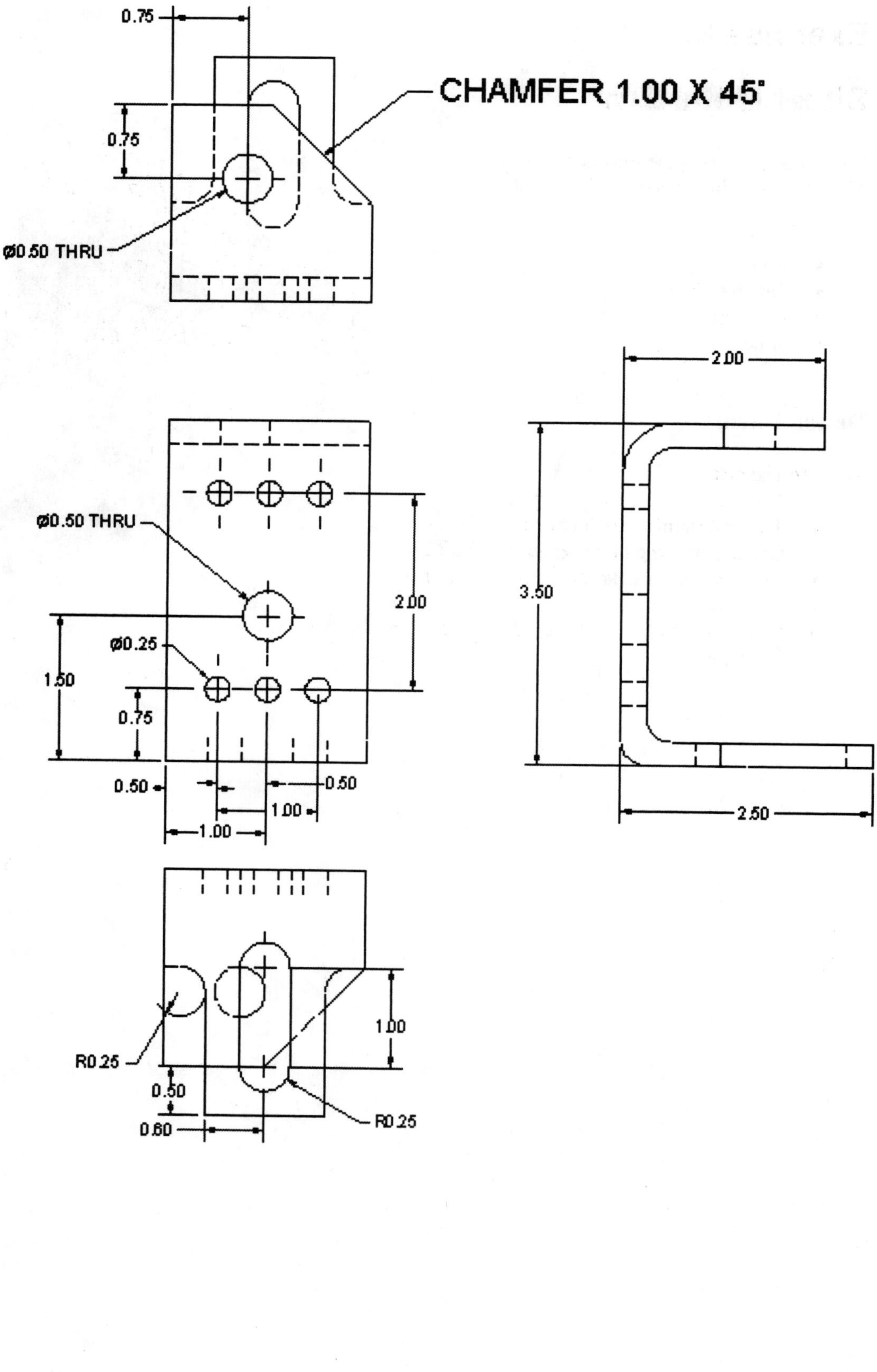
0.75
0.75
CHAMFER 1.00 X 45°
ø0.50 THRU
2.00
ø0.50 THRU
2.00
3.50
ø0.25
1.50
0.75
0.50
0.50
1.00
1.00
2.50
1.00
R0.25
0.50
0.60
R0.25

Exercise 9:

Circular Pattern

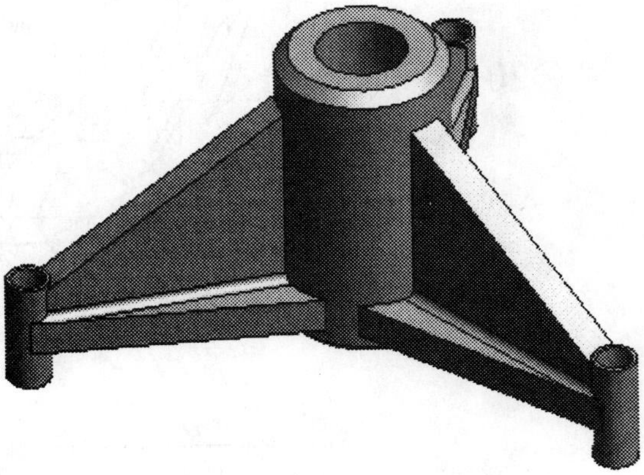

Create this part using the information provided.
This exercise reinforces the following skills:

- Fillet
- Circular Pattern
- Chamfer
- Hole
- Rib
- Work Plane, 2-Axis

Design Intent:

- The part is NOT symmetrical.
- The large hole is diameter 20 mm through
- The three small holes are 8 mm diameter through.
- Fillets are 2 mm.
- Chamfer both ends of the center cylinder 3 mm x 45 degrees.
- This is a metric part.

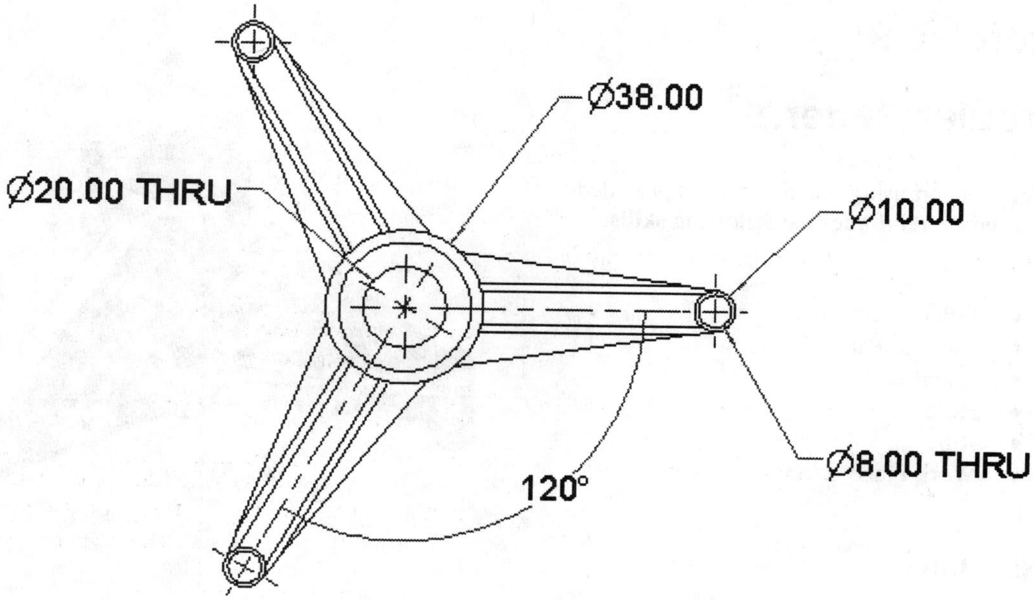
Ø38.00
Ø20.00 THRU
Ø10.00
Ø8.00 THRU
120°

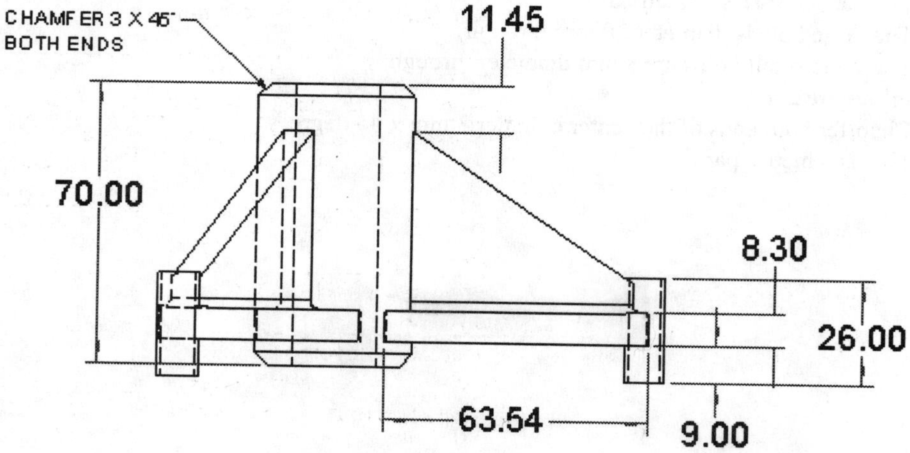
CHAMFER 3 X 45°
BOTH ENDS
11.45
70.00
8.30
26.00
63.54
9.00

APPENDIX A
TOOLBARS

Standard Toolbar

Button	Tool	Function	Special Instructions
	Parameters	Allows the user to create a part using a spreadsheet to control dimensions and features	
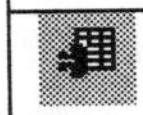	iPart Author	Creates a spreadsheet for an existing part	
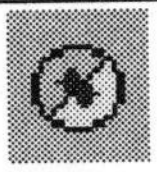	Create Interface	Allows the user to pre-set edges, faces, or axes to be used for assembly constraints	
	Zoom All	Zoom in or out so everything is visible in the graphics window	
	Zoom Window	Zoom in so the selected viewing area fills the graphics window	Pick two corners to designate the window
	Dynamic Zoom	Drag to zoom in or out	Use F3 to activate
	Pan	Drag to reposition the model in the graphics window – does not zoom in or out	Use F2 to activate
	Zoom Selected	Zooms in or out so selected geometry fits in graphics window	
	3D Rotate	Change the viewing perspective of the model	Use F4 to activate. Use spacebar to toggle rotation modes
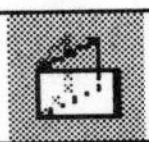	Look At	Select geometry for a PLAN view	
	Wire Frame display	Display the model as a wire frame	
	Hidden Edge display	Display the model as a shaded solid with hidden edges visible	
	Shaded Display	Display the model as a shaded solid	Default display setting
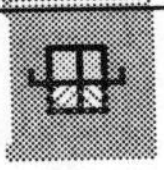	Section All Parts	Allows the user to create a sectioned 3D view of a part or assembly.	
	Help	Brings up Help	Use F1 to activate
	Visual Syllabus	Animated tutorials	
	Design Doctor	Diagnose and fix part and assembly errors and problems	Is grayed out unless errors occur

Feature Tools

Button	Tool	Function	Special Instructions
	Extrude	Extrude a profile normal to the sketch	Can be base feature
	Revolve	Revolve a profile around an axis	Can be base feature
	Hole	Create a hole in a part	Use hole points or line endpoints as hole centers
	Shell	Create a hollow part	Placed feature
	Rib	Creates a rib	Uses an open contour
	Loft	Construct a feature with varying cross sections; can follow a curved path	Requires multiple work planes
	Sweep	Extrude a profile along a curved path	Can be base feature
	Coil	Extrude a profile along a helical path	Can be base feature
	Thread	Maps a bitmap of a thread to a cylindrical face.	
	Fillet	Create a fillet or round edges	Placed feature
	Chamfer	Create a chamfer on selected edges	Placed feature
	Face Draft	Create a draft on selected faces	Placed feature
	Split	Part Split using parting line or spline	
	View Catalog	Open a Catalog of Design Elements	
	Insert Design Element	Add a Design Element	
	Create a Design Element	Create a Design Element from an Existing Feature	
	Derived Part	Create a new derived part from a base part	
	Rectangular Pattern	Creates a rectangular pattern of features	Pattern can be suppressed, items in the pattern can be individualized
	Circular Pattern	Creates a circular pattern around a center	Pattern can be suppressed, items in the pattern can be individualized
	Mirror Feature	Create a mirror image using a plane, line or axis as mirror line	
	Work Plane	Create a work plane	
	Work Axis	Create a work axis	
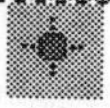	Work Point	Create a work point	Can be used to place holes on curved surfaces

Sketch Tools

Button	Tool	Function	Special Instructions
	Edit Coordinate System	Use for creating isometric or angled sketches	
	Line	Create line segment	Select NORMAL or CONSTRUCTION from the Style Menu
	Spline	Create spline	
	Circle	Create circle using center point and radius	Select NORMAL or CONSTRUCTION from the Style Menu
	Circle	Create circle tangent to three lines or arcs	
	Circle	Create ellipse	
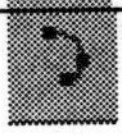	Arc	Create 3 point arc	Select NORMAL or CONSTRUCTION from the Style Menu
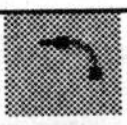	Arc	Create arc with center and two endpoints	
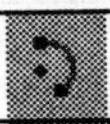	Arc	Create arc tangent to a line	
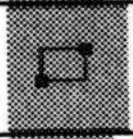	Rectangle	Use corner method to create rectangle	
	Rectangle	Create rectangle with three orthogonal points	
	Fillet	Create fillet by entering a radius and selecting two lines or arcs	Radius controlled by dialog box entry
	Chamfer	Create chamfer. Three options available: Equal Distance, Two Distances, and Distance-Angle	
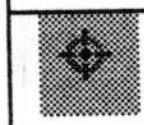	Point, Hole Center	Position the center point for a hole or sketch point	Select Hole Center (default) or Sketch Point from the Style Menu
	Mirror	Mirrors Geometry about a centerline	Requires Centerline
	Offset	Create parallel lines/curves at a specified distance	
	General Dimension	Apply dimensions to sketches	Use the Right click button to select the type of dimension to apply.
	Auto Dimension	Applies dimensions to selected sketch geometry	

Solids Editing Tools

Button	Tool	Function
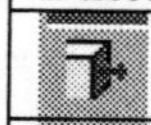	Move Face	Moves one or more faces on a solid
	Extend or Contract	Extend or contract a base solid symmetrically about a planar face or work plane
	Work Plane	Create a work plane
	Work Axis	Create a work axis
	Work Point	Create a work point
	Toggle Precise UI	Brings up the Precise Input Toolbar

Drawing Management Toolbar

Button	Tool	Function	Special Instructions
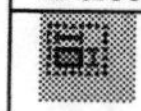	Create View	Creates a view of a 3D model	The user must select the 3D model file to be used
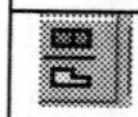	Projected Views	Creates an orthographic view	Requires a base view to have been defined
	Auxiliary View	Creates an auxiliary view	Select an edge to project a view
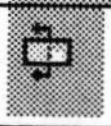	Section Views	Creates a section view	User must define a section line before the view can be created
	Detail View	Adds a detail view	
	New Sheet	Adds a new layout sheet	
	Draft View	Adds a sketch overlay to a drawing	Used to mark up or redline a drawing
	Property Field	Creates text field	Select source for text Only available when in Define New Title block mode
	Fill/Hatch Sketch Region	Adds color to profiles	Can be used to create logos or graphics Only available when in Define New Title block mode

Sheet Metal Tools

Button	Function	Settings/Options	Special Instructions
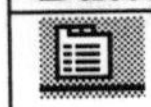	Styles	Sets sheet metals styles	Use the Variable Thickness to specify values under the Bend tab to boost productivity.
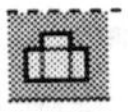	Flat Pattern	Creates a flat pattern of the sheet metal part.	
	Face	Creates a sheet metal face.	Similar to Extrude.
	Contour Flange	Uses an open profile to create a flange	
	Cut	Removes a profile from a sheet metal face.	
	Flange	Creates a flange on a sheet metal edge	
	Hem	Creates several different styles of hems	
	Fold	Creates a fold	Uses a single sketched line
	Corner Seam	Creates a corner seam between two sheet metal faces	
	Bend	Creates a bend between two sheet metal faces	
	Hole	Creates a Hole	This is the same as the Features tool
	Corner Round	Creates a fillet or round on a corner	
	Corner Chamfer	Creates a chamfer on a corner	
	View Catalog	Open a Catalog of Design Elements	
	Insert Design Element	Add a Design Element	
	Create a Design Element	Create a Design Element from an Existing Feature	
	Work Plane	Create a work plane	
	Work Axis	Create a work axis	
	Work Point	Create a work point	
	Rectangular Pattern	Create a rectangular pattern of one or more features	
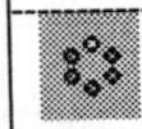	Circular Pattern	Create a circular pattern of one or more features	
	Mirror Feature	Mirror one or more features along a plane	

Drawing AnnotationTools

Button	Tool	Function	Special Instructions
	General Dimension	Creates a dimension between two points, lines, or curves.	Double click on a dimension to edit.
	Ordinate Dimension Set	Places a set of ordinate dimensions along an axis. The first dimension placed is automatically assumed to be the origin dimension.	To edit, select then right click to access the edit options
	Ordinate Dimension	Creates an ordinate dimension	Requires the user to select an Origin prior to placing the dimension
	Hole/Thread Notes	Adds a hole or thread note with leader	Hole notes can only be added to features created with the Hole tool.
	Center Mark	Creates a center mark	Style of center mark is set up in Drafting Standards under Format
	Center Line	Creates a center line	Right click to get assistance in placing the line
	Center line Bisector	Creates an angle bisector	Select two lines to bisect
	Centered Pattern	Creates a centerline for a circular pattern	
	Surface Texture Symbol	Creates a surface texture symbol	Some options not available in ANSI mode.
	Weld Symbol	Creates a weld symbol	Drafting Standards control the linetype, color, and gap
	Feature Control Frame	Creates a feature control symbol	Typing F can be used to initiate this command
	Feature Identifier Symbol	Creates a feature identifier symbol	NOT available in ANSI standard mode
	Datum Identifier Symbol	Creates a datum identifier symbol	
	Datum Targets	Datum Target with leader	
		Datum Target with circle	
		Datum Target with line	
		Datum Target with point	
		Datum Target with rectangle	
	Text	Creates a text block	Similar to MTEXT
	Leader text	Creates text with a leader attached.	
	Add balloon	Adds a reference balloon	Inventor assigns the reference numbers to parts automatically
	Balloon All	Adds balloons to all the parts in a view	
	Parts List	Creates a parts list	Customize the parts list using property fields

Assembly Tools

Button	Tool	Function
	Place Component	Places a link to an existing part of subassembly in an assembly. A change to any instance updates all other instances of a component.
	Create Component	Creates a new part or subassembly in an assembly
	Pattern Component	Creates copies of a component in a rectangular or circular pattern
	Place Constraint	Places an assembly constraint between two parts.
	Replace Component	Replaces a component in an assembly with another component
	Replace All	Replaces all occurrences of a component in an assembly
	Move Component	Enables a temporary translation of a constrained component. A constrained component returns to proper position when the user clicks Update. Enables permanent translation of a grounded component. A grounded component will remain in the placed position when Update is clicked.
	Rotate Component	Enables a temporary rotation of a constrained component. A constrained component returns to proper position when the user clicks Update. Enables permanent rotation of a grounded component. A grounded component will remain in the placed position when Update is clicked.
	Section Views	Displays a quarter section view of a model defined by hiding portions of components on one side of a defined cutting edge
		Displays a three quarter section view
		Displays a half section view
		Displays an unsectioned view of the model

NOTES:

Appendix B
Short Cut Keys

KEY	COMMAND
B	ADD BALLOON
C	ADD CENTER MARK
D	ADD DIMENSION
E	EXTRUDE
F	ADD FEATURE SYMBOL
H	ADD HOLE
L	CREATE LINE
O	ADD ORDINATE DIMENSION
R	REVOLVE
S	FINISH SKETCH/NEW SKETCH
T	ADD TWEAK

FUNCTION KEYS

F1	HELP
F2	PAN VIEW
F4	ROTATE VIEW
F5	PREVIOUS VIEW

About the Author

Elise Moss is currently a professor at DeAnza College in Cupertino, California teaching classes in Autodesk and SolidWorks software. She has worked as a mechanical engineer in Silicon Valley, primarily creating sheet metal designs for the last twenty years. She is a regular columnist for Autodesk's Toplines emagazine and AUGI's PaperSpace. She also is the owner of Moss Designs, a Registered Autodesk Developer, creating custom applications and designs for corporate clients. She holds a baccalaureate degree from San Jose State University.

She is married with two sons. Her older son, Benjamin, is currently studying electrical engineering at UC Santa Cruz. Her younger son, Daniel, is studying architecture at West Valley College. Her husband, Ari, is a computer scientist.

Elise is a third generation engineer. Her father, Bob Moss, is a metallurgical engineer, working in the aeronautic industry. Her grandfather, Solomon Kupperman, was a civil engineer for the City of Chicago.

She can be contacted via email at:
elise_moss@mossdesigns.com

More information about the author and her work can be found on her website at www.mossdesigns.com.

Index

A

B

C

C

D

D

E

F

G

H

I

L

M

N

O

P

P

R

S

T

T

U

V

W

Z